'The must-read history ... A masterw[...]

David Sexton, *Evening Standard*

'Already a classic – a gripping and thought-provoking study of the city whose modern religious, political and ethnic rivalries can be understood only in the context of its preceding 3,000 years of history. Montefiore writes with verve, sensitivity and a keen eye for the entertaining historical detail'

Tony Barber, *Financial Times* (Best Summer Reading)

'A fittingly vast and dazzling portrait of Jerusalem, utterly compelling from start to finish'

Christopher Hart, *Sunday Times*

'Astoundingly ambitious and triumphantly epic history ... tautly gripping ... a book with its gaze fixed on the stars [but] also with its feet firmly in the gutter ... A heavenly city Jerusalem may be; but it is also a relentlessly terrestrial one. The achievement of this marvellous book is to fuse them into one biography'

Tom Holland, *Daily Telegraph*

'Montefiore's book, packed with fascinating and often grisly detail, is a gripping account of war, betrayal, looting, rape, massacre, sadistic torture, fanaticism, feuds, persecution, corruption, hypocrisy and spirituality ... Montefiore's narrative is remarkably objective ... a reliable and compelling account'

Antony Beevor, *Guardian*

'Gripping ... This *meisterwerk* ... Montefiore has a great novelist's eye for human detail, a great journalist's nose for human frailty and a great historian's touch when it comes to selecting just the right primary source document to bring the past alive ... Supremely ambitious ... judicious, nuanced, balanced and sensitive ... when history is written this way one can never have too much'

Michael Gove, *The Times*

'*Jerusalem* is an extraordinary achievement, written with an imagination and energy that threatens to mesmerise and exhaust the reader at the same time. The sheer superabundance of condensed historical episodes, attended by collapsing walls, internecine punch-ups and blood-curdling carnage, pile up and press down on each other like the prodigious archaeological detritus of the city itself ... Read this book'

John Cornwell, *Financial Times*

'Monumental ... An enormous and enthralling epic, the prose equivalent of those sprawling Hollywood films such as *The Ten Commandments, Ben-Hur* or *The Fall of the Roman Empire*'

Peter Burton, *Daily Express*

'Simon Sebag Montefiore's history of Jerusalem is a labour of love and scholarship. It is a considerable achievement ... He has a wonderful ear for the absurdities and the adventurers of the past ... totally gripping ... vivid, compelling, engaged, engrossing, knowledgeable'

Barnaby Rogerson, *Independent*

'Outstanding ... superbly objective, elegantly written and highly entertaining'

Saul David, *Mail on Sunday*

'Montefiore really does give you the history of a living, breathing city ... Epic, challenging and possibly reckless ... a page-turner that any reader of any faith, or no faith at all, can relish ... Irresistible stuff'

Alyson Rudd, *The Times*

'Simon Sebag Montefiore's "biography" of the city of Jerusalem, eye-opening and hair-raising in equal measure, has outsold almost all the celebs ... his spectacular chronicle of unholy deeds in holy places ... his history of an ever-disputed ground, with its ebullient equal-opportunity account of the manifold crimes, perennial hypocrisy and very occasional generosity of all the powers and personalities who have invaded the city's sacred space'

Boyd Tonkin, *Independent*

'The story of Jerusalem gives as many examples of human cruelty, greed, hatred, pedantry, vanity, fanaticism and stark raving madness as the history of anything anywhere ... I recommend, of course, that you read the book from cover to cover. There is never a dull page'

Charles Moore, *Daily Telegraph*

'In his latest work, Simon Sebag Montefiore shows his talents and meticulousness in the service of a city of fury: Jerusalem. A masterpiece. What an achievement ... It is necessary to be Montefiore to give even to the knowledgeable reader the invigorating impression that he has never read anything about Jerusalem before. A dazzling fresco'

Christian Makarian, *L'Express*

'Spectacular. [Montefiore] really tells you what the life of the city has been like and why it means so much to everyone ... You fall in love with the city and it breaks your heart that people can't make peace over it ... It's a treasure. It's a wonderful book'

Bill Clinton, Book of the Year, *The Today Show* (NBC)

'Ambitious and arresting, *Jerusalem: The Biography* is a powerful achievement, erudite without pedantry, and intimate with the complex archaeology ... In the matter of the competing faiths, it is all but pitch-perfect ... *Jerusalem: The Biography* is double-headed: at once a scholarly record and an exuberantly written popular tour de force'

Colin Thubron, *New York Review of Books*

'Simon Sebag Montefiore's magnificent biography of Jerusalem has all the grandeur and sweep of her 3,000-year history. His masterful research and his gift for bringing it all to life make this fascinating work a treasure-trove for scholars and laymen alike'

Henry Kissinger

'Montefiore is that rarest of things: an historian who writes great weighty tomes that are as page-turning as the best thrillers. His biography of Stalin read like a successful HBO series. His new "biography" of Jerusalem is no less readable. Sebag has a visceral understanding of what makes history worth reading. He manages to bring people who have been dead for two millennia alive again and make them breathe. Sebag seems to have an insight into the mind of psychopathic tyrants that makes you wish he was working for the US Secretary of State'

Philip Kerr, *Newsweek*

'Sweeping and absorbing ... Montefiore is a master of colorful and telling details and anecdotes ... His account is admirably dispassionate and balanced'

Jackson Diehl, *Washington Post Book World*

'There have been many histories of Jerusalem ... but Mr. Montefiore's book is the city's first "biography" – a panoptic narrative of its rulers and citizens, heroes and villains, harlots and saints. In 550 pages, Mr Montefiore barely misses a trick or a character in taking us through the city's story with compelling, breathless tension'

Norman Lebrecht, *Wall Street Journal*

'Impossible to put down ... A vastly enjoyable chronicle [with] many fascinating asides ... Montefiore has a fine eye for the telling detail, and also a powerful feel for a good story ... For a book that spans 3,000 years, it does a remarkably inclusive job'

Jonathan Rosen, *New York Times Book Review*

'*Jerusalem: The Biography* reads like a richly drawn novel, with complex characters – kings, priests, philo-Semites, and anti-Semites – and riveting anecdotes. It also puts the region's contemporary conflict in perspective'

Dan Ephron, *Newsweek* and *Daily Beast*

'Magisterial ... [He has] been preparing all his life to write this particular book. And he has given much thought to how it should be approached. The story of Jerusalem is told chronologically through the lives of the men and women ... who shaped it ... and this straightforward approach works well. Mr Montefiore steers a clear path through the religious animosities and political intrigues ... adopting a strikingly apolitical tone. He adds richness by including sources not usually available in English ... As a writer, Mr Montefiore has an elegant turn of phrase and an unerring ear for the anecdote that will cut to the heart of a story ... It is this kind of detail that makes *Jerusalem* a particular joy to read'

Economist

'A dazzling historical encyclopaedia that brings alive the world of the three Abrahamic faiths ... Its splendid historical cast includes scheming kings and manipulative queens, bloodthirsty warlords and genocidal emperors, wild-eyed prophets and alluring harlots ... An excellent primer on the origins and histories of the three religions ... Anyone wishing to understand the religious forces and passions that shape much of our modern world would benefit from reading *Jerusalem* ... Scrupulously fair ... Wonderfully evocative'

Adam LeBor, *Literary Review*

'*Jerusalem: The Biography* – a wonderful mixture of biography, history, archaeology and brains'

Kate Mosse, *Woman & Home* magazine

'This book is not only immensely important it is immensely readable'

Bettany Hughes, *Daily Express*

'Admirably impartial ... Vivid, violent, anecdotal, and full of crazy, gung-ho, OTT characters'

Sue Arnold, *Guardian*

'Masterly, vastly entertaining and timely'

Victor Sebestyen, *Evening Standard*

'Ambitious and politically courageous ... a gripping read ... This magnificent history'

Rebecca Abrams, *New Statesman*

'A *tour de force*'

Philip Mansel, *Spectator*

'To write a "biography" of Jerusalem is a formidable undertaking. Simon Sebag Montefiore has risen to the challenge. His book can be commended to anyone who is planning a trip to Jerusalem, or who wants background on the Palestinian question – or who just enjoys a good read. The author is especially good on archaeology ... he can make the stones live and sing. He would be an excellent guide on an archaeological tour'

Bruce Anderson, *Prospect*

'He writes with elegance and authority'

Diarmaid MacCulloch, *London Review of Books*

'This superb book'

Paul Levy, *Wall Street Journal*

'Jerusalem deserves a great biographer, and Montefiore has provided the best in recent memory'

Seth J. Frantzman, *Jerusalem Post*

'As I think of the countless number of books I have read on the subject none even comes close to this one ... The book is utterly compelling ... *Jerusalem: The Biography* is a masterpiece that could only have been written by someone who has Jerusalem in his blood ... This is a history without political or religious bias ... This is simply a book that must be read by all who are serious about this great city'

Reverend Canon Andrew White, *Third Way*

'The book by the British historian and writer whose output includes two works about Stalin [*Young Stalin* and *Stalin: The Court of the Red Tsar*], is an incredibly ambitious project, and also – despite a great many footnotes and references – a piece of reading as exciting as a crime novel, full of dramatic scenes, unexpected turns, and vivid human portraits'

Tygodnik Powszechny (*Polish Catholic Weekly*)

'Simon Sebag Montefiore says that "the story of Jerusalem is the story of the world", because the city becomes more and more a centre of the world. He tells its story with impressive sweep and brilliance. This is a must-read'

Tomasz Bielecki, *Gazeta Wyborcza* (Poland)

'*Jerusalem: The Biography* by Simon Sebag Montefiore – I've been reading that from the end backwards, which is a slightly strange approach!'

David Cameron, Best Summer Books, *Spectator*

'An epic and utterly absorbing study of a city whose modern religious, political and ethnic rivalries can be understood only in the context of its preceding 3,000 years of history. Montefiore writes with tremendous verve, sensitivity to historical controversy and an exceptional eye for the entertaining detail'

Financial Times, Books of the Year

'One of the most ambitious and breathtakingly realised books of the year, *Jerusalem: The Biography*. The world's greatest city has found its perfect biographer in Montefiore. The city is brought to life not only through its wars but the people who made it. Spiritual, beastly and heroic, this is a gripping tale from first page to last'

Dan Jones, *Daily Telegraph*, Books of the Year

'This wonderfully vibrant account ... Balanced fair and above all colourful, Montefiore's narrative does justice to every religious tradition and confirms his reputation as one of our finest popular historians'

Dominic Sandbrook, *Sunday Times*, Books of the Year

'Triumphant biography of the city. It is the mark of his achievement that a fast-paced and relentlessly entertaining book should also be so true to the yearnings of those who have seen, shimmering beyond the earthly city of rock and dust, a celestial Jerusalem'

Tom Holland, *Guardian*, Books of the Year

'After his acclaimed biographies of Stalin, Catherine the Great and her lover, Potemkin, Simon Sebag Montefiore has finally turned to the book he was born to write'   *Economist*, Books of the Year

'I was utterly engrossed in its history of murder and religion'

Frances Osborne, *Evening Standard*, Books of the Year

'Vast, vigorous history with entertaining Gibbonian footnotes'

Hermione Eyre, *Evening Standard*, Books of the Year

Simon Sebag Montefiore was born in 1965 and read history at Gonville & Caius College, Cambridge University. *Catherine the Great & Potemkin* was shortlisted for the Samuel Johnson, Duff Cooper and Marsh Biography Prizes. *Stalin: The Court of the Red Tsar* won the History Book of the Year at the British Book Awards. *Young Stalin* won the Costa Biography Award (UK), the *LA Times* Book Prize for Biography (US), Le Grand Prix de la Biographie Politique (France) and the Kreisky Prize for Political Literature (Austria). Montefiore's books are published in more than thirty-five languages. He is also the author of the novel *Sashenka*. A Fellow of the Royal Society of Literature, he has been appointed Visiting Professor of the Humanities Research Institute, University of Buckingham. He has also written and presented a BBC series, *Jerusalem: The Making of a Holy City*. He lives in London with his wife, the novelist Santa Montefiore, and their two children. For more information or to contact the author, see: www.simonsebagmontefiore.com or follow him on Twitter @simonmontefiore

By Simon Sebag Montefiore

Catherine the Great & Potemkin
Stalin: The Court of the Red Tsar
Young Stalin
Jerusalem: The Biography

FICTION
Sashenka

JERUSALEM

THE BIOGRAPHY

Simon Sebag Montefiore

PHOENIX

A PHOENIX PAPERBACK

First published in Great Britain in 2011
by Weidenfeld & Nicolson
This paperback edition published in 2012
by Phoenix,
an imprint of Orion Books Ltd,
Orion House, 5 Upper St Martin's Lane,
London WC2H 9EA

An Hachette UK company

13

A CIP catalogue record for this book
is available from the British Library.

ISBN 978-1-7802-2025-3

Typeset by Input Data Services Ltd, Bridgwater, Somerset

Printed and bound by CPI Group (UK) Ltd, Croydon, CRO 4YY

www.orionbooks.co.uk

To my darling daughter
Lily Bathsheba

The view of Jerusalem is the history of the world; it is more; it is the history of heaven and earth.

Benjamin Disraeli, *Tancred*

The city has been destroyed, rebuilt, destroyed and rebuilt again. Jerusalem is an old nymphomaniac who squeezes lover after lover to death, before shrugging him off her with a yawn, a black widow who devours her mates while they are still penetrating her.

Amos Oz, *A Tale of Love and Darkness*

The Land of Israel is the centre of the world; Jerusalem is the centre of the Land; the Holy Temple is the centre of Jerusalem; the Holy of Holies is the centre of the Holy Temple; the Holy Ark is the centre of the Holy of Holies and the Foundation Stone from which the world was established is before the Holy Ark.

Midrash Tanhuma, *Kedoshim 10*

The sanctuary of the earth is Syria; the sanctuary of Syria is Palestine; the sanctuary of Palestine is Jerusalem; the sanctuary of Jerusalem is the Mount; the sanctuary of the Mount is the place of worship; the sanctuary of the place of worship is the Dome of the Rock.

Thaur ibn Yazid, *Fadail*

Jerusalem is the most illustrious of cities. Still Jerusalem has some disadvantages. Thus it is reported 'Jerusalem is a golden goblet full of scorpions'.

Muqaddasi, *Description of Syria including Palestine*

CONTENTS

PART EIGHT: EMPIRE

PART NINE: ZIONISM

ILLUSTRATIONS

Coin of Herod Antipas, *c.* AD 4–39, Israel Museum (AKG)

Coin of Herod Agrippa I, *c.* AD 43–39, Israel Museum (AKG)

Head of Titus, first century AD, Louvre Museum, Paris (Bridgeman Art Library)

Skeletal arm of young woman, AD 67 (Zev Radovan)

Rocks at the foot of the Wall, Jerusalem (author's photograph)

Detail from the Arch of Titus, Rome (AKG)

Coin minted to commemorate victory over Judaea, AD 81 (Zev Radovan)

Bronze bust of Hadrian, *c.* 135, Israel Museum (Bridgeman Art Library)

Silver coin issued by Simon bar Kochba, *c.* 132–5, Israel Museum (AKG)

Fourth-century pilgrim graffiti, Church of the Holy Sepulchre (Bridgeman Art Library)

Colossal head of Constantine the Great, Palazzo dei Conservatori, Rome (AKG)

SECTION TWO

Marble statue of Julian the Apostate, 362, Louvre Museum, Paris (AKG)

Justinian I and his retinue, *c.* 550, San Vitale, Ravenna (Bridgeman Art Library)

Theodora and her retinue, *c.* 550, San Vitale, Ravenna (Bridgeman Art Library)

Mosaic map of Palestine, Madaba (Bridgeman Art Library)

The Golden Gate (author's photograph)

Ascension of Muhammad, from a manuscript of Nizami's poem 'Khamza', 1539–43, British Library (AKG)

Umayyad dynasty gold dinar showing Abd al-Malik (The Trustees of the British Museum)

The Dome of the Rock (AKG)

Interior of the Dome of the Rock (Garo Nalbandian)

The looting of Jerusalem in 1099, illuminated miniature from a universal chronicle, Jean de Courcy, Bibliotèque Nationale, Paris (Bridgeman Art Library)

Baldwin I crosses the Jordan, illumination from *Roman de Godefroi de Bouillon*, Bibliotèque Nationale, Paris (AKG)

Medieval map of Jerusalem from Robert the Monk's *Chronicle of the Crusades* (Corbis)

Melisende marrying Fulk of Anjou from the *Histoire de la conquete de Jerusalem* by William of Tyre, Bibliotèque Nationale, Paris (Bridgeman Art Library)

Melisende's psalter, *c.* 1131–43, British Library (AKG)

Baldwin IV and William of Tyre, illumination from *Histoire de Outremer* by William of Tyre, British Library (AKG)

Portrait of Saladin, British Library (Bridgeman Art Library)

Frederick II entering Jerusalem, 1227, Vatican Library (AKG)

The Dome of Ascension (AKG)

Entrance to the Market of the Cotton Merchants

Qaitbay fountain (AKG)

Suleiman I, portrait attributed to school of Titian, *c.* 1530, Kunsthistorisches Museum, Vienna (Bridgeman Art Library)

Fountain of the Gate of the Chain (AKG)

Engraving of Sabbatai Zevi (AKG)

Detail from the exterior mosaics of the Dome of the Rock (Corbis)

SECTION THREE

Ibrahim Pasha, Charles-Philippe Larivière, Museum of French History at the Palace of Versailles (RMN)

Greek Church of the Holy Sepulchre, David Roberts, 1839 (AKG)

Sir Moses Montefiore (author's collection)

Montefiore windmill (Mishkenot Sha'ananim)

Photograph of the Church of the Holy Sepulchre, Patriarch Yessayi, 1861 (Armenian Partriarchate)

A group of Yemenite Jews (American Colony)

A group of Ashkenazi Jews, 1885, Hulton Archive (Getty)

Crowd of Russian pilgrims at the Church of the Holy Sepulchre (American Colony)

King David Street, Granger Collection (Topfoto)

Theodor Herzl and his family, Hulton Archive (Getty)

SECTION FOUR

FAMILY TREES

MAPS

PREFACE

The history of Jerusalem is the history of the world, but it is also the chronicle of an often penurious provincial town amid the Judaean hills. Jerusalem was once regarded as the centre of the world and today that is more true than ever: the city is the focus of the struggle between the Abrahamic religions, the shrine for increasingly popular Christian, Jewish and Islamic fundamentalism, the strategic battlefield of clashing civilizations, the front line between atheism and faith, the cynosure of secular fascination, the object of giddy conspiracism and internet myth-making, and the illuminated stage for the cameras of the world in the age of twenty-four-hour news. Religious, political and media interest feed on each other to make Jerusalem more intensely scrutinized today than ever before.

Jerusalem is the Holy City, yet it has always been a den of superstition, charlatanism and bigotry; the desire and prize of empires, yet of no strategic value; the cosmopolitan home of many sects, each of which believes the city belongs to them alone; a city of many names – yet each tradition is so sectarian it excludes any other. This is a place of such delicacy that it is described in Jewish sacred literature in the feminine – always a sensual, living woman, always a beauty, but sometimes a shameless harlot, sometimes a wounded princess whose lovers have forsaken her. Jerusalem is the house of the one God, the capital of two peoples, the temple of three religions and she is the only city to exist twice – in heaven and on earth: the peerless grace of the terrestrial is as nothing to the glories of the celestial. The very fact that Jerusalem is both terrestrial and celestial means that the city can exist anywhere: new Jerusalems have been founded all over the world and everyone has their own vision of Jerusalem. Prophets and patriarchs, Abraham, David, Jesus and Muhammad are said to have trodden these stones. The Abrahamic religions were born there and the world will also end there on the Day of Judgement. Jerusalem, sacred to the Peoples of the Book, *is* the city of the Book: the Bible is, in many ways, Jerusalem's own chronicle and its readers, from the Jews and early Christians via the Muslim conquerors and the Crusaders to today's American evangelists, have repeatedly altered her history to fulfil biblical prophecy.

When the Bible was translated into Greek then Latin and English, it became the universal book and it made Jerusalem the universal city. Every great king became a David, every special people were the new Israelites and every noble civilization a new Jerusalem, the city that belongs to no one and exists for everyone in their imagination. And this is the city's tragedy as well as her magic: every dreamer of Jerusalem, every visitor in all ages from Jesus' Apostles to Saladin's soldiers, from Victorian pilgrims to today's tourists and journalists, arrives with a vision of the authentic Jerusalem and then is bitterly disappointed by what they find, an ever-changing city that has thrived and shrunk, been rebuilt and destroyed many times. But since this is Jerusalem, property of all, only their image is the right one; the tainted, synthetic reality must be changed; everyone has the right to impose their 'Jerusalem' on Jerusalem – and, with sword and fire, they often have.

Ibn Khaldun, the fourteenth-century historian who is both participant and source for some of the events related in this book, noted that history is so 'eagerly sought after. The men in the street aspire to know it. Kings and leaders vie for it.' This is especially true for Jerusalem. It is impossible to write a history of this city without acknowledging that Jerusalem is also a theme, a fulcrum, a spine even, of world history. At a time when the power of internet mythology means that the hi-tech mouse and the curved sword can both be weapons in the same fundamentalist arsenal, the quest for historical facts is even more important now than it was for Ibn Khaldun.

A history of Jerusalem must be a study of the nature of holiness.

The phrase 'Holy City' is constantly used to describe the reverence for her shrines, but what it really means is that Jerusalem has become the essential place on earth for communication between God and man.

We must also answer the question: of all the places in the world, why Jerusalem? The site was remote from the trade routes of the Mediterranean coast; it was short of water, baked in the summer sun, chilled by winter winds, its jagged rocks blistered and inhospitable. But the selection of Jerusalem as the Temple city was partly decisive and personal, partly organic and evolutionary: the sanctity became ever more intense because she had been holy for so long. Holiness requires not just spirituality and faith but also legitimacy and tradition. A radical prophet presenting a new vision must explain the centuries that have gone before and justify his own revelation in the accepted language and geography of holiness – the prophecies of earlier revelations and the sites already long revered. Nothing makes a place holier than the competition of another religion.

Many atheistic visitors are repelled by this holiness, seeing it as infectious superstition in a city suffering a pandemic of righteous bigotry. But that is to deny the profound human need for religion without which it is impossible to understand Jerusalem. Religions must explain the fragile joys and perpetual anxieties that mystify and frighten humanity: we need to sense a greater force than ourselves. We respect death and long to find meaning in it. As the meeting-place of God and man, Jerusalem is where these questions are settled at the Apocalypse – the End of Days, when there will be war, a battle between Christ and anti-Christ, when the Kaaba will come from Mecca to Jerusalem, when there will be judgement, resurrection of the dead and the reign of the Messiah and the Kingdom of Heaven, the New Jerusalem. All three Abrahamic religions believe in the Apocalypse, but the details vary by faith and sect. Secularists may regard all this as antique gobbledegook, but, on the contrary, such ideas are all too current. In this age of Jewish, Christian and Muslim fundamentalism, the Apocalypse is a dynamic force in the world's febrile politics.

Death is our constant companion: pilgrims have long come to

Jerusalem to die and be buried around the Temple Mount to be ready to rise again in the Apocalypse, and they continue to come. The city is surrounded by and founded upon cemeteries; the wizened body-parts of ancient saints are revered – the desiccated blackened right hand of Mary Magdalene is still displayed in the Greek Orthodox Superior's Room in the Church of the Holy Sepulchre. Many shrines, even many private houses, are built around tombs. The darkness of this city of the dead stems not just from a sort of necrophilia, but also from necromancy: the dead here are almost alive, even as they await resurrection. The unending struggle for Jerusalem – massacres, mayhem, wars, terrorism, sieges and catastrophes – have made this place into a battlefield, in Aldous Huxley's words the 'slaughterhouse of the religions', in Flaubert's a 'charnel-house'. Melville called the city a 'skull' besieged by 'armies of the dead'; while Edward Said remembered that his father had hated Jerusalem because it 'reminded him of death'.

This sanctuary of heaven and earth did not always evolve providentially. Religions begin with a spark revealed to one charismatic prophet – Moses, Jesus, Muhammad. Empires are founded, cities conquered, by the energy and luck of one warlord. The decisions of individuals, starting with King David, made Jerusalem into Jerusalem.

There was surely scant prospect that David's little citadel, capital of a small kingdom, would become the world's cynosure. Ironically it was Nebuchadnezzar's destruction of Jerusalem that created the template for holiness because that catastrophe led the Jews to record and acclaim the glories of Zion. Such cataclysms usually led to the vanishing of peoples. Yet the Jews' exuberant survival, their obstinate devotion to their God and, above all, their recording of their version of history in the Bible laid the foundation for Jerusalem's fame and sanctity. The Bible took the place of the Jewish state and the Temple and became, as Heinrich Heine put it, the 'portable fatherland of the Jews, the portable Jerusalem'. No other city has its own book and no other book has so guided the destiny of a city.

The sanctity of the city grew out of the exceptionalism of the

Jews as the Chosen People. Jerusalem became the Chosen City, Palestine the Chosen Land, and this exceptionalism was inherited and embraced by the Christians and the Muslims. The paramount sanctity of Jerusalem and of the land of Israel was reflected in the growing religious obsession with the restoration of the Jews to Israel and the Western enthusiasm for Zionism, its secular equivalent, between the sixteenth-century Reformation in Europe and the 1970s. Since then, the tragic narrative of the Palestinians, with Jerusalem as their lost Holy City, has altered the perception of Israel. Thus Western fixation, this sense of universal ownership, can work both ways – it is a mixed blessing or a double-edged sword. Today it is reflected in the scrutiny of Jerusalem and the Israel–Palestine conflict, more intense, more emotional than any other on earth.

Yet nothing is quite as simple it seems. The history is often presented as a series of brutal changes and violent reversals but I want to show that Jerusalem was a city of continuity and co-existence, a hybrid metropolis of hybrid buildings and hybrid people who defy the narrow categorizations that belong in the separate religious legends and nationalist narratives of later times. That is why, wherever possible, I follow the history through families – the Davidians, Maccabees and Herodians, the Umayyads and the houses of Baldwin and Saladin, up to the Husseinis, Khalidis, Spaffords, Rothschilds and Montefiores – which reveal the organic patterns of life that defy the abrupt incidents and sectarian narratives of conventional history. There are not just two sides in Jerusalem but many interlinked, overlapping cultures and layered loyalties – a multi-faceted, mutating kaleidoscope of Arab Orthodox, Arab Muslims, Sephardic Jews, Ashkenazi Jews, Haredi Jews of legion courts, secular Jews, Armenian Orthodox, Georgians, Serbs, Russians, Copts, Protestants, Ethiopians, Latins and so on. A single individual often had several loyalties to different identities, the human equivalent of Jerusalem's layers of stone and dust.

In fact, the city's relevance has ebbed and flowed, never still, always in a state of transformation, like a plant that changes shape, size, even colour, yet always remains rooted in the same place. The latest, glib manifestation – Jerusalem as media 'Holy City sacred to three religions' and twenty-four-hour-news show – is relatively recent. There have been centuries when Jerusalem seemed to lose religious and political importance. In many cases, it was political necessity, not divine revelation, that again stimulated and inspired religious devotion.

Whenever Jerusalem has seemed most forgotten and irrelevant, it was often the bibliolatry, the devoted study of biblical truth by people in faraway lands – whether in Mecca, Moscow, Massachusetts – who projected their faith back on to Jerusalem. All cities are windows into foreign mindsets but this one is also a two-way mirror revealing her inner life while reflecting the world outside. Whether it was the epoch of total faith, righteous empire-building, evangelical revelation or secular nationalism, Jerusalem became its symbol, and its prize. But like the mirrors in a circus, the reflections are always distorted, often freakish.

Jerusalem has a way of disappointing and tormenting both conquerors and visitors. The contrast between the real and heavenly cities is so excruciating that a hundred patients a year are committed to the city's asylum, suffering from the Jerusalem Syndrome, a madness of anticipation, disappointment and delusion. But Jerusalem Syndrome is political too: Jerusalem defies sense, practical politics and strategy, existing in the realm of ravenous passions and invincible emotions, impermeable to reason.

Even victory in this struggle for dominance and truth merely intensifies the city's holiness for others. The greedier the possessor, the fiercer the competition, the more visceral the reaction. The law of unintended consequences reigns here.

No other place evokes such a desire for exclusive possession. Yet this jealous zeal is ironic since most of Jerusalem's shrines, and the stories that go with them, have been borrowed or stolen, belonging formerly to another religion. The city's past is often imaginary. Virtually every stone once stood in the long-forgotten temple of another faith, the victory arch of another empire. Most, but not all, conquests have been accompanied by the instinct to expunge the taint of other faiths while commandeering their traditions, stories, sites. There has been much destruction, but more often the conquerors have not destroyed what came before but reused and added to it. The important sites such as the Temple Mount, the Citadel, the City of David, Mount Zion and the Church of the Holy Sepulchre do not present distinct layers of history but are more like palimpsests, works of embroidery in which the silk threads are so interwoven it is now impossible to separate them.

The competition to possess the infectious holiness of others has led some shrines to become holy to all three of the religions successively then simultaneously; kings have decreed and men died for them – and yet they are now almost forgotten: Mount Zion has been the site of frenzied Jewish, Muslim and Christian reverence but now there are few Muslim or Jewish pilgrims, and it is mainly Christian again.

In Jerusalem, the truth is often much less important than the myth. 'In Jerusalem, don't ask me the history of *facts*,' says the eminent Palestinian historian Dr Nazmi al-Jubeh. 'Take away the fiction and there's nothing left.' History is so pungently powerful here that it is repeatedly distorted: archaeology is itself a historical force and archaeologists have at times wielded as much power as soldiers, recruited to appropriate the past for the present. A discipline that aims to be objective and scientific can be used to rationalize religious-ethnic prejudice and justify imperial ambitions. Israelis, Palestinians and the evangelical imperialists of the nineteenth century have all been guilty of commandeering the same events and assigning them contradictory meanings and facts. So a history of Jerusalem has to be a history of both truth and legend. But there are facts and this book aims to tell them, however unpalatable to one side or the other.

My aim here is to write the history of Jerusalem in its broadest sense for general readers, whether they are atheists or believers, Christians, Muslims or Jews, without a political agenda, even in today's strife.

I tell the story chronologically, through the lives of the men and women – soldiers and prophets, poets and kings, peasants and musicians – and the families who made Jerusalem. I think this is the best way to bring the city to life and to show how its complex and unexpected truths are the result of this history. It is only by chronological narrative that one avoids the temptation to see the past through the obsessions of the present. I have tried to avoid teleology – writing history as if every event were inevitable. Since each mutation is a reaction to the one that preceded it, chronology is the best way to make sense of this evolution, answer the question – why Jerusalem? – and show why people acted the way they did. I hope this is also the most entertaining way to tell it. Who am I to ruin a story that – to use a Hollywood cliché that is, in this case, merited – is the greatest ever told? Among thousands of books on Jerusalem, there are very few narrative histories. Four epochs – David, Jesus, the Crusades and the Arab–Israeli conflict – are familiar, thanks to the Bible, movies, novels and the news, but they are still frequently misunderstood. As for the rest, I dearly wish to bring much forgotten history to new readers.

This is a history of Jerusalem as the centre of world history, but it is not intended to be an encyclopaedia of every aspect of Jerusalem, nor a guidebook of every niche, capital and archway in every building. This is not a minute history of the Orthodox, Latins or Armenians, the Islamic Hanafi or Shafii schools of law, the Hasidic or the Karaite Jews, nor is it told from any specific point of view. The life of the Muslim city from Mamluks to the Mandate has been neglected. The Jerusalem Families have been studied by academics of the Palestinian experience, but scarcely covered by popular historians. Their histories have been and remain extremely important: some key sources are not yet available in English, but I have had them translated and I have interviewed the family members of all these clans in order to learn their stories. But they are only part of the mosaic. This is not a history of Judaism, Christianity or Islam, nor a study of the nature of God in Jerusalem: all these have been expertly done by others – most recently in Karen Armstrong's excellent *Jerusalem: One City, Three Faiths*. Nor is this a detailed history of the Israel–Palestine conflict: no subject today is so obsessively studied. But my daunting challenge is to cover all these things, I hope in proportion.

My task is to pursue the facts, not to adjudicate between the mysteries of different religions. I certainly do not claim the right to judge whether the divine wonders and sacred texts of the three great religions are 'true'. Anyone who studies the Bible or Jerusalem has to recognize that there are many levels of truth. The beliefs of other religions and other epochs seem strange to us, while the familiar customs of our own time and place always appear eminently reasonable. Even the twenty-first century, which many seem to regard as the very acme of secular reason and common sense, has its own conventional wisdoms and quasi-religious orthodoxies that will appear incomprehensibly absurd to our great-grandchildren. But the effect of the religions and their miracles on the history of Jerusalem is undeniably real, and it is impossible to know Jerusalem without some respect for religion.

There are centuries of Jerusalem's history when little is known and everything is controversial. Being Jerusalem, the academic and archaeological debates are always venomous and sometimes violent, even leading to riots and fighting. Events in the last half-century are so controversial that there are many versions of them.

In the early period, historians, archaeologists and cranks alike have squeezed, moulded and manhandled the very few sources available to fit every possible theory which they have then advocated with all the confidence of absolute certainty. In all cases, I have reviewed the original sources and the many theories and come to a conclusion. If I covered myself comprehensively in every case, the most common words in this book would be 'maybe', 'probably', 'might' and 'could'. I have therefore not included them on every appropriate occasion but I ask the reader to understand that behind every sentence is a colossal, ever-changing literature. Each section has been checked and read by an academic specialist. I am fortunate that I have been helped in this by some of the most distinguished professors at work today.

The most fraught of these controversies is that of King David, because its political implications are so charged and so contemporary. Even at its most scientific, this debate has been conducted more dramatically and with greater harshness than one would find in any other place on any other subject, except perhaps the natures of Christ or Muhammad. The source for the story of David is the Bible. His historical life was long taken for granted. In the nineteenth century, the imperialistic-Christian interest in the

Holy Land inspired the archaeological quest for David's Jerusalem. The Christian nature of this investigation was redirected by the creation of the State of Israel in 1948 which gave it passionate religious-political significance because of David's status as the founder of Jewish Jerusalem. In the absence of much evidence of the tenth century, revisionist Israeli historians downsized David's city. Some even questioned whether he was a historical character at all, much to the outrage of Jewish traditionalists and to the glee of Palestinian politicians, because it undermined the Jewish claim. But the discovery of the Tel Dan stele in 1993 proved that King David did exist. The Bible, though not written primarily as history, is nonetheless a historical source which I have used to tell the story. The extent of David's city and the trustworthiness of the Bible are discussed in the text and for the present conflict over the City of David, see the Epilogue.

Much later, it is impossible to write about the nineteenth century without feeling the shadow of Edward Said's *Orientalism*. Said, a Palestinian Christian born in Jerusalem who became a literary professor at Columbia University in New York and an original political voice in the world of Palestinian nationalism, argued that the 'subtle and persistent Eurocentric prejudice against Arabo-Islamic peoples and their culture', particularly among nineteenth-century travellers such as Chateaubriand, Melville and Twain, had diminished Arab culture and justified imperialism. However, Said's own work inspired some of his acolytes to try to airbrush these Western intruders out of the history: this is absurd. It is true, however, that these visitors saw and understood little of the real life of Arab and Jewish Jerusalem and, as explained above, I have worked hard to show the actual lives of the indigenous population. But this book is not a polemic and the historian of Jerusalem must show the dominating influence of Western romantic-imperial culture towards the city because it explains why the Middle East so mattered to the Great Powers.

Similarly, I have portrayed the progress of British pro-Zionism, secular and evangelical, from Palmerston and Shaftesbury to Lloyd George, Balfour, Churchill and their friend Weizmann for the simple reason that this was the single most decisive influence on the fate of Jerusalem and Palestine in the nineteenth and twentieth centuries.

I end the main body of the book in 1967 because the Six Day War essentially created the situation today and it provides a decisive stop. The Epilogue cursorily brings the politics up to the present and ends with a detailed portrait of a typical morning in the three Holy Places. But the situation is ever changing. If I were to continue the history in detail up to today, the book would lack any clear ending and have to be updated almost hourly. Instead I have tried to show why Jerusalem continues to be both the essence of and obstacle to a peace deal.

This work is a synthesis based on a wide reading of the primary sources, ancient and modern, on personal seminars with specialists, professors, archaeologists, families and statesmen, and on innumerable visits to Jerusalem, the shrines and archaeological digs. I have been fortunate to uncover some new or rarely used sources. My research has brought three special joys: that of spending much time in Jerusalem; that of reading the wondrous works of writers from Usamah bin Munqidh, Ibn Khaldun, Evliya Celebi and Wasif Jawhariyyeh to William of Tyre, Josephus and T. E. Lawrence; and, thirdly, that of being befriended and helped, with such trust and generosity, amid ferocious political crises, by Jerusalemites of all sects – Palestinians, Israelis and Armenians, Muslims, Jews and Christians.

I feel I have been preparing to write this book all my life. Since childhood, I have been wandering around Jerusalem. Because of a family connection, related in the book, 'Jerusalem' is my family motto. Whatever the personal link, I am here to recount the history of what happened and what people believed. To return to where we started, there have always been two Jerusalems, the temporal and the celestial, both ruled more by faith and emotion than by reason and facts. And Jerusalem remains the centre of the world.

Not everyone will like my approach – after all, this is Jerusalem. But in writing the book I always remembered Lloyd George's advice to his Governor of Jerusalem, Storrs, who was being savagely criticized by both Jews and Arabs: 'Well, if either one side stops complaining, you'll be dismissed.'

ACKNOWLEDGEMENTS

I have been helped in this huge project by a wide cast of scholars outstanding in their fields. I am deeply grateful to them for their help, advice and, where stated, reading and correcting of my text.

In the archaeological–biblical period, thank you, above all, to the following for reading and correcting this section: Professor Ronny Reich; Professor Dan Bahat, formerly the Chief Archaeologist of Jerusalem, who also gave me detailed tours of the city; Dr Raphael Greenberg, who likewise treated me to site visits; and Rosemary Eshel. Thanks for help and advice to Irving Finkel, Assistant Keeper of Ancient Iraq and magical-medical texts at the British Museum; and to Dr Eleanor Robson, Reader in Ancient Middle Eastern Science, Department of History and Philosophy of Science, Cambridge University, for her correction of the sections on Assyria–Babylon–Persia, and Dr Nicola Schreiber for her advice on the pottery implications for the dating of the gateways of Megiddo; to Dr Gideon Avni, Director of Excavations and Surveys Department, IAA; Dr Eli Shukron, for his regular tours of the dig in the City of David; Dr Shimon Gibson; Dr Renee Sivan of the Citadel. And special thanks to Dr Yusuf al-Natsheh, Director of the Department of Islamic Archaeology of the Haram al-Sharif, for his help throughout the project and for arranging access to closed sites on the Haram and tours with Khader al-Shihabi. On the Herodian–Roman– Byzantine period, I am immensely grateful to Professor Martin Goodman of Oxford University and to Dr Adrian Goldsworthy for the reading and correction of my text.

On the early Islamic period, Arabs, Turks and Mamluks, I owe huge thanks for his advice, guidance and detailed correction of my text to Hugh Kennedy, Professor of Arabic at the School of Oriental and African Studies (SOAS), and also to Dr Nazmi al-Jubeh, Dr Yusuf al-Natsheh and Khader al-Shihabi. On the Mamilla Cemetery, I thank Taufik De'adel.

On the Crusades: thanks to Professor Jonathan Riley-Smith, Professor of Ecclesiastical History, Cambridge University, and to Professor David Abulafia, Professor of Mediterranean History, Cambridge University, for reading and correcting the text.

On Jewish history from the Fatimids to the Ottomans: thanks to Professor Abulafia who gave me access to manuscript sections of his *Great Sea: A Human History of the Mediterranean*, to Professor Minna Rozen, Haifa University, and to Sir Martin Gilbert, who let me read the manuscript of *In Ishmael's House*.

On the Ottoman period and the Palestinian Jerusalem Families: thanks to Professor Adel Manna, who read and corrected the text of the sixteenth-, seventeenth- and eighteenth-century sections.

On the nineteenth-century–imperialist–early-Zionist periods: thanks to Yehoshoa Ben-Arieh; Sir Martin Gilbert; Professor Tudor Parfitt; Caroline Finkel; Dr Abigail Green, who let me read her manuscript *Moses Montefiore: Jewish Liberator, Imperial Hero*; and Bashir Barakat, for his private research on the Jerusalem Families. Kirsten Ellis generously gave me access to unpublished chapters of *Star of the Morning*. Dr Clare Mouradian gave me much advice and material. Professor Minna Rozen shared her research on Disraeli and other papers. On the Russian connection, thanks to Professor Simon Dixon, and to Galina Babkova in Moscow; and on the Armenians to George Hintlian and Dr Igor Dorfmann-Lazarev.

On the Zionist period, the twentieth century and the Epilogue: I owe the greatest thanks to Dr Nadim Shehadi, Associate Fellow of the Middle East Programme, Chatham House, and to Professor Colin Shindler, SOAS, both of whom read and corrected these entire sections. I am grateful to David and Jackie Landau of the *Economist* and *Haaretz* for their corrections. Thanks to Dr Jacques Gautier; to Dr Albert Aghazarian; to Jamal al-Nusseibeh for ideas and contacts; to Huda Imam for her tour of the Security Wall; to Yakov Loupo for his research on the ultra-Orthodox.

I owe much to Dr John Casey of Gonville and Caius College,

Cambridge, who nobly and mercilessly corrected the entire text, as did George Hintlian, historian of the Ottoman period, Secretary of the Armenian Patriarchate 1975–95. Special thanks to Maral Amin Quttieneh for her translation of Arabic materials into English.

Thanks for advice and family history to the following members of the Jerusalem Families interviewed or consulted: Muhammad al-Alami, Nasseredin al-Nashashibi, Jamal al-Nusseibeh, Zaki al-Nusseibeh, Wajeeh al-Nusseibeh, Saida al-Nusseibeh, Mahmoud al-Jarallah, Huda Imam of the Jerusalem Institute, Haifa al-Khalidi, Khader al-Shihabi, Said al-Husseini, Ibrahim al-Husseini, Omar al-Dajani, Aded al-Judeh, Maral Amin Quttieneh, Dr Rajai M. al-Dajani, Ranu al-Dajani, Adeb al-Ansari, Naji Qazaz, Yasser Shuki Toha, owner of my favourite Abu Shukri restaurant; Professor Rashid Khalidi of Columbia University.

Thanks to Shmuel Rabinowitz, Rabbi of the Western Wall and the Holy Sites; to Father Athanasius Macora of the Catholics, Father Samuel Aghoyan, Armenian Superior of the Church of the Holy Sepulchre, Father Afrayem Elorashamily of the Copts, Syriac Bishop Severius, Syriac Father Malke Morat.

I am grateful to Shimon Peres, the President of the State of Israel, and Lord Weidenfeld, both of whom shared memories and ideas; to Princess Firyal of Jordan for her memories of Jordanian Jerusalem; and to Prince and Princess Talal bin Muhammad of Jordan.

Thanks to HRH the Duke of Edinburgh for his advice and for checking the text on his mother Princess Andrew of Greece and his aunt Grand Duchess Ella; and to HRH the Prince of Wales. I am especially grateful for access to their private family archives to the Earl of Morley and to the Hon. and Mrs Nigel Parker for their charming hospitality.

Yitzhak Yaacovy was the man who introduced me to Jerusalem: survivor of Auschwitz, fighter in the 1948 War of Independence, man of letters, young aide in Ben-Gurion's office, he was the long-serving Chairman of the East Jerusalem Development Company under Mayor Teddy Kollek.

The envoys of both the State of Israel and the Palestinian Authority were immensely generous in time, ideas, information and conversation: thanks to Ron Prosor, the Israeli Ambassador to London, Rani Gidor, Sharon Hannoy and Ronit Ben Dor at the Israeli Embassy; Professor Manuel Hassassian, the Palestinian Authority Ambassador in London.

William Dalrymple and Charles Glass were both extremely generous throughout this project with ideas, materials and reading-lists. The Jerusalem Foundation was incredibly helpful: thanks to Ruth Chesin, Nurit Gordon, Alan Freeman and Uri Dromi, Director of Mishkenot Sha'ananim. No one helped as much with academic and other contacts as John Levy of the Friends of Israel Educational Foundation and of the Academic Study Group, and Ray Bruce, veteran television producer.

Thanks to Peter Sebag-Montefiore and his daughter Louise Aspinall for sharing Geoffrey Sebag-Montefiore's papers; to Kate Sebag-Montefiore for research into William Sebag-Montefiore's adventures.

Thanks for help, advice, encouragement to: Amos and Nily Oz, Paul Vester, Chairman of the American Colony Hotel, Rachel Lev, Archivist of the American Colony Archives, Paolo Fetz, General Manager, and Diana Aho of the American Colony Hotel, Munther Fahmi at the American Colony Bookshop, Philip Windsor-Aubrey, David Hare, David Kroyanker, Hannah Kedar, Fred Iseman, Lea Carpenter Brokaw, Danna Harman, Dorothy and David Harman, Caroline Finkel, Lorenza Smith, Professor Benjamin Kedar, Professor Reuven Amitai, Yaov Farhi, Diala Khlat, Ziyad Clot, Youssef Khlat, Rania Joubran, Rebecca Abram, Sir Rocco and Lady Forte, Professor Salim Tamari, Odd Karsten Tveit, Kenneth Rose, Dorrit Moussaieff and her father Shlomo Moussaieff, Sir Ronald and Lady Cohen, David Khalili, Richard Foreman, Ryan Prince, Tom Holland, Tarek Abu Zayyad, Professor Israel Finkelstein, Professor Avigdor Shinan, Professor Yair Zakovitch, Jonathan Foreman, Musa Klebnikoff, Arlene Lascona, Ceri Aston, Rev. Robin Griffith-Jones, the Master of the Temple, Hani Abu Diab, Miriam Ovits, Joana Schliemann, Sarah Helm, Professor Simon Goldhill, Dr Dorothy King, Dr Philip Mansel, Sam Kiley, John Micklethwait, editor of the *Economist*, Gideon Lichfield, Rabbi Mark Winer, Maurice Bitton, the Curator of Bevis Marks Synagogue, Rabbi

Abraham Levy, Professor Harry Zeitlin, Professor F. M. al-Eloischari, Melanie Fall, Rabbi David Goldberg, Melanie Gibson, Annabelle Weidenfeld, Adam, Gill, David and Rachel Montefiore, Dr Gabriel Barkey, Marek Tamm, Ethan Bronner of the *New York Times*, Henry Hemming, William Sieghart. Thanks to Tom Morgan for help with the research.

Thanks to my agent Georgina Capel and my international rights agents Abi Gilbert and Romily Must; to my British publishers Alan Samson, Ion Trewin and Susan Lamb, my brilliant editor Bea Hemming at Weidenfeld; and to Peter James, the master of copy-editors; to my most longstanding publishers: Sonny Mehta at Knopf; in Brazil to Luiz Schwarz and Ana Paula Hisayama at Companhía das Letras; in France, Mireille Paoloni at Calmann Lévy; in Germany, Peter Sillem at Fischer; in Israel, Ziv Lewis at Kinneret; in Holland, Henk ter Borg, at Nieuw Amsterdam; in Norway, Ida Bernsten and Gerd Johnsen at Cappelens; in Poland, Jolanta Woloszanska at Magnum; in Portugal, Alexandra Louro at Alêtheia Editores; in Spain, Carmen Esteban at Crítica; in Estonia, Krista Kaer of Varrak; and in Sweden, Per Faustino and Stefan Hilding at Norstedts.

My parents Dr Stephen and April Sebag-Montefiore have been superb editors of all my books. Above all I want to thank my wife Santa, who has been the patient, encouraging and loving sultana of this long process. Santa and my children Lily and Sasha have, like me, undoubtedly suffered the full effects of the Jerusalem Syndrome. They may never recover, but they probably know more about the Rock, the Wall and the Sepulchre than many a priest, rabbi or mullah.

NOTES ON NAMES,
TRANSLITERATIONS AND TITLES

This book inevitably contains a challenging diversity of names, languages and questions of transliteration. It is for general readers, so my policy is to use the most accessible and familiar names. I apologize to purists who are offended by these decisions.

In the Judaean period, I generally use the Greek not the Latin or Hebrew names for the Hasmonean kings – Aristobulos, for example. With minor characters such as Herod's brother-in-law I use his Hebrew name Jonathan instead of his Greek one, Aristobulos, to avoid confusion with the many other Aristobuloses. With household names, I use the familiar – Herod (not Herodes), Pompey, Mark Antony, Tamurlane, Saladin. For Persian names, if well known such as Cyrus, I use that version. The Maccabean family reigned as the Hasmonean dynasty, but I call them Maccabean throughout for the sake of clarity.

In the Arab period, the challenges are greater. I do not pretend to be consistent. I generally use familiar English forms – such as Damascus rather than Dimashq. I have dropped the Arabic article 'al-' before persons, groups and towns but kept it on the whole within compound names and for the first mention of names in the text and the notes and not thereafter. I do not use diacritical marks. Most of the Abbasid and Fatamid caliphs and Ayyubid sultans adopted a regnant name, a laqab, such as al-Mansur. Purely to ease reading, I drop in all cases the definite article. I use 'ibn' instead of 'bin' except in well-known names. In names such as Abu Sufyan, I do not use the Arabic genitive (which would give, for example, Muawiya ibn Abi Sufyan), again for facility. I generally call the Ayyubids the 'house of Saladin'.

There is no consistency in the Western historical use of Arab names – for example, the Abbasids are known by their ruling names apart from Harun al-Rashid because he is famous thanks to the Arabian Nights stories. All historians use the name Saladin for the twelfth-century sultan yet call his brother al-Adil. Saladin's birth name was Yusuf ibn Ayyub; his brother was Abu Bakr ibn Ayyub. Both men adopted honorific names Salah al-Din and Saif al-Din; and both later used regnant names al-Nasir (the Victor) for Saladin and al-Adil (the Just) for his brother. For ease, I use Saladin and Safedin respectively, partly to avoid confusion of Ayyubid names such as al-Adil, al-Aziz, al-Afdal, and partly to highlight the con-nection with Saladin.

During the Mamluk period, historians usually use the name Baibars, rather than using his regnant name al-Zahir, but then employ regnant names for most of the others – except for al-Nasir Muhammad where they use both. I follow this inconsistent tradition.

During the Ottoman period, in less well-known names, I try to use Turkish, not Arabic, spellings. I have simply chosen the most recognizable version: Jemal Pasha is Çemal in Turkish and often transliterated as Djemal. I use Mehmet Ali instead of Muhammad Ali.

In modern times, I call Hussein ibn Ali the Sherif of Mecca or King Hussein of the Hejaz; I call his sons Prince or Amir (until they too become kings) Faisal and Abdullah instead of Faisal and Abdullah ibn Hussein. I call them Sherifians in the early period and Hashemites later. I call the first king of Saudi Arabia Abdul Aziz al-Saud but more often use the Westernized version, Ibn Saud. Bertha Spafford married Frederick Vester: for consistency I call her Spafford throughout.

Canaan, Judah, Judaea, Israel, Palaestina, Bilad al-Shams, Pal-estine, Greater Syria, Coele Syria, the Holy Land, are just some of the names used to describe the country, with varying borders. There are said to be seventy names for Jerusalem. Within the city, the House of God, the Holy House, the Temple, all refer to the Jewish Temple. The Dome, the Qubbet al-Sakhra, Temple of the Lord, Templum Domini refer to the Dome of the Rock; the Aqsa is the

Temple of Solomon. Har HaBayit is the Hebrew and Haram al-Sharif is the Arabic for the Temple Mount, which I also call the sacred esplanade. The Sanctuary refers either to the Holy of Holies or later to the Temple Mount, which Muslims call the Noble Sanctuary (Haram); for Muslims, the Two Sanctuaries refer to Jerusalem and Hebron, another Herodian building: the tomb of Abraham and the patriarchs. The Anastasis, the Church, the Sepulchre and Deir Sultan refer to the Church of the Holy Sepulchre. The Rock is Sakhra in Arabic; the Foundation Stone is Even HaShtiyah in Hebrew; the Holy of Holies is Kodesh haKodeshim. The Wall, the Kotel, the Western and Wailing Wall and al-Buraq wall refer to the Jewish holy site. The Citadel and the Tower of David refer to the Herodian stronghold close to the Jaffa Gate. The Virgin's Tomb and St Mary of Jehoshaphat are the same place. The Valley of Jehoshaphat is the Kidron Valley. David's Tomb, Nabi Daoud, the Cenacle and Coenaculum describe the shrine on Mount Zion. Each of the gates has so many names which change so frequently that to list them would be worthless. Every street has at least three names: the Old City's main street is El Wad in Arabic; Ha-Gai in Hebrew and the Valley in English.

Constantinople and Byzantium refer to Eastern Rome and its empire; after 1453, I refer to the city as Istanbul. Catholics and Latins are used interchangeably; Orthodox and Greeks also. Iran and Persia are used interchangeably. I use Iraq instead of Mesopotamia for accessibility.

On titles: the Roman emperors were the *princeps* in Latin and later *imperator*; Byzantine emperors later became *basileos* in Greek. In early Islam, Muhammad's successors were variously Commanders of the Faithful and caliph. Sultan, padishah and caliph are all titles of the Ottoman rulers; in Germany, Kaiser and emperor and in Russia, tsar and emperor are used interchangeably.

PROLOGUE

On 8th of the Jewish month of Ab, in late July AD 70, Titus, the Roman Emperor Vespasian's son who was in command of the four-month siege of Jerusalem, ordered his entire army to prepare to storm the Temple at dawn. The next day happened to be the very day on which Babylonians had destroyed Jerusalem over 500 years before. Now, Titus commanded an army of four legions – a total of 60,000 Roman legionaries and local auxiliaries who were eager to deliver the final blow to the defiant but broken city. Within the walls, perhaps half a million starving Jews survived in diabolical conditions: some were fanatical religious zealots, some were freebooting bandits, but most were innocent families with no escape from this magnificent death-trap. There were many Jews living outside Judaea – they were to be found throughout the Mediterranean and Near East – and this final desperate struggle would decide not only the fate of the city and her inhabitants, but also the future of Judaism and the small Jewish cult of Christianity – and even, looking forward across six centuries, the shape of Islam.

The Romans had built ramps up against the walls of the Temple. But their assaults had failed. Earlier that day, Titus told his generals that his efforts to preserve this 'foreign temple' were costing him too many soldiers and he ordered the Temple gates set alight. The silver of the gates melted and spread the fire to the wooden doorways and windows, thence to the wooden fittings in the passageways of the Temple itself. Titus ordered the fire to be quenched. The Romans, he declared, should 'not avenge themselves on inanimate objects instead of men'. Then he retired for the night into his headquarters in the half-ruined Tower of Antonia overlooking the resplendent Temple complex.

Around the walls, there were gruesome scenes that must have resembled hell on earth. Thousands of bodies putrefied in the sun. The stench was unbearable. Packs of dogs and jackals feasted on human flesh. In the preceding months, Titus had ordered all prisoners or defectors to be crucified. Five hundred Jews were crucified each day. The Mount of Olives and the craggy hills around the city were so crowded with crucifixes that there was scarcely room for any more, nor trees to make them. Titus' soldiers amused themselves by nailing their victims splayed and spread-eagled in absurd positions. So desperate were many Jerusalemites to escape the city that, as they left, they swallowed their coins, to conceal their treasure, which they hoped to retrieve when they were safely clear of the Romans. They emerged 'puffed up with famine and swelled like men with dropsy', but if they ate they 'burst asunder'. As their bellies exploded, the soldiers discovered their reeking intestinal treasure troves, so they started to gut all prisoners, eviscerating them and searching their intestines while they were still alive. But Titus was appalled and tried to ban these anatomical plunderings. To no avail: Titus' Syrian auxiliaries, who hated and were hated by the Jews with all the malice of neighbours, relished these macabre games. The cruelties inflicted by the Romans and the rebels within the walls compare with some of the worst atrocities of the twentieth century.

The war had begun when the ineptitude and greed of the Roman governors had driven even the Judaean aristocracy, Rome's own Jewish allies, to make common cause with a popular religious revolt. The rebels were a mixture of religious Jews and opportunistic brigands who had exploited the decline of the emperor, Nero, and the chaos that followed his suicide, to expel the Romans and re-establish an independent Jewish state, based around the Temple. But the Jewish revolution immediately started to consume itself in bloody purges and gang-warfare.

Three Roman emperors followed Nero in rapid and chaotic succession. By the time Vespasian emerged as emperor and despatched Titus to take Jerusalem, the city was divided between three warlords at war with each other. The Jewish warlords had first fought pitched battles in the Temple courts, which ran with blood, and then plundered the city. Their fighters worked their way through the richer neighbourhoods, ransacking the houses, killing the men and abusing the women – 'it was sport to them'. Crazed by their power and the thrill of the hunt, probably intoxicated with looted wine, they 'indulged themselves in feminine wantonness, decked their hair and put on women's garments and besmeared themselves with ointments and had paints under their eyes'. These provincial cut-throats, swaggering in 'finely dyed cloaks', killed anyone in their path. In their ingenious depravity, they 'invented unlawful pleasures'. Jerusalem, given over to 'intolerable uncleanness', became 'a brothel' and torture-chamber – and yet remained a shrine.

Somehow the Temple continued to function. Back in April, pilgrims had arrived for Passover just before the Romans closed in on the city. The population was usually in the high tens of thousands, but the Romans had now trapped the pilgrims and many refugees from the war, so there were hundreds of thousands of people in the city. Only as Titus encircled the walls did the rebel chieftains halt their in-fighting to unite their 21,000 warriors and face the Romans together.

The city that Titus saw for the first time from Mount Scopus, named after the Greek *skopeo* meaning 'look at', was, in Pliny's words, 'by far the most celebrated city of the East', an opulent, thriving metropolis built around one of the greatest temples of the ancient world, itself an exquisite work of art on an immense scale. Jerusalem had already existed for thousands of years but this many-walled and towered city, astride two mountains amid the barren crags of Judaea, had never been as populous or as awesome as it was in the first century AD: indeed Jerusalem would not be so great again until the twentieth century. This was the achievement of Herod the Great, the brilliant, psychotic Judaean king whose palaces and fortresses were built on so monumental a scale and were so luxurious in their decoration that the Jewish historian Josephus says that they 'exceed all my ability to describe them'.

The Temple itself overshadowed all else in its numinous glory. 'At the first rising of the sun', its gleaming courts and gilded gates 'reflected back a very fiery splendour and made those who forced themselves to look upon it to turn their eyes away'. When strangers – such as Titus and his legionaries – saw this Temple for the first time, it appeared 'like a mountain covered with snow'. Pious Jews knew that at the centre of the courts of this city-within-a-city atop Mount Moriah was a tiny room of superlative holiness that contained virtually nothing at all. This space was the focus of Jewish sanctity: the Holy of Holies, the dwelling-place of God Himself.

Herod's Temple was a shrine but it was also a near-impregnable fortress within the walled city. The Jews, encouraged by Roman weakness in the Year of the Four Emperors and aided by Jerusalem's precipitous heights, her fortifications and the labyrinthine Temple itself, had confronted Titus with overweening confidence. After all, they had defied Rome for almost five years. However, Titus possessed the authority, the ambition, the resources and the talent necessary for the task. He set about reducing Jerusalem with systematic efficiency and overwhelming force. Ballistae stones, probably fired by Titus, have been found in the tunnels beside the Temple's western wall, testament to the intensity of Roman bombardment. The Jews fought for every inch with almost suicidal abandon. Yet Titus, commanding the full arsenal of siege engines, catapults and the ingenuity of Roman engineering, overcame the first wall within fifteen days. He led a thousand legionaries into the maze of Jerusalem's markets and stormed the second wall. But the Jews sortied out and retook it. The wall had to be stormed all over again. Titus next tried to overawe the city with a parade of his army – cuirasses, helmets, blades flashing, flags fluttering, eagles glinting, 'horses richly caparisoned'. Thousands of Jerusalemites gathered on the battlements to gawp at this show, admiring 'the beauty of their armour and admirable order of the men'. The Jews remained defiant, or too afraid of their warlords to disobey their orders: no surrender.

Finally, Titus decided to encircle and seal the entire city by building a wall of circumvallation. In late June, the Romans stormed the hulking Antonia Fortress that commanded the Temple itself and then razed it, except for one tower where Titus set up his command-post.

By mid-summer, as the blistered and jagged hills sprouted forests of fly-blown crucified cadavers, the city within was tormented by a sense of impending doom, intransigent fanaticism, whimsical sadism, and searing hunger. Armed gangs prowled for food. Children grabbed the morsels from their fathers' hands; mothers stole the tidbits of their own babies. Locked doors suggested hidden provisions and the warriors broke in, driving stakes up their victims' rectums to force them to reveal their caches of grain. If they found nothing, they were even more 'barbarously cruel' as if they had been 'defrauded'. Even though the fighters themselves still had food, they killed and tortured out of habit 'to keep their madness in exercise'. Jerusalem was riven by witch-hunts as people denounced each other as hoarders and traitors. No other city, reflected the eyewitness Josephus, 'did ever allow such miseries, nor did any age ever breed a generation more fruitful in wickedness than this was, since the beginning of the world'.

The young wandered the streets 'like shadows, all swollen with famine, and fell down dead, wherever their misery seized them'. People died trying to bury their families while others were buried carelessly, still breathing. Famine devoured whole families in their homes. Jerusalemites saw their loved ones die 'with dry eyes and open mouths. A deep silence and a kind of deadly night seized the city' – yet those who perished did so 'with their eyes fixed on the Temple'. The streets were heaped with dead bodies. Soon, despite Jewish law, no one buried the dead any more in this grandiose charnelhouse. Perhaps Jesus Christ had foreseen this when he predicted the coming Apocalypse, saying 'Let the dead bury their dead.' Sometimes the rebels just heaved bodies over the walls. The Romans left them to rot in putrescent piles. Yet the rebels were still fighting.

Titus himself, an unsqueamish Roman soldier, who had killed twelve Jews with his own crossbow in his first skirmish, was horrified and amazed: he could only groan to the gods that this was not his doing. 'The darling and delight of the human race', he was known for his generosity. 'Friends, I've lost a day,' he would say when he had not found time to give presents to his comrades. Sturdy and bluff with a cleft chin, generous mouth and round face, Titus was proving to be a gifted commander and a popular son of the new emperor Vespasian: their unproven dynasty depended on Titus' victory over the Jewish rebels.

Titus' entourage was filled with Jewish renegades including three Jerusalemites – a historian, a king and (it seems) a double-queen who was sharing the Caesar's bed. The historian was Titus' adviser Josephus, a rebel Jewish commander who had defected to the Romans and who is the sole source for this account. The king was Herod Agrippa II, a very Roman Jew, brought up at the court of the Emperor Claudius; he had been the supervisor of the Jewish Temple, built by his great-grandfather Herod the Great, and often resided in his Jerusalem palace, even though he ruled disparate territories across the north of modern Israel, Syria and Lebanon.

The king was almost certainly accompanied by his sister, Berenice, daughter of a Jewish monarch, and twice a queen by marriage, who had recently become Titus' mistress. Her Roman enemies later denounced her as 'the Jewish Cleopatra'. She was around forty but 'she was in her best years and at the height of her beauty', noted Josephus. At the start of the rebellion, she and her brother, who lived together (incestuously, claimed their enemies), had attempted to face down the rebels in a last appeal to reason. Now these three Jews helplessly watched the 'death-agony of a famous city' – Berenice did so from the bed of its destroyer.

Prisoners and defectors brought news from within the city that especially upset Josephus, whose own parents were trapped inside. Even the fighters started to run out of food, so they too probed and dissected the quick and the dead, for gold, for crumbs, for mere seeds, 'stumbling and staggering like mad dogs'. They ate cow dung, leather, girdles, shoes and old hay. A rich woman named Mary, having lost all her money and food, became so demented that she killed her own son and roasted him, eating half and keeping the rest for later. The delicious aroma crept across the city. The rebels savoured it, sought it and smashed into the house, but even those practised hatchetmen, on seeing the child's half-eaten body, 'went out trembling'.

Spymania and paranoia ruled Jerusalem the Holy – as the Jewish coins called her. Raving charlatans and preaching hierophants haunted the streets, promising deliverance and salvation. Jerusalem was, Josephus observed, 'like a wild beast gone mad which, for want of food, fell now upon eating its own flesh'.

That night of the 8th of Ab, when Titus had retired to rest, his legionaries tried to douse the fire spread by the molten silver, as he had ordered. But the rebels attacked the fire-fighting legionaries. The Romans fought back and pushed the Jews into the Temple itself. One legionary, seized 'with a divine fury', grabbed some burning materials and, lifted up by another soldier, lit the curtains and frame of 'a golden window', which was linked to the rooms around the actual Temple. By morning, the fire had spread to the very heart of holiness. The Jews, seeing the flames licking the Holy of Holies and threatening to destroy it, 'made a great clamour and ran to prevent it'. But it was too late. They barricaded themselves in the Inner Court then watched with aghast silence.

Just a few yards away, among the ruins of the Antonia Fortress, Titus was awakened; he jumped up and 'ran towards the Holy House to put a stop to the fire'. His entourage including Josephus, and probably King Agrippa and Berenice, followed, and after them ran thousands of Roman soldiers – all 'in great astonishment'. The fighting was frenzied. Josephus claims that Titus again ordered the fire extinguished, but this Roman collaborator had good reasons to excuse his patron. Nonetheless, everyone was shouting, the fire was racing and the Roman soldiers knew that, by the laws of warfare, a city that had resisted so obstinately expected to be sacked.

They pretended not to hear Titus and even shouted ahead to their comrades to toss in more firebrands. The legionaries were so impetuous that many were crushed or burned to death in the stampede of their bloodlust and hunger for gold, plundering so much that the price would soon drop across the East. Titus, unable to stop the fire and surely relieved at the prospect of final victory, proceeded through the burning Temple until he came to the Holy of Holies. Even the high priest was allowed to enter there only once a year. No foreigner had tainted its purity since the Roman soldier-statesman Pompey in 63 BC. But Titus looked inside 'and saw it and its contents which he found to be far superior', wrote Josephus, indeed 'not inferior to what we ourselves boasted of it'. Now he ordered the centurions to beat the soldiers spreading the fire, but 'their passions were too strong.' As the inferno rose around the Holy of Holies, Titus was pulled to safety by his aides – 'and no one forbade them to set fire to it' any more.

The fighting raged among the flames: dazed, starving Jerusalemites wandered lost and distressed through the burning portals. Thousands of civilians and rebels mustered on the steps of the altar, waiting to fight to the last or just die hopelessly. All had their throats cut by the exhilarated Romans as though it were a mass human sacrifice, until 'around the altar lay dead bodies heaped one upon another' with the blood running down the steps. Ten thousand Jews died in the burning Temple.

The cracking of vast stones and wooden beams made a sound like thunder. Josephus watched the death of the Temple:

> The roar of the flames streaming far and wide mingled with the groans of the falling victims and owing to the height of the hill and the mass of the burning pile, one would have thought the whole city was ablaze. And then the din – nothing more deafening or appalling could be conceived than that. There were the war cries of the Roman legions sweeping onward, the howls of the rebels encircled by fire and swords, the rush of the people who, cut off above, fled panic-stricken only to fall into the arms of the foe, and their shrieks as they met their fate, blended with lamentations and wailing [of those in the city]. Transjordan and the surrounding mountains contributed their echoes, deepening the din. You would have thought the Temple hill was boiling over from its base, being everywhere one mass of flame.

Mount Moriah, one of the two mountains of Jerusalem, where King David had placed the Ark of the Covenant and where his son

Solomon had built the first Temple, was 'seething hot full of fire on every part of it', while inside, dead bodies covered the floors. But the soldiers trampled on the corpses in their triumph. The priests fought back and some threw themselves into the blaze. Now the rampaging Romans, seeing that the inner Temple was destroyed, grabbed the gold and furniture, carrying out their swag, before they set fire to the rest of the complex.

As the Inner Courtyard burned, and the next day dawned, the surviving rebels broke out through the Roman lines into the labyrinthine Outer Courtyards, some escaping into the city. The Romans counter-attacked with cavalry, clearing the insurgents and then burning the Temple's treasury chambers, which were filled with riches drawn from the Temple tax paid by all Jews, from Alexandria to Babylon. They found there 6,000 women and children huddled together in apocalyptic expectation. A 'false prophet' had earlier proclaimed that they could anticipate the 'miraculous signs of their deliverance' in the Temple. The legionaries simply set the passageways alight, burning all these people alive.

The Romans carried their eagles on to the Holy Mountain, sacrificed to their gods, and hailed Titus as their *imperator* – commander-in-chief. Priests were still hiding out around the Holy of Holies. Two plunged into the flames, and one succeeded in bringing out the treasures of the Temple – the robes of the high priest, the two golden candelabra and heaps of cinnamon and cassia, spices that were burned every day in the Sanctuary. When the rest surrendered, Titus executed them as 'it was fitting for priests to perish with their Temple'.

Jerusalem was – and still is – a city of tunnels. Now the rebels disappeared underground while retaining control of the Citadel and the Upper City to the west. It took Titus another month to conquer the rest of Jerusalem. When it fell, the Romans and their Syrian and Greek auxiliaries 'poured into the alleys. Sword in hand; they massacred indiscriminately all whom they met and burned the houses with all who had taken refuge within.' At night when the killing stopped, 'the fire gained mastery of the streets'.

Titus parleyed with the two Jewish warlords across the bridge that spanned the valley between the Temple and the city, offering them their lives in return for surrender. But still they refused. He ordered the plundering and burning of the Lower City, in which virtually every house was filled with dead bodies. When the Jerusalemite warlords retreated to Herod's Palace and Citadel, Titus built ramparts to undermine them and on 7th of Elul, in mid-August, the Romans stormed the fortifications. The insurgents fought on in the tunnels until one of their leaders John of Gishala surrendered (he was spared, though he faced lifelong imprisonment). The other chieftain Simon ben Giora emerged in a white robe out of a tunnel under the Temple, and was assigned a starring role in Titus' Triumph, the celebration of the victory in Rome.

In the mayhem and the methodical destruction afterwards, a world vanished, leaving a few moments frozen in time. The Romans butchered the old and the infirm: the skeletal hand of a woman found on the doorstep of her burnt house reveals the panic and terror; the ashes of the mansions in the Jewish Quarter tell of the inferno. Two hundred bronze coins have been found in a shop on the street that ran under the monumental staircase into the Temple, a secret stash probably hidden in the last hours of the fall of the city. Soon even the Romans wearied of slaughter. The Jerusalemites were herded into concentration camps set up in the Women's Court of the Temple itself where they were filtered: fighters were killed; the strong were sent to work in the Egyptian mines; the young and handsome were sold as slaves, chosen to be killed fighting lions in the circus or to be displayed in the Triumph.

Josephus searched through the pitiful prisoners in the Temple courtyards, finding his brother and fifty friends whom Titus allowed him to liberate. His parents had presumably died. But he noticed three of his friends among the crucified. 'I was cut to the heart and told Titus,' who ordered them to be taken down and cared for by doctors. Only one survived.

Titus decided, like Nebuchadnezzar, to eradicate Jerusalem, a decision which Josephus blamed on the rebels: 'The rebellion destroyed the city and the Romans destroyed the rebellion.' The toppling of Herod the Great's most awesome monument, the Temple, must have been an engineering challenge. The giant ashlars of the Royal Portico crashed down on to the new pavements below and there they were found nearly 2,000 years later in a colossal heap, just as they had fallen, concealed beneath centuries of debris. The wreckage was dumped into the valley next to the Temple where it started to fill up the ravine, now almost invisible, between the Temple Mount and the Upper City. But the holding walls of the Temple Mount, including today's Western Wall, survived. The spolia, the fallen stones, of Herod's Temple and city are everywhere in Jerusalem, used and reused by all Jerusalem's conquerors and builders, from the Romans to the Arabs, from the Crusaders to the Ottomans, for over a thousand years afterwards.

No one knows how many people died in Jerusalem, and ancient historians are always reckless with numbers. Tacitus says there were 600,000 in the besieged city, while Josephus claims over a million. Whatever the true figure, it was vast, and all of these people died of starvation, were killed or were sold into slavery.

Titus embarked on a macabre victory tour. His mistress Berenice and her brother the king hosted him in their capital Caesarea Philippi, in today's Golan Heights. There he watched thousands of Jewish prisoners fight each other – and wild animals – to the death. A few days later, he saw another 2,500 killed in the circus at Caesarea Maritima and yet more were playfully slaughtered in Beirut before Titus returned to Rome to celebrate his Triumph.

The legions 'entirely demolished the rest of the city, and overthrew its walls'. Titus left only the towers of Herod's Citadel 'as a monument of his good fortune'. There the Tenth Legion made its headquarters. 'This was the end which Jerusalem came to', wrote Josephus, 'a city otherwise of great magnificence and of mighty fame among all mankind'.

Jerusalem had been totally destroyed six centuries earlier by Nebuchadnezzar, King of Babylon. Within fifty years of that first destruction, the Temple was rebuilt and the Jews returned. But this time, after AD 70, the Temple was never rebuilt – and, except for a few brief interludes, the Jews would not rule Jerusalem again for nearly 2,000 years. Yet within the ashes of this calamity lay the seeds not only of modern Judaism but also of Jerusalem's sanctity for Christianity and Islam.

Early during the siege, according to much later rabbinical legend, Yohanan ben Zakkai, a respected rabbi, had ordered his pupils to carry him out of the doomed city in a coffin, a metaphor for the foundation of a new Judaism no longer based on the sacrificial cult in the Temple.

The Jews, who continued to live in the countryside of Judaea and Galilee, as well as in large communities across the Roman and Persian empires, mourned the loss of Jerusalem and revered the city ever after. The Bible and the oral traditions replaced the Temple, but it was said that Providence waited for three and a half years on the Mount of Olives to see if the Temple would be restored – before rising to heaven. The destruction was also decisive for the Christians.

The small Christian community of Jerusalem, led by Simon, Jesus' cousin, had escaped from the city before the Romans closed in. Even though there were many non-Jewish Christians living around the Roman world, these Jerusalemites remained a Jewish sect praying at the Temple. But now the Temple had been destroyed, the Christians believed that the Jews had lost the favour of God: the followers of Jesus separated for ever from the mother faith, claiming to be the rightful heirs to the Jewish heritage. The Christians envisaged a new, celestial Jerusalem, not a shattered Jewish city. The earliest Gospels, probably written just after the destruction, recounted how Jesus had foreseen the siege of the city: 'ye shall see Jerusalem compassed with armies'; and the demolition of the Temple: 'Not one stone shall remain.' The ruined Sanctuary and the downfall of the Jews were proof of the new revelation. In the 620s, when Muhammad founded his new religion, he first adopted Jewish traditions, praying towards Jerusalem and revering the Jewish prophets, because for him too the destruction of the Temple proved that God had withdrawn his blessing from Jews and bestowed it on Islam.

It is ironic that the decision of Titus to destroy Jerusalem helped

make the city the very template of holiness for the other two Peoples
of the Book. From the very beginning, Jerusalem's sanctity did not
just evolve but was promoted by the decisions of a handful of men.
Around 1000 BC, a thousand years before Titus, the first of these
men captured Jerusalem: King David.

PART ONE
JUDAISM

The city of the Lord, the Zion of the Holy One of Israel … Awake, awake; put on thy strength, O Zion; put on thy beautiful garments, O Jerusalem, the holy city.

Isaiah 60.14, 52.1

My native city is Jerusalem, in which is situated the sacred shrine of the most high God. The holy city is the mother city not of one country, Judaea, but of most of the other neighbouring lands, as well as lands far away, most of Asia, [and] similarly Europe, to say nothing of the countries beyond the Euphrates.

Herod Agrippa I, King of Judaea, quoted in Philo,
De Specialibus Legibus

He who has not seen Jerusalem in her splendour has never seen a desirable city in his life. He who has not seen the Temple in its full construction has never seen a glorious building in his life.

Babylonian Talmud, Tractate of the Tabernacle

If I forget thee, O Jerusalem, let my right hand forget her cunning. If I do not remember thee, let my tongue cleave to the roof of my mouth; if I prefer not Jerusalem above my chief joy.

Psalm 137.5–6

Jerusalem is the most famous city of the East.

Pliny the Elder, Natural History, 5.70

I

THE WORLD OF DAVID

THE FIRST KING: CANAANITES

When David captured the citadel of Zion, Jerusalem was already ancient. But it was scarcely a city, just a small mountain stronghold in a land that would have many names – Canaan, Judah, Judaea, Israel, Palestine, the Holy Land to Christians, the Promised Land to Jews. This territory, just 100 by 150 miles, lies between the south-eastern corner of the Mediterranean and the River Jordan. Its lush coastal plain offered the best path for invaders and traders between Egypt and the empires of the east. Yet the isolated and remote town of Jerusalem, 30 miles from the nearest coast, far from any trade routes, stood high amid the golden-rocked desolation of the cliffs, gorges and scree of the Judaean hills, exposed to freezing, sometimes even snowy, winters and to witheringly hot summers. Nonetheless, there was security atop these forbidding hills; and there was a spring in the valley beneath, just enough to support a town.

The romantic image of David's city is far more vivid than any facts of verifiable history. In the fog of Jerusalem's pre-history, fragments of pottery, ghostly rock-cut tombs, sections of wall, inscriptions in the palaces of faraway kings and the holy literature of the Bible can provide only fleeting glints of human life in an invincible gloom, separated by hundreds of years. The sporadic clues that emerge cast a flickering light on some random moment of a vanished civilization, followed by centuries of life of which we know nothing – until the next spark illuminates another image. Only the springs, mountains and valleys remain the same, and even they have been redirected, resculpted, refilled by millennia of weather, debris and human endeavour. This much or little is certain: by the time of King David, holiness, security and nature had combined to make Jerusalem an ancient fastness that was regarded as impregnable.

People had lived there as early as 5000 BC. In the early Bronze Age, around 3200 BC, when the mother of cities, Uruk, in what became Iraq, was already home to 40,000 citizens, and nearby Jericho was a fortified town, people buried their dead in tombs in Jerusalem's hills, and started to build small square houses in what was probably a walled village on a hill above a spring. This village was then abandoned for many years. Jerusalem scarcely existed while the Egyptian pharaohs of the Old Kingdom reached the zenith of their pyramid building and completed the Great Sphinx. Then in the 1900s BC, at a time when Minoan civilization flourished in Crete, King Hammurabi was about to compile his legal code in Babylon and Britons worshipped at Stonehenge, some pottery, sherds of which were discovered near Luxor in Egypt, mentions a town named Ursalim, a version of Salem or Shalem, god of the evening star. The name may mean 'Salem has founded'.*

Back in Jerusalem, a settlement had developed around the Gihon Spring: the Canaanite inhabitants cut a channel through the rock leading to a pool within the walls of their citadel. A fortified underground passageway protected their access to the water. The latest archaeological digs on the site reveal that they guarded the spring with a tower and a massive wall, 23 feet thick, using stones weighing 3 tons. The tower could also have served as a temple celebrating the cosmic sanctity of the spring. In other parts of Canaan, priestly kings built fortified tower-temples. Further up the hill, remnants of a city wall have been found, the earliest in Jerusalem. The Canaanites turn out to have been builders on a scale more impressive than

---

* The Egyptian Pharaohs aspired to rule Canaan at this time but it is not clear whether they actually did. They may have used these pottery symbols to curse the defiant rulers of their enemies or to express their aspirations. The theories about these fragments have changed several times, showing how archaeology is as much interpretative as scientific. It was long believed that the Egyptians smashed these vases or figures to curse or execrate the places named on them – hence they are known as the Execration texts.

anyone in Jerusalem until Herod the Great almost 2,000 years later.

The Jerusalemites became subjects of Egypt which had conquered Palestine in 1458 BC. Egyptian garrisons guarded nearby Jaffa and Gaza. In 1350 BC, the frightened King of Jerusalem begged his overlord, Akhenaten, the pharaoh of the New Kingdom of Egypt, to send him help – even 'fifty archers' – to defend his small kingdom from the aggression of neighbouring kings and bands of marauding outlaws. King Abdi-Hepa called his citadel 'the capital of the Land of Jerusalem of which the name is Beit Shulmani', the House of Well-being. Perhaps the word Shulman is the origin of the 'Shalem' in the name of the city.

Abdi-Hepa was a paltry potentate in a world dominated by the Egyptians to the south, by the Hittites to the north (in today's Turkey) and to the north-west by the Mycenean Greeks who would fight the Trojan War. The king's first name is west Semitic – the Semites being the many Middle East peoples and languages, supposedly descended from Shem, son of Noah. Therefore Abdi-Hepa could have hailed from anywhere in the north-eastern Mediterranean. His appeals, found in the pharaoh's archive, are panic-stricken and sycophantic, the first known words of a Jerusalemite:*

At the feet of the King I have fallen 7 and 7 times. Here is the deed that Milkily and Shuwardatu have done against the land – they have led the troops of Gezer . . . against the law of the King . . . The land of the King has gone over to the Habiru [marauding outlaws]. And now a town belonging to Jerusalem has gone over to the men of Qiltu. May the King listen to Abdi-Hepa your servant and send archers.

* These are some of the 380 letters, written in Babylonian on baked clay tablets, by local chieftains to the heretic pharaoh Amenhotep IV (1352–1336), who instituted the worship of the sun, instead of the traditional pantheon of numerous Egyptian gods: he changed his name to Akhenaten. The royal archive of his foreign ministry, the House of Correspondence of Pharaoh, was discovered in 1887 at his new capital Akhetaten, now El-Amarna, south of Cairo. One theory suggests that the Habiru were the early Hebrews/Israelites, yet the word actually appears all over the Middle East at this time to describe these marauders – the word simply means 'vagrant' in Babylonian. It is possible that the Hebrews descended from a small group of Habiru.

We hear no more, but whatever happened to this beleaguered king, just over a century later the Jerusalemites built steep terraced structures above the Gihon Spring on the Ophel hill that survive today, the foundation of a citadel or temple of Salem. These powerful walls, towers and terraces were part of the Canaanite citadel known as Zion that David would capture. Some time during the thirteenth century BC, a people called the Jebusites occupied Jerusalem. But now the old Mediterranean world was being torn apart by waves of so-called Sea Peoples who came from the Aegean.

In this storm of raids and migrations, the empires receded. The Hittites fell, Mycenae was mysteriously destroyed, Egypt was shaken – and a people called the Hebrews made their first appearance.

ABRAHAM IN JERUSALEM: ISRAELITES

This new 'Dark Age', which lasted three centuries, allowed the Hebrews, also known as Israelites, an obscure people who worshipped one God, to settle and build a kingdom in the narrow land of Canaan. Their progress is illuminated by the stories about the creation of the world, their origins and their relationship with their God. They passed down these traditions which were then recorded in sacred Hebrew texts, later collated into the Five Books of Moses, the Pentateuch, the first section of the Jewish scriptures, the Tanakh. The Bible became the book of books, but it is not one document. It is a mystical library of interwoven texts by unknown authors who wrote and edited at different times with widely divergent aims.

This sacred work of so many epochs and so many hands contains some facts of provable history, some stories of unprovable myth, some poetry of soaring beauty, and many passages of unintelligible, perhaps coded, perhaps simply mistranslated, mystery. Most of it is written not to recount events but to promote a higher truth – the relationship of one people and their God. To the believer, the Bible is simply the fruit of divine revelation. To the historian, this is a contradictory, unreliable, repetitive,* yet invaluable source, often the only one available to us – and it is also, effectively, the first and paramount biography of Jerusalem.

The founding patriarch of the Hebrews was, according to Genesis the first book of the Bible, Abram – who is portrayed as travelling from Ur (in today's Iraq) to settle in Hebron. This was in Canaan, the land promised to him by God, who renamed him 'Father of Peoples' – Abraham. On his travels, Abraham was welcomed by Melchizedek, the priest-king of Salem in the name of El-Elyon, the Most High God. This, the city's first mention in the Bible, suggests that Jerusalem was already a Canaanite shrine ruled by priest-kings. Later God tested Abraham by ordering him to sacrifice his son Isaac on a mountain in 'the land of Moriah' – identified as Mount Moriah, the Temple Mount of Jerusalem.

Abraham's roguish grandson Jacob used trickery to clinch his inheritance, but redeemed himself in a wrestling match with a stranger who turned out to be God, hence his new name, Israel – He who Strives with God. This was the appropriate birth of the Jewish people, whose relationship with God was to be so passionate and tormented. Israel was the father of the founders of the twelve tribes who emigrated to Egypt. There are so many contradictions in the stories of these so-called Patriarchs that they are impossible to date historically.

After 430 years, the Book of Exodus portrays the Israelites, repressed as slaves building the pharaoh's cities, miraculously escaping Egypt with God's help (still celebrated by Jews in the festival of Passover), led by a Hebrew prince named Moses. As they wandered through Sinai, God granted Moses the Ten Commandments. If the Israelites lived and worshipped according to these rules, God promised them the land of Canaan. When Moses sought the nature of this God, asking 'What is thy name?', he received the majestically

---

* The Creation appears twice in Genesis 1.1–2.3 and 2.4–25. There are two genealogies of Adam, two flood stories, two captures of Jerusalem, two stories in which God changes Jacob's name to Israel. There are many anachronisms – for example, the presence of Philistines and Arameans in Genesis when they had not yet arrived in Canaan. Camels as beasts of burden appear too early. Scholars believe the early Biblical books were written by separate groups of writers, one who emphasized El, the Canaanite god, and another who stressed Yahweh, the Israelite one God.

forbidding reply, 'I AM THAT I AM,' a God without a name, rendered in Hebrew as YHWH: Yahweh or, as Christians later misspelt it, Jehovah.*

Many Semites did settle in Egypt; Ramses II the Great was probably the pharaoh who forced the Hebrews to work on his store-cities; Moses' name was Egyptian, which suggests at least that he originated there; and there is no reason to doubt that the first charismatic leader of the monotheistic religions – Moses or someone like him – did receive this divine revelation for that is how religions begin. The tradition of a Semitic people who escaped repression is plausible but it defies dating.

Moses glimpsed the Promised Land from Mount Nebo but died before he could enter it. It was his successor Joshua who led the Israelites into Canaan. The Bible portrays their journey as both a bloody rampage and a gradual settlement. There is no archaeo-logical evidence of a conquest but pastoral settlers did found many unwalled villages in the Judaean highlands.† A small group of Israelites, who escaped Egypt, were probably among them. They were united by their worship of their God – Yahweh – whom they revered in a moveable temple, a tabernacle that held the sacred wooden chest known as the Ark of the Covenant. They perhaps crafted their identity by telling the stories of their founding Patri-archs. Many of these traditions, from Adam and the Garden of Eden to Abraham, would later be revered not just by Jews but by Christians and Muslims too – and would be located in Jerusalem.

The Israelites were now very close to the city for the first time.

---

* When the Temple stood in Jerusalem, only the high priest, once a year, could utter the tetragram YHWH, and Jews, even today, are forbidden to say it, preferring to use Adonai (Lord), or just HaShem (the unspeakable Name).
† The Israelite invasion of Canaan is a battlefield of complex, usually unprovable theories. But it seems that the storming of Jericho, whose walls were crumbled by Joshua's trumpets, is mythical: Jericho was more ancient than Jerusalem. (In 2010, the Palestinian Authority celebrated its 10,000th anniversary – though the date is random.) However, Jericho was temporarily uninhabited and there is no evidence of collapsed walls. The Conquest Hypothesis is hard to take literally since the fighting (as recounted in the Book of Joshua) usually takes place in such a small area. Indeed Bethel near Jerusalem is one of the few conquered towns in the Book of Judges that *was* actually destroyed in the thirteenth century. The Israelites may have been far more peaceful and tolerant than they claimed.

2

THE RISE OF DAVID

YOUNG DAVID

Joshua set up his headquarters north of Jerusalem, at Shechem, where he built a shrine to Yahweh. Jerusalem was the home of the Jebusites, ruled by King Adonizedek, a name that suggests a priest-king. Adonizedek resisted Joshua but was defeated. Yet 'the sons of Judah could not drive out the Jebusites', who 'lived in Jerusalem side by side with the sons of Judah as they do today'. Around 1200 BC, Merneptah, the son of Ramses the Great and perhaps the pharaoh who was forced to release Moses' Israelites, faced attacks from the Sea Peoples – throwing the old empires of the Near East into flux. The pharaoh raided Canaan to restore order. When he returned home, he inscribed his triumph on the walls of his Theban temple, declaring that he had defeated the Sea Peoples, recaptured Ashkelon – and massacred a people who now appear in history for the first time: 'Israel is laid waste and his seed is not.'

Israel was not yet a kingdom; rather, the Book of Judges recounts, it was a confederation of tribes ruled by elders who were now challenged by a new enemy: the Philistines, part of the Sea Peoples, who originated in the Aegean. They conquered the coast of Canaan, building five rich cities where they wove clothes, crafted red and black pottery, and worshipped their many gods. The Israelites, hill shepherds from little villages, were no match for these sophisticated Philistines whose infantry wore Greek-style breastplates, greaves (leg armour) and helmets, and deployed close-combat weapons that challenged the cumbersome chariotry of the Egyptians.

The Israelites elected charismatic warlords – the Judges – to fight Philistines and Canaanites. At one point, a much neglected verse of the Book of Judges claims the Israelites took and burned Jerusalem; if so, they did not manage to keep the stronghold.

At the Battle of Ebenezer in about 1050 BC, the Philistines crushed the Israelites, destroyed their shrine at Shiloh, captured the Ark of the Covenant, the sacred symbol of Yahweh, and advanced into the hill country around Jerusalem. Faced with annihilation and wishing to be 'like other nations', the Israelites decided to elect a king, chosen by God. They turned to their ageing prophet, Samuel. Prophets were not predictors of the future but analysts of the present – *propheteia* in Greek means the interpreting of the will of the gods. The Israelites needed a military commander: Samuel chose a young warrior, Saul, whom he anointed with holy oil. Ruling from a hilltop citadel at Gibeon (Tell al-Ful), just three miles north of Jerusalem, this 'captain over my people Israel' justified his selection by defeating the Moabites, Edomites and Philistines. But Saul was not suited to the throne: 'an evil spirit from the Lord troubled him.'

Samuel, faced with a mentally unstable king, secretly looked elsewhere. He sensed the blessing of genius among the eight sons of Jesse of Bethlehem: David, the youngest, 'was ruddy, and withal of a beautiful countenance, and goodly to look to. And the Lord said, Arise, anoint him: for this is he.' David was also 'cunning in playing, a mighty valiant man, and a man of war, and prudent in matters'. He grew up to be the most remarkable yet rounded character in the Old Testament. The creator of sacred Jerusalem was a poet, conqueror, murderer, adulterer, the essence of the holy king and the flawed adventurer.

Samuel brought young David to court where King Saul appointed him as one of his armour-bearers. When the king was haunted by madness, David showed his first god-given gift: he played the harp 'so Saul was refreshed'. David's musical talents are an important part of his charisma: some of the Psalms ascribed to him may even be his.

The Philistines advanced to the valley of Elah. Saul and his army faced them. The Philistines produced a brobdingnagian champion,

Goliath from Gath,* whose full armour contrasted with the flimsy gear of the Israelites. Saul feared a pitched battle so he must have been relieved, if sceptical, when David demanded a shot at beating Goliath. David chose 'five smooth stones out of the brook' and, wielding his sling, he 'slang it and smote the Philistine in his forehead, that the stone sunk into his forehead'.† He beheaded the fallen champion and the Israelites pursued the Philistines all the way to their city of Ekron. Whatever its truth, the story signifies that as a boy David made his name as a warrior.‡

Saul promoted David but the women in the streets sang 'Saul hath slain his thousands; David, his ten thousands.' Saul's son Jonathan befriended David and his daughter Michal loved him. Saul allowed them to marry but was tormented by jealousy: he twice tried to kill his son-in-law with a javelin. Princess Michal saved David's life by letting him down from a palace window, and he was later granted asylum by the priests of Nob. The king pursued him, killing all the priests except one, but David escaped again, living on the run as the leader of 600 brigands. Twice he crept up on the sleeping king but spared his life, leading Saul to weep: 'Thou art more righteous than I.'

Finally David defected to the Philistine King of Gath who granted him his own city domain, Ziklag. The Philistines again invaded Judah and defeated Saul on Mount Gilboa. His son Jonathan was killed and the king himself fell on his sword.

* Just as the word 'Philistine' has, thanks to the Bible, entered the language to describe a lack of culture (despite their cultural sophistication), so the people of Gath, known at 'Gits', also entered the vernacular. But the Philistines gave their name to the land which became the Roman Palestina, hence Palestine.

† The sling was not then a child's toy but a powerful weapon: slingers are shown in inscriptions in Beni Hasan in Egypt standing beside the archers in battle. Royal inscriptions in Egypt and Assyria show contingents of slingers were regular units of the imperial armies of the ancient world. It is believed skilled slingers could project specially smoothed stones the size of tennis balls at 100–150mph.

‡ Was 'David' a nom de guerre or regal name? The Bible tells the Goliath story twice, and in the second version it names the Israelite boy-hero as Elhanan: was this David's real name?

3

THE KINGDOM AND THE TEMPLE

DAVID: THE ROYAL CITY

A young man appeared at David's camp claiming to have killed Saul: 'I have slain the Lord's anointed.' David killed the messenger and then lamented Saul and Jonathan in timeless poetry:

> The beauty of Israel is slain upon thy high places: how are the mighty fallen! Ye daughters of Israel, weep over Saul who clothed you in scarlet, with other delights, who put on ornaments of gold upon your apparel ... Saul and Jonathan were lovely and pleasant in their lives and in their death they were not divided: they were swifter than eagles, they were stronger than lions ... How are the mighty fallen and the weapons of war perished!

At this dark hour, the southern tribes of Judah anointed David as king with Hebron as his capital, while Saul's surviving son, Ishbosheth, succeeded Saul to rule the northern tribes of Israel. After a seven-year war, Ishbosheth was murdered and the northern tribes too anointed David as king. The monarchy was united yet the split between Israel and Judah was a schism healed only by David's charisma.

Jerusalem, known as Jebus after its Jebusite inhabitants, stood just south of Saul's stronghold, Gibeon. David and his army advanced on the citadel of Zion, facing the formidable fortifications which have been recently uncovered around the Gihon Spring.* Zion was said to be impregnable and how David captured it is a mystery. The Bible portrays the Jebusites lining the walls with the blind and the lame, a warning to any attacker of what would befall him. But the king somehow penetrated the city – through what the Hebrew Bible calls a *zinnor*. This may be a water-tunnel, one of the network now being excavated on the Ophel hill, or it may be the name of some magical spell. Either way, 'David took the stronghold of Zion: the same is the city of David.'

This capture may just have been a palace coup. David did not slaughter the Jebusites; instead he co-opted them into his cosmopolitan court and army. He renamed Zion the City of David, repaired the walls and summoned the Ark of the Covenant (recaptured in battle) to Jerusalem. Its awesome sanctity killed one of those moving it, so David placed it with a trusted Git until it was safe to bear. 'David and all the house of Israel brought up the ark of the Lord with shouting and the sound of the trumpet.' Donning the sacerdotal loincloth, 'David danced before the Lord with all his might.' In return, God promised David, 'thine house and thy kingdom shall be established for ever'. After the centuries of struggle, David was declaring that Yahweh had found a permanent home in a holy city.

Michal, Saul's daughter, mocked her husband's half-naked submission to God as a display of vulgar vanity. While the earlier books of the Bible are a mixture of ancient texts and backdated stories written much later, the rounded, unheroic portrait of David, buried within the second Book of Samuel and the first Book of Kings, reads so vividly that it may have been based on the memoir of a courtier.

David chose this stronghold for his capital because it belonged

---

* This is the world's most excavated archaeological site. The present dig around the Spring by Professor Ronny Reich is the twelfth on this site and has revealed the Canaanite fortifications described in chapter one. In 1867, the English archaeologist Charles Warren discovered a shaft leading from Ophel down to the spring. It was long believed that Warren's Shaft was man-made and that Jerusalemites lowered buckets to get water. But the most recent dig has changed all that: it seems Warren's Shaft was natural. In fact, the water flowed to a man-made rock-cut pool, guarded by an enormous tower and walls.

neither to the northern tribes nor to his own southern Judah. He brought the golden shields of his conquered enemies to Jerusalem, where he built himself a palace, importing cedarwood from his Phoenician allies in Tyre. David is said to have conquered a kingdom that stretched from Lebanon to the borders of Egypt, and eastwards into today's Jordan and Syria, even placing a garrison in Damascus. Our only source for David is the Bible: between 1200 and 850 BC, the empires of Egypt and Iraq were in eclipse and left meagre royal records, but they also left a power vacuum. David certainly existed: an inscription found in 1993 at Tel Dan in northern Israel dating from the ninth century BC shows that the kings of Judah were known as the House of David, proving that David was the kingdom's founder.

Yet David's Jerusalem was tiny. At this time, the city of Babylon, in today's Iraq, covered 2,500 acres; even the nearby town of Hazor covered 200. Jerusalem was probably no more than 15 acres, just enough to house about 1,200 people around the citadel. But the recent discoveries of fortifications above the Gihon Spring prove that David's Zion was much more substantial than previously thought, even if it was very far from an imperial capital.* David's kingdom, conquered with his Cretan, Philistine and Hittite mercenaries, is plausible too, however exaggerated by the Bible, and was only a tribal federation held together by his personality. The Maccabees would, much later, show how dynamic warlords could quickly conquer a Jewish empire during an imperial power vacuum.

One evening, David was relaxing on the roof of his palace: 'he saw a woman washing herself and the woman was very beautiful to look upon. And David sent and enquired after the woman. And one

---

* The scale of David's city is now much debated between the minimalists who claim that it was just a chieftain's small citadel and the maximalists who embrace the imperial capital of traditional Bible stories. Until the Tel Dan inscription was uncovered, the extreme minimalists even hinted that David himself never existed, pointing to the lack of any archaeological evidence except the Bible. In 2005 Dr Eilat Mazor announced that she had discovered King David's palace. This was widely doubted, but her excavations do seem to have uncovered a substantial tenth-century public building, which, along with the Canaanite fortifications and stepped structures, would have formed David's citadel.

said, Is this not Bathsheba?' The woman was married to one of his non-Israelite mercenary captains, Uriah the Hittite. David summoned her and 'she came in unto him and he lay with her', making her pregnant. The king ordered his commander Joab to send him her husband back from the wars in present-day Jordan. When Uriah arrived, David ordered him to go home to 'wash thy feet' though he really intended that Uriah should sleep with Bathsheba to cover up her pregnancy. But Uriah refused so David ordered him to take this letter back to Joab: 'Set ye Uriah in the forefront of the hottest battle ... that he may be smitten.' Uriah was killed.

Bathsheba became David's favourite wife, but the prophet Nathan told the king the story of a rich man who had everything but still stole a poor man's only lamb. David was appalled by the injustice: 'the man that hath done this thing shall surely die!' '*Thou art that man,*' replied Nathan. The king realized that he had committed a terrible crime. He and Bathsheba lost their first child born of this sin – but their second son, Solomon, survived.

Far from being some ideal court of a holy king, David presided over a bearpit that rings true in its details. Like many an empire built around one strongman, when he ailed, the cracks started to show: his sons struggled for the succession. His eldest, Amnon, may have expected to succeed David but the king's favourite was Amnon's half-brother, the spoiled and ambitious Absalom, with his lustrous head of hair and a physique without blemish: 'in all Israel there was none to be so much praised as Absalom for his beauty'.

ABSALOM: RISE AND FALL OF A PRINCE

After Amnon lured Absalom's sister Tamar to his house and raped her, Absalom had Amnon murdered outside Jerusalem. As David mourned, Absalom fled the capital and returned only after three years. The king and his favourite were reconciled: Absalom bowed to the ground before the throne and David kissed him. But Prince Absalom could not rein in his ambition. He paraded through Jerusalem in his chariot and horses with fifty men running before him.

He undermined his father's government – 'Absalom stole the heart of Israel' – and set up his own rebel court at Hebron.

The people flocked to the rising sun, Absalom. But now David regained some of his old spirit: he seized the Ark of the Covenant, the emblem of God's favour, and then abandoned Jerusalem. While Absalom established himself in Jerusalem, the old king rallied his forces. 'Deal gently for my sake with the young man,' David told his general, Joab. When David's forces massacred the rebels in the forest of Ephraim, Absalom fled on a mule. His gorgeous hair was his undoing: 'and the mule went under the thick boughs of a great oak, and his head caught hold of the oak and he was taken up between the heaven and the earth; and the mule that was under him went away.' When the dangling Absalom was spotted, Joab killed him and buried the body in a pit instead of beneath the pillar the rebel prince had built for himself.* 'Is the young man Absalom safe?' the king asked pathetically. When David heard that the prince was dead, he lamented: 'Oh my son, Absalom, my son, my son Absalom, would God I had died for thee, O Absalom, my son, my son!' As famine and plague spread across the kingdom, David stood on Mount Moriah and saw the angel of death threaten Jerusalem. He experienced a theophany, a divine revelation, in which he was ordered to build an altar there. There may already have been a shrine in Jerusalem whose rulers are described as priest-kings. One of the original inhabitants of the city, Araunah the Jebusite, owned land on Moriah which suggests that the city had expanded from the Ophel onto the neighbouring mountain. 'So David bought the threshing floor and the oxen for fifty shekels of silver. And David built there an altar unto the Lord and offered burnt offerings and peace offerings.' David planned a temple there and ordered cedarwood from Abibaal, the Phoenician King of Tyre. It was the crowning moment in his career, the bringing together of God and his

---

* The pyramid known as Absalom's Pillar in the Kidron Valley was first mentioned by Benjamin of Tudela in AD 1170 and it does not date from 1000 BC. It is actually a first-century BC tomb. In the Middle Ages, the Jews, banned from the city and even from the Western Wall, prayed close to the Pillar. Even into the early twentieth century, passing Jews used to spit or throw stones at it to signify their disgust for Absalom's disloyalty.

people, the union of Israel and Judah, and the anointment of Jerusalem herself as the holy capital. But it was not to be. God told
David: 'Thou shalt not build an house for my name, because thou
hast been a man of war and hast shed blood.'

Now that David was 'old and stricken', his courtiers and sons
intrigued for the succession. Another son Adonijah made a bid for
the throne, while a lissom virgin, Abishag, was brought in to distract
David. But the plotters underestimated Bathsheba.

SOLOMON: THE TEMPLE

Bathsheba claimed the throne for her son Solomon. David called in
Zadok the priest and Nathan the prophet, who escorted Solomon
on the king's own mule down to the sacred Gihon Spring. There
he was anointed king. The trumpet was blown and the people
celebrated. Adonijah, hearing the celebrations, sought refuge in the
sanctuary of the altar, and Solomon guaranteed his life.

After an extraordinary career that united the Israelites and cast
Jerusalem as God's city, David died, having ordered Solomon to
build the Temple on Mount Moriah. It was the authors of the Bible,
writing four centuries afterwards to instruct their own times, who
made the imperfect David into the essence of the sacred king. He
was buried in the City of David.* His son was very different.
Solomon would finish that sacred mission – but he started his
reign, in about 970 BC, with a bloody settling of scores.

Bathsheba, the queen mother, asked Solomon to allow his elder
half-brother, Adonijah, to marry King David's last concubine,
Abishag. 'Ask for him the kingdom too?' replied Solomon sar-
castically, ordering the murder of Adonijah and a purge of his
father's old guard. This story is the last from the court historian of

---

* Several hundred years later, John Hyrcanus, the Maccabean king, was said to have
plundered David's tomb to pay off a foreign conqueror. Two thousand years after
that, during the Crusader Kingdom, workmen repairing the Cenacle on Mount Zion,
where Jesus took his last supper, discovered a room that they thought was David's
tomb. This became a site revered by Jews, Christians and Muslims alike. But the
real site of David's tomb remains a mystery.

David but it is also really the first and only glimpse of Solomon as a man, for he becomes the inscrutably wise and splendid stereotype of a fabulous emperor. Everything Solomon had was bigger and better than any ordinary king: his wisdom generated 3,000 proverbs and 1,005 songs, his harem contained 700 wives and 300 concubines, and his army boasted 12,000 cavalry and 1,400 chariots. Those expensive showpieces of military technology were housed in his fortified towns, Megiddo, Gezer and Hazor, while his fleet was anchored at Ezion-Geber on the Gulf of Aqaba.

Solomon traded with Egypt and Cilicia in spices and gold, chariots and horses. He shared trading expeditions to Sudan and Somalia with his Phoenician ally King Hiram of Tyre. He hosted the Queen of Sheba (probably Saba, today's Yemen), who came to Jerusalem 'with a very great train with camels that bore spices and very much gold and precious stones'. The gold came from Ophir, probably India; the bronze from his own mines. His wealth embellished Jerusalem: 'The king made silver to be in Jerusalem as stones and cedars made he to be as the sycamore trees that are in the vale, for abundance.' The most telling mark of his international prestige was his marriage to a pharaoh's daughter. Pharaohs almost never married their daughters to foreign princes – especially not parvenu Judaeans only recently graduated from hill shepherd chieftains. Yet once-haughty Egypt was in such shameful chaos that Pharaoh Siamun raided Gezer not far from Jerusalem and, perhaps finding himself exposed far from home, offered the spoils to Solomon along with his daughter, an unthinkable honour at any other time. But the Temple of Jerusalem, planned by his father, was his masterpiece.

The 'house of God' was to stand right next to Solomon's royal palace in an imperial-sacred acropolis, described in the Bible, that boasted halls and palaces of astonishing grandeur covered in gold and cedarwood, including the House of the Forest of Lebanon and the Hall of Pillars where the king adjudicated.

This was not just an Israelite achievement. The Phoenicians, who lived in independent city states along the Lebanese coast, were the most sophisticated artisans and seafaring traders of the Mediterranean, famed for their Tyrian purple dye from which they derived their name and for creating the alphabet. King Hiram of

Tyre provided not only the cypress and cedarwood but also the craftsmen who carved the silver and gold ornamentation. Everything was 'pure gold'.

The Temple was not just a shrine, it was the home of God himself, a complex made up of three parts, standing about 33 by 115 feet, in a walled enclosure. First there was a gateway with two bronze pillars, Yachin and Boaz, 33 feet high, decorated with pomegranates and lilies, that led into a huge pillared courtyard open to the skies and surrounded on three sides with two-storey chambers that may have contained the royal archives or treasury. The portico opened into a sacred hall: ten golden lamps stood along walls. A golden table for shewbread was placed in front of an incense altar for sacrifices, a water pool and wheeled lavers with bowls on top for purification, and a bronze pool known as the Sea. Steps led up towards the Holy of Holies,* a small chamber guarded by two winged cherubim, 17 feet high, made of olive wood covered with gold foil.

Yet Solomon's own magnificence came first. He took seven years to finish the Temple, and thirteen to build his own palace, which was larger. There had to be silence in God's house, so 'there was neither hammer nor axe nor any tool of iron heard in the house': his Phoenician craftsmen dressed the stones, carved the cedar and cypress, and crafted the silver, bronze and gold decorations in Tyre before shipping them to Jerusalem. King Solomon fortified Mount Moriah by expanding the old walls: henceforth the name 'Zion'

---

* Where was the Holy of Holies? This is now a politically explosive question and an intractable challenge for any Israeli–Palestinian peace deal sharing Jerusalem. There are many theories, depending on the size of the Temple Mount which was later extended by Herod the Great. Most scholars believe it stood atop the rock within the Islamic Dome of the Rock. Some argue that this mysterious yellow, twisted cavern was originally a burial cave of around 2000 BC, and there seem to be folk memories of this: when exiles returned from Babylon around 540 BC, they were said to have found Araunah the Jebusite's skull. The Mishnah, the compilation of oral Jewish traditions of the second century AD, calls it the Tomb of the Abyss, hollowed for 'fear of any grave in the depths'. The Muslims called it the Well of Souls. Jews and Muslims believe this was where Adam was created and Abraham almost sacrificed Isaac. It is likely that in AD 691, the caliph Abd al-Malik chose the site for the Dome at least partly to create an Islamic successor to the Temple. Jews regard the Rock as the foundation stone of the Temple.

described both the original citadel and the new Temple Mount.

When all was finished, Solomon assembled the people to watch the priests bear the acacia wood chest of the Ark of the Covenant from its tent on the citadel of Zion, the City of David, to the Temple on Mount Moriah. Solomon sacrificed at the altar and then the priests took the Ark into the Holy of Holies and placed it beneath the wings of the two immense gold cherubim. There was nothing in the Holy of Holies except the cherubim, and the Ark, and nothing within the Ark – just 4 by $2\frac{1}{2}$ feet – except the tablets of Moses' law. Its holiness was such that it was not designed for public worship: In this emptiness resided the austere, imageless divinity of Yahweh, an idea unique to the Israelites.

As the priest came out, the 'cloud' of the Divine Presence, 'the glory of the Lord, filled the house of the Lord.' Solomon consecrated the Temple before his people, declaring to God: 'I have surely built thee a house to dwell in, a settled place for thee to abide for ever,' God replied to Solomon, 'I will establish the throne of thy kingdom upon Israel for ever, as I promised to David thy father.' This became the first of the festivals that developed into the great pilgrimages of the Jewish calendar: 'three times a year did Solomon offer burnt offerings upon the altar'. At that moment, the concept of sanctity in the Judaeo-Christian-Islamic world found its eternal home. Jews and the other Peoples of the Book believe that the Divine Presence has never left the Temple Mount. Jerusalem would become the superlative place for divine-human communication on earth.

SOLOMON: THE DECLINE

All the ideal Jerusalems, new and old, celestial and temporal, were based on the Bible's description of Solomon's city. But there is no other source to confirm it, and nothing has been found of his Temple.

This is less surprising than it sounds. It is impossible to excavate the Temple Mount for political and religious reasons, but even if such excavations were allowed we would probably find no traces of Solomon's Temple because it was obliterated at least twice, cut down to bedrock at least once and remodelled countless times. Yet the Temple is plausible in size and design even if the biblical writers exaggerated its splendour. Solomon's Temple was a classic shrine of its time. The Phoenician temples, on which Solomon's was partly based, were thriving corporations run by hundreds of officials, temple prostitutes whose fees contributed to corporate income, and even in-house barbers for those who dedicated their hair to their gods. The layout of Syrian temples, discovered all over the region, along with their sacred paraphernalia such as their lavers, were very similar to the biblical descriptions of Solomon's Sanctuary.

Its bounty of gold and ivory is completely credible. A century later, the kings of Israel reigned from sumptuous palaces in nearby Samaria where their ivory has been found by archaeologists. The Bible says Solomon dedicated 500 gold shields to the Temple in an era when other sources prove that gold was plentiful – imported from Ophir, the Egyptians also mined it in Nubia. Just after Solomon's death, the pharaoh Sheshonq was paid off with the Temple's treasury of gold when he threatened Jerusalem. King Solomon's mines were long thought to be mythical, but copper mines have been found in Jordan that were working during his reign. The size of his army, too, was feasible given that we know a king of Israel would field 2,000 chariots just over a century later.*

Solomon's magnificence may be exaggerated, but his decline rings only too true: the king of wisdom became an unpopular tyrant who funded his monumental extravagances through high taxes and the 'chastisement of whips'. To the disgust of the monotheistic

---

* The Bible cites the fortresses of Megiddo, Gezer and Hazor as Solomon's store-cities. But in the debates of the twenty-first century, revisionists, led by Professor Israel Finkelstein, argue that they are actually Syrian-style palaces built a hundred years later, leaving Solomon without any buildings. Other archaeologists challenge the revisionist dating. The black-on-red pottery found at these sites belongs in the late tenth century BC, roughly the time of Solomon's reign and Pharaoh Sheshonq's invasion, nine years after the king's death, while exciting new analysis of the buildings suggests they were indeed huge, tenth-century stables, and therefore plausibly evidence of Solomon's cavalry power and Mediterranean horse-trading operations. The debate continues.

biblical authors, writing two centuries later, Solomon prayed to Yahweh and other local gods, and furthermore he 'loved many strange women'.

Solomon faced rebellions from Edom in the south and Damascus in the north, while his general, Jeroboam, started to plan a revolt among the northern tribes. Solomon ordered Jeroboam's assassination but the general fled to Egypt where he was backed by Sheshonq, the Libyan pharaoh of a resurgent empire. The Israelite kingdom was tottering.

4

THE KINGS OF JUDAH

930–626 BC

REHOBOAM VERSUS JEROBOAM: THE SPLIT

When Solomon died in 930 BC after a reign of forty years, his son Rehoboam summoned the tribes to Shechem. The northerners chose the general, Jeroboam, to tell the young king that they would no longer tolerate Solomon's taxes, 'I will add to your yoke: my father hath chastised you with whips,' replied the brash Rehoboam, 'I will chastise you with scorpions.' The ten northern tribes rebelled, anointing Jeroboam as king of a new breakaway kingdom of Israel.

Rehoboam remained king of Judah; he was David's grandson and he possessed the Temple of Jerusalem, the home of Yahweh. But the more experienced Jeroboam, who made his capital at Shechem, faced up to this: 'If this people go up to do sacrifice in the house of the Lord at Jerusalem, then shall the heart of this people turn again unto Rehoboam King of Judah and they shall kill me.' So he built two mini-temples at Bethel and Dan, traditional Canaanite shrines. Jeroboam's reign was long and successful, but he could never match Rehoboam's Jerusalem.

The two Israelite kingdoms were sometimes at war with each other, sometimes close allies. For around four centuries after 900 BC, the Davidic dynasty ruled Judah, the small rump around the royal Temple city of Jerusalem, while the much richer Israel became a local military power in the north, usually dominated by charioteer generals who seized the throne in bloody coups. One of these usurpers killed so many of the ruling family that 'he left him not one that pisseth against a wall'. The authors of the Books of Kings and Chronicles, writing two centuries later, were not concerned with personal detail or strict chronology but judged the rulers by their loyalty to the one God of Israel. Fortunately, however, the Dark Age was over: the inscriptions of the empires of Egypt and Iraq now illuminate – and often confirm – the furiously righteous pontifications of the Bible.

Nine years after Solomon's death, Egypt and history returned to Jerusalem. The pharaoh Sheshonq, who had encouraged the breakup of the Israelite united monarchy, marched up the coast, swerving inland towards Jerusalem. The Temple was rich enough to make such a detour lucrative. King Rehoboam had to buy off Sheshonq with the Temple treasury – Solomon's gold. Attacking both Israelite kingdoms, the pharaoh devastated Megiddo on the coast where he left an inscription on a stele boasting of his conquests: a tantalizing fragment survives. On his return, he advertised his successful raid at his Temple of Amun in Karnak. A hieroglyphic text at Bubastis, then the pharaoh's capital, shows that soon afterwards Sheshonq's heir Osorkon dedicated 383 tons of gold to his temples, probably the loot from Jerusalem. Sheshonq's invasion is the first biblical event confirmed by archaeology.

After fifty years of fighting, the two Israelite kingdoms made peace. King Ahab of Israel had made a prestigious marriage to a Phoenician princess, who became the Bible's arch-monstress, a corrupt tyrant and worshipper of Baal and other idols. Her name was Jezebel and she and her family came to rule Israel – and Jerusalem. They brought butchery and disaster to both.

JEZEBEL AND DAUGHTER, QUEEN OF JERUSALEM

Jezebel and Ahab had a daughter named Athaliah whom they married to king Jehorah of Judah: she arrived in a Jerusalem that was thriving – Syrian merchants traded in their quarter, a Judaean fleet sailed the Red Sea and the Canaanite idols had been expelled from the Temple. But Jezebel's daughter did not bring luck or happiness.

The Israelites had flourished only while the great powers were in abeyance. Now in 854, Assyria, based around Nineveh in modern Iraq, rose again. When the Assyrian king Shalmaneser III started the conquest of the Syrian kingdoms, Judah, Israel and Syria formed a coalition to resist him. At the Battle of Karkar, King Ahab, fielding 2,000 chariots and 10,000 infantry and backed by the Judaeans and the various Syrian kings, halted the Assyrians. But afterwards, the coalition fell apart. The Judaeans and Israelites fought with the Syrians; their subject peoples rebelled.* King Ahab of Israel was killed by an arrow – 'dogs licked up his blood'. A general named Jehu rebelled in Israel, slaughtered the royal family – stacking the heads of Ahab's seventy sons in a heap at the gate of Samaria, and assassinated not only the new king of Israel but the visiting king of Judah too. As for Queen Jezebel, she was tossed out of her palace window, to be pulverized under chariot-wheels.†

Jezebel's carcass was fed to the dogs in Israel but in about 841 BC, Jezebel's daughter, Queen Athaliah, seized power in Jerusalem, killing all the Davidian princes (her own grandchildren) that she could find. Only one baby prince, Jehoash, was saved. The second

---

* The Kings of Israel and Judah marched together against Mesha, the rebellious Moabite king who, in a stele, declared that he sacrificed his own son and successfully repelled the invaders. Almost 3,000 years later, in 1868, some Bedouin showed a German missionary a black basalt stone which unleashed an archaeological race between Prussia, France and England, whose agents intrigued to win this prestigious imperial prize. One tribe of Bedouin tried to destroy the stone, but finally the French won. It was worth the struggle. Sometimes contradicting, sometimes confirming the Bible, Mesha admits that Israel had conquered Moab but states that he rebelled against King Ahab and then defeated Israel and Judah – which (according to the latest translation) he calls 'House of David', again confirming David's existence. He then boasts that he took from a captured Israelite town 'the vessels of Yahweh,' the first mention of the Israelite God outside the Bible.

† The Bible portrays King Jehu of Israel as the restorer of Yahweh and smasher of the idols of Baal. But the Bible is more interested in his relations with God than in the power politics now revealed by archaeology: Jehu probably had help from Damascus because its king Hazael left the stele at Tel Dan in northern Israel boasting that he had defeated previous kings of the House of Israel and the House of the David, the archaeological proof that King David existed. But Jehu also had to become a vassal of the Assyrian king Shalmaneser III. On the Black Obelisk, found at Nimrud, now in the British Museum, Jehu makes his low obeisance to Shalmaneser who sits, with his braided beard, diadem, embroidered robes and sword, before the winged symbol of Assyrian power, sheltered by a parasol held by a courtier. 'I received', says Shalmaneser, 'silver, gold, a gold bowl, a gold vase, gold buckets, tin, a staff, hunting spears.' This kneeling Jehu is the first historical image of an Israelite.

Book of Kings – and some new archaeological finds – here deliver the first glimpse of life in Jerusalem.

The princeling was hidden in the Temple complex while Jezebel's half-Phoenician, half-Israelite daughter attracted cosmopolitan trade and Baalist worship to her small mountain capital. An exquisite ivory dove perched atop a pomegranate, less than an inch high, was found in Jerusalem, it was probably used to decorate a piece of furniture in a grand Jerusalem house. Phoenician clay seals – known as *bullae*, the headed notepaper of the day – have been found around the rock pool below the City of David with images of their ships and holy totems such as a winged sun over a throne, along with 10,000 fishbones, probably imported from the Mediterranean by these ocean-going traders. But Athaliah was soon as hated as Jezebel. Her idolatrous priests set up Baal and other gods in the Temple. After six years, the Temple's priest called Jerusalem's grandees to a secret meeting and revealed the existence of the little prince, Jehoash – to whom they immediately swore loyalty. The priest armed the guards with the spears and shields of King David, still stored in the Temple, and then publicly anointed the child, crying 'God save the king' and blowing trumpets.

The Queen heard 'the noise of the guard and the people' and rushed through the acropolis from the palace into the neighbouring Temple, now packed with people. 'Treason! Treason!' she cried, but the guards seized her, dragged her off the holy mountain and killed her outside the gates. The priests of Baal were lynched, their idols smashed.

King Jehoash ruled for forty years until about 801 when he was defeated in battle by the Syrian king, who marched on Jerusalem and forced him to pay out 'all the gold in the treasures' of the Temple. He was murdered. Thirty years later, a king of Israel raided Jerusalem and plundered the Temple. From now on the growing wealth of the Temple made it a tempting prize.

Yet Jerusalem's remote prosperity was no match for Assyria, energized under a new king: that carnivorous empire was again on the march. The kings of Israel and of Aram-Damascus tried to put together a coalition to resist the Assyrians. When King Ahaz of Judah refused, the Israelites and Syrians besieged Jerusalem. They could not break through the newly fortified walls, but King Ahaz despatched the Temple treasury and an appeal for help to Tiglath-Pileser III of Assyria. In 732, the Assyrians annexed Syria and ravaged Israel. In Jerusalem, King Ahaz agonized over whether to submit to Assyria or fight.

ISAIAH: JERUSALEM AS BEAUTY AND HARLOT

The king was advised by Isaiah, prince, priest and political consigliere, to wait: Yahweh would protect Jerusalem. The king, said Isaiah, would have a son named Emmanuel – meaning 'God with us' – 'For unto us a child is born' who would be 'the Mighty God, the everlasting Father, the Prince of Peace', bringing 'peace without end'.

There were at least two authors of the Book of Isaiah – one of them wrote over 200 years later – but this first Isaiah was not just a prophet but a visionary poet who, in an age of voracious Assyrian aggression, was the first to imagine life beyond the destruction of the Temple, in a mystical Jerusalem. 'I saw the Lord sitting upon a throne high and lifted up and his train filled the temple ... and the house was filled with smoke.'

Isaiah loved the 'holy mountain', which he saw as a beautiful woman, 'the mount of the daughter of Zion, the hill of Jerusalem', sometimes righteous, sometimes a harlot. The possession of Jerusalem was nothing without godliness and decency. But if all was lost and 'Jerusalem is ruined', there would be a new mystical Jerusalem for everyone 'upon every dwelling-place', preaching loving-kindness: 'Learn to do well; seek judgement; relieve the oppressed; judge the fatherless; plead for the widow.' Isaiah foresaw an extraordinary phenomenon: 'the mountain of the Lord's house shall be established in the top of the mountains ... and all nations shall flow to it'. The laws, values and stories of this remote and perhaps vanquished mountain city would rise again: 'And many people shall go and say, Come ye and let us go up to the mountain of the Lord, to the House of the God of Jacob; and he will teach us of his ways ... Out of Zion shall go forth the law, and the word of the Lord from

Jerusalem. And he shall judge among the nations.' Isaiah predicted a mystical Day of Judgement when an anointed king – the Messiah – would come: 'they shall beat their swords into ploughshares and spears into pruning-hooks ... and neither shall they learn war any more.' The dead would rise again. 'The wolf also shall dwell with the lamb and the leopard shall lie down with the kid.'

This incandescent poetry first expressed the apocalyptic yearnings that would run throughout Jerusalem's history until today. Isaiah would help shape not only Judaism but Christianity. Jesus Christ studied Isaiah, and his teachings – from the destruction of the Temple and the idea of a universal spiritual Jerusalem to the championing of the underdog – derive from this poetical vision. Jesus himself would be seen as Isaiah's Emmanuel.

King Ahaz travelled to Damascus to make obeisance to Tiglath-Pileser, returning with an Assyrian-style altar for the Temple. When the conqueror died in 727 BC, Israel rebelled, but the new Assyrian king Sargon II besieged Samaria the capital for three years and then swallowed Israel, deporting 27,000 of its people to Assyria. Ten of the Twelve Tribes, who had lived in the northern kingdom, almost vanish from history.* The modern Jews are descended from the last two tribes who survived as the Kingdom of Judah. The baby whom Isaiah had hailed as Emmanuel was King Hezekiah, who was no Messiah but nonetheless possessed the most priceless of all political qualities, luck. And traces of his Jerusalem survive today.

SENNACHERIB: THE WOLF ON THE FOLD

Hezekiah waited twenty years for a chance to revolt against Assyria: first he purged the idols, shattering the bronze snake that stood in the Temple, and summoned his people to celebrate an early version

* The ancient Jewish communities of Iran and Iraq claim descent from the Ten Tribes of Israel deported by the Assyrians as well as from those deported later by the Babylonians. The latest genetic research proves that these Jews were indeed separated from other Jewish communities around 2,500 years ago. Yet the quest for these vanished Israelites has spawned a thousand fantasies and theories: the Ten Tribes have been 'discovered' in various unlikely places – from the Native Americans of North America to the English.

of Passover in a Jerusalem which was expanding for the first time on to the western hill.* The city filled with refugees from the fallen northern kingdom, and they probably brought with them some of their ancient scrolls of early Israelite history and legend. Jerusalem's scholars started to fuse together the Judaean traditions with those of the northern tribes: ultimately these scrolls, written just as the Greeks were recording Homer's epic poem the *Iliad*, would become the Bible.

When Sargon II was killed in battle in 705, the Jerusalemites, even Isaiah, hoped it marked the fall of the evil empire. Egypt promised support; the city of Babylon rebelled and sent ambassadors to Hezekiah, who felt his moment had come: he joined a new coalition against Assyria and prepared for war. But, unfortunately for the Judaeans, the new Great King of Assyria was a warlord of apparently endless confidence and energy: his name was Sennacherib.

He called himself 'King of the World, King of Assyria' at a time when the titles were synonymous. Assyria ruled from the Persian Gulf to Cyprus. Its landlocked heartland in today's Iraq was defended by mountains to the north and the Euphrates in the west but was vulnerable to attack from south and east. The empire resembled a shark that could survive only by constant consumption. For the Assyrians, conquest was a religious duty. Each new king swore at his accession to expand what they called 'the land of God Ashur' – the country was named after its patron god. The kings were both high priests and commanders who led their 200,000-strong armies in person, and like the tyrants of modern times, they cowed their subjects using not just terror but vast deportations of peoples from one end of the empire to another.

---

* Two new suburbs developed outside the walled City of David and the Temple Mount: the Makhtesh in the Tyropaean Valley that ran between Mount Moriah and the western hill, and another, the Mishneh, on the western hill itself, today's Jewish Quarter. High officials were buried in the tombs around the city: 'This is [the tomb] of [...]yahu, the Royal Steward,' reads a tomb in Silwan village. 'There is no gold or silver here, only his bones and the bones of his slavewife – cursed be anyone who opens this tomb.' The curse did not work: the tomb was plundered and is today a chicken coop. But this royal steward may actually have been Hezekiah's courtier criticized by Isaiah for building a grandiose tomb: the name could read 'Shebnayahu'.

The body of Sennacherib's father was never recovered from the battlefield, a terrible sign of divine displeasure, and the empire started to break up. But Sennacherib smashed all the rebellions and when he recaptured Babylon, he destroyed the entire city. But once order was restored, he tried to consolidate, extravagantly rebuilding his capital Nineveh, city of Ishtar, goddess of war and passion, with canals irrigating its gardens and his massive Palace Without Rival. The Assyrian kings were avid propagandists, whose triumphalist decorations on the walls of their palaces advertised Assyrian victories and the gruesome deaths of their enemies – mass-impalings, flayings and beheadings. The courtiers of conquered cities paraded through Nineveh wearing the heads of their kings on ghoulish necklaces around their necks. But their depredations were probably no more vicious than other conquerors: the Egyptians, for example, collected the hands and penises of their enemies. Ironically Assyria's most brutal era was over; Sennacherib preferred to negotiate if possible.

Sennacherib buried records of his achievements in the foundations of his palaces. In Iraq, archaeologists have found the remains of his city, revealing Assyria at its apogee, made rich by conquest and agriculture, administered by scribes whose records were preserved in royal archives. Their libraries contained collections of omens to aid royal decision-making, and of incantations, rituals and hymns to maintain divine support, but also tablets of literary classics such as the *Epic of Gilgamesh*. Worshipping many gods, revering magical figurines and spirits and calling upon the power of divination, the Assyrians studied medicine, writing prescriptions on tablets that read: 'If the man is suffering from the following symptoms, the problem is ... Take the following drugs ...'

Israelite prisoners, toiling far from home in the resplendently gaudy cities of Assyria with their Babel-like ziggurat towers and painted palaces, saw them as metropolises 'of blood, full of lies, full of plunder, never without victims!' The prophet Nahum described 'the crack of whips, the clatter of wheels, galloping horses and jolting chariots!' Now those eight-spoked chariots, those vast armies and Sennacherib himself were marching on Jerusalem, swooping down, says Deuteronomy, 'as swift as the eagle flieth'.

HEZEKIAH'S TUNNEL

Hezekiah knew what horrors had befallen Babylon; he frantically built fortifications around Jerusalem's new quarters. Sections of his 'broad wall', 25 feet wide, survive today in several places but most impressively in the Jewish Quarter. He prepared for a siege by ordering two groups of craftsmen to hack a tunnel 1,700 feet through the rock to link the Gihon Spring outside the city to the Siloam Pool, south of the Temple Mount below the City of David, which now, thanks to his new fortifications, lay inside the walls. When the two teams met up deep in the rock, they celebrated by carving an inscription to record their amazing achievement:

[When the tunnel] was driven through. And this was the way in which it was cut through. While [they were] still [excavating with their] axes, each man toward his fellow, and while there were still three cubits to cut through, [they heard] the voice of a man calling to his fellows, for there was a fissure in the rock on the right [and the left]. And when the tunnel was driven through, the quarrymen hewed [the rock], each man toward his fellow, axe against axe; and the water flowed from the spring toward the reservoir for 1,200 cubits and the height of the rock above the heads of the quarrymen was 100 cubits.*

* In 1880, Jacob Eliahu, aged sixteen, son of Jewish converts to Protestantism, invited a school friend to dive the length of the Siloam Tunnel. They were both fascinated by the biblical story of 2 Kings 20.20: 'And the rest of the acts of Hezekiah, and all his might, and how he made a pool, and a conduit, and brought water into the city, are they not written in the book of the chronicles of the kings of Judah?' Jacob started from one end and his friend from the other, feeling the workers' ancient chisel-marks with their fingers. When the marks changed direction Jacob realized he was at the place where the two teams had met and there he found the inscription. He emerged at the other end to find that his friend had long since given up; and he terrified the local Arabs who believed the Tunnel contained a djinn or dragon. When he told his headmaster, word spread and a Greek trader crept into the Tunnel and roughly cut out the inscription, breaking it. But the Ottoman police caught him; and the inscription is now in Istanbul. Jacob Eliahu then joined the evangelical American Colonists and was adopted by the Colony's founding family, the Spaffords. Jacob Spafford became a teacher at their school, instructing his pupils about the Tunnel, never mentioning that *he* was the boy who had found the inscription.

North of the Temple Mount, Hezekiah dammed a valley to create one of the Bethesda Pools to deliver more water into the city, and he seems to have distributed food – oil, wine, grain – to his forces, ready for siege and war. Jar handles have been found at sites across Judah marked *lmlk* – 'for the king' – stamped with his emblem, the four-winged scarab.

'The Assyrian came down like the wolf on the fold,' wrote Byron. Sennacherib and his vast armies were now very close to Jerusalem. The Great King would have travelled, like most Assyrian kings, in a hulking three-horse chariot, shaded under the royal parasol, horses splendidly caparisoned with shimmering headcrests while he himself would have worn a long embroidered robe, a flat hat with a pointed peak, a square-cut, long, braided beard and rosette bracelets, and often carried a bow in his hands and a sword at his belt in a scabbard decorated with lions. He saw himself more as a lion than a biblical vulture or Byronic wolf – Assyrian kings wore lionskins to celebrate their victories in the Temple of Ishtar, decorated their palaces with lion sphinxes and avidly hunted lions as the sport of great kings.

He bypassed Jerusalem to besiege Hezekiah's second city, fortified Lachish, to the south. We know from the bas-reliefs at his Nineveh palace what his troops (and the Judaeans) looked like: the Assyrians, a polyglot imperial army, wore their hair braided, and dressed in tunics and chainmail, with plumed and pointed helmets, arrayed in contingents of charioteers, spearmen, archers and slingers. They built siege-ramps; sappers undermined the walls, a fearsomely spiked siege-engine shattered the fortifications. Archers and slingers laid down withering fire as Sennacherib's infantry stormed up scaling ladders to take the city. Archaeologists have excavated a mass grave of 1,500 men, women and children, some impaled or skinned, just as the bas-relief shows; throngs of refugees fled the mayhem. Jerusalem knew what to expect.

Sennacherib swiftly defeated an Egyptian army that had come to aid Hezekiah, ravaged Judah and then closed on Jerusalem, camping to the north, the same place chosen by Titus over five hundred years later.

Hezekiah poisoned any wells outside Jerusalem. His troops,

manning his new walls, wore turbans fastened with headbands and long earflaps, short kilts, leg armour and boots. As the siege set in, there must have been panic in the city. Sennacherib sent his generals to parley – resistance was hopeless. The prophet Micah foresaw the destruction of Zion. However, old Isaiah counselled patience: Yahweh would provide.

Hezekiah prayed in the Temple. Sennacherib bragged that he had surrounded Jerusalem 'like a bird in a cage'. But Isaiah was right: God intervened.

MANASSEH: CHILD SACRIFICE IN THE VALLEY OF HELL

'The angel of the Lord went out and smote in the camp of the Assyrians . . . and when they arose in the morning, they were all dead corpses.' The Assyrians suddenly packed up their camp, probably to suppress a rebellion in the east. 'So Sennacherib king of Assyria departed.' Yahweh told Sennacherib that 'The daughter of Jerusalem hath shaken her head at thee.' This was the Jerusalem version, but Sennacherib's annals describe Hezekiah's crushing tribute, including 30 talents of gold and 800 of silver: he seems to have paid them to leave. Sennacherib reduced Judah to a rump not much larger than the district of Jerusalem and boasted that he had deported 200,150 people.

When Hezekiah died soon after the siege, his son Manasseh became a loyal Syrian vassal. He brutally crushed any opposition in Jerusalem, married an Arabian princess, overturned his father's reforms and installed ritual male prostitutes and the idols Baal and Asherah in the Temple. Most dreadful of all, he encouraged the sacrifice of children at the roaster – the *tophet* – in the Valley of Hinnom,* south of the city. Indeed 'he made his own son pass

---

* There are hints of child sacrifice in Genesis and Exodus, including Abraham's willingness to sacrifice Isaac. Human sacrifice was long associated with Canaanite and Phoenician ritual. Much later, Roman and Greek historians ascribed this dastardly practice to the Carthaginians, those descendants of the Phoenicians. Yet very little evidence was discovered until the early 1920s, when two French colonial officials in Tunisia found a *tophet*, with buried urns and inscriptions in a field. They bore the letters MLK (as in *molok*, offering) and contained the burned bones of

through the fire ...' Children were said to be taken there as priests beat drums to hide the shrieks of the victims from their parents.

Thanks to Manasseh, the Valley of Hinnom became not just the place of death, but Gehenna, 'hell' in Jewish and later Christian and Islamic mythology. If the Temple Mount was Jerusalem's own heaven, Gehenna was her own Hades.

Then in 626, Nabopolassar, a Chaldean general, seized control of Babylon and started to destroy the Assyrian empire, recording his exploits in the Babylonian Chronicles. In 612, Nineveh fell to an alliance of Babylonians and Medes. Manasseh was succeeded by his eight-year-old grandson, Josiah, whose long and momentus reign seemed to herald a golden age ruled by a Messiah.

children and the telling message of a victim's father reading: 'It was to Baal that Bomilcar vowed this son of his own flesh. Bless him!' These finds may have coincided with the time of Manasseh, implying that the biblical stories were plausible. *Molok* (offering) was distorted into the biblical 'moloch', the definition of the cruel idolatrous god and, later in Western literature, particularly in John Milton's *Paradise Lost*, one of Satan's fallen angels. Gehenna in Jerusalem became not just hell, but the place where Judas invested his ill-gotten silver pieces and during the Middle Ages the site of mass charnel-houses.

5

THE WHORE OF BABYLON

586–539 BC

JOSIAH: THE REVOLUTIONARY SAVIOUR

It was a miracle: the evil empire of Assyria had fallen apart and the kingdom of Judah was free. King Josiah may have extended his kingdom northwards into the former lands of Israel, southwards towards the Red Sea and eastwards towards the Mediterranean, and then, in the eighteenth year of his reign, Hilkiah the chief priest found a forgotten scroll stored in the chambers of the Temple.

Josiah recognized the power of this document, an early version of the Book of Deuteronomy ('Second Law' in Greek), probably one of the scrolls brought southwards from Israel after its fall and hidden in the Temple during Manasseh's persecutions. Having assembled the Judaeans in the Temple, Josiah stood by that totemic symbol, the royal pillar, and announced his covenant with the one God to keep the Law. The king set his scholars to retell the ancient history of the Judaeans, linking the mythical Patriarchs, the sacred kings David and Solomon and the story of Jerusalem into a single past, to illuminate the present. This was another step towards the creation of the Bible. Indeed these laws were backdated and attributed to Moses, but the biblical portrait of the Temple of Solomon surely reflected the real but later Jerusalem of Josiah, the new David. Henceforth the holy mountain became nothing less than *ha-Makom* in Hebrew: the Place.

The king had the idols burned in the Kidron Valley, and expelled the male prostitutes from the Temple; he smashed the child-roasters of the Valley of Hell and killed the idolatrous priests, grinding their bones into their altars.* Josiah's revolution sounds violent, frenzied and puritanical. He then held a Passover festival to celebrate. 'And like unto him was there no king before him.' Yet he was playing a dangerous game. When Necho, the Egyptian pharaoh, marched up the coast, Josiah, fearing he was about to swap Assyrian for Egyptian dominion, rushed to stop him. In 609 BC, the pharaoh crushed the Judaeans and killed Josiah at Megiddo. Josiah had failed, but his optimistic, revelatory reign was more influential than any other between David and Jesus. The dream of independence, however, ended at Megiddo, which became the very definition of catastrophe: Armageddon.

The pharaoh advanced on Jerusalem and placed Josiah's brother Jehoiakim on the throne of Judah. But Egypt failed to stop the rise of a new Near Eastern empire. In 605, the Babylonian king's son, Nebuchadnezzar, routed the Egyptians at Carchemish. Assyria vanished; Babylon inherited Judah. But in 597, King Jehoiakim saw his chance in the midst of this instability to liberate Judah and called a national fast to win God's protection. His adviser and prophet Jeremiah warned, in the first jeremiad, that God would destroy Jerusalem. King Jehoiakim publicly burned Jeremiah's writings.[†] He allied Judah with Egypt, but no Egyptian help came as a new conqueror descended on Jerusalem.

NEBUCHADNEZZAR

'In the seventh month of Kislev,' declared Nebuchadnezzar's chronicle, preserved on a clay inscription, 'the Babylonian king marched

---

* Josiah's reforms were a vital step in the development of Judaism. Two tiny silver scrolls were found in a Valley of Hinnom tomb of this period: inside was etched the priestly prayer of Numbers 6.24–6 which remains part of the Jewish service today. 'For YHWH is our restorer and rock. May YHWH bless you and keep you and make his face shine.'

† Royal courtiers lived and worked atop the City of David. An archive of forty-five *bullae* – clay seals hardened by being burned in the destruction of the city – has been found in a house there, which archaeologists call the House of the Bullae. This was obviously a secretariat of the king: one *bulla* bears the inscription 'Gemaraiah son of Shaphan', the name of the royal scribe of King Jehoiakim in the Book of Jeremiah. Some time during the crisis, the king died, to be succeeded by his son, Jehoiachin.

to the land of Hatti [Syria], besieged the City of Judah [Jerusalem] and on the second day of the month of Adar [16 March 597] took the city and captured the king.' Nebuchadnezzar plundered the Temple and deported the king and 10,000 nobles, artisans and young men to Babylon. There, Jehoiakim joined his vanquisher's court.

Nebuchadnezzar was the son of a usurper but he was a dynamic empire-builder, who regarded himself as the viceroy on earth of Babylon's patron god Bel-Marduk. Inheriting the Assyrian style of ferocious imperial repression, he promoted himself as a paragon of piety and virtue. At home 'the strong used to plunder the weak', but Nebuchadnezzar 'did not rest night or day but with counsel and deliberation he persisted' in giving justice. His Judaean victims might not have recognized the soi-disant 'King of Justice'.

The exiles from Judah found themselves in a city that made Zion look like a village. While a few thousand lived in Jerusalem, Babylon boasted a quarter of a million in a metropolis so majestic and hedonistic that the goddess of love and war Ishtar was said to tiptoe through the streets, kissing her favourites in the inns and alleyways.

Nebuchadnezzar stamped Babylon with his own aesthetic flair: grandiose gigantism tinted in his favourite colour, divine sky-blue, reflected in the canals of the mighty Euphrates. The four towers of the Ishtar Gate were faced with blue-glazed bricks, illustrated with bulls and dragons in yellow and ochre, leading into the city's triumphal boulevard, the Processional Way. His palace, in his words an 'edifice to be admired, a gleaming sanctuary, my royal abode', was decorated with towering lions. Hanging Gardens embellished his summer palace. Honouring Babylon's patron god Marduk, Nebuchadnezzar raised a ziggurat, an immense seven-storey, stepped tower with a flat top: his Foundation Platform of Heaven and Earth was the real Tower of Babel, its many languages reflecting the cosmopolitan capital of the entire Near East.

In Jerusalem, Nebuchadnezzar placed the exiled king's uncle, Zedekiah, on the throne. In 594, Zedekiah visited Babylon to make obeisance to Nebuchadnezzar, but on his return he launched a rebellion, haunted by the prophet Jeremiah, who warned that the Babylonians would destroy the city. Nebuchadnezzar marched southwards. Zedekiah appealed to the Egyptians, who sent meagre forces that were soon defeated. Inside Jerusalem, Jeremiah, observing the panic and paranoia, tried to escape but was arrested at the gates. The king, torn between asking his advice and executing him for treason, imprisoned him in the dungeons under the royal palace. For eighteen months, Nebuchadnezzar ravaged Judah,* leaving Jerusalem until last.

In 587, Nebuchadnezzar encircled Jerusalem with forts and a siege wall. 'The famine', wrote Jeremiah, 'was sore in the city'. Young children 'faint for hunger at the top of every street', and there were hints of cannibalism: 'the daughter of my people is become cruel ... The hands of the pitiful women have sodden their own children: they were their meat in the destruction'. Even the rich were soon desperate, wrote the author of Lamentations: 'they that were brought up in scarlet embrace dunghills', searching for food. People wandered the streets, dazed, 'like blind men'. Archaeologists have found a sewer pipe that dated from the siege: the Judaeans usually lived on lentils, wheat and barley, but the pipe's contents showed that people were living on plants and herbs, diseased with whipworm and tapeworm.

On the 9th of the Jewish month of Ab, August 586, after eighteen months, Nebuchadnezzar broke into the city, which was set on fire, probably with flamed torches and burning arrows (arrowheads were discovered in today's Jewish Quarter in a layer of soot, ashes and charred wood). Yet the fire that consumed the houses also baked the clay *bullae*, the seals of the bureaucracy, so hard that they have survived to this day among the burned houses.

---

* Shattered sherds bearing messages – known as *ostraca* – have been found by archaeologists buried in layers of ashes at the city gate of the fortress of Lachish: they give a human glimpse of the unstoppable Babylonian advance. Lachish and another fortress, Azekah, held out the longest, communicating with each other and Jerusalem by fire-signals. At Lachish, the beleaguered Judaean commander Yaush received reports from his outposts as they were gradually destroyed. His officer Hoshayahu soon noted that the fire-signals no longer came from Azekah. Then Lachish too was destroyed in heavy fighting.

Jerusalem suffered the infernal depredations of fallen cities. Those that were killed were luckier than those who starved: 'Our skin was black like the oven because of the famine. They ravished the women in Zion; princes were hanged up by their hand.' Edomites from the south poured into the city to loot, party and gloat in the wreckage: 'Rejoice and be glad, O daughter of Edom ... thou shalt be drunken and shalt make thyself naked.' The Edomites, according to Psalm 137, encouraged the Babylonians to 'rase it, rase it, even to the foundation thereof ... Happy shall he be, that taketh and dasheth thy little ones against the stones.' The Babylonians ravaged Jerusalem while, beneath the royal palace, Jeremiah survived in his dungeon.

NEBUCHADNEZZAR: THE ABOMINATION OF DESOLATION

Zedekiah broke out through the gate close to the Siloam Pool, heading for Jericho, but the Babylonians captured the king and brought him before Nebuchadnezzar 'where sentence was pronounced on him. They killed the sons of Zedekiah before his eyes. Then they put out his eyes, bound him with bronze shackles and took him to Babylon.' The Babylonians must have found Jeremiah in the king's prison for they brought him to Nebuchadnezzar, who apparently interviewed him and gave him to the commander of the imperial guard, Nebuzaradan, who was in charge of Jerusalem. Nebuchadnezzar deported 20,000 Judaeans to Babylon, though Jeremiah says he left many of the poor behind.

A month later Nebuchadnezzar ordered his general to obliterate the city. Nebuzaradan 'burned the House of the Lord, the king's palace and all the houses of Jerusalem' and 'brake down the walls'. The Temple was destroyed, its gold and silver vessels plundered, and the Ark of the Covenant vanished for ever. 'They have cast fire into thy Sanctuary,' recounted Psalm 74. The priests were killed before Nebuchadnezzar. As with Titus in AD 70, Temple and palace must have been toppled into the valley beneath: 'How is the gold become dim! How is the most fine gold changed!

The stones of the Sanctuary are poured in the top of every street.'*

The streets were empty: 'How doth the city sit solitary that was full of people.' The well-off were impoverished: 'they that did feed delicately are desolate in the streets'. Foxes loped across the barren mountain of Zion. The Lamentations of the Judaeans mourned their bleeding 'Jerusalem . . . as a menstruous woman': 'She weepeth sore in the night and her tears are on her cheeks: among her lovers, she hath none to comfort her.'

The destruction of the Temple must have seemed to be the death not just of a city but of an entire nation. 'The ways of Zion do mourn because none come to the solemn feasts: all her gates are desolate: her priests sigh ... And from the daughter of Zion all her beauty is departed. The crown is fallen from our head.' This seemed to be the end of the world, or, as the Book of Daniel explained it, 'the abomination that maketh desolate'. The Judaeans would surely vanish like other peoples whose gods had failed them. But the Jews somehow transformed this catastrophe into the formative experience that redoubled the sanctity of Jerusalem and created a prototype for the Day of Judgement. For all three religions, this inferno made Jerusalem the venue of the Last Days and the coming of the divine kingdom. This was the Apocalypse – based on the Greek word for 'revelation' – that Jesus would prophesy. For Christians it became a defining and perennial expectation, while Muhammad would see Nebuchadnezzar's destruction as the withdrawal of divine favour from the Jews, making way for his Islamic revelation.

In Babylonian exile, some of the Judaeans kept their

---

* Nothing has been found of the Temple. But Jeremiah was surprisingly accurate: Nebuchadnezzar's henchmen set up headquarters at the city's Middle Gate to organize Judah, and their names in the Book of Jeremiah are confirmed by a text found in Babylon. Nebuchadnezzar appointed a royal minister, Gedaliah, as puppet ruler over Judah, but as Jerusalem was in ruins he ruled from Mizpah to the north, advised by Jeremiah. Judaeans rebelled and murdered Gedaliah, and Jeremiah had to flee to Egypt, where he vanishes from the story.

commitment to God and Zion. At the same time as Homer's poems were becoming the national epic of the Greeks, the Judaeans started to define themselves by their own biblical texts and their faraway city: 'By the rivers of Babylon, there we sat down, yea, we wept when we remembered Zion. We hanged our harps upon the willows in the midst thereof.' Yet even the Babylonians, according to Psalm 137, appreciated the Judaean songs: 'For there they that carried us away captive required of us a song; and they that wasted us required of us mirth, saying, Sing us one of the songs of Zion. How shall we sing the Lord's song in a strange land?'

Yet it was there that the Bible began to take shape. While young Jerusalemites such as Daniel were educated in the royal household and the more worldly exiles became Babylonians, Judaeans developed new laws to emphasize that they were still distinct and special – they respected the Sabbath, circumcised their children, adhered to dietary laws, adopted Jewish names – because the fall of Jerusalem had demonstrated what happened when they did not respect God's laws. Away from Judah, the Judaeans were becoming Jews.*

The Exiles immortalized Babylon as 'the mother of prostitutes and the abominations of the earth', yet the empire prospered and their nemesis, Nebuchadnezzar, ruled for over forty years. However, Daniel claims the king went insane: he was 'driven away from the people and ate grass like cattle, his nails growing like claws of a bird' – a suitable punishment for his crimes (and wonderful inspiration for William Blake's paintings). If vengeance was not complete, the exiles could at least wonder at the ironies of life in

---

* Between 586 and 400 BC, the mysterious writers of the Bible, scribes and priests living in Babylon, refined and collated the Five Books of Moses, known as the Torah in Hebrew, combining the different traditions of God, Yahweh and El. The so-called Deuteronomists retold the history and recast the law to show the fecklessness of kings and the supremacy of God. And they incorporated stories inspired by Babylon such as the Flood, so similar to the Epic of Gilgamesh, the origins of Abraham in nearby Ur and of course the Tower of Babel. The Book of Daniel was written over a long period: some parts were definitely written in the early Exile, other parts later. We do not know if there was an individual named Daniel or whether he is a composite. But the book is also full of historical confusions that archaeologists have clarified with the help of the evidence found in Babylon during nineteenth-century excavations.

Babylon: Nebuchadnezzar's son Amel-Marduk was such a disappointment that his father threw him in prison, where he became acquainted with Jehoiachin, King of Judah.

BELSHAZZAR'S FEAST

When Amel-Marduk became king of Babylon, he freed his royal Judaean friend from prison. But in 556 the dynasty was overthrown: the new king, Nabonidus, rejected Bel-Marduk, god of Babylon, in favour of Sin the moon-god and eccentrically left the city to live at Teima, far away in the Arabian desert. Nabonidus was struck by a mysterious disease, and it was surely he (not Nebuchadnezzar, as Daniel claimed) who went mad and 'ate grass like cattle'.

In the king's absence, the regent, his son Belshazzar, according to the Bible, held the depraved feast at which he used the 'gold and silver goblets that Nebuchadnezzar had taken from the Temple in Jerusalem' and suddenly saw on the wall God's words: 'MENE MENE TEKEL UPHARSIN'. Decoded, these were measurements warning that the days of the empire were numbered. Belshazzar trembled. For the Whore of Babylon, 'the writing was on the wall'.

In 539 BC, the Persians marched on Babylon. Jewish history is filled with miraculous deliverances. This was one of the most dramatic. After forty-seven years 'by the rivers of Babylon', the decision of one man, in its way as seminal as that of David, restored Zion.

6

THE PERSIANS

539–336 BC

CYRUS THE GREAT

Astyges, King of Media in western Persia, dreamed that his daughter was urinating a golden stream which squirted out the whole of his kingdom. His magi, the Persian priests, interpreted this to mean that his grandsons would threaten his rule. Astyges married his daughter to a weak, unthreatening neighbour to the east, the King of Anshan. This marriage spawned an heir, Kourosh, who became Cyrus the Great. Astyges dreamed again that a vine was growing from between his daughter's fecund thighs until it overshadowed him – a sexual-political version of Jack and the Beanstalk. Astyges ordered his commander Harpagus to murder little Cyrus, but the boy was hidden with a shepherd. When Astyges discovered that Cyrus was not dead, he butchered and cooked Harpagus' son and served him to his father as a stew. It was not a meal that Harpagus would easily forget or forgive.

On the death of his father in about 559 BC, Cyrus returned and seized his kingdom. Astyges' pungent dreams, as recounted by the Greek historian Herodotus, who liked to believe all Persian business was decided with the help of sexual or urinary auguries, came true: Cyrus, backed by Harpagus, defeated his grandfather, uniting the Medes and Persians. Leaving Belshazzar's Babylon to the south, Cyrus confronted another potentate, Croesus, wealthy King of Lydia in western Turkey. Cyrus force-marched his cameleer army to surprise Croesus in his capital. The Lydian horses bolted when they detected the smell of charging camels. Then Cyrus turned on Babylon.

Nebuchadnezzar's blue-glazed metropolis opened its gates to Cyrus, who shrewdly paid homage to Bel-Marduk, the neglected Babylonian god. The fall of Babylon elated the Jewish exiles: 'For the Lord hath done it; shout . . . break forth into singing, ye mountains, O forest, and every tree therein; for the Lord hath redeemed Jacob, and glorified himself in Israel.' Cyrus inherited the Babylonian empire, including Jerusalem: 'every king on earth', he said, 'brought me heavy tribute and kissed my feet when I sat in Babylon'.

Cyrus had a fresh vision of empire. While the Assyrians and Babylonians built empires on slaughter and deportation, Cyrus offered religious tolerance in return for political dominance to 'unite peoples into one empire'.*

Soon after, the King of Persia issued a decree that must have astonished the Jews: 'The Lord God hath given me all the kingdoms of the earth and he hath charged me to build him a house at Jerusalem. Who is there among you of all his people? Let him go up to Jerusalem and build the house of the Lord God of Israel.'

Not only was he sending the Judaean exiles home, and guaranteeing their rights and laws – the first ruler ever to do so – but he returned Jerusalem to them and offered to rebuild the Temple. Cyrus appointed Sheshbazzar, son of the last king, to govern Jerusalem, returning to him the Temple vessels. No wonder a Judaean prophet hailed Cyrus as the Messiah. 'He is my shepherd, and shall perform all my pleasure: even saying to Jerusalem, Thou shalt be built; and to the temple, Thy foundation shall be laid.'

---

* One of Cyrus' decrees of tolerance, later found inscribed on a cylinder, won him the soubriquet Father of Human Rights, and a copy now stands at the entrance of the United Nations in New York. But he was no liberal. For instance, when the Lydian capital of Sardis rebelled, he slaughtered thousands of its inhabitants. Cyrus himself believed in Ahura Mazda, the winged Persian god of life, wisdom and light in whose name the prophet of the Aryan Persians, Zoroaster, had decreed that life was a battle between truth and lie, fire versus darkness. But there was no state religion, just this polytheistic vision of light and dark that was not incompatible with Judaism (and later Christianity). Indeed the Persian word for heaven – *paridaeza* – became our own 'paradise'. Their priests – the magi – gave us the word 'magic', and the three eastern priests said to have heralded the birth of Christ.

Sheshbazzar led 42,360 exiles back to Jerusalem in the province of Yehud – Judah.* The city was a wasteland after the magnificence of Babylon, but 'Awake, awake, put on thy strength, O Zion,' wrote Isaiah, 'put on thy beautiful garments, O Jerusalem, the holy city . . . Shake thyself from the dust . . . O captive daughter of Zion.' However, the plans of Cyrus and the returning exiles were obstructed by the locals who had remained in Judaea and particularly Samaria.

Just nine years after the return from exile, Cyrus, still in his prime, was killed in battle in Central Asia. It was said that his victorious enemy dropped his head into a blood-filled wineskin to satiate his greedy thirst for the lands of others. His heir redeemed his body and buried him in a golden sarcophagus at Pasargadae (in southern Iran) where his tomb still stands. 'He eclipsed all other monarchs, before him and since,' wrote the Greek soldier Xenophon. Jerusalem had lost her protector.

DARIUS AND ZERUBBABEL: THE NEW TEMPLE

The fate of Cyrus' empire, already larger than anything that had gone before, was decided close to Jerusalem. Cyrus' son Cambyses II – Kambujiya – succeeded to the throne and in 525 marched through Gaza and across Sinai to conquer Egypt. Far away in Persia, his brother rebelled. On his way home to save his throne, Cambyses died mysteriously near Gaza; there, seven noble conspirators met on horseback to plan the seizure of the empire. They had not decided who would be their candidate, so they agreed that 'the one

---

* This is a biblical exaggeration. Many thousands chose to live as Jews in Iraq and Iran. Babylonian Jews remained a rich, powerful and numerous community under the Seleucids, Parthians and Sassanids up to the Abbasid caliphate and the Middle Ages. Babylon became a centre of Jewish leadership and learning almost as important as Jerusalem until the Mongol invasion. The community recovered under the Ottomans and British. But persecutions started in the 1880s in Baghdad (which was said to be one third Jewish) and intensified under the Hashemite monarchy. In 1948, there were 120,000 Jews in Iraq. When the shah was overthrown in 1979, there were 100,000 Iranian Jews. The majority of both communities emigrated to Israel. Twenty-five thousand Iranian Jews and a mere fifty Iraqi Jews remain today.

whose horse was first to neigh after dawn should have the throne'. The horse of Darius, a young scion of one of the noble clans and Cambyses' lance-bearer, was the first to neigh. Herodotus claimed that Darius cheated by ordering his groom to dip his fingers into a mare's vulva: he then gave Darius' horse a thrilling whiff at the vital moment. Thus Herodotus gleefully attributed the rise of an eastern despot to a venereal sleight of hand.

Aided by his six co-conspirators, Darius galloped eastwards, and succeeded in reconquering the entire Persian empire, suppressing rebellions in virtually every province. But the civil war 'ceased the work of the house of God in Jerusalem unto the second year of the reign of Darius'. In about 520, Prince Zerubbabel, grandson of the last king of Judah, and his priest, Joshua, son of the last priest of the old Temple, set off from Babylonia to rescue Jerusalem.

Zerubbabel rededicated the altar on the Temple Mount, hiring artisans and buying Phoenician cedarwood to rebuild the Temple. Excited by the rising edifice, encouraged by the disorder in the empire, the Jews could not help but entertain messianic dreams of a new kingdom. 'In that day, saith the Lord of hosts, I will take thee, O Zerubbabel, my servant . . . and make thee as a signet', wrote the prophet Haggai, citing the Davidic signet-ring lost by Zerubbabel's grandfather. Jewish leaders arrived from Babylon with gold and silver, hailing Zerubbabel (which means 'Seed of Babylon') as the 'Shoot' that 'shall assume majesty and rule upon his throne'.

The local people, who lived around the city and to the north in Samaria, now wanted to join in with this sacred task and offered Zerubbabel their help, but the returning Exiles practised a new Judaism. They regarded these locals as half-heathens, disdaining them as the Am Ha-Aretz, 'the people of the land'. Alarmed by the revival in Jerusalem or bribed by the locals, the Persian governor stopped the building.

Within three years, Darius had defeated all challenges and emerged as one of the most accomplished rulers of the ancient world, establishing a tolerant world empire that stretched from Thrace and Egypt to the Hindu Kush – the first to extend across three continents.* The new Great King turned out to be a rare combination of conqueror and administrator. From his image carved in rock to commemorate his victory, we know that this Darius – Darayavaush – presented himself as a classic Aryan with high brow and straight nose, shown as 5 feet 10 inches tall, wearing a war crown of gold studded with oval jewels, his fringe frizzed, his drooping moustache twirled, his hair tied in a bun and his square beard arranged in four rows of curls alternating with straight strands. In his majesty, he wore a long robe over trousers and shoes, and carried a duck-headed bow.

This was the awesome ruler to whom Zerubbabel appealed, citing the decree of Cyrus. Darius ordered a check of the imperial rolls and found the decree, commanding, 'Let the governor of the Jews build this house of God. I, Darius, have a decree. Let it be done with speed.' In 518, he marched westwards to restore order in Egypt, probably passing through Judaea to settle the over-excited Jews of Jerusalem: he may have executed Zerubbabel, who now disappeared without explanation – the last of the Davidians.

In March 515, the Second Temple was dedicated joyfully by the priests with the sacrifice of 100 bullocks, 200 rams, 400 lambs and twelve goats (to expiate the sins of the Twelve Tribes). The Judaeans thus celebrated the first Passover since the Exile. But when the old men who remembered Solomon's Temple saw this modest building, they burst into tears. The city remained tiny and deserted.

Over fifty years later, the cup-bearer of Darius' grandson, King Artaxerxes I, was a Jew named Nehemiah. The Jerusalemites appealed to him for help: 'The remnant are in great affliction. The wall of Jerusalem is broken down.' Nehemiah was heartbroken: 'I sat down and wept and mourned.' When he was next serving at

---

* Darius raided Central Asia east of the Caspian, and probed India and Europe, attacking Ukraine and annexing Thrace. He built his sumptuous palace-capital of Persepolis (in southern Iran), promoted the religion of Zoroaster and Ahura Mazda, organized the first world currency (the Daric), raised a navy of Greeks, Egyptians and Phoenicians, and created the first real postal service, setting up inns every 15 miles along the 1,678 miles of the King's Road from Susa to Sardis. The achievements of his thirty-year reign make him the Augustus of the Persian empire. But even Darius reached his limits. Shortly before his death in 490 BC, he tried to push into Greece, where he was defeated at the Battle of Marathon.

court in Susa, the Persian capital, King Artaxerxes asked, 'Why is thy countenance sad?' 'Let the king live for ever,' replied this Jewish courtier, 'why should not my countenance be sad, when the city, the place of my father's sepulchres, lieth waste? ... If it please the king ... send me unto Judah ... that I may build it.' Nehemiah was 'sore afraid' as he awaited the answer.

NEHEMIAH: THE DECLINE OF THE PERSIANS

The Great King appointed Nehemiah governor and granted him funds and a military escort. But the Samaritans, north of Jerusalem, were ruled by their own hereditary governor, Sanballat, who distrusted this secretive courtier from faraway Susa and the schemes of the returning Exiles. By night Nehemiah, who feared assassination, inspected Jerusalem's broken walls and burned gates. His memoir, the only political autobiography in the Bible, tells how Sanballat 'laughed us to scorn' when he heard the plans to rebuild the walls until Nehemiah revealed his appointment as governor. Landowners and priests were each given sections of the wall to rebuild. When they were attacked by Sanballat's ruffians, Nehemiah set guards 'so the wall was finished in fifty and two days', enclosing just the City of David and the Temple Mount, with a small fortress north of the Temple.

Now Jerusalem 'was large and great', Nehemiah said, but 'the people were few therein'. Nehemiah persuaded the Jews outside the city to draw lots: one out of every ten would settle in Jerusalem. After twelve years Nehemiah travelled to Persia to report to the king, but when he returned to Jerusalem he found that Sanballat's cronies were lucratively running the Temple while the Jews were marrying with the locals. Nehemiah expelled these interlopers, discouraged intermarriage and imposed his new pure Judaism.

As the Persian kings lost control over their provinces, the Jews developed their own semi-independent statelet of Yehud. Based around the Temple, and funded by growing numbers of pilgrims, Yehud was ruled by the Torah and governed by a dynasty of high priests supposedly descended from King David's priest Zadok. Once again, the Temple treasury became a coveted prize. One of the high priests was murdered inside the Temple by his own avaricious brother, Jesus (the Aramaic for Joshua), a sacrilege that gave the Persian governor the pretext to march on Jerusalem and loot its gold.

While the Persian courtiers were distracted by their own homicidal intrigues, King Philip II of Macedon trained a formidable army, conquered the Greek city-states and prepared to launch a sacred war against Persia to avenge the invasions of Darius and his son Xerxes. When Philip was assassinated, his twenty-year-old son Alexander seized the throne and launched the attack on Persia that would bring Greece to Jerusalem.

7

THE MACEDONIANS

336–166 BC

ALEXANDER THE GREAT

Within three years of his father's murder in 336 BC, Alexander had twice defeated the Persian king Darius III, who decided to withdraw eastwards. Alexander did not pursue him at first, but instead marched along the coast towards Egypt, and ordered Jerusalem to contribute provisions for his army. The high priest initially refused. But not for long: when Tyre resisted him, Alexander besieged the city and when it fell, he crucified all its survivors.

Alexander 'hurried to go up to Jerusalem', wrote the Jewish historian Josephus much later, claiming that the conqueror was welcomed at the gates by the high priest in his purple and scarlet robes and all the Jerusalemites in white. They led him into the Temple where he sacrificed to the Jewish God. This story was probably wishful thinking: it is more likely that the high priest, along with the leaders of the semi-Jewish Samaritans, paid court to Alexander on the coast at Rosh Ha Ayim and that, emulating Cyrus, he recognized their right to live by their own laws.* He then pushed

* The Samaritans were already developing their separate semi-Jewish cult, based on a Judaism formed before the introduction of the new Babylonian rules. Under the Persians, Samaria was ruled by Sanballat's dynasty of governors. Their exclusion from Jerusalem encouraged them to set up their own Temple at Mount Gerizim and they embarked on a feud with the Jews and Jerusalem. Like all family rivalries, it was based on the hatred of tiny differences. The Samaritans became second-class citizens, despised by the Jews as heathens, hence Jesus' surprising revelation that there was such a thing as a 'good Samaritan'. Around a thousand Samaritans still live in Israel: long after the destruction of the end of the Jewish cult of sacrifice, the Samaritans in the twenty-first century still annually sacrifice the Passover lamb on Mount Gerizim.

on to conquer Egypt, where he founded the city of Alexandria before heading east, never to return.

After finishing off the Persian empire and expanding his hegemony as far as Pakistan, Alexander began his great project, the fusing of the Persians and Macedonians into a single elite to rule his world. If he did not quite succeed, he changed the world more than any other conqueror in history by spreading his version of Hellenikon – Greek culture, language, poetry, religion, sport and Homeric kingship – from the deserts of Libya to the foothills of Afghanistan. The Greek way of life became as universal as the British during the nineteenth century or the American today. From now on, even the monotheistic Jewish enemies of this philosophical and polytheistic culture could not help but see the world through the lens of Hellenism.

On 13 June 323, eight years after conquering the known world, Alexander lay in Babylon dying either of fever or of poison, aged just thirty-three. His devoted soldiers filed past his bed with tears pouring down their faces. When they asked him to whom he had left his kingdom, he replied: 'To the strongest.'

PTOLEMY: THE SABBATH SACKING

The tournament to find the strongest was a twenty-year war between Alexander's generals. Jerusalem was tossed between these Mace-donian warlords who 'multiplied the evils in the earth'. In the duel between the two leading contenders, Jerusalem changed hands six times. She was ruled for fifteen years by One-Eyed Antigonos, until in 301 he was killed in battle and the victor, Ptolemy, arrived outside the walls to claim Jerusalem.

Ptolemy was Alexander's cousin, a veteran general who had fought his way from Greece to Pakistan, where he had commanded the Macedonian fleet on the Indus. Just after Alexander's death, he was granted Egypt. When he heard that Alexander the Great's cortège was on its way back to Greece, he rushed up through Palestine to seize it and carried it back to rest in his capital, Alexandria. The guardian of the ultimate Greek talisman, Alexander's body, became the keeper of his flame. Ptolemy was not just a warlord: the soldier's strong chin and blunt nose on his coins belied his subtlety and common sense.

Now Ptolemy told the Jerusalemites that he wished to enter the city on the Sabbath to sacrifice to the Jewish God. The resting Jews believed this ruse and Ptolemy seized the city, thus revealing the fanaticism of Jewish observance. But when the sun set on the Sabbath, the Jews fought back. Ptolemy's troops then rampaged through Jerusalem – 'the houses rifled, the women ravished; and half the city go forth into captivity'. Ptolemy probably posted Macedonian garrisons in the Baris Fortress, built by Nehemiah just north of the Temple, and he deported thousands of Jews to Egypt. These founded the Greek-speaking Jewish community in Ptolemy's splendid capital Alexandria. In Egypt, Ptolemy and his successors became pharaohs; in Alexandria and the Mediterranean they were Greek kings. Ptolemy Soter – the 'Saviour' as he was known – adopted the local gods, Isis and Osiris, and Egyptian traditions of kingship, promoting his dynasty as both Egyptian god-kings and semi-divine Greek monarchs. He and his sons conquered Cyprus, Cyrenaica and then swathes of Anatolia and the Greek Islands. He understood that not just magnificence but also culture would give him legitimacy and greatness. So he made Alexandria the world's paramount Greek city, opulent and sophisticated, founding its Museum and the Library, recruiting Greek scholars and commissioning the Pharos lighthouse, one of the Wonders of the World. His empire endured for three centuries down to the last of his family – Cleopatra.

Ptolemy lived into his eighties, and wrote a history of Alexander. Ptolemy II Philadelphos favoured the Jews, freeing 120,000 Jewish slaves and sending gold to embellish the Temple. He understood the power of pageantry and spectacle. In 275 he held a parade for a small number of special guests in the name of Dionysus, god of wine and abundance, in which a vast wineskin made of leopard pelts held 200,000 gallons of wine and a phallos 180 feet long and 9 feet wide was paraded along with elephants and subjects from every corner of his empire. He was also an avid book collector. When the high priest sent the twenty or so books of the Jewish

Tanakh* to Alexandria, the king ordered it to be translated into Greek. He respected the scholarship of his Alexandrian Jews and invited them to a dinner to discuss the translation: 'everything', promised the king, 'will be served in compliance with your habits and for me also.' It was said that in seventy days the seventy scholars each produced an identical translation. The Septuagint Bible changed the history of Jerusalem and later made possible the spread of Christianity. Thanks to Alexander, Greek was the international language; now, for the first time, the Bible could be read by virtually everyone.

JOSEPH THE TOBIAD

Jerusalem remained a semi-independent statelet within Ptolemy's empire, and Judah issued its own coins, inscribed 'Yehud'. She was not just a political entity but God's own city ruled by the high priests. These scions of the Oniad family, claiming descent from the biblical priest Zadok, enjoyed the opportunity to amass fortunes and power, provided they paid tribute to the Ptolemies. In the 240s, High Priest Onias II tried to hold back the 20 silver talents he owed Ptolemy III Euergetes. This created an opportunity for a well-connected young Jew who decided to outbid the high priest not just for Jerusalem but for the entire land.

This adventurer was the high priest's own nephew, Joseph,† who set off for Alexandria where the king was holding an auction: bidders promised the highest tribute in return for the power to rule and tax their territories. The Syrian grandees mocked young Joseph but he outplayed them with outrageous chutzpah. He managed to see the king first and charmed him. When Ptolemy III asked for offers, the bumptious Joseph outbid his rivals for

---

* Tanakh was a Hebrew acronym for Law, Prophets and Writings, the books which the Christians later called The Old Testament.

† Joseph's family were Jews of mixed origin, perhaps descendants of a Tobiah the Ammonite who had opposed Nehemiah. His father Tobiah was a magnate close to Ptolemy II – the papyrus archive of a royal official named Zenon shows him trading with the king – and ruled huge estates in Amnon (today's Jordan).

all of Coele-Syria, Phoenicia, Judah and Samaria. The king asked Joseph for the usual hostages to guarantee his promised tribute. 'I give you no other persons, O King,' replied the cocky Jerusalemite, 'than yourself and your wife.' Joseph could have been executed for this impertinence but Ptolemy laughed and agreed.

Joseph returned to Jerusalem with 2,000 Egyptian infantry. He had much to prove. When Ashkelon refused to pay its taxes, he murdered its twenty leading citizens. Ashkelon paid.

Joseph, like his namesake in Genesis, had played at the highest level in Egypt and won. In Alexandria, where he hobnobbed with the king, he fell in love with an actress. When he set up the seduction, his brother replaced her with his own daughter. During the night, Joseph was too drunk to notice and when he was sober, he fell in love with his niece and their marriage strengthened the dynasty. However, their son Hyrcanus grew up to be as much of a rogue as Joseph himself. Living grandly, ruling severely and taxing exorbitantly, Joseph was nonetheless 'a good man of great magnanimity', according to Josephus, admired for his 'gravity, wisdom and justice. He brought the Jews out of a state of poverty and meanness to one that was more splendid.'

Joseph the Tobiad was important to the kings of Egypt because they were now continuously fighting a rival Macedonian dynasty, the Seleucids, for control of the Middle East. In about 241, Ptolemy III showed his gratitude, after a victory over his enemies, by visiting Jerusalem and there sacrificing respectfully in the Temple, hosted no doubt by Joseph. When the king died, however, the Egyptians found themselves challenged by a teenaged Seleucid king of irrepressible ambition.

ANTIOCHUS THE GREAT:
CLASH OF THE ELEPHANTS

The challenger was the Macedonian king of Asia, Antiochus III. In 223, this peripatetic eighteen-year-old inherited a grandiose title and a disintegrating empire,* but he possessed the gifts to reverse this decay. Antiochus regarded himself as the heir to Alexander and, like all the Macedonian kings, he associated himself with Apollo, Hercules, Achilles and, above all, Zeus. In a dizzying succession of campaigns, Antiochus reconquered Alexander's eastern empire as far as India, earning the soubriquet 'the Great'. He repeatedly attacked Palestine but the Ptolemies repelled his invasions and the ageing Joseph the Tobiad continued to rule Jerusalem. But his son Hyrcanus betrayed him and attacked the city. Shortly before his death, Joseph defeated his son, who went on to carve out his own principality in today's Jordan.

In 201, Antiochus the Great, now in his forties, returned from his triumphs in the east. Jerusalem was 'tossed like a ship in a storm between both sides'. Finally, Antiochus routed the Egyptians, and Jerusalem welcomed a new master. 'The Jews, when we came into their city,' declared Antiochus, 'gave us a splendid reception and met us with their senate, and also helped us expel the Egyptian garrison.' A Seleucid king and army were an impressive sight. Antiochus would have worn a diadem of royalty, laced boots of crimson embroidered with gold, a broad-brimmed hat and a dark-blue cloak spangled with gold stars, brooched at the throat in crimson. The Jerusalemites provisioned his multinational army that included Macedonian phalanxes bearing their sarissa lances, Cretan mountain fighters, Cilician light infantry, Thracian slingers, Mysian bowmen, Lydian javelineers, Persian bowmen, Kurdish infantry, Iranian heavy-armoured cataphracts on war horses and, most prestigious of all, elephants – probably a first for Jerusalem.†

* Antiochus was the heir of the other great dynasty descended from the generals who carved up Alexander the Great's empire. When Ptolemy I secured his own kingdom in Egypt, he backed Antiochus' ancestor Seleucos, one of Alexander's officers, in his bid to seize Babylon. As gifted as Ptolemy, Seleucos reconquered most of Alexander's Asian territories – hence the Seleucid title King of Asia. Seleucos ruled from Greece to the Indus – only to be assassinated at his apogee. The family had been promised Coele-Syria, but Ptolemy had refused to hand it over: the result was a century of Syrian wars.

† This was the age of the war elephant. Ever since Alexander had returned from his Indian campaign with a corps of elephants, these armoured pachyderms had become the most prestigious (and expensive) weapons for any self-respecting Macedonian

Antiochus promised to repair the Temple and the walls, repopulate the city and confirmed the Jews' right to rule themselves 'in accordance with the laws of their fathers'. He even banned foreigners from entering the Temple or bringing 'into the city the flesh of horses or mules or wild or tame asses or leopards, foxes or hares'. Simon, the high priest, had certainly backed the right side: never had Jerusalem enjoyed such an indulgent conqueror. Jerusalemites looked back at this time as a golden age ruled by the ideal high priest who, they said, resembled 'the morning star in the midst of a cloud'.

SIMON THE JUST: THE MORNING STAR

When Simon* emerged from the Holy of Holies on the Day of Atonement, the High Priest 'was clothed in the perfection of glory, when he went up to the holy altar'. He was the paragon of the high priests who ruled Judah as anointed princes, a combination of monarch, pope and ayatollah: he wore gilded robes, a gleaming breastplate and a crown-like turban on which he sported the *nezer*, a golden flower, the symbol of life and salvation, a relic of the headdress of the kings of Judah. Jesus Ben Sira, the author of Ecclesiasticus and the first writer to capture the sacred drama of

king – though they often trampled their own infantry instead of the enemy's. Meanwhile in the west, the Carthaginians, descendants of Phoenicians from Tyre, and the Romans, were fighting for mastery of the Mediterranean. Hannibal, the brilliant Carthaginian general, invaded Italy, having marched his elephants over the Alps. Antiochus deployed Indian elephants, the Ptolemies had African elephants and Hannibal used the smaller, now extinct species from the Atlas Mountains in Morocco.

* Some historians believe Simon actually ruled under Ptolemy I. The sources are contradictory but he was, most likely, Antiochus the Great's contemporary Simon II, who rebuilt the fortifications, repaired the Temple and added a giant cistern on the Temple Mount. His tomb stands north of the Old City in the Palestinian Sheikh Jarrah neighbourhood. During the Ottoman centuries, a 'Jewish picnic' was held there annually which was celebrated by Muslims, Jews and Christians together, one of the festivals shared by all sects in the days before nationalism. Today, the tomb is a Jewish shrine at the centre of Israeli plans to build a nearby settlement. Yet the tomb, like so many sites in Jerusalem, is itself a myth: it is neither Jewish nor the resting-place of Simon the Just. Built 500 years later, it was the tomb of a Roman lady, Julia Sabina.

the flourishing city, described Simon as 'a cypress tree which groweth up to the clouds'.

Jerusalem had become a theocracy – the very word was invented by the historian Josephus to describe this statelet with its 'entire sovereignty and all authority in the hands of God'. Harsh rules regulated every detail of life, for there was no distinction between politics and religion. In Jerusalem there were no statues nor graven images. The observance of the Sabbath was an obsession. All crimes against religion were punished with death. There were four forms of execution – stoning, burning, beheading and strangling. Adulterers were stoned, a punishment inflicted by the whole community (though the condemned were first thrown down a cliff so that they were usually unconscious by the time of the stoning). A son who struck his father was garrotted. A man who fornicated with both a mother and her daughter was burned.

The Temple was the centre of Jewish life: the high priest and his council, the Sanhedrin, met there. Every morning, the trumpets announced the first prayer, like the muezzin of Islam. Four times a day, the blaring of the seven silver trumpets called the worshippers to prostrate themselves in the Temple. The two daily sacrifices of a male sheep, cow or dove without blemish at the Temple altar, morning and evening, always accompanied by an offering of incense on the altar of perfumes, were the chief rituals of Jewish worship. The word 'holocaust', derived from the Hebrew *olah* meaning to 'go up', refers to the burning of the whole animal whose smoke 'goes up' to God. The city must have smelt of the Temple altar, the censers with their delicious cinnamon and cassia mixing with the reek of burning flesh. Small wonder the people wore much myrrh, nard and balm as perfumes.

Pilgrims poured into Jerusalem for the festivals. At the Sheep Gate to the north of the Temple, sheep and cattle were herded and wrangled, ready for sacrifice. At Passover, 200,000 lambs were slaughtered. But Tabernacles was the holiest and most exuberant week of the Jerusalem year, when men and girls in white costumes danced in the Temple courtyards, singing, waving lighted torches and feasting. They gathered palms and branches to build huts on the rooftops of their houses or in the Temple courts.*

Yet even under the pure Simon, there were many worldly Jews who probably looked like rich Greeks, living in their new Grecian palaces on the western hillside known as the Upper City. What the fanatical Jewish conservatives regarded as heathen pollution, these cosmopolitans saw as civilization. This was the start of a new pattern in Jerusalem: the more sacred she became, the more divided. Two ways of life existed in the closest proximity with the intimate loathing of a family feud. Now the city – and the very existence of the Jews – was threatened by the most infamous monster since Nebuchadnezzar.

ANTIOCHUS EPIPHANES: THE MAD GOD

Jerusalem's benefactor, Antiochus the Great, could not rest: he now turned to the conquest of Asia Minor and Greece. But the over-confident King of Asia underestimated the rising power of the Republic of Rome, which had just defeated Hannibal and Carthage to dominate the western Mediterranean. Rome repelled Antiochus' bid for Greece, forcing the Great King to surrender his fleet and elephant corps and send his son to Rome as a hostage. Antiochus headed east to replenish his treasury but, while looting a Persian temple, he was assassinated.

Jews, from Babylon to Alexandria, now paid an annual tithe to the Temple, and Jerusalem was so rich that her treasures intensified power struggles among the Jewish leaders and started to attract the cash-strapped Macedonian kings. The new king of Asia, named Antiochus like his father, rushed to the capital at Antioch and seized the throne, killing any other family claimants. Brought up in Rome

---

* The chief Jewish festivals – Passover, Weeks and Tabernacles – were still developing. Passover was the spring festival that now combined the two old feasts of the Unleavened Bread and the story of the Exodus. Gradually Passover replaced Tabernacles as the main Jewish festival in Jerusalem. Tabernacles survives today as Sukkot, when Jewish children still build a harvest hut decorated with fruit. Temple duties were divided by rota between the Levites, descendants of the tribe of Levi, and the priests (descendants of Moses' brother Aaron, themselves a sub-group of the Levites).

and Athens, Antiochus IV inherited the irrepressible, glittering talents of his father but his cackling menace and manic flamboyance more resembled the demented exhibitionism of Caligula or Nero.

As the son of a Great King laid low, he had too much to prove. As beautiful as he was unhinged, Antiochus relished the pageantry of court ritual yet was bored by its constraints, priding himself on his absolute right to surprise. In Antioch, the young king got drunk in the main square and bathed and was massaged in public with expensive unguents, befriending grooms and porters in the baths. When a spectator complained about his extravagant use of myrrh, Antiochus ordered the pot smashed over the man's head, causing a riot as the mob tried to salvage this priceless lotion while the king just laughed hysterically. He enjoyed dressing up, appearing in the streets in a crown of roses with a golden cloak, but when his subjects stared he threw stones at them. At night, he plunged in disguise into the stews of Antioch's backstreets. Spontaneously friendly to strangers, his caresses were panther-like for he could suddenly turn nasty, as pitiless as he was genial.

The potentates of the Hellenic age usually claimed descent from Hercules and other gods, but Antiochus took it a step further. He called himself Epiphanes – the God-manifest – though his subjects nicknamed him Epumanes – the Madman. But there was method in his madness for he hoped to bind his empire together around the worship of one king, one religion. He fully expected his subjects to worship their local gods and merge them into the Greek pantheon and his own cult. But it was different for the Jews, who had a love–hate relationship with Greek culture. They craved its civilization but resented its dominance. Josephus says they regarded Greeks as feckless, promiscuous, modernizing lightweights, yet many Jerusalemites were already living the fashionable lifestyle, using Greek and Jewish names to show they could be both. Jewish conservatives disagreed; for them, the Greeks were simply idolators, whose nude athletics disgusted them.

The first instinct of the Jewish grandees was to race each other to Antioch to bid for power in Jerusalem. The crisis started with a family feud about money and influence. When High Priest Onias III made his bid to the king, his brother Jason offered an extra eighty talents and returned as high priest with a programme to rebrand Jerusalem as a Greek *polis*: he renamed her Antioch-Hierosolyma (Antioch-in-Jerusalem) in honour of the king, downgraded the Torah and built a Greek gymnasium probably on the western hill facing the Temple. Jason's reforms were quite popular. Young Jews were painfully keen to appear fashionable at the gymnasium, where they exercised naked except for a Greek hat. Somehow they managed to reverse their circumcisions, the mark of the covenant with God, giving the appearance of restoring their foreskins, surely a triumph of fashion over comfort. But Jason himself was outbid for Jerusalem: he sent his henchman Menelaos to Antioch to deliver his tribute. But instead the thuggish Menelaos stole the Temple funds, outbid Jason and bought the high priesthood, even though he lacked the required Zadokite lineage. Menelaos seized Jerusalem. When the Jerusalemites sent delegates to the king to protest, he executed them, and he even allowed Menelaos to arrange the murder of the ex-High Priest Onias.

Antiochus was most concerned to raise funds to reconquer his empire – and he was about to pull off an astonishing coup: the uniting of the Ptolemaic and Seleucid empires. In 170 BC Antiochus conquered Egypt, but the Jerusalemites undermined his triumph, rebelling under the deposed Jason. The Madman marched back across Sinai, and stormed Jerusalem deporting 10,000 Jews.* Accompanied by his henchman Menelaos, he entered the Holy of Holies, an unforgivable sacrilege, and stole its priceless artefacts – the golden altar, the candlestick of light and the shewbread table. Worse, Antiochus ordered the Jews to sacrifice to him as God-manifest, testing the loyalty of the many Jews who were probably attracted to Greek culture – and then, his coffers filled with Temple gold, he rushed back to Egypt to crush any resistance.

Antiochus liked to play the Roman, sporting a toga and holding

* Jason fled again, taking refuge with his backer, Hyrcanus the Tobiad prince. Hyrcanus had ruled much of Jordan for forty years, remaining an ally of the Ptolemies even when they lost Jerusalem. He fought campaigns against the Arabians and built a luxurious fortress at Araq e-Emir with beautiful carvings and ornamental gardens. When Antiochus conquered Egypt and retook Jerusalem, Hyrcanus ran out of options: the last of the Tobiads committed suicide. The ruins of his palace are now a tourist site in Jordan.

mock elections in Antioch, while he secretly rebuilt his banned fleet and elephant corps. But Rome, determined to dominate the eastern Mediterranean, would not tolerate Antiochus' new empire. When the Roman envoy Popillius Laenas met the king in Alexandria, he brashly drew a circle in the sand around Antiochus, demanding he agree to withdraw from Egypt before stepping out of it – the origin of the phrase 'draw a line in the sand'. Antiochus, 'groaning and in bitterness of heart', bowed before Roman power.

Meanwhile the Jews refused to sacrifice to Antiochus the God. To ensure that Jerusalem would not rebel a third time, the Madman decided to eradicate the Jewish religion itself.

ANTIOCHUS EPIPHANES:
ANOTHER ABOMINATION OF DESOLATION

In 167, Antiochus captured Jerusalem by a ruse on the Sabbath, slaughtered thousands, destroyed her walls and built a new citadel, the Acra. He handed the city over to a Greek governor and the collaborator Menelaos.

Then Antiochus forbade any sacrifices or services in the Temple, banned the Sabbath, the Law and circumcision on pain of death, and ordered the Temple to be soiled with pigs' flesh. On 6 December, the Temple was consecrated as a shrine to the state god, Olympian Zeus – the very abomination of desolation. A sacrifice was made to Antiochus the God-King, probably in his presence, at the altar outside the Holy of Holies. 'The Temple was filled with riot and revelling by Gentiles who dallied with harlots,' fornicating 'in the holy places'. Menelaos acquiesced in this, people processed through the Temple wearing ivy crowns, and, after prayers, even many of the priests descended to watch the naked games at the gymnasium.

Those practising the Sabbath were burned alive or suffered a gruesome Greek import: crucifixion. An old man perished rather than eat pork; women who circumcised their children were thrown with their babies off the walls of Jerusalem. The Torah was torn to shreds and burned publicly: everyone found with a copy was put to death. Yet the Torah, like the Temple, was worth more than life.

These deaths created a new cult of martyrdom and stimulated expectation of the Apocalypse. 'Many of them that sleep in the dust of the earth shall awake and come to everlasting life' in Jerusalem, evil would fail, and goodness triumph with the arrival of a Messiah – and a Son of Man, invested with eternal glory.*

Antiochus progressed back to Antioch, where he celebrated his flawed victories with a festival. Gold-armoured Scythian horsemen, Indian elephants, gladiators and Nisaean horses with gold bridles paraded through the capital, followed by young athletes with gilded crowns, a thousand oxen for sacrifice, floats bearing statues, and women spraying perfume on to the crowds. Gladiators fought in the circuses and fountains ran red with wine while the king entertained a thousand guests at his palace. The Madman supervised everything, riding up and down the procession, ushering in guests, joking with his comedians. At the end of the banquet, the comedians carried in a figure swaddled in cloth. They laid it on the ground where, at the first notes of a symphonia, it suddenly threw off its coverings and out burst the king naked and dancing.

Far to the south of this delirious debauch, Antiochus' generals were enforcing his persecutions. In the village of Modin, near Jerusalem, an old priest called Mattathias, father of five sons, was ordered to make the sacrifice to Antiochus to prove he was no longer a Jew, but he replied: 'If all the nations of the King's dominion hearken unto him yet will I and my sons walk in the Covenant of our fathers.' When another Jew stepped forward to make the sacrifice, Mattathias' 'zeal was kindled, his veins trembled', and, drawing his sword, he killed first the traitor, then Antiochus' general, and pulled down the altar. 'Whoever maintaineth the Covenant,' he said, 'let him come forth after me.' The old man and his five sons fled into the mountains, joined by extremely pious Jews known as the Righteous – Hasidim. Initially they were so pious that they observed the Sabbath even (disastrously) in battle: the Greeks presumably tried to fight all their battles on Saturdays.

* The Book of Daniel is a collection of stories, some from the Babylonian Exile, others from the persecutions of Antiochus: the fiery furnace may describe his tortures. Daniel's new vision of an enigmatic 'Son of Man' inspired Jesus. The cult of martyrdom would be replayed in the early centuries of Christianity.

Mattathias died soon afterwards, but his third son Judah, assuming command in the hills around Jerusalem, defeated three Syrian armies in a row. Antiochus initially did not take the Jewish revolt seriously for he marched east to conquer Iraq and Persia, ordering his viceroy Lysias to crush the rebels. But Judah defeated him too.

Even Antiochus, campaigning in faraway Persia, realized that Judah's victories threatened his empire, and cancelled the terror. The Jews, he wrote to the pro-Greek members of the Sanhedrin, could 'use their own proper meats and observe their own laws'. But he was too late, and soon afterwards Antiochus Epiphanes suffered an epileptic fit and fell dead from his chariot. Judah had already earned the heroic moniker that would give its name to a dynasty: the Hammer.

8

THE MACCABEES

164–66 BC

JUDAH THE HAMMER

In the winter of 164 BC, Judah the Hammer conquered all of Judaea and Jerusalem apart from Antiochus' newly built Acra Fortress. When Judah saw the Temple overgrown and deserted, he lamented. He burned incense, rededicated the Holy of Holies, and on 14 December presided as sacrifices resumed. In the ravaged city, there was a shortage of oil to light the candelabra in the Temple, but somehow the candles never went out. The liberation and resanctification of the Temple are still celebrated in the Jewish festival of Hanukkah – the Dedication.

The Hammer – Maqqabah* in Aramaic – campaigned across the Jordan and sent his brother Simon to rescue the Jews in Galilee. In Judah's absence, the Jews were defeated. The Maccabee struck back, captured Hebron and Edom and smashed the pagan shrine in Ashdod before besieging the Acra in Jerusalem. But the Seleucid

---

* His family is correctly known as the Hasmonean dynasty, but for simplicity they are identified in this book as the Maccabeans. The Maccabee became the medieval prototype for Christian chivalry alongside King Arthur and Charlemagne. Charles 'Martel' – the Hammer – who defeated the Arabs at the Battle of Tours in 732; Richard the Lionheart in the twelfth century and Edward I (1272–1303) promoted themselves as latterday Maccabees. Later, Rubens painted Judah the Maccabee; Handel wrote an oratorio dedicated to him. The Maccabees have especially inspired Israel, where many of the football teams are named after them. As the heroes of Hanukkah, Jews traditionally regard them as freedom-fighters against a genocidal tyrant, a precursor of Hitler. But some have suggested another view, inspired by today's struggle between American democracy and jihadist terrorism, in which the Greeks are the civilized ones fighting Maccabee religious fanatics who resemble a Jewish Taleban.

regent defeated the Maccabees at Beth-Zacharia, south of Beth-lehem, then besieged Jerusalem, until he had to withdraw to face a revolt in Antioch. He therefore granted the Jews the right to live 'after their own laws' and worship in their Temple. Four centuries after Nebuchadnezzar, Jewish independence was restored.

But the Jews were not yet safe. The Seleucids, beset by civil wars, diminished but still formidable, were determined to crush the Jews and retain Palestine. This vicious, complicated war lasted twenty years. There is no need to recount every detail, with its many similarly named Seleucid pretenders, but there were moments when the Maccabees were close to annihilation. Yet this endlessly resourceful, gifted family always managed to recover and strike back.

The Acra Fortress, overlooking the Temple, remained to torment the divided Jerusalem. As the trumpets blew and the priests again performed the sacrifices, Acra's pagan mercenaries and renegade Jews sometimes 'rushed out suddenly', says Josephus, 'and destroyed those going up to the Temple'. The Jerusalemites executed the high priest, Menelaos, 'the cause of all evils', and elected a new one.* But the Seleucids rallied again. Their general Nicanor recaptured Jerusalem. Pointing at the altar, the Greek issued a threat: 'unless Judah and his host be now delivered in my hands, I will burn up this House.'

Judah, fighting for his life, appealed to Rome, that enemy of the Greek kingdoms, and Rome effectively recognized Jewish sovereignty. In 161, the Hammer routed Nicanor, ordering his head and his arm to be cut off and brought to Jerusalem. At the Temple, he presented these ghoulish trophies – the hand and the excised tongue that had threatened the Temple were shredded and hung out for the birds while the head lolled atop the fortress. Jerusalemites celebrated Nicanor Day as a festival of deliverance. The Seleucids

* This new high priest was not even a member of the Zadokite House of Onias. Its rightful heir was Onias IV, who now fled with his followers to Egypt where he was welcomed by King Ptolemy VI Philometer. Philometer allowed him to build a Jewish temple on the site of a disused Egyptian shrine at Leontopolis in the Nile Delta, and there he created his own Jerusalem, still known as Tell al-Jahudiya – Hill of the Jews. These Jewish princes became powerful military commanders in Egypt. Onias' temple lasted until Titus ordered its destruction in AD 70.

then defeated and killed the Maccabee himself; Jerusalem fell.
Judah was buried in Modin. All seemed lost. But he was survived
by his brothers.

SIMON THE GREAT: TRIUMPH OF THE MACCABEES

After two years on the run, Jonathan, Judah's brother, emerged
from the deserts to rout the Seleucids again, setting up his court at
Michmas, north of Greek-held Jerusalem. Jonathan, known as the
Diplomat, played off the rival kings of Syria and Egypt to regain
Jerusalem. He then restored the walls, resanctified the Temple and,
in 153, persuaded the Seleucid king to appoint him to the gold-
clasped rank of 'king's friend' – and High Priest. The Maccabee
was anointed with the oil and bedecked with the royal flower and
the priestly robes at the most raucous of festivals, Tabernacles. Yet
Jonathan was descended from a provincial priest with no connection
to Zadok. At least one Jewish sect saw him as the 'Wicked Priest'.

First Jonathan was backed by the Egyptian king Ptolemy VI
Philometer, who marched up the coast to Joppa (Jerusalem's nearest
port, Jaffa), to meet Jonathan, in their respective pharaonic and
priestly magnificence. At Ptolemais (now Acre), Philometer
achieved the dream of every Greek king since Alexander the Great:
he was crowned king of Egypt and Asia. But at the very moment of
his triumph, his horse reared at the sight of the Seleucid elephants,
and he was killed.*

As rival Seleucids fought for power, Jonathan the Diplomat
repeatedly switched sides. One of the Seleucid pretenders, besieged

---

* Philometer's successor was hostile to the Jews because Onias and the Alexandrian
Jews had supported Philometer. Even by the family's vicious standards, Ptolemy
VIII Euergetes, nicknamed Fatso (Physkon) by the Alexandrian mob, was a monster.
Fatso took revenge on the Jews in Egypt, massing his elephants to trample them,
but, perhaps in a divine miracle, the elephants trampled the king's entourage instead.
The climax of his cruelties was the murder of his own fourteen-year-old son who
totally trusted his father: Fatso had the boy's head, legs and hands cut off and sent
to his own mother, Cleopatra II. When another of the family, Cleopatra Thea who
married the Syrian king Demetrius II, decided to murder her own son, she offered
him a cup of poison. But the son forced the mother to drink it. Such was family life
among the Ptolemies.

in his Antioch palace, appealed for Jonathan's help in return for full Jewish independence. Jonathan marched his 2,000 men all the way from Jerusalem, through what is now Israel, Lebanon and Syria, to Antioch. The Jewish soldiers, firing arrows from the palace then leaping from roof to roof across the burning city, rescued and restored the king. Returning to Judaea, Jonathan conquered Ashkelon, Gaza, and Beth-Zur – and started to besiege the Acra Fortress in Jerusalem. But he was lured to Ptolemais without his bodyguards to meet his latest Greek ally who seized him and marched on Jerusalem.

The Maccabee family was not yet exhausted: there was still one more brother. This was Simon, who refortified Jerusalem and rallied his army. Along with a sudden snowstorm, this forced the Greek to retreat, but he had his revenge: he executed Simon's captive brother, Jonathan. In spring 141, Simon stormed and demolished the Acra,* razing the very hill on which it stood before celebrating in Jerusalem 'with praise, palm branches, harps, cymbals, viols and hymns.' The 'yoke of the heathen was taken away from Israel' and a Great Assembly hailed Simon as hereditary ruler, clothing him in royal purple buckled with gold, king in all but name. 'The people began to write in their contracts: "In the first year of Simon the Great, High Priest, Commander-in-Chief and Leader of the Jews".'

JOHN HYRCANUS: EMPIRE-BUILDER

Simon the Great was at the height of his popularity when, in 134 BC, he was invited to dinner by his son-in-law. There, the last of the first generation of Maccabees was assassinated, and the son-in-law then seized Simon's wife and two of his sons. Assassins tried to

---

* No trace has been found of the Acra. Some scholars believe it stood just south of Temple Mount. Herod the Great was to extend the Temple Mount, so probably the razed hill of the Acra is now beneath the Temple platform where al-Aqsa Mosque stands. For those who question why so little survives from the reign of, say, King David, this demonstrates that enormous constructions can leave no archaeological trace.

catch his other son John – Yehohanan in Hebrew – but he made it
to Jerusalem and held the city.

John faced disaster on every side. When he pursued the conspirators to their stronghold, his mother and brothers were torn to
pieces before him. As the third son, John had not expected to reign
but he possessed all the family talents to become the ideal Jewish
ruler, with 'charismatic-Messianic traits'. Indeed, wrote Josephus,
God granted John 'three of the greatest privileges – the rule of the
nation, the office of High Priest and the gift of prophecy'.

The Seleucid king, Antiochus VII Sidetes, exploited this Jewish
civil war to regain Palestine and besiege Jerusalem. The Jerusalemites were starting to starve, when King Sidetes signalled his
willingness to negotiate by sending in 'a magnificent sacrifice' of
bulls with gilded horns for the Feast of Tabernacles. John sued for
peace, agreeing to surrender Maccabee conquests outside Judaea,
to pay 500 silver talents and to demolish the walls.

John had to support his new master on campaign against the
rising power in Iran and Iraq, the Parthians. The expedition
proved a disaster for the Greeks but a blessing for the Jews. John
may have secretly negotiated with the Parthian king, who had
many Jewish subjects. The Greek king was killed and somehow
John escaped from this quagmire, returning with his independence restored.*

The great powers were distracted by their own internecine
intrigues, so John was free to embark on conquests on a scale
unseen since David, who ironically helped fund his wars: John
plundered his rich tomb, presumably in the old City of David. He
conquered Madaba across the Jordan, forced the conversion of the
Edomites (who became known as the Idumeans) to the south, and
destroyed Samaria before taking Galilee. In Jerusalem, John built
the so-called First Wall around the growing city.† His kingdom was

---

* And with a new nickname, Hyrcanus, surely the result of his Parthian adventures,
even though he never reached Hyrcania on the Caspian. He consolidated his power
abroad with a new Roman alliance and in Jerusalem through the backing of the rich
Temple elite, the Sadducees, descendants of the house of Zadok – hence their name.
† The city wall extended from the Temple Mount to the Siloam Pool and thence to
the Citadel, where the foundations of his towers remain today, and where one can
see little residential houses of Maccabean Jerusalem. Sections of his wall survive at

a regional power, and its Temple was the centre of Jewish life, though the growing communities around the Mediterranean conducted their daily prayers in local synagogues. It was probably in this newly confident time that the twenty-four books became the agreed text of the Jewish Old Testament.

After John's death, his son Aristobulos declared himself king of Judaea, the first monarch in Jerusalem since 586, and conquered Iturea in today's northern Israel and southern Lebanon. But the Maccabeans were now almost as Greek as their enemies, using both Greek and Hebrew names. They started to behave with all the ferocity of Greek tyrants. Aristobulos threw his mother into jail and murdered his more popular brother, a crime that drove him mad with guilt. Yet as he died vomiting blood, he feared that his arrogant surviving brother, Alexander Jannaeus, was a monster who would destroy the Maccabees.

ALEXANDER THE THRACIAN:
THE FURIOUS YOUNG LION

As soon as he had secured Jerusalem, King Alexander (Jannaeus was the Greek version of his Hebrew name Yehonatan) married his brother's widow and set about conquering a Jewish empire. Alexander was spoilt and heartless – soon the Jews loathed him for his debauched sadism. But Alexander enjoyed his freedom to wage war on his neighbours – the Greek kingdoms were collapsing, the Romans had not yet arrived. Alexander always managed to survive

various places: on the south slope of Mount Zion, just west of the Catholic Cemetery, there is a place where John's wall still stands next to the bigger stones of Hezekiah's and the much later ones of the Byzantine empress Eudocia. In 1985, Israeli archaeologists discovered a subterranean aqueduct and large pool built by John and the Maccabees. British, German and French archaeologists in the nineteenth century had uncovered this Struthion Pool underground in 1870 when the Sisters of Zion convent was built on the Via Dolorosa. The aqueduct reveals how the Struthion Pool was supplied and, beneath the Convent, close to the Via Dolorosa, visitors can walk along this aqueduct, now part of the Temple Tunnel. The Maccabees also built a bridge across the deep valley between the Temple Mount and the Upper City. John himself resided in his Baris stronghold, north of the Temple, but he also probably started to build a palace in the expanding Upper City.

his frequent defeats thanks to the luck of the devil* and tenacious savagery: the Jews nicknamed him the Thracian for his barbarism and his army of Greek mercenaries.

Alexander conquered Gaza and Raphia on the borders of Egypt and the Gaulanitis (Golan) in the north. Ambushed by the Nabataean Arabs in Moab, Alexander fled back to Jerusalem. When he officiated as high priest at the Feast of Tabernacles, the people bombarded him with fruit. Encouraged by the more religious Pharisees (who followed oral traditions as well as the written Torah), they taunted him with the claim that, since his mother had been a prisoner, he was unfit to be high priest. Alexander responded by unleashing his Greek mercenaries, who massacred 6,000 people in the streets. The Seleucids exploited the rebellion to attack Judaea. Alexander fled to the hills.

He bided his time, planning his revenge. When the king re-entered Jerusalem, he slaughtered 50,000 of his own people. He celebrated his victory by cavorting with his concubines at a feast while he watched 800 rebels being crucified around the hills. The throats of their wives and children were slit before their eyes. 'The furious young lion', as his enemies called him, died of alcoholism, leaving his wife Salome Alexandra a Jewish empire that included parts of today's Israel, Palestine, Jordan, Syria and Lebanon. He advised her to conceal his death from the soldiers until she had secured Jerusalem, then to govern with the Pharisees.

The new queen was the first woman to rule Jerusalem since Jezebel's daughter. But the genius of the dynasty was exhausted. Salome Alexandra (Salome being the Greek version of Sha-lomzion – Peace in Zion), shrewd widow of two kings, ruled her little empire into her sixties with the help of the Pharisees, but she struggled to control her two sons: the elder, the high priest John

* When he attacked the Greek city Ptolemais, Ptolemy IX Soter, then ruling in Cyprus, intervened and defeated Alexander. But he was rescued by Jewish con-nections: Soter was at war with his mother Cleopatra III, Queen of Egypt, who feared her son's power in Judaea. Cleopatra's commander was the Jewish Ananias, the son of the ex-high priest Onias, who rescued the Maccabean king. Cleopatra considered annexing Judaea, but her Jewish general advised against this, and she was in no position to take on her own army.

Hyrcanus II, was not energetic enough, while the younger Aristobulos was too energetic by far.

To the north, Rome advanced relentlessly around the Mediterranean, swallowing first Greece then today's Turkey, where Roman power was resisted by Mithridates, the Greek King of Pontus. In 66 BC, the Roman general Pompey defeated Mithridates, and moved south to fill the vacuum. Rome was coming to Jerusalem.

9

THE ROMANS ARRIVE

66–40 BC

POMPEY IN THE HOLY OF HOLIES

When Queen Salome died, her sons fought. Hyrcanus II was defeated near Jericho by his brother Aristobulos II. The brothers were reconciled, embracing before the Jerusalemites in the Temple, and Aristobulos became king. Hyrcanus retired, but he was advised and controlled by a cunning outsider, Antipater. This Idumean potentate* was the future. His son would become King Herod. Their talented and depraved family would dominate Jerusalem for over a century and essentially create the Temple Mount and Western Wall as they are today.

Antipater helped Hyrcanus flee to Petra, the 'rose red city half as old as time', the Nabataean Arab capital. King Aretas (Harith in Arabic), fabulously rich from the Indian spice trade and related to Antipater's Arab wife, helped them defeat King Aristobulos, who fled back to Jerusalem. The Arab king gave chase, besieging Aristobulos in the fortified Temple Mount. But all this sound and fury signified nothing, because to the north Pompey was setting up headquarters in Damascus. Gnaeus Pompeius, the most powerful man in Rome, was a maverick commander who without official position had led his private army to victory in the Roman civil wars in Italy, Sicily and North Africa. He had celebrated two Triumphs and won vast wealth. He was a cautious general with a cherubic

* The Idumeans, the Biblical Edomites, tough pagan warriors based to the south of Jerusalem, had been converted en masse to Judaism by John Hyrcanus. Antipater was the son of a convert to Judaism who had been appointed Governor of Edom by King Alexander, though the family originated from the Phoenician coastal cities.

face – 'nothing was more delicate than Pompey's cheeks' – but this was deceptive: Pompey was, wrote the historian Sallust, 'honest in face, shameless in heart', and his early sadism and greed in the civil wars had earned him the nickname 'the young butcher'. Now he had established himself in Rome but the laurels of a Roman strongman required constant refreshment. His nickname 'Magnus' – the Great – was at least partly sarcastic. As a boy he had worshipped Alexander the Great, and his Homeric, heroic kingship, along with the unconquered provinces and prizes of the East, would henceforth prove irresistible to every Roman oligarch on the make.

In 64 BC, Pompey terminated the Seleucid kingdom, annexed Syria and was happy to mediate between the warring Jews. Delegations arrived from Jerusalem representing not only both the feuding brothers but also the Pharisees, who begged Pompey to rid them of Maccabeans. Pompey ordered both princes to await his judgement, but Aristobulos, who had not quite grasped the steely power of Rome, rashly double-crossed him.

Pompey swooped on Jerusalem. He captured Aristobulos, but the Maccabean's retainers occupied the fortified Temple Mount, breaking down the bridge that linked it to the Upper City. Pompey, encamped north of the Bethesda Pool, besieged the Temple for three months, using catapults to bombard it. Once again taking advantage of Jewish piety – it was the Sabbath and a fast – the Romans stormed the Temple from the north, cutting the throats of the priests who guarded the altar. Jews set alight their own houses; others threw themselves from the battlements. Twelve thousand were killed. Pompey destroyed fortifications, abolished the monarchy, confiscated most of the Maccabean kingdom and appointed Hyrcanus as high priest, ruling just Judaea with his minister Antipater.

Pompey could not resist the opportunity of seeing inside the famous Holy of Holies. The Romans were intrigued by Eastern rites yet proud of their many gods and disdainful of the primitive superstition of Jewish monotheism. The Greeks sneered that the Jews in secret worshipped a golden ass's head or fattened up a human sacrifice to cannibalize later. Pompey and his entourage entered the Holy of Holies, an unspeakable sacrilege given that even the high priest visited it only once a year. The Roman was probably only the second gentile (after Antiochus IV) ever to penetrate the Sanctuary. Yet he respectfully examined the golden table and the holy candelabra – and realized that there was nothing else there, no godhead, just an intense sanctity. He stole nothing.

Pompey hurried back to Rome to enjoy the Triumph celebrating his Asian conquests. Hyrcanus meanwhile was tormented by the rebellions of Aristobulos and his sons, but the real ruler, his minister Antipater, possessed a genius for winning support in Rome which was now the source of all power. However, even that most serpentine of politicians was challenged by the twists of Roman politics. Pompey was forced to share power in a triumvirate with two other leaders, Crassus and Caesar, the latter soon to make his name conquering Gaul. In 55 BC, Crassus, the next Roman oligarch looking for glory in the east, arrived in Syria, keen to equal the conquests of his rivals.

CAESAR AND CLEOPATRA

Crassus, known in Rome as Dives, the Rich Man, was notorious for his avarice and cruelty. He had added victims to the Roman dictator Sulla's death-lists purely to seize their money, while he had celebrated his suppression of the Spartacus rebellion by crucifying 6,000 slaves along the Appian Way. Now he planned an expedition to throw back the new Parthian kingdom that had replaced the Persians and Seleucids in today's Iraq and Iran.

Crassus funded his invasion by raiding the Temple in Jerusalem, whence he stole 2,000 talents untouched by Pompey and the 'beam of solid gold' in the Holy of Holies. But the Parthians annihilated Crassus and his army. The Parthian king Orad II was watching a Greek play when Crassus' head was tossed on stage. Orad had molten gold poured into Crassus' mouth, saying, 'Be satisfied now with thy life's desire.'

Now Rome's two strongmen, Caesar and Pompey, competed for supremacy. In 49 BC, Caesar crossed the Rubicon from Gaul and invaded Italy, defeating Pompey eighteen months later. Pompey fled to Egypt. Elected dictator of Rome, Caesar gave chase, arriving in Egypt two days after the Egyptians had murdered Pompey. He was horrified yet relieved to receive Pompey's pickled head as a welcoming gift. He had campaigned in the East thirty years earlier. Now he found Egypt divided in a vicious struggle between King Ptolemy XIII and his sister-wife Cleopatra VII to secure for Rome the richest prize of the East: Egypt. But he could not have foreseen how this young queen, deposed from the throne and in desperate straits, would shape his will to her own ends.

Cleopatra demanded a secret audience with the master of the Roman empire. This accomplished impresario of sexual-political pantomime had herself carried into Caesar's palace wrapped in a laundry bag (not a carpet) – perhaps divining that he was susceptible to such theatrical excitement. Gaius Julius Caesar, battleworn and grizzled, was fifty-two and self-conscious about his balding pate. But this astounding if somewhat chilling life-force, possessed of all the talents of war, letters and politics, and the remorseless energy of a younger man, was also a sexual adventurer who had slept with the wives of both Crassus and Pompey. Cleopatra was twenty-one: 'her beauty was absolutely not without parallel but her physical attractions, combined with her persuasive charm and the aura she projected' exerted a powerful fascination, even if, as coins and statues suggest, she possessed the aquiline nose and pointed chin of her forebears. She had a kingdom to reclaim and a peerless lineage to live up to. Both Caesar and Cleopatra were keen practitioners of the adventurous school of politics. They embarked on an affair – she soon bore him a child, Caesarion – but, more importantly, he was now committed to back her.

Caesar soon found himself trapped in Alexandria as the Egyptians rose against Cleopatra and her Roman patron. Meanwhile in Jerusalem, Antipater, Pompey's ally, saw a chance of redeeming himself with Caesar. He marched on Egypt with 3,000 Jewish troops, persuaded the Egyptian Jews to back him, and attacked Caesar's opponents. Caesar triumphed and restored Cleopatra. Before returning to Rome, the grateful Caesar reappointed Hyrcanus as high priest and ethnarch – ruler – of the Jews and let him repair Jerusalem's walls, but he granted all the power to Antipater as procurator of Judaea with his sons as the local tetrarchs: the elder one, Phasael, ran Jerusalem; the younger, Herod, got Galilee.

Herod, aged just fifteen, immediately showed his mettle when he hunted down and killed a band of fanatical religious Jews. In Jerusalem, the Sanhedrin were incensed by young Herod's unauthorized killings and summoned him for trial. However, the Romans appreciated that Antipater and his sons were the sort of allies required to govern this turbulent people. The Roman governor of Syria ordered Herod's acquittal and awarded him greater powers.

Herod was already exceptional. He was, wrote Josephus, 'blessed with every gift of looks, body and mind'. Named to be a hero, he was sophisticated enough to charm and impress the pre-eminent Romans of the era. He was sexually voracious – or, as Josephus put it, 'slave to his passions' – yet he was not crude. He had taste in architecture, was highly educated in Greek, Latin and Jewish culture and, when not busy with politics and pleasure, he enjoyed debates on history and philosophy. Yet power always came first and this craving would poison every relationship he had. Son of a second-generation Idumean convert to Judaism and an Arab mother (hence his brother was called Phasael – Faisal), Herod was a cosmopolitan who could play the Roman and the Greek and the Jew. But the Jews never quite forgave his mongrel origins. Raised in a rich but vigilant and ruthless household, he would see the destruction of his closest family and sense the fragility of power and the facility of terror. He grew up using death as a political tool: paranoid, over-sensitive, almost hysterical, this tough teenager, a 'man of great barbarity' as well as sensitivity, played to survive and dominate at all costs.

After Caesar was assassinated in 44, Cassius (who was one of his killers) arrived to govern Syria. Herod's father Antipater switched sides. But the somersaults of intrigue finally caught up with him, and he was poisoned by a rival, who managed to occupy Jerusalem – until Herod had him murdered. Soon afterwards, Cassius and his fellow assassin Brutus were defeated at Philippi. The victors were Caesar's great-nephew and adopted son Octavian, twenty-two years old, and the swashbuckling general Mark Antony. They split the empire, Antony receiving the East. As Antony processed towards Syria, two young potentates, with radically opposite interests, rushed to meet the Roman strongman. One wanted to restore the Jewish kingdom, the other to swallow it into her ancestral empire.

ANTONY AND CLEOPATRA

Cleopatra came to Antony, as a queen at the height of her charisma, scion of the Ptolemies, the most prestigious dynasty in the known world, and, as Isis-Aphrodite to meet her Dionysus, who could grant her the provinces of her forefathers.

Their meeting was fateful for both. Antony was fourteen years older than her but in his prime: he was hard-drinking, thick-necked, barrel-chested, lantern-jawed and prided himself on his muscular legs. He was dazzled by Cleopatra and keen to embrace the Greek culture and sybaritic splendour of the East, seeing himself as the heir of Alexander, descendant of Hercules – and Dionysus of course. But he also required Egyptian money and provisions for his planned Parthian invasion. Thus they needed each other, and necessity is so often the mother of romance. Antony and Cleopatra celebrated their alliance and affair by murdering Cleopatra's sister (she had already murdered her brother).

Herod, too, had ridden hastily to Antony. As a young cavalry commander in Egypt, the general had been cultivated by Herod's father. He therefore appointed Herod and his brother as the real rulers of Judaea with High Priest Hyrcanus as the figurehead. Herod celebrated his rising power with a royal engagement. His fiancée was Mariamme, a Maccabean princess who, by family intermarriage, was the granddaughter of two kings. Her body, wrote Josephus, was as beautiful as her face. This relationship, played out in Jerusalem, would be passionately destructive.

Antony followed Cleopatra, now pregnant with his twins, to her capital, Alexandria. But, just as it appeared that Herod's rise was assured, the Parthians invaded Syria. Antigonos, a Maccabean prince who was Hyrcanus' nephew, offered the Parthians 1,000 talents and a harem of 500 girls in exchange for Jerusalem.

PACORUS: PARTHIAN SHOT

The Jewish city rose against the Roman puppets Herod and his brother Phasael. Besieged in the royal palace opposite the Temple, the brothers defeated the rebellion – but the Parthians were a different matter. Jerusalem was crowded with pilgrims – it was the Feast of Weeks – as Maccabean supporters opened the gates for the Parthian prince Pacorus* and his protégé Antigonos. Jerusalem celebrated the return of the Maccabees.

The Parthians pretended to play the honest broker between Herod and Antigonos. Instead they lured Herod's brother Phasael into a trap. Herod faced elimination as the Parthians looted the city and then handed power to Antigonos as king of Judaea and high priest.† He mutilated his uncle Hyrcanus, cutting off his ears, to disqualify him from the high priesthood. As for Herod's brother Phasael, he was either murdered or dashed out his own brains.

Herod had lost Jerusalem and his brother. He had backed the Romans, but it was the Parthians who had conquered the Middle East. A mercurial man, he was surely cyclothymic, if not a manic depressive. But his will to power, pungent intelligence, greed for life and instinct for survival were ferocious. He almost cracked up, but he overcame his nerves. By night, he gathered his entourage for a desperate escape, and a bid for power.

---

* Pacorus was the son and heir-apparent of the Arsacid King of Kings, Orad II, who had defeated Crassus. The Parthians had expanded from their homeland east of the Caspian, breaking away from the Seleucids around 250 BC, to create a new empire that challenged Roman power. Pacorus' army was spearheaded by his Pahlavan knights, who wore heavy armour and loose trousers and wielded 12-foot lances, axes and maces. Charging at full tilt, these cataphracts had smashed the Roman legions at Carrhae. They were supported by mounted archers famous for the speed and accuracy of their over-the-shoulder marksmanship – the 'Parthian shot'. But Parthia had a feudal flaw: its kings were often at the mercy of its overmighty, insubordinate nobles.

† Antigonos, son of the late king Aristobulos II, used Greek and Hebrew names. His coins show the Temple menorah – the candelabra, his family's symbol – with 'King Antigonos' in Greek; the reverse has the Temple shewbread table with 'Mattathias the High Priest' in Hebrew.

HEROD: ESCAPE TO CLEOPATRA

Herod, accompanied by his retinue – 500 concubines, his mother, sister, and, most importantly, his fiancée, the Maccabee princess Mariamme – galloped out of Jerusalem into the barren Judaean hills. King Antigonos, furious that Herod had escaped with his concubines (clearly the harem offered as payment to the Parthians) sent his cavalry in pursuit. As he fled through the hills, Herod again broke down and tried to commit suicide, but his guards snatched his raised sword. Soon afterwards Antigonos' horsemen caught up with his caravan. Herod recovered his confidence and defeated them. Leaving his entourage in the impregnable mountain fortress of Masada, he himself escaped to Egypt.

Antony had already left for Rome, but Herod was welcomed by Queen Cleopatra, who offered him employment in a bid to keep him in Alexandria. Instead Herod sailed for Rome, accompanied by his fiancée's little brother, Jonathan, a Maccabean prince who was his candidate for the Judaean throne. But Antony, who was now planning a war to expel the Parthians, realized that this was no job for a child; it would require Herod's ruthless competence.

Antony and Octavian, his partner in ruling the empire, escorted Herod to the Senate where he was declared king of Judaea and Roman ally: *rex socius et amicus populi Romani*. The newly minted King Herod walked out of the Senate flanked by Octavian and Antony, the two pillars of the world, quite a moment for a half-Jew half-Arab from the mountains of Edom. His relationship with these two men would be the foundation of his forty-year reign of terror and magnificence. However, he was a long way from ruling a kingdom: the Parthians still occupied the east; Antigonos reigned in Jerusalem. To the Jews, Herod was a Roman stooge and Idumean mongrel. He would have to fight for every inch of his kingdom, and then Jerusalem.

10

THE HERODS

40 BC–AD 10

THE FALL OF ANTIGONOS: LAST OF THE MACCABEANS

Herod sailed to Ptolemais, mustered an army and started to conquer his kingdom. When rebels held out in impregnable caves in Galilee, he lowered his troops in chests held by chains and, armed with hooks, these soldiers fished out his opponents and sent them hurtling into the canyons below. But Herod needed Antony's support to take Jerusalem.

The Romans were driving back the Parthians. In 38 BC, Antony himself was besieging a Parthian fortress at Samosata (southeastern Turkey) when Herod marched north to offer, and ask for, help. The Parthians had ambushed Antony when Herod counterattacked and saved the baggage-train. The bluff Antony welcomed Herod like an old comrade, affectionately hugging him in front of his army, paraded in honour of the young king of Judaea. The grateful Antony despatched 30,000 infantry and 6,000 cavalry to besiege Jerusalem in Herod's name. As the Romans pitched camp just north of the Temple, Herod married the seventeen-year-old Mariamme. After a forty-day siege, the Romans stormed the outer wall. Two weeks later, they burst into the Temple, ravaging the city 'like a company of madmen', cutting down the Jerusalemites in the narrow streets. Herod had to bribe the Romans to stop the slaughter – and then sent the captured Antigonos to Antony who solicitously beheaded the last Maccabean king. The Roman strongman then set off to invade Parthia with 100,000 troops. His military prowess was much exaggerated; his expedition was a near-disaster, and he lost a third of his army. The survivors were saved by

Cleopatra's delivery of provisions. Antony's reputation in Rome never quite recovered.

King Herod celebrated his conquest of Jerusalem by liquidating forty-five of the seventy-one members of the Sanhedrin. Demolishing the Baris Fortress north of the Temple, he built a square fortified tower with four turrets, the Antonia, named after his patron, and colossal enough to dominate the city. Nothing is left of the Antonia except traces of its stone-cut base, but we know what it must have been like because many of Herod's fortresses survive: each of his mountain strongholds was designed to combine impregnable security with peerless luxury.* Yet he never felt secure, and now he had to defend his kingdom from the intrigues of two queens, his own wife Mariamme – and Cleopatra.

HEROD AND CLEOPATRA

Herod may have been feared but he himself was wary of the Maccabeans, and the most dangerous of them was in his own bed. The king, now aged thirty-six, had fallen in love with Mariamme, who was cultured, chaste and haughty. But her mother, Alexandra, a real-life version of the stereotype of the mother-in-law from hell, immediately started to conspire with Cleopatra to destroy Herod. The Maccabean women were proud of their lineage and she resented her daughter having married into the mongrel Herodians. Yet Alexandra did not realize that, even by the feral standards of first-century politics, the psychotic Herod was more than a match for her.

Since the mutilated old Hyrcanus could no longer officiate in the Temple, Alexandra wanted her teenaged son Jonathan, Mariamme's younger brother, to become high priest, an eminence

---

* The murdered counsellors were probably buried in the ornate Sanhedrin tomb that still stands north of the Old City, decorated with pomegranates and acanthus leaves. As for his mountain strongholds, the most famous are: Masada, where the last Jewish fighters against Rome committed mass suicide in AD 73; Machaerus, where John the Baptist was beheaded by one of Herod's sons; and the man-made mountain of Herodium, where Herod and his sons were buried.

to which Herod, the half-Arab Idumean parvenu, could not aspire. Jonathan happened to be not only the rightful king but also of arresting beauty in an age when appearances were believed to reflect divine favour. He was mobbed wherever he went. Herod feared the teenager and solved this problem by raising an obscure Babylonian Jew to the high priesthood. Alexandra secretly appealed to Cleopatra. Antony had increased Cleopatra's kingdom with lands in Lebanon, Crete and north Africa and also gave her one of Herod's most valuable possessions – the balsam and date groves of Jericho.* Herod rented them back from her but it was obvious that she coveted Judaea, the territory of her forefathers.

Dangling the pretty Jonathan like a tasty morsel, Mariamme and her mother Alexandra sent a painting of the boy to Antony who, like most men of his era, appreciated male as much as female beauty. Cleopatra promised to support his claim to be king. So when Antony summoned the boy, Herod was thoroughly alarmed and refused to let him go. Herod placed his mother-in-law under close surveillance in Jerusalem, while Cleopatra offered asylum to her and her son. Alexandra had two coffins made to smuggle them out of the palace.

At last Herod, unable to resist Maccabean popularity and the entreaties of his wife, appointed Jonathan as high priest at the Feast of Tabernacles. When Jonathan went up to the altar in his gorgeous robes and royal-priestly headdress, the Jerusalemites loudly praised him. Herod solved his problem in Herodian style: he invited the high priest to join him at his sumptuous palace in Jericho. Herod was alarmingly kind; the night was steamy; Jonathan was encouraged to swim. In the pleasure pools, Herod's henchmen held him under water, and his body was found floating there in the morning. Mariamme and her mother were heartbroken and outraged; Jerusalem grieved. At Jonathan's funeral, Herod himself broke down in tears.

* These were some of the most valuable luxury brands of the ancient Mediterranean: Jericho palms produced date wine; the balsam groves produced Balsam of Gilead, prized for its cures for headaches and cataracts but also for its most expensive scent. Cleopatra also annexed most of the coast including Joppa (Jaffa), leaving Herod with Gaza as his only port.

Alexandra reported the murder to Cleopatra, whose sympathy was purely political: she had killed at least two and probably three of her own siblings. She persuaded Antony to summon Herod to Syria. If Cleopatra got her way, he would not return. Herod prepared for this risky encounter – and showed his love for Mariamme in his own sinister way: he placed her under the guardianship of his uncle Joseph, viceroy in his absence, but ordered that if he was executed by Antony, Mariamme must be instantly put to death. When Herod was gone, Joseph repeatedly told Mariamme how much the king loved her, so much, he added, that he would rather kill her than let her live without him. Mariamme was shocked. Jerusalem seethed with rumours that Herod was dead. In Herod's absence, Mariamme lorded it over the king's sister, Salome, one of the most vicious players in a viperous court.

In Laodicea, Herod, that expert at handling Roman potentates, charmed Antony who forgave him; the two banqueted together day and night. On Herod's return Salome told her brother how their uncle Joseph had seduced Mariamme while his mother-in-law was planning rebellion. Somehow Herod and Mariamme were reconciled. He now declared his love for her. 'They both fell into tears and embraced' – until she let on that she knew about his plan to execute her. Herod, tormented with jealousy, placed Mariamme under house arrest and executed his uncle Joseph.

In 34 BC, Antony reasserted Roman power, after his early bungled expedition, by successfully invading Parthian Armenia. Cleopatra accompanied him to the Euphrates and, on the way home, visited Herod. These two beguiling monsters spent days together, flirting and considering how to kill one another. Herod claimed that Cleopatra tried to seduce him: this was probably her usual manner with any man who could do something for her. It was also a deadly snare. Herod resisted and decided to kill the serpent of old Nile, but his counsellors advised strongly against it.

The Egyptian queen progressed home to Alexandria. There Antony, in a spectacular ceremony, raised Cleopatra to 'Queen of Kings'. Caesarion, her son by Caesar, now thirteen years old, became her co-pharaoh, while her three children by Antony became kings of Armenia, Phoenicia and Cyrene. In Rome, this Oriental posing appeared unRoman, unmanly and unwise. Antony tried to justify his Eastern wassails by writing his only known work of literature entitled 'On His Drinking' – and he wrote to Octavian, 'Why have you changed? Is it because I'm screwing the queen? Does it really matter where or in whom you dip your wick?' But it did matter. Cleopatra was seen as a *fatale monstrum*. Octavian was becoming ever stronger as their partnership fell apart. In 32 BC, the Senate revoked Antony's *imperium*. Next Octavian declared war on Cleopatra. The two sides met in Greece: Antony and Cleopatra mustered his army and her Egyptian-Phoenician fleet. It was a war for the world.

AUGUSTUS AND HEROD

Herod had to back the winner. He offered to join Antony in Greece but instead he was ordered to attack the Arab Nabataeans in today's Jordan. By the time Herod returned, Octavian and Antony were facing each other at Actium. Antony was no match for Octavian's commander, Marcus Agrippa. The sea battle was a debacle. Antony and Cleopatra fled back to Egypt. Would Octavian also destroy Antony's Judaean king?

Herod again prepared for death, leaving his brother Pheroras in charge and, just to be safe, having old Hyrcanus strangled. He placed his mother and sister in Masada while Mariamme and Alexandra were kept in Alexandrium, another mountain fortress. If anything happened to him, he again ordered that Mariamme was to die. Then he sailed for the most important meeting of his life.

Octavian received him in Rhodes. Herod handled the meeting shrewdly and frankly. He humbly laid his diadem crown at Octavian's feet. Then instead of disowning Antony, he asked Octavian not to consider *whose* friend he had been but '*what sort* of friend I am'. Octavian restored his crown. Herod returned to Jerusalem in triumph, then followed Octavian down to Egypt, arriving in Alexandria just after Antony and Cleopatra had committed suicide, he by blade, she by asp.

Octavian now emerged as the first Roman emperor, adopting the name Augustus. Still only thirty-three, this punctilious manager, delicate, unemotional and censorious, became Herod's most loyal patron. Indeed the emperor and his deputy, almost his partner-in-power, the plain-spoken Marcus Agrippa, became so close to Herod that, in Josephus' expression, 'Caesar preferred no one to Herod besides Agrippa and Agrippa made no one his greater friend than Herod besides Caesar.'

Augustus increased Herod's kingdom to include swathes of modern Israel, Jordan, Syria and Lebanon. Like Augustus, Herod was an icily competent manager: when famine struck, he sold his own gold and bought Egyptian grain to import, saving the Judaeans from starvation. He presided over a half-Greek, half-Jewish court, serviced by pretty eunuchs and concubines. Many of his entourage were inherited from Cleopatra. His secretary Nikolaus of Damascus had been the tutor to her children,* and his bodyguard of 400 Galatians had been her personal bodyguard: Augustus gave them to Herod as a present and they joined his own Germans and Thracians. These blond barbarians handled torture and murder for this most cosmopolitan king: 'Herod was Phoenician by descent, Hellenized by culture, Idumean by place of birth, Jewish by religion, Jerusalemite by residence and Roman by citizenship.'

In Jerusalem, he and Mariamme resided at the Antonia Fortress. There he was a Jewish king, reading Deuteronomy every seven years in the Temple and appointing the high priest, whose robes he kept in the Antonia. But outside Jerusalem he was a munificent Greek monarch whose new pagan cities – chiefly Caesarea on the coast and Sebaste (being the Greek for Augustus) on the site of Samaria – were opulent complexes of temples, hippodromes, and

---

* This Syrian Greek scholar became Herod's confidant as well as Augustus' personal friend. He must have been a supple courtier indeed to survive the murderous courts of both Cleopatra and Herod. He later wrote biographies of both Augustus and Herod, for which his chief source was Herod himself. Nikolaus' Herodian biography has vanished but it provided Josephus' main source and it is hard to imagine a better one. As for Nikolaus' former royal pupils, Augustus had Caesarion, the son of Caesar and Cleopatra, murdered. But the other three children were brought up in Rome by the emperor's sister, Antony's ex-wife Octavia. The eventual fate of the boys is unknown but the girl, Cleopatra Selene, married Juba II, King of Mauretania. Her son King Ptolemy of Mauretania was executed by Caligula. There ended the Ptolemaic dynasty 363 years after Alexander the Great.

palaces. Even in Jerusalem, he built a Greek-style theatre and hippo-drome where he presented his Actian Games to celebrate Augustus' victory. When this pagan spectacle provoked a Jewish conspiracy, the plotters were executed. But his beloved wife did not celebrate his success. The court was poisoned by the struggle between the Maccabean and Herodian princesses.

MARIAMME: HEROD IN LOVE AND HATRED

While Herod had been away, Mariamme had once again charmed her guardian into revealing her husband's plans for her if he did not return. Herod found her personally irresistible yet politically toxic: she openly accused him of killing her brother. Sometimes she made it humiliatingly obvious to the entire court that she was denying him sex; at other times they were passionately reconciled. She was the mother of two of his sons, yet she was also planning his destruction. She taunted Salome, Herod's sister, with her com-monness. Herod was 'entangled between hatred and love', his obsession all the more intense because it was mixed up with his other reigning passion: power.

His sister Salome ascribed Mariamme's hold on him to magic. She brought him evidence that the Maccabean had beguiled him with a love-potion. Mariamme's eunuchs were tortured until they revealed her guilt. The guardian who had watched Mariamme in his absence was killed. Mariamme herself was imprisoned in the Antonia then put on trial. Salome kept up the momentum of reve-lations, determined that the Maccabean queen should die.

Mariamme was sentenced to death, whereupon her mother Alex-andra denounced her, hoping to save her own skin. In response, the crowd booed her. As Mariamme was led to execution, she behaved with astonishing 'greatness of soul', saying that it was a shame her mother should expose herself in that way. Probably strangled, Mariamme died like a real Maccabean 'without changing the colour of her face', displaying a grace that 'revealed the nobility of her descent to the spectators'. Herod went berserk with grief, believing that his love for Mariamme was a divine vengeance

The Temple Mount – Har haBayit in Hebrew, Haram al-Sharif in Arabic, known in the Bible as Mount Moriah – is the centrepiece of Jerusalem. The Western Wall, the holiest shrine of Judaism, is part of Herod's western supporting wall of the esplanade, the setting for the Islamic shrines, the Dome of the Rock and the Aqsa Mosque. To many, these 35 acres remain the centre of the world.

Below In 1994, archaeologists found this stele at Tel Dan on which Hazael, King of Aram-Syria, boasts of his victory over Judaea, the 'house of David', thereby confirming David's existence.

Left In 701 BC, King Hezekiah fortified the city against the approaching Assyrian army. His so-called broad wall can be seen in today's Jewish Quarter.

Below Meanwhile two teams of his engineers started digging the 533-metre-long Siloam Tunnel to provide water for the city: when they met in the middle, they celebrated with this inscription, which was discovered by a schoolboy in 1891.

Before he turned to Jerusalem, Sennacherib, master of the mighty, rapacious Assyrian empire, stormed Hezekiah's second city Lachish. The bas-reliefs in his Nineveh palace depict the bloody siege and the punishments suffered by its citizens. Here Judaean families are led away by an Assyrian.

King Darius, seen here in a relief from his Persepolis palace, was the real creator of the Persian Empire that ruled Jerusalem for over two centuries. He allowed the Jewish priests to govern themselves, even issuing this Yehud (Judaea) coin.

After Alexander the Great's early death, two Greek families vied to control his empire. Ptolemy I Soter (*above left*) hijacked Alexander's corpse, founded a kingdom in Egypt and stormed Jerusalem. After a century under the Ptolemies, their Seleucid rivals grabbed Jerusalem. The effete, flamboyant King Antiochus IV (*above right*) polluted the Temple and tried to annihilate Judaism, provoking a revolt by Judah the Maccabee (shown here in a fanciful Medieval engraving, *left*), whose family created the new Jewish kingdom that lasted until the arrival of the Romans.

The Roman strongman of the east, Mark Antony (*below left*), backed a new ruler, Herod, but his mistress Cleopatra, the last Ptolemaic queen, (*below right*) wanted Jerusalem for herself.

Ruthless, murderous and brilliant, Herod the Great, half-Jewish and half-Arab, conquered Jerusalem, rebuilt the Temple (shown here in a model reconstruction) and created the city at its most splendid.

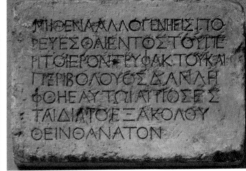

Above left This ossuary, marked 'Simon the builder of the Sanctuary', probably contained the bones of his architect. *Above right* The inscription in Greek from the Temple warning gentiles not to enter the inner courts on pain of death.

Most of the southern and western walls of the Temple Mount, including the shrine, the Wall, are Herodian. The impregnable south-eastern corner was the Pinnacle where Jesus was tempted by Satan. A seam in the wall (just visible on the far right of this picture) seems to show Herod's giant ashlars to the left and the older, smaller Maccabean stones to the right.

Jesus' Crucifixion, depicted by van Eyck in this painting, was almost certainly a Roman measure, backed by the Temple elite, to destroy any messianic threat to the status quo.

Herod the Great's son Herod Antipas, ruler of Galilee, mocked Jesus but refused to judge him.

King Herod Agrippa was an urbane, happy-go-lucky adventurer and the most powerful Jew in Roman history. His friendship with the psychotic Emperor Caligula saved Jerusalem, and he later helped raise Claudius to the throne.

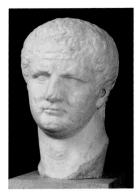

After four years of independence, Titus (*left*), the son of the new Roman Emperor Vespasian, arrived to besiege Jerusalem. *Centre* The city and its Temple were destroyed in the savage fighting: archaeologists have discovered the skeletal arm of a young girl trapped in a burned house and the heap of Herodian stones pushed off the Temple Mount by the Roman soldiers as they smashed Herod's Royal Portico. *Bottom* The Arch of Titus in Rome celebrates his Triumph in which the candelbra, or menorah, symbol of the Maccabees, was displayed, and this coin, inscribed 'Judaea Capta', commemorates the victory.

Left Restless, petulant and talented, Emperor Hadrian banned Judaism and refounded Jerusalem as a Roman town, Aelia Capitolina, which provoked a Jewish rebellion led by Simon Bar Kochba (who issued this coin depicting the restored Temple, *below*).

Above This graffiti (Domine Ivimus 'We go to the Lord') was discovered by the Armenians beneath the Church of the Holy Sepulchre in 1978. Possibly dating from around AD 300, does it show that Christian pilgrims prayed beneath Hadrian's pagan temple?

Right Constantine the Great was no saint – he murdered his wife and son – but he embraced Christianity and transformed Jerusalem, ordering the building of the Church of the Holy Sepulchre, which he sent his mother Helena to supervise.

designed to destroy him. He shrieked for her around the palaces, ordered his servants to find her, and tried to distract himself with banquets. But his parties ended with him weeping for Mariamme. He fell ill and erupted in boils, at which Alexandra made a last bid for power. Herod had her killed, and then murdered four of his most intimate friends who perhaps had been close to the charming queen. He never quite recovered from Mariamme, a curse that was to return to destroy another generation. The Talmud later claimed that Herod preserved Mariamme's body in honey, and this may have been true – for it was fittingly sweet, suitably macabre.

Soon after her death, Herod started to work on his masterpiece: Jerusalem. The Maccabean Palace opposite the Temple was not grand enough for him. The Antonia must have been haunted by the ghost of Mariamme. In 23 BC, he expanded his western fortifications by building a new towered citadel and palace complex, a Jerusalem-within-Jerusalem. Surrounded by a wall 45 feet high, the Citadel boasted three sentimentally named towers, the highest, the Hippicus (after a youthful friend killed in battle), 128 feet high, its base 45 feet square, the Phasael (after his dead brother) and the Mariamme.* While the Antonia dominated the Temple, this fortress ruled the city.

To the south of the Citadel, Herod built his Palace, a pleasure dome containing two sumptuous apartments named after his patrons, Augustus and Agrippa, with walls of marble, cedarwood beams, elaborate mosaics, gold and silver decorations. Around the palace were constructed courtyards, colonnades and porticoes complete with green lawns, lush groves and cool pools and canals set off by cascades, above which perched dovecotes (Herod probably communicated with his provinces by pigeon post). All this was funded by Herod's Croesian wealth: he was, after the emperor, the

---

* This might have been named after a later wife, also called Mariamme. But it must have reminded him and everyone else of the Maccabean princess. Today's Tower of David, which has nothing to do with David, is based on Herod's Hippicus Tower. After Titus' destruction of the city, it remained until Ottoman times the chief stronghold of Jerusalem. No other building in Jerusalem so reveals the embroidered nature of the city's development as the Citadel, where archaeologists have uncovered Judaean, Maccabean, Herodian, Roman, Arab, Crusader, Mamluk and Ottoman ruins.

richest man in the Mediterranean* The bustle of the palace, with the trumpets of the Temple and the rumble of the city in the distance, must have been pacified by the cooing of birds and tinkle of fountains.

But his court was anything but tranquil. His brothers were pitiless intriguers: his sister Salome ranks as a peerless monstress and his own harem of women were all apparently as ambitious and as paranoid as the king himself. Herod's priapic tastes complicated the politics – he was, wrote Josephus, 'a man of appetites'. He had married one wife, Doris, before Mariamme; and, after her, he married at least another eight, choosing beauties for love or lust, never again for their pedigree. As well as his 500-strong harem, his Greek tastes extended to the pages and eunuchs of his household. But his burgeoning family of half-spoiled, half-neglected sons, each backed by a power-hungry mother, became a devil's brood. Even the masterful puppeteer himself struggled to manage all this hatred and jealousy. Yet the court did not distract him from his most cherished project. Knowing that the prestige of Jerusalem was linked to his own, Herod decided to equal Solomon.

HEROD: THE TEMPLE

Herod pulled down the existing Second Temple and built a wonder of the world in its place. The Jews were afraid he would destroy the old Temple and never finish the new one, so he called a city meeting to persuade them, preparing every detail. A thousand priests were trained as builders. Lebanese cedar forests were felled, the beams

---

* Herod's wealth came from his landholdings all over the Middle East. These produced sheep, cattle (raised in Jordan and Judaea), wheat and barley from Galilee and Judaea, fish, olive oil, wine and fruit, lilies and onions from Ashkelon (hence shallots are Ashkelon onions), pomegranates from Geba, north of Jerusalem, figs from Joppa, date palms and balsam from Jericho. Herod owned a half to two-thirds of his kingdom; he taxed and exported Nabataean spices; and he was also a mining magnate, paying Augustus 300 talents for rights to half the copper mines of Cyprus. While he exported his local wines, he himself drank the Italian vintages. Even on his death, after a lifetime of building and giving Rome huge sums, he still left over 1,000 talents or a million drachmas to Augustus, and there was much more than that for his family.

floated down the coast. At quarries around Jerusalem, the massive ashlar stones, gleaming yellow and almost white limestone, were marked and cut out. A thousand wagons were amassed, but the stones were gargantuan. In the tunnels alongside the Temple Mount, there is one stone, 44.6 feet long, 11 feet high, that weighs 600 tons.* No din, no hammering had polluted the building of Solomon's Temple, so Herod ensured that everything was readied offsite and silently slotted into place. The Holy of Holies was ready in two years, but the entire complex was not completed for eighty.

Herod dug down to the foundation rock and built from there, so he would have destroyed any remnants of Solomon's and Zerubbabel's Temples. Though limited to the east by the steepness of the Kidron Valley, he expanded the esplanade of the Temple Mount to the south, filling the space with a substructure held up by eighty-eight pillars and twelve vaulted arches, now called Solomon's Stables, to create a 3-acre platform, twice as large as the Roman Forum. Today, it is easy to see the seam in the eastern wall, visible 105 feet from the south-western corner of the city, with Herodian ashlars to the left and smaller Maccabean stones to the right.

The courts of the Temple led in diminishing size to ever-increasing sanctity. Gentiles and Jews alike could enter the huge Court of Gentiles, but a wall encircled the Court of Women with this warning inscription:

FOREIGNER! DO NOT ENTER WITHIN THE GRILLE
AND PARTITION SURROUNDING THE TEMPLE
HE WHO IS CAUGHT
WILL HAVE ONLY HIMSELF TO BLAME
FOR HIS DEATH WHICH WILL FOLLOW

* Herod would have used the latest technology. The Egyptians had known how to move vast stones to build the pyramids as early as 4000 BC. The Roman engineer Vitruvius had created enormous devices – wheels, sledges and cranes – to transport such stones. Large wheels over 13 feet in diameter served as axles pulled by teams of oxen. Then there were winches – horizontal rotating beams with attached poles and cranks which enabled teams of ten men or fewer to use them. This way, eight men could lift 1½ tons.

Fifty steps led up to a gate that opened into the Court of Israel, open to any male Jew, which led to the exclusive Court of Priests. Within that stood the Sanctuary, the Hekhal itself, containing the Holy of Holies. This rested upon the rock where Abraham was said to have almost sacrificed Isaac, and where David built his altar. Here the sacrifices were conducted on the Altar of Burnt Offering, which faced the Court of Women and the Mount of Olives.

Herod's Antonia Fortress guarded the Temple Mount in the north. There, Herod constructed his own secret tunnel into the Temple. In the south the Temple was reached by monumental stairs passing through the Double and Triple Gates, to underground passages decorated with doves and flowers that led into the Temple. On the west, a monumental bridge, doubling as an aqueduct bringing water into huge hidden cisterns, stretched across the valley into the Temple. In its sheer eastern wall stood the Shushan Gate, used exclusively by the high priest to progress to the Mount of Olives to sanctify the full moon, or to sacrifice that rarest, holiest of victims, the unblemished red heifer.*

There were pillared porticoes on all four sides but the greatest of these was the Royal Portico, a vast basilica which dominated the whole mountain. About 70,000 people lived in Herod's city but during the festivals hundreds of thousands arrived on

---

* 'Speak unto the children of Israel,' said God to Moses and Aaron in Numbers 19, 'that they bring thee a red heifer without spot, wherein is no blemish.' The heifer would be sacrificed on a pyre of cedar and hyssop overlaid with a strand of scarlet thread and its ashes mixed with holy water. According to the Mishnah, this had only happened nine times, and on the tenth, the Messiah would come. Since the millennial excitement of the Israeli conquest of Jerusalem in 1967, fundamentalist Christian evangelists and Jewish redemptionists believe that two of the three essential preconditions for the Apocalypse and coming of the Messiah (or the Second Coming for the Christians) have been met: Israel has been restored and Jerusalem is Jewish. The third precondition is the restoration of the Temple. Some Christian fundamentalists and the tiny factions of redemptionist Orthodox Jews, such as those of the Temple Institute, believe that this is possible only when the Temple Mount is purified with the sacrifice of the red heifer. Therefore even today a Pentecostal preacher from Mississippi named Clyde Lott is, in alliance with Rabbi Richman of the Temple Institute, trying to breed the red heifer from a herd of 500 Red Angus imported from Nebraska to a farm in the Jordan Valley. They believe they will breed the 'heifer that will change the world'.

pilgrimage. Like any bustling shrine, even today, the Temple needed a gathering place for friends to meet and for rituals to be arranged. This was the Royal Portico. When visitors arrived, they could shop on the busy shopping street that ran beneath the monumental arches along the western walls. When it was time to visit the Temple, pilgrims took purifying baths in the many *mikvahs* – ritual pools – that have been found around the southern entrances. They would climb one of the monumental staircases that led into the Royal Portico where they saw all the sights of the city, before it was time to pray.

At the south-eastern corner, the towering walls and cliff of the Kidron Valley created a precipitous peak, the Pinnacle, where the Gospels say the Devil tempted Jesus. At the south-western corner, facing the wealthy Upper City, priests announced the start of festivals and Sabbaths on Friday nights with trumpet blasts that must have echoed across the desolate gorges. A stone, thrown down by Titus in AD 70, proclaims 'The Trumpeting Place'.

The design of the Temple, supervised by the king and his anonymous architects (an ossuary has been found inscribed 'Simon builder of the Temple'), showed a brilliant understanding of space and theatre. Dazzling and awe-inspiring, Herod's Temple was 'covered all over with plates of gold and at the first rising of the sun reflected back a fiery splendour' so bright that visitors had to look away. Arriving in Jerusalem from the Mount of Olives, it reared up 'like a mountain covered with snow'. This was the Temple that Jesus knew and that Titus destroyed. Herod's esplanade survives as the Islamic Haram al-Sharif supported on three sides by Herodian stones that still gleam today, particularly in the Western Wall revered by the Jews.

Once the Sanctuary and the esplanade were complete – it was said there was no rain in the daytime, so that work was never delayed – Herod, who could not enter the Holy of Holies since he was not a priest, celebrated by sacrificing 300 oxen. He had reached his apogee. But his undeniable greatness was to be challenged by his own children when the crimes of the past returned to haunt the heirs of the future.

HEROD'S PRINCES: THE FAMILY TRAGEDY

Herod now had at least twelve children by his ten wives. He seemed
to ignore most of them except for his two sons by Mariamme,
Alexander and Aristobulos. They were half-Maccabee, half-
Herodian and they would be his successors. He sent them to Rome
where Augustus himself supervised their education. After five
years, Herod brought the two teenage princes home to marry:
Alexander wed the daughter of the King of Cappadocia while
Aristobulos married Herod's niece.*

In 15 BC, Marcus Agrippa arrived to inspect Herod's Jerusalem,
accompanied by his new wife, Julia, Augustus' nymphomaniacal
daughter. Agrippa, Augustus' partner and victor of Actium, was
already friends with Herod, who proudly showed him Jerusalem.
He stayed in his eponymous apartments in the Citadel and there
gave banquets in Herod's honour. Augustus already paid for a daily
sacrifice to Yahweh in the Temple, but now Agrippa sacrificed a
hundred oxen. He managed to behave with such tact that even the
prickly Jews gave him the accolade of laying palms in his path and
the Herodians named their children after him. Afterwards, the pair
toured Greece with their fleets. When local Jews appealed against
Greek repression, Agrippa backed Jewish rights, Herod thanked
him and the two embraced as equals. But on his return from
hobnobbing with the Roman potentate, Herod was challenged by
his own children.

Princes Alexander and Aristobulos, polished by a Roman education, inheriting the looks and arrogance of both parents, soon
blamed their father for their mother's fate and, like her, disdained

* Herod's family tree is complicated because the family were so endogamous,
repeatedly intermarrying and remarrying within the Herodian and Maccabee clans
trying to reconcile them: he married his brother Pheroras to Mariamme's sister and
his eldest son Antipater to the daughter of the last King Antigonos (beheaded at his
request by Antony). But the marriages were interspersed with executions: Salome's
first two husbands were killed by Herod. Herodians also married into the royal
families of Cappadocia, Emesa, Pontus, Nabataea and Cilicia, all Roman allies. At
least two marriages were cancelled because the husband would not convert to
Judaism and be circumcised.

the half-breed Herodians. Alexander, being married to a king's daughter, was particularly snobbish; both boys mocked Aristobulos' Herodian wife, thus insulting her mother, their dangerous aunt Salome. They boasted that when they were kings they would put Herod's wives to labour with the slaves and use Herod's other sons as clerks.

Salome reported all this to Herod, who was infuriated by the ingratitude and alarmed by the betrayal of these spoilt princelings. He had long ignored Antipater, his eldest son, by his first wife Doris. But now in 13 BC, Herod recalled Antipater and asked Agrippa to take him to Rome with a sealed document for the emperor: it was his will, disinheriting the two boys and instead bequeathing the kingdom to Antipater. But his new heir, probably in his mid-twenties, was embittered by paternal neglect and fraternal envy. He and his mother conspired to destroy the disinherited princes, whom they accused of treason.

Herod asked Augustus, staying at Aquileia on the Adriatic, to judge the three princes. Augustus reconciled father and sons, with the result that Herod sailed home, called a meeting in the court of the Temple and announced that his three sons would share the kingdom. Doris, Antipater and Salome set about reversing this reconciliation for their own purposes, but they were helped by the arrogance of the boys: Prince Alexander told everyone that Herod dyed his hair to look younger and confided that he deliberately missed his targets out hunting to make his father feel better. He also seduced three of the king's own eunuchs, giving him access to his father's secrets. Herod arrested and tortured Alexander's servants until one confessed that his master planned to assassinate him out hunting. Alexander's father-in-law, the King of Cappadocia, who was visiting his daughter, managed to reconcile father and sons again. Herod expressed his gratitude by presenting the Cappadocian with a very Herodian gift: a courtesan who gloried in the name Pannychis – All-Night-Long.

The peace did not last long: the torture of servants now revealed a letter from Alexander to the commander of the Alexandrium Fortress that said: 'When we have achieved all we set out to do, we'll come to you.' Herod dreamed that Alexander was raising a dagger over him, a nightmare so vivid that he arrested both boys, who admitted they were planning to escape. Herod had to consult Augustus, by now tiring of his old friend's excesses – though the emperor himself was no stranger to naughty children and tangled successions. Augustus ruled that, if the boys had plotted against Herod, he had every right to punish them.

Herod held the trial in Berytus (Beirut), outside his formal jurisdiction – and therefore supposedly a fair place for the trial. The boys were sentenced to death as Herod wished, which was hardly surprising since he had generously embellished the city. Herod's counsellors advised mercy – but when one hinted that the boys were suborning the army, Herod liquidated 300 officers. The princes were taken back to Judaea and garrotted. The tragedy of their mother Mariamme, the curse of the Maccabees, had come full circle. Augustus was not amused. Knowing that Jews eschewed pork, he commented drily: 'I'd rather be Herod's pig than his son.' But this was just the beginning of the Grand Guignol decay of Herod the Great.

HEROD: THE LIVING PUTREFACTION

The king, now in his sixties, was ailing and paranoid. Antipater was the sole named heir, but there were many other sons available to inherit the kingdom, and Herod's sister Salome started to plot against him; she found a servant who claimed that Antipater was planning to poison Herod with a mysterious drug. Antipater, who was in Rome meeting with Augustus, rushed home and galloped to the palace in Jerusalem, but he was arrested there before he could reach his father. At his trial, the suspect drug was given to a convict who dropped down dead. More torture revealed that a Jewish slave belonging to the Empress Livia, Augustus' own wife and herself an expert on poisons, had forged letters to frame Salome.

Herod sent the evidence to Augustus and drew up his third will, leaving the kingdom to another of his sons, Antipas, the Herod who would later encounter John the Baptist and Jesus. Herod's illness distorted his judgement and weakened his grip on the Jewish opposition. He placed a gilded bronze eagle on the great gate of the Temple. Some students climbed on to the roof, abseiled down in front of the crowded courtyard and cut it down. The troops of the Antonia Fortress rushed into the Temple to arrest them. Paraded before Herod on his sickbed, they insisted they were obeying the Torah. The culprits were burned alive.

Herod collapsed, suffering an agonizing and gruesome putre-faction: it started as an itching all over with a glowing sensation within his intestines, then developed into a swelling of his feet and belly, complicated by ulceration of the colon. His body started to ooze clear fluid, he could scarcely breathe, a vile stench emanated from him, and his genitals swelled grotesquely until his penis and scrotum burst out into suppurating gangrene that then gave birth to a seething mass of worms.

The rotting king hoped he would recover in the warmth of his Jericho palace but, as his suffering increased, he was borne out to the warm sulphur baths at Callirhoe, which still exist on the Dead Sea, only for the suphur to aggravate the agony.* Treated with hot oil, he passed out and was carried back to Jericho where he ordered the summoning of the Temple elite from Jerusalem, whom he had locked en masse in the hippodrome. It is unlikely that he planned to slaughter them. Probably he wanted to finesse the succession while holding all troublemaking grandees in custody.

At around this time, a child named Joshua ben Joseph, or (in Aramaic) Jesus, was born. His parents were a carpenter, Joseph, and his teenaged betrothed, Mary (Mariamme in Hebrew), based in Nazareth, up in Galilee. They were not much richer than

---

* Doctors have debated his symptoms ever since. The most likely diagnosis is that Herod suffered hypertension and arteriosclerosis complicated by progressive dementia and by congestive heart and kidney failure. The arteriosclerosis led to venous congestion, aggravated by gravity, so that fluid collected in his feet and genitals, becoming so severe that the fluid bubbled through the skin; the blood flow became so poor that necrosis of the flesh – gangrene – developed. The bad breath and itching were caused by kidney failure. The penile/scrotal gangrene provided ideal material for the laying of eggs by flies that hatched as maggots. It is possible that the genital worms were hostile propaganda, symbolizing divine vengeance on an evil king: Antiochus IV Epiphanes, Herod's grandson, Agrippa I, and many other sinners including Judas Iscariot, were assigned similar worm-infested, bowel- and scrotum-exploding exits.

peasants, but it was said they were descended from the old Davidian house. They travelled down to Bethlehem where a child, Jesus, was born 'that shall rule my people Israel'. After he had been circumcised on the eighth day, according to St Luke, 'they brought him to Jerusalem, to present him to the Lord' and make the traditional sacrifice in the Temple. A wealthy family would sacrifice a sheep or even a cow, but Joseph could afford only two turtledoves or pigeons.

As Herod lay dying, Matthew's Gospel claims, he ordered his forces to liquidate this Davidian child by massacring all newborn babies, but Joseph took refuge in Egypt until he heard that Herod had died. There were certainly messianic rumours afoot and Herod would have feared a Davidian pretender, but there is no evidence that the king ever heard of Jesus or massacred any innocents. It is ironic that this monster should be particularly remembered for the one crime he neglected to commit. As for the child from Nazareth, we do not hear of him again for about thirty years.*

---

* Jesus' birth is historically challenging, the Gospels contradictory. No one knows the date but it was probably before Herod's death, in 4 BC which means Jesus died in his early thirties if he was crucified in AD 29–30, forty if it was AD 36. The story of the census summoning the family to Bethlehem is not historical because Quirinius' census took place after Herod's successor, Archelaus, was deposed in AD 6, almost ten years *after* Jesus' birth. In recounting the journey to Bethlehem and his Davidic genealogy, Matthew's Gospel provides Jesus with royal birth and fulfilment of prophecy – 'for thus it is written by the prophet.' The Massacre of the Innocents and the escape to Egypt are clearly inspired by the Passover story: one of the Ten Plagues was the Killing of the First Born. Wherever Jesus was born, it is likely that the family did travel to the Temple for the sacrifice. Muslim tradition, expanded on by the Crusaders, believes that Jesus was raised in the chapel beneath al-Aqsa Mosque, Jesus' Cradle. Jesus' family is mysterious: after the birth, Joseph simply disappears from the Gospels. Matthew and Luke state that Mary remained a virgin and Jesus was fathered by God (an idea familiar in Roman and Greek theology, and also suggested in Isaiah's prophecy of Emmanuel). But Matthew, Mark and John name Jesus' brothers: James, Joses, Judas and Simon along with a sister, Salome. When Mary's virginity became Christian dogma, the existence of these other children became inconvenient. John mentions 'Mary the wife of Cleophas'. If Joseph died young, Mary may have married this Cleophas and had more children because, after the Crucifixion, Jesus was succeeded as leader first by his brother James then by 'Simon son of Cleophas'.

ARCHELAUS: MESSIAHS AND MASSACRES

Emperor Augustus sent his reply to Herod: he had had Livia's slave girl beaten to death and Herod was free to punish Prince Antipater. Yet Herod was now in such torment, he seized a dagger to kill himself. This fracas convinced Antipater, in his nearby cell, that the old tyrant was dead. He exuberantly called in his jailer to unlock the cell. Surely, finally, Antipater was King of the Jews? The jailer had heard the cries too. Hurrying to court, he found Herod was not dead, just demented. His servants had seized the knife from him. The jailer reported Antipater's treason. This pustulous but living carcass of a king beat his own head, howled and ordered his guards to kill the hated son immediately. Then he rewrote his will, dividing the kingdom between three of his teenaged sons – with Jerusalem and Judaea going to Archelaus.

Five days later, in March 4 BC, after a reign of thirty-seven years, Herod the Great, who had survived 'ten thousand dangers', died. The eighteen-year-old Archelaus danced, sang and made merry as if an enemy, not a father, had died. Even Herod's grotesque family were shocked. The body, wearing the crown and gripping the sceptre, was borne on a catafalque of purple-draped, bejewelled gold in a parade – led by Archelaus and followed by the German and Thracian guards, and by 500 servants carrying spices (the stink must have been pungent) – the 24 miles to the mountain fortress of Herodium. There Herod was buried in a tomb* that was lost for 2,000 years.

Archelaus returned to secure Jerusalem, ascending a golden throne in the Temple, where he announced the softening of his father's severity. The city was filled with Passover pilgrims, many

---

* Herod's tomb was discovered in 2007 by Professor Ehud Netzer who found an ornate red sarcophagus, decorated with flowers, smashed to pieces almost certainly by the anti-Herodian Jewish rebels of AD 66–70. Two other sarcophagi are white, decorated with flowers: do they belong to his sons? Herodium was another miracle of Herod's construction – a man-made mountain 210 feet in diameter with a massive luxurious palace on top containing a domed bathhouse, towers, frescoes and pools. Herod's pyramidal tomb was on the Herodium Hill below the eastern tower of the fortress, also destroyed in 66–70.

of whom, certain that the king's death heralded an apocalyptic deliverance, ran amok in the Temple. Archelaus' guards were stoned. Archelaus, although he had just promised an easing of the repression, sent in the cavalry: 3,000 people were slaughtered in the Temple.

This teenage despot left his steady brother Philip in charge and sailed for Rome to confirm his succession with Augustus. But his younger brother, Antipas, raced him to Rome, hoping to win the kingdom for himself. As soon as Archelaus was gone, Augustus' local steward, Sabinus, ransacked Herod's Jerusalem Palace to find his hidden fortune, sparking more riots. The Governor of Syria, Varus, marched down to restore order but gangs of Galileans and Idumeans, arriving for Pentecost, seized the Temple and massacred any Romans they could find as Sabinus cowered in Phasael's Tower.

Outside Jerusalem, three rebels – ex-slaves – declared themselves king, burned Herodian palaces and marauded in a 'wild fury'. These self-appointed kings were pseudo-prophets, proving that Jesus was indeed born at a time of intense religious speculation. Having spent all of Herod's reign awaiting such leaders in vain, the Jews found that three arrived at once: Varus defeated and killed all three pretenders,* but henceforth pseudo-prophets kept coming and the Romans kept killing them. Varus crucified 2,000 rebels around Jerusalem.

In Rome, Augustus, now sixty, listened to the squabbles of the Herodians and confirmed Herod's will but, withholding the title of king, appointed Archelaus as ethnarch of Judaea, Samaria and Idumea with Antipas as tetrarch of Galilee and Peraea (part of

---

* One of these 'kings' was Simon, a hulking slave belonging to Herod, soon beheaded by the Romans. Simon may be the subject of the so-called Gabriel's Revelation, a stone inscription found in southern Jordan in which the Archangel Gabriel acclaims a 'prince of princes' called Simon who will be killed but will rise again 'in three days' when 'you will know that evil will be defeated by justice. In three days you will live, I, Gabriel, command you.' The details – resurrection and judgement three days after a prophet's death – predate Jesus' crucifixion by over thirty years. After killing Simon, Publius Quinctilius Varus commanded the German frontier. Some ten years later, in AD 9, he was ambushed, losing three legions. This disaster spoiled the last years of Augustus, who supposedly wandered his palace crying, 'Varus, give me back my legions!'

today's Jordan), and their half-brother Philip as tetrarch of the rest.*
The life of the rich in the Roman villas of Archelaus' Jerusalem was
louche, Grecian and extremely unJewish: a silver goblet, buried
nearby, lost for two millennia before it was bought in 1911 by an
American collector, depicts explicit homosexual couplings – on one
side, a man lowers himself using a pulley onto a catamite as a
voyeur slave peeps through the door, while on the other two lithe
boys intertwine on a couch. But Archelaus turned out to be so
vicious, inept and extravagant that, after ten years, Augustus
deposed him, exiling him to Gaul. Judaea became a Roman province, and Jerusalem was ruled from Caesarea on the coast by a
series of low-ranking prefects; it was now that the Romans held a
census to register taxpayers. This submission to Roman power was
humiliating enough to provoke a minor Jewish rebellion and was
the census recalled by Luke, probably wrongly, as the reason that
Jesus' family came to Bethlehem.

For thirty years, Herod Antipas ruled Galilee, dreaming of his
father's kingdom which he had almost inherited, until John the
Baptist, a charismatic new prophet, burst out of the desert to mock
and challenge him.

---

* All three sons adopted the name 'Herod', causing much confusion in the Gospels.
Archelaus was married but fell in love with Glaphyra, that daughter of the King of
Cappadocia who had been married to Herod and Mariamme's son Alexander. After
Alexander was executed, she married King Juba of Mauretania and after his death
returned to Cappadocia. Now she married Archelaus.

II

JESUS CHRIST

AD 10–40

JOHN THE BAPTIST AND THE FOX OF GALILEE

John's parents, Zacharias, a priest in the Temple, and Elizabeth lived in the village of Ein Kerem, just outside the city. Zacharias was probably one of the humble priests who drew lots for their duties in the Temple, a far cry from the Temple grandees. But John would often have visited the Temple as a boy. There were many ways to be a good Jew and he chose to live ascetically in the wilderness as Isaiah had urged: 'Prepare the way of Yahweh in the desert.'

In the late 20s AD, John started to win a following first in the deserts not far from Jerusalem – 'all men mused in their hearts of John whether he were the Christ or not' – and then later further north in Herod Antipas' Galilee, where he had family. Mary was a cousin of John's mother. When she was pregnant with her son Jesus, she stayed with John's parents. Jesus came from Nazareth to hear his cousin preach and John baptized him in the Jordan. The cousins started to preach together, offering remission of sin in baptism, their new ceremony adapted from the Jewish tradition of ritual bathing in the *mikvah*. However, John also started to denounce Herod Antipas.

The Tetrarch of Galilee lived majestically, his luxuries funded by tax-collectors who were widely hated. Antipas constantly lobbied the new Roman emperor, Tiberius, Augustus' morose stepson, to grant him his father's full kingdom. He named his capital 'Livias' after Augustus' widow, Tiberius' mother, a friend of the family. Then in AD 18, he founded a new city on the Sea of Galilee named

Tiberias. Jesus, like John, despised Antipas as a venal debauchee and Roman stooge: 'that fox', Jesus called him.

Antipas had married the daughter of the Nabataean Arab king Aretas IV, an alliance designed to ensure peace between Jewish and Arab neighbours. After thirty years on his little throne, the middle-aged Antipas fell fatally in love with his niece, Herodias. She was the daughter of Herod the Great's executed son Aristobulos and was already married to a half-brother. Now she demanded that Antipas divorce his Arab wife. Antipas foolishly agreed, but the Nabataean princess did not go quietly. To huge crowds, John the Baptist taunted this adulterous couple as a latter-day Ahab and Jezebel until Antipas ordered his arrest. The prophet was imprisoned in Herod the Great's Machaerus Fortress across the Jordan, 2,300 feet above the Dead Sea. John was not alone in these dungeons for there was another celebrity prisoner: Antipas' Arab wife.

Antipas and his courtiers celebrated his birthday at a banquet with Herodias and her daughter, Salome, who was married to the tetrarch Philip. (The mosaic floors of Machaerus' banqueting hall are still partly intact – as are some of the cells beneath.) Salome 'came in and she danced and pleased Herod', perhaps even performing a striptease of the seven veils,* so gracefully that he said: 'Ask of me whatsoever thou wilt and I will give it thee.' Prompted by her mother, Salome replied, 'The head of John the Baptist.' Moments later, the head was brought up from the dungeons, borne into the banquet on a charger and given 'to the damsel and the damsel gave it to her mother'.

Jesus, realizing that he was in danger, escaped to the desert, but

---

* Salome the dancer symbolizes cold-hearted caprice and female depravity, but the two Gospels Mark and Matthew never give her name. Josephus gives us the name of Herodias' daughter in another context but simply recounts that Antipas ordered John's execution without any terpsichorean encouragement. The dance of the seven veils was a much later elaboration. There were many Herodian Salomes (Jesus' sister was also named Salome). But most probably the dancer was the wife of Herod Philip, Tetrarch of Trachonitis, until his death when she married another cousin who was later appointed king of Lesser Armenia: the dancer ended up as a queen. Ultimately John's head would become one of the most prized of Christian relics. There would be at least five shrines claiming to have the original: the shrine of John's head in the Umayyad Mosque in Damascus is revered by Muslims.

he frequently visited Jerusalem – the only founder of the three
Abrahamic religions to have walked her streets. The city and the
Temple were central to his vision of himself. The life of a Jew
was based on study of the prophets, observance of the Laws and
pilgrimage to Jerusalem, which Jesus called 'the City of the Great
King'. Although the first three decades of Jesus' life are unknown
to us, it is clear that he was steeped in knowledge of the Jewish
Bible and everything he did was a meticulous fulfilment of its
prophecies. As he was a Jew, the Temple was a familiar part of
Jesus' life and he was obsessional about the fate of Jerusalem. When
he was twelve his parents took him to the Temple for Passover. As
they left, Luke says he slipped away from them and after three
worrying days 'they found him in the temple sitting in the midst of
the doctors, hearing them and asking them questions'. When he
was tempted, the devil 'setteth him on the pinnacle of the temple'.
As he unveiled his mission to his followers, he stressed that the
playing-out of his own destiny had to take place in Jerusalem: 'From
that time forth began Jesus to shew unto his disciples how he must
go unto Jerusalem and suffer many things ... and be killed and be
raised again on the third day.' But Jerusalem would pay for this:
'And when ye shall see Jerusalem compassed with armies, then
know that the desolation thereof is nigh ... Jerusalem shall be
trodden down of the Gentiles, until the times of the Gentiles be
fulfilled.'

Supported by his Twelve Apostles (including his brother James),
Jesus emerged again in his Galilean homeland, moving southwards
as he preached what he called 'the good news', in his own subtle
and homespun style, often using parables. But the message was
direct and dramatic: 'Repent: for the kingdom of heaven is at hand.'
Jesus left no writings and his teachings have been endlessly ana-
lysed, but the four Gospels reveal that the essence of his ministry
was his warning of the imminent Apocalypse – Judgement Day and
the Kingdom of Heaven.

This was a terrifying and radical vision in which Jesus himself
would play a central part as the mystical semi-messianic Son of
Man, a phrase taken from Isaiah and Daniel: 'The Son of Man shall
send forth his angels, and they shall gather out of his kingdom all

things that offend, and them which do iniquity; and shall cast them into a furnace of fire: there shall be wailing and gnashing of teeth. Then shall the righteous shine forth as the sun in the kingdom of their Father.' He foresaw the destruction of all human ties: 'And the brother shall deliver up the brother to death, and the father the child: and the children shall rise up against their parents, and cause them to be put to death ... Think not that I am come to send peace on earth: I came not to send peace, but a sword.'

This was not a social or nationalistic revolution: Jesus was most concerned with the world after the Last Days; he preached social justice not so much in this world as in the next: 'Blessed are the poor in spirit: for theirs is the kingdom of heaven.' Tax-collectors and harlots would enter God's kingdom before grandees and priests. Jesus shockingly evoked the Apocalypse when he showed that the old laws would no longer matter: 'Let the dead bury their dead.' When the world ended, 'the Son of Man shall sit in the throne of his glory' and all the nations would gather before him for judgement. There would be 'everlasting punishment' for the evil and 'life eternal' for the righteous.

However, Jesus was careful, in most cases, to stay within Jewish law and in fact his entire ministry emphasized that he was fulfilling biblical prophecies: 'Think not that I am come to destroy the law, or the prophets: I am not come to destroy, but to fulfil.' Rigid adherence to the Jewish law though was not enough: 'except your righteousness shall exceed the righteousness of the scribes and Pharisees, ye shall in no case enter into the kingdom of heaven'. Yet he did not make the mistake of directly challenging the Roman emperor, or even Herod. If the Apocalypse dominated his preaching, he offered a more direct proof of his sanctity: he was a healer, he cured cripples and raised people from the dead and 'great multitudes were gathered together unto him'.

Jesus visited Jerusalem at least three times for Passover and other festivals before his final visit, according to John, and had two lucky escapes. When he preached in the Temple during Tabernacles, he was hailed by some as a prophet and by others as the Christ – though snobbish Jerusalemites sneered, 'Shall Christ come out of Galilee?' When he debated with the authorities, the crowd challenged him: 'Then they took up stones to cast at him but Jesus hid himself and went out of the temple, going though the midst of them.' He came back for Hanukkah (the Festival of Dedication), but when he claimed 'I and my Father are one, then the Jews took up stones again to stone him ... but he escaped'. He knew what a visit to Jerusalem would mean.

Meanwhile in Galilee, Antipas' discarded Arab wife escaped from the dungeons of Machaerus to the court of her father, Aretas IV, the wealthiest King of Nabataea, the builder of the remarkable Khazneh shrine and royal tomb in 'rose-red' Petra. Furious at this insult, Aretas invaded Antipas' principality. Herodias had first caused the death of a prophet and had now started an Arab–Jewish war which Antipas lost. Roman allies were not permitted to launch private wars: the Emperor Tiberius, who bathed in increasingly senile debauchery in Capri, was irritated by Antipas' folly but backed him.

Herod Antipas now heard about Jesus. People wondered who he was. Some thought him 'John the Baptist but some say Elias and others, one of the prophets', while his disciple Peter believed he was the Messiah. Jesus was especially popular among women, and some of these were Herodians – the wife of Herod's steward was a follower. Antipas knew of the connection to the Baptist: 'It is John, whom I beheaded: he is risen from the dead.' He threatened to arrest Jesus, but significantly some of the Pharisees, evidently friendly towards him, warned him: 'Depart hence: for Herod will kill thee.'

Instead Jesus defied Antipas. 'Go ye, and tell that fox' that he would continue healing and preaching for two days and on the third he would visit the only place where a Jewish Son of Man could fulfil his destiny: 'It cannot be that a prophet perish out of Jerusalem.' His sublimely poetical message to the son of the king who had built the Temple is steeped in Jesus' love for the doomed city: 'O Jerusalem, Jerusalem, which killest the prophets, and stonest them that are sent unto thee: how often would I have gathered thy children together, as a hen doth gather her brood under her wings, and ye would not! Behold, your house is left unto you desolate.'

JESUS OF NAZARETH: THREE DAYS IN JERUSALEM

At the Passover of AD 33,* Jesus and Herod Antipas arrived in Jerusalem at almost the same time. Jesus led a procession to Bethany on the Mount of Olives, with its spectacular view of the gleaming snowy mountain of the Temple. He sent his Apostles into the city to bring back an ass – not one of our donkeys but the sturdy mount of kings. The Gospels, our only sources, each give slightly different versions of what happened in the next three days. 'All this was done', explains Matthew, 'that the scriptures of the prophets might be fulfilled'.

The Messiah was prophesied to enter the city on an ass, and as Jesus approached, his followers laid down palms before him and hailed him as 'Son of David' and 'King of Israel'. He probably entered the city, like many visitors, through the southern gate near the Siloam Pool and then climbed to the Temple up the monumental staircase of Robinson's Arch. His Apostles, Galilean provincials who had never visited the city, were dazzled by the grandeur of the Temple: 'Master, see what manner of stones and what buildings are here!' Jesus, who had often seen the Temple, replied, 'Seest thou these great buildings? There shall not be left one stone upon another, that shall not be thrown down.'

Jesus expressed his love for and disappointment in Jerusalem but he foresaw the abomination of desolation. Historians believe that these prophecies were added later, because the Gospels were written after Titus had destroyed the Temple. Yet Jerusalem had been smashed and rebuilt before, and Jesus was reflecting the

---

* No one knows exactly when Jesus came to Jerusalem. Luke starts Jesus' ministry with his baptism by John, around AD 28–29, saying he was about thirty, suggesting that his death was between AD 29 and say AD 33. John says his ministry lasted one year; Matthew, Mark and Luke say it lasted three years. Jesus may have been killed in 30, 33 or 36. But his historical existence is confirmed not only in the Gospels but in Tacitus and Josephus, who also mentions John the Baptist. At the very least, we know that Jesus came to Jerusalem at Passover after Pilate's arrival as prefect (26) and before his departure (36) during the reigns of Tiberius (died 37) and Antipas (before 39) and the high priesthood of Caiaphas (18–36): most likely between 29 and 33. Pilate's character is confirmed by both Josephus and Philo Judaeus of Alexandria, and his existence confirmed by an inscription found in Caesarea.

popular anti-Temple traditions.* 'Destroy this Temple and I shall build another not made by human hands,' he added, echoing his prophetic inspiration, Isaiah. Both saw beyond the real city to a heavenly Jerusalem that would have the power to shake the world, yet Jesus promised to rebuild the Temple himself in three days, perhaps showing that it was the corruption, not the Holy House itself, that he opposed.

By day, Jesus taught, and healed sick people at the Bethesda Pool just north of the Temple and at the Siloam Pool to its south, both crowded with Jewish pilgrims purifying themselves to enter the Holy House. At night he returned to his friends' home in Bethany. On the Monday morning, he again entered the city but this time he approached the Royal Portico of the Temple.

At Passover, Jerusalem was at its most crowded and dangerous. Power was founded on money, rank and Roman connections. But the Jews did not share the Roman respect for military kudos or cold cash. Respect in Jerusalem was based on family (Temple magnates and Herodian princelings), scholarship (the Pharisee teachers) and the wild card of divine inspiration. In the Upper City, across the valley from the Temple, the grandees lived in Grecian-Roman mansions with Jewish features: the so-called Palatial Residence

---

* Such as those of the Essenes, probably an offshoot of the pious Hasidim who had originally backed the Maccabees. Josephus explained that they were one of the three sects of Judaism in the first century AD, but we learned more in the Dead Sea Scrolls, discovered in eleven caves at Qumran near the Dead Sea in 1947–56. These contain the earliest Hebrew versions of some of the biblical books. Christians and Jews had long debated the differences between the Septuagint Bible (translated into Greek, from a vanished Hebrew original and the basis of the Christian Old Testament, between the third and first centuries BC) and the earliest surviving Hebrew Bible (the Masoretic, dating from the seventh to the tenth or early eleventh centuries AD). The Aleppo Codex is the oldest Masoretic text, but incomplete; the St Petersburg Codex, dated 1008, is the oldest complete text. The Scrolls revealed differences but confirm that the Masoretic was fairly accurate. The Scrolls prove, however, that there were many versions of the biblical books in circulation as late as Jesus' time. The Essenes were austere Jews who developed the apocalyptic ideas of Jeremiah and Daniel and saw the world as a struggle between good and evil ending in war and judgement. Their leader was a mystical 'Teacher of Righteousness'; their enemy was the 'Wicked Priest' – one of the Maccabees. They feature in many crackpot theories about the origins of Christianity, but we can only say that John the Baptist may have lived with them in the desert and that Jesus may have been inspired by their hostility to the Temple and by their apocalyptic scenarios.

excavated there has spacious receiving-rooms and *mikvahs*. Here stood the palaces of Antipas and the high priest Joseph Caiaphas. But the real authority in Jerusalem was the prefect, Pontius Pilate, who usually ruled his province from Caesarea on the coast but always came to supervise Passover, staying at Herod's Citadel.

Antipas was not the only Jewish royalty in Jerusalem. Helena, the Queen of Adiabene, a small kingdom in today's northern Iraq,* had converted to Judaism and moved to Jerusalem, building a palace in the City of David, donating the golden candelabra over the doorway of the Temple sanctuary and paying for food when there were bad harvests. Queen Helena too would have been there for Passover, probably wearing the sort of jewellery recently discovered in Jerusalem: a large pearl inlaid in gold with two drop pieces, each with an emerald set in gold.

Josephus guessed that two and a half million Jews came for Passover. This is an exaggeration but there were Jews 'out of every nation,' from Parthia and Babylonia to Crete and Libya. The only way to imagine this throng is to see Mecca during the haj. At Passover, every family had to sacrifice a lamb, so the city was jammed with bleating sheep – 255,600 lambs were sacrificed. There was much to do: pilgrims had to take a dip in a *mikvah* every time they approached the Temple as well as buy their sacrificial lambs in the Royal Portico. Not everyone could stay in the city. Thousands lodged in the surrounding villages, like Jesus, or camped around the walls. As the smell of burning meat and heady incense wafted – and the trumpet blasts, announcing prayers and sacrifices, ricocheted – across the city, everything was focused on the Temple, nervously watched by the Roman soldiers from the Antonia Fortress.

Jesus now walked into the towering, colonnaded Royal Portico,

---

* This Iraqi kingdom remained Jewish well into the next century. Queen Helena and her sons were buried just outside the old city of Jeruslaem under three pyramids; the ornate King's Tomb survives today, north of the Damascus Gate on the Nablus Road that leads past the American Colony Hotel. In the nineteenth century, a French archaeologist excavated the site and announced it had belonged to King David. Adiabene was not the only Jewish fiefdom in that area: two Jewish rebels against Parthia, Asinaeus and Anilaeus, created an independent Jewish state around Babylon that lasted about fifteen years.

the bustling, colourful, crowded centre of all life, where pilgrims gathered to organize their accommodation, to meet friends, and to change money for the Tyrian silver used to buy sacrificial lambs, doves, or, for the rich, oxen. This was not the Temple itself nor one of its inner courts but the most accessible and public section of the entire complex, designed to serve like a forum. In the Portico, Jesus attacked the Temple establishment: 'Is this house, which is called by thy name, become a den of robbers?' he said, overturning the tables of the money-changers while quoting and channelling the prophecies of Jeremiah, Zachariah and Isaiah. His demonstration attracted attention but not enough to warrant any intervention by Temple guards or Roman soldiers.

After another night in Bethany, he returned to the Temple* the next morning to debate with his critics. The Gospels cite the Pharisees as Jesus' enemies, but this probably reflected the situation fifty years later when their authors were writing. The Pharisees were the more flexible and populist sect, and some of their teachings may have been similar to those of Jesus. His real enemies were the Temple aristocracy. The Herodians now challenged him about paying taxes to Rome, but he replied adeptly, 'Render unto Caesar the things that are Caesar's and to God the things that are God's.'

Yet he did not call himself the Messiah, emphasizing the Shema, the basic Jewish prayer to the one God, and the love of his fellow men: he was very much a Jew. But then he warned the excited crowds of the imminent Apocalypse that would of course take place in Jerusalem: 'You are not far from the Kingdom of God.' While

* The Golden Gate is the traditional gate by which Jesus entered the Temple, and in Jewish, Muslim and Christian mysticism, the Messiah will enter Jerusalem there. But Jesus would not have entered this way: the Gate was not built for another 600 years and the nearby Shushan Gate was not open to the public and only rarely used by the high priest himself. Another Christian tradition says Jesus entered through the Beautiful Gate, on the other side, today probably close to the Bab al-Silsila (Gate of the Chain) on the west. This is more likely. But the Beautiful Gate is also the place where Peter and John performed a miracle after Jesus' death. The very name Golden Gate may be a muddled version of 'beautiful' since golden in Latin (*aurea*) and beautiful in Greek (*oreia*) are so similar. Jerusalem's holiness is criss-crossed with such misunderstandings, and multiple legends applied to the same sites to enforce and embellish their sanctity.

Jews held various views on the coming of the Messiah, most agreed that God would preside over the end of the world, which would be followed by the creation of the Messiah's kingdom in Jerusalem: 'Sound in Zion the trumpet to summon the saints,' declared the Psalms of Solomon, 'announce in Jerusalem the voice of one bringing good news for the God of Israel has been merciful.' Hence his followers asked him: 'Tell us what shall be the sign of your coming and of the end of the world?' 'Watch therefore for ye know not what hour your Lord will come,' he answered, but then he spelt out the coming Apocalypse: 'Nation shall rise against nation, and kingdom against kingdom, and there shall be famines and pestilences and earthquakes,' before they saw 'the Son of Man coming in clouds of heaven with power and great glory'. Jesus' inflammatory gambit would have seriously alarmed the Roman prefect and high priests, who, he warned, could expect no mercy in the Last Days: 'Ye serpents, ye generation of vipers, how can ye escape the damnation of hell?'

Jerusalem was always tense at Passover but the authorities were even more jumpy than usual. Mark and Luke state, in a couple of neglected verses, that there had just been some sort of Galilean rebellion in Jerusalem, suppressed by Pilate, who had killed eighteen Galileans around the 'tower of Siloam' south of the Temple. One of the surviving rebels, Barabbas, whom Jesus would soon encounter, had 'committed a murder in the insurrection'. The high priests decided to take no chances with another Galilean predicting their destruction in an imminent Apocalypse: Caiaphas and Annas, the influential former high priest, discussed what to do. Surely it was better, argued Caiaphas in John's Gospel, 'that one man should die for the people and that the whole nation perish not'. They made their plans.

The next day Jesus prepared for Passover at the Upper Room – the Cenacle, or Coenaculum – on the western hill of Jerusalem (later known as Mount Zion). At the supper, Jesus somehow learned that his Apostle, Judas Iscariot, had betrayed him for thirty pieces of silver, but he did not change his plan to walk around the city to the tranquil olive groves of the Garden of Gethsemane just across the Kidron Valley from the Temple. Judas slipped away. We do not know if he betrayed Jesus out of principle – for being too radical or not radical enough – or out of greed or envy.

Judas returned with a posse of senior priests, Temple guards and Roman legionaries. Jesus was not instantly recognizable in the dark, so Judas betrayed him by identifying him with a kiss and received his silver. In a chaotic torchlit drama, the Apostles drew their swords, Peter lopped off the ear of one of the high priest's lackeys and a nameless boy ran off stark naked into the night, a touch so eccentric, it rings of truth. Jesus was arrested and the Apostles scattered except for two who followed at a distance.

It was now almost midnight. Jesus, guarded by Roman soldiers, was marched around the southern walls through the Siloam Gate to the palace of the city's *éminence grise* Annas, in the Upper City.* Annas dominated Jerusalem and personified the rigid, incestuous network of Temple families. Himself a former high priest, he was the father-in-law of the present incumbent Caiaphas and no less than five of his sons would be high priests. But he and Caiaphas were despised by most Jews as venal, thuggish collaborators, whose servants, complained one Jewish text, 'beat us with staves'; their justice was a corrupt money-making scam. Jesus, on the other hand, had struck a popular chord and had admirers even among the Sanhedrin. The trial of this popular and fearless preacher would have to be conducted shiftily, by night.

Some time after midnight, as the guards built a fire in the courtyard (and Jesus' disciple Peter thrice denied knowing his

* Every event in this story was to develop its own geography in Jerusalem, though many of these sites are probably historically wrong. The Upper Room (Cenacle) on Mount Zion is the traditional site of the Last Supper; the real site was maybe closer to the cheaper houses around the Siloam Pool since Mark mentions 'a man carrying a jar of water' there. The Last Supper tradition developed later in the fifth century and even more strongly under the Crusaders. A stronger tradition suggests this site was where the Holy Spirit descended on the Apostles at Pentecost, after Jesus' death: this is certainly one of the most ancient Christian shrines. Its holiness was so infectious that Jews and Muslims later revered it too. The traditional but plausible site of Annas' mansion is under the Church of Holy Archangels in the Armenian Quarter. A stone weight inscribed 'belonging to the house of Caiaphas' in Aramaic has been uncovered in Jerusalem and in 1990 builders found a sealed burial case in which one ossuary was inscribed 'Joseph son of Caiaphas' – so these are possibly the high priest's bones. The Gethsemane Garden with its ancient olive grove is believed to be the correct site.

master), Annas and his son-in-law assembled their loyal Sanhedrin members – but not all of them, because at least one, Joseph of Arimathea, was an admirer of Jesus and never approved his arrest. Jesus was cross-examined by the high priest: had he threatened to destroy the Temple and rebuild it in three days? Did he claim to be the Messiah? Jesus said nothing but finally admitted, 'ye shall see the Son of Man sitting on the right hand of power, and coming in the clouds of heaven'.

'He hath spoken blasphemy,' said Caiaphas.

'He is guilty of death,' answered the crowd who had gathered despite the late hour. Jesus was blindfolded and spent the night being taunted in the courtyard until dawn, when the real business could begin. Pilate was waiting.

PONTIUS PILATE: THE TRIAL OF JESUS

The Roman prefect, guarded by his auxiliary troops and watched by a tense crowd, held court on the Praetorium, the raised platform outside Herod's Citadel, the Roman headquarters near today's Jaffa Gate. Pontius Pilate was an aggressive, tactless martinet out of his depth in Judaea. He was already loathed in Jerusalem, notorious for his 'venality, violence, theft, assaults, abuse, endless executions and savage ferocity'. Even one of the Herodian princes called him 'vindictive with a furious temper'.

He had already outraged the Jews by ordering his troops to march into Jerusalem displaying their shields with images of the emperor. Herod Antipas led delegations requesting their removal. Always 'inflexible and cruel', Pilate refused. When more Jews protested, he unleashed his guards, but the delegates lay on the ground and bared their necks. Pilate then removed the offending images. More recently he had killed the Galilean rebels 'whose blood Pilate had mingled with their sacrifices'.

'Art thou the King of the Jews?' Pilate asked Jesus. After all, Jesus' followers had acclaimed him king when he entered Jerusalem. But he answered, 'Thou sayest it,' and refused to add anything more. But Pilate did learn he was a Galilean. 'As soon as he knew that he belonged unto Herod's jurisdiction', Pilate sent his prisoner to Herod Antipas as a courtesy to the ruler of Galilee, who had a special interest in Jesus. It was a short walk to Antipas' palace. Herod Antipas, says Luke, 'was exceeding glad' for he had wanted to meet John the Baptist's successor for a long time 'and he hoped to have seen some miracle done by him'. But Jesus so despised the 'fox', killer of John, that he did not even deign to speak to him.

Antipas played with Jesus, asking him to perform his tricks, presented him with a royal robe and called him 'king'. The tetrarch was hardly likely to try to save John the Baptist's successor, but he appreciated the opportunity to interview him. Pilate and Antipas had long been enemies but now they 'made friends together'. Nonetheless, Jesus was a Roman problem. Herod Antipas sent him back to the Praetorium. There, Pilate tried Jesus, two so-called thieves and Barabbas, who, says Mark, 'lay bound with them that had made insurrection with him'. This suggests that a handful of rebels, who perhaps included the two 'thieves', were being tried with Jesus.

Pilate toyed with releasing one of these prisoners. Some of the crowd called for Barabbas. According to the Gospels, Barabbas was released. The story sounds unlikely: the Romans usually executed murderous rebels. Jesus was sentenced to crucifixion while, according to Matthew, Pilate 'took water and washed his hands before the multitude, saying, I am innocent of the blood of this just person'.

'His blood be upon us and our children,' replied the crowd.

Far from being a mealy-mouthed vacillator, the violent and obstinate Pilate had never previously felt the need to wash his hands before his blood-letting. In an earlier dispute with the Jews, he had sent his troops in civilian disguise among a peaceful Jerusalem crowd; at Pilate's signal, they had drawn their swords and cleared the streets, killing many. Now Pilate, already faced with the Barabbas rebellion that week, clearly feared any resurgence of the 'kings' and 'pseudo-prophets' who had plagued Judaea since Herod's death. Jesus was inflammatory in his oblique way, and he was undoubtedly popular. Even many years later, Josephus, himself a Pharisee, described Jesus as a wise teacher.

The traditional account of the sentencing therefore does not ring true. The Gospels claim that the priests insisted they did not have the authority to pass death sentences, but it is far from clear that this is true. The high priest, writes Josephus, 'will adjudicate in cases of dispute, punish those convicted of crime'. The Gospels, written or amended after the destruction of the Temple in 70, blamed the Jews and acquitted the Romans, keen to show loyalty to the empire. Yet the charges against Jesus, and the punishment itself, tell their own story: this was a Roman operation.

Jesus, like most crucifixion victims, was scourged with a leather whip tipped with either bone or metal, a torment so savage that it often killed the victim. Wearing a placard reading 'KING OF THE JEWS' prepared by the Roman soldiers, many of them Syrian-Greek auxiliaries, and bleeding heavily after his flagellation, Jesus was led away, on what was probably the morning of 14th of Nisan or Friday 3 April 33. Along with the other two victims, he carried the *patibulum*, crossbar, for his own crucifixion, out of the Citadel prison and through the streets of the Upper City. His followers persuaded a certain Simon of Cyrene to help bear the crossbar while his women admirers lamented. 'Daughters of Jerusalem,' he said, 'weep not for me but weep for yourselves and your children,' because the Apocalypse was imminent – 'the days are coming'.

Jesus left Jerusalem for the last time, turning left through the Gennath (Gardens) Gate into an area of hilly gardens, rock-cut tombs and Jerusalem's execution hill, the aptly named Place of the Skull: Golgotha.*

---

* This is a totally different route from the traditional Via Dolorosa. The Gennath Gate, mentioned by Josephus, was identified by the Israeli archaeologist Nahman Avigad in the northern part of the Jewish Quarter in a section of the First Wall. In the Muslim period, Christians wrongly believed that the Antonia Fortress was the Praetorium where Pilate had made his judgements. Medieval Franciscan monks developed the tradition of the Stations of the Cross along the Via Dolorosa, from the Antonia site to the Church of the Holy Sepulchre – almost certainly the wrong route. Golgotha derives from the Aramaic for 'skull', Calvary from the Latin for 'skull', *calva*.

JESUS CHRIST: THE PASSION

A crowd of enemies and friends followed Jesus out of the city to watch the macabre and technical business of execution, always a spectacle that fascinated. The sun had risen when he arrived at the execution place where the upright post awaited him: it would have been used before him and would be used again after him. The soldiers offered Jesus the traditional drink of wine and myrrh to steady his nerves, but he refused it. He was then attached to the crossbar and hoisted up the stake.

Crucifixion, said Josephus, was 'the most miserable death',* designed to demean the victim publicly. Hence Pilate ordered Jesus' placard to be attached to his cross – KING OF THE JEWS. Victims could be tied or nailed. The skill was to ensure victims did not bleed to death. The nails were usually driven through the forearms – not the palms – and ankles: the bones of a crucified Jew have been found in a tomb in north Jerusalem with a 4½-inch iron nail still sticking through a skeletal ankle. Nails from crucifixion victims were popularly worn as charms, around the neck, by both Jews and gentiles to ward off illness, so the later Christian fetish for crucificial relics was actually part of a long tradition. Victims were usually crucified naked – with men facing outwards, women inwards.

The executioners were experts at either prolonging the agony or ending it quickly. The aim was to not kill Jesus too quickly but to demonstrate the futility of defying Roman power. He was most

---

* Indeed, in 74 BC, the young Julius Caesar was captured by pirates. After he was ransomed and released, he returned to arrest and crucify them. But, in recognition of their politeness, he did so as humanely as possible: he graciously slit their throats *before* crucifixion. Crucifixion originated in the east – Darius the Great crucified Babylonian rebels – and was adopted by the Greeks. As we have seen, Alexander the Great crucified the Tyrians; Antiochus Epiphanes and the Jewish king Alexander Jannaeus crucified rebellious Jerusalemites; the Carthaginians crucified insubordinate generals. In 71 BC the Roman suppression of the Spartacus slave revolt culminated in a mass crucifixion. The wood for the cross is said to have come from the site of the fortified eleventh-century Monastery of the Cross, near today's Israeli Knesset. The monastery was long the headquarters of the Georgian Orthodox Church in Jerusalem.

probably nailed to the cross with his arms outstretched as shown in Christian art, supported by a small wedge, *sedile*, under the buttocks and a *suppedaneum* ledge under the feet. This arrangement meant he could survive for hours, even days. The quickest way to expedite death was to break the legs. The body weight was then borne by the arms and the victim would asphyxiate within ten minutes.

Hours passed; his enemies mocked him; passers-by jeered. His friend Mary of Magdala kept vigil alongside his mother Mary and the unnamed 'disciple whom he loved', possibly his brother James. His supporter Joseph of Arimathea visited him too. The heat of the day came and went. 'I thirst,' Jesus said. His female followers dipped a sponge into vinegar and hyssop, and raised it to his lips on a reed so that he could suck on it. Sometimes he seemed to despair: 'My God, my God, why hast thou forsaken me?' he called out, quoting the appropriate scripture, Psalm 22. Yet what did he mean by God forsaking him? Was Jesus expecting God to unleash the End of Days?

As he weakened, he saw his mother. 'Behold thy son,' he said, asking the beloved disciple to care for her. If it was his brother, this made sense, for the disciple escorted Mary away to rest. The crowds must have dispersed. Night fell.

Crucifixion was a slow death from heat stroke, hunger, suffocation, shock or thirst, and Jesus was probably bleeding from the flagellation. Suddenly he gave a sigh. 'It is finished,' he said, and lost consciousness. Given the tension in Jerusalem and the imminent Sabbath and Passover holiday, Pilate must have ordered his executioners to accelerate matters. The soldiers broke the legs of the two bandits or rebels, allowing them to suffocate, but when they came to Jesus he already seemed dead, so 'one of the soldiers with a spear pierced his side and forthwith came blood and water'. It may have actually been the spear that had killed him.

Joseph of Arimathea hurried to the Praetorium to ask Pilate for the body. Victims were usually left to rot on their crosses, the prey of vultures, but Jews believed in swift burial. Pilate agreed.

Jewish dead were not buried in the earth during the first century but laid in a shroud in a rock tomb, which their family always checked, partly to ensure that the deceased were indeed dead and not merely comatose: it was rare but not unheard of to find that the 'dead' were awake the next morning. The bodies were then left for a year to desiccate, then the bones were placed in a bone-box, known as an ossuary, often with the name carved on the outside, in a rock-cut tomb.

Joseph and Jesus' family and followers brought down the body and quickly found an unused tomb in a nearby garden where they laid him. The body was sweetened by expensive spices and wrapped in a shroud – like the first-century shroud found in a tomb a little south of the city walls in the Field of Blood, still bearing clumps of human hair (but unlike the famous Turin Shroud, which has now been dated to between 1260 and 1390). It is likely that the present Church of the Holy Sepulchre, which encloses both the place of crucifixion and the tomb, is the genuine site since its tradition was kept alive by local Christians for the next three centuries. Pilate posted guards around Jesus' tomb at Caiaphas' request 'lest his disciples come by night and steal him away and say unto the people, He is risen from the dead'.

Up to this point, the story of Jesus' Passion – from the Latin *patior*, to suffer – is based on our sole source, the Gospels, but no faith is required to believe in the life and death of a Jewish prophet and thaumaturge. However, three days after his crucifixion, on Sunday morning, according to Luke, some of Jesus' female family and followers (including his mother and Joanna, the wife of Herod Antipas' steward) visited the tomb: 'They found the stone rolled away from the sepulchre and they entered in and found not the body of the Lord Jesus ... As they were much perplexed, behold two men stood by them in shining garments and as they were afraid ... they said unto them: Why seek ye the living among the dead? He is not here but is risen.' The frightened disciples were in hiding on the Mount of Olives during the Passover week, but Jesus appeared several times to them and to his mother, saying to them, 'Be not afraid.' When Thomas doubted the Resurrection, Jesus showed him the wounds on his hands and in his side. After some days, he led them up to the Mount of Olives where he ascended to heaven. This Resurrection, which turned a sordid death into a transforming triumph of life over death, is the defining moment of Christian faith, celebrated on Easter Sunday.

For those who do not share this faith, the facts are impossible to verify. Matthew reveals what was surely the contemporary alternative version of events, 'commonly reported among the Jews to this day': the high priests immediately paid off the soldiers who were meant to be guarding the tomb and ordered them to tell everyone that 'his disciples came by night and stole him away while we slept'.

Archaeologists tend to believe that the body was simply removed and buried by friends and family in another rock-cut tomb somewhere around Jerusalem. They have excavated tombs, with ossuaries that bear names such as 'James brother of Jesus' and even 'Jesus son of Joseph'. These have generated media headlines. Some have been exposed as forgeries but most are genuine first-century tombs with very common Jewish names – and with no connection to Jesus.*

Jerusalem celebrated Passover. Judas invested his silver in real estate – the Potter's Field on the Akeldama south of the city, appropriately in the Valley of Hell – where he then 'burst asunder in the midst and all his bowels gushed out'.† When the disciples emerged from hiding, they met for Pentecost in the Upper Room, the Cenacle on Mount Zion, 'and suddenly there came from heaven a rushing mighty wind' – the Holy Spirit that allowed them to speak in

---

* The Gospel of Peter, a Gnostic codex dating from the second or third century, discovered in nineteenth-century Egypt, contains a mysterious story about the removal of the body. The oldest Gospel, Mark, written forty years later around AD 70, ends with Jesus being laid in his tomb, never mentioning the Resurrection. Mark's account of the resurrection was a later addition. Matthew, written about AD 80, and Luke are based on Mark and another unknown source. Hence these three are known as the Synoptics – from the Greek meaning 'seen together'. Luke minimized the role of Jesus' family at the Crucifixion, but Mark mentions Mary mother of James, Joses and Jesus' sister. John, the latest Gospel, written probably at the end of the century, portrays a more divine Jesus than the others but has other sources, giving more detail on Jesus' earlier visits to Jerusalem.

† Acts of the Apostles tells this story, but Matthew has another version: the remorseful Judas threw away his silver in the Temple at which the high priest (who could not put it into the Temple treasury because it was blood money) invested it in the Potter's Field 'to bury strangers in'. Then he hanged himself. The Akeldama – Field of Blood – remained a burial place into the Middle Ages.

tongues to the many nationalities who were in Jerusalem and to perform healing in the name of Jesus. Peter and John were entering the Temple through the Beautiful Gate for their daily prayers when a cripple asked for alms. 'Rise up and walk,' they said, and he did.

The Apostles elected Jesus' brother as 'Overseer of Jerusalem', leader of these Jewish sectaries known as the Nazarenes. The sect must have grown because not long after Jesus' death, 'there was a great persecution against the church at Jerusalem'. One of Jesus' Greek-speaking followers, Stephen, had denounced the Temple, saying that 'the Most High dwelleth not in temples made with hands'. Proving that the high priest could order capital punishment, Stephen was tried by the Sanhedrin and stoned outside the walls, probably to the north of today's Damascus Gate. He was the first Christian 'martyr' – an adaptation of the Greek word for 'witness'. Yet James and his Nazarenes remained practising Jews, loyal to Jesus, but also teaching and praying in the Temple for the next thirty years. James was widely admired there as a Jewish holy man. Jesus' Judaism was clearly no more idiosyncratic than that of the many other preachers who came before and after him.

Jesus' enemies did not prosper. Soon after his crucifixion, Pilate was sunk by a Samaritan pseudo-prophet who preached to excited crowds that he had found Moses' urn on Mount Gerizim. Pilate sent in the cavalry who culled many of his followers. The prefect had already driven Jerusalem to the edge of open revolt; now the Samaritans too denounced his brutality.

The Governor of Syria had to restore order in Jerusalem. He sacked both Caiaphas and Pilate, who was sent back to Rome. This was so popular that the Jerusalemites jubilantly welcomed the Roman governor. Pilate vanishes from history. Tiberius was meanwhile tiring of Herod Antipas. But this was not the end of that dynasty: the Herodians were about to enjoy an extraordinary restoration thanks to the most adventurous of the Jewish princes, who would befriend Rome's demented emperor and regain Jerusalem.

12

THE LAST OF THE HERODS

AD 40–66

HEROD AGRIPPA: CALIGULA'S FRIEND

Young Herod Agrippa grew up in Rome amid the imperial family and became best friends with the emperor Tiberius' son Drusus. This charming, high-rolling extrovert – the grandson of Herod the Great and Mariamme, child of their executed son Aristobulos – amassed huge debts to keep up with the emperor's son and the fast crowd.

When Drusus died young in AD 23, the heartbroken emperor could no longer face his son's friends and Herod Agrippa, now broke, retreated to Galilee, ruled by Antipas who was married to his sister Herodias. Antipas gave him a drab job in Tiberias, but drabness was not Agrippa's style and he fled to Idumea, the family's homeland, and there contemplated suicide. With this prodigal rogue, however, something always turned up.

Around the time of Jesus' crucifixion, Philip, the tetrarch of the family's northern lands, died. Antipas asked the emperor to expand his principality. Tiberius had always liked Herod Agrippa; so he rushed to the emperor's residence on Capri to stake his own claim and undermine his uncle's. He found Tiberius residing gloomily at the Jupiter Villa, his jaded appetites, according to the historian Suetonius, fed by boys known as his 'minnows', trained to suck his privates as he swam in the pool.

Tiberius welcomed Agrippa – until he heard about the string of unpaid debts he had left around the Mediterranean. But Agrippa, a born gambler, persuaded his mother's friend Antonia to lend him money and appeal to the emperor. Severe and chaste, Antonia, daughter of Mark Antony, was respected by Tiberius as the ideal Roman aristocrat. He took her advice and forgave the Jewish rascal. Agrippa used the cash not to pay off his debts but to give a generous present to another bankrupt princeling, Caligula, who with the child Gemellus, son of Agrippa's late friend Drusus, was Tiberius' joint heir. The emperor asked the Herodian to look after Gemellus.

Instead the opportunistic Agrippa became best friends with Gaius Caligula, who ever since being paraded before the legions as a child mascot in a mini-military uniform (including army boots, *caligae* – hence the nickname 'Bootkins'), was beloved for being the son of the popular general Germanicus. Now twenty-five, balding and gangly, Caligula had grown up spoilt, dissolute and quite possibly insane, but he remained the people's darling and he was impatient to inherit the empire. Caligula and Herod Agrippa are likely to have shared a life of extravagant debauchery, a million miles from the piety of the latter's brethren in Jerusalem. As they rode around Capri, the two fantasized about Tiberius' death, but their charioteer was listening. When Agrippa had him arrested for stealing, the charioteer snitched to the emperor. Agrippa was thrown into jail and bound in chains but, protected by his friend Caligula, he was allowed to bathe, receive friends and relish his favourite dishes.

When Tiberius finally died in March 37, Caligula, having murdered young Gemellus, succeeded as emperor. He at once released his friend, presented him with gold fetters to commemorate his time in real shackles and promoted him to king, giving him Philip's northern tetrarchy. Quite a reversal of fortune. Simultaneously Agrippa's sister Herodias and Jesus' hated 'fox', Antipas, travelled to Rome to undo this decision and win their own kingdom. But Agrippa framed them, alleging that they were planning a rebellion. Caligula deposed Antipas, the killer of John the Baptist – who later died in Lyons – and gave all his lands to Herod Agrippa.

The new king scarcely visited his kingdom, preferring to stay close to Caligula whose homicidal eccentricities rapidly turned him from Rome's favourite to its oppressor. Lacking the military kudos of his predecessors, Caligula tried to bolster his prestige by ordering his own image to be worshipped across the empire – and in the

Holy of Holies of the Temple. Jerusalem was defiant; the Jews prepared to rebel, with delegations telling the Governor of Syria that 'he must first sacrifice the entire Jewish nation' before they would tolerate such a sacrilege. Ethnic fighting broke out in Alexandria between Greeks and Jews. When the two parties sent delegations to Caligula, the Greeks claimed that the Jews were the only people who would not worship Caligula's statue.

Fortunately, King Agrippa was still in Rome, ever more intimate with the increasingly erratic Caligula. When the emperor launched an expedition to Gaul, the Jewish king was one of his entourage. But, instead of fighting, Caligula declared victory over the sea, collecting seashells for his Triumph.

Caligula ordered Petronius, the Governor of Syria, to enforce his orders and crush Jerusalem. Jewish delegations, led by Herodian princes, begged Petronius to change his mind. Petronius hesitated, knowing that it was war to proceed and death to refuse. But King Herod Agrippa, the prodigal time-server, suddenly showed himself to be the surprising champion of the Jews, writing courageously to Caligula in one of the most astonishing letters written on behalf of Jerusalem:

I, as you know, am by birth a Jew and my native city is Jerusalem in which is situated the sacred shrine of the most high God. This Temple, my Lord Gaius, has never from the first admitted any figure wrought by men's hands, because it is the sanctuary of the true God. Your grandfather [Marcus] Agrippa visited and paid honour to the Temple and so did Augustus. [He then thanks Caligula for favours granted but] I exchange all [those benefits] for one thing only – that the ancestral institutions be not disturbed. Either I must seem a traitor to my own or no longer be counted your friend as I have been; there is no other alternative.*

* 'It fell to me', Agrippa wrote as a Maccabee and a Herodian, 'to have for my grandparents and ancestors, kings, most of whom had the title High Priest, who considered their kingship inferior to the priesthood. Holding the office of High Priest is as superior in excellence to that of king as God surpasses men. For the office of one is to worship God, of the other to have charge of men. As my lot is cast in such a nation, city and Temple, I beseech you for them all.'

Even if the stark bravado of this 'death or freedom' is exaggerated, this was a risky letter to write to Caligula – yet the king's intervention did apparently save Jerusalem.

At a feast, the emperor thanked King Agrippa for the help he had given him before his accession, offering to grant him any request. The king asked him not to place his image in the Temple. Caligula agreed.

HEROD AGRIPPA AND EMPEROR CLAUDIUS: ASSASSINATION, GLORY AND WORMS

After recovering from a strange illness in late 37, the emperor became increasingly unbalanced. During the next years, the sources claim he committed incest with his three sisters, prostituted them to other men and appointed his horse as a consul. It is hard to assess the truth of these scandals, though his actions certainly alienated and terrified much of the Roman elite. He married his sister, then, when she became pregnant, supposedly ripped the baby out of her womb. Kissing his mistresses, he mused, 'And this beautiful throat will be cut whenever I please' and told the consuls, 'I only have to give one nod and your throats will be cut on the spot.' His favourite bon mot was 'if only Rome had one neck', but unwisely he also liked to tease his macho Praetorian Guards with saucy passwords such as 'Priapus'. It could not go on.

At midday on 24 January 41, Caligula, accompanied by Herod Agrippa, was leaving the theatre through a covered walkway when one of the Praetorian tribunes drew his sword and cried, 'Take this!' The swordblow hit Caligula's shoulder, almost filleting him in half, but he kept shouting, 'I'm still alive.' The conspirators cried, 'Strike again,' and finished him off. His German bodyguards marauded through the streets, the Praetorian Guardsmen ransacked the imperial palace on the Palatine Hill and murdered Caligula's wife, dashing out the brains of his baby. The Senate meanwhile tried to restore the republic, ending the despotism of the emperors.

Herod Agrippa took control of Caligula's body, winning time by declaring that the emperor was still alive but wounded, while he led a squad of Praetorians to the palace. They noticed a stirring behind a curtain and discovered the lame, stammering scholar, Claudius, Caligula's uncle and son of Agrippa's family friend Antonia. Together, they acclaimed him as emperor, carrying him to their camp on a shield. Claudius, a republican, tried to refuse the honour, but the Jewish king advised him to accept the crown and persuaded the Senate to offer it to him. No practising Jew, before or since, even in modern times, has ever been so powerful. The new Emperor Claudius, who proved a steady, sensible ruler, rewarded his friend by presenting him with Jerusalem and the whole of Herod the Great's kingdom, as well as granting him the rank of consul. Even Agrippa's brother received a kingdom.

Herod Agrippa had left Jerusalem as a penniless ne'er-do-well; he returned as king of Judaea. He made a sacrifice in the Temple, and dutifully read Deuteronomy to the gathered people. The Jews were moved when he wept for his own mixed origins and dedicated Caligula's gold fetters, the symbol of his good fortune, to the Temple. 'The holy city', which he saw as 'the mother-city' not just of Judaea but of Jews across Europe and Asia, was won over by this new Herod, whose coins called him 'Great King Agrippa, Friend of Caesar'. Outside Jerusalem he lived like a Roman-Greek king, but when he was in the city he lived as a Jew and sacrificed each day in the Temple. He beautified and fortified the expanding Jerusalem, adding a Third Wall to enclose the new Bezetha suburb – the northern section of which has been excavated.

Yet even Agrippa struggled to manage Jerusalem's tensions: he appointed three successive high priests in two years and acted against the Jewish Christians. This may have coincided with Claudius' crackdown on the Jewish Christians in Rome – they were expelled for disorders 'at the instigation of Chrestus' (Christ). 'Now about this time', says the Acts of the Apostles, 'Herod the king stretched forth his hands to vex certain of the church,' and had James beheaded (not Jesus' brother but the disciple of that name). He also arrested Peter, whom he planned to execute after Passover. Peter somehow survived: the Christians hailed this as a miracle but other sources suggest that the king simply released him, possibly as a gift to the crowds.

Agrippa's making of emperors had gone to his head, for he called a summit of local kings to Tiberias without asking Roman permission. The Romans were alarmed and ordered the kings to disperse. Claudius halted the building of any more Jerusalem fortifications. Afterwards, Agrippa was holding court like a Greek godking in gold-encrusted robes in the forum of Caesarea when he was taken ill with stomach pains: 'he was eaten of worms', says the Acts of the Apostles. The Jews sat in sackcloth praying for his recovery but in vain. Agrippa had the charisma and sensitivity to conciliate Jewish moderates, Jewish fanatics and Romans; there died the only man who might have saved Jerusalem.

HEROD AGRIPPA II: NERO'S FRIEND

The king's death unleashed riots. Though his son and namesake Agrippa II was only seventeen, Claudius wanted to give him the kingdom, but he was advised that the boy was too young to govern his inflammable inheritance. Instead the emperor restored direct rule by Roman procurators and granted the late Agrippa's brother, King Herod of Chalcis, the right to appoint high priests and manage the Temple. For the next twenty-five years, Jerusalem was run in an ambiguous partnership between Roman procurators and Herodian kings but they could not soothe the turbulence caused by a succession of prophetic charlatans, ethnic conflicts between Greeks, Jews and Samaritans, and the widening gap between the rich, pro-Roman grandees and the poorer, religious Jews.

The Jewish Christians, the Nazarenes, led by Jesus' brother James, and their so-called *presbyteroi* or elders, survived in Jerusalem where the original disciples worshipped as Jews in the Temple. But Jesus was far from the last of the preachers who challenged Roman order: Josephus lists the eruption of one pseudo-prophet after another, most of them executed by the Romans.

The procurators did not help matters. Like Pilate, their reaction to this efflorescence of prophets was to massacre their followers while squeezing the province for profit. One year, at Passover in Jerusalem, a Roman soldier exposed his bottom to the Jews, causing a riot. The procurator sent in soldiers who started a stampede in which thousands suffocated in the narrow streets. A few years later, when fighting broke out between Jews and Samaritans, the Romans crucified many Jews. Both sides appealed to Rome. The Samaritans would have succeeded but young Herod Agrippa, who was being educated in Rome, won over Claudius' powerful wife, Agrippina: the emperor not only backed the Jews but ordered the Roman tribune at fault to be humiliated in Jerusalem and then executed. Like his father with Caligula, Agrippa II was popular not only with Claudius but with his heir, Nero. When his uncle Herod of Chalcis died, Agrippa was made king of that Lebanese fiefdom with special powers over the Temple in Jerusalem.

In Rome, the now senile Claudius was poisoned by Agrippina,* supposedly with a plateful of mushrooms. The new teenaged emperor Nero awarded Agrippa II more territories in Galilee, Syria and Lebanon. Agrippa gratefully renamed Caesarea Philippi, his capital, Neronias and advertised his warm relations with Nero on his coins with the legend 'Philo-Caesar'. However, Nero's procurators tended to be corrupt and clumsy. One of the worst was Antonius Felix, a venal Greek freedman who, writes the historian Tacitus, 'practised every kind of cruelty and lust, wielding the power of a king with the instincts of a slave'. As he was the brother of the secretary to Claudius and (for a time) to Nero, the Jews could no longer appeal to Rome. King Agrippa's scandalous sisters personified the corruption of the elite. Drusilla, who 'exceeded all women in beauty', was married to the Arab king Azizus of Emesa, but Felix 'conceived a passion for her. She being unhappy and wishing to escape the malice of her sister Berenice' eloped with Felix. Berenice, who had been Queen of Chalcis (married to her uncle), left her latest husband, the King of Cilicia, to live with her brother: Roman rumours suggested incest. Felix milked Judaea for

* Claudius was unlucky in his four marriages, especially his last two: he killed one wife and the other killed him. He executed his unfaithful teenaged wife Messalina for treason then married his niece, Julia Agrippina, the sister of Caligula, who started to promote Nero, her son by an earlier marriage, as heir. Claudius made Nero joint heir with his own son Britannicus, named to celebrate his conquest of Britain. On his accession, Nero murdered Britannicus.

money while 'a new species of bandit' known as the Sicarii (after their short Roman daggers – the origin of the word 'sickle') started to assassinate Jewish grandees at festivals in the middle of Jerusalem – their first success was the killing of an ex-high priest. Faced with ethnic slaughter and repeated 'pseudo-prophets', Felix struggled to keep the peace while enriching himself.

Amid this apocalyptic turbulence, the small sect of Jesus was now split between its Jewish leaders in Jerusalem and its gentile followers in the wider Roman world. Now the most dynamic radical of all Jesus' followers, who more than anyone else would forge a new world religion, returned to plan the future of Christianity.

PAUL OF TARSUS: THE CREATOR OF CHRISTIANITY

Jerusalem was recovering from her latest spasm of apocalyptic violence. An Egyptian Jew had just led a mob up the Mount of Olives, announcing, with echoes of Jesus, that he was going to bring down the walls and take Jerusalem. The pseudo-prophet tried to storm the city, but the Jerusalemites joined the Romans in repelling his followers. Felix's legions then killed most of them. There was a manhunt for the 'sorcerer' himself, as Paul arrived in the city he knew well.

Paul's father was a Pharisee who prospered enough to become a Roman citizen. He sent his son – born about the same time as Jesus but in Cilicia (today's Turkey) – to study in the Temple in Jerusalem. When Jesus was crucified, Saul, as he then was, supported the 'threatenings and slaughter': he held the cloaks of those who stoned Stephen 'and was consenting to his death'. A tentmaker, this Greek-speaking Roman Pharisee served as an agent of the high priest until, around AD 37, on the road to Damascus, he experienced his 'apocalypse': 'Suddenly there shined round him a light from heaven' and he heard a voice 'saying unto him: Saul, Saul, why persecutest thou me?' The risen Christ commissioned him to become a thirteenth apostle to preach the good news to the gentiles.

James and the Christians in Jerusalem were understandably

suspicious of this new convert, but Paul felt compelled to teach his message with all his obessional energy: 'Woe is unto me if I preach not the Gospel.' Finally, 'James, the Lord's brother' accepted this new colleague. For the next fifteen years, this irrepressible firebrand travelled the east, dogmatically preaching his own version of Jesus' Gospel that fiercely rejected the exclusivity of the Jews. 'The Apostle to Gentiles' believed that 'for our sake' God had made Jesus 'a sin offering, who knew no sin, so that in him, we might become the righteousness of God'. Paul focused on the Resurrection, which he saw as the bridge between humanity and God. Paul's Jerusalem was the Heavenly Kingdom, not the real Temple; his 'Israel' was any follower of Jesus, not the Jewish nation. He was, in some ways, strangely modern, for, contrary to the harsh ethos of the ancient world, he believed in love, equality and inclusiveness: Greeks and Jews, women and men, all were one, all could achieve salvation just by faith in Christ. His letters dominate the New Testament, forming a quarter of its books. His vision was boundless, for he wished to convert all people.

Jesus had won a few non-Jewish followers, but Paul was particularly successful among gentiles and the so-called God-fearers, those non-Jews who had embraced aspects of Judaism without undergoing circumcision. Paul's Syrian converts in Antioch were the first to be known as 'Christians'. Around AD 50, Paul returned to Jerusalem to persuade James and Peter to allow non-Jews into the sect. James agreed a compromise, but in the following years he learned that Paul was turning Jews against Mosaic Law.

An unmarried puritanical loner, Paul endured shipwrecks, robberies, beatings and stonings on his travels, yet nothing distracted him from his mission – to remodel the rustic Jewish Galilean into Jesus Christ, the saviour of all mankind who would imminently return in the Second Coming – the Kingdom of Heaven. Sometimes he was still a Jew himself and he may have returned to Jerusalem as many as five times, but sometimes he presented Judaism as the new enemy. In the earliest Christian text, his First Letter to the Thessalonians (Greek gentiles who had converted to Christianity), he ranted against the Jews for killing Jesus and their own prophets. He believed that circumcision, the Jewish Covenant with God, was a Jewish duty but irrelevant for gentiles: 'Look out for the dogs! Look out for those who cut off the flesh! For we are the true circumcision who worship God in spirit and glory in Christ Jesus,' he raged at Christian gentiles considering circumcision.

By now James and the elders in Jerusalem disapproved of Paul. They had known the real Jesus, yet Paul insisted: 'I have been crucified with Christ. The life I live now is not my life but the life Christ lives in me.' He claimed, 'I bear the marks of Jesus branded on my body.' James, that respected holy man, accused him of rejecting Judaism. Even Paul could not ignore Jesus' own brother. In AD 58, he came to make peace with the Jesus dynasty.

THE DEATH OF JAMES THE JUST:
THE JESUS DYNASTY

Paul accompanied James to the Temple to purify himself and pray as a Jew, but he was recognized by some Jews who had seen him preach on his travels. The Roman centurion, charged with keeping order in the Temple, had to rescue him from lynching. When Paul again started preaching, the Romans thought he was the fugitive Egyptian 'sorcerer', so he was clapped in chains and marched to the Antonia castle to be scourged. 'Is it lawful for you to scourge a man that is a Roman?' Paul asked. The centurion was dumbfounded to find that this wild-eyed visionary was a Roman citizen with the right to appeal to Nero for judgement. The Romans allowed the high priest and Sanhedrin to question Paul, watched by an irate crowd. His answers were so insulting that again he was almost lynched. The centurion calmed the mob by sending him off to Caesarea.

Paul's exploits may have tainted the Jewish Christians. In 62, the high priest Ananus, son of Annas who had tried Jesus, arrested James, tried him before the Sanhedrin and had him tossed off the wall of the Temple, probably from the Pinnacle where his brother had been tempted by the Devil. James was then stoned and given the *coup de grâce* with a mallet.* Josephus, who was living in Jerusalem, denounced Ananus as 'savage', explaining that most Jews were appalled: Jesus' brother had been universally respected. King Agrippa II instantly sacked Ananus. Yet the Christians remained a dynasty: Jesus and James were succeeded by their cousin or half-brother Simon.

Meanwhile, Paul arrived as a prisoner in Caesarea: Felix the procurator received Paul alongside his Herodian wife, the former queen Drusilla, and offered to free him in return for a bribe. Paul refused. Felix had more pressing worries. Fighting broke out between Jews and Syrians. He slaughtered a large number of Jews and was recalled to Rome,† leaving Paul in jail. Herod Agrippa II and his sister Berenice, ex-queen of both Chalcis and Cilicia (and supposedly his incestuous lover), visited Caesarea to greet the new procurator, who offered the Christian case to the king, as Pilate had sent Jesus to Antipas before him.

Paul preached the Christian Gospel to the royal couple who reclined in 'great pomp', cleverly adapting his message for the moderate king: 'I know thee to be an expert in all customs among the Jews. King Agrippa, believest thou the prophets? I know thou believest.'

'Almost thou persuadest me to be a Christian,' replied the king. 'This man might have been set at liberty if he had not appealed to Caesar.' But Paul *had* appealed to Nero – and to Nero he must go.

JOSEPHUS: THE COUNTDOWN TO REVOLUTION

Paul was not the only Jew awaiting judgement from Nero. Felix had also despatched some unfortunate priests from the Temple to be

---

* James' head was buried alongside another Jacobite head – that of the St James killed by Agrippa I – in what became the Cathedral of the Armenian Quarter. Hence its name is the very plural St Jameses' Cathedral. Saintly heads tended to proliferate in the reliquaries of Europe: another head (plus a headless body) of St James the Apostle was discovered in tenth-century Spain and became the focus of the cult of Santiago (St James) de Compostela, which remains a vibrant shrine today.
† Felix and Drusilla had a son who lived in Pompeii. When the town was destroyed by the volcano in 79, the son and his mother Drusilla died in the ash.

judged by the emperor. Their friend, a twenty-six-year-old named Joseph ben Matthias, decided to sail to Rome and save his fellow priests. Better known as Josephus, he was to be many things – rebel commander, Herodian protégé, imperial courtier – but above all, he was to be Jerusalem's supreme historian.

Josephus was a priest's son, descended from the Maccabeans, a Judaean landowner, raised in Jerusalem, where he was admired for his learning and wit. As a teenager he had experimented with the three major Jewish sects, even joining some ascetics in the desert, before returning to Jerusalem.

When he arrived in Rome, Josephus made contact with a Jewish actor in favour with the pernicious but thespian emperor. Nero had killed his wife and fallen in love with Poppaea, a married beauty with red hair and pale skin. Once she was empress, Poppaea gave Nero the confidence to kill his own malignant mother Agrippina. Yet Poppaea also became one of the semi-Jewish 'God-fearers'. Through his actor friend, Josephus reached the empress, who helped free his friends. Josephus had done well, but when he and his friends returned home, they found Jerusalem pervaded 'with high hopes of a revolt against the Romans.' Yet revolt was not inevitable: Josephus' acquaintance with Poppaea shows how the lines between Rome and Jerusalem were still open. The city filled annually with vast numbers of Jewish pilgrims with little sign of trouble despite the presence of only one auxiliary Roman cohort (600–1,200 men) in the Antonia. The rich Temple city existed 'in a state of peace and prosperity', run by a Jewish high priest appointed by a Jewish king. It was only now that the Temple was finally completed, causing the unemployment of 18,000 builders. So King Agrippa created more work for them by commissioning new streets.*

At any time, a more diligent emperor, a more just procurator, could have restored order among the Jewish factions. While the empire was run by Nero's efficient Greek freedmen, his posturings as actor and athlete, even his blood purges, were tolerable. But when the economy started to fail, Nero's ineptitude spread down to

---

* The street that survives right beside the Western Wall was his – and so was another pavement that can be seen on Mount Zion.

Judaea, where there was now 'no form of villainy' that his procurators 'omitted to practise'. In Jerusalem, the latest incumbent ran
a protection-racket, taking bribes from the grandees whose thuggish
retinues competed with the Sicarii to terrorize the city. No wonder
another prophet, ironically named Jesus, loudly cried in the Temple,
'Woe to Jerusalem!' Judged insane, he was scourged but not killed.
Yet Josephus recounts little anti-Roman sentiment.

In 64, Rome caught fire. Nero probably oversaw the fire-fighting
and he opened his gardens to those who had lost their homes. But
conspiracists claimed that Nero had started the fire to enable him
to build a larger palace and that he had neglected to fight the fire
because he was plucking on his lyre. Nero blamed the fast-spreading
semi-Jewish sect, the Christians, many of whom he caused to be
burned alive, torn to pieces by wild animals or crucified. Among
his victims were two arrested in Jerusalem years earlier: Peter was
said to have been crucified head down; Paul beheaded. Nero's anti-
Christian pogrom earned him his place in the Christian Book of
Revelation, the last in the canon of what became the New Testament: Satan's 'beasts' are Roman emperors and 666, the number
of the beast, probably a code for Nero.*

The 'exquisite tortures' he devised for the Christians did not save
Nero. At home, he kicked his pregnant empress Poppaea in the
stomach, accidentally killing her. As the emperor killed enemies
real and imagined while promoting his acting career, his latest
procurator in Judaea, Gessius Florus, 'ostentatiously paraded his
outrages upon the nation'. The catastrophe started in Caesarea:
Syrian Greeks sacrificed a cockerel outside a synagogue; the Jews
protested. Florus was bribed to support the gentiles and then
marched down to Jerusalem, demanding a tax of seventeen talents
from the Temple. When he appeared at the Praetorium in the spring
of 66, Jewish youths collected pennies and tossed them at him.

---

* If the Greek form of 'Nero Caesar' is transliterated into Hebrew consonants and
the consonants are replaced by their numerical equivalent, the resulting figures
added together equal 666. Revelation was probably written during the persecutions
of Emperor Domitian in 81–96. In 2009, papal archaeologists discovered a hidden
tomb beneath the Church of St Paul Outside the Walls in Rome, always reputed to
be the place of Paul's burial. The bones were carbon-dated to the first to third
centuries – they could be the remains of Paul.

Florus' Greek and Syrian troops attacked the crowds. Florus demanded that the Temple grandees hand over the hooligans, but they refused. His legionaries ran amok, 'plunged into every house and slaughtered the inhabitants'. Florus flagellated and crucified his prisoners, including Jewish grandees who were Roman citizens. This was the last straw: the Temple aristocrats could no longer count on Roman protection. The brutality of Florus' local auxiliaries inflamed Jewish resistance. As his cavalry clattered through the streets with 'a degree of madness,' they even attacked King Agrippa's sister, Queen Berenice. Her guards bundled her back into the Maccabean Palace but she resolved to save Jerusalem.

13

JEWISH WARS: THE DEATH OF JERUSALEM

AD 66–70

BERENICE THE BAREFOOT QUEEN: REVOLUTION

Berenice walked barefoot to the Praetorium herself – the same route Jesus would have taken from Herod Antipas back to Pilate thirty years earlier. The beautiful Berenice – daughter and sister of kings, and twice a queen – was on a pilgrimage to Jerusalem, to thank God for her recovery from an illness, fasting for thirty days and shaving her head (surprising in this Romanized Herodian). Now she threw herself before Florus and begged him to stop, but he wanted vengeance and booty. As his reinforcements approached Jerusalem, the Jews were divided between those keen on reconciliation with the Romans and the radicals who were preparing for war, perhaps in the hope of winning a limited independence under Roman suzerainty.

The priests in the Temple paraded the holy vessels, sprinkling the dust of mourning in their hair, in a bid to restrain the young rebels. The Jews marched out peacefully to greet the Roman cohorts, but on Florus' instructions the cavalry rode them down. The crowds ran for the gates but many suffocated in the stampede. Florus then charged towards the Temple Mount, hoping to seize the commanding Antonia Fortress. In response the Jews bombarded the Romans with spears from the rooftops, occupied the Antonia and cut down the bridges that led into the Temple, turning it into a fortress of its own.

Just as Florus left, Herod Agrippa arrived from Alexandria. The king called an assembly of the Jerusalemites in the Upper City beneath his Palace. As Berenice listened from the safety of the roof,

Agrippa begged the Jews to stay the rebellion: 'Don't venture to oppose the entire empire of the Romans. War, if it be once begun, is not easily laid down. The power of the Romans is invincible in all parts of the habitable earth. Have pity, if not on your women and children, yet upon this metropolis – spare the Temple!' Agrippa and his sister wept openly. The Jerusalemites shouted that they wished only to fight Florus. Agrippa told them to pay their tribute. The people agreed and Agrippa led them to the Temple to arrange these peaceful gestures. But on the Temple Mount, King Agrippa insisted the Jews obey Florus until a new procurator arrived, outraging the crowd all over again.

The priests, including Josephus, met in the Temple and debated whether to stop the daily sacrifice to the Roman emperor that signified loyalty to Rome. This decisive act of rebellion was approved – 'the foundation of war with the Romans', wrote Josephus, who himself joined the revolt. As the rebels seized the Temple and the moderate grandees took the Upper City, the Jewish factions bombarded each other with slingshot and spears.

Agrippa and Berenice left Jerusalem, sending 3,000 cavalry to back the moderates, but it was the extremists who triumphed. The Zealots, a popular party based around the Temple, and the Sicarii, the dagger-wielding brigands, stormed the Upper City and drove out King Agrippa's troops. They burned the palaces of the high priest and the Maccabees as well as the archives where debts were recorded. For a short moment, their leader, a 'barbarous, cruel' warlord ruled Jerusalem until the priests assassinated him and the Sicarii escaped to the Masada fortress near the Dead Sea and played no further part until Jerusalem had fallen.

The priests were back in nominal control but from now on, the factions in Jerusalem and their warlords, often provincial opportunists and local adventurers as well as religious fanatics, embarked on a savage and chaotic Jewish civil war. Even Josephus, our sole source, fails to clarify who formed these factions and what they believed. But he traces the strain of religious anti-Roman zealotry all the way back to the Galilean rebellions after Herod the Great's death: 'they have a passion for liberty, which is almost unconquerable since they are convinced God alone is their leader'. They 'sowed the seed from which sprang life'. During the next few years, he says, Jew fought Jew 'in a perpetual slaughter'.

The Roman garrison of 600, still holding Herod the Great's Citadel, agreed to give up their arms in return for safe passage out of the city but these Syrians and Greeks who had massacred so many innocent Jews were then 'savagely butchered'. King Agrippa abandoned his attempts to mediate and threw in his hand with Rome. In November 66, the Roman Governor of Syria, backed by Agrippa and allied kings, marched down from Antioch and fought his way into Jerusalem. Yet he abruptly retired, perhaps having been bribed, and his retreat under ferocious Jewish attack cost the lives of more than 5,000 Roman soldiers, and the eagle of a legion.

The die was cast. Roman pride had to be avenged. The rebels chose the former high priest, Ananus, as the leader of independent Israel. He strengthened the walls, while the city echoed to the hammering and forging of armour and weapons. He also appointed generals, among them Josephus, the future historian, who now left the city as the commander of Galilee, where he found himself fighting a warlord, John of Gischala, more viciously than either of them fought the Romans.

The new Jewish coins celebrated 'The Freedom of Zion' and 'Jerusalem the Holy' – yet it seemed this was a liberation that not many had wanted and the city waited like 'a place doomed to destruction'. Nero was in Greece to perform his songs and compete in chariot-races in the Olympic Games (he won even though he fell out of his chariot), when he heard that Israel had rebelled.

JOSEPHUS' PROPHECY: THE MULETEER AS EMPEROR

Nero feared victorious generals, so he chose as the commander of his Jewish War a dogged veteran from his own entourage. Titus Flavius Vespasianus was in his late fifties and often annoyed the emperor by falling asleep during his theatrical performances. But he had made his name in the conquest of Britain and his nickname – The Muleteer – revealed his unglamorous dependability and the fortune he had made by selling mules to the army.

Sending his son Titus to Alexandria to collect reinforcements, Vespasian mustered an army of 60,000, four legions plus Syrian slingers, Arab archers and the cavalry of King Herod Agrippa. Then he marched down the coast to Ptolemais (Acre). In early 67, he methodically started to reconquer Galilee, resisted fanatically by Josephus and his Galileans. Finally, Vespasian besieged Josephus in his fortress of Jotapata. On 29 July that year, Titus crept through the shattered walls and seized the city. The Jews fought to the death, many of them committing suicide.

Josephus and some other survivors hid in a cave. When the Romans trapped them, they decided to kill themselves and drew lots to determine who would kill whom. 'By the providence of God' (or by cheating), Josephus drew the last lot and emerged alive from the cave. Vespasian decided to send him as a prize to Nero, which would entail an atrocious death. Josephus asked to speak to the general. When he stood before Vespasian and Titus, he said: 'Vespasian! I come to you as a messenger of greater tidings. Do you send me to Nero? Why? It is you, Vespasian, who are and shall be Caesar and Emperor, you and your son.' The dour Vespasian was flattered, keeping Josephus in prison but sending him presents. Titus, who was almost the same age as Josephus, befriended him.

As Vespasian and Titus advanced towards Judaea, Josephus' rival, John of Gischala, escaped to Jerusalem – 'a city without a governor' engaged in a frenzy of self-destructive butchery.

JERUSALEM THE BROTHEL:
THE TYRANTS JOHN AND SIMON

The gates of Jerusalem remained open to Jewish pilgrims, so religious fanatics, battle-hardened cut-throats and thousands of refugees poured into the city, where the rebels expended their energies in gang warfare, orgiastic pleasure-seeking and vicious witch-hunts for traitors.

Young, brash brigands now challenged the rule of the priests. They seized the Temple, overthrowing the high priest himself, electing by lot in his stead a 'mere rustic'. Ananus rallied the

Jerusalemites and attacked the Temple, but he hesitated to storm the inner courts and Holy of Holies. John of Gischala and his Galilean fighters saw an opportunity to win the entire city. John invited in the Idumeans, that 'most barbarous and bloody nation' from south of Jerusalem. The Idumeans broke into the city, stormed the Temple, which 'overflowed with blood', and then rampaged through the streets, killing 12,000. They murdered Ananus and then his priests, stripped them and stamped on the naked bodies, before tossing them over the walls to be eaten by dogs. 'The death of Ananus', says Josephus, 'was the beginning of the destruction of the city.' Finally, laden with booty and sated with blood, the Idumeans left a Jerusalem dominated by a new strongman, John of Gischala.

Even though the Romans were not far away, John gave free rein to his Galileans and Zealots to enjoy their prizes. The Holy House became a bawdy-house; but some of John's supporters soon lost faith in this tyrant and defected to the rising power outside the city, a young warlord named Simon ben Giora, 'not as cunning as John but superior in strength and courage'. Simon 'was a greater terror to the people than the Romans themselves'. The Jerusalemites, hoping to save themselves from one tyrant, invited in a second – Simon ben Giora – who soon occupied much of the city. But John still held the Temple. Now the Zealots rebelled against him, seizing the Inner Temple so that, in the words of Tacitus, 'there were three generals, three armies' fighting each other for one city – even though the Romans were getting closer. When nearby Jericho fell to Vespasian, all three Jewish factions ceased fighting each other and worked to fortify Jerusalem, digging trenches and strengthening Herod Agrippa I's Third Wall in the north. Vespasian prepared to besiege Jerusalem. But then all at once he stopped.

Rome had lost its head. On 9 June 68, Nero, beset by rebellions, committed suicide with the words: 'What an artist the world is losing in me!' In quick succession, Rome acclaimed and destroyed three emperors while three False Neros arose and foundered in the provinces – as if one real one had not been enough. Finally, the legions of Judaea and Egypt hailed Vespasian as their own emperor. The Muleteer remembered Josephus' prophecy and freed him, granting him citizenship and appointing him as his adviser, almost his mascot, as he conquered first Judaea – and then the world. Berenice pawned her jewels to help fund Vespasian's bid for the throne of Rome: the Muleteer was grateful. The new emperor headed via Alexandria to Rome and his son Titus, commanding 60,000 troops, advanced on the Holy City, knowing that his dynasty would be made or broken by the fate of Jerusalem.

PART TWO

PAGANISM

How doth the city sit solitary, that was full of people! how is she become as a widow! she that was great among the nations, and princess among the provinces, how is she become tributary! She weepeth sore in the night, and her tears are on her cheeks: among all her lovers she hath none to comfort her.

Lamentations, 1.1–2

Even while Jerusalem was still standing and the Jews at peace with us, the practice of their sacred rites was at variance with the glory of our empire and the customs of our ancestors.

Cicero, *Pro L. Flacco*

It is better for a person to live in the Land of Israel in a city entirely of non-Jews than to live outside the Land in a city entirely Jewish. He who is buried there it is as if he were born in Jerusalem and he who is buried in Jerusalem, it is as though he were born under the throne of glory.

Judah haNasi, *Talmud*

Ten measures of beauty descended upon the world, nine were given to Jerusalem and one to the rest of the world.

Midrash Tanhuma, *Kedoshim 10*

For the freedom of Jerusalem.

Simon bar Kochba, coins

Thus was Jerusalem destroyed on the very day of Saturn, the day which even now the Jews reverence most.

Dio Cassius, *Roman History*

14

AELIA CAPITOLINA

AD 70–312

TITUS' TRIUMPH: JERUSALEM IN ROME

A few weeks later, once the city had been destroyed and he had completed his round of bloody spectacles, Titus again passed through Jerusalem, comparing her melancholy ruins with her vanished glory. He then sailed for Rome, taking with him the captured Jewish leaders, his royal mistress Berenice, his favourite renegade Josephus, and the treasures of the Temple – to celebrate the conquest of Jerusalem. Vespasian and Titus, crowned with laurel and clothed in purple, emerged from the Temple of Isis, were greeted by the Senate and took their places in the Forum to review one of the most extravagant Triumphs in the history of Rome.

The pageant of divine statues and gilded floats, three or even four storeys high, heaped with treasure, afforded the spectators both 'pleasure and surprise', noted Josephus drily, 'for there was to be seen a happy country laid waste'. The fall of Jerusalem was acted out in *tableaux vivants* – legionaries charging, Jews massacred, Temple in flames – and on top of each float stood the Roman commanders of every town taken. There followed what was for Josephus the cruellest cut of all, the splendours of the Holy of Holies: the golden table, the candelabra and the Law of the Jews. The star prisoner, Simon ben Giora, was paraded with a rope around his neck.

When the procession stopped at the Temple of Jupiter, Simon and the rebel chieftains were executed; the crowds cheered; sacrifices were consecrated. There died Jerusalem, mused Josephus: 'Neither its antiquity, nor its deep wealth, nor its people spread over the whole habitable world nor yet the great glory of its religious rites, were sufficient to prevent its ruin.'

The Triumph was commemorated by the construction of the Arch of Titus, which still stands in Rome.* Jewish spoils paid for the Colosseum and the Temple of Peace, where Vespasian displayed the prizes of Jerusalem – except for the Law scrolls and the purple veils of the Holy of Holies that were placed in the imperial palace itself. The Triumph and remodelling of central Rome celebrated not just a new dynasty but a rededication of the empire itself and victory over Judaism. The tax paid by all Jews to the Temple was replaced by the Fiscus Judaicus, paid to the Roman state to fund the rebuilding of the Temple of Jupiter, a humiliation fiercely enforced.† Yet most Jews, surviving in Judaea and Galilee, and in the populous communities of the Mediterranean and Babylonia, lived as they had lived before, accepting Roman or Parthian rule.

The Jewish War was not quite over. The Masada Fortress held out for three years, under Eleazar the Galilean, as the Romans raised a ramp to storm it. In April 73, their leader addressed his men and their families about the realities of this dark new world: 'Where is this city that was believed to have God himself inhabiting therein?' Jerusalem was gone and now they faced slavery:

> We long ago my generous friends resolved never to be servants to the Romans nor to any other than God Himself. We were the first that revolted against them; we are the last that fight against them

* As for Vespasian, he is best remembered in Italy for creating public lavatories, which are still known as *vespasiani*.

† Vespasian's coins boasted 'JUDAEA CAPTA' with the female figure of Judaea seated, bound, at the foot of a palm tree while Rome leaned on his spear above her. The fate of the Jerusalem treasures is mysterious. In 455, Genseric, King of the Vandals, sacked Rome and took the Temple treasures to Carthage, where they were later captured by Emperor Justinian's general Belisarius, who in turn brought them to Constantinople. Justinian sent the candelabra back to Jerusalem, but it must have been looted by the Persians in 614; at any rate, it vanished. The Arch of Titus, completed by Titus' brother Domitian, shows the arms of the candelabra lengthened and turned upwards to resemble a trident: it may have been altered or it may be the artist's mistake. Ironically the Romanized candelabra (except the pagan symbols) became the basis for the modern Jewish menorah, the candelabra used at Hanukkah and as the insignia of Israel.

and I cannot but esteem it as a favour that God has granted us that it is still in our power to die bravely and in a state of freedom, in a glorious manner, together with our dearest friends. Let our wives die before they are abused and our children before they have tasted slavery.

So the 'husbands tenderly embraced their wives, and took their children into their arms, giving the longest parting kisses to them with tears in their eyes'. Each man killed his wife and children; ten men were chosen by lot to slay the rest until all 960 were dead.

To most Romans, the Masada suicide confirmed Jews as demented fanatics. Tacitus, though writing thirty years later, expressed the conventional view that the Jews were 'sinister and revolting' bigots, with bizarre superstitions including monotheism and circumcision, who despised Roman gods, 'rejected patriotism' and 'have entrenched themselves by their very wickedness'. Yet Josephus collected the details of Masada from the handful of survivors who hid during the suicide and could not conceal his admiration for Jewish courage.

BERENICE: THE JEWISH CLEOPATRA

Josephus lived in Vespasian's old house in Rome. Titus gave him some of the scrolls from the Temple, a pension and lands in Judaea, and commissioned his first book, *The Jewish War*. The emperor and Titus were not Josephus' only source. 'When you come to me,' wrote his 'dear friend' King Herod Agrippa, 'I'll inform you of a great many things.' But Josephus realized that 'my privileged position exacted envy and brought danger': he needed the imperial protection he received up to the reign of Domitian, who solicitously executed some of his enemies. Yet even as Josephus basked in Flavian favour in his last years – he died around AD 100 – he hoped the Temple would be rebuilt, and his pride in the Jewish contribution to civilization surged: 'We've introduced the rest of the world to a very large number of beautiful ideas. What greater beauty than inviolable piety? What higher justice than obedience to the Laws?'

Berenice, the Herodian princess, stayed in Rome with Titus but she offended the Romans with her flashy diamonds, her royal airs and the stories of her incest with her brother. 'She dwelt in the palace cohabiting with Titus. She expected to marry him and was already behaving in every respect as if she were his wife.' It was said that Titus had the general Caecina murdered for flirting with her. Titus loved her but the Romans compared her to Antony's femme fatale, Cleopatra – or worse, since the Jews were now despised and defeated. Titus had to send her away. When he succeeded his father in 79, she returned to Rome, now in her fifties, but such was the outcry that he again separated from the Jewish Cleopatra, aware that the Flavians were far from secure on the throne. Perhaps she rejoined her brother, almost the last of the Herodians.*

Titus' reign was short. He died two years later with the words: 'I have only done one thing wrong.' The destruction of Jerusalem? The Jews believed his early death was God's punishment. For forty years, a tense exhaustion reigned over blighted Jerusalem before Judaea again exploded in a final and disastrous spasm of rage.

DEATH OF THE JESUS DYNASTY:
THE FORGOTTEN CRUCIFIXION

Jerusalem was the headquarters of the Tenth Legion, whose camp was set up in the present-day Armenian Quarter around the three towers of Herod's Citadel – the base of the last of them, the Hippicus, stands today. The Legion's rooftiles and bricks, always emblazoned with its anti-Jewish emblem, the boar, have been found all over the city. Jerusalem was not totally deserted but had been settled

* Herod Agrippa II was rewarded with an expanded kingdom in Lebanon. Perhaps he was not tempted to rule the ruins of Judaea but he may have played with the idea of a political career in Rome. When he visited in 75 for the inauguration of the Temple of Peace (exhibiting some of the Temple vessels), he was granted the rank of praetor. Having reigned under ten emperors, he died around AD 100. His relatives became kings of Armenia and Cilicia and ultimately even Roman consuls.

with Syrian and Greek veterans, who traditionally hated the Jews. This barren moonscape of gigantic rockheaps must have been eerie. But Jews must have hoped that the Temple would be rebuilt as it had been once before.

Vespasian allowed the rabbi Yohanan ben Zakkai, who had escaped Jerusalem in a coffin, to teach the Law at Yavneh (Jamnia) on the Mediterranean, and the Jews were not formally banned from Jerusalem. Indeed many of the wealthier Jews had probably joined the Romans, as Josephus and Agrippa had done. Nonetheless, they were not allowed onto the Temple Mount. Instead, pilgrims bitterly mourned the Temple, praying next to the Tomb of Zechariah* in the Kidron Valley. Some hoped for the Apocalypse to restore God's kingdom, but for ben Zakkai the vanished city assumed an immaterial mysticism. When he visited the ruins, his pupil cried, 'Woe to us!' 'Be not grieved,' replied the rabbi (according to the Talmud, compiled several centuries later). 'We have another atonement. It is acts of loving-kindness.' No one realized it at this time, but this was the beginning of modern Judaism – without the Temple.

The Jewish Christians, led by Simon son of Cleophas, Jesus' half-brother or cousin, returned to Jerusalem where they started to honour the Upper Room, on today's Mount Zion. Beneath the present building lies a synagogue, built probably with Herodian debris from the Temple. Yet the growing number of gentile Christians around the Mediterranean no longer revered the real Jerusalem. The defeat of the Jews separated them for ever from the mother-religion, proving the truth of Jesus' prophecies and the succession of a new revelation. Jerusalem was just the wilderness of a failed faith. The Book of Revelation replaced the Temple with Christ the Lamb. At the End of Days, golden, bejewelled Jerusalem would descend from heaven.

These sects had to be careful: the Romans were on guard against any signs of messianic kingship. Titus' successor, his brother Domitian, maintained the anti-Jewish tax and persecuted the Christians, as a way of rallying support for his own faltering regime. On his

---

* This is an unfinished family tomb. Its family probably perished in the siege, so it was an appropriate place for Jews to gather to mourn the Temple. These pilgrims carved the Hebrew inscriptions that are still visible today.

assassination, the pacific, elderly Emperor Nerva relaxed the repression and the Jewish tax. Yet this was a false dawn. Nerva had no sons, so he chose his pre-eminent general as heir. Trajan, tall, athletic, stern, was the ideal emperor, perhaps the greatest since Augustus. But he saw himself as a conqueror of new lands and a restorer of old values – bad news for the Christians, and worse for the Jews. In 106 he ordered the crucifixion of Simon, the Overseer of the Christians in Jerusalem, because, like Jesus, he claimed descent from King David. There ended the Jesus dynasty.

Trajan, proud that his father had made his name fighting the Jews under Titus, restored the Fiscus Judaicus, but he was another Alexander hero-worshipper: he invaded Parthia, expanding Roman power into Iraq, home of the Babylonian Jews. During the fighting, they surely appealed to their Roman brethren. As Trajan advanced into Iraq, the Jews of Africa, Egypt and Cyprus, led by rebel 'kings', massacred thousands of Romans and Greeks, vengeance at last, possibly co-ordinated by the Jews of Parthia.

Trajan, fearing Jewish treason in his rear and attack from Babylonian Jews as he advanced into Iraq, 'was determined if possible to destroy the nation utterly'. Trajan ordered Jews to be killed from Iraq to Egypt, where, wrote the historian Appian, 'Trajan was destroying totally the Jewish race.' The Jews were now seen as hostile to the Roman Empire: they 'regard as profane everything we hold sacred,' wrote Tacitus, 'while they permit all we abhor'.

Rome's Jewish problem was witnessed by the new Governor of Syria, Aelius Hadrian, who was married to Trajan's niece. When Trajan died unexpectedly without an heir, his empress announced that he had adopted a son on his deathbed: the new emperor was Hadrian, who devised a solution to end the Jewish problem once and for all. He was a remarkable emperor, one of the makers of Jerusalem and one of the supreme monsters of Jewish history.

HADRIAN: THE JERUSALEM SOLUTION

In 130, the emperor visited Jerusalem, accompanied by his young lover Antinous, and decided to abolish the city, even down to its very name. He ordered a new city to be built on the site of the old one, to be named Aelia Capitolina, after his own family and Jupiter Capitolinus (the god most associated with the empire), and he banned circumcision, the sign of God's covenant with the Jews, on pain of death. The Jews, realizing that this meant the Temple would never be rebuilt, smarted under these blows, while the oblivious emperor travelled on to Egypt.

Hadrian, now aged fifty-four, born in Spain to a family rich from the production of olive oil, was a man seemingly designed to rule the empire. Blessed with a photographic memory, he could dictate, listen and consult simultaneously; he designed his own architecture and composed his own poetry and music. He existed in perpetual movement, restlessly travelling the provinces to reorganize and consolidate the empire. He was criticized for withdrawing from Trajan's hard-won conquests in Dacia and Iraq. Instead he envisaged a stable empire, united by Greek culture, a taste so marked that he was nicknamed the Greekling. (His Greek beard and hairstyle were groomed with curling irons by specially trained slaves.) In 123, on one of his tours in Asia Minor, he met the love of his life, the Greek boy Antinous, who became almost his consort.* Yet this perfect emperor was also an unpredictable control-freak. In a rage, he once stabbed a slave in the eye with a pen; and he opened and closed his reign with blood purges.

Now in Jerusalem, on the wreckage of the Jewish city, he planned a classic Roman town, built around the worship of Roman, Greek and Egyptian gods. A splendid three-gated entrance, the Neapolis (today's Damascus) Gate, built with Herodian stones, opened into a circular space, decorated with a column, whence the two main streets, the Cardines – axes – led down to two forums, one close to the demolished Antonia Fortress and the other south of today's Holy Sepulchre. There Hadrian built his Temple of Jupiter with a statue of Aphrodite outside it, on the very rock where Jesus had

* This displeased the Romans. Greek love was conventional and not regarded as effeminate: Caesar, Antony, Titus and Trajan were all what we would call bisexual. However, in a reversal of morality today, Romans believed it was acceptable to have sex with boys but not with adults. Yet even when Antinous became a man, Hadrian ignored his wife and treated his lover as his partner.

been crucified, possibly a deliberate decision to deny the shrine to the Jewish Christians. Worse, Hadrian planned a shrine on the Temple Mount, marked by a grandiose equestrian statue of himself.* Hadrian was deliberately eradicating Jerusalem's Jewishness. Indeed he had studied that other Philhellenic showman, Antiochus Epiphanes, reviving his plan to build an Olympian temple in Athens.

On 24 October, the festival in which the Egyptians celebrated the death of their god Osiris, Hadrian's lover Antinous mysteriously drowned in the Nile. Did he kill himself? Did Hadrian or the Egyptians sacrifice him? Was it an accident? The usually inscrutable Hadrian was heartbroken, deifying the boy as Osiris, founding a town Antinopolis and an Antinous cult, spreading statues of his graceful face and magnificent physique all over the Mediterranean.

On his way home from Egypt, Hadrian passed through Jerusalem, where he probably ploughed the furrow around the city-limits of Aelia Capitolina. Outraged by the repression, the paganization of Jerusalem and the obligatory nudes of the boy Antinous, the Jews stashed weapons and prepared underground complexes in the Judaean hills.

Once Hadrian was safely on his way, a mysterious leader known as the Prince of Israel launched the most terrible of the Jewish wars.

---

* Hadrian's buildings survive in some odd places: Zalatimo's Sweet Shop, 9 Hanzeit Street, incorporates the remains of the gate of Hadrian's Temple of Jupiter and the entrance to the main forum. The shop was opened in 1860 by Muhammad Zalatimo, an Ottoman sergeant; it is still run by the family patriarch of this Palestinian cake dynasty, Samir Zalatimo. Hadrian's walls continue into another old Palestinian family business – the fruit-juice store of Abu Assab – and then into the Russian Alexander Nevsky Church. The archway of Hadrian's lesser forum survives on the Via Dolorosa, which many Christians mistakenly believe is where Pilate presented Jesus to the crowd with the words 'Ecce homo' (Here is the man). In fact, the arch did not exist until a hundred years later. The base of the Damascus Gate has been excavated to reveal its Hadrianic glory. Today's main street Ha-Gai or El Wad follows the route of Hadrian's Cardo, which has been excavated in the Western Wall plaza. But the strangest of these pagan remnants are in the Church of the Holy Sepulchre. The historian Cassius Dio and the later Christian source Chronicon Paschale suggest that a Temple of Jupiter was built on the Temple Mount. This is possible, but no traces have been found.

SIMON BAR KOCHBA: THE SON OF THE STAR

'At first the Romans took no account of the Jews,' but this time the Jews were well prepared under one capable commander, Simon bar Kochba, self-declared Prince of Israel and Son of the Star, the same mystical sign of kingship that marked the birth of Jesus, prophesied in Numbers: 'There shall come forth a star out of Jacob, and a sceptre shall rise out of Israel and shall smite Moab.' Many hailed him as the new David. 'This is the King Messiah,' insisted the respected rabbi Akiba (in the fourth-century Talmud), but not everyone agreed. 'Grass will sprout on your chin, Akiba,' answered another rabbi, 'and the Son of David will still not have appeared.' Kochba's real name was bar Kosiba; sceptics punned that he was bar Koziba, the Son of the Lie.

Simon swiftly defeated the Roman governor and his two legions. His orders, discovered in a Judaean cave, reveal his harsh competence: 'I shall deal with the Romans' – and he did. He wiped out an entire legion. 'He caught missiles on his knee then hurled them back and killed some of the enemy.' The prince tolerated no dissent: 'Simon bar Kosiba to Yehonatan and Masabala. Let all men from Tekoa and other places who are with you, be sent to me without delay. And if you shall not send them, you shall be punished.' A religious zealot, he supposedly 'ordered Christians to be punished severely if they did not deny Jesus was the Messiah', according to Justin, a contemporary Christian. He 'killed the Christians when they refused to help him against the Romans', added a Christian, Eusebius, writing much later. 'The man was murderous and a bandit but relied on his name, as if dealing with slaves, and claimed to be a giver of light.' He was said to have tested his fighters' dedication by asking each to cut off a finger.

The Son of the Star ruled his State of Israel from the fort of Herodium, just south of Jerusalem: his coins announced 'Year One: The Redemption of Israel'. But did he rededicate the Temple and restore the sacrifice? His coins boasted 'For the Freedom of Jerusalem', and were emblazoned with the Temple, but none of his coins have been found in Jerusalem. Appian wrote that Hadrian, like Titus, destroyed Jerusalem, implying that there was something to demolish, and the rebels, sweeping all before them, would surely have besieged the Tenth Legion in the Citadel and worshipped on the Temple Mount if they had had the chance, but we do not know if they did.

Hadrian hastened back to Judaea, summoned his best commander Julius Severus all the way from Britain, and mustered seven or even twelve legions who 'moved out against the Jews, treating their madness without mercy,' according to Cassius Dio, one of the few historians of this obscure war. 'He destroyed in heaps thousands of men, women and children and under the law of war enslaved the land.' When Severus arrived, he adopted Jewish tactics, 'cutting off small groups, depriving them of their food and shutting them in' so that he could 'crush and exterminate them'. As the Romans closed in, bar Kochba needed severe threats to enforce discipline: 'If you maltreat the Galileans with you,' he told a lieutenant, 'I will put fetters on your feet as I did to ben Aphlul!'

The Jews retreated to the caves of Judaea, which is why Simon's letters and their poignant belongings have been found there. These refugees and warriors carried keys to their abandoned houses, the consolation of those doomed never to return, and their luxuries – a glass plate, a vanity mirror in a leather case, a wooden jewellery box, an incense shovel. There, they perished, for the possessions lie beside their bones. Their fragmented letters record the terse semaphores of catastrophe: 'Till the end . . . they have no hope . . . my brothers in the south . . . these were lost by the sword . . .'

The Romans moved in on bar Kochba's last fortress, Betar, 6 miles south of Jerusalem. Simon himself died in the last stand at Betar, with a snake around his neck according to Jewish legend. 'Bring his body to me!' said Hadrian, and was impressed by the head and the snake. 'If God had not slain him, who would have overcome him?' Hadrian had probably already returned to Rome but, either way, he wreaked an almost genocidal vengeance.

'Very few survived,' wrote Cassius Dio. 'Fifty of their outposts and 985 villages were razed to the ground. 585,000 were killed in battles' and many more by 'starvation, disease and fire'. Seventy-five known Jewish settlements simply vanished. So many Jews were enslaved that at the Hebron slave market they fetched less than a horse. Jews continued to live in the countryside, but Judaea itself never recovered from Hadrian's ravages. Hadrian not only enforced the ban on circumcision but banned the Jews from even approaching Aelia, on pain of death. Jerusalem had vanished. Hadrian wiped Judaea off the map, deliberately renaming it Palaestina, after the Jews' ancient enemies, the Philistines.

Hadrian received acclamation as *imperator*, but this time there was no Triumph: the emperor was tarnished and exhausted by his losses in Judaea. When he reported to the Senate, he was unable to give the usual reassurance, 'I am well, and so is the army.' Suffering from the arteriosclerosis (flagged by the split earlobes depicted on his statues), swollen with dropsy, Hadrian killed any possible successors, even his ninety-year-old brother-in-law, who cursed him: 'May he long for death but be unable to die.' The curse came true: unable to die, Hadrian tried to kill himself. But no autocrat has ever written as wittily and wistfully about death as Hadrian:

> Little soul, little wanderer, little charmer,
> Body's guest and companion,
> To what places will you set out for now?
> To darkling, cold and gloomy ones —
> And you won't be making your usual jokes.

When he eventually died – 'hated by all' – the Senate refused to deify him. Jewish literature never mentions Hadrian without adding, 'May his bones rot in hell!'

His successor, Antoninus Pius, slightly relaxed the persecution of Jews, allowing circumcision again, but Antoninus' statue joined Hadrian's on the Temple Mount* to emphasize that the Temple would never be rebuilt. The Christians, now fully separated from

* Upside down just above the decorated section of the Double Gate in the southern wall of the Temple Mount is an inscription that reads 'TO THE EMPEROR CAESAR TITUS AELIUS HADRIANUS ANTONINUS AUGUSTUS PIUS', almost certainly the base of the equestrian statue of Antoninus Pius that also stood on the Temple Mount. It must have been looted and then reused by the Umayyad caliphs who built the gate.

the Jews, could not help but crow. 'The House of Sanctuary', wrote the Christian Justin to Antoninus, 'has become a curse, and the glory which our fathers blessed is burned with fire.' Unfortunately for the Jews, the settled politics of the empire for the rest of the century discouraged any change in Hadrian's policy.

Aelia Capitolina was a minor Roman colony of 10,000, without walls, just two-fifths of its former size, extending only from today's Damascus Gate to the Gate of the Chain, with two forums, the Temple of Jupiter on the site of Golgotha, two thermal baths, a theatre, a nymphaeum (statues of nymphs around pools) and an amphitheatre, all decorated with colonnades, tetrapylons and statues, including a large one of the Tenth Legion's very unkosher boar. Gradually the Tenth Legion was moved away from Jerusalem as the Jews, no longer a threat, came to be regarded more as an irritant. When the emperor Marcus Aurelius passed through on his way to Egypt, 'being often disgusted with the malodorous and disorderly Jews', he jokingly compared them to other rebellious tribes: 'Oh Quadi, oh Samaritans, at last I have found a people more unruly than you!' Jerusalem had no natural industries except holiness – and the absence of the Tenth Legion must have made her even more of a backwater.

When the peaceful succession in Rome ended in civil war in 193, the Jews, who now lived mainly in Galilee and around the Mediterranean coast, began to stir, either fighting their local enemies the Samaritans or perhaps rising in support of the ultimate winner of the throne, Septimus Severus. This led to a softening of anti-Jewish policy: the new emperor and his son Caracalla visited Aelia in 201 and seem to have met the Jewish leader, Judah haNasi, known as 'the Prince'. When Caracalla succeeded to the throne, he rewarded Judah with estates in the Golan and Lydda (near Jerusalem) and with the hereditary power to adjudicate religious disputes and set the calendar, recognizing him as the community leader – the Patriarch of the Jews.

The wealthy Judah, who seems to have combined rabbinical scholarship with aristocratic luxury, held court in Galilee with a bodyguard of Goths while he compiled the Mishnah, the oral traditions of post-Temple Judaism. Thanks to Judah's imperial connections, and to the passing of time, Jews were allowed, after bribing the garrison, to pray opposite the ruined Temple on the Mount of Olives or in the Kidron Valley. There, they believed, the *shekinah* – the holy spirit – resided. It is said that Judah won permission for a small 'holy community' of Jews to live in Jerusalem, praying in the one synagogue on today's Mount Zion. Nonetheless, the Severan emperors never reconsidered Hadrian's policy.

Yet the Jewish longing for Jerusalem never faltered. Wherever they lived in the following centuries, Jews prayed three times a day: 'May it be your will that the Temple be rebuilt soon in our days.' In the Mishnah, they compiled every detail of Temple ritual, ready for its restoration. 'A woman may put on all her ornaments,' instructed the Tosefta, another compilation of oral traditions, 'but should leave out one small thing in remembrance of Jerusalem.' The Passover *seder* dinner ended with the words: 'Next Year in Jerusalem'. If they ever approached Jerusalem, they devised a ritual of rending their garments on catching sight of the ruined city. Even Jews who lived far away wanted to be buried close to the Temple so that they would be the first to rise again on Judgement Day. Thus began the Jewish cemetery on the Mount of Olives.

There was every chance that the Temple would be rebuilt – indeed it had been before and very nearly was again. While the Jews were still formally banned from Jerusalem, it was now the Christians who were seen as the clear and present danger to Rome.

From 235, the empire suffered a thirty-year crisis, shattered from inside and out. In the east, a vigorous new Persian empire, replacing Parthia, challenged the Romans. During the crisis, the Roman emperors blamed the Christians for being atheists who refused to sacrifice to their gods and savagely persecuted them, even though Christianity was not so much a single religion as a bundle of different traditions.* But Christians agreed on the

* The Gnostics were one of these strands: they believed that the divine spark was released only to an elite few with special knowledge. In 1945, the discovery by Egyptian peasants of thirteen codices hidden in a jar and dating from the second or third centuries has revealed much more – and generated many bad movies and novels. In the Apocalypse of Peter and the First Apocalypse of James, it is a substitute who is crucified in place of Jesus. In the Gospel of Philip, there are fragmentary references to Jesus kissing Mary Magdalene, encouraging the idea that they may

basics: redemption and life after death for those saved by Jesus Christ, confirming the ancient Jewish prophecies which they had commandeered and adopted as their own. Their founder had been killed by the Romans as a rebel, but the Christians rebranded themselves as a faith hostile to the Jews, not to the Romans. Hence Rome became their holy city; most Christians in Palestine lived in Caesarea on the coast; Jerusalem became 'the heavenly city', while the actual place, Aelia, was just an obscure town where Jesus had died. Yet local Christians kept alive the tradition of the site of the Crucifixion and Resurrection, now buried under Hadrian's Temple of Jupiter, even creeping inside to pray and scratch graffiti.*

At Rome's nadir in 260, the Persians captured the emperor (who was forced to drink molten gold, and was then gutted and stuffed with straw) while the entire East, including the unwalled town of Aelia, was lost to a short-lived Palmyran empire led by a young woman, Zenobia. But within twelve years Rome had recovered the East. At the end of the century, the emperor Diocletian successfully restored Roman power and revived the worship of the old gods. But the Christians seemed to be undermining this resurgence. In 299, Diocletian was sacrificing to the gods at a parade in Syria when some Christian soldiers made the sign of the cross, at which the pagan diviners declared that the divination had failed. When Diocletian's palace burned down, he blamed the Christians and

---

have married. The Gospel of Judas, which emerged in 2006, appears to present Judas as Jesus' assistant in accomplishing the Crucifixion, rather than traitor. The texts were probably hidden in the fourth century when the Christian emperors started to crack down on heretics, but the word 'Gnostic', based on the Greek for knowledge, was coined in the eighteenth century. The Jewish Christians survived in tiny numbers as the Ebionites – the Poor Ones – rejecting the Virgin Birth and revering Jesus the Jewish prophet into the fourth century. As for the mainstream Christians, though relatively small in numbers, their sense of community and mission gave them a growing disdain for the gentiles whom they called bumpkins – *pagani*, hence pagan.

* While excavating the ancient Armenian Chapel of St Helena, Armenian archaeologists opened up a space (now the Varda Chapel) which contained the most intriguing graffito: a sketch of a boat and a phrase in Latin: '*Domine ivimus*' (Lord we have come), a reference to Psalm 122 which starts '*In domum domini ibimus*' (We'll go the house of the Lord). This dates from the second century, proving that Christians were secretly praying beneath the Temple of Jupiter in pagan Aelia.

unleashed a vicious persecution, martyring Christians, burning their books, destroying their churches.

When Diocletian abdicated in 305, dividing the empire, Galerius, new emperor of the East, intensified the butchery of Christians by axe, roasting and mutilation. But the emperor of the West was Constantius Chlorus, a sturdy Illyrian soldier, who assumed the purple in York. Already ill, he died soon afterwards but in July 306 the British legions hailed his young son, Constantine, as emperor. It would take him fifteen years to conquer first the West and then the East, but Constantine, like King David, would change the history of the world and the fate of Jerusalem with a single decision.

PART THREE

CHRISTIANITY

Jerusalem – it is the city of the great King.

Jesus, St Matthew, 5.35

O Jerusalem, Jerusalem, thou that killest the prophets and stonest them which are sent unto thee.

Jesus, St Matthew, 23.37

Destroy this temple and in three days I will raise it up.

Jesus, St John, 2.19

As Judaea is exalted above all other provinces so is this city exalted above all Judaea.

St Jerome, Epistles

Jerusalem is now made a place of resort from all parts of the world, and there is such a throng of pilgrims of both sexes that all temptation is here collected together.

St Jerome, Epistles

15

THE APOGEE OF BYZANTIUM

312–518 AD

CONSTANTINE THE GREAT: CHRIST, GOD OF VICTORY

In 312, Constantine invaded Italy and attacked his rival Maxentius just outside Rome. The night before battle, Constantine saw before him 'in the sky the sign of a cross of light' superimposed on the sun with the slogan: 'By this sign you will conquer!' So he emblazoned the shields of his soldiers with the Chi-Rho symbol, the first two letters of 'Christ' in Greek. The next day at the Battle of Milvian Bridge, he won the West. In this age of auguries and visions, Constantine believed he owed his power to the Christian 'Supreme God'.

Constantine was a rough soldier, a holy visionary, a murderous autocrat and a political showman who slashed his way to power but, once at the pinnacle of human supremacy, he envisioned an empire unified under one religion, one emperor. He was a bundle of contradictions – he was bullnecked, aquiline-nosed and his paranoia often exploded in the sudden killing of friends and family. He wore his hair shoulder-length, sported gaudy bracelets and bejewelled robes, and relished the pageantry of power, the debates of philosophers and bishops and schemes of architectural beauty and religious boldness. No one knows why he embraced Christianity at that moment, though, like many brutally confident men, he adored his mother, Helena, and she was an early convert. If his personal conversion was as dramatic as Paul's on the road to Damascus, his political embrace of Christianity was gradual. Most importantly, Christ had delivered victory in battle, and that was a language that Constantine understood: Christ the Lamb became the god of victory. Not that Constantine was in any way lamb-like himself: he soon presented himself as the Equal of the Apostles. There was nothing remarkable in his promotion of himself as a military commander with divine protection. Roman emperors, like Greek kings, always identified themselves with divine patrons. Constantine's own father revered the Unconquered Sun, a step towards monotheism. But the choice of the Christ was not inevitable – it depended purely on Constantine's personal whim. In 312, Manichaeanism and Mithraism were no less popular than Christianity. Constantine could just as easily have chosen one of these – and Europe might today be Mithraistic or Manichaean.*

In 313, Constantine and the Eastern emperor Licinius granted toleration and privileges to the Christians in their Edict of Milan. But it was only in 324 that Constantine, now aged fifty-one, defeated Licinius to unite the empire. He tried to impose Christian chastity across his domains and banned pagan sacrifices, sacred prostitution, religious orgies, and gladiatorial shows, replacing them with chariot-racing. That year, he moved his capital eastwards, founding his Second Rome on the site of a Greek town called Byzantium on the Bosphorus, a gateway between Europe and Asia. This soon became known as Constantinople with its own patriarch, who now joined the bishop of Rome and the patriarchs of Alexandria and Antioch as the ruling powers of Christianity. The new faith suited Constantine's new style of kingship. Christianity had from the earliest days of James, Overseer of Jerusalem, developed a hierarchy of elders (*presbyteroi*) and overseers / bishops (*episkopoi*) in charge of regional dioceses. Constantine saw that Christianity, with its hierarchy, paralleled the organization of the Roman empire: there would be one emperor, one state, one faith.

Yet he had no sooner bound his supremacy to his imperial

* Initially, Constantine identified the Unconquered Sun with the Christian God, placing crosses on some of his coins, the Sun on others, and remaining Pontifex Maximus (High Priest) of the pagan cults. In 321, Constantine declared Sunday – the day of the Sun – as the Christian version of the Sabbath. Mithraism was a Persian mystery religion with a following among Roman troops. As for Manichaeanism, the Parthian prophet Mani preached that existence was a perpetual struggle of light and dark, ultimately judged and enlightened by Jesus Christ. Now only the word survives to describe a world-view that sees life as a tournament between good and evil.

religion than he discovered that Christianity was divided: the Gospels were vague about Jesus' nature and his relationship to God. Was Jesus a man with some divine characteristics or God inhabiting the body of a man? Now that the Church was established, Christology became paramount, more important than life itself, for the right definition of Christ would decide whether a man would achieve salvation and enter heaven. In our secular era, the debates on nuclear disarmament or global warming are the closest equivalents in their passion and intensity. Christianity now became a mass religion in an age of fanatical faith and these questions were debated in the streets as well as in the palaces of the empire. When Arius, an Alexandrian priest who preached to huge crowds using popular jingles, argued that Jesus was subordinate to God and therefore more human than divine, this upset the many who regarded Christ as more God than man. When the local governor tried to suppress Arius, his followers rioted in Alexandria.

In 325 Constantine, infuriated and bemused by this doctrinal tumult, called the bishops to the Council of Nicaea and tried to impose his solution: that Jesus was divine and human, 'of one substance' with the Father. It was at Nicaea (present-day Isnik in Turkey), that Macarius, the Bishop of Aelia Capitolina (once called Jerusalem), brought the fate of his small and neglected town to Constantine's attention. Constantine knew Aelia, probably having visited it as a boy of eight when he was in Emperor Diocletian's entourage. Now keen to celebrate his success at Nicaea and project the sacred glory of his empire, he decided to restore the city and create what Eusebius (Bishop of Caesarea and the emperor's biographer) called 'The New Jerusalem built over against the one so famous of old'. Constantine commissioned a church that befitted Jerusalem as the cradle of the Good News. But the work was accelerated by the emperor's murderous domestic troubles.

CONSTANTINE THE GREAT: THE FAMILY KILLINGS

Soon after Constantine's victory, his wife Fausta denounced his eldest son (by an earlier marriage) Crispus Caesar for a sexual offence. Did she play on Constantine's new Christian chastity by claiming that Crispus had tried to seduce her or that he was a rapist? Was it actually an affair turned sour? Crispus would not have been the first young man to have an affair with his stepmother nor the last to want one, but perhaps the emperor was already jealous of Crispus' military successes. Certainly Fausta had every reason to dislike this obstacle to the rise of her own sons.

Whatever the truth, Constantine, outraged by his son's immorality, ordered his execution. The emperor's Christian advisers were disgusted and the most important woman in his life, his mother, now intervened. Helena had been a Bithnian barmaid and possibly never married his father, but she was an early convert to Christianity and was now the Augusta – empress – in her own right.

Helena convinced Constantine that he had been manipulated. Perhaps she revealed that Fausta had actually tried to seduce Crispus, not vice versa. Redeeming one unforgivable murder with another, Constantine ordered the execution of his wife, Fausta, for adultery: she was either scalded to death in boiling water or suffocated in an overheated steamroom, a particularly unChristian solution to a highly unChristian dilemma. But Jerusalem would benefit from this double murder,* scarcely mentioned by the embarrassed Christian eulogists.

Soon afterwards, Helena, securing carte blanche to embellish Christ's city, set off for Jerusalem.† Her glory would be Constantine's penance.

---

* In killing his son, Constantine joined an unsavoury crew of royal filicides that includes Herod the Great, Ivan the Terrible, Peter the Great, Suleiman the Magnificent. Herod, the emperor Claudius and Henry VIII also executed their own wives.

† But she was not the first lady of Constantine's family to be there. Eutropia, Fausta's Christian mother, was already in Jerusalem, perhaps to supervise the emperor's plans, when her daughter was killed. She shared her daughter's downfall and was almost written out of history.

HELENA: THE FIRST ARCHAEOLOGIST

Helena, septuagenarian empress, whose coins show her sharp face and her braided coiffuer and tiara, arrived in Aelia 'with all the energy of youth', and generous funds, to become Jerusalem's most monumental builder and miraculously successful archaeologist.

Constantine knew that the place of Jesus' Crucifixion and burial lay beneath Hadrian's Temple with its statue of that 'impure demon called Aphrodite, a dark shrine of lifeless idols', as Eusebius put it. He had ordered Bishop Macarius to purify the place, demolish the pagan temple, excavate the original tomb within and build there a basilica that would be 'the finest in the world' with 'the most beautiful structures, columns and marbles, the most precious and serviceable, ornamented in gold'.

Helena determined to find the actual tomb. The pagan temple had to be smashed, the paving stones lifted, the earth removed and the holy place located. The empress's quest must have created an excited and lucrative search in small Aelia. A Jew, perhaps one of the remaining Christian Jews, produced documents that led to the discovery of the cave that was declared to be Jesus' tomb. Helena also sought the site of the Crucifixion and even the Cross itself.

No archaeologist has ever approached her success. She discovered three wooden crosses, a wooden plaque that read 'Jesus of Nazareth, King of Jews', and the actual nails. But which cross was the right one? The empress and bishop are said to have borne these pieces of wood to the bedside of a dying woman. When the third was placed beside her, the invalid 'suddenly opened her eyes, regained her strength and sprang well from her bed'. Helena 'sent part to her son Constantine together with the nails', which the emperor had set into the bridle of his horse. From now on, all Christendom craved the holy relics that usually originated in Jerusalem, and this Life-Giving Tree begat a forest of splinters of the True Cross, which started to replace the earlier Chi-Rho as the symbol of Christianity.

Helena's discovery of the Cross was possibly a later invention, but she certainly changed the city for ever. She built churches of

the Ascension and of the Eleona on the Mount of Olives. Her
third church, that of the Holy Sepulchre, which took ten years to
complete, was not one building but a complex of four parts, its
façade facing eastwards, which was entered from the main Roman
street, the Cardo. (Today's church faces south.) The visitor climbed
steps into an atrium that led via three entrances into the Basilica or
Martyrium, a huge 'church of wondrous beauty', with five aisles
and rows of pillars, which led in turn, through its apse, into the
Holy Garden, a colonnaded courtyard where, in the south-eastern
corner, stood the hill of Golgotha enclosed in an open chapel. The
gold-domed Rotunda (the Anastasis) opened to the sky so that
the light shone down on to Jesus' tomb. Its splendour dominated
Jerusalem's sacred space, mocking the Temple Mount, where
Helena levelled any pagan shrine and 'ordered filth thrown in its
place' to show the failure of the Jewish God.*

Just a few years later, in 333, one of the first new pilgrims, an
anonymous visitor from Bordeaux, found Aelia already transformed
into a bustling Christian temple-city. The 'wondrous' Church was
not finished but was rising fast, yet Hadrian's statue still stood amid
the ruins of the Temple Mount.

Empress Helena visited all the sites of Jesus' life, creating the
first roadmap for the pilgrims who slowly began to flock to Jerusalem to experience its special holiness. Helena was nearly eighty
by the time she returned to Constantinople where her son kept
parts of the Cross, despatching another splinter and the plaque to
her aptly named Roman church, Santa Croce in Gerusalemme.

Eusebius, Bishop of Caesarea, was jealous of Jerusalem's new

---

* We do not know the exact sequence of these buildings and discoveries. Eusebius
of Caesarea, who provides the contemporary record, mentions only the orders of the
emperor and the actions of Bishop Macarius in building the Church of the Holy
Sepulchre (but nothing about Helena's role in finding the Cross). Yet he gives her
credit for the Ascension Church on the Mount of Olives. The story of Helena and
the Cross is told later by Sozomen (also a local Christian). Some of Constantine's
walls can still be seen, within the Russian Alexander Nevsky Church: the stones
contain the niches by which Constantine's architects attached the marble. Constantinian churches were based not on pagan temples but the secular basilica, the
audience-halls of emperors. Church rituals and clerical costumes were based on the
imperial court to promote for the representatives of the King of Heaven a hierarchy
parallel to that of the emperor.

eminence, doubting that this Jewish city, 'which after the bloody murder of the Lord had paid the penalty of its wicked inhabitants', could be the city of God. After all, the Christians had paid little attention to Jerusalem for three centuries. Yet Eusebius had a point: Constantine had to confront the heritage of the Jews just as the creator of the New Jerusalem had to divert the holiness of the Jewish sites towards his new shrines.

When the Romans worshipped many gods, they tolerated others, providing they did not threaten the state, but a monotheistic religion demanded the recognition of one truth, one god. The persecution of the Jewish Christ-killers whose wretchedness proved Christian truth, thus became essential. Constantine ordered that any Jews who tried to stop their brethren from converting to Christianity were to be instantly burned.* Yet a small Jewish community had been living in Jerusalem, praying at a synagogue on Mount Zion, for over a century and Jews discreetly prayed on the deserted Temple Mount. Now 'the detestable mob of Jews', as Constantine called them, were banned from Jerusalem except once a year when they were allowed on to the Temple Mount, where the Bordeaux pilgrim saw them 'mourn and rend their garments' over the 'perforated stone' – the foundation-stone of the Temple, today enclosed by the Dome of the Rock.

Constantine decided to celebrate the thirtieth anniversary of his accession in Jerusalem but was still struggling to control the controversy stirred up by the troublesome priest Arius – even after he had departed this world in a fecally explosive incident.† When

* Up until Nicaea, Easter still fell on Passover, since it was at Passover that Jesus had been crucified. Now Constantine's hatred of the Jews informed his decision to change this for ever. Constantine decreed that Easter should be fixed on the first full moon Sunday after the vernal equinox. This system remained universal until 1582 when the Eastern and Western calendars diverged.

† Arius was on his way through Constantinople after a meeting with Constantine when he felt a 'relaxation of the bowels'. Before he could reach a convenience, wrote Socrates Scholasticus, Arius' bowels burst in the middle of the Forum with his intestines, liver and spleen haemorrhaging out of him, a clear demonstration of the evil of his heresy. Yet Arianism lived on after Constantine's death, supported by his heir Constantius II until condemned again by Theodosius I, who in 381 decreed that Jesus was equal to the Father in the Trinity of Father, Son and Holy Spirit and of the same substance.

Constantine ordered a synod 'to free the Church from blasphemy and lighten my cares', once again the Arians defied him, overshadowing the first Christian festival in Jerusalem, a gathering of bishops from across the world. But the emperor was too ill to come. Finally baptized on his deathbed in 337, he divided the empire among his three sons and two nephews. The only things on which they agreed were the continuation of the Christian empire and the promulgation of more anti-Jewish laws: in 339, they banned intermarriage with Jews, whom they called a 'savage, abominable disgrace'.

Constantine's heirs fought for twenty years, a civil war finally won by his second son Constantius. This turbulence unsettled Palaestina. In 351, an earthquake in Jerusalem led all the Christians to rush to the Church of the Holy Sepulchre 'seized with awe'. When the Galilean Jews rebelled, led by a messianic king, they were so wantonly slaughtered by the emperor's cousin Gallus Caesar that even the Romans were sickened. Yet the Jews now found sympathy in a surprising place: the Emperor decided to overturn Christianity – and rebuild the Jewish Temple.

JULIAN THE APOSTATE: JERUSALEM RESTORED

On 19 July 362, the new emperor, Constantine's nephew Julian, who was in Antioch on his way to invade Persia, asked a Jewish delegation: 'Why do you not sacrifice?'

'We aren't allowed,' replied the Jews. 'Restore us to the city, rebuild the Temple and the Altar.

'I shall endeavour with the utmost zeal', replied Julian, 'to set up the Temple of the Most High God.' The emperor's astonishing reply was greeted with such Jewish enthusiasm that it was 'as if the days of their kingdom had already arrived'.

Julian reversed the Hadrianic and Constantinian persecutions, restored Jerusalem to the Jews, returned their property, revoked the anti-Jewish taxes and granted power of taxation and the title praetorian prefect to their patriarch Hillel. Jews must have poured into Jerusalem from all over the Roman and Persian worlds to celebrate this miracle. They reclaimed the Temple Mount, probably removing the statues of Hadrian and Antoninus to raise a provisional synagogue, perhaps around the stones that the Bordeaux Pilgrim called the House of King Hezekiah.

Julian was shy, cerebral and awkward. A biased Christian recalled his 'oddly disjointed neck, hunched and twitching shoulders, wild darting eye, swaying walk, haughty way of breathing down that prominent nose, that nervous and uncontrolled laughter, ever-nodding head and halting speech'. But the bearded, burly emperor was also decisive and single-minded. He restored paganism, favouring the family's old divine patron, the Sun, encouraging the traditional sacrifices in pagan temples and dismissing Galilean (as he called Christian) teachers in order to diminish their effete, unRoman values.

Julian had never expected to rule the empire. He was just five when Constantius murdered his father and most of his family; only two survived, Gallus and Julian. In 349, Constantius appointed Gallus as Caesar only to behead him, partly for his inept suppression of a Jewish revolt. Yet he needed a Caesar in the West and there was now only one candidate left. Julian, then a student of philosophy in Athens, became Caesar, ruling from Paris. Understandably, he was nervous when the unpredictable emperor summoned him. Inspired by a dream about Zeus, he accepted the imperial crown from his troops. As he marched eastwards, Constantius died and Julian found himself ruler of the entire empire.

Julian's rebuilding of the Jewish Temple was not just a mark of his tolerance but a nullification of the Christian claim to have inherited the true Israel, a reversal of the fulfilment of the prophecies of Daniel and Jesus that the Temple would fall, and a sign that he was serious in the overturning of his uncle's work. It would also win the support of the Babylonian Jews during his planned Persian war. Julian saw no contradiction between Greek paganism and Jewish monotheism, believing that the Greeks worshipped the Jewish 'Most High God' as Zeus: Yahweh was not unique to the Jews.

Julian appointed Alypius, his representative in Britain, to rebuild the Jewish Temple. The Sanhedrin were nervous: was this too good to be true? To reassure them, Julian, setting off for the Persian front, wrote 'To the Community of Jews', repeating his promise. In Jerusalem, exhilarated Jews 'sought out the most skilled artisans, collected materials, cleared the ground and embarked so earnestly on the task that even women carried heaps of earth and brought their necklaces to defray the expenses'. Building materials were stored in the so-called Stables of Solomon. 'When they had removed the remains of the former building, they cleared the foundation.'

As the Jews took control of Jerusalem, Julian invaded Persia with 65,000 troops. But on 27 May 363 Jerusalem was struck by an earthquake that somehow ignited the building materials.

The Christians were delighted by this 'wonderful phenomenon', though they may well have helped it along with arson. Alypius could have continued the work, but Julian had crossed the Tigris into Iraq. In tense Jerusalem, Alypius decided to await Julian's return. The emperor, however, was already in retreat. On 26 June in a confused skirmish near Samara, an Arab soldier (possibly a Christian) stabbed him in the side with a spear. Pierced in the liver, Julian tried to pull it out, shredding the sinews of his hand. Christian writers claimed that he died saying, 'Vicisti, Galilaee!', 'Thou has conquered, Galilean!'. He was succeeded by the commander of his guard, who restored Christianity, reversed all Julian's acts and again banned the Jews from Jerusalem: henceforth there would again be one religion, one truth. In 391–2 Theodosius I made Christianity the empire's official religion and started to enforce it.*

---

* Nothing remains of this very short Jewish blossoming, but there may be one small clue. High on the Western Wall, a Hebrew inscription has been discovered reading: 'And when you see this, your heart will rejoice, and your bones shall flourish like young grass.' It was too high on the wall for the Second Temple but in this period the ground was much higher. Some scholars believe this expresses the joy of the Jews at Jerusalem's restoration. More likely, it refers to a tenth-century cemetery: bones were found below this spot.

JEROME AND PAULA:
SAINTHOOD, SEX AND THE CITY

In 384, a splenetic Roman scholar named Jerome arrived in Jerusalem with an entourage of wealthy Christian women. Obsessively pious, they nonetheless travelled under a cloud of sexual scandal.

Now in his late thirties, the Illyrian Jerome had lived as a hermit in the Syrian desert, always tormented with sexual longings: 'Although my only companions were scorpions, I was mingling with the dances of girls, my mind throbbing with desires.' Jerome then served as the secretary to Damasus I, the Bishop of Rome, where the nobility had embraced Christianity. Damasus felt confident enough to declare that the bishops of Rome served with divine blessing in direct apostolic succession from St Peter, a big step in their development into the supreme, infallible popes of later times. But now the Church had such patrician support, Damasus and Jerome found themselves entangled in some very worldly scandals: Damasus was accused of adultery, dubbed 'the tickler of the ears of middle-aged women', while Jerome was said to be having an affair with the rich widow Paula, one of the many such ladies who had embraced Christianity. Jerome and Paula were exonerated – but they had to leave Rome and so they set out for Jerusalem, accompanied by her daughter Eustochium.

The very presence of this teenaged virgin seemed to inflame Jerome who smelled sex everywhere and spent much of the trip writing tracts warning of its dangers. 'Lust', he wrote, 'tickles the senses and the soft fire of sensual pleasure sheds its pleasing glow.' Once in Jerusalem, Jerome and his pious millionairesses found a new city that was an entrepot of sanctity, trade, networking and sex. The piety was intense and the richest of these ladies, Melania (who enjoyed an annual income of 120,000 pounds of gold), founded her own monastery on the Mount of Olives. But Jerome was horrified by the sexual opportunities offered by the mixing of so many strange men and women crowded together in this theme park of religious passion and sensory excitement: 'all temptation is collected here', he wrote, and all humanity – 'prostitutes, actors and clowns'. Indeed 'there is no sort of shameful practices in which they don't indulge', observed another saintly but sharp-eyed pilgrim, Gregory of Nyssa. 'Cheating, adultery, theft, idolatry, poisoning, quarrels and murder are everyday occurrences.'

Imperial patronage, monumental building and the stream of pilgrims now created a new calendar of festivals and rituals around the city, climaxing with Easter, and a new spiritual geography of Jerusalem, based on the sites of Jesus' Passion. Names were changed,* traditions muddled, but all that matters in Jerusalem is what is believed to be true. Another female pioneer, Egeria, a Spanish nun, who visited in the 380s, described the ever-expanding panoply of relics in the Holy Sepulchre† that now included King Solomon's ring and the horn of oil that had anointed David. These joined Jesus' crown of thorns and the lance that pierced his side.

The theatre and sanctity drove some pilgrims into a delirium special to Jerusalem: the True Cross had to be specially guarded because pilgrims tried to bite off chunks when they kissed it. That curmudgeon Jerome could not bear all this theatrical screaming – hence he settled in Bethlehem to work on his

---

* Zion was originally the name of the citadel of David's City, south of the Temple, but became synonymous with the Temple Mount. Now 'Zion' became the Christian name for the western hill. In 333, the Bordeaux Pilgrim already called it Zion. In 390, the Bishop of Jerusalem built the magnificent and colossal Zion, Mother of Churches there on the site of the Coenaculum. Jerusalem's gift for dynamic reinvention and cultural theft is endless – but it does make names very confusing. Take this example: Hadrian's Neapolis Gate with the huge column standing before it now became St Stephen's Gate for some centuries before the Arabs called it the Gate of the Column, and later the Nablus Gate (Neapolis being today's Nablus); the Jews called it the Shechem Gate; the Ottomans called it today's name, Damascus Gate. (Today's St Stephen's Gate is on the eastern side of the city.)
† The Byzantines moved most of the Jewish traditions of the Temple Mount to the Church of the Holy Sepulchre. The reddish stone of the Temple Mount had been known as the 'Blood of Zacharias' (the priest murdered there as told in 2 Chronicles 24.21), but this site now moved to the Church as did the Creation, the burial place of Adam, the altars of Melchizedek and Abraham and Solomon's devil-catching silver bowl. These joined the platter for John the Baptist's head, the sponge that soothed Jesus on the cross, the column where he was scourged, the stone that killed St Stephen and, of course, the True Cross. The Temple had been the 'centre of the world' for Jews; no wonder this one-stop shrine of all biblical holiness, the Church, was now itself regarded as 'a navel of the world'.

masterpiece, translating the Hebrew Bible into Latin. But he visited frequently and was never shy about expressing his views. 'It's as easy to find the way to Heaven in Britain as in Jerusalem,' he snarled in reference to the vulgar crowds of British pilgrims. When he watched his friend Paula's emotive prayers before the Cross in the Holy Garden, he cattily claimed that she looked 'as though she saw the Lord hanging upon it' and kissed the tomb 'like a thirsty man who had waited long and at last comes to water'. Her 'tears and lamentations' were so loud that they 'were known to all Jerusalem or to the Lord himself whom she called upon'.

Yet one drama that he did appreciate took place on the Temple Mount, kept in desolation to confirm Jesus' prophecies. On each 9th of Ab Jerome gleefully watched the Jews commemorating the destruction of the Temple: 'Those faithless people who killed the servant of God – that mob of wretches congregates and, while the Church of Resurrection glows and the banner of His Cross shines forth from the Mount of Olives, those miserable people groan over the ruins of the Temple. A soldier asks for money to allow them to weep a little longer.' Despite his fluent Hebrew, Jerome hated the Jews, who raised children 'just like worms', and relished this gratifying freak show that confirmed Christ's victorious truth: 'Can anyone harbour doubts when he looks upon this scene about the Day of Tribulation and Suffering?' The very tragedy of the Jews' plight redoubled their love for Jerusalem. For Rabbi Berekhah this scene was a ritual as sacred as it was poignant: 'They come silently and go silently, they come weeping and go weeping, they come in darkness of the night and depart in darkness.'

Yet now Jewish hopes were to be raised again by the Empress who came to rule Jerusalem.

BARSOMA AND THE PARAMILITARY MONKS

Empresses tended to be described by chauvinistic historians as hideous, vicious whores or serene saints, but unusually Empress

Eudocia was especially praised for her exquisite looks and artistic nature. In 438, this beautiful wife of the Emperor Theodosius II came to Jerusalem and relaxed the rules against the Jews. At the same time, a synagogue-burning ascetic, Barsoma of Nisibis, arrived on one of his regular pilgrimages with a thuggish retinue of paramilitary monks.

Eudocia was a protector of pagans and Jews because she had been pagan herself. The striking daughter of an Athenian sophist, educated in rhetoric and literature, she came to Constantinople to appeal to the emperor after her brothers stole her inheritance. Theodosius II was a malleable boy, ruled by his pious and graceless sister, Pulcheria. She introduced Eudocia to her brother, who was instantly smitten and married her. Pulcheria dominated her brother's government, intensifying the persecution of the Jews, who were now excluded from the army and public life, and condemned to be second-class citizens. In 425, Theodosius ordered the execution of Gamaliel VI, the last Jewish patriarch, to punish him for building more synagogues, and abolished the office for ever. Gradually, Eudocia became powerful and Theodosius promoted her to Augusta, equal in rank to his sister. A coloured stone inlay of her in a Constantinople church shows her regal style, black hair, slim elegance and delicate nose.

In Jerusalem, the Jews, facing intensifying repression from Constantinople, begged Eudocia for more access to the Holy City, and she agreed that they could openly visit the Temple Mount for their chief festivals. This was wonderful news, and the Jews declared that they should all 'hasten to Jerusalem for the Feast of Tabernacles for our kingdom will be established'.

However, Jewish joy disgusted that other visitor to Jerusalem, Barsoma of Nisibis, a Syrian monk who was one of the new breed of militant monastic leaders. During the fourth century, certain ascetics started to react against the worldly values of society and the splendour of the clerical hierarchs and founded monasteries in the desert in order to return to the values of the earliest Christians. The hermits – from the Greek word for 'wilderness' – believed it was not enough to know the right formula for Christ's nature, it was also necessary to live righteously, so they existed in hair-shirted, celibate simplicity in the deserts of Egypt and Syria.* Their self-flagellating feats of ostentatious holiness were celebrated, their biographies were written (the first hagiographies), their hermitages were visited and their discomforts became sources of wonder. The two St Simeons lived for decades, thirty feet up, atop columns and were known as the stylites (from *stylos* meaning 'column'). One stylite, Daniel, was asked how he defecated: drily, like a sheep, he replied. Indeed, Jerome thought they were more interested in filth than in holiness. But these monks were far from peaceful. Jerusalem, which was now surrounded by new monasteries and contained many of its own, was at the mercy of these squadrons of street-fighting fanatics.

Barsoma, who was said to be so holy that he never sat or lay down, was offended by the survival of Jewish and Samaritan 'idolators' and determined to cleanse Palaestina of them. He and his monks killed Jews and burned synagogues. The emperor banned the violence for reasons of order, but Barsoma ignored him. Now, in Jerusalem, Barsoma's coenobite shock-troopers, armed with swords and clubs under monks' robes, ambushed the Jews on the Temple Mount, stoning and killing many of them, tossing their bodies into water cisterns and courtyards. The Jews fought back, arrested eighteen attackers and handed them over to the Byzantine governor who charged them with murder. 'These brigands in the respectable habits of monks' were brought to Eudocia, the pilgrim empress. They were guilty of murder but when they implicated Barsoma, he spread rumours that noble Christians were to be burned alive. The mob turned in Barsoma's favour, especially when he cited a timely earthquake as a sign of divine approval.

If the empress planned to execute Christians, Barsoma's followers cried, then 'we will burn the empress and all those with her'. Barsoma terrorized officials into testifying that the Jewish victims

---

* Monastic women often had to disguise themselves as eunuchs, which led to some entertaining stories: a certain Marina shaved her head, donned a male tunic and joined a monastery as Marinos but was accused of fathering a child and expelled. She brought up the child and only on her death did the monks discover that she was unequipped to perpetrate the sin of which she had been accused.

had no wounds: they had died of natural causes. Another earthquake added to the widespread fear. The city was slipping out of control. Eudocia had little choice but to acquiesce. 'Five hundred groups' of paramilitary monks patrolled the streets and Barsoma announced that 'The Cross has triumphed', a cry repeated across the city 'like the roar of a wave' as his followers anointed him with expensive perfumes, and the murderers were freed.

Despite this violence, Eudocia cherished Jerusalem, commissioning an array of new churches, and she returned to Constantinople laden with new relics. But her sister-in-law Pulcheria was plotting to destroy her.

EUDOCIA: EMPRESS OF JERUSALEM

Theodosius sent Eudocia a Phrygian apple. She gave it to her protégé, Paulinus, Master of the Offices, who then sent it as a present to the emperor. Theodosius, hurt by this, confronted his wife who lied and insisted that she had not given his present away to anyone but had eaten it. At that, the emperor produced the apple. This white lie suggested to Theodosius that what his sister had been whispering was true: Eudocia was having an affair with Paulinus. The story is mythical – apples symbolize life and chastity – but in its very human details it chronicles just the sort of accidental chain of events that can end badly in the hothouse courts of fraught autocracies. Paulinus was executed in 440, but the imperial couple negotiated a way for Eudocia to retire from the capital with honour. Three years later, she arrived in Jerusalem to rule Palaestina in her own right.

Even then Pulcheria tried to destroy her, despatching Saturnius, Count of the Imperial Bodyguard, to execute two of her entourage. Eudocia quickly had Saturnius murdered. Once this imperial skulduggery had died down, she was left to her own devices: she built palaces for herself and the city's bishop and a hospice next to the Sepulchre that survived for centuries. She built the first walls since Titus, enclosing Mount Zion and the City of David – her sections of wall can be seen today in both places. The pillars of her multi-levelled church around the Siloam Pool still stand in the waters there.*

The empire was now disturbed by the reignited Christological dispute. If Jesus and the Father were 'of one substance', how could Christ combine both divine and human natures? In 428, Nestorius, the new Patriarch of Constantinople, tactlessly stressed Jesus' human side and dual nature, claiming that the Virgin Mary should be considered not Theotokos, Bearer of God, but merely Christokos, Bearer of Christ. His enemies, the Monophysites, insisted that Christ had one nature which was simultaneously human and divine. Dyophysites fought their Monophysite protagonists in the imperial palaces and in the backstreets of Jerusalem and Constantinople with all the violence and hatred of Christological football hooligans. Everyone, noticed Gregory of Nyssa, had an opinion: 'You ask a man for change, he'll give you a piece of philosophy concerning the Begotten and the Unbegotten; if you enquire the price of a loaf, he replies "The Father is greater and the Son inferior"; or if you ask whether the bath is ready, the answer you receive is that the Son was made out of nothing.'

When Theodosius died, his two empresses faced each other across the Christological divide. Pulcheria, who had seized power in Constantinople, backed the Dyophysites, but Eudocia, like most Eastern Christians, was a Monophysite. Pulcheria duly expelled her from the Church. When Juvenal, the Bishop of Jerusalem, backed Pulcheria, the Monophysite Jerusalemites mobilized their monkish shock-troopers who drove him out of the city, a predicament he exploited. Christianity had long been ruled by the four great metropolitan bishoprics – Rome and the eastern

---

* Eudocia was inspired by Psalm 51: 'Do good in thy good pleasure [Greek: *eudocia*] unto Zion: build the walls of Jerusalem.' She was advised by the celebrated Armenian monk Euphemius whose protégé Sabas later founded the hauntingly beautiful Mar Saba Monastery, today inhabited by twenty monks, in the Judaean mountains not far from Jerusalem. Armenia, in the Caucasus, had been the first kingdom to convert to Christianity in 301 (after the mythical conversion of King Abgar of Edessa), followed by its neighbour Georgia (known as Iberia) in 327. Eudocia was joined by her own protégé, Peter the Georgian, the king of Iberia's son, who built a monastery outside the walls. This was the start of the Caucasian presence in Jerusalem that endures today.

patriarchates. But Jerusalem's bishops had always campaigned for promotion to patriarch. Now Juvenal won this promotion as the prize for the loyalty that almost cost him his life. Finally in 451, at the Council of Chalcedon, Pulcheria enforced a compromise: in the Union of Two Natures, Jesus was 'perfect in divinity, and perfect in humanity'. Eudocia agreed and became reconciled with Pulcheria. This compromise has lasted to this day in the Orthodox, Catholic and Protestant Churches, but it was flawed: the Monophysites and Nestorians, for precisely opposite reasons, rejected it and split off from Orthodoxy for ever.*

At a time when the Western Roman empire was being terrorized by Attila the Hun and hurtling toward its fatal collapse, the ageing Eudocia was writing Greek poetry and building her St Stephen's basilica, now vanished, but just north of the Damascus Gate, where in 460 she was buried alongside the relics of the first martyr.

---

* Nestorianism became popular in the East through the Assyrian Church of the East that converted some of the royal family of Sassanid Persia and later many of Genghis Khan's family. Simultaneously, Monophysite Eastern Christians, rejecting Chalcedon, formed the Egyptian Coptic, Syriac Orthodox (known also as Jacobite after its founder Jacob Baradeus) and Ethiopian Churches. The latter developed a special link with Judaism – *The Book of Glory of Kings* celebrates the union of King Solomon and Sheba, as the parents of the 'Lion of Judah' King Menelik who brought the Ark of the Covenant to Ethiopia, where it is now said to rest in Axum. This link later created the House of Israel (Beta Israel), the Falashas, black Ethiopian Jews, who existed at least from the fourteenth century; in 1984, the Israelis airlifted them to Israel.

16

SUNSET OF THE BYZANTINES:
PERSIAN INVASION

518–630

JUSTINIAN AND THE SHOWGIRL EMPRESS:
BYZANTINE JERUSALEM

In 518, aged thirty-five, Justinian found himself the real ruler of
the eastern empire when his uncle Justin was raised to the throne.
The elderly new emperor was an illiterate Thracian peasant and
depended on his clever nephew Peter, who adopted the name
Justinian.* He did not come to power alone: his mistress Theodora
was the daughter of the Blue chariot-racing team's bear-trainer,
raised among the sweaty charioteers, louche bathhouses and
bloody bearpits of the Constantinople hippodrome. Starting as a
pre-pubescent burlesque showgirl, she was said to be a gym-
nastically gifted orgiast whose speciality was to offer all three
orifices to her clients simultaneously. Her nymphomaniacal party
piece was to spread-eagle herself on stage while geese pecked
grains of barley from 'the calyx of this passion flower'. The sexual
details were no doubt exaggerated by their court historian, who

* One of Justinian's earliest decisions in his uncle's reign was to destroy the Arabian
Jewish kingdom of Yemen. In the early fifth century, the Kings of Yemen (Himyara)
had converted to Judaism. In 523, in response to Byzantine threats, the Jewish king
Joseph – Dhu Nuwas Zurah Yusuf – massacred Christians in Yemen and forced
neighbouring principalities to convert to Judaism. Justinian ordered the Christian
king Kaleb of Axum (Ethiopia) to invade Yemen. King Joseph was defeated in 525
and committed suicide by riding into the sea on horseback. Yet many Jews remained
in Yemen and Judaism did not disappear in Arabia: many of its tribes remained
Jewish in Muhammad's day; Yemenite Jews would start to settle in Jerusalem in the
nineteenth century and emigrate to Israel after 1948. Only one village of Jews
remains in Yemen in 2010.

must secretly have resented the sycophancy of his day job. Whatever the truth, Justinian found her life-force irresistible and changed the law so that he could marry her. Though her intrigues complicated Justinian's life, Theodora often provided the will he lacked. When he had almost lost Constantinople during the Nika riots and was ready to flee, she said she would prefer to die in imperial purple than live without it and despatched his generals to massacre the rebels.

Thanks to their realistic portraits in the San Vitale Church at Ravenna, we know that Justinian was thin-faced and unprepossessing with a reddish complexion, while Theodora, delicate, pale and glacial, with dazzling eyes and pursed lips, stares at us witheringly as ropes of pearls bedeck her head and breast. They were a supreme political double-act. Whatever their origins, both were humourlessly, mercilessly serious about empire and religion.

Justinian, the last Latin-speaking emperor of the east, believed that his life's mission was to restore the Roman empire and reunite Christendom: shortly before he was born, the last emperor of Rome had been driven from the city by a Germanic chieftain. Ironically, this enhanced the prestige of the bishops of Rome, soon to be known as popes, and the differences between east and west. Justinian achieved astounding success in promoting his universal Christian empire by war, faith and art. He reconquered Italy, north Africa and southern Spain, though he faced repeated invasions by the Persians who at times almost overran the East. The imperial couple promoted their Christian empire as 'the first and greatest blessing of all mankind', suppressing homosexuals, pagans, heretics, Samaritans and Jews. Justinian demoted Judaism from a permitted religion and banned Passover if it fell before Easter, converted synagogues into churches, forcibly baptized Jews, and commandeered Jewish history: in 537, when Justinian dedicated his breathtaking domed Church of Hagia Sofia ('Holy Wisdom') in Constantinople, he is said to have reflected, 'Solomon, I have surpassed thee.' Then he turned to Jerusalem to trump Solomon's Temple.

In 543, Justinian and Theodora started to build a basilica, the

Nea (New) Church of St Mary Mother of God,* almost 400 feet long and 187 feet high, with walls 16 feet thick, facing away from the Temple Mount and designed to overpower Solomon's site. When Justinian's general Belisarius conquered the Vandal capital of Carthage, he found there the candelabra, pillaged from the Temple by Titus. After being paraded through Constantinople in Belisarius' Triumph, it was sent to Jerusalem, probably to embellish Justinian's Nea Church.

The Holy City was ruled by the rituals of Orthodox Christianity.† Pilgrims entered through Hadrian's gateway in the north and walked down the Cardo, a paved and colonnaded street, 40 feet wide, enough for two wagons to pass, lined with covered shops, extending down to the Nea Church. The well-to-do lived south and south-west of the Temple Mount in two-storeyed mansions set around courtyards. 'Happy are those who live in this house' was written in one of them. The houses, churches, even the shops, were decorated gloriously with mosaics: the Armenian kings probably commissioned the incandescent mosaic of herons, doves and eagles (dedicated 'For the memory and salvation of all the Armenians whose names only God knows'). More mysterious is the vivid semi-Christian mosaic of a puckish Orpheus playing his lyre found at the turn of the century north of the Damascus Gate. Rich Byzantine women wore long Greek robes bordered in gold, red and green, red shoes, strings of pearls, necklaces and

---

* For years this immense complex was lost, but its foundations, stretching from the Jewish Quarter under the present walls to outside the Old City, were discovered in excavations by the archaeologist Nahman Avigad in 1973. Justinian built on a series of vaults constructed along the slope to support its weight. This inscription was found among them: 'And this is the work carried out by the generosity of our most gracious Emperor Flavius Justinianus.'

† In 1884, a colourful mosaic was found on the floor of a Byzantine church in Madaba (in Jordan), inscribed 'The Holy City of Jerusalem', the first Jerusalem map to show the Byzantine view of the city with its six main gates, churches and the Temple Mount scarcely worth showing at all. Yet the Temple Mount was not completely empty. It has never been excavated by archaeologists, but in the 1940s British engineers, restoring the Islamic holy sites, made shallow probes and found Byzantine traces. Optimists hoped these might be the foundations of Emperor Julian's (unbuilt) Jewish Temple. But these may be traces of the only Byzantine shrine on this site – the small Church of the Pinnacle marking Jesus' temptation by the devil.

earrings. A gold ring has been unearthed in Jerusalem decorated with a gold model of the Church of the Holy Sepulchre.

The city was set up to host thousands of pilgrims: the grandees stayed with the patriarch; poor pilgrims in the dormitories of Justinian's hospices which had beds for 3,000; and ascetics, in caves, often old Jewish tombs, in the surrounding hills. When the rich died, they were buried in sarcophagi; the sides of which were decorated with frescoes and equipped with bells for the dead to ward off demons. The cadavers of the poor were pushed into the anonymous mass tomb of the Field of Blood. The temptations that had outraged Jerome were always available: there was chariot-racing in the hippodrome, supported by the rumbustious Blue and Green factions of supporters. 'Fortune of the Blues wins!' cries an inscription found in Jerusalem. 'Live long!'

Theodora died of cancer soon after the Nea was finished, but Justinian lived on into his eighties until 565, having ruled for almost fifty years. He had expanded the empire more than anyone except Augustus and Trajan, but by the end of the century it was overstretched and vulnerable. In 602, a general seized the throne and tried to hold on to it by unleashing the Blue chariot-racing faction against his enemies, who were supported by the Greens, and ordering the forcible conversion of the Jews. The Blues and Greens, always a dangerous combination of sporting fans and political bullyboys, fought for Jerusalem: 'evil, malicious men filled the city with crime and murder.' The Greens won, but Byzantine troops retook the city and crushed their rebellion.

This turbulence was irresistibly tempting to Khusrau II, the Persian shah. As a boy he had been helped back on to his throne by the Byzantine emperor Maurice, but when the latter was murdered, Khusrau had his pretext to invade the East, hoping to destroy Constantinople once and for all. Jerusalem was about to suffer a rollercoaster epoch that would see her ruled by four different religions in twenty-five years: Christian, Zoroastrian, Jewish and Muslim.

THE SHAH AND THE ROYAL BOAR:
THE FURY OF MAD DOGS

The Persians, spearheaded by the mailed fist of their heavy cavalry, conquered Roman Iraq and then swooped into Syria. The Jews of Antioch, so long persecuted by the Byzantines, rebelled and, as the brilliant Persian commander, who gloried in the name Shahrbaraz – the Royal Boar – marched south, 20,000 Jews from Antioch and Tiberias joined him to besiege Jerusalem. Inside, the patriarch Zacharias tried to negotiate, but the chariot-racing bully-boys ruled the streets and refused. Somehow the Persians and Jews broke into the city.

Jerusalem, and virtually the entire Roman East, now belonged to the young Persian King of Kings, the Shah-in-Shah Khusrau II, whose new empire extended from Afghanistan to the Mediterranean. This shah was the grandson of the greatest of the Sassanid rulers who had burned Antioch during Justinian's reign. But he had spent a humiliating boyhood as the helpless pawn of rival noble families and had grown up into a paranoid megalomaniac who imposed his power with extravagant gigantism: his tiger-skin banner was 130 feet long, 20 feet wide; he held court on the King's Spring, a carpet of 1,000 square feet, inlaid in gold and brocade and depicting an imaginary royal garden; his *shabestan* – the cool underground apartments where the shahs kept their women – contained 3,000 concubines; and it was possibly he who built the colossal palace at his capital Ctesiphon (close to present-day Baghdad) with the world's largest audience-hall. Riding his black horse, Midnight, his robes were woven in gold, encrusted in jewels, his armour gold-trimmed.

The shah, whose polyglot subjects included many Jews and Christians, was Zoroastrian, but he had married a lovely Nestorian Christian, Shirin, whom he had won, according to legend, by sending his rival to perform the impossible task of carving stairs out of the Behustan mountains.

Once Jerusalem had been taken, the shah's general, the Royal

Boar, moved on to conquer Egypt, but no sooner was he gone than the Jerusalemites rebelled against the Persians and Jews. The Royal Boar galloped back and besieged Jerusalem for twenty days, destroying the churches on the Mount of Olives and Gethsemane. The Persians and Jews mined under the north-eastern wall, always the most vulnerable place, and on the twenty-first day, in early May 614, they stormed Jerusalem 'in great fury, like infuriated wild beasts', according to the eyewitness Strategos, a monk. 'The people hid in churches and there they destroyed them in great wrath, gnashing their teeth and slew all they found like mad dogs.'

In three days, thousands of Christians were massacred. The patriarch and 37,000 Christians were deported to Persia. As the survivors stood on the Mount of Olives 'and gazed upon Jerusalem, a flame, as out of a furnace, reached up to the clouds and they fell to sobbing and lamenting', dropping ashes in their hair for they saw the Church of the Holy Sepulchre, the Nea, the Mother of Churches on Mount Zion and the Armenian cathedral of St Jameses, consumed by the inferno. The Christian relics – the Lance, the Sponge and the True Cross – were sent to Khusrau, who gave them to his queen Shirin. She preserved them in her church in Ctesiphon.

Then, 600 years after Titus had destroyed the Temple, the Royal Boar gave Jerusalem to the Jews.

NEHEMIAH II:

THE JEWISH TERROR

After centuries of repression, the Jews, led by a shadowy figure named Nehemiah, were keen to avenge themselves on the Chris-tians who until weeks earlier had been persecuting them. The Persians imprisoned thousands of less valuable prisoners in the Mamilla Pool, a large reservoir, where, according to Christian sources, they were offered the same choice recently offered to the Jews: convert or die. Some monks converted to Judaism; others were martyred.* The joyous Jews may have started to reconsecrate the Temple Mount, for the Jews now 'made sacrifices'† and messianic fervour vibrated through the Jewish world, inspiring the enthusiasm of the Book of Zerubbabel.

The Persian shah had conquered Egypt, Syria, Iraq and Asia Minor all the way to Constantinople. Only the city of Tyre still held out against the Persians, who ordered the Jewish commander Nehemiah to capture it. The Jewish army failed in this mission and fled from Tyre, but the Persians surely already realized that the more numerous Christians were more useful. In 617, after three years of Jewish rule, the Royal Boar expelled the Jews from Jerusalem. Nehemiah resisted but was defeated and executed at Emmaus near Jerusalem.

The city was returned to the Christians. Once again it was the Jewish turn to suffer. The Jews left the city by an eastern gate like the Christians before them, marching away towards Jericho. The Christians found the Holy City ravaged: Modestos, the priest in charge during the absence of the patriarch, energetically restored the shattered Holy Sepulchre, but the city never regained the magnificence of Constantine and Justinian.

Three times since Titus the Jews had grasped moments of free prayer among the rock heaps of the Temple – probably under bar Kochba, certainly under Julian and Khusrau – but Jews would not control the Temple again for 1,350 years. As for the triumphant Persians, they now faced a dynamic young Byzantine emperor who seemed to merit the name of Hercules.

---

* Christian accounts make the exaggerated claim that 10,000 to 90,000 Christians were murdered by the Jews and buried by Thomas the Gravedigger. Christian legend claims the victims were buried in the Mamilla cemetery of the Lions' Cave, so named because survivors hid in the cave until they were saved by a lion. The Jews claim that it was Jewish victims of a Christian massacre who were saved by the lion.

† Some traces of a building at the Temple Mount's south-west corner seem to show a menorah painted over a cross, possibly a Christian shrine inherited for a short time by Jews. But this may date from the early Islamic period.

HERACLIUS: THE FIRST CRUSADER

Blond and tall, he looked the part of imperial saviour. The son of the governor of Africa and of Armenian descent, Heraclius had seized power in 610 when much of the east was already in Persian hands and it seemed that things could scarcely get worse – but they did. When Heraclius counterattacked, he was defeated by the Royal Boar who then conquered Syria and Egypt before attacking Constantinople itself. Heraclius sued for a humiliating peace that gave him time to rebuild Byzantine strength and plan his vengeance.

On Easter Monday 622, Heraclius sailed with an army, not (as expected) through the Black Sea to the Caucasus, but around the Ionian coast of the Mediterranean to the Bay of Issus whence he marched inland and defeated the Royal Boar. Even as the Persians threatened Constantinople, Heraclius was taking the war into their homeland. The next year, he repeated the trick, marching through Armenia and Azerbaijan towards Khusrau's palace at Ganzak. The shah retreated. Heraclius wintered in Armenia and then in 625, in a Herculean display of military virtuosity, prevented three Persian armies uniting, before defeating each in turn.

In this war of wild gambles and global ambition, the shah turned the tables once again, despatching one general to seize Iraq and the Boar to link up with the Avars, a marauding, nomadic tribe, and take Constantinople. The shah, calling himself 'Noblest of the Gods, King and Master of the Whole Earth', wrote to Heraclius: 'You say you trust in God; why then has He not delivered out of my hand Caesarea, Jerusalem, Alexandria? Could I not also destroy Constantinople? Have I not destroyed you Greeks?' Heraclius despatched one army to fight in Iraq, another to defend the capital, while he himself hired 40,000 nomadic Turkic horsemen, the Khazars, to form a third.

Constantinople was besieged by the Persians and Avars on either side of the Bosphorus, but the shah was jealous of the Royal Boar. The overweening arrogance and creative cruelties of the Master of the Whole Earth were already alienating his own noblemen. The shah sent a letter to the Royal Boar's deputy ordering him to kill the general and take command. Heraclius intercepted it. Inviting the Boar to a meeting, he showed him the letter; they made a secret alliance. Constantinople was saved.

The Royal Boar withdrew to Alexandria to rule Syria, Palestine and Egypt. Heraclius sailed his army to the Caucasus via the Black Sea, and with his Khazar horsemen invaded Persia. He out-manoeuvred the Persian forces, challenged and killed three Persian champions in duels, then defeated their main army, stopping just outside the shah's capital. Khusrau's deluded intransigence destroyed him. He was arrested and placed in the dungeon, the House of Darkness, where his favourite son was butchered in front of him before he was himself tortured to death. The Persians agreed to restore the *status quo ante bellum*. The Royal Boar agreed to marry Heraclius' niece and revealed the hiding-place of the True Cross. After tortuous intrigues, the Royal Boar seized the Persian throne – but was soon assassinated.

In 629, Heraclius set out from Constantinople with his wife (also his niece) to return the True Cross to Jerusalem. He pardoned the Jews of Tiberias, where he stayed in the mansion of a rich Jew, Benjamin, who accompanied him to Jerusalem, converting to Christianity on the way. The Jews were promised that there would be no vengeance and that they could reside in Jerusalem.

On 21 March 630, Heraclius, now fifty-five, exhausted and grey, rode up to the Golden Gate, which he had built for this special occasion. This exquisite gate became, for all three Abrahamic religions, Jerusalem's most potently mystical gateway for the arrival of the Messiah on the Day of Judgement.* There the emperor dismounted to carry the True Cross into Jerusalem. It was said that when Heraclius tried to enter in his Byzantine robes the gate became a solid wall, but when he humbled himself it opened for his imperial procession. Carpets and aromatic herbs were spread

---

* The Golden Gate, actually two gates, is directly and precisely aligned with the Tomb itself in the Church of the Holy Sepulchre, the place to which Heraclius took the Cross. The place had further symbolism, as we have seen, because the Byzantines mistakenly believed it also marked the Beautiful Gate where Jesus entered on Palm Sunday and where his apostles performed a miracle after his death. Nonetheless some scholars believe the gate was actually built by the Ummayad caliphs. The Gate soon assumed mystical significance for the Jews who called it the Gate of Mercy.

as Heraclius delivered the True Cross to the Holy Sepulchre, now cleaned up by the patriarch Modestos. The catastrophe that had befallen the empire and the emperor's return played into a new variant of the ever malleable vision of the Apocalypse in which a messianic Last Emperor would smash the enemies of Christianity and then hand power to Jesus who would rule until Judgement Day.

The Christians demanded vengeance on the Jews, but Heraclius refused until the monks took the sin of his broken oath to the Jews upon themselves as a fast of atonement. Heraclius then expelled any remaining Jews; many were massacred; he later ordered the forcible conversion of all Jews.

Far away to the south, the Arabians had noticed not so much Heraclius' victory as his weakness. 'The Romans have been defeated,' declared Muhammad, the leader who had just united the Arabian tribes, in what became the sacred text of his new revelation, the Koran. While Heraclius was in Jerusalem, Muhammad despatched a raid up the King's Highway to probe Byzantine defences. The Arabs encountered a Byzantine detachment – but they would soon return.

Heraclius would not have been too alarmed: the divided Arab tribes had been raiding Palaestina for centuries. The Byzantines and Persians had both hired Arab tribes as buffer states between the empires, and Heraclius had fielded large squadrons of Arab cavalry in his armies.

The next year, Muhammad sent another small detachment to attack Byzantine territory. But he was now old and his spectacular life was near its end. Heraclius left Jerusalem and headed back to Constantinople.

There seemed little to fear.

PART FOUR

ISLAM

Glory to Him who made His servant travel by night from the sacred place of worship to the furthest place of worship.

The Koran, 17.1

The Apostle of Allah, accompanied by Gabriel, was transported to Jerusalem where he found Abraham and Moses and the other Prophets.

Ibn Ishaq, *Sirat Rasul Allah*

A ruler was not considered a caliph unless he reigned over both the Holy Mosque [Mecca] and the Jerusalem Mosque.

Sibani, *Fadail*

One day in Jerusalem is like a thousand days, one month like a thousand months, and one year like a thousand years. Dying there is like dying in the first sphere of heaven.

Kaab al-Ahbar, *Fadail*

A sin committed [in Jerusalem] is equal to a thousand sins and a good deed there to a thousand good deeds.

Khalid bin Madan al-Kalai, *Fadail*

Allah, may he be praised, said of Ierusalem. You are my Garden of Eden, my hallowed and chosen land.

Kaab al-Ahbar, *Fadail*

O Jerusalem, I shall send you my servant Abd al-Malik to rebuild and adorn you.

Kaab al-Ahbar, *Fadail*

17

THE ARAB CONQUEST

630–60

MUHAMMAD: THE NIGHT JOURNEY

Muhammad's father died before he was born and his mother died when he was just six. But he was adopted by his uncle, who took him on trading trips to Bosra in Syria. There he was taught about Christianity by a monk, studied the Jewish and Christian scriptures, coming to venerate Jerusalem as one of the noblest of sanctuaries. In his twenties, a wealthy widow named Khadija, much older than he, employed him to manage her caravan trading and then married him. They lived in Mecca, the home of the Kaaba and its black stone, the sanctuary of a pagan god. The city thrived on the pilgrims attracted by this cult and by caravan trading. Muhammad was a member of the Quraysh tribe, who provided its leading merchants and custodians of the sanctuary, but his Hashemite clan was not one of the more powerful.

Muhammad, described as handsome with curly hair and beard, possessed both an all-conquering geniality – it was said that when he shook someone's hand he never liked to be the one to let go first – and a charismatic spirituality. He was admired for his integrity and intelligence – as his warriors later put it, 'He was the best among us' – and he was known as al-Amin, the Reliable.

As with Moses, David or Jesus, it is impossible now for us to divine the personal essence of his success, but like them, he came at the time he was needed. In the Jahiliya, the Time of Ignorance before his revelation, 'there was nobody more destitute than we were,' wrote one of his soldiers later. 'Our religion was to kill one another and raid. There were those among us who would bury their daughters alive not wanting them to eat our food. Then God sent us a well-known man.'

Outside Mecca was the Cave of Hira where Muhammad liked to meditate. In 610, according to tradition, the Archangel Gabriel visited him there with his first revelation from the one God who had chosen him to be his Messenger and Prophet. When the Prophet received God's revelations, his face was said to become flushed, he fell silent, his body lying limp on the ground, sweat poured down his face; he was engulfed by humming sounds and visions – and then he would recite his poetical, divine revelations. Initially he was terrified by this, but Khadija believed in his vocation and he started to preach.

In this rough military society where every boy and man bore arms, the literary tradition was not written but consisted of a rich spoken poetry that celebrated the deeds of honourable warriors, passionate lovers, fearless hunters. The Prophet was to harness this poetical tradition: his 114 *sura* – chapters – were initially recited before they were collated into the Koran, 'The Recitation', a compendium of exquisite poetry, sacred obscurity, clear instruction and bewildering contradiction.

Muhammad was an inspirational visionary who preached submission – Islam – to the one God in return for universal salvation, the values of equality and justice, and the virtues of pure living, with easily learned rituals and rules for life and death. He welcomed converts. He revered the Bible, and regarded David and Solomon, Moses and Jesus as prophets, but his revelation superseded the earlier ones. Importantly for the fate of Jerusalem, the Prophet stressed the coming of the Apocalypse that he called the Judgement, the Last Day or just the Hour, and this urgency inspired the dynamism of early Islam. 'The knowledge of it is only with God,' says the Koran, 'but what will make you realize the Hour is near?' All the Judaeo-Christian scriptures stressed that this could take place only in Jerusalem.

One night, his followers believed that, as he slept beside the Kaaba, Muhammad had a vision. The Archangel Gabriel awoke him and together they embarked on a Night Journey mounted on Buraq, a winged steed with a human face, to the unnamed 'Furthest

Sanctuary'. There Muhammad met his 'fathers' (Adam and Abraham) and his 'brothers' Moses, Joseph and Jesus, before ascending by a ladder to heaven. Unlike Jesus, he just called himself the Messenger or Apostle of God, claiming no magical powers. Indeed the Isra – Night Journey – and the Miraj – Ascension – were his only miraculous exploits. Jerusalem and the Temple are never actually mentioned but Muslims came to believe that the Furthest Sanctuary was the Temple Mount.

When his wife and uncle died, Muhammad was exposed to the disapproval of the richer families of Mecca, who depended on the Kaaba stone for their livelihoods. The Meccans tried to kill him. But he was contacted by a group from Yathrib, a date-palm oasis to the north founded by Jewish tribes but also the home of pagan artisans and farmers. They asked him to make peace between its feuding clans. He and his inner circle of believers departed on the Migration – Hijra – to Yathrib, which became Madinat un-Nabi, the city of the Prophet – Medina. There he fused his first devotees, the Emigrants, and new followers, the Helpers, and their Jewish allies, into a new community, the *umma*. It was 622, the beginning of the Islamic calendar.

Muhammad was a skilled conciliator of men and co-opter of ideas. Now in Medina, with its Jewish clans, he created the first mosque,* adopting the Jerusalem Temple as the first *qibla*, the direction of prayer. He prayed at Friday sundown – the Jewish Sabbath – fasted on the Day of Atonement, banned pork and practised circumcision. The oneness of Muhammad's God rejected the Christian Trinity but other rituals – the prostration on prayer mats – owed much to Christian monasteries; his minarets were perhaps inspired by the pillars of the stylites; the festival of Ramadan resembled Lent. Yet Islam was very much his own.

Muhammad created a small state with its own laws, but he faced resistance from Medina and his old home Mecca. His new state needed to defend itself and to conquer: jihad – struggle – was both internal mastery of self and holy war of conquest. The Koran promoted not only the destruction of infidels but also tolerance if

* The word 'mosque' derives from the Arabic *masjid*, which led to the Spanish *mezquita* and the French *mosquée*.

they submitted. This was relevant because the Jewish tribes resisted Muhammad's revelations and his control. Hence he changed the *qibla* to Mecca and rejected the Jewish way: God had destroyed the Jewish Temple because the Jews had sinned so 'they will not follow your *qibla*, Jerusalem'.

When he fought the Meccans, he could not afford disloyalty in Medina so he expelled the Jews and made an example of one Jewish clan: its 700 men were beheaded, its women and children enslaved. In 630, Muhammad finally took Mecca, spreading his monotheism across Arabia by conversion and force. Muhammad's followers became ever more militant as they strove to live righteously to prepare for the Last Judgement. Now, having conquered Arabia, they encountered the sinful empires beyond. The Prophet's early followers, the Emigrants and Helpers, formed his entourage – but he also welcomed former enemies and talented opportunists with equal enthusiasm. Meanwhile Muslim tradition recounts his personal life: he had many wives – Aisha, daughter of his ally Abu Bakr was his favourite – and took numerous concubines, including beautiful Jewesses and Christians; and he had children, most importantly a daughter named Fatima.

In 632 Muhammad, aged about sixty-two, died and was succeeded by his father-in-law, Abu Bakr, who was acclaimed Amir al-Muminin, Commander of the Believers.* Muhammad's realm tottered after his death, but Abu Bakr managed to pacify Arabia. Then he turned to the Byzantine and Persian empires, which the Muslims regarded as evanescent, sinful and corrupt. The Commander despatched contingents of warriors on camels to raid Iraq and Palestine.

* Muhammad's successors used the title Commander of the Believers. Later the Heads of State were known as *Khalifat Rasul Allah* – Successor to the Messenger of God – or caliph. Abu Bakr may have used this title but there is no evidence it was used again for another seventy years, until the reign of Abd al-Malik. Then it was applied retrospectively: the first four rulers became known as the Righteous Caliphs.

KHALID IBN WALID: SWORD OF ISLAM

Somewhere near Gaza, 'there was a battle between the Romans and the nomads of Muhammad', writes Thomas the Presbyter, a Christian who in 640 was the first independent historian to mention the Prophet.* 'The Romans fled.' The Emperor Heraclius, still in Syria, prepared to smash these Arab armies who in turn asked Abu Bakr for reinforcements. He called for his best general, Khalid ibn Walid, who was raiding Iraq. Riding six days across the waterless desert, Khalid arrived in Palestine just in time.

Khalid was one of the Meccan aristocrats who had fought against Muhammad but when he finally converted, the Prophet welcomed this dynamic commander and called him the Sword of Islam. Khalid was one of those swaggering generals who pay little attention to the orders of their political masters. The sequence of events is unclear but he joined up with the other Arab warlords, assumed command and then defeated a Byzantine detachment south-west of Jerusalem before storming Damascus. Far to the south in Mecca, Abu Bakr died and was succeeded by Omar, one of the Prophet's first converts and closest confidants. The new Commander of the Believers distrusted Khalid, who was amassing a fortune, and a legend, and recalled him to Mecca: 'Khalid,' he said, 'take your property out of our arse.'

Heraclius despatched an army to stop the Arabs. Omar appointed a new commander, Abu Ubayda, and Khalid rejoined the armies as his subordinate. After months of skirmishing, the Arabs finally lured the Byzantines to battle amidst the impenetrable gorges of the Yarmuk river between today's Jordan, Syria and Israeli Golan. 'This is one of God's battles,' Khalid told his men – and on 20 August 636, God delivered a duststorm that blinded the Christians who panicked and bolted helter-skelter

---

* The early history of Islam, including the surrender of Jerusalem, is mysterious and contested. The pre-eminent Islamic historians wrote one or two centuries later and far from Jerusalem or Mecca: Ibn Ishaq, Muhammad's first biographer, wrote in Baghdad, dying in 770; al-Tabari, al-Baladhuri and al-Yaqubi all lived in late-ninth-century Persia or Iraq.

over the cliffs of the Yarmuk. Khalid cut off their retreat and by the end of the battle, the Christians were so exhausted that the Arabs found them lying down in their cloaks, ripe for the slaughter. Even the emperor's brother was killed and Heraclius himself never recovered from this defeat, one of the decisive battles of history, that lost Syria and Palestine. Byzantine rule, weakened by the Persian war, seems to have collapsed like a house of cards and it is unclear whether the Arab conquest was more a triumphant series of raids. However intense the conquest really was, it was an astonishing achievement that these tiny contingents of Arabian cameleers, some of them as small as 1,000 men, had smashed the legions of the Eastern Rome. But the Commander of the Believers did not rest; he sent another army northwards to conquer Persia which also fell to the Arabs.

In Palestine, Jerusalem alone held out under Patriarch Sophronius, a Greek intellectual who praised her in his poetry as 'Zion, radiant Zion of the Universe'. He could scarcely believe the disaster that had befallen the Christians. Preaching in the Church of the Sepulchre, he denounced the sins of the Christians and the atrocities of the Arabs, whom he called Sarakenoi in Greek – Saracens: 'Whence come these wars against us? Whence multiply barbarian invasions? The slime of the godless Saracens has captured Bethlehem. The Saracens have risen up against us with a beastly impulse because of our sins. Let us correct ourselves.'

It was too late for that. The Arabs converged on the city which they called Ilya (Aelia, the Roman name). The first of their commanders to besiege Jerusalem was Amr ibn al-As, who after Khaled was their best general and another irrepressibly larger-than-life adventurer from the Meccan nobility. Amr, like the other Arab leaders, knew the area very well: he even owned land nearby and had visited Jerusalem in his youth. But this was not just a quest for booty.

'The Hour has drawn nigh,' says the Koran. The early Muslim Believers' militant fanaticism was stoked by their belief in the Last Judgement. The Koran did not state this specifically but they knew from the Jewish-Christian prophets that it had to take place in Jerusalem. If the Hour was upon them, they needed Jerusalem.

Khaled and the other generals joined Amr around the walls but the Arab armies were probably too small to storm the city and there does not seem to have been much fighting. Sophronius simply refused to surrender without a guarantee of tolerance from the Commander of the Believers himself. Amr suggested solving this problem by passing off Khaled as the Commander but he was recognized so Omar was summoned from Mecca.

The Commander inspected the rest of the Arab armies at Jabiya in the Golan and Jerusalemites probably met him there to negotiate their surrender. The Monophysite Christians, who were the majority in Palestine, hated the Byzantines and it seems the early Moslem Believers were happy to allow freedom of worship to their fellow monotheists.* Following the Koran, Omar offered Jerusalem a Covenant – *dhimma* – of Surrender that promised religious tolerance to the Christians in return for payment of the *jizya* tax of submission. Once this was agreed, Omar set out for Jerusalem, a giant in ragged, patched robes riding a mule, with just one servant.

OMAR THE JUST: TEMPLE REGAINED

When he saw Jerusalem from Mount Scopus, Omar ordered his muezzin to give the call to prayer. After praying, he donned the white robes of the pilgrim, mounted a white camel and rode down to meet Sophronius. The Byzantine hierarchs awaited the conqueror, their bejewelled robes contrasting with his puritanical simplicity. Omar, the hulking Commander of the Believers, a wrestler in his youth, was an implacable ascetic who always carried a whip. It was said that when Muhammad entered a room, women and children would continue to laugh and chat, but when they saw Omar they

* The early Muslims seem to have called themselves 'Believers' – the word appears 1,000 times in the Koran while 'Muslim' appears about 75 times – and as we will see in Jerusalem, they were certainly not yet hostile to their fellow monotheists, Christians or Jews. Professor Fred M. Donner, an authority on early Islam, takes this further: 'There is no reason to believe', he writes, 'that the Believers viewed themselves as a new or separate religious confession. Some of the early Believers were Christians or Jews.'

fell silent. It was he who started to collate the Koran, created the Muslim calendar and much Islamic law. He enforced far more severe rules on women than the Prophet himself. When his own son got drunk, Omar had him scourged with eighty lashes which killed him.

Sophronius presented Omar with the keys of the Holy City. When the patriarch saw Omar and his ragged hordes of Arab cameleers and horsemen, he muttered that this was 'the abomination of desolation'. Most of them were tribesman from the Hejaz or the Yemen; they travelled light and fast, draped in turbans and cloaks, living on *ilhiz* (ground camel hair mixed with blood and then cooked). A far cry from the heavily armoured Persian and Byzantine cataphract cavalry, only the commanders wore chainmail or helmets. The rest 'rode shaggy stumpy horses, their swords highly polished but covered in a shabby cloth scabbard'. They carried bows and spears that were bound with camel sinews, and red cowhide shields resembling 'a thick red loaf of bread'. They cherished their broadswords, their *sayf*, gave them names and sang poems about them.

Priding themselves on their uncouthness, they wore 'four locks of hair' stuck up like 'the horns of a goat'. When they encountered rich carpets, they rode on to them and cut them up to make spear coverings, enjoying the booty – human and material – like any other conquerors. 'Suddenly, I sensed the presence of a human form hidden under some covers,' wrote one of them. 'I tear them away and what do I find? A woman like a gazelle, radiant like the sun. I took her and her clothes and surrendered the latter as booty but put in a request that the girl should be alotted to me. I took her as a concubine.'* The Arab armies had no technical advantages, but they were fanatically motivated.

Sophronius, say the traditional Muslim sources, dating from much later, escorted the Saracen Commander to the Holy Sepulchre, hoping his visitor would admire or even embrace the perfect sanctity of Christianity. When Omar's muezzin called his soldiers

---

* There is no contemporary account of the fall of Jerusalem but the Arab historians describe the armies that simultaneously invaded Persia and this is based on those sources.

to prayer, Sophronius invited the Commander to pray there, but he is said to have refused, warning that this would make it a place of Islamic worship. Omar knew that Muhammad had revered David and Solomon. 'Take me to the sanctuary of David,' he ordered Sophronius. He and his warriors entered the Temple Mount, probably through the Prophets' Gate in the south, and found it contaminated by 'a dungheap which the Christians had put there to offend the Jews.'

Omar asked to be shown the Holy of Holies. A Jewish convert, Kaab al-Ahbar, known as the Rabbi, replied that, if the Commander preserved 'the wall' (perhaps referring to the last Herodian remains, including the Western Wall), 'I will reveal to him where are the ruins of the Temple.' Kaab showed Omar the foundation-stone of the Temple, the rock which the Arabs called the Sakhra.

Aided by his troops, Omar began to clear the debris to create somewhere to pray. Kaab suggested he place this north of the foundation-stone 'so you will make two qiblas, that of Moses and that of Muhammad.' 'You still lean towards the Jews,' Omar supposedly told Kaab, placing his first prayer house south of the rock, roughly where al-Aqsa Mosque stands today, so that it clearly faced Mecca. Omar had followed Muhammad's wish to reach past Christianity to restore and co-opt this place of ancient holiness, to make the Muslims the legitimate heirs of Jewish sanctity and outflank the Christians.

The stories of Omar in Jerusalem date from over a century later when Islam had formalized its rituals in ways that were very distinct from those of Christianity and Judaism. Yet the story of Kaab and other Jews, which later formed the Islamic literary tradition of *Israiliyyat*, much of it about Jerusalem's greatness, proves that many Jews and probably Christians joined Islam. We will never know exactly what happened in those early decades but the relaxed arrangements in Jerusalem and elsewhere suggest that there may have been a surprising amount of mingling and sharing amongst the Peoples of the Book.*

---

* Jews and most Christians would not have had a problem with the earliest versions of the Muslim statement of faith – the *shahada* – which read 'There is no God but God', as it may not have been until 685 that they added 'Muhammad is the apostle of

The Muslim conquerors were initially happy to share shrines with the Christians. In Damascus, they shared the Church of St John for many years and the Umayyad Mosque there still contains the tomb of St John the Baptist. In Jerusalem, there are also accounts of them sharing churches. The Cathisma Church outside the city was actually equipped with a Muslim prayer-niche. Contrary to the Omar legend, it seems that the early Muslims first prayed in or beside the Church of the Holy Sepulchre before arrangements could be made on the Temple Mount.

The Jews too welcomed the Arabs after centuries of Byzantine repression. It is said that Jews, as well as Christians, rode in the Muslim armies. Omar's interest in the Temple Mount understandably excited Jewish hopes, because the Commander of the Believers not only invited the Jews to maintain the Temple Mount but also allowed them to pray there with the Muslims. A well-informed Armenian bishop, Sebeos, who wrote thirty years later, claims that 'the Jews planned to build the Temple of Solomon and, locating the Holy of Holies, they built (the Temple) without a pedestal' – and adds that Omar's first governor of Jerusalem was Jewish. Omar certainly invited the leader of Tiberias' Jewish community, the Gaon, and seventy Jewish families to return to Jerusalem where they settled in the area south of the Temple Mount.*

God'. Jewish and Muslim names for Jerusalem overlap: Muhammad called Palestine 'The Holy Land' in the Judaeo-Christian tradition. The Jews called the Temple *Beyt ha-Miqdash* (the Holy House) which the Muslims adapted: they called the city herself *Bayt al-Maqdis*. The Jews called the Temple Mount *Har ha-Beyt* (the Mount of the Holy House); Muslims initially called it *Masjid Bayt al-Maqdis*, the Mosque of the Holy House, and later also *Haram al-Sharif*, the Noble Sanctuary. Ultimately Muslims had seventeen names for Jerusalem; Jews claimed seventy, and both agreed 'a multiplicity of names is a sign of greatness'.

* The traditional text of the Covenant or Pact of Omar with the Christians claims Omar agreed to ban the Jews from Jerusalem. This is Christian wishful thinking or a later forgery because we know that Omar welcomed the Jews back in Jerusalem, that he and the early caliphs allowed Jewish worship on the Temple Mount and that the Jews did not leave again as along as Islam held sway. The Armenians were already a large Christian community in Jerusalem with their own bishop (later patriarch). They established close relations with the Muslims and received their own Covenant. For the next millennium and a half, Christians and Jews were *dhimmi*, people of the Covenant, tolerated but inferior, sometimes left to themselves, sometimes viciously persecuted.

Jerusalem was still impoverished and plague-ridden after the Persian depredations and it remained overwhelmingly Christian for many years. Omar also settled Arabs here, especially the more sophisticated Quraysh who liked Palestine and Syria, which they called Bilad al-Shams. Some of the Prophet's closest followers, known as the Companions, came to Jerusalem and were buried in the first Muslim cemetery just outside the Golden Gate, ready for the Day of Judgement. Two of the famous Jerusalem Families, who play such a prominent role in this story right into the twenty-first century, trace their descent from these earliest Arab grandees.*

In Jerusalem, Omar was accompanied not only by his generals Khalid and Amr but also by a pleasure-loving but competent young man who could not have been more different from the whip-wielding Commander. Muawiya ibn Abi Sufyan was a son of Abu Sufyan, the Meccan aristocrat who had led the opposition to Muhammad. Muawiya's mother ate the liver of the Prophet's uncle Hamza after the Battle of Uhuh. When Mecca surrendered to Islam, Muhammad appointed Muawiya as his secretary and married his sister. After Muhammad's death, Omar appointed Muawiya as governor of Syria. The Commander gave him a backhanded compliment: Muawiya, he said, was the 'Caesar of the Arabs'.

---

* Omar ordered the retirement of Khaled, victor of Yarmuk, after hearing about a wine-soaked bathhouse orgy in which a poet sang of the general's heroics. Khaled died of plague though today's Khalidi family claim descent from him. One of Muhammad's early supporters had been a woman named Nusaybah who lost two sons and a leg fighting for the Prophet. Now Nusaybah's brother, Ubadah ibn al-Samit, arrived with Omar, who is said to have appointed him as a judge in Jerusalem, and custodian of the Holy Sepulchre and of the Rock. His descendants, the Nusseibeh family, are still Custodians of the Holy Sepulchre in 2010 (see the Epilogue).

18

THE UMAYYADS: THE TEMPLE RESTORED

660–750

MUAWIYA: ARAB CAESAR

Muawiya ruled Jerusalem for forty years, first as governor of Syria and then as the monarch of the vast Arab empire which was expanding eastwards and westwards with astounding speed. But in the midst of all of this success, a civil war about the succession almost destroyed Islam and it created a schism that still divides it today.

In 644, Omar was assassinated and his successor was Othman, a cousin of Muawiya. After more than ten years, Othman was hated for his nepotism. When he too was assassinated, the Prophet's first cousin, Ali, who was also married to his daughter Fatima, was chosen as Commander of the Believers. Muawiya demanded that Ali punish the assassins – but the new Commander refused. Muawiya feared that he would lose his domain in Syria. He won the ensuing civil war, Ali was killed in Iraq, and there ended the reign of the last of the so-called Righteous Caliphs.

In July 661, the grandees of the Arab empire gathered on the Temple Mount in Jerusalem to acclaim Muawiya as Commander of the Believers and pledge allegiance in the traditional Arab way – the *bayah*.* Afterwards the new Commander visited the Holy Sepulchre and the Virgin Mary's Tomb, not as a pilgrim but to show the continuity of religions and his imperial role as protector of the holy places. He ruled from Damascus, but he adored Jerusalem which he advertised on his coins as 'Iliya Filastin' – Aelia Palestina.

* This was a handshake which meant a contract to render obedience: the word comes from *baa* – to sell.

He was tempted to make her his capital and it is likely that he often resided here in one of the luxurious palaces just south of the Temple which he may have built. Muawiya borrowed Jewish traditions about the Temple Mount to declare that Jerusalem was the 'land of ingathering and resurrection on Judgement Day', and he added, 'The area between the two walls of this mosque are dearer to God than the rest of the earth.'

Christian writers hailed his reign as just, peaceful and tolerant; Jews called him a 'lover of Israel'. His armies contained Christians; indeed he cemented his alliance with Christian Arab tribes by marrying Maysun, the daughter of their sheikh, and she was allowed to remain Christian. Moreover, he ruled through Mansur ibn Sanjun (the Arab for Sergius), a Christian bureaucrat inherited from Heraclius. Muawiya had grown up beside the Jews of Arabia, and it is said that when he was visited by one of their delegations he first asked them if they could cook the delicious *haris* dish which he had so savoured back home. Muawiya settled more Jews in Jerusalem, permitting them to pray there on the site of the Holy of Holies; the traces of a menorah on the Temple Mount, dating from the seventh century, may be evidence of this.

Muawiya was probably the real creator of today's Islamic Temple Mount. It was he who actually built the first mosque there, flattening the rock of the old Antonia Fortress, extending the esplanade and adding an open-sided hexagon, the Dome of the Chain: no one knows what it was for but since it is in the precise middle of the Temple Mount, it may celebrate the centre of the world. Muawiya, writes a contemporary, 'hews Mount Moriah and makes it straight and builds a mosque there on the holy rock'. When a Gallic bishop named Arculf visited Jerusalem, he saw that 'in the former place where the Temple stood, the Saracens now frequent an oblong house of prayer pieced together with upright planks and large beams over some ruined remains, said to hold 3,000 people.' It was scarcely yet recognizable as a mosque but it probably stood where al-Aqsa stands today.*

---

* The modern mosque contains both a *mihrab*, a prayer-niche facing Mecca, and a *minbar*, the pulpit. Muawiya's prayer-hall had the *mihrab* but probably not yet a *minbar* because early Islam was too egalitarian to have a pulpit. However, according

Muawiya personified *hilm*, the wisdom and patience of the Arab sheikh: 'I apply not my sword when my lash suffices nor my lash when my tongue suffices. And even if but one hair is binding me to my fellow men, I don't let it break. When they pull, I loosen, if they loosen I pull.' This is almost a definition of statesmanship and Muawiya, the creator of Arab monarchy and the first of the Umayyad dynasty, is a much-neglected paragon of how absolute power does not have to corrupt absolutely. He expanded his realm into eastern Persia, Central Asia and north Africa and he took Cyprus and Rhodes, making the Arabs a maritime power with his new navy. He launched annual assaults on Constantinople, and on one occasion besieged it by land and sea for three years.

Yet Muawiya never lost the ability to laugh at himself, a quality that is rare amongst politicians, let alone conquerors. He became very fat (perhaps for this reason he became the first Arab monarch to recline on a throne instead of sitting on cushions) and teased another fat old grandee: 'I'd like a slavegirl with legs like yours.'

'And a bottom like yours, Commander of the Believers,' retorted the old man.

'Fair enough,' laughed Muawiya. 'If you start something, you have to take the consequences.' He never lost his pride in his legendary sexual prowess but even there he could take some mockery: he was cavorting with a Khurasani girl in his harem when he was presented with another whom he took without further ado. When she had left, he turned back to the Khurasani girl, proud of his leonine performance: 'How do you say "lion" in Persian?' he asked her.

'*Kaftar*,' she replied.

'I'm a *kaftar*, the Commander boasted to his courtiers until someone asked him if he knew what a *kaftar* was.

'A lion?'

'No, a lame hyena!'

'Well done,' Muawiya chuckled, 'that Khurasani girl knew how to get her own back.'

to the historian Ibn Khaldun, Muawiya's imperial reign changed that. His Egyptian governor, the general Amr, invented the *minbar* in his mosque in Egypt and Muawiya started to use it to give the Friday sermon, adding a latticed enclosure around it to protect him from assassins.

When he died in his eighties, his heir Yazid, a debauchee always accompanied by a pet monkey, was acclaimed Commander on the Temple Mount but soon faced two rebellions in Arabia and Iraq, the start of Islam's second civil war. His enemies taunted him: 'Yazid of liquors, Yazid of whoring, Yazid of dogs, Yazid of monkeys, Yazid of wine-swoons.'

The Prophet's grandson Hussein rebelled to avenge his father Ali's death, but was beheaded at Karbala in Iraq, his martyrdom creating Islam's great schism between the majority of Sunni and the Shia, 'the party of Ali'.* But in 683 Yazid died young, at which the Syrian armies summoned his shrewd old kinsman Marwan to become the Commander. When Marwan died in April 685, his son Abd al-Malik was acclaimed as Commander in Damascus and Jerusalem. But his empire was fragile: Mecca, Iraq and Persia were controlled by rebels. Yet it was Abd al-Malik who gave Islamic Jerusalem the jewel in her crown.

ABD AL-MALIK: THE DOME OF THE ROCK

Abd al-Malik did not suffer fools gladly. When a sycophant complimented him, he snapped, 'Don't flatter me. I know myself better than you.' According to the image on his rare coins, he was severe, thin and hook-nosed. His hair was curly, shoulder length, and he wore long brocaded robes with a sword at his belt, but his critics later claimed that he had big eyes, eyebrows grown together, a protruding nose, a cleft lip and halitosis so noxious that he was nicknamed the 'fly-killer'. Yet here was another royal lover who liked to muse on eroticism: 'He who wishes to take a slave girl for pleasure, let him take a Berber; to produce a child, take a Persian; as a domestic servant, a Byzantine.' Abd al-Malik

* Iran remains a Shiite theocracy. Shiites are a majority in Iraq and a large minority in Lebanon. Hussein's brother Hasan bin Ali remained in retirement, though he too may have been murdered. His direct descendants include today's royal dynasties of Morocco's Alouite and of Jordan's Hashemite kings. The Twelve Shiite Imams, the Fatimid dynasty, the Aga Khans and the Jerusalemite Family the Husseinis all trace their roots back to Hussein. Their descendants are often known as the Nobility, the Ashraf (the singular is Sherif usually addressed as *Sayyid*).

grew up in a rough school. At sixteen, he was commanding an army against the Byzantines; he witnessed the murder of his cousin, Commander of the Believers Othman; and matured into a sacred monarch never afraid to get his hands dirty. He started by reconquering Iraq and Iran. When he captured a leading rebel, he publicly tortured him in front of the Damascene crowds, placed a silver collar around his neck and led him around like a dog before 'straddling his chest, butchering him and tossing his head out to his supporters'.

Mecca remained for the moment beyond his control, but he possessed Jerusalem, which he revered as much as Muawiya had. Abd al-Malik envisaged the creation of a united Islamic empire out of a second civil war, with Bilad al-Shams – Syria–Palestine – as its heart: he planned a highway between Jerusalem and Damascus.* Muawiya had planned to build over the Rock: now Abd al-Malik assigned seven years' worth of his Egyptian revenues to create the Dome of the Rock.

The plan was exquisitely simple: a dome, 65 feet in diameter supported by a drum, all resting on octagonal walls. The Dome's beauty, power and simplicity are equalled by its mystery: we do not know exactly why Abd al-Malik built it – he never said. It is not actually a mosque but a shrine. Its octagonal shape resembles a Christian martyrium, indeed its dome echoes those of the Holy Sepulchre and Hagia Sofia in Constantinople yet its circular walkways designed for circumambulation recall the Kaaba of Mecca.

The Rock was the site of Adam's paradise, Abraham's altar, the place where David and Solomon planned their Temple later visited by Muhammad on his Night Journey. Abd al-Malik was rebuilding the Jewish Temple for the true revelation of God, Islam.

The building has no central axis but is encircled thrice – first by

* In 1902, one of Abd al-Malik's milestones was found east of Jerusalem with an inscription that defined the way the caliph saw his power in relation to that of God: 'There is no God but God alone. Muhammad is the messenger of God ... Abd al-Malik, the Commander of the Faithful and servant of God, had ordered the repair of this road and construction of this milestone. From Ilya [Jerusalem] to here is seven miles ...'

the outside walls, next by the octagonal arcade and then right under the dome, bathed in sunlight, the arcade around the Rock itself: this declared that this place was the centre of the world. The dome itself was heaven, the link to God in human architecture. The golden dome and the lush decorations and gleaming white marble declared this was the new Eden, and the place for the Last Judgement when Abd al-Malik and his Umayyad dynasty, would surrender their kingdom to God at the Hour of the Last Days. Its wealth of images – jewels, trees, fruit, flowers and crowns – make it a joyful building even for non-Muslims – its imagery combined the sensuality of Eden with the majesty of David and Solomon.

The Dome's message was therefore also imperial: since he had not regained Mecca from his rebels, he was declaring the grandeur and permanence of his dynasty to the Islamic world – and possibly, if he had not retaken the Kaaba, he might have made this his new Mecca. The gold dome projected his glory as an Islamic emperor. But it had a wider audience: just as Justinian's Hagia Sofia in Constantinople had surpassed Solomon, so Abd al-Malik was surpassing Justinian, and Constantine the Great too, a rebuke of the Christian claim to be the new Israel. Ironically, the mosaics were probably the work of Byzantine craftsmen, lent to the Commander by Justinian II during a rare peace between the empires.

After it was finished in 691/2, Jerusalem was never the same again: Abd al-Malik's astonishing vision seized the skyline of Jerusalem for Islam by building on the mountain, disdained by the Byzantines, which ruled the city. Physically the Dome dominated Jerusalem and overshadowed the Church of the Holy Sepulchre – and that was Abd al-Malik's purpose, believed later Jerusalemites such as the writer al-Muqaddasi. It worked: henceforth right up into the twenty-first century, the Muslims mocked the Church of the Holy Sepulchre – the *Kayamah* in Arabic – calling it the *Kumamah* – the Dungheap. The Dome both complemented and vanquished the rival yet related claims of Jews and Christians, so Abd al-Malik confronted both with the superior novelty of Islam. Circling the building, he placed 800 feet of inscriptions that denounce the idea of the divinity of Jesus with a directness that hints at the close relationship between the two faiths of monotheists: they shared much but not the Trinity. The inscriptions are fascinating because they are our first glimpse at the text of the Koran which Abd al-Malik was having collated into its final form.

The Jews were less important imperially but more important theologically. The Dome was maintained by 300 black slaves assisted by twenty Jews and ten Christians. The Jews could not help but see the Dome with hope: was it their new Temple? They were still allowed to pray there and the Umayyads created an Islamic version of the Temple rituals of purification, anointment and circumambulation of the stone.*

The Dome has a power beyond all this: it ranks as one of the most timeless masterpieces of architectural art; its radiance is the cynosure of all eyes wherever one stands in Jerusalem. It shimmers like a mystical palace rising out of the airy and serene space of the esplanade which immediately became an enormous open-air mosque, sanctifying all the space around it. The Temple Mount became instantly – and still remains – a place for recreation and relaxation. Indeed the Dome created an earthly paradise that combined the tranquillity and sensuality of this world with the sanctity of the hereafter, and that was its genius. Even in its earliest years, there was, wrote Ibn Asakir, no greater pleasure than 'eating a banana in the shade of the Dome of the Rock'. It ranks with the Temples of Solomon and Herod as one of the most successful

* 'O People of the Book do not go beyond the bounds of your religion and do not speak anything about God except the truth ' read the inscriptions around the Dome. 'Indeed the Messiah Jesus son of Mary was only a messenger of God so believe in God and in his messengers and do not say "three" ... It is not for God to take a son.' This seems more an attack on Trinitarianism than on Christianity as a whole. As for the Jews, the bi-weekly service there referred strongly to the Jewish Temple: 'On every Tuesday and Thursday, they order saffron and they prepare with musk, ambergris and sandalwood perfumed with rosewater. Then the servants (who were Jews and Christians) eat and enter the bath to purify themselves. They go to the wardrobe and come out with new red and blue clothes and bands and belts. Then they go to the Stone and anoint.' As the scholar Andreas Kaplony writes, this was 'a Muslim service, the Temple service as the Muslims think it should be. To cut a long story short, this is the Former Temple rebuilt, the Koran is the new Torah and the Muslims are the true people of Israel.'

sacred-imperial edifices ever built and, in the twenty-first century, it has become the ultimate secular touristic symbol, the shrine of resurgent Islam and the totem of Palestinian nationalism: it still defines Jerusalem today.

Soon after the Dome was built, Abd al-Malik's armies recaptured Mecca and resumed the jihad to spread God's kingdom against the Byzantines. He expanded this colossal empire westward across northern Africa and eastward into Sind (today's Pakistan). But within his realm, he needed to unify the House of Islam as a single Muslim religion with an emphasis on Muhammad, expressed in the double *shahada* that now appeared on many inscriptions: 'There is no God but God, and Muhammad is the apostle of God.' The Prophet's sayings – *hadith* – were collected and Abd al-Malik's full edition of the Koran became the invincible source of legitimacy and holiness. Rituals became more rigidly defined; graven images banned – he stopped minting coins bearing his own image. Abd al-Malik now called himself Khalifat Allah, God's Deputy, and henceforth Islamic rulers became the caliphs. The official versions of Muhammad's earliest biography and the Muslim Conquest excluded the Christians and Jews from Islam. The administration was Arabized. Like Constantine, Josiah and St Paul rolled into one, Abd al-Malik believed in a universal empire of one monarch, one God, and it was he more than anyone who oversaw the evolution of Muhammad's community into today's Islam.

WALID: APOCALYPSE AND LUXURY

Jerusalem had a shrine in the Dome but not an imperial mosque, so Abd al-Malik and his son Walid, who succeeded him, next built the Further Mosque, al-Aqsa, Jerusalem's mosque for ordinary Friday prayers, at the southern boundary of the Temple Mount. The caliphs saw the Temple Mount as the centrepiece of Jerusalem just as Herod had. For the first time since AD 70, they built a new Great Bridge across the valley for pilgrims to enter the Temple Mount from the west, over Wilson's Arch, today's Gate of the Chain. To enter from the south, they created the domed Double Gates, which matched the Golden Gate in style and beauty.*

This was a vibrant moment in Jerusalem. In the space of a few years, the caliphs had turned the Temple Mount into a holy Islamic shrine and Jerusalem into an imperial-Umayyad city and this once again unleashed the infectious competition for shrines and stories that characterizes Jerusalem even today. The Christians had commandeered many of the Jewish myths which were gradually placed at their central shrine, the Sepulchre. But now the raising of the Dome and al-Aqsa reinvigorated the old myths all over again: a footprint on the Rock that had once been shown to Christian pilgrims as the mark of Jesus became the footprint of Muhammad. The Umayyads covered the Temple Mount with new domes all linked to Biblical traditions from Adam and Abraham via David and Solomon to Jesus. Their scenario of the Last Judgement took place on the Temple Mount when the Kaaba would come to Jerusalem.†
And it was not just the Temple Mount: the Muslims came to revere anything associated with David, so now they regarded the Citadel, which the Christians called David's Tower, as David's Mihrab (prayer-niche): they were not the last to mistake Herod's grandeur for David's. The Umayyads did not just build for God but also for themselves.

* As always in Jerusalem, the builders borrowed from elsewhere, so Aqsa's wooden beams were taken from a Christian site, still marked in Greek with the name of a sixth-century Patriarch (now in the Rockefeller and Haram Museums). The Double and Triple Gates to the south, matching the Golden Gate to the east, all of them now closed, are the most beautiful in Jerusalem, built using the stones of earlier Herodian and Roman buildings. It was there that the wall contains the upside-down inscription to Emperor Antoninus Pius from his equestrian statue on the Temple Mount.

† 'Every soul shall taste death and you will be paid in full only on the Day of Resurrection,' says the Koran. The Muslims created a geography of Apocalypse around Jerusalem. The forces of evil perish at the Golden Gate. The Mahdi – the Chosen – dies when the Ark of the Covenant is placed before him. At the sight of the Ark, the Jews convert to Islam. The Kaaba of Mecca comes to Jerusalem with all those who ever made the pilgrimage to Mecca. Heaven descends on the Temple Mount with Hell in the Valley of Hinnom. The people assemble outside the Golden Gate on the Plain – al-Sahira. Israfil the Archangel of Death (one of the Dome's gates is named after him) blows his trumpet: the dead (especially those buried close to the Golden Gate) are resurrected and pass through the Gate, the portal to the End of Days (with its two little domed Gates of Mercy or that of Repentance), to be judged in the Dome of the Chain where the scales of justice hang.

These caliphs were pleasure-loving and cultured: this was the apogee of their Arab empire – even Spain was now theirs – and though Damascus was their capital, they spent much time in Jerusalem. Just south of the Temple Mount, Walid I and his son built a complex of palaces, unknown until they were uncovered in the late 1960s: they stood three or four storeys high around cool courtyards and the caliphs even had a special royal entrance to al-Aqsa via a rooftop bridge. The remains reveal nothing more than the size of the palaces, but the survival of their desert palaces reveal how opulently they would have lived here.

The most luxurious desert palace or *qasr* survives at Amra, in today's Jordan, where the caliphs relaxed in private quarters and bathhouses decorated with mosaic floors and graphic paintings depicting hunting scenes, nude or half-dressed women, athletes, cupids, satyrs and a bear playing the lute. Walid I appears in the colourful fresco of Six Kings showing monarchs defeated by the Umayyads such as the emperors of Constantinople and China. These decadent, Hellenistic paintings seem distinctly unIslamic, but, like the Herods, they perhaps lived differently in public. Walid I ended the sharing arrangement with the Christians in Damascus, creating the glorious Umayyad Mosque there, and the language of government now changed from Greek to Arabic. Yet Jerusalem remained overwhelmingly Christian. Muslims and Christians mixed freely: both celebrated the feast of the Dedication of the Holy Sepulchre in September, attracting 'a great crowd to Jerusalem', the streets filling with 'camels and horses, asses and oxen'. Christian pilgrims, now more Armenian and Georgian than Greek, scarcely noticed the Muslim sites, while Jews hardly mention the Christians. Henceforth visitors tended to be increasingly blinkered and uncurious pilgrims who saw no more than their own religion.

In 715, Walid's brother, Suleiman, received the acclamation on the Temple Mount: 'Never had one seen such richness that greeted the new Caliph. Seated under one of the domes that ornament the platform, he held an audience' on a sea of carpets and cushions with his treasury piled around him to pay his soldiers. Suleiman, who made the last full-scale Arab assault on Constantinople (and almost captured it), 'conceived the plan of living in Jerusalem and making it his capital and bringing together there great wealth and a considerable population'. He founded the city of Ramla as an administrative centre, but died before he could move to Jerusalem.

Jews, many of them from Iran and Iraq, settled in the Holy City, living together south of the Temple Mount, retaining the privilege of praying on (and maintaining) the Temple Mount. But in about 720, after almost a century of freedom to pray there, the new Caliph Omar II, who was, unusually in this decadent dynasty, an ascetic stickler for Islamic orthodoxy, banned Jewish worship – and this prohibition would stand for the rest of Islamic rule. Instead the Jews started to pray around the four walls of the Temple Mount and in a subterranean synagogue called ha-Meara – the Cave – at Warren's Gate, almost beneath the Temple Mount near the Holy of Holies.

While the Umayyad caliphs enjoyed their Hellenistic palaces and dancing girls, the empire reached its limits for the first time. Islamic forces in Spain were already probing France, but in 732, a Frankish nobleman, Charles, Mayor of the Palace of the Merovingian kings, defeated a Muslim raid at Tours. Hailed as a Maccabee, he became Charles Martel – the Hammer.

'Dynasties,' writes the Arab historian Ibn Khaldun, 'have a natural lifespan like individuals' and now the decadent, worldly Umayyads had reached the end of theirs. In a village east of the Jordan lived the descendants of Abbas, the Prophet's uncle who had long secretly opposed the hedonistic rule of the Umayyads, who were totally unrelated to Muhammad. 'Woe to the House of Umayya,' declared their leader Abu al-Abbas, 'they preferred the ephemeral to the eternal, crime obsessed them; they possessed forbidden women.' The discontent spread fast. Even the tribes of the loyal Syrian heartland rebelled – even Jerusalem. The last caliph had to storm the city and raze her walls. An earthquake shook Jerusalem damaging al-Aqsa and the palaces as if God was angry with the Umayyads. Christians and Jews dreamed that this was the Apocalypse. But so did Muslims, and the real threat to the Umayyads came from far away to the east.

In 748, in Khorasan, today's eastern Iran and Afghanistan, a charismatic mystic named Abu Muslim demanded a sterner Islam and the rule by one of Muhammad's descendants. The new Muslims of the borderlands joined his puritanical army, which dressed all in black and marched under black banners and hailed the coming of the imam, precursor of the Mahdi,* to redeem Islam. Abu Muslim led his triumphant armies westwards but he had not yet decided whether to back the family of Ali or the family of Abbas – and there were still many Umayyad princes around too. But it was Abu al-Abbas who defeated the last Umayyad ruler and solved this problem in a way that earned him his nickname.

* An imam is the leader of a mosque or community but in Shia, imams can be spiritual leaders, chosen by God and blessed with infallibility. The Twelver Shiites of Iran believe in the first twelve imams descended from Muhammad's son-in-law Ali and his daughter Fatima and that the Twelfth Imam was 'occulted' – hidden by God – and will return as the Madhi, the Chosen messianic redeemer of Judgement Day. The Islamic Republic of Iran was founded by Ayatollah Khomeini on this millenarian expectation: the clergy rule only until the Imam's return.

19

THE ABBASIDS: DISTANT MASTERS

750–969

CALIPH SAFFAH: THE SLAUGHTERER

Abu al-Abbas declared himself caliph and invited the Umayyads to a banquet to declare his peaceful intentions. In the midst of the feast, the waiters drew out clubs and swords and butchered the entire family, tossing the bodies into the lamb stew. The Slaughterer himself died soon afterwards but his brother Mansur, the Victorious, systematically murdered the Alid family and then liquidated the overmighty Abu Muslim too. His perfumier, Jamra, later told how Mansur kept the keys of a secret storeroom which was to be opened only on his death. There his son later found a vaulted chamber filled with the bodies, each meticulously labelled, of the family of Ali from old men to infants, whom Mansur had killed, all preserved in the hot dry air.

Wiry with brown, weather-beaten skin and saffron-dyed hair, Mansur was the real father of the Abbasid dynasty that ruled for many centuries, but his power-base was to the east: he moved his capital to his new Round City, Baghdad.

Soon after seizing power, Mansur visited Jerusalem. There he repaired the damaged Aqsa, but paid for this work by melting the gold and silver doors of the Dome of the Rock given by Abd al-Malik. Mansur's successors no longer bothered to visit. Just as the city diminished in the Islamic world,* a western emperor revived the Christian fascination with Jerusalem.

---

* Jerusalem's importance lessened as Mecca's grew: if Jerusalem had perhaps at one point approached Mecca and Medina as part of the *haj* – 'You shall only set out for the three mosques Mecca, Medina, and al-Aqsa,' declared one of the *hadith* of al-Khidri – now under the Abbasids, Jerusalem was reduced to a *ziyara*, a pious visit.

THE EMPEROR AND THE CALIPH:
CHARLEMAGNE AND HAROUN AL-RASHID

On Christmas Day 800, Charles the Great, known as Charlemagne, the King of the Franks, who ruled most of modern France, Germany and Italy, was crowned emperor of the Romans by the pope in Rome. This ceremony marked the new confidence of the popes and their western Latin-based Christianity that would become Catholicism – and their growing differences with the Greek-speaking Orthodox of Constantinople. Charlemagne was a merciless warrior-king hacking his way to ever-greater power, yet he was also fascinated with history, and as devout as he was ambitious: he saw himself as the heir to the missions of Constantine and Justinian to become the universal holy Roman emperor, and as a latter-day King David – and both these aspirations led to the Holy City. So earlier on the same Christmas Day, it was said that a delegation sent by the Patriarch of Jerusalem had presented him with the keys of the Holy Sepulchre. Rome and Jerusalem in one day was no mean feat.

This was not a bid for possession because the patriarch had the blessing of Jerusalem's ruler, Caliph Haroun al-Rashid whose reign, recounted in the *Thousand and One Nights*, was the apogee of the Abbasid empire. Charlemagne and the caliph had been exchanging envoys for three years: Haroun was probably keen to play off the Franks against his enemies in Constantinople and Jerusalem's Christians needed Charlemagne's help.

The caliph sent Charlemagne an elephant and an astrolabe water clock, a sophisticated device that showed off Islamic superiority – and alarmed some of the primitive Christians as a contraption of diabolical sorcery. The two emperors did not sign a formal treaty, but Christian property in Jerusalem was listed and protected, while Charlemagne paid the entire poll tax for the city's Christians – 850 dinars. In return Haroun allowed him to create a Christian quarter around the Holy Sepulchre, with a convent, library and pilgrims' hostel, staffed by 150 monks and seventeen nuns. 'The Christians and pagans', noted one pilgrim, 'have this kind of peace between them.' This generosity generated the story that Charlemagne had covertly visited Jerusalem, making him the heir of Heraclius, and playing into the mystical legend of the Last Emperor whose reign would herald the End Days. This was widely believed, particularly in the age of the Crusades, but Charlemagne never did visit Jerusalem.

When Haroun died, the civil war between his sons was won by Maamun. The new caliph was an enthusiastic student of science, founding the famous literary-scientific academy, the House of Wisdom, commissioning a world map and ordering his sages to calculate the circumference of the globe.* In 831, arriving in Syria to organize a campaign against Constantinople, Maamun probably visited Jerusalem, where he built new gates on the Temple Mount, but he erased Abd al-Malik's name in the Dome to emphasize the superiority of the Abbasids and had it replaced with his own. He did not just take his name, he also purloined his gold from the Dome which remained a grey lead colour for over a thousand years. It got its gold back in the 1960s – but Abd al-Malik never got his name back and Maamun's remains there to this day.

This sleight of hand did not alter the slippage of Abbasid power. Just two years later, a peasant rebel leader was welcomed in Jerusalem by all three religions until, in 841, he pillaged the city, at which most of the inhabitants fled. The Sepulchre was saved only by a bribe from the patriarch. But the Arab caliphs had lost their grip. In 877, Ahmed ibn Tulun, the son of a Turkish slave who had become ruler of Egypt under the nominal aegis of the caliph, retook Jerusalem.

---

* The Abbasids, particularly Maamun, regularly requested copies of Greek classics from the Byzantines, securing for posterity Plato, Aristotle, Hippocrates, Galen, Euclid and Ptolemy of Alexandria. The Arabs developed an entire new vocabulary of science that entered the English language: alcohol, alembic, alchemy, algebra, almanac are just some of the words thus borrowed. Al-Nadim's famous *Index* shows that they also produced 6,000 new books. Paper was now replacing parchment scrolls: in one of history's decisive battles, the Abbasids had defeated an invasion by the Chinese Tang emperors, ensuring the Middle East would be Islamic not Chinese and also capturing the secrets of Chinese paper-makers.

KAFUR: THE SCENTED EUNUCH

Ibn Tulun was one of the Turks who gradually replaced the Arabs as the power in the Islamic empire. Maamun's successor Mustasim had started to recruit slave boys – they were known as *ghulam*, pageboy – from among the newly Muslim Turkish horse-archers of Central Asia. These warriors of Asiatic appearance became first the praetorian guard, then the strongmen of the caliphate.

After Ibn Tulun's son and heir was assassinated by his eunuchs, a Turkish strongman Muhammad ibn Tughj, known by the Central Asian title of prince – al-Ikhshid – came to rule Egypt and Jerusalem. The political instability intensified religious competition. In 935, an annexe to the Holy Sepulchre was forcibly converted into a mosque. Three years later, Muslims attacked Christians celebrating Palm Sunday, looting and damaging the Church. The Jews were now split between the traditional Rabbanites, led by the scholar-judges known as the gaons, who lived by the Talmud, the oral traditions, and the Karaites, a new sect who rejected any law except the Torah (hence their name means the 'readers') and believed in a return to Zion.* These Turkish rulers favoured the Karaites, and just to complicate matters there was also a new community of Khazars†

---

* The Jewish communities of the world were ruled by the two hereditary gaons of the Jerusalem Academy and the Babylonian/Iraqi Academy, whose seat was in Baghdad. The Karaites spread throughout the Jewish world, building up large communities from the Crimea to Lithuania that survived up to the Holocaust, when most of them were annihilated. This led to one of the strangest anomalies of the Nazi repression: in the Crimea, some Karaites were of Turkic rather than Semitic origin, so the Nazis actually ordered the protection of this Jewish sect.

† The Khazars – shamanist Turkic nomads, ruling the steppes from the Black Sea to Central Asia – formed the last Jewish state before the creation of Israel. In about 805, their kings converted to Judaism, taking names such as Manasseh and Aaron. When the Jerusalemite writer Muqaddasi passed through Khazaria he laconically observed, 'Sheep, honey and Jews exist [there] in large quantities.' By the 960s, this Jewish empire was in decline. However, writers from Arthur Koestler to the recent Shlomo Sand have claimed that much of European Jewry are actually descended from these Turkic tribesmen. If true, this would undermine Zionism. But modern genetics refutes the theory: the two latest surveys suggest that modern Jews, both Sephardic and Ashkenazi, are around 70 per cent descended from Middle Eastern genes of 3,000 years ago and around 30 per cent from European stock.

with their own synagogue in the Jewish Quarter. When the Ikhshid died in 946, aged sixty-four, he was buried in Jerusalem and his power passed to a negro eunuch whose soubriquet derived from his taste for perfume and make-up.

Abul-Misk Kafur, who was to rule Egypt, Palestine and Syria for over twenty years, was an Ethiopian slave bought as a child by the Ikhshid. Deformed, obese and malodorous, he splashed on so much white camphor and black musk that his master renamed him after them. His rise began when some exotic animals arrived for the Ikhshid. All the other servants rushed to admire them, but the African boy never took his eyes off his master, awaiting the slightest command. The Ikhshid appointed him tutor to his sons, then commander of the armies that conquered Palestine and Syria, and finally regent with the title of the Master. Once in power, the eunuch cultivated Islamic piety, restoring the walls of the Temple Mount, while patronizing the arts. However, to the north, the Byzantines had been reinvigorated by a succession of outstanding soldier-emperors who raided southwards towards Syria, threatening to take Jerusalem, which set off anti-Christian riots. In 966, Kafur's governor started to squeeze the Christians, demanding ever-greater payments from Patriarch John, who appealed to Kafur. But when John was caught corresponding with Constantinople, the governor, supported by the Jews (who hated Byzantines), attacked the Sepulchre and burned the patriarch at the stake.

In Cairo, the fragrant eunuch was now ailing. After the death of the last of the Ikhshids, Kafur ascended the throne in his own right. The first Muslim king to be born a slave – or for that matter to be a eunuch – employed a jewish minister who would become the mastermind of an Islamic revolution and of a new empire over Jerusalem.

20

THE FATIMIDS: TOLERANCE AND LUNACY

969–1099

IBN KILLIS: THE JEWISH VIZIER AND THE
FATIMID CONQUEST

The son of a Jewish merchant from Baghdad, Yaqub ben Yusuf, known as Ibn Killis, had enjoyed a rollercoaster career, from bankrupt mountebank in Syria to financial adviser to Kafur in Egypt. 'Were he a Muslim,' said Kafur, 'he'd have been the right man for vizier [chief minister].' Ibn Killis took the hint and converted, but the eunuch died, being buried in Jerusalem,* and Ibn Killis was imprisoned. Having bribed his way out of jail, he secretly travelled westwards to the Shiite kingdom in modern Tunisia ruled by the Fatimid family. The ever-flexible Ibn Killis converted to Shia and advised the Fatimid caliph Muizz that the time was ripe to take Egypt. In June 969, Muizz's general Jawhar al-Siqilli conquered Egypt and then advanced north to take Jerusalem.

---

* Recent rulers of Jerusalem had also been buried there, believing, like the Jews, that burial in Jerusalem would mean they would be resurrected first on the Day of Judgement. The closer to the Temple Mount, the sooner they would rise again. The Ikhshid tombs have never been found but are believed to have been just on the northern edge of the Temple Mount. A Palestinian historian showed this author how History has so often been invented in Jerusalem by all three religions for political reasons only to gain its own sacred momentum. When there was talk of Israeli building just north of the Temple Mount, the historian suggested simply putting up a plaque identifying this as the site of the Ikhshid tombs, which has become the accepted shrine. The new building was cancelled.

PALTIEL AND THE FATIMIDS: JEWISH DOCTOR-PRINCES
AND THE LIVING IMAMS

The messianic Fatimids, the new masters of Jerusalem, were unlike any other Islamic dynasty for they not only declared themselves caliphs, they were also sacred kings, the Living Imams, almost suspended between man and heaven. Visitors to their courts were shown through courtyards of increasingly eye-watering luxury before they came to a gold-curtained throne at which they prostrated themselves and the curtains were drawn to reveal the Living Imam in golden robes. Their sect was secretive, their beliefs mystical, redemptionist and esoteric, and their rise to power mysterious, clandestine and filled with adventure. In 899, a rich merchant in Syria, Ubayd Allah, declared himself the Living Imam, direct descendant of Ali and Fatima, the Prophet's daughter, via the Imam Ismail, hence they were known as Ismaili Shiites. His secret agents, the so-called *dawa*, fanned out across the east, conquering Yemen and converting some Berber tribesmen in Tunisia; but the Abbasids tried to kill him, so he vanished. Some years later, he or someone claiming to be him reappeared in Tunisia as al-Mahdi, the Chosen, founding his own caliphate which started to conquer a new empire with a sacred mission: to overthrow the false Abbasids of Baghdad and redeem the world. In 973, the Caliph Muizz, now ruler of swathes of north Africa, Sicily, Egypt, Palestine and Syria, moved to his new capital, al-Qahira al-Muizziyya – the Conquest of Muizz, known today as Cairo.

His successor, Aziz, appointed their consigliere Ibn Killis, as grand vizier, chief minister of the empire which he ruled until his death almost twenty years later. Apart from his immense wealth – he owned 8,000 female slaves, he was a scholar who debated religion with Jewish and Christian clerics and his career personifies the tolerance of the Fatimids, being sectarians themselves, towards Jews and Christians that was immediately felt in Jerusalem.

The Jews in Jerusalem were divided, poor and desperate, while their Egyptian brethren flourished under the Fatimids. They started to provide the doctors for the caliphs of Cairo: these were more than just royal physicians. They tended to be scholar-merchants who became influential courtiers and were usually appointed chief of the Jews of the Fatimid empire, a post known as the *nagid*, the prince. A Jew of mysterious origins named Paltiel was probably the first of these doctor-courtier-princes. A protégé of Jawhar, the Fatimid conqueror of Jerusalem, he immediately intervened to help the Jews in the Holy City.

After years of Abbasid neglect and the inconsistent patronage of Turkish rulers, Jerusalem was diminished and unstable. The constant wars between the caliphs of Cairo and Baghdad discouraged pilgrims; Bedouin raids sometimes overran the city for short periods; and in 974, the dynamic Byzantine Emperor John Tzimiskes captured Damascus and galloped into Galilee, promising his 'intent to deliver the Holy Sepulchre of Christ our God from the bondage of the Muslim'. He was close; Jerusalem waited, but he never came.

The Fatimids encouraged the pilgrimages of their fellow Ismailis and Shiites to the Mosque of Jerusalem but the wars against Baghdad cut off the city from Sunni pilgrims. The very isolation of Jerusalem somehow intensified her sanctity: Islamic writers now compiled more popular anthologies of Jerusalem's 'merits' – the *Fadail* – and they gave her new names: she was still Iliya and Bayt al-Maqdis, the Holy House, but she now became al-Balat, the Palace, too. Yet Christian pilgrims were becoming richer and more numerous than the ruling Muslims – Franks sailed from Europe and rich caravans arrived every Easter from Egypt.

The Jews too looked to their saviours in Cairo where Paltiel now persuaded the Caliph to pay a subsidy to the impoverished gaon and Academy of Jerusalem. He won the right for Jews there to buy a synagogue on the Mount of Olives, to gather close to Absalom's Pillar and also to pray at the Golden Gate on the eastern wall of the Temple Mount. At festivals the Jews were allowed to encircle the old Temple seven times but their main synagogue remained 'the inner altar of the sanctuary at the western wall': the Cave. The Jews had been scarcely tolerated under the Abbasids but now, poor as they were, they had more freedom than they had enjoyed for two centuries. Sadly, the Rabbanites and Karaites, who were specially favoured by the Fatimids, fellow sectarians, held separate services on the Mount of Olives that led to scuffles and soon these threadbare scholars were at war with each other in the dusty, ramshackle synagogues and holy underground caverns of Jerusalem. And their freedoms only exacerbated Muslim frustration.

When Paltiel died in 1011, his son brought his body to be buried in Jerusalem but the rich cortège was attacked by Muslim ruffians. Even after Paltiel, the Jews of Cairo despatched caravans with money to fund the Academy and a mystical sect called the Mourners of Zion who prayed for the restoration of Israel, in effect, religious Zionists. But the help was never enough: 'the city is widowed, orphaned, deserted and impoverished with its few scholars,' wrote a Jewish Jerusalemite in a fundraising letter. 'Life here is extremely hard, food scarce. Help us, save us, redeem us.' Now the Jews were 'a pitiful assembly, constantly harassed'.

Yet the Sunni Muslims were increasingly scandalized by the excesses and liberties of the infidels. 'Everywhere, the Christians and Jews have the upper hand,' grumbled Muqaddasi, the travel writer whose very name means 'Born in Jerusalem'.

MUQADDASI: THE JERUSALEMITE

'All the year round, never are her streets empty of strangers.' Around 985, at the height of Fatimid rule, Muhammad ibn Ahmed Shams al-Din al-Muqaddasi had come home to the city he called al-Quds, the Holy.* Now in his forties, he had been travelling for twenty years, 'seeking knowledge through travel that was so much part of the training of every Islamic savant, combining piety with the scientific observation practised in the House of Wisdom. In his masterpiece *The Soundest Divisions for Knowledge of the Regions*, he reveals his irrepressible curiosity and sense of adventure:

> There is nothing that befalls travellers of which I did not have my
> share except begging and grievous sin. At times I've been pious,

* Al-Quds first appeared on Maamun's coins in 832. Henceforth Jerusalemites were known as people from Quds: qudsi, or in slang, 'utsi'.

at times I've eaten impure foods. I've been close to drowning, my caravans have been waylaid on the highroad. I've spoken to kings and ministers, accompanied the licentious, been accused of being a spy, thrown into jail, I've eaten porridge with mystics, broth with monks and pudding with sailors. I've seen war in battleships against the Romans [Byzantines] and the ringing of church bells at night. I've worn the robes of honour of kings and many times I've been destitute. I've owned slaves and carried baskets on my head. What glory and honour I've been granted. Yet my death was plotted more than once.

Wherever he was, nothing dimmed his pride in Jerusalem:

One day, I sat in the council of the judge in Basra [in Iraq]. Egypt [Cairo] was mentioned. I was asked: which city is nobler? I said: 'Our city.' They said: Which one is sweeter? 'Ours.' They said: Which is better? 'Ours.' They said: Which is more bountiful? 'Ours.' The council were surprised at this. They said, 'You are a man of conceit. You have claimed that which we cannot accept from you. You are like the owner of the camel during the Haj.

Yet he was honest about Jerusalem's faults: he admitted that 'the meek are molested and the rich are envied. You won't anywhere find baths more filthy than those in the Holy City, nor heavier fees for their use.' But Jerusalem produced the best raisins, bananas and pinenuts; she was the city of many muezzins calling the faithful to prayer – and no brothels. 'There's no place in Jerusalem where you cannot get water or hear the call to prayer.'

Muqaddasi described the holy places on the Temple Mount dedicated to Mary, Jacob and the mystical saint, Khidr.* Al-Aqsa

---

* Khidr is the most fascinating of Islamic saints, closely associated with Jerusalem where he was said to celebrate Ramadan. Khidr the Green Man was a mystical stranger, eternally young but with a white beard, cited in the Koran (18.65) as Moses' guide. In Sufism – Islamic mysticism – Khidr is the guide and illuminator of the holy path. The Green Man seems to have inspired the Green Knight in the Arthurian epic *Sir Gawain and the Green Knight*. But he is chiefly identified with the Jewish Elijah and the Christian St George, a Roman officer executed by Diocletian. His shrine at Beit Jala near Bethlehem is still revered by Jews, Muslims and Christians.

was 'even more beautiful' than the Church of the Holy Sepulchre but the Dome was peerless: 'At the dawn when the light of the sun first strikes the Dome and the drum catches the rays, then is this edifice a marvellous sight and one such that in all of Islam I have not seen the equal, neither in pagan times.' Muqaddasi was only too aware that he lived in two Jerusalems – the real and the celestial – and this was the place of the Apocalypse: 'Is she not the one that unites the advantages of This World with those of the Next? Is this not to be the *sahira* – the plain – of marshalling on the Day of Judgement where the Gathering Together and the Appointment will take place? Truly Mecca and Medina have their superiority but on the Day of Judgement, they will both come to Jerusalem and the excellence of them all will be united here.'

Yet Muqaddasi still complained about the lack of Sunnis and the noisy confidence of Jews and Christians: 'scholars are few and Christians numerous and rude in public places.' The Fatimids after all were sectarians and local Muslims even joined in with Christians' festivals. But things were about to take a terrifying turn: by the time Muqaddasi died at the age of fifty in 1000, a child had succeeded to the throne of the Living Imam who would seek to destroy Christian and Jewish Jerusalem.

HAKIM: THE ARAB CALIGULA

When the Caliph Aziz lay dying, he kissed his son and then sent him away to play. Soon afterwards he died, and no one could find the eleven-year-old Living Imam. After frantic searching, he was discovered inauspiciously at the top of a sycamore tree. 'Come down, my boy,' a courtier begged the child. 'May God protect you and us all.'

The gorgeously clad courtiers gathered at the bottom of the tree. 'I descended,' recalled the new caliph, Hakim, and the courtier 'placed on my head the turban adorned with jewels, kissed the ground before me, and said: "Hail to the Commander of the Believers, with the mercy of God and his blessing." He then led me out in that attire and showed me to all the people, who kissed the ground before me and saluted me with the title of Caliph.'

Son of a Christian mother whose brothers were both patriarchs, Hakim grew into a broad-shouldered youth, his blue eyes speckled with gold. At first, advised by ministers, he pursued his family's Ismaili mission, tolerating Jews and Christians. He adored poetry and founded his own House of Wisdom in Cairo for the study of astronomy and philosophy. He prided himself on his asceticism, eschewing the diamond turban for a plain scarf, and he even traded jokes with poor Cairenes in the streets. But when he started to rule in his own right, there were soon signs that this mystical autocrat was unbalanced. He ordered the killing of all the dogs in Egypt, followed by all the cats. He forbade the eating of grapes, watercress and fish without scales. He slept by day and worked at night, ordering all Cairenes to follow his strange hours.

In 1004, he started arresting and executing Christians, closing churches in Jerusalem and converting them into mosques. He banned Easter and the drinking of wine, a measure aimed at Christians and Jews. He ordered Jews to wear a wooden cow necklace to remind them of the Golden Calf, and bells to alert Muslims of their approach. Christians had to wear iron crosses. Jews were forced to choose between conversion or leaving the country. Synagogues were destroyed in Egypt and in Jerusalem. But it was the growing popularity of a Christian ritual that drew Hakim's attention to Jerusalem. Every Easter Christian pilgrims from the West and East poured into Jerusalem to celebrate the city's own Easter miracle: the Descent of the Holy Fire.

On Holy Saturday, the day after Good Friday, thousands of Christians spent the night in the Church of the Holy Sepulchre where the Tomb was sealed and all lamps extinguished until, amid emotional scenes, the patriarch entered the Tomb in the darkness. After a long interval of spine-tingling anticipation, a spark seemed to descend from above, a flame flickered, brightness flared and the patriarch emerged with a mysteriously lit lamp. This sacred flame was distributed from candle to candle through the crowd to screams of joy and acts of wild abandon. The Christians regarded this relatively new ritual, first mentioned by a pilgrim in 870, as divine confirmation of Jesus' Resurrection. The Muslims believed this was a spectacle of fairground hucksterism achieved by trickery – the smearing of the wire holding the lamp with resinous oil. 'These abominations', wrote a Muslim Jerusalemite, 'make one shudder with horror.'

When Hakim heard about this and observed the sheer wealth of the Christian caravan setting out for Jerusalem, he burned the Jewish Quarter of Cairo – and ordered the total destruction of the Church of the Holy Sepulchre. In September 1009, his henchmen obliterated the Church 'stone by stone', 'razed it completely except those parts impossible to destroy', and started to demolish the city's synagogues and churches. Jews and Christians pretended to convert to Islam.

The caliph's antics convinced some Ismailis that 'Hakim had the personified God within him'. In the frenzy of his own holy revelations Hakim did not discourage this new religion, and started to persecute Muslims; he banned Ramadan and terrorized Shiites as well as Sunnis. He became so hated by Muslims that he needed the support of the Christians and Jews in Cairo, whom he allowed to rebuild their synagogues* and churches.

By this time, the psychopathic caliph was wandering in trances through the streets of Cairo, often heavily medicated by doctors. Hakim purged his court, ordering the killing of his own tutors,

---

* Not all the synagogues had been destroyed. The Jewish synagogue in Fustat, Old Cairo, contained one of the key historical resources of the Middle Ages, the Cairo Geniza. In those times, all three Peoples of the Book revered the paper on which holy language was written because words had spiritual life like people. The Jews kept papers received in synagogues in a *geniza* or storehouse for seven years at which point they were buried in a cemetery or stowed in a special attic. For over 900 years, the Cairo Geniza was not emptied, preserving 100,000 papers showing Jewish Egyptian life, its connections with Jerusalem, and the Mediterranean world in all its aspects, sealed and forgotten until 1864 when a Jerusalemite scholar first penetrated it. In the 1890s, Geniza documents started to emerge, bought by English, American and Russian scholars, but it was only in 1896 that two eccentric Scottish ladies showed some Geniza documents to Professor Solomon Schechter, who recognized the earliest Hebrew text of Ben Sira's Ecclesiasticus. Schechter collected the priceless hoard, which enabled S. D. Goitein to produce his six-volume *Mediterranean Society*.

judges, poets, cooks and cousins, and the cutting off of the hands of female slaves, often himself playing the butcher.

HAKIM: THE VANISHING

Finally, in the middle of one night in February 1021, the demented caliph, still only thirty-six years old, rode out of Cairo into the hills and vanished so mysteriously that his devotees were convinced 'Hakim was not born of woman and did not die'. Since his donkey and some bloodied rags were discovered, he had probably been murdered by his sister who arranged the succession of his little son, Zahir. Hakim's devotees were slaughtered by the Fatimid troops, but a few escaped to found a new sect which survives to this day as the Druze of Lebanon.

The scars of Hakim's insanity never healed in Jerusalem: the Church of Constantine was never fully rebuilt in its original form. As if Hakim was not bad enough, an earthquake in 1033 devastated the city, shattering the Byzantine walls and the Umayyad palaces; the old Umayyad Aqsa collapsed in ruins; the Jewish Cave was damaged.

Caliph Zahir, who revered Jerusalem, restored the tolerance of his ancestors, promising protection to both the Jewish sects, and on the Temple Mount he rebuilt al-Aqsa, the inscription on its delicately decorated triumphal arch linking himself, his Jerusalem and the Night Journey of the Prophet, though his mosque was far smaller than the original. He rebuilt the city walls, but around a smaller city, roughly as we see it today, leaving Mount Zion and the ruined Umayyad palaces outside.

Zahir and his successor welcomed Byzantine help to fund the rebuilding of the Church. Emperor Constantine IX Monomachus created a new Holy Sepulchre, finished in 1048, with its entrance now facing south: 'a most spacious building capable of holding 8,000 people, built most skilfully of coloured marbles adorned with Byzantine brocade working in gold with pictures,' wrote Nasir-i-Khusrau, a Persian pilgrim. But it was much smaller than the Byzantine basilica. The Jews never managed to rebuild all their destroyed synagogues, even though the Jewish grand vizier in Cairo, Tustari,* supported the Jerusalem community.

Hakim's persecutions seemed to inspire a fresh passion for Jerusalem – now a flourishing pilgrim city of 20,000. 'From the countries of the Greeks and other lands,' noted Nasir, 'Christians and Jews come up to Jerusalem in great numbers.' Twenty thousand Muslims assembled annually on the Temple Mount instead of making the *haj* to Mecca. Jewish pilgrims arrived from France and Italy.

It was the changes in Christendom that helped make Jerusalem so alluring for Franks from the west, Greeks from the east. The Christianity of the Latins under the Catholic popes of Rome and the Orthodox Greeks under the emperors and patriarchs of Constantinople were now dramatically different. It was not just that they prayed in different languages and bickered about abstruse theological formulae. Orthodoxy, with its icons and elaborate theatricality, was more mystical and passionate; Catholicism, with its concept of original sin, believed in a greater divide between man and God. On 16 July 1054, in the middle of a service in Hagia Sofia, a Papal legate excommunicated the Byzantine Patriarch who furiously excommunicated the pope. This Great Schism, that still divides Christendom, encouraged competition between east and west for Jerusalem.

The Byzantine emperor Constantine X Doukas sponsored the first real Christian Quarter around the Church. Indeed there were so many Byzantine pilgrims and artisans in Jerusalem that Nasir

---

* This was the age of Jewish ministers for Islamic monarchs. In Egypt, the scion of a trading family of Persian Karaites, Abu Saad al-Tustari became a purveyor of luxuries to Zahir, to whom he then sold a black slave girl. On the caliph's death in 1036, she became the Walida, mother of Caliph Mustansir, with Tustari as the power behind the throne. He amassed colossal wealth, once giving al-Walida a silver ship and tent worth 130,000 dirhams. He never converted to Islam. The poet Rida ibn Thawb wrote: 'People of Egypt, I have good advice for you / Turn Jew, for Heaven itself has become Jewish.' In 1048, Tustari was murdered by Turkish troops, much mourned by the Goan of Jerusalem. Meanwhile the vizier of Islamic Granada in Spain was another patron of Jerusalem: Samuel ibn Nagrela, 'The Prince', a polymathic doctor, poet, Talmudic scholar and general, perhaps the only practising Jew to command Islamic armies in battle. His son succeeded him but was murdered in 1066 in a massacre of Jews in Granada.

heard mystical murmurings that the Emperor of Constantinople was in Jerusalem incognito. But there were also many western pilgrims – the Muslims called them all 'Franks' after Charlemagne's people, though they were actually from all over Europe – that Amalfitan merchants built hostels and monasteries to house them. It was widely believed that the pilgrimage redeemed the sins of the baronial wars and as early 1001, Fulk the Black, Count of Anjou and founder of the Angevin dynasty that later ruled England, came on pilgrimage after he had burned his wife alive in her weddingdress having found her guilty of adultery with a swineherd. He came three times. Later in the century, the sadistic Earl Sweyn Godwinson, brother of King Harold of England, set out barefoot for Jerusalem having raped the virginal Abbess Edwiga, while Robert, duke of Normandy, the father of William the Conqueror, abandoned his duchy to pray at the Sepulchre. But all three of them perished on the road: death was never far from the pilgrimage.

The Fatimids, beset with court intrigues, struggled even to hold Palestine, let alone Jerusalem, and the bandits preyed on the pilgrims. Death was so common that the Armenians created a title – *mahdesi* – for pilgrims who had seen death on the way, their equivalent of the Muslim *haj*.

In 1064, a rich caravan of 7,000 German and Dutch pilgrims led by a bishop of Bamberg approached the city but was attacked by Bedouin tribesmen just outside the walls. Some of the pilgrims swallowed their gold to hide it from the brigands who eviscerated them to retrieve it. Five thousand pilgrims were slaughtered. Even though the Holy City had now been Muslim for four centuries, such atrocities suddenly seemed to place the Church of the Holy Sepulchre in peril.

In 1071, the new strongman of the east, Alp Arslan – Heroic Lion – defeated and captured the Byzantine emperor at Manzikert.*

* When the captive emperor was brought before the victorious Alp Arslan, whose moustaches were so long he draped them over his shoulders, asked, 'What would you do if I was brought before you as a prisoner?' 'Perhaps I'd kill you, or exhibit you in the streets of Constantinople,' replied Romanos IV Diogenes. 'My punishment is far heavier,' replied Alp Arslan. 'I forgive you, and set you free.' But the Lion did not last long himself. When he saw the approach of an assassin, he waved aside his bodyguards in order to display his skill as an archer by bringing down the attacker.

Alp Arslan was the leader of the Seljuks, Turkoman horsemen who had come to dominate the Baghdad caliphate and had been granted the new title of sultan – meaning 'the power'. Now Heroic Lion, conquering an empire from Kashgar to modern Turkey, despatched his general Atsiz ibn Awak al-Khwarazmi, to gallop south – towards a terrified Jerusalem.

ATSIZ: THE BEASTLY SACKING

The Gaon and many of the Jews, who had been well treated under the Fatimids, fled Jerusalem to the Fatimid stronghold of Tyre. Atsiz camped outside the new walls but, as a pious Sunni Muslim, he claimed he would not harm Jerusalem. 'It is God's sanctuary,' he insisted. 'I will not fight it.' Instead, in June 1073, he starved Jerusalem into surrender. He then headed south to Egypt, where he was defeated. This encouraged the Jerusalemites to rebel. They besieged the Turkomans (and Atsiz's harem) in the Citadel.

Atsiz returned and when he was ready to attack, his concubines crept out of the Citadel and opened a gate for him. His Central Asian horde killed 3,000 Muslims, even those who had hidden in the mosques. Only those who sheltered on the Temple Mount were spared. 'They robbed and murdered and ravished and pillaged the storehouses; they were a strange and cruel people, girt with garments of many colours, capped with helmets black and red, with bow and spear and full quivers,' reported a Jewish poet who encountered Atsiz's men in Egypt. Atsiz and his horsemen ravaged Jerusalem: 'They burned the heaped corn, cut down the trees and trampled the vineyards, and despoiled the graves and threw out the bones. They don't resemble men, they resemble beasts, and also harlots and adulterers and they inflame themselves with males [and] cut off ears and noses and stole the garments, leaving them stark naked.'

But his foot slipped, and the asssassin stabbed him. Dying, he warned his son Malik Shah, 'Remember well the lessons learned, and do not allow your vanity to overreach your good sense.' His tomb in Merv reads with Ozymandian irony: 'O those who saw the sky-high grandeur of Alp Arslan, behold! He is under the black soil now.'

The Heroic Lion's empire immediately disintegrated as his family and generals seized their own fiefdoms. Atsiz was murdered and Jerusalem fell into the hands of another Turkish warlord, Ortuq bin Aksab. On arrival, he fired an arrow into the dome of the Sepulchre to show that he was the master. Yet he proved surprisingly tolerant, even appointing a Jacobite Christian as governor, and he invited Sunni scholars to return to Jerusalem.*

Ortuq's sons Suqman and Il-Ghazi inherited Jerusalem. In 1093 'someone revolted against the governor', wrote Ibn al-Arabi, a Spanish scholar, 'and entrenched himself in the Tower of David. The governor attempted to assault him using his archers.' While Turkoman soldiers fought pitched battles through the streets, 'no one else cared. No market was closed, no ascetic left his place in al-Aqsa Mosque; no debate was suspended.'† But the monstrosities of Hakim, the defeat of the Byzantine emperor, the fall of Jerusalem to the Turkomans and the slaughter of pilgrims shook Christendom: the pilgrimage was in danger.

In 1098, the Egyptian vizier was surprised to learn that a powerful army of Christian Europeans was advancing on the Holy Land. He presumed they were just Byzantine mercenaries, so he offered them a carve-up of the Seljuk empire: the Christians could take Syria; he would regain Palestine. When he discovered their object was Jerusalem, the vizier besieged the city 'for forty days with forty catapults' until the two sons of Ortuq fled to Iraq. Appointing one

---

* A dispute over the Fatimid succession gave rise to a murderous breakaway sect of Ismaili Shiites led by Hassan al-Sabbah. He and his Nizaris fled to Persia, where he seized the mountain fortress of Alamut and later they gained fortresses in Lebanon. He made up for his small numbers by launching a spectacular campaign of terrorism against his Sunni enemies. His team of killers, who terrorized the Middle East for over a century, were supposedly under the influence of hashish, and came to be called the Hashishim, or Assassins. The Muslims, though, called them Batini, seekers after secret esoteric knowledge.

† In 1095, the Sunni philosopher Abu Hamid al-Ghazali sought refuge in Jerusalem from the Assassins. 'I shut myself up in the precinct of the Dome of the Rock,' he said, in a tiny chamber atop the Golden Gate, to write the *Revivification of the Science of Religion*. This reinvigorated Sunni Islam by separating the logic of philosophy – Greek metaphysics – from the ecstatic revelation of religious truth, while giving each its due. Ultimately his demolition of scientific cause and effect (in his *Incoherence of the Philosophers*) in favour of divine revelation ended the golden age of Arabic learning in Baghdad and helped undermine Arab science and philosophy.

of his generals as *iftikhar al-dawla* or governor of Jerusalem with a garrison of Arabs and Sudanese, the vizier returned to Cairo. The negotiations with the Franks continued into the summer of 1099 – the Christian envoys celebrated Easter in the Sepulchre.

The timing of the Frankish invasion was fortuitous: the Arabs had lost their empire to the Seljuks. The glory of the Abbasid Caliphate was now a distant memory. The Islamic world had fragmented into small warring baronies ruled by princelings dominated by Turkish generals – amirs – and regents known as atabegs. Even as the Christian armies marched south, a Seljuk princeling attacked Jerusalem but was repelled. Meanwhile the great city of Antioch had fallen to the Franks, who marched down the coast. On 3 June 1099, the Franks took Ramla and closed in on Jerusalem. Thousands of Muslims and Jews took refuge within the walls of the Holy City. On the morning of Tuesday 7 June, the Frankish knights reached the tomb of Nabi (the Prophet) Samuel, four miles north of Jerusalem. Having travelled all the way from western Europe, they now gazed down from Montjoie – the Mount of Joy – on the City of the King of all Kings. By nightfall, they were camped around Jerusalem.

MAXIMI

Above Emperor and philosopher Julian overturned Christianity, restored paganism and gave the Temple Mount back to the Jews, before he was killed fighting the Persians.

Top right The Byzantine emperor Justinian I and his wife Theodora (*right*), once a promiscuous showgirl, promoted themselves as universal Christian monarchs and built the colossal Nea Church in Jerusalem.

The Madaba Map shows the magnificence of Byzantine Jerusalem and ignores the Temple Mount which was kept as the symbolic rubbish-heap of Judaism. After the East fell to the Persians, Emperor Heraclius entered the city in 630 through the Golden Gate (*below*), which Jews, Muslims and Christians believe to be the setting for the Apocalypse.

Above Arab conquest: this illustration from Nizami's poem *Khamza* shows Muhammad's Night Flight (Isra) to Jerusalem, riding Buraq, his steed with the human face, followed by his Ascension (Miraj) to converse with Jesus, Moses and Abraham.

Right Caliph Abd al-Malik (seen here in one of the last Islamic coins to show human features) was the real formulator of Islam and a visionary statesman – yet it was said that his breath was so vile it could kill flies. In 691 he built the first surviving Muslim shrine, the Dome of the Rock, inscribed with the earliest quotations from the Koran.

Abd al-Malik's Dome affirmed the supremacy of Islam and his Umayyad empire, challenged Christianity, outshone the Church of the Holy Sepulchre and emphasized the Muslims as successors to the Jews by building on the Rock, the foundation stone of the Jewish Temple (*left*).

Above In 1099, after four hundred years of Islamic rule, the Crusaders stormed Jerusalem with an orgy of killing. The city still stank of putrescent flesh six months later.

King of Jerusalem Baldwin I was a tireless warrior and worldly politician, but also a bigamist who was accused of indulging his fleshly appetites.

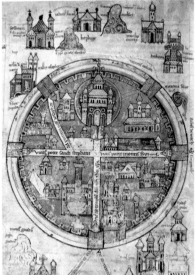

For the Christians of the Crusader era, Jerusalem was the centre of the world – as shown in many twelfth-century maps, such as this one from Robert the Monk's Chronicle.

Crusader splendour: the city reached its apogee under Queen Melisende, here seen marrying Fulk of Anjou. He accused her of an affair with Hugh of Jaffa. This exquisite Psalter (*below left*) may have been his marital peace offering.

Above The curse of Jerusalem: the boy Baldwin IV shows his tutor William of Tyre how he feels no pain during games played with friends, the first sign of leprosy. The Leper King symbolized the decline of the kingdom.

Above left Merciless when he needed to be, patient and tolerant when he could afford to be, Saladin created an empire embracing Syria and Egypt, annihilated the army of Jerusalem and then took the city.

Above right Emperor Frederick II, known as Stupor Mundi – the Wonder of the World to some, the Anti-Christ to others – is seen here entering the Holy City. He negotiated a peace deal that divided Jerusalem between Christians and Muslims.

Above left Saladin and his family re-Islamized Jerusalem often using Crusader spolia. Muslims regard the Dome of the Ascension, built in 1200 on the Temple Mount, as the site of Muhammad's Miraj, yet it started life as the Crusader Templar baptistery. But it was the Mamluks who really created today's Muslim Quarter. Sultan Nasir al-Muhammad built the Market of the Cotton Merchants in the distinctive Mamluk style (*above centre*); Sultan Qaitbay commissioned this fountain on the Temple Mount (*above right*).

Left Suleiman the Magnificent: a Sultan to the Arabs, a Caesar to the Christians. He never visited Jerusalem but, regarding himself as the second Solomon, he rebuilt most of the walls and gates that we see today.

Below left & right Suleiman used a Crusader sarcophagus and decoration to build the Fountain of the Gate of the Chain and asserted Ottoman splendour and legitimacy by adding mosaics to the Dome of the Rock.

Left Charismatic, schizhophrenic, Sabbatai Zevi was rejected in Jerusalem, but the self-declared Jewish Messiah excited Jewish hopes – until the Ottoman Sultan forced his conversion to Islam.

PART FIVE

CRUSADE

Enter on the road to the Holy Sepulchre; wrest that land
from the wicked race and subject it to ourselves.

> Pope Urban II, Address at Clermont

Jerusalem is for us an object of worship that we could
not give up even if there were only one of us left.

> Richard the Lionheart, Letter to Saladin

Jerusalem is ours as much as yours – indeed it's even
more sacred to us.

> Saladin, Letter to Richard the Lionheart

Have we any heritage save the sanctuaries of God?
Then how should we forget His Holy Mount?
Have we either in the East or the West
A place of hope wherein we may trust
Except the land that is full of gates
Towards which the gates of Heaven open.

> Judah Halevi

When I took up my theme and said
When I to Zion from Spanish exile went
My soul from depths to heaven made ascent
Greatly rejoicing that day, God's hill to see
The day for which I longed since I had come to be.

> Judah al-Harizi

21

THE SLAUGHTER

1099

DUKE GODFREY: THE SIEGE

It was the high summer of 1099 in the arid Judaean hills; the Holy City was well defended by Egyptian troops backed by a militia of Jerusalemite Jews and Muslims. They were well stocked with provisions and the cisterns were full of water, whereas the wells of the parched countryside had been poisoned. Jerusalem's Christians were expelled. The citizens, 30,000 at the most, could comfort themselves that the Egyptian vizier was marching north to rescue them, and they were well armed: they even possessed the secret flame-throwing weapon, Greek Fire.* Behind Jerusalem's formidable walls, they must have disdained their attackers.

The Frankish army was too small, just 1,200 knights and 12,000 soldiers, to surround the walls. In open battle, the lightly armoured Arab and Turkish cavaliers could not withstand the awesome charges of the Frankish knights, who formed a fist of thundering steel mounted on hulking destrier warhorses. The knights each wore a helmet, a cuirass and hauberk chain-mail over a gambeson (a padded quilt undergarment) and were armed with lance, broadsword, mace and shield.

Yet their Western horses had long since perished or been eaten

---

* 70,000 is the traditional figure for Jerusalem's population but this is an implausible exaggeration. In the eleventh century, Constantinople had 600,000 inhabitants; Baghdad and Cairo, the great cities of Islam: 400,000–500,000; Rome, Venice and Florence 30,000–40,000; Paris and London 20,000. As for the Greek Fire, 'God's flame', a petroleum-based concoction fired through siphons, had once saved Constantinople. Now the Muslims, not the Christians, had it.

by the hungry army. In the blistered gorges around Jerusalem, charges were impossible, horses useless and armour too hot: this exhausted force of Franks had to fight on foot, while their leaders feuded constantly. There was no supreme commander. Pre-eminent among them, and also the richest, was Raymond, Count of Toulouse. A courageous but uninspiring leader, noted for obstinacy and lack of tact, Raymond initially set up camp in the west opposite the Citadel but after a few days moved south to besiege the Zion Gate.

Jerusalem's weak spot was always in the north: the young, capable Count Robert of Flanders, the son of a veteran Jerusalem pilgrim, camped opposite what is now Damascus Gate; Duke Robert of Normandy (son of William the Conqueror), brave but ineffectual and nicknamed Curthose (short-shanks) or just Fatlegs, covered Herod's Gate. But the driving spirit was Godfrey of Bouillon, the strapping, blond Duke of Lower Lorraine, aged thirty-nine, 'the ideal picture of a northern knight', admired for his piety and chastity (he never married). He took up positions around today's Jaffa Gate. Meanwhile the twenty-five-year-old Norman Tancred de Hauteville, eager to conquer a principality of his own, galloped off to seize Bethlehem. When he had returned, he joined Godfrey's forces at the north-western corner of the city.

The Franks had lost legions of men and travelled thousands of miles across Europe and Asia to reach the Holy City. All realized that this would either be the apogee or the apotheosis of the First Crusade.

POPE URBAN II: GOD WILLS IT

The Crusade had been the idea of one man. On 27 November 1095, Pope Urban II had addressed a gathering of grandees and ordinary folk at Clermont to demand the conquest of Jerusalem and the liberation of the Church of the Holy Sepulchre.

Urban saw his life's mission as the restoration of the power and reputation of the Catholic Church. He devised a new theory of holy war to reinvigorate Christendom and the papacy, justifying the cleansing liquidation of the infidel in return for the remission of sins. This was an unprecedented indulgence that created a Christian version of Muslim jihad, but it dovetailed with the popular reverence for Jerusalem. In an age of religious fervour, a time of holy signs, Jerusalem was Christ's city, seen as both supreme shrine and celestial kingdom, yet familiar to every Christian, evoked in sermons, in tales of pilgrimages, in passion plays, paintings and relics. But Urban also passionately stoked the rising anxiety about the security of the Holy Sepulchre, citing the massacre of pilgrims and the Turkoman atrocities.

The moment was ripe for thousands of people, high and low, to answer Urban's call: 'violence held sway among the nations, fraud, treachery and chicanery overshadowed all things,' observed the Jerusalemite historian William of Tyre. 'All virtue had departed, every kind of fornication was practised openly, luxury, drunkenness and games of chance.' The Crusade offered personal adventure, the removal of thousands of troublemaking knights and freebooters, and escape from home. But the modern idea, promoted in Hollywood movies and in the backlash after the disaster of the 2003 Iraqi war, that crusading was just an opportunity for enrichment with sadistic dividends, is wrong. A handful of princes created new fiefdoms and a few Crusaders made their careers, whereas the costs were punishing and many lives and fortunes were lost in this quixotic and risky but pious enterprise. A spirit was abroad that is hard for modern people to grasp: Christians were being offered the opportunity to earn the forgiveness of all sins. In short, these warrior-pilgrims were overwhelmingly believers seeking salvation on the battlements of Jerusalem.

The crowds at Clermont answered the pope: '*Deus le volt!* God wills it!' Raymond of Toulouse was one of the first to take the Cross. Eighty thousand people, some in disciplined contingents led by princes, some in rampaging gangs led by adventurers, and others in pious crowds of peasants under holy hermits, took the Cross. As the first wave crossed Europe heading for Constantinople, they forced the conversion or massacred thousands of Jews in vengeance for the killing of Christ.

The Byzantine Emperor Alexios, half-horrified by these Latin ruffians, welcomed them – and hurried them on towards Jerusalem. Once in Anatolia, hordes of European peasants were killed by the Turks, but the organized, committed and experienced knights of the main armies routed the Seljuks. The enterprise was a triumph of faith over experience and reason: from the beginning but with rising intensity as they neared the Holy Land, the military campaign was guided and encouraged by divine visions, angelic visitations and the discovery of sacred signs that were just as important as military tactics. But fortunately the Europeans were attacking a region that was fatally divided between warring caliphs, sultans and amirs, Turks and Arabs, who placed their own rivalries above any concept of Islamic solidarity.

The fall of Antioch was the Crusaders' first real success, but they were then besieged inside the city. Faced with starvation and stalemate, the Crusade almost ended there. At the height of the crisis at Antioch, Peter Bartholomew, one of Count Raymond's men, dreamed that the Holy Lance lay under a church: they dug down and duly found the Lance. Its discovery boosted morale. When Bartholomew was accused of being a fraud, he underwent an ordeal by fire. He survived his walk across what was usually nine feet of red hot irons and claimed no ill effects. But he died twelve days later.

The Crusaders survived Antioch and, as they marched south-wards, the Turkish and Fatimid amirs of Tripoli, Caesarea and Acre made deals with them. The Fatimids abandoned Jaffa, and the Crusaders cut inland towards Jerusalem. When the contingents were establishing themselves around the walls, a hermit on the Mount of Olives, inspired by a vision, told the Crusader warlords to attack immediately. On 13 June, they attempted to storm the walls but were easily repulsed, suffering heavy losses. The princes realized that success required better planning, more ladders, catapults and siege-engines, but there was not enough wood to build them. They got lucky. On the 17th, Genoese sailors docked at Jaffa and hauled the timbers of their dismantled ships to Jerusalem to build wheeled siege-machines equipped with catapults.

The princes were already bickering over the spoils. The two ablest had grabbed their own principalities: Bohemond of Taranto had been left to hold Antioch while Godfrey's dynamic brother Baldwin had seized Edessa, far away on the Euphrates. Now the rapacious Tancred demanded Bethlehem for himself, but the Church laid claim to the site of the Nativity. The heat was unforgiving, the sirocco blew, water was short, men too few, morale low, and the Egyptians were approaching. There was no time to lose.

A divine message saved the day. On 6 July, a visionary priest announced that he had (not for the first time) been visited by Adhemar of Le Puy, a revered bishop who had died at Antioch, but whose spirit now urged the Franks to hold a procession around the walls as Joshua had around Jericho. The army fasted for three days then on 8 July, led by priests bearing holy relics, they marched barefoot around the walls of Jerusalem, 'with trumpets, banners and arms', as the Jerusalemites mocked them from the battlements, hurling insults at the crucifixes. The Joshuan circuit completed, they assembled on the Mount of Olives to be addressed by their chaplains and to witness the reconciliations of their leaders. Ladders, siege-engines, mangonels, missiles, arrows, fascines – everything had to be ready, and everyone worked day and night. Women and old men joined the effort by sewing the animal hides for the siege-engines. The choice was stark: death or victory on the ramparts of the Holy City.

TANCRED: CARNAGE ON THE TEMPLE MOUNT

By night on 13 July, the Crusaders were ready. Their priests preached them into a ferment of ferocious and sanctimonious determination. Their mangonels catapulted cannonballs and missiles at the walls, from which the defenders had suspended sacks of cotton and hay to soften the blows until the ramparts resembled giant washing lines. The Muslims fired their own mangonels. When the Christians discovered a spy in their midst, they catapulted him alive over the walls.

The Crusaders worked all night to fill the ditches with fascines. Three siege-machines were brought forward in parts, then assembled like giant flatpacks, one for Raymond on Mount Zion, the other two in the north. Raymond was the first to position his siege-machine against the walls, but the Egyptian governor, commanding the southern sector, put up determined resistance. At almost the last moment, Godfrey of Bouillon identified the weakest point in the defences (east of today's Herod's Gate, opposite the Rockefeller Museum). The Duke of Normandy and Count of Flanders, along with Tancred, swiftly moved their forces to the north-eastern corner. Godfrey himself ascended his siege-tower as it was pushed forward at the ideal spot: he emerged at the top wielding a crossbow as the armies traded salvoes of arrows and bolts, and the mangonels rained missiles on the walls.

As the sun rose, the princes used flashing mirrors on the Mount of Olives to co-ordinate their moves. Simultaneously Raymond attacked to the south and the Normans in the north. At dawn on Friday the 15th, they renewed their attacks. Godfrey rode the rickety wooden tower, shooting bolts over the walls while the defenders unleashed their Greek Fire – but not enough to stop the Franks.

At midday, Godfrey's engine finally closed on the walls. The Franks threw planks across and two brothers climbed into the city, with Godfrey following them. They claimed to have seen the late Bishop Adhemar fighting among them: 'Many testified he was the first to scale the wall!' The dead bishop ordered them to open the Gate of the Column (Damascus Gate). Tancred and his Normans burst into the narrow streets. To the south, on Mount Zion, the Count of Toulouse heard the cheering. 'Why do you loiter,' Raymond scolded his men. 'Lo, the Franks are even now within the city!' Raymond's men broke into Jerusalem and pursued the governor and garrison to the Citadel. The governor agreed to surrender to Raymond in return for the lives of his garrison. Citizens and soldiers fled to the Temple Mount, pursued by Tancred and his men. In the fray, the Jerusalemites slammed shut the gates of the Temple Mount and fought back, but Tancred's warriors smashed their way on to the sacred esplanade, crowded with desperate people.

The fighting raged there for hours; the Franks went berserk, and killed anyone they encountered in the streets and alleyways. They cut off not only heads but hands and feet, glorying in the spurting fountains of cleansing infidel blood. Although carrying out a massacre in a stormed city was not unprecedented, the sanctimonious pride with which the perpetrators recorded it possibly was. 'Wonderful sights were to be seen,' enthused one eyewitness, Raymond of Aguilers, the Count of Toulouse's chaplain: 'Our men cut off the heads of their enemies, others shot them with arrows so that they fell from the towers, others tortured them longer by casting them into the flames. Piles of heads, hands and feet were to be seen on the streets. It was necessary to pick one's way over the bodies of men and horses.'

Babies were seized from their mothers, their heads dashed against the walls. As the barbarity escalated, 'Saracens, Arabs and Ethiopians' – meaning the black Sudanese troops of the Fatimid army – took refuge on the roofs of the Dome of the Rock and al-Aqsa. But, as they fought their way towards the Dome, the knights hacked a path across the crowded esplanade, killing and dicing through human flesh until 'in the Temple [of Solomon, as the Crusaders called al-Aqsa], they rode in blood up to their bridles. Indeed it was a just and splendid judgement of God that this place should be filled with the blood of unbelievers.'

Ten thousand people, including many Muslim clergy and Sufi ascetics, were killed on the Temple Mount, including 3,000 packed into al-Aqsa. 'Our gladiators', wrote the chronicler Fulcher of Chartres, started shooting down the Muslims on the roof of al-Aqsa with their bows. 'What more shall I relate? None were left alive, neither women nor children were spared.' But Tancred sent his banner to the remaining three hundred people on the roof of al-Aqsa, signifying protection. He halted the killing, took some valuable prisoners and was shown the treasures of the Temple Mount. He then plundered the huge golden lanterns that hung in the shrines there. The Jews sought refuge in their synagogues, but the Crusaders set them on fire. The Jews were burned alive, almost a climactic burnt offering in Christ's name. Godfrey of Bouillon took off his sword and with a small entourage circled the city and prayed, before making his way to the Holy Sepulchre.

Next morning, to Tancred's fury, Raymond's men nervously climbed onto the roof of al-Aqsa, surprised the huddled Muslims and beheaded the men and women in another spasm of killing.

Some of the Muslims leaped to their deaths. A respected female scholar from Shiraz in Persia took refuge with a crowd of women in the Dome of the Chain – they too were slaughtered. A ghoulish delight was taken in the dismemberment of the victims, which was treated almost as a sacrament. 'Everywhere lay fragments of human bodies, headless bodies and mutilated limbs, strewn in all directions.' There was something even more dreadful in the wild-eyed, gore-spattered Crusaders themselves, 'dripping with blood from head to foot, an ominous sight that brought terror to all who met them'. They searched the streets of the bazaars, dragging out more victims to be 'slain like sheep'.

Each Crusader had been promised possession of any house marked by his 'shield and arms': 'consequently the pilgrims searched the city most carefully and boldly killed the citizens', culling 'wives, children, whole households,' many of them 'dashed headlong to the ground' from high windows.*

On the 17th, the pilgrims (as these slaughterers called themselves) were finally sated with butchery and 'refreshed themselves with the rest and food they greatly needed'. The princes and priests made their way to the Holy Sepulchre where they sang in praise of Christ, clapping joyously and bathing the altar in tears of joy, before parading through the streets to the Temple of the Lord (the Dome of the Rock) and the Temple of Solomon. Those streets were strewn with body parts, decaying in the summer heat. The princes forced the surviving Jews and Muslims to clear the remains away and burn them in pyres, after which they were themselves butchered and presumably joined their brethren on the fires. The Crusaders who died were buried in the Cemetery of the Lion at

---

* The laws of warfare stated that no quarter was expected after bitter sieges, yet the Frankish eyewitnesses went further in advertising their butchery and claiming that no one was spared. But some of their descriptions are inspired directly by the Book of Revelation. They did not specify numbers. Later, Muslim historians claimed 70,000 or even 100,000 were killed, but the latest research suggests that the massacre was smaller, perhaps around 10,000, considerably less than the future Muslim massacres of Edessa and Acre. The best-placed contemporary, Ibn al-Arabi, who had recently lived in Jerusalem and was in Egypt in 1099, cited 3,000 as killed in al-Aqsa. Nor were all the Jews killed. There were certainly Jews and Muslims left alive. Unusually, it seems that the Crusader chroniclers, for propaganda and religious purposes, hugely exaggerated the scale of their own crimes. Such was holy war.

Mamilla or in the sacred earth just outside the Golden Gate, already a Muslim cemetery, ready to arise at the Last Day.

Jerusalem was so full of treasures, 'gems, raiments, gold and silver' and valuable prisoners that the Franks held slave-auctions for two days. Some respected Muslims had been saved for ransom: a thousand dinars was demanded for the Shafii scholar Sheikh Abd al-Salam al-Ansari, but when no one paid he was killed. Surviving Jews and 300 Hebrew books (including the Aleppo Codex, one of the earliest Hebrew Bibles that partially survives today) were ransomed to Egyptian Jews. The ransoming of prisoners was to be one of the most lucrative industries of the Kingdom of Jerusalem. But not all the human giblets could be collected, and Jerusalem literally stank for long afterwards – even six months later, when Fulcher of Chartres returned: 'Oh what a stench there was around the walls, within and without, from the rotting bodies of the Saracens, lying wherever they had been hunted down.' Jerusalem was not yet secure: the Egyptian army was approaching. The Crusaders urgently needed a commander-in-chief – the first King of Jerusalem.

GODFREY: ADVOCATE OF THE HOLY SEPULCHRE

The higher nobles and clergy made inquiries into the morals of the candidates for the crown. They felt they had to offer the throne to the senior prince, the unpopular Raymond, but did so grudgingly. Raymond obligingly turned it down, insisting he could not be a king in Jesus' city. They then offered it to their real choice, the chaste and worthy Duke Godfrey, who accepted a newly coined title: Advocate of the Holy Sepulchre.

This outraged Raymond who, realizing he had been tricked, refused to give up the Tower of David until the bishops mediated. Triumphant as their arms were, these warrior-pilgrims did not find it easy to enforce the morality expected in a city ruled by Jesus himself. They elected the Norman chaplain, Arnulf, as patriarch but he soon had to defend himself for adultery and fathering a child by an Arab woman.

Arnulf placed bells in the churches (the ringing of church bells had always been banned by the Muslims). This was to be a Latin, Catholic Jerusalem. Now he demonstrated how vicious the schism was: he placed the Latin priests in charge of the Holy Sepulchre, banishing the Greek patriarch and clergy. He thereby started the unseemly conflict among Christian sects that continues to scandalize and amuse visitors to this day. Yet Arnulf could not find the main section of the True Cross and the Orthodox priests refused to reveal its hiding-place. The patriarch tortured them; a Christian torturing Christians to procure the Life-Giving Tree of the Lamb of God. They finally conceded.

On 12 August, leaving Jerusalem almost undefended, Advocate Godfrey led the entire Crusader army out towards Ashkelon where he defeated the Egyptians. When Ashkelon offered to surrender to Raymond, Godfrey refused to accept unless it was ceded to him: Ashkelon was lost – only the first of many self-inflicted wounds caused by the feuding of Jerusalem's leaders. But Jerusalem was secure – if empty.

The Duke of Normandy, Count of Flanders and many of the Crusaders now returned home, leaving Godfrey with a putrid, devastated city peopled by just 300 knights and 2,000 infantry, and scarcely enough citizens to fill a quarter. Raymond of Toulouse recovered from his sulk and set about reducing the Lebanese coast, finally founding his own dynasty as Count of Tripoli. There were four Crusader states – the Principality of Antioch, the Counties of Edessa and Tripoli, and the Kingdom of Jerusalem. This idiosyncratic patchwork of interrelated fiefdoms became known as the land of Outremer, 'Across the Sea'.

Yet the reaction of the Islamic world – divided between the weakened caliphs of Sunni Baghdad and Shiite Cairo – was surprisingly muted. Only a few preachers called for jihad to liberate Jerusalem, and there was little reaction among the all-powerful Turkish amirs, who remained preoccupied with their personal feuds.

On 21 December, Baldwin, Godfrey's brother, who was Count of Edessa, and the flaxen-haired Prince Bohemond of Antioch arrived to spend Christmas in Jerusalem. But Godfrey struggled to defend himself against the Church. The pope's representative, an over-weening Pisan named Daimbert, was now appointed patriarch (to replace the sinful Arnulf). Determined to establish a theocracy to be ruled by himself, he forced Godfrey to cede the city and Jaffa to the Church. In June 1100, Godfrey collapsed in Jaffa, probably with typhoid. Borne home to Jerusalem, he died on 18 July and was buried five days later, like all his successors, at the foot of Calvary in the Church of the Holy Sepulchre.

Daimbert took control of the city, but Godfrey's knights refused to surrender the Citadel, and instead summoned the late advocate's brother, Baldwin. The Count of Edessa was fighting to defend northern Syria, however, and received no message until late August. On 2 October Baldwin set out with 200 knights and 700 troops, and found that he had to fight all the way to Jerusalem, facing repeated Islamic ambushes. On 9 November, with less than half his original force, he at last entered the Holy City.

22

THE RISE OF OUTREMER

1100–1131

BALDWIN THE BIG: THE FIRST KING

Two days later, Baldwin was acclaimed king and Daimbert was forced to recognize his accession. Almost at once Baldwin set off to raid Egypt. On his return, he was crowned 'King of the Latins in Jerusalem' in the Church of the Nativity in Bethlehem by Patriarch Daimbert.

The first King of Jerusalem was not as saintly as his brother but he was far more able. Baldwin had an aquiline nose, light skin, dark beard and hair, a prominent upper lip and a slightly receding chin. He had studied for holy orders as a boy and never lost the contemplative air of a clergyman, always wearing a clerical cloak around his shoulders. He married out of political necessity, risking bigamy for the sake of expediency, left no children and may not have consummated any of his marriages. However, he 'struggled in vain against the lustful sins of the flesh yet so circumspectly did he conduct himself in the indulgence of these vices' that he offended no one. Some have claimed he was gay, but the nature of his peccadilloes remains mysterious.

Relentless war was his urgent duty and true passion. His chaplain called him 'the arm of his people, the terror of his enemies'. This wily warrior of almost superhuman energy devoted himself to securing and expanding the kingdom, repeatedly fighting the Egyptians outside Ramallah. Once they defeated him, but he escaped on his horse, Gazala, to the coast and, hitching a lift with a passing English pirate, sailed to Jaffa where he landed, mustered his knights and vanquished the Egyptians again. His forces were so small, probably no more than 1,000 knights and 5,000 infantry, that he recruited local auxiliaries (some possibly Muslim) who were known as Turcopoles. A flexible diplomat, he played on the rivalries of the Muslim chieftains, and allied himself with Genoese, Venetian and English fleets to conquer the Palestinian coast from Caesarea to Acre and Beirut.

In Jerusalem, Baldwin managed to depose the overmighty Daimbert as patriarch, defeating the main challenge to his authority. The Crusaders had destroyed the people of Jerusalem but mercifully they commandeered the sacred places of al-Quds rather than razing them – probably because they believed they were the biblical originals. Baldwin fortified the Citadel, long known to Christians as the Tower of David, which became palace, treasury, prison, and garrison: its Crusader arches are still visible. When in 1110 and again in 1113 Egyptian raids threatened the city, the trumpets blared from the Tower of David to call the citizens to arms. In 1104, Baldwin made al-Aqsa Mosque into the royal palace.

Many Crusaders believed that the Dome and al-Aqsa really had been built by King Solomon or at least by Constantine the Great, though some knew perfectly well that they were Islamic. A cross was placed atop the Dome of the Rock which was now known as Templum Domini, the Temple of the Lord. Like every conqueror of Jerusalem, the Franks used the spolia of other builders to create their own monuments: Baldwin stripped the lead roof of his Aqsa palace to refit the Holy Sepulchre.

In 1110, Sigurd, the teenage King of Norway, who had fought his way around the Mediterranean massacring infidels, landed at Acre with his 60-ship fleet. Baldwin escorted Sigurd, the first king to visit, into what the Norsemen called Jorsalaborg on roads covered with carpets and palms. Baldwin offered Sigurd a splinter of the True Cross if he would help him storm Sidon with his fleet. Sidon fell – and the Norwegians spent the winter in Jerusalem.

Baldwin repelled invasions by the atabegs of Damascus and Mosul: it was a life of unending warfare and wheeler-dealing for which this king was well suited. Early in the Crusade, he had married Arda, daughter of an Armenian potentate, an alliance that had helped him seize Edessa as his own county. But Arda was excess to requirements in Jerusalem. He confined her to St Anne's monastery just north of the Temple Mount, unchivalrously claiming that she had seduced (or been raped by) Arab pirates on the way to Antioch. She decamped to Constantinople, where her subsequent pleasures suggest it was the former rather than the latter that was the true account.

Baldwin negotiated a profitable marriage with the rich Adelaide, widow of the Norman Count of Sicily.* Baldwin agreed with Adelaide that if the marriage was childless (which was likely since Baldwin had no children and she was no longer young), her son Roger II of Sicily should become King of Jerusalem. Pirates attacked her flotilla, but she finally arrived in Acre displaying all the wealth of Norman Sicily in Cleopatran style with two triremes, each bearing five hundred warriors, and seven ships filled with jewels and gold. Her own trireme boasted gilded masts, prows and poop, all guarded by Saracen archers. Outremer had never seen anything as magnificent as her cavalcade. The streets were bannered and carpeted as Baldwin escorted this ageing Cleopatra into a rejoicing Jerusalem. However, her haughtiness proved inconvenient, her charm insufficient and her wealth all too exhaustible. She disliked provincial Jerusalem, missing the luxuries of Palermo. When Baldwin fell dangerously ill, his bigamy began to trouble him and he despatched the Queen back to Sicily. When Baldwin renounced Adelaide, he also broke his promise that her son Roger II would succeed him. This 'imbued him forever with a violent hatred of Jerusalem and its people'.

---

* Adelaide was the third wife of Roger de Hauteville, one of the remarkable Norman brothers, led by Robert Guiscard, who had conquered their own empire in southern Italy and then Sicily. There, Roger, now Count of Sicily, created a uniquely cosmopolitan kingdom, extending from Sicily to north Africa: while the Crusaders were massacring Moslems, Roger practised tolerance, commanded a Saracen army, ruled from Arabesque palaces and employed Arab ministers. Indeed, his chief minister was called the Amir of Amirs (or Amiratus), who often commanded his formidable fleet: this is the origin of the word 'admiral'. (No wonder Roger was dubious about the Crusade – though Bohemond, Prince of Antioch and young Tancred, Prince of Galilee were Hautevilles.) On his death, his Italian widow Adelaide became Regent, bringing up her son Roger II, who became the brilliantly successful King of Norman Sicily at its apogee, overseeing a blossoming of a fused Arab–Norman–Greek culture and science, naval power and Mediterranean trade.

Meanwhile the king found a solution to the emptiness of Jerusalem. In 1115, he raided across the Jordan, building castles there but also encountering the poverty-stricken Syrian and Armenian Christians, whom he invited to settle in Jerusalem, ancestors of today's Palestinian Christians.

The Crusaders of Jerusalem faced a strategic dilemma: should they expand northwards into Syria and Iraq or southwards into the fraying caliphate of Egypt? To secure the kingdom, Baldwin and his successors knew they had to conquer one of these territories. Their strategic nightmare was a union of Syria and Egypt. So in 1118 Baldwin raided Egypt, but, halting to catch fish in the Nile, he fell ill again. Carried back in a litter, he died at the border town of El-Arish, where the Bardawil lagoons are named after him. He was a gifted adventurer who had become a Levantine king, now surprisingly mourned by 'Franks, Syrians and even the Saracens'.

On Palm Sunday, the Jerusalemites were solemnly parading their palms in the Kidron Valley when they were heartened to see from the north the arrival of the Count of Edessa. Only then did they observe, approaching from the south, the catafalque of their dead king, weaving closely through the Judaean hills guarded by his mourning army.

BALDWIN II THE LITTLE

Once Baldwin was laid in the Church, the barons reviewed the candidates for the throne. But one faction simply elected the Count of Edessa and seized Jerusalem. The kingdom was fortunate in its choice. Baldwin II, the dead king's cousin, known as the Little, in contrast to his lanky predecessor, had ruled Edessa through eighteen years of constant warfare and even survived four years of prison after being captured by the Turks. Wearing a long beard down to his chest, blond now streaked with silver, he was wholesomely married to an Armenian heiress, Morphia, with four daughters, and was so saintly that his knees were calloused from prayer. Baldwin was, even more than his predecessor, a Levantine as well as a Frankish king: he was at home in the Middle East, holding court in robes, seated cross-legged on cushions. The Muslims regarded him as 'rich in experience' with 'good sense and the gift of kingship' – high praise for an infidel.

In Jerusalem, Baldwin the Little lent his Temple of Solomon to a new military order of 'God-fearing' knights, 'professing the wish to live perpetually in poverty, chastity and obedience', who would take their name from their new home. The Templars started as nine guardians of the pilgrim route from Jaffa but grew into a crack military-religious order of 300 knights, wearing the red cross, granted them by the pope, and commanding hundreds of sergeants and thousands of infantry. The Templars converted the Islamic Haram al-Sharif into a Christian complex of shrine, arsenal and accommodation:* al-Aqsa was already divided up into rooms and apartments but they added a capacious Templar Hall (of which traces still exist) around the south wall. Near the Rock, the Dome of the Chain became St James's Chapel. The underground Mosque of Jesus' Cradle became the Christian St Mary's. Herod's sub-terranean halls, which they called the Stables of Solomon, housed the Order's 2,000 horses and 1,500 pack camels, accessed through a new single gate in the southern wall, all this protected to the south by a fortified barbican. North of the Dome, they built a canons' cloister, their own bathhouse and a crafts workshop. On top of al-Aqsa, they created, says the German monk Theodorich who visited in 1172, 'an abundance of gardens, courtyards, antechambers, vestibules and rainwater cisterns'.

A little earlier in 1113, Pope Paschal II granted the area just south of the Holy Sepulchre to another new order, the Hospitallers, who later became a holy army even richer than the Templars. At first they wore black tunics with white crosses; later the pope granted them the red surcoat with a white cross. They built their own quarter including a hostel with a thousand beds and the huge Hospital,

* The round Temple Church in London, consecrated by Heraclius, the Patriarch of Jerusalem, in 1185 and made famous in Dan Brown's novel *The Da Vinci Code*, is surely modelled on the Temple of the Lord, the Dome of the Rock, which is believed to have been built by Solomon. But there are scholars who assert it is based on the double-domed Church of the Holy Sepulchre.

where four doctors inspected the sick twice a day, checked their urine and let their blood. New mothers each received a cot. But there were limits to its comforts, so each patient received a sheepskin coat and boots to wear to the latrine. Jerusalem echoed with many languages including French, German and Italian – Baldwin granted the Venetians trading privileges – but it was still a Christian reserve: he allowed Muslim traders into the city, but they were not permitted to spend the night in Christ's capital.

Soon afterwards, Il-Ghazi, once ruler of Jerusalem, now master of Aleppo, attacked Antioch and killed its prince. King Baldwin raced north, bearing the True Cross* with his army, and defeated him. But in 1123 the king was captured by Il-Ghazi's nephew Balak.

While Baldwin remained a prisoner of the Ortuq family and the Crusader armies besieged Tyre, the Egyptians advanced from Ashkelon hoping to seize a Jerusalem bereft of king and defenders.

---

* At times of crisis the Life-Giving Tree, which was tended in the church by the *scriniarius*, the relic-keeper, in a bejewelled chest, was carried before the king by four bearers.

23

THE GOLDEN AGE OF OUTREMER

1131-42

MELISENDE AND FULK: A ROYAL WEDDING

The Jerusalemites, commanded by the constable, Eustace of Grenier, twice saw off the Egyptians. To universal joy, Baldwin was ransomed: on 2 April 1125, the entire city turned out to welcome the king home. Baldwin's imprisonment had concentrated his mind on the succession. His heiress was his daughter Melisende, whom he now married to the capable and experienced Fulk, Count of Anjou, descendant of the depraved serial-pilgrim Fulk the Black and son of the delightfully named Fulk the Repulsive, and himself already a veteran Crusader.

In 1131, Baldwin fell ill in Jerusalem, and, withdrawing to die in the Patriarch's Palace as a humble supplicant, he abdicated in favour of Fulk, Melisende and their baby son, the future Baldwin III. Jerusalem had evolved its own coronation ritual. Assembling at the Temple of Solomon, wearing embroidered dalmatics, stoles and the crown jewels, Fulk and Melisende mounted gorgeously caparisoned horses. Led by the chamberlain brandishing the king's sword, followed by the seneschal with the sceptre and the constable with the royal standard, they rode through the cheering city – the first Jerusalemite monarchs to be crowned in the rotunda of the Holy Sepulchre, already being rebuilt.

The patriarch administered the royal oath then asked the congregation thrice to confirm that these were the lawful heirs: *Oill!* Yes! shouted the crowd.* The two crowns were borne towards the

---

* The original Crusaders overwhelmingly spoke the northern French dialect *langue d'oie*, totally different from the Provençal *langue d'oc*. But it was *langue d'oc* that became Outremer's chief dialect.

altar. The royal couple were anointed from a horn of oil before Fulk was given the ring of loyalty, the orb of dominion and the sceptre for punishment of sinners, and girded with the sword of war and justice. They were then both crowned and kissed by the patriarch. Outside the Sepulchre, the marshal helped King Fulk mount his horse and they rode back to the Temple Mount. At the banquet in Templum Domini, the king offered to return the crown and then retrieved it, a tradition based on the story of Jesus' circumcision when it was said that Mary brought him to the Temple, offered him to God and bought him back for two pigeons. Finally the burgesses brought the food and wine, served to the royals by the seneschal and chamberlain as the marshal held the banner over them. After much singing, music and dancing, the constable escorted the king and queen to their suite.

Melisende was the queen regnant but at first Fulk expected to rule in his own name. He was a squat forty-year-old soldier with red hair, 'like King David' as William of Tyre put it, and a poor memory, always a flaw in kings. Accustomed to ruling his own realm, he found it hard to manage, let alone charm, his imperious queen. Melisende, slim, dark and intelligent, was soon spending too much time with her handsome cousin and childhood playmate Count Hugh of Jaffa, the richest magnate in Jerusalem. Fulk accused them of having an affair.

QUEEN MELISENDE: THE SCANDAL

Melisende's flirtation started as gossip but rapidly became a political crisis. As queen she was unlikely to be punished; but, by Frankish law, if a couple were found guilty of adultery, the woman suffered rhinotomy (nose-slitting), the man castration. One way to prove innocence was single combat: now a knight challenged Count Hugh to prove his innocence by duel. But Hugh fled to Egyptian territory, where he stayed until the Church negotiated a compromise by which he would go into exile for three years.

On his return to Jerusalem, Hugh was sitting playing dice in a tavern on Furriers Street one day when a Breton knight stabbed him.

Somehow he survived, but Jerusalem was 'shaken at the outrage; a great crowd assembled' and the rumour spread that Fulk had ordered his rival's murder. Now it was the king who needed to prove his innocence: the Breton was tried and sentenced to be dismembered and have his tongue cut out. But Fulk ordered that his tongue remain intact to show he was not being silenced. Even when the Breton had been totally dismembered with only head, torso (and tongue) left, he still asserted Fulk's innocence.

It is not surprising that the evident sleaziness of Outremer politics became notorious in Europe. Ruling Jerusalem was a challenge: the kings were really first among equals, contending with Crusader princelings, ambitious magnates, thuggish adventurers, ignorant new arrivals from Europe, independent military-religious orders of knights and intriguing churchmen, before they were even able to face their Islamic enemies.

The royal marriage became extremely frosty, but if Melisende had lost her love, she had regained her power. To thaw the queen, Fulk gave her a special present – the sumptuous Psalter that bears her name.* But as the kingdom enjoyed its golden age, Islam was mobilizing.

ZANGI THE BLOODY: THE FALCON PRINCE

In 1137, Zangi, Atabeg of Mosul and Aleppo (in today's Iraq and Syria), attacked first the Crusader city of Antioch and then Muslim Damascus: the fall of either of these cities would be a blow for Jerusalem. For nearly four decades, the loss of Jerusalem had made surprisingly little impression on the divided and distracted Islamic world. As so often in Jerusalem's history, religious fervour was inspired by political necessity. Zangi now started to harness a rising fury, religious and political, at Jerusalem's loss, calling himself 'Fighter of Jihad, tamer of atheists, destroyer of heretics'.

* The Melisende Psalter, with its carved ivory covers, studded with turquoise, ruby and emerald stones, was crafted by Syrian and Armenian artists in the Holy Sepulchre scriptorium. Its Byzantine, Islamic and Western styles show how Crusader and Eastern art fused during the reign of this half-Armenian, half-Frankish queen.

The caliph awarded this Turkish atabeg the title 'King of Amirs' for restoring Islamic pride. For the Arabs he called himself the Pillar of the Faith; for fellow-Turks, the Falcon Prince. Poets, vital ornaments for every ruler in that poetry-loving society, flocked to his court to sing of his glories, but the feral Zangi was a harsh master. He skinned and scalped important enemies, hanged minor ones, and crucified any of his troops who trampled on crops. He castrated his boy lovers to preserve their beauty. When he exiled his generals, he reminded them of his power by castrating their sons. Demented with drink, he divorced one of his wives and then had her gang-raped by his grooms in the stables – while he watched. If one of his soldiers deserted, remembered one of his officers, Usamah bin Munqidh, Zangi would order the two neighbouring men to be cut in half. His cruelties are recorded by Muslim sources. As for the Crusaders, they (in a pun worthy of a tabloid-newspaper headline) nicknamed him Zangi the Sanguine.

Fulk hurried to confront him but Zangi defeated the Jeru-salemites, trapping the king in a nearby fortress. William, the Patri-arch of Jerusalem, led the army to his rescue, brandishing the True Cross. Zangi, realizing that relief was on its way, offered to free Fulk in return for the fortress. After this close escape, Fulk and Melisende were reconciled, but Zangi, now in his early fifties, kept up the pressure, threatening not only the Crusader cities of Antioch and Edessa but renewing his attack on Damascus, which was so alarmed that its ruler, Unur, allied himself with infidel Jerusalem.

In 1140, Unur, the Atabeg of Damascus, set off for Jerusalem accompanied by his worldly adviser, a Syrian aristocrat and the century's finest Muslim writer.

USAMAH BIN MUNQIDH:
GREAT EVENTS AND CALAMITIES

Usamah bin Munqidh was one of those ubiquitous players who know everyone who matters at a certain time or place in history and always find themselves at the centre of events. During his long career, this Zeligesque courtier, warrior and writer managed to serve all the great Islamic leaders of his century, from Zangi and the Fatimid caliphs to Saladin, and to know at least two of the kings of Jerusalem.

A member of the dynasty that ruled the Syrian fortress of Shaizar, Usamah lost the succession, and his family was then wiped out in an earthquake. After these blows, he became a cavalier – a *faris* – ready to serve whichever ruler offered him the best opportunities, and, now aged forty-five, he was serving Unur of Damascus. Usamah lived for fighting, hunting and literature. His accident-prone pursuit of power, wealth and glory was both bloody and farcical: the phrase 'yet another disaster' appears frequently in his memoirs, which are entitled *Great Events and Calamities*. But he was also a natural chronicler: one senses that, even as his schemes collapsed, this aesthetic Arab Quixote knew the stories would make great material for his witty, sharp, melancholic writings. Usamah was a master *adib* – the refined Arab belle-lettrist par excellence – writing books and poems on the delights of women, male manners (*The Kernels of Refinement*), eroticism and warfare. In his hands, a history of walking sticks was really an essay on ageing.

Atabeg Unur now arrived in Jerusalem with his exuberant courtier, Usamah: 'I used to travel frequently to visit the King of the Franks during the truce,' wrote Usamah, whose relations with Fulk were surprisingly courteous.* King and cavalier bantered about the nature of knighthood. 'They told me you were a great knight,' said Fulk, 'but I hadn't really believed it.' 'My lord, I am a knight of my race and people,' answered Usamah. We do not know anything about Usamah's appearance, but it seems that the Franks were impressed with his physique.

During his trips to Jerusalem, Usamah enjoyed studying the inferiority of the Crusaders, whom he regarded as 'mere beasts, possessing no other virtues but courage and fighting' – even though his works reveal that many Muslim traditions were just as savage and primitive. Like every good reporter, he recorded opposites –

* Fulk was not the first king of Jersualem Usamah had known. In 1124, Baldwin II had been a prisoner at Shaijar, Usamah's family castle. He was treated so hospitably that the Crusaders came to respect Usamah and the family. The ruins of Shaijar castle can still be seen in Syria.

good and bad things about both sides. When he looked back as an old man at the court of Saladin, he must have reflected that he saw Jerusalem at the height of the Crusader kingdom's glory.

MELISENDE'S JERUSALEM: HIGH LIFE AND LOW LIFE

Melisende's Jerusalem was regarded by many Christians as the true centre of the world, very different from the empty, stinking Frankish conquest of forty years before. Indeed, in the maps of the city from this time, Jerusalem is shown as a circle with the two main streets serving as the arms of the cross with its centre on the Church of the Holy Sepulchre, emphasizing the Holy City as the navel of the world.

The king and queen held court in the Tower of David and its neighbouring palace, while the Patriarch's Palace was the centre of Church affairs. Life for ordinary barons in Outremer Jerusalem was probably better than for kings in Europe, where even potentates wore unlaundered wool and lived in bare-stone draughty keeps with rough furniture. If few Crusader barons could live as grandly as John of Ibelin, later in the century, his palace in Beirut reveals the style: mosaic floors, marble walls, painted ceilings, fountains and gardens. Even bourgeois townhouses boasted rich carpets, damask wall-hangings, delicate faience, carved, inlaid tables and porcelain dishes.

Jerusalem combined the rough edges of the frontier town with the luxurious vanities of a royal capital. Even in Jerusalem the less reputable women, such as the patriarch's mistress, flaunted their jewels and silks to the disapproval of the more respectable. With her 30,000 inhabitants and streams of pilgrims, she was Holy City, Christian melting-pot and a military headquarters – dominated by war and God. The Franks, men and women, now bathed regularly – there were public baths on Furriers Street; the Roman sewerage was still working and it is likely most houses had lavatories. Even the most Islamophobic of Crusaders had to adapt to the east. At war, the knights wore linen robes and Arab *keffiyeh* over their armour to prevent the steel heating up in the sun. At home, the knights dressed like the locals, in silk burnous and even turbans. Jerusalemite ladies wore long underrobes with a short tunic or long robe-coats embroidered with gold thread; their faces were heavily painted; and they were usually veiled in public. Both sexes wore furs in winter, though this luxury was specifically banned for the austere Templars, who personified this capital of Christian holy war. The Knights of the Orders set the tone: the Templars in their belted and hooded red-crossed mantles, Hospitallers in their black mantles with white crosses on the breast. Every day, the 300 Templars clattered out of the Stables of Solomon to train outside the city. In the Valley of Kidron, the infantry practised their archery.

The city thronged not only with French, Norwegian, German and Italian soldiers and pilgrims, but also with eastern Christians – short-bearded Syrians and Greeks, Armenians and Georgians with long beards and high hats, who stayed in the dormitories of hostels or the many small taverns. Street life was centred around the Roman Cardo, leading from St Stephen's (now Damascus) Gate, passing the Sepulchre and Patriarch's Quarter on the right and then entering the three parallel covered market streets, joined by crisscrossing alleyways, smelling of spices and cooked food. Pilgrims bought takeaways and sherbet drinks from the Street of Bad Cooking, Malcuisinat; changed money on Syrian Moneychangers Street close to the Sepulchre; bought trinkets from the Latin Goldsmiths, furs on Furriers Street.

Even before the Crusades it was said that 'No travellers are as evil as pilgrims to Jerusalem.' Outremer was the medieval version of the Wild West: murderers, adventurers and whores came out to make their fortunes, but the prim chroniclers tell us little about Jerusalem's night life. However, the local half-caste soldiers, the Turcopoles, second-generation poor and orientalized Latins known as *poulains*, Venetian and Genoese merchants and newly arrived knights needed the taverns and pleasures of any military town. Each tavern had a clunking chain across the entrance to stop boisterous knights riding into the bar. Soldiers could be seen gambling and rolling dice in the doorways of shops. European harlots were shipped out to service the soldiers of Outremer. Later the secretary of the sultan Saladin would gleefully describe one such boatload from the Muslim point of view:

> Lovely Frankish women, foulfleshed and sinful, appearing proudly in public, ripped open and patched up, lacerated and mended, making love and selling themselves for gold, callipygian and graceful, like tipsy adolescents, they dedicated as a holy offering what they kept between their thighs, each trailed the train of her robe behind her, bewitched with her effulgence, swayed like a sapling, and longed to lose her robe.

Most of them ended up in the ports of Acre and Tyre, with their streets filled with Italian sailors, and Jerusalem would have been policed by officials keen to enforce Christian morals, but all humanity was there.

When pilgrims fell ill, the Hospitallers nursed them in the Hospital, which could hold 2,000 patients. Surprisingly, they also nursed Muslims and Jews and even had a kosher/halal kitchen so that they could eat meat. But death was always on their minds: Jerusalem was a necropolis where old or sick pilgrims were content to die and be buried until the Resurrection. For the poor, there were free charnel-pits in the Mamilla graveyard and the Akeldama in the Valley of Hell. During one epidemic later in the century, fifty pilgrims died each day and carts collected bodies each night after vespers.*

Life revolved physically around the two temples – the Holy Sepulchre and the Temple of the Lord – and chronologically around a calendar of rituals. In this 'intensely theatrical age in which every technique was used to heighten public feelings through display,' writes the historian Jonathan Riley-Smith, Jerusalem's shrines resembled stage-sets and were constantly remodelled and improved

---

* An Orthodox and a Latin church were built atop their respective Akeldama charnel-houses where bodies were dropped through holes in the roof: it was believed that the bodies decomposed within twenty-four hours with no smell. Last used for burials in 1829, the Latin charnel-house is filled with earth but the Greek Orthodox pit is visible today. Peering through a small opening, one can see the white bones. Neither of the churches exists, probably destroyed by Saladin.

to intensify the effect. The capture of the city was celebrated every 15 July when the patriarch led virtually the entire city from the Sepulchre to the Temple Mount where he prayed outside the Temple of Solomon and then led his procession through the Golden Gate – through which that first Crusader, Emperor Heraclius, had borne the True Cross in 630 – to the place on the northern wall, crowned with a huge cross, where Godfrey had broken into the city. Easter was the most exciting set piece. Before sunrise on Palm Sunday, the patriarch and clergy, holding the True Cross, walked from Bethany towards the city, while another procession bearing palms came from the Temple Mount to meet the patriarch in the Valley of Jehoshaphat. Together they then opened the Golden Gate* and processed around the sacred esplanade before praying in the Temple of the Lord.

On Holy Saturday, Jerusalemites gathered at the Church for the Holy Fire. A Russian pilgrim watched 'the crowd rush in, jostling and elbowing', weeping, wailing and shouting, 'Will my sins prevent the Holy Fire from descending?' The king walked from the Temple Mount but, when he arrived, the crowd was so tightly packed, overflowing even the courtyard, that his soldiers had to clear a path for him. Once inside, the king, shedding 'torrents of tears', took his place on a rostrum before the Tomb, surrounded by his weeping courtiers, waiting for the Holy Fire. As the priest chanted vespers, the ecstasy intensified in the darkening church, until suddenly 'the Holy Light illumined the Sepulchre, stunningly bright and splendid'. The patriarch emerged brandishing the fire, with which he kindled the royal lamp. The fire spread across the

---

* The holy Golden Gate was opened just twice a year. The cemetery outside the Golden Gate, probably attached to the Templar convent, was a special resting-place. It was here that the murderers of Thomas Becket were reported buried. A few important Frankish knights were buried inside on the Temple Mount. In 1969, James Fleming, an American Bible student, was photographing the Gate when the earth gave way and he fell into a hole 8 feet deep. He found himself standing on a heap of human bones. The hole revealed what appeared to be a neat arch of Herodian ashlars. The bones may belong to Crusaders (Frederick of Regensburg was buried there in 1148; the archaeologist Conrad Schick found bones there in 1891). Before and after the Crusades, the Muslims used this as a special cemetery. Either way, Fleming was unable to check because the Muslim authorities swiftly cemented it over.

crowd, lantern to lantern – and was then borne across town like an Olympic flame across the Great Bridge to the Temple of the Lord.

Melisende embellished Jerusalem as both Temple shrine and political capital, creating much that we see today. The Crusaders had developed their own style, a synthesis of Romanesque, Byzantine and Levantine with round-headed arches, massive capitals, all carved with delicate, often floral motifs. The queen built the monumental St Anne's Church, north of the Temple Mount, on the site of the Bethesda Pool – it stands today as the simplest and starkest example of Crusader architecture. Already used as a repository for discarded royal wives and more recently the home of Melisende's sister Princess Yvette, its convent became the most richly endowed in Jerusalem. A few of the shops in the market-places are still marked 'ANNA' to show where their profits went; other shops, perhaps Templar-owned, are marked 'T' for the Temple.

A small chapel, St Giles, was built on the Great Bridge into the Temple Mount. Outside the walls, Melisende added to the Church of Our Lady of Jehoshaphat, the Virgin Mary's tomb where she was later buried (her grave survives today), and built the Bethany Monastery, appointing Princess Yvette as abbess. In the Temple of the Lord, she added an ornate metal grille to protect the Rock (now mostly in the Haram Museum though a small section, still in situ, may have held a portion of Jesus' foreskin,* and later enclosed hair from Muhammad's beard).

On their state visit to see Fulk and Melisende, Usamah bin Munqidh and his master, the Atabeg of Damascus, were allowed to pray on the Temple Mount, where they encountered both the insularity and cosmopolitanism of their Frankish hosts.

---

* The Holy Prepuce was just one of a panoply of medieval relics. Charlemagne presented a section to Pope Leo before his coronation in 800, but there were soon between eight and eighteen such relics in the Christian world. Baldwin I sent one to Antwerp in 1100 but Melisende possessed another section. Most of the relics were lost or destroyed in the Reformation.

USAMAH BIN MUNQIDH AND JUDAH HALEVI:
MUSLIMS, JEWS AND FRANKS

Usamah had become friends with some of the Templars whom he had met in war and peace. Now they escorted him and Atabeg Unur on to the sacred esplanade, the thoroughly Christianized headquarters of the Templars.

Some Crusaders now spoke Arabic and built houses with courtyards and fountains like Muslim potentates; some even ate Arabic food. Usamah met Franks who did not eat pork and 'presented a very fine table, extremely clean and delicious'. Most Franks disapproved of anyone going too native: 'God has transformed the Occident into the Orient', wrote Fulcher. 'He who was a Roman or a Frank has in this land been made into a Galilean or a Palestinian.' Similarly, there were limits to Usamah's friendship with the Templars and to their open-mindedness. When one Templar was returning home, he cheerfully invited Usamah to send his son to be educated in Europe so that 'when he returns he will be a truly rational man'. Usamah could scarcely contain his disdain.

As they prayed in the Dome of the Rock, one of the Franks approached the atabeg to ask: 'Would you like to see God when he was young?'

'Why yes,' said Unur, at which the Frank led him and Usamah to an icon of Mary and the boy Jesus.

'This is God when he was young,' said the Frank, much to Usamah's amused contempt.

Usamah then walked over to pray in the Temple of Solomon, formerly al-Aqsa, welcomed by his Templar friends, even though he was openly reciting 'Allahu Akhbar – God is Greatest'. But then there was an unsettling incident when 'a Frank rushed up to me and grabbed me and turned my face towards the east, "Pray like this!"' The 'Templars hurried towards him and took him away from me. "This man is a stranger," the Templars explained, apologetically, "and has just arrived from the Frankish lands."' Usamah realized that 'anyone recently arrived' is 'rougher in character than those who have become acclimatized and frequented the company of Muslims'. These new arrivals remained 'an accursed race that will not become accustomed to anyone not of their own race'.

It was not only Muslim leaders who visited Melisende's Jerusalem. Muslim peasants came into town daily to sell their fruit and left in the evening. By the 1140s, the rules banning Muslims and Jews from Christ's city had been relaxed – hence the travel writer Ali al-Harawi said, 'I lived long enough in Jerusalem at the time of the Franks to know how the trick of the Holy Fire was achieved.' There were already a few Jews in Jerusalem, but pilgrimage was still dangerous.

Just at this time, in 1141, Judah Halevi, a Spanish poet, philosopher and doctor, is said to have arrived from Spain. In his love songs and religious poetry, he craved 'Zion perfect in beauty' while suffering because 'Edom [Islam] and Ishmael [Christianity] riot in the Holy City'. The Jew in exile was 'the dove in a strange land.' All his life, Halevi, who wrote poetry in Hebrew but spoke Arabic, believed in the return of the Jews to Zion:

> O city of the world, most chastely fair,
> In the far West, behold I sigh for thee.
> Oh! had I eagles' wings, I'd fly to thee,
> And with my falling tears make moist thine earth.

Halevi, whose poems are still part of the synagogue liturgy, wrote as poignantly as anyone has ever written about Jerusalem: 'When I dream of the return of thy captivity, I am a harp for thy songs.' It is not clear if he actually made it to Jerusalem, but according to legend, as he walked through the gates, he was ridden down by a horseman, probably a Frank, and killed, a fate perhaps foreseen in his words: 'I would fall with my face upon thine earth, and take delight in thy stones and be tender to thy dust.'

This death would not have surprised Usamah, who studied the violence of Frankish laws. On his way to Jerusalem he had watched two Franks solving a legal question by combat – one smashed in the skull of another. 'That was but a taste of their jurisprudence and their legal procedure.' When a man was accused of murdering pilgrims, his trial was to be trussed up and dipped in a pool of water. If he sank he was innocent, but since he floated he was found guilty and, as Usamah put it, 'they applied some kohl to his eyes' – he was blinded.

As for their sexual customs, Usamah gleefully recounted how one Frank found another in bed with his wife but let him off with a mere warning, and how another ordered his male barber to shave off his wife's pubic hair. In medicine Usamah described how while an Eastern doctor was treating a Frank's leg abscess with a poultice, a Frankish doctor burst in with an axe and hacked off the leg, with the immortal question – would he prefer to live with one leg or die with two? But he died with one. When the Eastern doctor prescribed a special diet to a woman suffering 'dryness of humours', the same Frankish doctor, diagnosing a 'demon inside her head', carved a cross into her skull, killing her too. The best doctors were Arab-speaking Christians and Jews: even the kings of Jerusalem now preferred Eastern doctors. Yet Usamah was never simplistic – he cites two cases where Frankish medicine miraculously worked.

The Muslims regarded the Crusaders as brutish plunderers. But the cliché that the Crusaders were barbarians and the Muslims aesthetes can be taken too far. After all, Usamah had served the sadist Zangi and, if read in full, his account presents a picture of Islamic violence no less shocking to modern sensibilities: the collecting of Christian heads, the crucifying and bisections of their own soldiers and heretics, the severe punishments of Islamic sharia – and the story of how his father, in a rage, lopped off the arm of his page. Violence and similarly brutal laws ruled on both sides. The Frankish knight and the Islamic *faris* had much in common: they were both led by self-made adventurers such as the Baldwins and Zangi, who founded warrior dynasties. Both systems depended on the granting of fiefs of property or income-streams to leading warriors. The Arabs used poetry to show off, to entertain and to spread propaganda. When Usamah served the Damascene atabeg, he negotiated with the Egyptians in verse, while Crusader knights spun the poems of courtly love. Both knight and *faris* lived by similar codes of noble behaviour and shared the same obsessions – religion, war, horses – and the same sports.

Few soldiers, few novelists have captured the excitement and fun

of war like Usamah. To read him is to ride in the skirmishes of
Holy War in the Kingdom of Jerusalem. He gloried in his battlefield
anecdotes of derring-do, devil-may-care cavaliers, miraculous
escapes, terrible deaths, and the exhilaration of wild charges, flashing steel, sweating horses and spurting blood. But he was also a
philosopher of Fate and God's mercy: 'Even the smallest and most
insignificant of things can lead to destruction.' Above all, both sides
believed that, in Usamah's words, 'victory in war is from God alone.'
Religion was everything. Usamah's highest praise for a friend was:
'a genuine scholar, a real cavalier and a truly devout Muslim'.

Now the tranquillity of Melisende's Jerusalem was suddenly
shattered by an accident caused by the sport shared by both Muslim
and Frank grandees.

24

STALEMATE

1142–1174

ZANGI: HUBRIS AND NEMESIS

When he was not fighting or reading, Usamah hunted deer, lions, wolves, hyenas with cheetahs, hawks and dogs – and in this, he was no different from Zangi or King Fulk, who hunted as often as they could. When Usamah and the Atabeg of Damascus visited Fulk, they admired a goshawk, so the king gave it to them as a present.

On 7 November 1142, soon after Usamah's visit to Jerusalem, King Fulk was riding near Acre when he spotted a hare and, spurring his horse, gave chase. His saddle girth suddenly snapped and he was thrown. The saddle flew over his head and fractured his skull. He died three days later. The Jerusalemites marched out to escort Fulk's cortège to burial in the Sepulchre. On Christmas Day, Melisende had her twelve-year-old son crowned as Baldwin III, but she was the real ruler. In an age dominated by men, she was a 'woman of great wisdom' who, writes William of Tyre, 'had risen so far above the normal status of women that she dared undertake important measures, and ruled the kingdom with as much skill as her ancestors'.*

---

* Melisende was the third queen to rule Jerusalem in her own right – after Athaliah, Jezebel's daughter, and Alexandra, widow of Alexander Jannaeus in Maccabean times. She was crowned three times, once with her father in 1129, then with Fulk in 1131 and again with her son in 1143. Despite the low status of women on both sides, Usamah bin Munqidh tells of both Islamic and Crusader women who in times of peril pulled on armour and fought the enemy in battle. Melisende did not forget her Armenian roots. After the fall of Edessa, she settled its Armenian refugees in Jerusalem and in 1141 the Armenians started to rebuild St James's Cathedral near the royal palace.

At this bittersweet moment, disaster struck. In 1144, Zangi the Bloody captured Edessa, slaughtering Frankish men, enslaving Frankish women (though protecting Armenian Christians), and thereby destroying the first Crusader state and the cradle of the Jerusalem dynasty. The Islamic world was exultant. The Franks were not invincible and surely Jerusalem was next. 'If Edessa is the high sea,' wrote Ibn al-Qaysarani, 'Jerusalem is the shore.' The Abbasid caliph awarded Zangi the titles Ornament of Islam, Auxiliary of the Commander of the Believers, Divinely Aided King. Yet Zangi's hard-drinking perversity caught up with him in his own boudoir.

At a siege in Iraq, a humiliated eunuch, perhaps one of those castrated for Zangi's pleasure, crept into his heavily guarded tent and stabbed the drunken potentate in his bed, leaving him scarcely alive. A courtier found him bleeding, helplessly begging for his life: 'He thought I was intending to kill him. He gestured to me with his index finger, appealing to me. I halted in awe of him and said, "My Lord, who's done this to you?"' There died the Falcon Prince.

His staff pillaged his belongings around the still-warm corpse and his two sons divided his lands: the younger of them, the twenty-eight-year-old Nur al-Din, tugged his father's signet ring off his finger and seized the Syrian territories. Talented but less ferocious than his father, Nur al-Din intensified the jihad against the Franks. Shocked by the fall of Edessa, Melisende appealed to Pope Eugenius II, who called the Second Crusade.

ELEANOR OF AQUITAINE AND KING LOUIS: SCANDAL AND DEFEAT

Louis VII, the saintly young King of France, accompanied by his wife Eleanor, Duchess of Aquitaine, and Conrad III, King of Germany, a veteran pilgrim, answered the pope's call. But their German and French armies were mauled by the Turks as they crossed Anatolia. Louis VII only just made it to Antioch after a disastrous fighting march that must have been terrifying for Queen

Eleanor, who lost much of her baggage – and any respect for her sanctimonious, inept husband.

Prince Raymond of Antioch urged Louis to help him to capture Aleppo but Louis was determined to make his pilgrimage to Jerusalem first. The worldly Raymond was Eleanor's uncle and 'the handsomest of princes'. After the miserable journey, Eleanor 'disregarded her marriage vows and was unfaithful to her husband', according to William of Tyre. Her husband was puppyishly besotted with her, but regarded sex, even in marriage, as indulgent. No wonder Eleanor called him 'more monk than man'. Yet Eleanor, acutely intelligent, dark-haired, dark-eyed and curvaceous, was the richest heiress in Europe, brought up at the sensual Aquitanian court. Priestly chroniclers claimed that the blood of sin coursed through her veins because her grandfather was William the Troubadour, a promiscuous warrior-poet, while her grandmother on the other side was her grandfather's mistress, nicknamed La Dangereuse. This came about because the Troubadour had facilitated his access to La Dangereuse by marrying her daughter to his son.

Whether Eleanor and Raymond committed adultery or not, their behaviour was provocative enough to humiliate the husband and launch an international scandal. The King of France solved his marital problem by kidnapping Eleanor and heading off to join the German king who had arrived in Jerusalem. When Louis and Eleanor approached the city, 'all the clergy and people went out to meet him' and escort him to the Sepulchre 'to the accompaniment of hymns and chants'. The French couple stayed along with Conrad in the Temple of Solomon, but Eleanor must have been carefully watched by the French courtiers. She was stranded there for months.

On 24 June 1148, Melisende and her son Baldwin III called a council at Acre that approved the target of the Crusade: Damascus. The city had recently been Jerusalem's ally, but it was still a sensible target because it would only be a matter of time before it fell to Nur al-Din. On 23 July, the kings of Jerusalem, France and Germany fought their way into the orchards on the west side of Damascus but two days later mysteriously moved camp to the east. Four days after that, the Crusade fell apart and the three kings ignominiously retreated.

Unur, Atabeg of Damascus, may have bribed the Jerusalemite barons, convincing them that the Western Crusaders wanted the prize for themselves. Such duplicitous venality was all too credible but, more likely, the Crusaders simply learned that Nur al-Din, Zangi's son, was advancing with a relief army. Now Jerusalem wilted under the strain of this disaster. Conrad sailed home; Louis, bathing in ascetic penitence, stayed to celebrate Easter in the Holy City. They could not leave fast enough for Eleanor: the marriage was annulled on their return.*

When they had gone, Queen Melisende celebrated her greatest triumph and suffered her greatest humiliation. On 15 July 1149, she and her son reconsecrated their new Church of the Holy Sepulchre, then – and now – the masterpiece and dazzling holy stage-set of Crusader Jerusalem. The architects, finding a cluttered labyrinth of chapels and shrines in the complex built in 1048 and restored in 1119, solved this challenge with astonishing boldness. They roofed over the compound with a soaring rotunda and united all its sites in one magnificent Romanesque building, expanding into the old Holy Garden in the east. They opened up the eastern wall of the Rotunda to add chapels and a huge ambulatory. On the site of Constantine's Basilica, they placed a large cloister. They kept the 1048 southern entrance, creating a Romanesque façade with two portals (one is now bricked up) topped with sculpted lintels (now in the Rockefeller Museum). The peerless carvings of the staircase leading up to the Chapel of the Hill of Calvary are perhaps the most exquisite of all Crusader art. A surprising feature of the façade is the two elaborate balustrades, at the top and in the middle, which were somehow discovered and rescued by the Crusaders: they once stood in Hadrian's pagan temple that was destroyed by Constantine the Great.

Melisende's son resented her and demanded his full powers.

---

* As soon as she was free, Eleanor married Henry, Duke of Normandy and Count of Anjou, the grandson of King Fulk of Jerusalem, who soon succeeded to the English throne as Henry II. Their children included King John and the future Crusader, King Richard the Lionheart.

Now twenty years old and acclaimed for his brains and flaxen-haired brawn, Baldwin III was said to be the perfect Frankish king – with a few vices. He was also known as a gambler and seducer of married women. But a northern crisis showed that Jerusalem needed an active warrior-king in the saddle: Zangi's son, Nur al-Din, defeated the Antiochenes and killed Eleanor's uncle Raymond.

Baldwin raced northwards in time to save Antioch but when he returned his mother Melisende, now forty-seven, resisted his demand that he be crowned at Easter. The king decided to fight.

MOTHER VERSUS SON: MELISENDE VERSUS BALDWIN III

Melisende offered him the rich ports of Tyre and Acre, but kept Jerusalem for herself. The 'still smouldering fire was rekindled' when Baldwin raised his own forces to seize the kingdom. Melisende sped from Nablus to Jerusalem with Baldwin in pursuit. Jerusalem opened its gates to the king. Melisende retreated into the Tower of David where Baldwin besieged her. He 'set up his engines for assault', firing bolts and ballista stones at her for several days. Finally the queen resigned power – and Jerusalem.

Baldwin had scarcely seized his birthright when Antioch was again attacked by Nur al-Din. While the king was once more in the north, the Ortuq family that had ruled Jerusalem from 1086 to 1098 marched from their Iraq fiefdom to seize the Holy City, massing on the Mount of Olives, but the Jerusalemites sortied out and massacred them on the Jericho road. Morale boosted, Baldwin led his army and the True Cross to Ashkelon, which fell after a long siege. But in the north, Damascus finally succumbed to Nur al-Din, who became the master of Syria and eastern Iraq.

Nur al-Din, 'a tall swarthy man with a beard, no moustache, a fine forehead and pleasant appearance enhanced by melting eyes', could be as cruel as Zangi, but he was more measured, more subtle. Even the Crusaders called him 'valiant and wise'. He was beloved by his courtiers who now included that political weathervane Usamah bin Munqidh. Nur al-Din so enjoyed polo that he played at night by the light of candles. But it was he who channelled the Islamic fury at the Frankish conquest into a Sunni resurgence and a new military confidence. A fresh stream of *fadail* works extolling Jerusalem promoted Nur al-Din's jihad to 'purify Jerusalem from the pollution of the Cross' – ironically since the Crusaders had once called the Muslims 'polluters of the Holy Sepulchre'. He commissioned an elaborately carved *minbar* or pulpit to stand in al-Aqsa when he conquered the city.

Baldwin was locked in stalemate with Nur al-Din. They agreed a temporary truce while the king sought Byzantine help: he married the emperor Manuel's niece, Theodora. At the marriage and crowning in the Church, 'the bridal outfit of the maiden in gold and gems, garments and pearls' brought the exotic splendour of Constantinople to Jerusalem. The marriage was still childless when Baldwin fell ill in Antioch, finally dying a few weeks later on 10 February 1162.

The funeral cortège travelled from Beirut to Jerusalem amid unprecedented scenes of 'deep and poignant sorrow'. The kings of Jerusalem, like the other veteran Crusader families, had become Levantine grandees so that now, observed William of Tyre, 'there came down from the mountains a multitude of infidels who followed the cortège with wailing'. Even Nur al-Din said that the 'Franks have lost such a prince that the world has not known his like'.

AMAURY AND AGNES:
'NO QUEEN FOR A CITY AS HOLY AS JERUSALEM'

The disreputable reputation of a woman now almost derailed the succession of Jerusalem. Baldwin's brother Amaury, Count of Jaffa and Ashkelon, was the heir, but the patriarch refused to crown him unless he annulled his marriage to Agnes, claiming that they were too closely related – even though they already had a son together. The real problem was that 'she was no queen for a city as holy as Jerusalem', noted one prissy chronicler. Agnes had a bad reputation for promiscuity, but it is impossible to know if she deserved it since the historians were all so prejudiced against her. Nonetheless, she was clearly a much-desired trophy and, at various times, her lovers were said to include the seneschal, the patriarch and four husbands.

Amaury dutifully divorced her and was crowned at the age of twenty-seven. Already awkward in manner – he stammered and had a gurgling laugh – he soon became 'excessively fat with breasts like those of a woman hanging down to his waist'. Jerusalemites mocked him in the streets, which he ignored 'as if he had not heard the things said'. Despite the man-breasts, he was both an intellectual and a warrior who now faced the most daunting strategic challenge since the founding of the kingdom. Syria was lost to Nur al-Din, but Baldwin III's conquest of Ashkelon had opened the gateway to Egypt. Amaury would need all his energy and manpower to fight Nur al-Din for that supreme prize.

This was one reason why he welcomed to Jerusalem the most notorious rogue of the day, Andronikos Komnenos, a Byzantine prince 'attended by a large retinue of knights', useful reinforcements. At first his knights were 'a source of much comfort' in Jerusalem. A cousin of the Emperor Manuel, Andronikos had seduced the emperor's niece, was almost murdered by her furious brothers and spent twelve years in jail before being forgiven and appointed Governor of Cilicia. He was then sacked for incompetence and disloyalty, and fled to Antioch where he seduced Philippa, the daughter of the ruling prince, and had to flee again – to Jerusalem. 'But like a snake in the bosom or a mouse in the wardrobe,' recalled Amaury's courtier, William of Tyre, 'he proved the truth of the saying, "I fear the Greeks even when bearing gifts."'

Amaury gave him Beirut as his lordship, but Andronikos, now almost sixty, dumped Princess Philippa and seduced Baldwin III's lissom widow, Theodora, the Dowager Queen of Jerusalem, who was only twenty-three. Jerusalem was outraged: Andronikos had to escape yet again. Abducting Theodora, he defected with her to Nur al-Din in Damascus.* No one was sorry to see this 'snake' go, least

---

* At least he seems to have loved Theodora longer than the others. When she was captured by the emperor, Andronikos surrendered and was forgiven. Then the emperor died, and the preposterous cad seized power in 1182 and became one of

of all Amaury's favourite clergyman, William of Tyre, who had been born in Jerusalem. After studying in Paris, Orleans and Bologna, William returned to become Amaury's most trusted adviser. Over twenty years, as Archbishop of Tyre and later Chancellor, William was the intimate witness of the unbearable royal tragedy that now coincided with Jerusalem's most grievous crisis.

WILLIAM OF TYRE: THE BATTLE FOR EGYPT

King Amaury commissioned William to write the histories of the Crusader and the Islamic kingdoms, quite a project. William had no problem writing the history of Outremer but, though he knew some Arabic, how was he to write about Islam?

By now, Fatimid Egypt was falling apart. There were rich pickings for the sharp opportunist – so naturally Usamah bin Munqidh was in Cairo. There, the power games were lethal but lucrative. Usamah made his fortune and built up a library; inevitably, however, it went wrong and he had to flee for his life. But he sent his family, his gold and his cherished library by ship. When it was shipwrecked off Acre, his treasure was lost and his library confiscated by the King of Jerusalem: 'The news that my children and our women were safe made it easier to take the news about all the wealth lost. Except the books: 4,000 volumes. A heartache that lasted all my life.' Usamah's loss proved to be William's gain for he inherited Usamah's books and made good use of them to write his Islamic history.

Meanwhile Amaury plunged into the battle for Egypt, launching no fewer than five invasions. The stakes were high. In the second invasion, Amaury seemed to have conquered Egypt. If he had succeeded in keeping the riches and resources of that country, the Christian Kingdom of Jerusalem would probably have endured and

---

the most despicable emperors in the history of Constantinople. During his reign of terror, he killed most of the imperial family including the women. Aged sixty-five but still boyishly handsome, he married a thirteen-year-old princess. When he was overthrown, the mob tortured him to death in the most horrible way, an arm cut off, an eye gouged, hair and teeth torn out, his face burned with boiling water to ruin his famous looks. Theodora's fate is unknown.

the entire history of the region would have been different. Instead the deposed Egyptian vizier fled to Nur al-Din, who sent his Kurdish general, the vigorous yet rotund Shirkuh, to conquer Egypt. Amaury defeated Shirkuh, taking Alexandria, but instead of consolidating he accepted tribute and returned to Jerusalem.

Thanks to his Egyptian booty, Amaury's capital flourished. The elegant Gothic room in the Cenacle on Mount Zion was built at this time and the king raised a new royal palace, porticoed with a gabled roof, a small domed tower and a large circular one, south of the Tower of David.* But Egypt was far from cowed.

Mired in this expensive conflict, Amaury sought help from the emperor Manuel in Constantinople, marrying his great-niece Maria and despatching his historian William to negotiate military co-operation – but the timing of war and aid never dovetailed. In Egypt, Amaury and his Egyptian allies were about to take Cairo when Nur al-Din's commander Shirkuh returned. The king retreated on the promise of further payments.

When Amaury sickened in Gaza, he asked his Egyptian allies to send him their best doctor – the king was an admirer of Eastern medicine. The Egyptians offered this job to one of the caliph's Jewish doctors, who by chance had just returned from Jerusalem.

MOSES MAIMONIDES: THE GUIDE FOR THE PERPLEXED

Maimonides refused to treat the Crusader king, probably a shrewd move since he had only recently arrived in Fatimid Egypt, where the alliance with Jerusalem was short-lived. Maimonides was a refugee from Muslim persecution in Spain, where the golden age of Jewish–Muslim civilization was very much over. It was now split between aggressive Christian kingdoms in the north, and the Muslim south, which had been conquered by fanatical Berber

---

* This palace appears on the fairly realistic map of Jerusalem created in Cambrai around this time. Theodorich saw the palace in 1169. It was given to the German Crusaders in 1229, but it vanished, probably destroyed by the raiding Khwarizmian Turks in 1244. Archaeologists found parts of its foundations in 1971 and 1988 under the Armenian Garden and the Turkish barracks.

tribesmen, the Almohads. They had offered Jews the choice of conversion or death. Young Maimonides pretended to convert but in 1165, he escaped and set off on pilgrimage to Jerusalem. On 14 October, during Tishri, the month of the Jewish New Year and the Day of Atonement, a favourite season for pilgrimages to Jerusalem, Maimonides stood on the Mount of Olives with his brother and father. There he first set eyes on the mountain of the Jewish Temple, and ritually rent his garments – he later specified exactly how much tearing (and later restitching) should be practised by the Jewish pilgrim and when it should be done.

Entering the city through the eastern Jehoshaphat Gate, he found a Christian Jerusalem from which Jews were still officially banned – though there were actually four Jewish dyers living near the Tower of David, under royal protection.* Maimonides grieved for the Temple: 'in ruins, its sanctity endures'. Then 'I entered the great and holy temple and prayed.' It sounds as if he was allowed to pray at the Rock in the Temple† of the Lord (just as Muslims such as Usamah bin Munqidh had been), though he later forbade any visit to the Temple Mount, a rule still obeyed by some Orthodox Jews.

Afterwards, he settled in Egypt where, known to the Arabs as Musa ibn Maymun, he won fame as a polymathic scholar, producing works on subjects varying from medicine to Jewish law, among them the masterpiece *The Guide for the Perplexed*, which wove together philosophy, religion and science; he also served as

* The Jewish traveller Benjamin of Tudela visited Jerusalem just after Maimonides. While he was there, workmen refurbishing the Cenacle on Mount Zion discovered a mysterious cavern that was hailed as King David's Tomb. The Crusaders added a cenotaph which, in the contagious religious atmosphere of Jerusalem, made this Christian site holy for Jews and Muslims too. Benjamin claimed he travelled on to Iraq. Either way, he recorded the drama playing out in Baghdad where a young Jew named David el-Rey (the King) or Alroy declared himself the Messiah, promising to fly the local Jews on wings 'to conquer Jerusalem.' The Jews of Baghdad waited on their rooftops but never achieved lift-off, much to the amusement of their neighbours. Alroy was later murdered. When Benjamin Disraeli visited Jerusalem in the nineteenth century, he started to write his novel, *Alroy*.

† After four centuries as a Jewish synagogue under Islam, the Crusaders sealed up the 'Cave' in the tunnels next to the western wall, turning it into a cistern. So it is unlikely Maimonides prayed there.

royal doctor. But Egypt was in chaos as Amaury and Nur al-Din fought for supremacy over the beleaguered Fatimid caliphate. Amaury was tireless – but unlucky.

In 1169, the master of Syria, Nur al-Din completed the encircle-ment of Jerusalem when his amir Shirkuh won the Battle of Egypt. Shirkuh was aided by his young nephew: Saladin. When the obese Shirkuh died in 1171, Saladin took over Egypt for himself, appointing Maimonides as Rais al-Yahud, Chief of the Jews – and his personal physician. Back in Jerusalem, the plight of the royal heir placed medicine centre-stage.

25

THE LEPER-KING

1174–87

WILLIAM OF TYRE: THE ROYAL TUTOR

King Amaury appointed William of Tyre as tutor to his son, Baldwin. William adored the prince:

> The boy, then about nine, was committed to my care to be instructed in liberal studies. I devoted myself to my royal pupil. He was comely of appearance and continued to make progress in pursuit of letters and gave ever-increasing promise of developing a loveable disposition. He was an excellent horseman. His intellect was keen. He had a retentive memory.

'Like his father,' added William, 'he eagerly listened to history and was well-disposed to follow good advice' – William's advice no doubt. The boy was playful and that was how his tutor discovered his plight.

> He was playing with his companions when they began, as playful boys often do, to pinch each other's arms and hands with their nails. But Baldwin endured it altogether too patiently as if he felt nothing. After this had occurred several times, it was reported to me. When I called him, I discovered that his right arm and hand were particularly numb. I began to be uneasy. The lad's father [the king] was informed, physicians consulted. In the process of time, we recognized the early symptoms. It is impossible to refrain from tears.

THE DISEASE OF BALDWIN IV

William's delightful pupil was a leper* – and the heir to an embattled kingdom. On 15 May 1174, the strongman of Syria and Egypt, mastermind of the new jihad, Nur al-Din, died. Even William admired him as a 'just prince and a religious man'.

King Amaury sped north to exploit Nur al-Din's death but he caught dysentery. He was just thirty-eight but, as Arab and Frankish doctors argued about remedies, he died in Jerusalem on 11 July. The 'loveable' new king Baldwin IV excelled at his studies with William, but he had to endure a variety of treatments – bloodlettings, oil-rubs in 'saracenic ointment' and enemas. His health was supervised by an Arab doctor, Abu Sulayman Dawud, whose brother taught Baldwin to ride with one hand as the disease advanced.

It is hard to find a case of nobler courage and grace under fire than this doomed young king who was closely watched by his devoted tutor: 'Day by day, his condition became worse, the extremities of his face were especially attacked so that his faithful followers were moved with compassion when they looked at him.' He had been brought up apart from his mother but now the louche Agnes returned to support her son, always accompanying him on campaign. She unwisely placed the king in the hands of an arrogant minister who served as seneschal. When he was assassinated in Acre, Jerusalem politics began to assume the menace of a Mafia family in decline.

The king's cousin Count Raymond III of Tripoli demanded the regency and restored stability, appointing the royal tutor, William, as chancellor. But the strategic nightmare that had always haunted Jerusalem now materialized: Saladin, strongman of Cairo, seized

* Leprosy was common. Indeed Jerusalem had its own Order of St Lazarus for leprous knights. Leprosy is hard to catch: the child must have had months of contact, perhaps with a wetnurse suffering mild symptoms. The disease is caused by bacteria passed through droplets in sweat and touch. Baldwin's adolescence triggered lepromatous leprosy. In the film *Kingdom of Heaven* he is shown wearing an iron mask to conceal his utterly ravaged, noseless face, but actually he refused to hide himself as king even as the disease consumed him.

Damascus, gradually but steadily uniting Syria, Egypt, Yemen and much of Iraq into one powerful sultanate, encircling Jerusalem. Raymond of Tripoli, one of those urbane Levantine dynasts who spoke Arabic, bought time by agreeing a truce with Saladin. But it bought time for Saladin too.

Baldwin showed his mettle by raiding up into Syria and Lebanon, but during his frequent illnesses the magnates feuded around the sickbed. The Master of the Templars was increasingly insubordinate, while the Hospitallers were waging a private war against the patriarch, even firing arrows inside the Sepulchre. Meanwhile a new arrival, the veteran knight Reynald of Chatillon, Lord of Kerak and Outrejourdain, across the Jordan, was both asset and liability, radiating aggressive confidence and reckless swagger.

Saladin started to probe the kingdom, attacking Ashkelon and riding towards Jerusalem, whose citizens panicked and fled into the Tower of David. Ashkelon was about to fall when in late November 1177 the leper-king, Reynald and a few hundred knights attacked Saladin's 26,000 troops at Montgisard, north-west of Jerusalem. Inspired by the presence of the True Cross and sightings of St George on the battlefield, Baldwin won a famous victory.

GRACE UNDER PRESSURE:
VICTORY OF THE LEPER-KING

The leper-king returned in triumph while Saladin only just escaped on a camel. But the sultan was still master of Egypt and Syria, and he soon raised new armies.

In 1179, during a raid into Saladin's Syria, Baldwin was ambushed, his horse bolted and he escaped thanks only to the courage of the old Constable of the Kingdom who gave his life to save the boy. Recovering with characteristic pluck, he again led his forces against Saladin's raiders. Close to the Litani river, he was unhorsed and horribly exposed: his spreading paralysis prevented him mounting again. A knight had to carry him off the battlefield on his back. The young king could never marry – it was thought that leprosy could be passed sexually and now he could scarcely lead his armies. He expressed his personal distress – and the need for a strong new king from Europe – to Louis VII of France: 'To be deprived of the use of one's limbs is little help to one in carrying out the work of government. If only I could be cured of the disease of Naaman but I have found no Elisha to heal me. It's not fitting that a hand so weak should hold power when Arab aggression presses upon the Holy City.' The sicker the king, the hotter the fight for power. The king's decline matched the political and moral rot. When Count Raymond of Tripoli and Prince Bohemond of Antioch rode towards the city with a cavalry squadron, the king angrily suspected a coup d'état, again buying time with a truce with Saladin.

When the patriarch died, the queen mother Agnes passed over William, Archbishop of Tyre, and appointed Heraclius of Caesarea, said to be her lover. Favouring rich silks, glittering with jewellery and wafting on a cloud of expensive scent, this ecclesiastical gigolo kept a Nablusite draper's wife, Paschia de Riveri, as his mistress. She now moved to Jerusalem, and even bore him a daughter: Jerusalemites called her Madame la Patriarchesse.

The King would soon die. Agnes had to settle the succession.

GUY: FLAWED HEIR

Agnes therefore arranged a marriage between the king's sister-heiress Sibylla and Guy of Lusignan, the attractive twenty-seven-year-old brother of her latest lover, the Constable of the Kingdom. Princess Sibylla, a young widow who had a son by her first marriage, was the only person who was delighted with the match. To most of the barons, her new husband seemed neither experienced nor high born enough to handle Jerusalem's existential crisis. Guy, now Count of Jaffa and Ashkelon, was a well-born Poitevin baron, but he certainly lacked authority. He divided the kingdom just as it most needed to be united.

Reynald of Kerak broke the truce by attacking the caravans of pilgrims en route to Mecca. There was no duty more sacred for a Muslim ruler than the protection of the *haj*. Saladin was incandescent. But Reynald next outfitted a fleet and raided down the Red

Sea, landing on the coast nearest to Mecca and Medina. Taking the war to the enemy was an impressive but also dangerous game. Reynald was defeated on land and sea and Saladin ordered the throats of captured Frankish sailors to be cut in public outside Mecca. He then raised another army from his ever-expanding empire. As for Reynald, Saladin swore, in his own words, 'to shed the blood of the tyrant of Kerak'.

Baldwin, his 'extremities diseased and damaged, unable to use hands and feet', fell ill with a fever: he appointed Guy as regent, keeping Jerusalem as his royal fief.* Guy could not but glory in his rise, until in September 1183, Saladin invaded Galilee. Guy mustered 1,300 knights and 15,000 infantry near the fountain of Sephoria but either feared – or was unable – to attack Saladin, who finally marched away to attack the fortress of Kerak across the Jordan. Baldwin ordered the beacon lit on the Tower of David to signal to Kerak that help was on its way. Valiantly, heartbreakingly, the leper-king – borne on a litter, blind, grotesque and decaying – led out his army to rescue Kerak.

On his return, the king sacked Guy, appointed Raymond as regent and had his eight-year-old nephew, son of Sibylla, crowned as Baldwin V. After the coronation, the child was carried from the Sepulchre to the Temple on the shoulders of the tallest magnate, Balian of Ibelin. On 16 May 1185, Baldwin IV died aged twenty-three. But the new child-king Baldwin V reigned just a year, buried in an ornate sarcophagus depicting Christ flanked by angels and decorated with wetleaf acanthus.

---

* It was now that William of Tyre 'wearied by the sad disasters, in utter detestation of the present, resolved to abandon the pen and commit to the silence of the tomb the chronicle of events that can serve only to draw forth lamentations and tears. We lack the courage to continue. It is therefore time to hold our peace.' His Outremer chronicle survives, his Islamic history is lost. He argued with Patriarch Heraclius, who excommunicated him. William appealed to Rome but died just as he was leaving for Italy. Possibly he was poisoned. In 1184, Heraclius, bearing the keys of Jerusalem, toured England and France in a quest for an heir to the leper-king or at least more funds and knights. He tried to interest Henry II of England. Instead his youngest son John wanted to accept the throne of Jerusalem, but his father refused to let him. It is hard to imagine that John, later known as Softsword and one of England's most inept kings, would have saved Jerusalem.

Jerusalem needed an adult commander-in-chief. In Nablus, Raymond of Tripoli and the barons gathered to prevent Guy's return, but in Jerusalem the throne belonged to Sibylla, now queen regnant – and she was married to the despised Guy. Sibylla persuaded Patriarch Heraclius to crown her, promising to divorce Guy and nominate another king. But during the coronation, she summoned Guy to be crowned as king beside her. She had outwitted everyone, but the new king and queen were unable to restrain Reynald of Kerak and the Master of the Templars, who were both spoiling for a fight with Saladin. Despite the truce, Reynald ambushed a *haj* caravan from Damascus, capturing Saladin's own sister, mocking Muhammad and torturing his prisoners. Saladin appealed for compensation to King Guy, but Reynald refused to pay it.

In May, Saladin's son raided Galilee. The Templars and the Hospitallers recklessly attacked him, but they were slaughtered at the springs of Cresson, the Master of the Templars and three knights being the only ones to escape. This disaster brought temporary unity.

KING GUY: TAKING THE BAIT

On 27 June 1187, Saladin, at the head of an army of 30,000, marched on Tiberias, hoping to lure the Franks out and strike 'a tremendous blow in the jihad'.

King Guy mustered 12,000 knights and 15,000 infantry at Sephoria in Galilee, but, at a council in the red tent of the kings of Jerusalem, he agonized over the unpalatable alternatives facing him. Raymond of Tripoli urged restraint even though his wife was besieged in Tiberias. Reynald and the Master of the Templars responded by calling Raymond a traitor and demanded battle. Finally Guy took the bait. He led the army across the baking-hot Galilean hills for a day until, harassed by Saladin's troops, overwhelmed by scorching heat and paralysed by thirst, he pitched camp on the volcanic plateau of the twin-peaked Horns of Hattin. They then went looking for water – but the well there was dry. 'Ah

Lord God,' said Raymond, 'the war is over; we are dead men; the kingdom is finished.'

When the Crusaders awoke on the morning of Saturday 4 July, they could hear prayers in the Muslim camp below. They were already thirsty in the summer heat. The Muslims lit the scrubland. Soon it was burning all around them.

26

SALADIN

1187–1189

SALADIN: THE BATTLE

Saladin did not sleep, but spent the night organizing his forces and supplies, positioning his two wings. He had surrounded the Franks. The Sultan of Egypt and Syria was determined not to waste this opportunity. His multinational army, with its contingents of Kurds, Arabs, Turks, Armenians and Sudanese, was an awesome sight, relished by Saladin's excitable secretary, Imad al-Din:

> A swelling ocean of whinnying chargers, swords and cuirasses, iron-tipped lances like stars, crescent swords, Yemenite blades, yellow banners, standards red as anemones and coats of mail glittering like pools, swords polished white as streams of water, feathered bows blue as birds, helmets gleaming over slim curvetting chargers.

At dawn, Saladin, commanding the centre on horseback, accompanied by his young son Afdal, and protected as always by his bodyguard of devoted Turkish mamluks (slave-soldiers), started his attack, showering the Franks with arrows and directing the charges of his cavaliers and horse-archers to keep the heavily armoured Franks at bay. For Guy, everything depended on maintaining the shield of infantry around his mounted knights; for Saladin, everything depended on separating them.

As the Bishop of Acre raised the True Cross before the king, Guy's army repelled the first charges, but soon the thirsty Frankish soldiers fled to higher ground, leaving the knights exposed. Guy's knights launched their charges. As Raymond of Tripoli and Balian of Ibelin galloped towards the sultan's forces, Saladin simply ordered his nephew Taki al-Din, commanding the right wing, to open his ranks: the Crusaders galloped through. But the Muslim ranks closed again, tightening the net. Their archers, mostly Armenians, picked off the Frankish horses with 'clouds of arrows like locusts', stranding the knights, and 'their lions became hedgehogs'. On that 'burningly hot day', unhorsed and exposed, swollen-mouthed with thirst, tormented by the infernal brushwood, unsure of their leadership, Guy's soldiers perished, fled or surrendered as his order of battle disintegrated.

He retreated to one of the Horns and there pitched his red tent. His knights surrounded him for a last stand. 'When the Frankish king had withdrawn to the hilltop,' recalled Saladin's son Afdal, 'his knights made a valiant charge and drove the Muslims back upon my father.' For a moment, it seemed as if Frankish courage would threaten Saladin himself. Afdal saw his father's dismay: 'He changed colour and pulled at his beard then rushed forward crying, "Give the devil the lie!"' at which the Muslims charged again, breaking the Crusaders, 'who retreated up the hill. When I saw the Franks fleeing, I cried out with glee, "We've routed them!"' But 'tortured by thirst', they 'charged again and drove our men back to where my father stood'. Saladin rallied his men, who broke Guy's charge. 'We've routed them,' cried Afdal again.

'Be quiet,' snapped Saladin, pointing at the red tent. 'We haven't beaten them so long as that tent stands there!' At that moment, Afdal saw the tent overturned. The Bishop of Acre was killed, the True Cross was captured. Around the royal tent, Guy and his knights were so exhausted that they lay in their armour helpless on the ground. 'Then my father dismounted,' said Afdal, 'and bowed to the ground, giving thanks to God with tears of joy.'

Saladin held court in the lobby of his resplendent tent, which was still being pitched as his amirs delivered their prisoners. Once the tent was up, he received the King of Jerusalem and Reynald of Kerak. Guy was so desiccated that Saladin offered him a glass of sherbet iced with the snows of Mount Hermon. The king slaked his thirst then handed it to Reynald at which Saladin said: 'You're the one who gave him the drink. I give him no drink.' Reynald was not offered the protection of Arab hospitality.

Saladin rode out to congratulate his men and inspect the battlefield, with the 'limbs of the fallen, naked on the field, scattered in pieces, lacerated and disjointed, dismembered, eyes gouged out, stomachs disembowelled, bodies cut in half,' the carnage of medieval battle. On his return, the sultan recalled Guy and Reynald. The king was left in the vestibule; Reynald taken inside: 'God has given me victory over you,' said Saladin. 'How often have you broken your oaths?'

'This is how princes have always behaved,' replied the defiant Reynald.

Saladin offered him Islam. Reynald refused disdainfully, at which the sultan sprang up, drew a scimitar and sliced off his arm at the shoulder. The guards finished him off. The headless Reynald was dragged feet first past Guy and thrown out at the tent door.

The King of Jerusalem was led inside. 'It's not customary for kings to kill kings,' said Saladin, 'but this man crossed the limits so he suffered what he suffered.'

In the morning, Saladin bought all the 200 Templars and Hospitaller knights from his men, for fifty dinars each. The Christian warriors were offered conversion to Islam, but few accepted. Saladin called for volunteers from the Sufi mystics and Islamic scholars, to whom he gave the order to kill all the knights. Most begged for the privilege, though some appointed substitutes out of fear that they would be mocked for bungling the job. As Saladin watched from his dais, this messy and amateurish butchery now destroyed what remained of the might of Jerusalem. The bodies were left where they fell. Even a year later, the battlefield remained 'covered with their bones'.

Saladin sent the King of Jerusalem to Damascus along with the True Cross, hung impotently upside down on a lance, along with prisoners so plentiful that one of Saladin's retainers saw 'a single person holding a tent-rope pulling by himself thirty prisoners'. Frankish slaves cost just three dinars and one was bought for a shoe.

The sultan himself advanced to conquer the rest of Outremer, capturing the coastal cities of Sidon, Jaffa, Acre and Ashkelon but failing to take Tyre when the courageous Conrad, Marquis of Montferrat (whose brother had been briefly married to Sibylla) arrived just in time to rescue this key fortress-port. Instead, Saladin's Egyptian viceroy, his brother, Safadin, advised him to go post-haste towards Jerusalem in case he fell ill before taking the Holy City: 'If you die of a colic tonight, Jerusalem will stay in the hands of the Franks.'

SALADIN'S SIEGE: SLAUGHTER OR SURRENDER?

On Sunday 20 September 1187, Saladin surrounded Jerusalem, first setting up camp on the west outside the Tower of David then moving to the north-east, where Godfrey had stormed the walls.

The city was crowded with refugees but there were only two knights left to fight under the patriarch and the two queens of Jerusalem, Sibylla and King Amaury's widow Maria, now married to the magnate Balian of Ibelin. Heraclius could scarcely find fifty men to guard the walls. Fortunately Balian of Ibelin arrived, under Saladin's safe-conduct, to rescue his wife Queen Maria and their children. Balian had promised Saladin not to fight, but now the Jerusalemites begged him to take command. Balian could not refuse and writing as one knight to another, he apologized to Saladin, who forgave this bad faith. The sultan even arranged an escort for Maria and the children. Giving them bejewelled robes and treating them to feasts, the sultan sat the children on his knees and began to weep, knowing they were seeing Jerusalem for the last time. 'The things of this world are merely lent to us,' he mused.

Balian* knighted every noble boy over sixteen and thirty bourgeois, armed every man, launching sorties. As Saladin started to attack, the women prayed at the Sepulchre, shaving their heads in penance, and monks and nuns paraded barefoot under the walls. By 29 September, Saladin's sappers were undermining the wall. The Franks prepared to die as holy martyrs, but Heraclius

* A fictional version of Balian (played by Orlando Bloom) is the hero of the movie *Kingdom of Heaven*, where he has an affair with Queen Sibylla (Eva Green).

discouraged them, saying that this would leave the women to be harem slaves. Syrian Christians, who resented the Latins, agreed to open the gates for Saladin. On the 30th, as the Muslim forces attacked the city, Balian visited Saladin to negotiate. The sultan's flag was even raised on the walls, but his troops were repulsed.

'We shall deal with you just as you dealt with the population of Jerusalem [in 1099] with murder and enslavement and other savageries,' Saladin told Balian.

'Sultan,' replied Balian, 'there are very many of us in the city. If we see death is inevitable, we shall kill our children and our wives, and pull down the Sanctuary of the Rock and al-Aqsa Mosque.'

At this, Saladin agreed on terms. He graciously freed Queen Sibylla and even the widow of Reynald, but the rest of the Jerusalemites had to be either ransomed or sold into slavery.

SALADIN: THE MAN

Saladin was never quite the liberal gentleman, superior in manners to the brutish Franks, portrayed by Western writers in the nineteenth century. But by the standards of medieval empire-builders he deserves his attractive reputation. When he gave one of his sons advice about how he had built an empire, he told him: 'I have only achieved what I have by coaxing people. Hold no grudge against anyone for Death spares nobody. Take care in your relations with people.' Saladin did not look impressive and lacked vanity. When his silken robes were spattered by a courtier riding through a puddle in Jerusalem, Saladin just burst out laughing. He never forgot that the twists of fate that had brought him such success could just as easily be reversed. While his rise had been bloody, he disliked violence, advising his favourite son Zahir: 'I warn you against shedding blood, indulging in it and making a habit of it, for blood never sleeps.' When Muslim raiders stole a baby from a Frankish woman, she crossed the lines to appeal to Saladin who, moved to tears, immediately had the baby found and returned it to its mother. On another occasion, when one of his sons asked to be allowed to kill some Frankish prisoners, he reprimanded him and refused, lest he get a taste for killing.

Yusuf ibn Ayyub, son of a Kurdish soldier of fortune, was born in 1138 in Tikrit (today's Iraq – Saddam Hussein was also born there). His father and his uncle, Shirkuh, served Zangi and his son Nur al-Din. The boy grew up in Damascus, enjoying the life of wine, cards and girls. He played nocturnal polo by candlelight with Nur al-Din, who made him police chief of Damascus. He studied the Koran but also the pedigrees of horseflesh. In the struggle for Egypt, Nur al-Din despatched Shirkuh, who took along his nephew, Yusuf, now aged twenty-six.

Together, leading a mere 2,000 foreign horsemen and over-coming desperate odds, this Kurdish uncle and nephew managed to steal Egypt from the armies of the Fatimids and Jerusalem. In January 1169, Yusuf, who took the honorific name Saladin,* assassinated the vizier whom his uncle then succeeded. But Shirkuh died of a heart attack. At thirty-one, Saladin became the last Fatimid vizier. In 1071, when the last caliph died, Saladin dismantled the Shiite caliphate in Egypt (which has remained Sunni ever since), and massacred the overmighty Sudanese guards in Cairo, while adding Mecca, Medina, Tunisia and Yemen to his growing realm.

When Nur al-Din died in 1174, Saladin headed north and took Damascus, gradually expanding his empire to embrace much of Iraq and Syria as well as Egypt, but the link between the two territories was today's Jordan, which was partly controlled by the Crusaders. War with Jerusalem was not just good theology, but good imperial politics too. Saladin preferred Damascus, regarding

---

* Saladin was the Crusaders' shorthand for Salah al-Dunya al-Din (the Goodness of the World and the Faith). Saladin's brother, known by the Crusaders as Safadin, was born Abu Bakr ibn Ayyub, adopting the honorific Safah al-Din (Sword of the Religion) and later the royal name al-Adil (The Just) by which he is called in most histories. Two of Saladin's courtiers wrote biographies: Imad ad-Din, his secretary, wrote *The Lightning of Syria* and then *Ciceronian Eloquence on the Conquest of the Holy City*, characterized by purple passages. In 1188, Baha al-Din Ibn Shaddad, an Islamic scholar from Iraq, visited Jerusalem and was appointed by Saladin first as qadi (judge) of the army and then as overseer of Jerusalem. On Saladin's death he served as chief qadi for two of his sons. His biography, *Sultanly Anecdotes and Josephly Virtues* (a reference to his first name Yusuf, Joseph), is a rounded portrait of a warlord under pressure.

Egypt as his cash-cow: 'Egypt was a whore,' he joked, 'who'd tried to part me from my faithful wife [Damascus].'

Saladin was no dictator.* His empire was a patchwork of greedy amirs, rebellious princelings and ambitious brothers, sons and nephews, to whom he doled out fiefdoms in return for loyalty, taxes and warriors. He was always short of cash and soldiers. Only his charisma held it all together. Frequently defeated by the Crusaders, he was not an outstanding general, but 'shunning his womenfolk and all his pleasures', he was tenacious. He spent most of his life fighting other Muslims but now his personal mission, the Holy War to win back Jerusalem, became his ruling passion. 'I've given up earthly pleasures,' he said. 'I've had my fill of them.'

Once when walking by the sea during the war, he told his minister Ibn Shaddad, 'I have it in my mind that, when God has allowed me to conquer the rest of the coast, I shall divide my lands, make my testament and set sail on this sea to pursue them there until there no longer remain on the face of the earth any who deny God – or die in the attempt.' But he enforced Islam more strictly than the Fatimids. When he heard of a young Islamic heretic preaching in his lands, he had him crucified and left hanging for days.

He was happiest sitting up at night with his entourage of generals and intellectuals, receiving messengers while chatting. He admired scholars and poets, and his court was not complete without Usamah bin Munqidh, now ninety, who recalled how 'he sought me out across the land. By his goodwill, from misfortune's fangs was I snatched. He treats me like family.' Saladin was lame and often ill, cared for by twenty-one doctors – eight Muslim, eight Jewish (including Maimonides) and five Christian. When the sultan rose for prayer or ordered the candles, his courtiers recognized the sign that the evening was over. If he himself was above reproach, his hedonistic and ambitious relatives more than made up for his restraint.

---

* In Jerusalem an old man had the temerity to sue the sultan himself over some property. Saladin came down from his throne to be judged equally, and won the case, but then loaded the claimant with gifts.

DANCING-GIRLS AND APHRODISIACS:
THE COURT OF SALADIN

The young princes, according to the satirist al-Wahrani, held orgies where the hosts ran naked on all fours howling like dogs and sipped wine from the navels of singing girls while cobwebs took over in the mosques. In Damascus, the Arabs grumbled about Saladin's rule. The writer Ibn Unain mocked Saladin's Egyptian officials, particularly the black Sudanese: 'If I were black with a head like an elephant, bulky forearms and a huge penis, then you would see to my needs.' Saladin exiled him for this impertinence.

Saladin's nephew Taki al-Din was his most talented general, but also the most ambitious and debauched of the princes. His hobbies were so notorious that it was said his words were 'sweeter than a beating with a prostitute's slipper'. The satirist Wahrani suggested ironically, 'If you resign from the government, you could turn away from repentance and collect the prostitutes of Mosul, the panders of Aleppo and the singing-girls of Iraq.'

Such was Taki's priapic over-indulgence that he started losing weight, energy and erection. He consulted his Jewish doctor Maimonides, who advised his own community against excessive 'eating, drinking and copulation' but treated his princely patients differently. The royal doctor wrote Saladin's nephew a special work entitled *On Sexual Intercourse*, prescribing moderation, limited alcohol, women not too old nor too young, a cocktail of oxtongue plant and wine and, finally, a 'wondrous secret' of medieval Viagra: massage the royal penis for two hours before intercourse with oils mixed with saffron-coloured ants. Maimonides promised the erection would last long after the act.

Saladin loved Taki, whom he promoted to viceroy of Egypt, but was then exasperated by his nephew's attempt to create his own fiefdom. He moved him to rule swathes of Iraq instead. Now this exuberant nephew and most of Saladin's family arrived to enjoy the liberation of Jerusalem.

SALADIN'S CITY

Saladin watched the Latin Christians leave Jerusalem for ever: the Jerusalemites had to pay a ransom of ten dinars per man, five per woman, one per child. No one could leave without a receipt of payment, but Saladin's officials made fortunes as bribes were paid and Christians were lowered from the walls in baskets or escaped in disguise. Saladin himself had no interest in money and, though he received 220,000 dinars, much of the cash went astray.

Thousands of Jerusalemites could not afford their ransom. They were led away into slavery and the harem. Balian paid 30,000 dinars to ransom 7,000 poor Jerusalemites, while the Sultan's brother Safadin asked for a thousand unfortunates and freed them. Saladin gave 500 each to Balian and to Patriarch Heraclius. The Muslims were shocked to see the latter pay his ten dinars and leave the city laden with carts of gold and carpets. 'How many well-guarded women were profaned, nubile girls married, virgins dishonoured, proud women deflowered, lovely women's red lips kissed, untamed ones tamed,' recalled Saladin's secretary Imad al-Din with a rather creepy glee. 'How many noblemen took them as concubines, how many great ladies sold at low prices!'

Under the eyes of the sultan, the two columns of Christians looked back one last time and wept at the loss of Jerusalem, reflecting, 'She who was named the mistress of other cities had become a slave and handmaid.'

On Friday 2 October, Saladin entered Jerusalem and ordered the Temple Mount, known to Muslims as the Haram al-Sharif, to be cleansed of the infidel. The Cross over the Dome of the Rock was thrown down to cries of 'Allahu Akhbar', dragged through the city and smashed, the Jesus paintings torn out, the cloisters north of the Dome demolished, the cubicles and apartments within the Aqsa removed. Saladin's sister arrived from Damascus with a camel caravan of rosewater. The sultan himself and his nephew Taki personally scrubbed the courts of the Haram with rosewater, accompanied by a cleaning-party of princes and amirs. Saladin brought Nur al-Din's carved wooden *minbar* from Aleppo and set it up in al-Aqsa Mosque where it remained for seven centuries.

The sultan did not so much destroy and rebuild as adapt and embroider, reusing the gorgeous spolia of the Crusaders with their foliate patterns, capitals and wetleaf acanthus; his own architecture is thus constructed with the very symbols of his enemies, which makes it hard to distinguish between the buildings of the Crusaders and Saladin.

Every respected member of the *ulema*, Muslim clergy and scholars, from Cairo to Baghdad, wanted to preach at Friday prayers, but Saladin chose the Qadi of Aleppo, giving him a black robe to wear: his sermon in al-Aqsa praised the *fadail* – the merits – of Islamic Jerusalem. Saladin himself had become the 'light that shines in every dawn that brings darkness to the believers' by 'liberating the brother shrine of Mecca'. Saladin then walked to the Dome to pray in what he called 'the jewel of the signet-ring of Islam'. Saladin's love for Jerusalem was 'as great as mountains'. His mission was to create an Islamic Jerusalem and he considered whether to destroy the Dungheap – the Holy Sepulchre. Some of his grandees called for its demolition, but he mused that the place would still remain holy whether or not the Church stood there. Citing Omar the Just, he closed the Church for only three days and then gave it to the Greek Orthodox, though he bricked up one entrance to control the movement (and profits) of pilgrims more easily. Overall, he tolerated most churches, but aimed to diminish the Christian Quarter's non-Islamic character. Church bells were again banned. Instead, for hundreds of years right up until the nineteenth century, the muezzin held the monopoly of sound and the Christians announced prayers with the clack of wooden clappers and the clash of cymbals. He destroyed some churches outside the walls and commandeered many prominent Christian buildings for his own Salahiyya endowments – which still exist today.*

---

* Saladin held court sometimes in the Hospital and sometimes in the Patriarch's Palace, where there was a wooden hut on the roof where he liked to sit up late at night with his entourage. His brother Safadin resided in the Cenacle complex on Mount Zion. Saladin decided to give the Patriarch's Palace to his own Salahiyya Sufi convent, or *khanqah*. Today it remains the Salahiyya *khanqah* (as its inscription declares) and the bedroom with its fine Crusader capitals where Saladin (and the patriarchs) slept is today the bedroom of Sheikh al-Alami, a member of one of

Saladin brought many Muslim scholars and mystics to the city; but Muslims alone could not repopulate Jerusalem, so he invited back many Armenians, who became a special community that endures today (they call themselves the Kaghakatsi); and many Jews – 'the entire race of Ephraim' – from Ashkelon, Yemen and Morocco.

Saladin was exhausted but he reluctantly left Jerusalem to mop up the last Crusader fortresses. He took the great sea base of Acre. Yet he never finished off the Crusaders: he chivalrously released King Guy and failed to conquer Tyre, which left the Christians with a vital seaport from which to plan a counter-attack. Perhaps he underestimated the reaction of Christendom but the news of Jerusalem's fall had shocked Europe, from kings and popes to knights and peasants, and mobilized a powerful new Crusade, the Third.

Saladin's mistakes would cost him dear. In August 1189, King Guy appeared before Acre with a small force and proceeded to besiege the city. Saladin did not take Guy's brave exploit too seriously but sent a contingent to swat his little army. Instead Guy fought Saladin's men to a standstill and rallied the Crusader fightback. Saladin besieged Guy but Guy besieged Acre. When Saladin's Egyptian fleet was defeated, Guy was joined by shiploads of German, English and Italian Crusaders. In Europe, the kings of England and France and the German Emperor took the Cross; fleets were being collected; armies mustered to join the battle for Acre. This was the start of a grindingly bloody two-year struggle, soon joined by the greatest kings of Europe who were determined to win back Jerusalem.

First came the Germans. When Saladin heard that the red-bearded Emperor Frederick Barbarossa was already marching to the Holy Land with a German army, he finally summoned his forces and called for a jihad. But then came better news.

Jerusalem's prominent families. The patriarchs had special entrances from their Palace to the Church of the Holy Sepulchre and Saladin blocked these though they can still be seen behind the tills of today's shops. He also took over St Mary's Latina for his Salahiyya Hospital and commandeered St Anne's as his Salahiyya madrassa, religious school. Now it is a church again but it is still inscribed to Saladin as 'Reviver of the Empire of the Commander of the Believers'.

In June 1190, Barbarossa drowned in a Cilician river; his son, Duke Frederick of Swabia, boiled the body and pickled it in vinegar, burying the flesh in Antioch. But he then marched to Acre with his army and his father's bones which he planned to bury in Jerusalem. Barbarossa's death played into the eschatalogical legend, that the Emperor of the Last Days was asleep, one day to rise again. The Duke of Swabia himself died of scurvy outside Acre and the German Crusade was broken. But after many months of desperate fighting with thousands killed by the plague (including Heraclius the patriarch and Sibylla, Queen of Jerusalem),* Saladin received the bad news that the outstanding warrior of Christendom was on his way.

* The new Queen of Jerusalem was Sibylla's half-sister, Isabella, daughter of King Amaury and Queen Maria. Isabella divorced her husband to marry Conrad of Montferrat. He thus became by marriage the titular king of Jerusalem.

27

THE THIRD CRUSADE:
SALADIN AND RICHARD

1189–93

LIONHEART: CHIVALRY AND SLAUGHTER

On 4 July 1190, Richard the Lionheart, King of England, and Philip II Augustus, King of France, set out on the Third Crusade to liberate Jerusalem. The thirty-two-year-old Richard had just inherited his father Henry II's Angevin empire – England and half of France. Possessed of abundant vitality, red-haired and athletic, he was as brash and extrovert as Saladin was patient and subtle. He was a man of his time, both a writer of saucy troubadour songs and a pious Christian who, overcome with his sinfulness, threw himself naked before his clergy and scourged himself with whips.

Eleanor of Aquitaine's favourite son showed little interest in women, but the nineteenth-century claim that he was homosexual has been discredited. War was his real love and he ruthlessly squeezed the English to pay for his Crusade, joking, 'I'd have sold London if there'd been a buyer.' As England vibrated with Crusader revivalism,* the Jews were targeted in the cull that culminated in the mass-suicide of York, the English Masada. By then, Richard had departed. He sailed for Jerusalem and wherever he landed he presented himself as the personification of the royal warrior. He always wore scarlet, the colour of war, and brandished a sword that he claimed was Excalibur. In Sicily, he rescued his sister, the widowed Queen Joanna, from the new king, and sacked Messina. When he reached Cyprus, ruled by a Byzantine prince, he simply

---

* The oldest pub in England, Ye Olde Trip to Jerusalem, in Nottingham, dates from Richard's Crusade.

conquered the island and then sailed for Acre with twenty-five galleys.

On 8 June 1191, Richard landed and joined the King of France at the siege, where bouts of fighting alternated with interludes of fraternizing between the camps. Saladin and his courtiers watched his arrival and were impressed with the 'great pomp' of 'this mighty warrior' and with his 'passion for war'.

The battlefield had become a plague-ridden shanty encampment of royal marquees, filthy huts, soup kitchens, markets, bathhouses and brothels. That the prostitutes fascinated the Muslims is evident from the account of Imad, Saladin's secretary, who visited Richard's camp and exhausted even his reservoir of pornographic metaphors as he ogled these 'singers and coquettes, tinted and painted, blue-eyed with fleshy thighs', who 'plied a brisk trade, brought their silver anklets up to touch their golden earrings, invited swords to sheath, made javelins rise toward shields, gave birds a place to peck with their beaks, caught lizard after lizard in their holes, [and] guided pens to inkwells'.

If even Imad admitted that 'a few foolish mamluks slipped away' to sample these Frankish coquettes, many must have done so. Richard's energy changed the nature of the war. Saladin was already ill; soon both the European kings fell sick too, but even on his sickbed Richard brandished a crossbow, firing bolts at the enemy camp while fleet after fleet delivered the cream of European knighthood.

Saladin, like 'a bereft mother, on horseback urging people to perform their jihad duty' was outmanned and outfought. After the early departure of the jealous Philip Augustus, Richard took command – 'I rule and nobody rules me' – but his forces too were suffering. He opened negotiations, Saladin sending his worldly but more aloof brother Safadin as his envoy, though these pragmatists were still shadow-boxing with everything to play for. They were evenly matched, each fielding 20,000 men, both struggling to impose their will on their insubordinate, troublesome grandees and polyglot armies.

Meanwhile Acre could hold out no longer and its governor started to negotiate surrender. 'More affected than a distracted lovesick girl', Saladin had little choice but to acquiesce in Acre's capitulation, promising the return of the True Cross and the release of 1,500 prisoners. But his priority was to defend Jerusalem. He dragged his feet on the terms in order to encourage divisions among the Crusaders, save money and delay their campaign. But Lionheart meant business and called Saladin's bluff.

On 20 August, he shepherded 3,000 bound Muslim prisoners on to the plain in view of Saladin's army and then butchered the men, women and children. So much for the legend of chivalry. The horrified Saladin sent in his cavalry, but it was too late. Afterwards, he beheaded all Frankish prisoners who fell into his hands.

Five days later, Richard marched down the coast towards Jaffa, the port of Jerusalem, his army chanting '*Sanctum Sepulchrum adjuva!* Help us, Holy Sepulchre!' On 7 September, Lionheart found Saladin and his army blocking the way at Arsuf. Richard's challenge was to use massed infantry to exhaust Saladin's waves of charging, curveting cavaliers and horse-archers until he could unleash the thundering power of his knights. Richard held back until a Hospitaller galloped forward. Then he led the full charge that smashed into the Muslims. Saladin desperately threw in his royal guard of mamluks – known as the Ring. Faced with a 'complete rout', the sultan withdrew just in time, his army 'conserved for the protection of Jerusalem'. At one point, he was guarded by just seventeen men. Afterwards he was wrung out and too downhearted even to eat.

Saladin rode to Jerusalem to celebrate Ramadan and prepare her defences. Richard knew that while Saladin's army and empire were intact, the Crusaders could not hold Jerusalem even if they captured her – which made it sensible to negotiate. 'The Muslims and the Franks are done for,' Richard wrote to Saladin, 'the land is ruined at the hands of both sides. All we have to talk about is Jerusalem, the True Cross and these lands. Jerusalem is the centre of our worship which we shall never renounce.' Saladin explained what al-Quds meant to the Muslims: 'Jerusalem is ours just as much as yours. Indeed for us it is greater than it is for you, for it is where Our Prophet came on his Night Journey and the gathering place of the angels.'

Richard was willing to learn. Flexible and imaginative, he now proposed a compromise: his sister Joanna would marry Safadin.

The Christians would get the coast and access to Jerusalem; the Muslims the hinterland, with Jerusalem the capital of King Safadin and Queen Joanna under Saladin's sovereignty. Saladin agreed to this in order to draw out Richard but Joanna was indignant: 'How could she possibly allow a Muslim to have carnal knowledge of her?' Richard claimed it was a joke, and then told Safadin: 'I shall marry you to my niece.' Saladin was bemused: 'Our best course is to fight on with the jihad – or die ourselves.'

On 31 October, Richard set off slowly towards Jerusalem while continuing to negotiate with the urbane Safadin. They met in magnificent tents, exchanged gifts and attended each other's feasts. 'We must have a foothold in Jerusalem,' insisted Richard. When he was criticized for the negotiations by his French knights, he beheaded some Turkish prisoners and ghoulishly posed their heads around the camp.

At this fraught moment, Saladin received bad news: his dissolute nephew, Taki al-Din, who had been trying to build his own private empire, was dead. Saladin hid the letter, ordered his tent cleared, then 'wept bitterly, choked by his tears', before washing his face with rosewater and returning to the command: it was no time to show weakness. He inspected Jerusalem and her new Egyptian garrison.

On 23 December, Richard advanced to Le Thoron des Chevaliers (Latrun) where he, his wife and his sister celebrated Christmas in splendour. On 6 January 1192, amid rain, cold and mud, Richard had reached Bayt Nuba, 12 miles from the city. The French and English barons wanted Jerusalem at any cost but Richard tried to convince them that he did not have the men for a siege. Saladin waited in Jerusalem hoping that the rain and snow would discourage the Crusaders. On 13 January, Richard retreated.*

It was stalemate. Saladin used fifty stonemasons and 2,000

---

* In April 1192, Richard finally realized that Guy, who had been king of Jerusalem only by marriage to his late wife, was a busted flush. Instead he recognized Conrad of Montferrat, husband of Queen Isabella, as king of Jerusalem. But days later, Conrad was killed by the Assassins. Henry, Count of Champagne, a nephew of both Richard of England and Philip of France, married Queen Isabella of Jerusalem, still aged only twenty-one, pregnant with Conrad's child and already on her third husband. He became King Henry of Jerusalem. In order to compensate Guy, Richard sold him Cyprus, which his family ruled for three centuries.

Frankish prisoners to refortify Jerusalem, demolishing the higher
floors of Our Mary of Jehoshaphat at the foot of the Mount of Olives
and the Coenaculum on Mount Zion to provide the stones. Saladin,
Safadin and their sons themselves worked on the walls.

Richard meanwhile captured and fortified Ashkelon, the gateway
to Egypt, offering Saladin a partition of Jerusalem, with Muslims
keeping the Haram and Tower of David. But these talks, almost
comparable in complexity to those between Israelis and Palestinians
in the twenty-first century, were in vain: both still hoped to possess
Jerusalem totally. On 20 March, Safadin and his son Kamil visited
Richard with an offer of access to the Sepulchre and the return of
the True Cross: in the classic *beau geste* of chivalry, Lionheart dubbed
young Kamil, girding him with the belt of knighthood.

Yet this theatre of chivalry was unpopular with the mutinous
French knights, who demanded the immediate storming of Jerusalem. On 10 June Richard led them back to Bayt Nuba, where they
proceeded to set up camp in the parching heat and for three weeks
argued about what to do next. Richard relieved the tension by riding
out on reconnaissance, at some point reaching Montjoie, where he
dismounted to say his prayers but held up his shield to hide the
glory of Jerusalem, supposedly saying, 'Lord God, I pray thee not to
let me see thy Holy City that I could not deliver from thine enemies!'

Lionheart employed spies in the sultan's army who now
informed him that one of Saladin's princes was leading a caravan
of reinforcements from Egypt. Richard, sporting Bedouin dress, led
out 500 knights and 1,000 light cavalry, to ambush the Egyptians.
He dispersed the troops, captured the caravan, bagging 3,000
camels and ample packhorses of supplies – enough perhaps to
march on Jerusalem or Egypt. 'This was grievous to Saladin's heart,'
said his minister Ibn Shaddad, 'but I tried to calm him.' Within a
fraught Jerusalem, Saladin was close to panic, his stress unbearable.
He poisoned the wells around the city and positioned his meagre
contingents under the command of his sons. His armies were
inadequate and he anxiously recalled Safadin from Iraq.

On 2 July, he convened a council of war, but his amirs were just
as unreliable as Richard's barons. 'The best thing we can do,' said
Ibn Shaddad, opening the meeting, 'is assemble at the Dome of the

Rock to prepare ourselves for death.' Then there was silence, the amirs sitting so still it was 'as though there were birds on their heads'. The council debated whether the leader should make a last stand within the city or avoid being trapped in a siege. The sultan himself knew that without his own presence his henchmen would soon surrender. Finally Saladin said, 'You're the army of Islam. Turn your reins away and they'll roll up these lands like a scroll. It's your responsibility – that's why you've been funded by the treasury all these years.' The amirs agreed to fight, but the next day they returned to say they feared a siege like that of Acre. Was it not better to fight outside the walls and at worst, temporarily lose Jerusalem? The generals insisted that Saladin or one of his sons had to stay in Jerusalem or else his Turks would fight his Kurds.

Saladin stayed – and his spies kept him well informed about Richard's problems. As 15 July, the anniversary of the capture of Jerusalem in 1099, approached, the Crusaders discovered yet another fragment of the True Cross, a timely miracle which elated the ranks. But the French under the Duke of Burgundy and the Anglo-Angevins under Richard were almost at daggers drawn, taunting each other with silly slogans and filthy ditties. Richard, the troubadour, penned a jingle of his own.

Saladin was almost sick with the tension: on the night of Thursday 3 July, Ibn Shaddad was so worried that he prescribed the comfort of prayer: 'We are in the most blessed place we could be on this day.' At Friday prayers the sultan should make two ritual *rakas*, bows from the waist then two full prostrations. Saladin performed these rituals and openly wept. By nightfall, his spies reported that the Franks were packing up. On 4 July, Richard led the retreat.

Saladin was exuberant, riding out to meet his favourite son Zahir, kissing him between the eyes and escorting him into Jerusalem, where the prince stayed with his father in the palace of the Master of the Hospitallers. But both sides were exhausted: Richard was receiving reports that back in England his brother John was close to open rebellion. If he wished to save his lands, he needed to return home soon.

Encouraged by Richard's problems, on 28 July Saladin sprang a surprise attack on Jaffa, which he swiftly captured after a bombardment by his mangonels. While Ibn Shaddad was negotiating the surrender, his son Zahir fell asleep on watch. Suddenly Richard the Lionheart appeared offshore in a scarlet-flagged galley. He had arrived just in time: some Franks were still holding out. Firing an arbalest crossbow, he waded on to the beach – 'red haired, his tunic red, his banner red.' Without even time to take off his waders and don his armour, wielding a Danish battleaxe, accompanied by just seventeen knights and a few hundred infantry, Richard managed to retake the town in a stupendous display of flamboyant shock-fighting.

Afterwards, he teased Saladin's minister: 'This sultan of yours is a great man [yet] how is it he departed merely because I arrived? I only had my seaboots on and not even my breastplate!' Saladin and Safadin were said to have sent Arabian horses to Lionheart as a gift, but such chivalry was often a delaying tactic for they soon counter-attacked. Richard repulsed them and then challenged the Saracens to single combat. He galloped with his lance up and down the ranks – but there were no takers.

Saladin ordered another attack, but his amirs refused. He was so enraged that he considered a Zangi-style crucifixion of his mutinous generals. However, he calmed himself and then invited them to share some juicy apricots that had just arrived from Damascus.

The king and the sultan had fought themselves to a standstill. 'You and we together are ruined,' Richard confided to Saladin. As they negotiated, both the warlords collapsed, desperately ill, their resources and wills utterly exhausted.

28

THE SALADIN DYNASTY

1193–1250

THE DEATH OF THE SULTAN

On 2 September 1192, sultan and king agreed the Treaty of Jaffa, the first partition of Palestine: the Christian kingdom received a new lease of life with Acre as its capital, while Saladin kept Jerusalem, granting full Christian access to the Sepulchre.

On the way back to Jerusalem, Saladin met his brother Safadin who kissed the ground to thank God, and they prayed together at the Dome of the Rock. Though Richard refused to visit Islamic Jerusalem, his knights flocked there to make their pilgrimages and were received by Saladin. The sultan showed them the True Cross, but afterwards the largest part of that ultimate relic was lost – and vanished for ever.* When the king's adviser Hubert Walter was in Jerusalem, he discussed Richard with Saladin who offered the view that Lionheart lacked wisdom and moderation. Thanks to Walter, Saladin allowed Latin priests back into the Sepulchre. When the Byzantine emperor Isaac Angelus demanded it for the Orthodox, Saladin decided that they must share it under his supervision and appointed Sheikh Ghanim al-Khazraji as Custodian of the Church, a role still performed today by his descendants, the Nusseibeh family.

The two protagonists never met. On 9 October, Richard sailed

---

* In 1187, Saladin himself sent a small piece of the Cross as a gift to Emperor Isaac Angelos in a Venetian ship. The ship was captured by a Pisan pirate named Fortis, who killed the entire crew and took the relic to Bonafacio in Corsica, whence it was seized by Genoese pirates. Sections of the Cross still survive in the reliquaries of Europe.

for Europe.* Saladin appointed Ibn Shaddad, whose memoirs have been such a vivid source, to oversee his plans in Jerusalem. Presently Saladin left for Damascus.

There, the joys of family life awaited him – he had seventeen sons – but he was now fifty-four and worn out. His son Zahir could not bear to leave his father, perhaps sensing they would never meet again: touchingly, he kept saying goodbye, then riding back to kiss Saladin again. At the palace, Ibn Shaddad found the Sultan playing with one of his baby sons in a portico amid his gardens while Frankish barons and Turkish amirs awaited an audience.

A few days later, after welcoming the *haj* caravan from Mecca, he was struck down by a fever, probably typhoid. His doctors bled him, but he grew worse. When he asked for warm water, it was too cold. 'Heavens above!' he exclaimed. 'Is nobody able to get the water just right!' At dawn on 3 March 1193, he died listening to recitations of the Koran. 'I and others would have given our lives for him,' said Ibn Shaddad who reflected:

Then these years and their players passed away
As though they all had been merely dreams.

MUAZZAM ISA: THE OTHER JESUS

Saladin's sons spent the next six years fighting among themselves in ever-changing combinations, mediated by their shrewd uncle Safadin. The three eldest sons, Afdal, Zahir and Aziz received Damascus, Aleppo and Egypt, while Safadin ruled Outrejourdain and Edessa.

Afdal, now twenty-two, inherited Jerusalem, which he cherished. He built the Mosque of Omar right next to the Church and settled

---

* On his way home, Richard was captured and handed over to the German emperor Henry VI, who imprisoned him for over a year, until England had paid a large ransom. He returned to fighting the French king, bringing home some Saracen soldiers and the secret of the Greek Fire. In 1199, besieging a minor French castle, he was killed by an archer's bolt. 'He was', writes Steven Runciman, 'a bad son, a bad husband and a bad king but a gallant and splendid soldier.'

north Africans in a Maghrebi quarter where he built the Afdaliyya Madrassa within a few metres of the Western Wall.

Afdal, drunk and inept, found it hard to inspire loyalty and Jerusalem was tossed between the warring brothers. Just when Aziz had won the war and emerged as sultan, he was killed out hunting. The surviving brothers Afdal and Zahir ganged up on their uncle, but Safadin defeated both and seized the empire, ruling as sultan for twenty years. Cold, elegant and dour, Safadin was no Saladin: not one contemporary describes him with affection, but everyone respected him. He was 'brilliantly successful, probably the ablest of his line'. In Jerusalem, Safadin commissioned the double-gate – the Gate of the Chain and the Gate of Divine Presence, probably the site of the Crusaders' Beautiful Gate – using exquisite Frankish spolia from the Templar cloister and featuring a twin-domed porch and capitals with carvings of animals and lions: this still forms the main western entrance to the Temple Mount. But even before he became sultan, in 1198, his second son, Muazzam Isa (Isa being the Arabic for Jesus), was given Syria.

In 1204, Muazzam made Jerusalem his capital, and Amaury's palace his home. The most popular member of the family since his uncle Saladin, Muazzam was easy-going and open-minded. When he visited scholars to study philosophy and science, he simply walked to their houses like an ordinary student. 'I saw him in Jerusalem,' recalled the historian Ibn Wasil. 'Men, women and boys were jostling him and no one pushed them away. In spite of his boldness and high sense of honour, he had little taste for ostentation. He rode without being accompanied by the royal standards, with only a small escort. On his head he wore a yellow cap and made his way through the markets and streets without a pathway being cleared for him.'

One of Jerusalem's most prolific builders, Muazzam restored the walls, built seven hulking towers and converted the Crusader structures on the Temple Mount into Muslim shrines.* In 1209, he

---

* The foundations of six of his towers can be seen today. On the Temple Mount, he built the domed Grammar School and the glorious arches and domed entrance to al-Aqsa. He may have used Frankish spolia to built the octagonal Dome of Solomon,

settled 300 Jewish families from France and England in Jerusalem. When the Jewish poet of Spain, Judah al-Harizi, made his pilgrimage, he praised the dynasty of Muazzam and Saladin even as he mourned the Temple: 'We went out every day to weep for Zion, we grieved her destroyed palaces, we ascended the Mount of Olives to prostrate ourselves before the Eternal One. What torment to see our holy courts converted into an alien temple.' Suddenly, in 1218, Muazzam's achievements were thrown into peril when John of Brienne, titular King of Jerusalem,* led the Fifth Crusade to attack Egypt. The Crusaders besieged the port of Damietta. Safadin, now seventy-four years old, led out his armies but died when he heard that the Chain Tower of Damietta had fallen. Muazzam hastened from Jerusalem to Egypt to help his elder brother Kamil, the new Sultan of Egypt. But the brothers panicked and twice offered Jerusalem to the Crusaders if they would leave Egypt. In the spring of 1219, with the family empire in jeopardy, Muazzam took the heartbreaking decision to destroy all his fortifications in Jerusalem, arguing that 'if the Franks took it, they would kill everyone there and dominate Syria'.

Jerusalem was left defenceless and half-empty – her inhabitants fled in droves. 'Women, girls and old men gathered on the Haram, tore their hair and clothes and scattered in all directions' as if it were 'the Day of Judgement'. Yet the Crusaders foolishly refused the brothers' offers of Jerusalem – and the Crusade itself fell apart.

Once the Crusaders had departed, Kamil and Muazzam, who had co-operated so well during the ultimate crisis, embarked on a

also known as the Kursi Isa – the Throne of Jesus (the Jesus may be Isa himself) – and the Dome of the Ascension; the latter has an inscription dating it to 1200–1. But it is more likely that both were original Crusader buildings: indeed the baptismal font of the Dome of the Ascension with its Frankish capitals, topped with an elegant Frankish false lantern, may have originated in the Templum Domini. It was Muazzam who walled up the Golden Gate.

* Queen Isabella of Jerusalem was unlucky in marriage: her third husband Henry of Champagne ruled Acre as king of Jerusalem and fathered two more daughters by her – but, reviewing German Crusaders in 1197, he was distracted by his dwarf and stepped backwards out of a window. Then she married Amaury of Lusignan, King of Cyprus, who died of a surfeit of white mullet in 1205. On her death, her daughter Maria – now queen of Jerusalem – married the knight John of Brienne, and they had a daughter Yolande.

vicious fraternal war for supremacy. Jerusalem did not really recover until the nineteenth century. Fabled before and afterwards for her walls, she was to be without them for three centuries. Yet the city was about to change hands again in a most unlikely peace deal.

EMPEROR FREDERICK II:
WONDER OF THE WORLD, BEAST OF THE APOCALYPSE

On 9 November 1225, at the cathedral in Brindisi, Frederick II, Holy Roman Emperor and King of Sicily, married Yolande, fifteen-year-old Queen of Jerusalem. As soon as the wedding was over, Frederick assumed the title of king of Jerusalem ready to set off on his Crusade. His enemies claimed that he proceeded to seduce his new wife's ladies-in-waiting while cavorting with his harem of Saracen odalisques. This appalled his father-in-law John of Brienne and upset the pope. But Frederick was already the most powerful monarch in Europe – he was later to be known as Stupor Mundi, the Wonder of the World – and he did everything in his own way.

Frederick of Hohenstaufen, green-eyed and ginger-haired, half-German and half-Norman, had been raised in Sicily and there was nowhere else in Europe quite like his court in Palermo, which combined Norman, Arab and Greek cultures in a unique blend of the Christian and the Islamic. It was this upbringing that made Frederick so unusual and he certainly flaunted his eccentricities. His entourage usually featured a sultanic harem, a zoo, fifty falconers (he wrote a book called *The Art of Hunting with Birds*), an Arab bodyguard, Jewish and Muslim scholars and often a Scottish magician and hierophant. He was certainly more Levantine in culture than any other king in Christendom but that did not stop him ruthlessly suppressing Arab rebels in Sicily – he used his own spur to rip open the belly of their captured leader. He deported the Arabs from Sicily but built them a new Arab town in Lucera with its own mosques and a palace which became his favourite residence. Similarly he enforced anti-Jewish laws while he patronised Jewish savants, welcomed Jewish settlers and insisted they be fairly treated.

Yet it was power not exotica that consumed Frederick, who

devoted his life to defending his vast inheritance, stretching from the Baltic to the Mediterranean, against envious popes who excommunicated him twice, denounced him as the Anti-Christ and blackened him with the most outlandish calumnies. He was alleged to be a secret atheist or Muslim who said Moses, Jesus and Muhammad were frauds. He was portrayed as a medieval Dr Frankenstein who had sealed a dying man in a barrel to see if his soul could escape; who had disembowelled a man to study his digestion; and locked children in isolation-cells to see how they developed language.

Frederick took himself and his family's rights very seriously: he was actually a conventional Christian who was convinced that as emperor he should be a universal holy monarch on the Byzantine model and that as the descendant of generations of Crusaders and the heir to Charlemagne, he must liberate Jerusalem. He had already taken the Cross twice but kept delaying his departure.

Now that he was king of Jerusalem, he planned his expedition in earnest – but of course after his own fashion. He deposited his pregnant queen of Jerusalem in his Palermo harem, promising the pope that he was departing on Crusade – but Yolande, aged sixteen, died after giving birth to a son. Since Frederick was king of Jerusalem by marriage, his son now assumed the title. But he was not going to let that detail interfere with his new approach to crusading.

The Emperor hoped to win Jerusalem by exploiting the rivalries of the House of Saladin. Indeed Sultan Kamil offered him Jerusalem in return for help against Muazzam who held the city. Frederick finally set off in 1227, only to fall ill and return – at which Pope Gregory IX excommunicated him, which was more than an inconvenience for a Crusader. He sent his Teutonic Knights and infantry on ahead and by the time he joined them in Acre in September 1228, Muazzam was dead and Kamil had occupied Palestine – and withdrawn his offer.

However, Kamil was now having to fight Muazzam's sons as well as Frederick and his army. He could not handle both threats. Emperor and sultan were too weak to fight for Jerusalem so they opened secret negotiations.

Kamil was as unconventional as Frederick. As a boy, Safadin's son had been knighted by the Lionheart himself. While emperor and sultan negotiated the sharing of Jerusalem, they debated Aristotelian philosophy and Arab geometry. 'I've no real ambition to hold Jerusalem,' Frederick told Kamil's envoy, 'I simply want to safeguard my reputation with the Christians.' The Muslims wondered if Christianity was 'a game to him'. The sultan sent the emperor 'dancing girls' while the latter entertained his Muslim guests with Christian dancers. Patriarch Gerold denounced Frederick's singing girls and jugglers as 'persons not only of ill-repute but unworthy to be mentioned by Christians', which of course he then proceeded to do. Between negotiating sessions, Frederick hunted with his falcons and seduced new mistresses, playing the troubadour to write to one of them: 'Alas I didn't think that separation from my lady would be so hard remembering her sweet companionship. Happy song, go to the flower of Syria, to her who holds my heart in prison. Ask that most loving lady to remember her servant who shall suffer from love of her until he has done all she wills him to do.'

When the negotiations wavered, Frederick marched his troops down the coast to Jaffa in the footsteps of Richard, threatening Jerusalem. This did the trick and on 11 February 1229, he achieved the undreamable: in return for ten years' peace, Kamil ceded Jerusalem and Bethlehem with a corridor to the sea. In Jerusalem, the Muslims kept the Temple Mount with freedom of entry and worship under their qadi. The deal ignored the Jews (who had mostly fled the city), but this treaty of shared sovereignty remains the most daring peace deal in Jerusalem's history.

Yet both worlds were horrified. In Damascus, Muazzam's son Nasir Daud ordered public mourning. The throng sobbed at the news. Kamil insisted, 'we've only conceded some churches and ruined houses. The sacred precincts and venerated Rock remain ours.' But the deal worked for him – he was able to reunite Saladin's empire under his crown. As for Frederick, Patriarch Gerold banned the excommunicate from visiting Jerusalem, and the Templars denounced him for not gaining the Temple Mount.

On Saturday 17 March, Frederick, escorted by his Arab bodyguards and pages, his German and Italian troops, the Teutonic

Knights, and two English bishops, was met at the Jaffa Gate by the sultan's representative, Shams al-Din, the Qadi of Nablus, who handed him the keys of Jerusalem.

The streets were empty, many Muslims had left, the Orthodox Syrians were sullen at this Latin resurgence – and Frederick's time was short: the Bishop of Caesarea was on his way to enforce the patriarch's ban and place the city under interdict.

THE CROWNING OF FREDERICK II: GERMAN JERUSALEM

After spending the night in the palace of the Master of the Hospitallers, Frederick held a special Mass in the Holy Sepulchre, empty of priests but filled with his German soldiery. He rested his imperial crown on the altar of Calvary then placed it on his own head, a crown-wearing ceremony designed to project himself as the universal and paramount monarch of Christendom. He explained to Henry III of England: 'We being a Catholic Emperor wore the crown which Almighty God provided for us from the throne of His Majesty when of His especial grace He exalted us on high among the princes of the world in the house of His servant David.' Frederick was not one to underestimate his own importance: his eerie, magnificent mise-en-scène was the crowning of a sacred king, a mystical Emperor of the Last Days, in the Church that he saw as King David's temple.

Afterwards, the emperor toured the Temple Mount, admiring the Dome and al-Aqsa, praising its beautiful *mihrab*, climbing on to Nur al-Din's *minbar*. When he spotted a priest holding a New Testament trying to enter al-Aqsa, he knocked him over, shouting 'Swine! By God if one of you comes here again without permission, I shall have his eyes!'

The Muslim custodians did not know what to make of this gingerhaired maverick: 'Had he been a slave, he wouldn't have been worth 200 dirhams,' mused one of them tactlessly. That night Frederick noticed the silence of the muezzins: 'O Qadi,' he said to the sultan's representative, 'why didn't the muezzins give the call to prayer last night?'

'I recommended the muezzins not to give the call out of respect for the king,' said the qadi.

'You did wrong,' replied Frederick. 'My chief aim in passing the night in Jerusalem was to hear the muezzins and their cries of praise to God during the night.' If his enemies saw this as Islamophilia, Frederick was probably more interested in making sure his unique deal worked. When the muezzins called the midday prayer, 'all his valets and pages as well as his tutor' prostrated themselves to pray.

That morning, the Bishop of Caesarea arrived with his interdict. The emperor left his garrison in the Tower of David and headed back to Acre where he was faced with the ungrateful hostility of barons and Templars. Now under papal attack in Italy, the emperor planned a secret departure, but at dawn on 1 May the Acre mob, collecting the offal of Butchers Street, bombarded him with entrails and giblets. On his ship home to Brindisi, Frederick pined for his 'flower of Syria': 'Ever since I went away, I've never endured such anguish as I did on board the ship. And now I believe I shall surely die if I don't return to her soon.'

He had not stayed long and he never returned, but Frederick remained officially the master of Jerusalem for ten years. Frederick gave the Tower of David and Royal Palace to the Teutonic Knights. He ordered their master, Hermann of Salza and Bishop Peter of Winchester, to repair the Tower (some of this work survives today) and fortify St Stephen's (today's Damascus) Gate. Franks reclaimed 'their churches and had their old possessions restored to them'. The Jews were again banned. Without walls, Jerusalem was insecure: weeks later, the imams of Hebron and Nablus led 15,000 peasants into the city while the Christians cowered in the Tower. Acre sent an army to eject the Muslim invaders and Jerusalem remained Christian.*

* Frederick and Kamil maintained their friendship: the sultan sent the emperor a bejewelled planetarium, which was both a clock and a moving map of the heavens – and an elephant; Frederick sent Kamil a polar bear. Frederick spent the rest of his life in a constant war with the popes to defend his dual inheritance in Germany and Italy. It was the popes who stigmatized him as the Beast of the Apocalypse. His eldest son Henry King of the Romans betrayed him; Frederick imprisoned him for the rest of his life, appointing Conrad King of Jerusalem, his son by Yolande, as his

In 1238, Sultan Kamil died, throwing the Saladin dynasty into further internecine wars, exacerbated by a new crusade under Count Thibault of Champagne. When the Crusaders were defeated, Muazzam's son, Nasir Daud, galloped into Jerusalem and besieged the Tower of David for twenty-one days until it fell on 7 December 1239. He then destroyed the new fortifications, and the warring princes of the Saladin family took an oath of peace on the Temple Mount. But familial strife and the arrival of an English Crusade under Henry III's brother, Richard, Earl of Cornwall, again forced the surrender of Jerusalem to the Franks. This time the Templars expelled the Muslims and regained the Temple Mount: the Dome and al-Aqsa became churches again. 'I saw monks in charge of the Sacred Rock,' recalled Ibn Wasil. 'I saw on it bottles of wine for mass.' The Templars started to fortify the Holy City – but not fast enough: in order to fight his family rivals, the new sultan Salih Ayyub had hired a horde of freebooting Tartars, nomadic Central Asian horsemen displaced by the new Mongol empire. But he could not control them. To the horror of the Christians of Acre, 10,000 Khwarizmian Tartars rode towards Jerusalem.

BARKA KHAN AND THE TARTARS: CATASTROPHE

On 11 July 1244, the Tartar horsemen led by Barka Khan clattered into Jerusalem, fighting and hacking their way through the streets, smashing into the Armenian convent and murdering the monks and nuns. They destroyed churches and houses, plundering the Holy Sepulchre and setting it on fire. Coming upon the priests as they celebrated Mass the Tartars beheaded and disembowelled them at the altar. The bodies of the kings of Jerusalem were disinterred and burned, yet their elaborate sarcophagi were somehow spared; the stone at the door of Jesus' tomb was shattered. The Franks,

---

heir. The Wonder died of dysentery in 1250, and was buried in Palermo. Conrad died young, the crown of Jerusalem being inherited by Conrad's baby son, Conradin who was himself beheaded aged sixteen. But Frederick's reputation grew: as time passed, liberals celebrated his modern tolerance; while Hitler and the Nazis admired him as a Nietzschean superman.

besieged in the Tower, appealed to Nasir Daud, who persuaded Barka to allow the garrison to leave in safety.

Six thousand Christians left for Jaffa but, seeing Frankish flags on the battlements and believing help had arrived, many turned back. The Tartars massacred 2,000 of them. Only 300 Christians reached Jaffa. When they had thoroughly destroyed Jerusalem, the Tartars galloped away.* Smouldering and smashed, Jerusalem would not be Christian again until 1917.

In 1248, King Louis XI led the last effective Crusade and once again, the Crusaders hoped to win Jerusalem by conquering Egypt. In November 1249 the Crusaders advanced on Cairo, where Sultan Salih Ayyub was already dying. His widow, the sultana, Shajar al-Durr, took control, summoning her stepson Turanshah back from Syria. The Crusaders overreached themselves and were routed by the mamluks, the crack regiments of military slaves. Louis was captured. But the new sultan Turanshah neglected his own soldiers: on 2 May 1250, he was holding a banquet to celebrate the victory, attended by many of the Crusader prisoners, when mamluks, led by a blond giant named Baibars, then aged twenty-seven, burst in, swords drawn.

Baibars slashed at the sultan who fled bleeding down to the Nile as the mamluks fired arrows into him. He stood wounded in the river begging for his life until a mamluk waded in, cut off his head and sliced open his chest. His heart was cut out and shown to King Louis of France at a banquet; no doubt he lost his appetite.

There ended the dynasty of Saladin in Egypt, a downfall that condemned Jerusalem, now half-deserted, half-ruined, to ten

---

* These Tartars were finally defeated by Saladin's descendants in 1246. Drunk in battle, Barka Khan was beheaded, his head displayed in Aleppo. But his daughter married the Mamluk strongman Baibars, future sultan; his sons became powerful amirs who between 1260 and 1285 built the fine tomb, *turba*, that still stands on the Street of the Chain. There they buried their father: 'This is the tomb of the servant needful of God's mercy Barka Khan.' His sons were later buried with him. But when archaeologists inspected the tomb, there was no Barka inside. Perhaps his body never arrived from Aleppo. In 1846–7, the wealthy Khalidi family bought this building and indeed the entire street. Barka's tomb is now the reading room of the Khalidi library, founded in 1900. It is still the home of Mrs Haifa al-Khalidi and has a fine view of the Western Wall. As a quaint reminder of Jerusalem's span of history, the extended house also contains a red British postbox from the Mandate.

chaotic years tossed between different warlords and princelings as they fought for power* while a fearsome shadow fell across the Middle East. In 1258, the Mongols, the shamanist hordes from the Far East who had already conquered the largest empire the world had ever known, sacked Baghdad, massacring 80,000 people and killing the caliph. They took Damascus and galloped as far as Gaza, raiding Jerusalem on the way. Islam would need a ferocious champion to defeat them. The man who rose to the challenge was Baibars.

* At times, Jerusalem was ruled from Syria, at times from Cairo where Shajar al-Durr made herself sultana in her own right. This was a feminine achievement unique in Islam and the source of many legends. As a young concubine, she had won the eye of the sultan by wearing a dress made entirely of pearls, hence Shajar al-Durr, Tree of Pearls. Now she needed male support so she married a mamluk officer, Aibeg, who became sultan. But the couple soon fell out and she had him stabbed in his bath. After eighty days' reign the mamluks deposed her. Before she tried to escape, she ground her famous diamonds to dust so no other woman could wear them. When she was caught, Aibeg's concubines (perhaps furious not to inherit the jewels) beat her to death with their clogs – the mamluk equivalent of death by stiletto.

PART SIX

MAMLUK

Before the end of the world, all prophecies have to be fulfilled – and the Holy City has to be given back to the Christian Church.

Christopher Columbus, Letter to King Ferdinand and Queen Isabella of Spain

And she [the Wife of Bath] had thrice been to Jerusalem.

Geoffrey Chaucer, *The Canterbury Tales*

In Jerusalem, there is not a place one calls truly sacred.

Ibn Taymiyya, *In Support of Pious Visits to Jerusalem*

The practice [of the Holy Fire] is still going on. There occur under the eyes of Muslims a number of hateful things.

Mujir al-Din, *History of Jerusalem and Hebron*

The Greeks [are] our worst and atrocious enemies, the Georgians are the worst heretics, like the Greeks and equal in malice; the Armenians are very beautiful, rich and generous, [and] the deadly enemies of the Greeks and Georgians.

Francesco Suriano, *Treatise on the Holy Land*

We beheld the famous city of our delight and we rent our garments. Jerusalem is mostly desolate and in ruins and without walls. As for the Jews, the poorest have remained [living] in heaps of rubbish, for the law is that a Jew may not rebuild his ruined house.

Rabbi Obadiah of Bertinoro, *Letters*

29

SLAVE TO SULTAN

1250–1339

BAIBARS: THE PANTHER

Baibars was a fair-haired and blue-eyed Turk from Central Asia sold as a child to a Syrian prince. But, despite his towering barrel-chested physique, he had an unsettling defect: a white cataract on the iris of one of his eyes which led his owner to sell him on to the sultan in Cairo. Salih Ayyub, Saladin's great-nephew, bought Turkish slaves 'in batches like sandgrouse' to form his mamluk regiments. He could not trust his own family but thought 'one slave is more loyal than 300 sons'. Baibars, like all these pagan slaveboys, was converted to Islam and trained as a slave-soldier, a mamluk. He excelled with the arbalest steel crossbow, winning the nickname the Arbalestier and joined the Bahriyya regiment, the crack soldiers who defeated the Crusaders and became known as the Turkish Lions and the Islamic Templars.

When Baibars had won the trust of his master, he was manumitted – released from slavery – and climbed the ranks. The mamluks were loyal to their masters and even more loyal to each other – but ultimately each of these orphan-warriors owed nothing to anyone except himself and Allah. After his role in the killing of the sultan, Baibars lost out in the power struggle and fled to Syria where he offered his crossbow to the highest bidder in the civil wars raging between the local princelings. At one point, he seized and plundered Jerusalem. But the power was in Egypt and Baibars was finally recalled there by the latest general to seize the crown, Qutuz.

When the Mongols raided Syria in force, Baibars commanded the vanguard that hurried north to stop them. On 3 September

1260, Baibars defeated the Mongol army at Goliath's Spring (Ain Jalut) near Nazareth. The Mongols would return and even reach Jerusalem again, but they had been halted for the first time. Much of Syria fell under Cairo's rule and Baibars was hailed as the Father of Victory and the Lion of Egypt. He expected a reward – the governorship of Aleppo – but Sultan Qutuz refused. One day, while the sultan was hunting, Baibars (literally) stabbed him in the back. The junta of mamluk amirs granted him the crown as the man who had killed the monarch.

As soon as he took power, Baibars set about the destruction of the rump Crusader kingdom surviving on the Palestinian coast. In 1263, on his way to war, he arrived in Jerusalem. The Mamluks revered the city and Baibars began the Mamluk mission to resanctify and embellish the Temple Mount and the area around it, today's Muslim Quarter. He ordered the Dome and al-Aqsa to be renovated and in order to compete with Christian Easter, he promoted a new festival, possibly started under Saladin, by building a dome over the tomb of the Prophet Moses near Jericho. For the next eight centuries, Jerusalemites celebrated Nabi Musa with a procession from the Dome of the Rock to Baibars' shrine where they would gather for prayers, picnics and parties.

Just north-west of the walls, the Sultan built a lodge for his favourite order of Sufis. Like many of the Mamluks, he was a patron of the populist mysticism of the Sufis who believed that passion, chants, saintly cults, dances and self-mortification could bring Muslims closer to God than rigid traditional prayer. Baibars' closest adviser was a Sufi sheikh with whom he would recite and dance the Sufi *zikr*. Baibars implicitly trusted the sheikh and did nothing without his approval while allowing him to organize the looting of churches and synagogues and the lynching of Jews and Christians.* It was a new era: Baibars and his Mamluk successors, who were to rule Jerusalem for the next 300 years, were harsh, intolerant military

---

* Baibars' Sufi guru, Sheikh Khadir, became so powerful that he was able to seduce the wives, sons and daughters of the Mamluk generals in a reign of terror. It only ended when they presented Baibars with such full evidence that he had to order Khadir's arrest for sodomy and adultery. He was spared death only because he predicted that Baibars' death would rapidly follow his own.

dictators or juntas. The old age of Islamic chivalry, personified by Saladin, was gone. The Mamluks were a Turkish master-caste who forced Jews to wear yellow turbans, while the Christians had to wear blue. For both, but especially the Jews, their days as protected *dhimmi* were past. The Turkish-speaking Mamluks disdained Arabs too and only Mamluks were allowed to wear furs or armour or ride a horse in towns. At their gaudy court, the sultans awarded their courtiers colourful titles such as Bearer of the Royal Polo Stick and Amir-to-be-Serenaded-by-Music – the game of politics there was as often lethal as it was lucrative.

Baibar's symbol was a prowling panther which he used to mark his victories – eighty of them have been found on inscriptions between Egypt and Turkey and in Jerusalem, and they still prowl the Lions' Gate. No symbol was more appropriate for this terrifying predator with the white eye who now embarked on a spree of conquests.

When he had inspected Jerusalem, he attacked Acre which withstood the attack but he was to return often. Meanwhile, one by one, he stormed the other Crusader cities, killing with deranged, sadistic rapture. He received Frankish ambassadors surrounded by Christian heads, crucified, bisected and scalped his enemies, and built heads into the walls of fallen towns. He enjoyed taking risks like scouting incognito into enemy cities, negotiating with his enemies in disguise, and even when he was in Cairo he inspected his offices in the middle of the night, so restless and paranoid that he suffered insomnia and stomach-aches.

Acre alone defied him* but he marched north to conquer Antioch, whence he chillingly wrote to its prince 'to tell you what

---

* By 1268, the rump Kingdom was in such peril that the pope called a new Crusade. In May 1271, the heir to the English throne, Edward Longshanks, arrived at Acre which he helped defend against Baibars. But when Acre negotiated a truce with the sultan, Edward objected and it seems Baibars ordered his assassination: he was stabbed with a poisoned dagger. Having survived this, Edward tried in vain to organize a new alliance: the Crusaders would help the Mongols fight Baibars in return for Jerusalem. When he returned to England as Edward I, he promoted himself as Hammer of the Scots, illustrating his Painted Chamber at Westminster with scenes of the Maccabees. Yet he forced English Jews to wear yellow stars and finally expelled them from England. They did not return for three centuries. At his death, Edward was mourned as 'Jerusalem's flower of chivalry'.

we've just done. The dead were heaped up, you should have seen your Muslim enemy trample on the place you celebrate mass, cutting the throats of the monks on the altar, the fire running through your palaces. If you'd been there to see it, you'd have wished you'd never been alive!' He marched into Anatolia and crowned himself Sultan of Rum. But the Mongols had returned and Baibars rushed back to defend Syria.

On 1 June 1277, he fell victim to his own macabre ingenuity, when he prepared a drink of poisoned *qumiz* – fermented mare's milk, relished by Turks and Mongols – for a guest, but then forgetfully drank it himself. His successors finished his work.

On 18 May 1291, the Mamluks stormed the Frankish capital Acre and slaughtered most of the defenders, enslaving the rest (girls were sold for just one drachma each). The title King of Jerusalem was now united with that of King of Cyprus. But it survived only as a picturesque ornament – and it remains so today. There ended the Kingdom of Jerusalem.* Even the real Jerusalem only just survived – less a city, more of a senescent village, unwalled and half-deserted, raided at will by Mongol horsemen.

In 1267, a pilgrim, the old Spanish rabbi known as Ramban, mourned her eclipse:

> I compare you, my mother, to the woman whose son died in her lap and painfully there is milk in her breasts and she suckles the pups of dogs. And despite all that, your lovers abandoned you and your enemies desolated you, but faraway they remember and glorify the Holy City.

---

* Many of the royal houses of Europe, including the Bourbons, the Habsburgs and the Savoyards, claimed the title. In 1277, Charles of Anjou bought it from Mary of Antioch, one of its claimants, after which kings of Naples or Sicily claimed it and it descended via the Savoyards to the Italian kings. The King of Spain still uses it. Only one English monarch used the title. When Mary I, daughter of Henry VIII, married Philip II of Spain, in Winchester in 1554, she was declared, among other Habsburg titles, to be queen of Jerusalem. The title was used by the Habsburg emperors until 1918.

RAMBAN

Rabbi Moses ben Nachman, known by his Hebrew acronym
RAMBAN or just Nahmanides, was amazed to find that there were
only 2,000 inhabitants left in Jerusalem, just 300 Christians and
only two Jews, brothers, who were dyers like the Jews under the
Crusades. The sadder Jerusalem seemed to the Jews, the more
sacred it became, the more poetical: 'Whatever is more holy',
thought Ramban, 'is more ruined.'

The Ramban was one of the most inspiring intellectuals of his
time, a doctor, philosopher, mystic and Torah scholar. In 1263,
he had defended Barcelona's Jews so adeptly against Dominican
accusations of blasphemy that King James of Aragon remarked,
'I've never seen a man defend a wrong cause so well,' and gave
Ramban 300 gold pieces. But the Dominicans then tried to have
Ramban executed. As a compromise, the septuagenarian was
banished – and set out on his pilgrimage.

He believed that Jews should not just mourn Jerusalem but
return, settle and rebuild before the coming of the Messiah – what
we might call religious Zionism. Only Jerusalem could soothe his
homesickness:

> I left my family, I forsook my home, my sons and daughters. I left my
> soul with the sweet and dear children whom I've brought up on my
> knee. But the loss of all else is compensated for by the joy of a day in
> thy courts, O Jerusalem! I wept bitterly but I found joy in my tears.

The Ramban commandeered 'a broken-down house built with
marble columns and a handsome dome.* We took it for a prayer

* Its fate tells the story of the Jews in Jerusalem. The first synagogue was probably
on Mount Zion but soon moved to the Jewish Quarter. Under the Mamluks, a
mosque and al-Yehud (Jewish) minaret were built next to it, extended in 1397. When
the synagogue collapsed in 1474, Muslims demolished it and refused to permit its
reconstruction. But the penultimate Mamluk sultan Qaitbay allowed it to be rebuilt.
It was closed again by the Ottomans in 1587. A synagogue was then opened in the
neighbouring building until the Ramban and the next-door synagogue were united
and reopened in 1835. But in the early twentieth century the Ramban was taken over
by the Muslims and used as storage until it again became a synagogue. It was
deliberately destroyed by the Arab Legion in 1948. In 1967, it was reopened.

house because the city is a shambles and whoever wants to appropriate ruins does so.' He also retrieved the Torah scrolls hidden from the Mongols, but soon after his death, the raiders were back.

But this time there was a difference: some of them were Christians. In October 1299, the Christian King of Armenia, Hethoum II, galloped into Jerusalem with 10,000 Mongols. The city quaked before yet another barbaric sacking and the few Christians 'hid in caverns out of fright.' The Mongol Il-Khan had recently converted to Islam yet the Mongols had little interest in Jerusalem for they left her to Hethoum who rescued the Christians, held 'festivities in the Holy Sepulchre' and ordered the Armenian St Jameses and the Virgin's Tomb to be repaired – and then, strangely, after just two weeks, he headed back to see his Mongol master in Damascus. However the century-long duel between Mamluks and Mongols was over and once again the magneticism of Jerusalem's sanctity drew the world back. In Cairo, a new sultan came to the throne who revered Jerusalem – amongst other things, he called himself 'Sultan al-Quds.' Nasir Muhammad dubbed himself The Eagle; his people called him The Exquisite – and as the leading historian of this period writes, 'he was perhaps the greatest Mamluk sultan' but also 'the nastiest.'

NASIR MUHAMMAD: THE EXQUISITE EAGLE

Ever since he was eight, he had been humiliatingly tossed like a royal doll between the warlords of the Mamluk junta. Twice he had been raised to the throne and twice discarded. He was the younger son of a slave who had risen to become a great sultan and his elder brother, the conqueror of Acre, had been assassinated, so when Nasir Muhammad seized the throne for the third time at the age of twenty-six, he was determined to keep it. His sultanic eagle suited his style – aesthetic splendour, aquiline paranoia and the swoop of sudden death. His companions were promoted and enriched – but then strangled, bisected, poisoned without warning and he seemed to prefer horses to people: the limping sultan could supposedly cite the bloodlines of all his 7,800 racehorses and often paid more for a horse than for the most gorgeous slaveboy. Yet everything The Exquisite did – his marriage to a descendant of Genghis Khan, his twenty-five children, his 1,200 concubines – he did with the meticulous magnificence he brought to Jerusalem.

In 1317, he himself arrived on pilgrimage and proceeded to demonstrate to his generals that their sacred duty was to embellish the Temple Mount and the streets around it. Assisted by his best friend and Syrian viceroy, Tankiz, the sultan refortified the Tower of David, adding a Friday mosque for the garrison, and raised monumental colonnades and madrassas on the Temple Mount, reroofing the Dome and al-Aqsa, adding the minaret at the Gate of the Chain, and the Gate of the Cotton-sellers and Cotton-Sellers Market – all of which can be seen today.

Nasir favoured the Sufi route to reach God and built five convents for his orders of mystics. In their gleaming new lodges, they restored some of the holy magic to Jerusalem with their dancing, singing, trances and sometimes even self-mutilation, all to achieve the soaring emotion necessary to reach up towards God.

The sultan's men got the message: he and his successors exiled out-of-favour amirs to Jerusalem where they were expected to spend their ill-gotten wealth on sumptuous complexes that contained palaces, madrassas and tombs. The closer to the Temple Mount, the sooner they would arise on Judgement Day. They constructed enormous arched substructures and then built on top of them. These buildings* were ingeniously squeezed onto the roofs of earlier ones around the gates of the Noble Sanctuary.†

* It was now that most of Herod's wall along the west side of the Temple disappeared behind the new Mamluk buildings. But it reappears once, down a hidden alleyway in a courtyard of the Muslim Quarter: it is one of Jerusalem's secret places. Just as Jews revered the famous Western Wall to the south, so small numbers of Jews prayed and still pray at this, the Little Wall.

† The Mamluks built in a distinctive style that can be seen all over the Muslim Quarter: stalactite corbelling called *muqarna* and the alternating of dark and light stones known as *ablaq*. Perhaps the finest example of the Mamluk style is Tankiz's Tankiziyya palace-madrassa built over the Gate of the Chain: altogether there are twenty-seven madrassas, all marked with the blazons of the Mamluk amirs – Tankiz as Cupbearer marks his buildings with a cup. The typical Mamluk amir in Jerusalem

Nasir found Jerusalem – or at least the Muslim Quarter – in dust and cobwebs and left her in marble, so when Ibn Battutah visited, he discovered a city that was 'large and imposing'. Islamic pilgrims poured into al-Quds, exploring from the hell of Gehenna to the paradise of the Dome and reading the books of *fadail* that told them 'a sin committed in Jerusalem is the equivalent of a thousand sins and a good work there equal to a thousand'. He who lived there 'is like a warrior in the jihad' while to die there 'is like dying in heaven'. Jerusalem's mysticism blossomed to such an extent that Muslims started to circumambulate, kiss and anoint the Rock as they had not done since the seventh century. The fundamentalist scholar Ibn Taymiyya railed against Nasir and these Sufi superstitions, warning that Jerusalem ranked only as a pious visit – a *ziyara* – not the equivalent of the *haj* to Mecca. The sultan imprisoned this puritanical dissident six times but to no avail and Ibn Taymiyya provided the inspiration for the harsh Wahabiism of Saudi Arabia and today's Jihadists.

The Exquisite sultan no longer trusted the Turkish Mamluks who had become the elite so he started to buy Georgian or Circassian slaveboys from the Caucasus to provide his bodyguard and they influenced his decisions in Jerusalem: he granted the Church of the Holy Sepulchre to the Georgians. But the Latins had not forgotten her either: in 1333, he allowed King Robert of Naples (and Jerusalem) to repair parts of the Church and take possession of the Cenacle on Mount Zion where he started a Franciscan monastery.

The ailing tiger is the most dangerous. The sultan fell ill but he had made his friend Tankiz 'so powerful he became afraid of him'. In 1340, Tankiz was arrested and poisoned. Nasir himself died a year later, succeeded by his many sons. But ultimately, the new Caucasian slaves overthrew the dynasty, founding a new line of sultans who favoured the Georgians in Jerusalem. On the other

would endow a charitable trust, a *waqf*, partly to maintain his madrassa, partly to provide a home and job for his descendants in case his power and wealth were lost in the frequent power struggles. Each tomb or *turba* was usually downstairs in a room with green-latticed windows so that passers-by could hear the prayers being recited – and they too can be seen. These buildings were much later assigned to Jerusalem's Arab families who endowed them as trusts so that today many are still family homes.

hand, the Catholic Latins – the heirs of the hated Crusaders – were there on sufferance under the repressive Mamluks whose paroxysms of violence terrorized Christians and Jews alike. When the Cypriot king attacked Alexandria in 1365, the Church was closed down and the Franciscans dragged off to be publicly executed in Damascus. The Franciscan order was allowed to return but the Mamluks built minarets overshadowing the Church and the Ramban Synagogue to emphasize the supremacy of Islam.

In 1399, the dread Central Asian conqueror Tamurlane captured Baghdad and smashed into Syria just as a Mamluk boy-sultan and his tutor set out on their pilgrimage to Jerusalem.

30

DECLINE OF THE MAMLUKS

1399–1517

TAMURLANE AND THE TUTOR: PILGRIM CITY

The royal tutor was the most celebrated scholar in the Islamic world. Now aged around seventy, Ibn Khaldun had served the monarchs of Morocco, then (after a spell in prison) Granada, Tunisia and finally (after another spell in prison) the Mamluk sultan. In between spells in power and in prison, he wrote his masterpiece, the *Muqaddimah*, a world history that still sparkles today. The sultan therefore appointed him tutor to his son, Faraj, who succeeded to the throne as a child.

Now, as the peppery historian showed Jerusalem to the ten-year-old sultan, Tamurlane besieged Mamluk Damascus. Timur the Lame – known as Tamurlane – had risen to power in 1370 as a local warlord in Central Asia. In thirty-five years of incessant warfare, this harsh genius, of Turkic descent, had conquered much of the Near East, which he ruled from the saddle, promoting himself as the heir to Genghis Khan. In Delhi, he slaughtered 100,000; at Isfahan, he killed 70,000, building twenty-eight towers of 1,500 heads each, and he had never been defeated.

Yet Tamurlane was not just a warrior. His palaces and gardens in Samarkand displayed his sophisticated taste; he was an ace chess-player and a history-buff who enjoyed debates with philosophers. Not surprisingly, he had always wanted to meet Ibn Khaldun.

Yet the Mamluks were in a state of panic: if Damascus fell, so would Palestine and perhaps Cairo too. The old pedagogue and the boy-sultan hurried back to Cairo but the Mamluks decided to send the pair into Syria to negotiate with Tamurlane – and save the empire. At the same time, the Jerusalemites were debating what to do: how to save the Holy City from the invincible predator known as the Scourge of God?

In January 1401, Tamurlane, encamped around Damascus, heard that Sultan Faraj and Ibn Khaldun awaited his pleasure. He had no interest in the boy but he was fascinated by Ibn Khaldun whom he immediately summoned. As a politician, Ibn Khaldun represented the sultan, but as a historian, he naturally longed to meet the supreme man of the era – even if he was not sure if he would emerge dead or alive. The two were almost the same age: the grizzled conqueror received the venerable historian in his palatial tent.

Ibn Khaldun was awed by this 'greatest and mightiest of kings' whom he found 'highly intelligent and perspicacious, addicted to debate and argumentation about what he knows and also what he does not know'. Ibn Khaldun persuaded Tamurlane to release some Mamluk prisoners, but the Scourge of God would not negotiate: Damascus was stormed and sacked in what Ibn Khaldun called 'an absolutely dastardly and abominable deed'. The road to Jerusalem was now open. The city's *ulema* decided to surrender the city to Tamurlane and despatched a delegation with the keys of the Dome of the Rock. But when the Jerusalemites arrived in Damascus, the conqueror had instead ridden north to rout the rising power in Anatolia, the Ottoman Turks. Then, in February 1405, en route to conquer China, Tamurlane died and Jerusalem remained Mamluk. Ibn Khaldun, who had made it home to Cairo from his meeting with Tamurlane, died in his bed a year later. His pupil Sultan Faraj never forgot his eventful cultural tour: he frequently returned to Jerusalem, holding court on the Temple Mount, beneath the royal parasol, amid the yellow banners of the sultanate, handing out gold to the poor.

There were only 6,000 Jerusalemites, with just 200 Jewish and 100 Christian families, in a small city with outsized passions. The city was dangerous and unstable: in 1405 Jerusalemites rioted against exorbitant taxes and chased the Mamluk governor out of town. The archives of the Haram give us a feel for Jerusalem's dynasties of religious judges and Sufi sheikhs, exiled Mamluk amirs, and wealthy merchants in a world of Koran study, book-collecting, trade in olive oil and soap, and crossbow and sword practice. But now that Crusades were no longer a threat, Christian pilgrims were milked as the chief source of income. However, they were scarcely welcomed: they were frequently arrested on trumped-up charges until they paid arbitrary fines. 'You will either have to pay,' one interpreter explained to his imprisoned Christian charges, 'or be beaten to death.'

It was hard to say who was the more dangerous – the venal Mamluks, the disreputable pilgrims, the feuding Christians or the greedy Jerusalemites. Many pilgrims were so villainous that the locals and travellers were warned, 'Protect yourself from anyone travelling to Jerusalem', while even Muslims liked to say 'no one is so corrupt as the residents of holy cities'.

Meanwhile Mamluk sultans sometimes swept down on the city to repress Christians and Jews who already faced periodic lynchings by the Jerusalemite crowds.

The corruption and disorder started at court in Cairo: the empire was still ruled by Caucasian sultans so, even though the Catholic Franciscans enjoyed European support, Christian Jerusalem was dominated by the Armenians and the Georgians who hated one another – and of course the Catholics. The Armenians, who were aggressively expanding their Quarter around St Jameses, managed to bribe the Mamluks to wrest Calvary from the Georgians, who then outbid them and won it back. But not for long. In the course of thirty years, Calvary changed hands five times.

The bribes and profits were enormous because the pilgrimage had become wildly popular in Europe. Europeans did not feel that the Crusades were over – after all, the Catholic reconquest of Islamic Spain was a Crusade – but while there were no expeditions to liberate Jerusalem, all Christians felt they knew Jerusalem even if they had never been. Jerusalem appeared in sermons, paintings and tapestries. Many towns featured Jerusalem Chapels, founded by Jerusalem Brotherhoods made up of ex-pilgrims or people who could not make the trip. The Palace of Westminster had its Jeru-salem Chamber and from Paris in the west to Prussia and Livonia in the east, many places now boasted these local Jerusalems. The only Jerusalem in England, a tiny village in Lincolnshire, dates from this revived enthusiasm. But thousands did travel there every year* and many of them were notoriously unsaintly: Chaucer's saucy Wife of Bath had been to Jerusalem three times.

Pilgrims had to pay repeated fines and tolls just to enter Jerusalem and then the Church where the Mamluks also controlled the Sepulchre inside. They sealed the Church every night so pilgrims, for a price, could be locked inside for days and nights if they wished. The pilgrims found that the Church resembled a bazaar-cum-barbershop with stalls, shops, beds and large quantities of human hair: many believed that illness would be cured if they shaved themselves and placed the hair in the Sepulchre. Many of the pilgrims spent much time carving their initials into every shrine they visited while artful Muslims serviced the relic industry: pilgrims claimed that stillborn Muslim babies were embalmed and then sold to rich Europeans as the victims of the Massacre of the Innocents.

Some pilgrims were convinced that children conceived within the Church were specially blessed, and of course there was alcohol, so that the dark hours often became a candlelit, hard-drinking orgy in which good-natured hymn singing gave way to ugly brawls. The Sepulchre, said one disgusted pilgrim, was 'a complete brothel.' Another pilgrim, Arnold von Harff, a mischievous German knight, spent his time learning phrases in Arabic and Hebrew that give some clues to his preoccupations:

How much will you give me?
I will give you a gulden.
Are you a Jew?
Woman, let me sleep with you tonight.
Good madam, I am ALREADY in your bed.

---

* In 1393, Henry Bolingbroke came on pilgrimage to Jerusalem and when he seized the throne as Henry IV, he was told that he would return there to die. He managed to fulfil this prophecy on his deathbed: he had himself placed in the Jerusalem Chamber at Westminster. His son Henry V shared this devotion: on his deathbed, the victor of Agincourt wished he had made the pilgrimage to rebuild the walls of Jerusalem.

The Franciscans guided and welcomed Catholic visitors: their itinerary, retracing the footsteps of Christ, started at what they believed was Pilate's Praetorium, on the site of the Mamluk governor's mansion. This became the first station of The Lord's Way, later the Via Dolorosa. Pilgrims were shocked to find Christian sites had been Islamicized, such as St Anne's Church – the birthplace of the Virgin Mary's mother – occupied by Saladin's madrassa. The German friar Felix Fabri sneaked into this shrine, while Harff risked his life by penetrating the Temple Mount in disguise – and both recorded their adventures. Their entertaining travelogues revealed a new tone of inquisitive lightheartedness as well as reverence.

However, Christians and Jews were never quite safe from the capricious Mamluk repression – and sanctity in Jerusalem was so infectious that when the two older religions started to fight for David's Tomb on Mount Zion, the sultans claimed it for the Muslims.

There was now a settled Jewish community of about 1,000 in what became the Jewish Quarter. They prayed in their Ramban synagogue, as well as around the gates of the Temple Mount (particularly at their study house by the Western Wall) and on the Mount of Olives, where they began to bury their dead ready for Judgement Day. But they had come to revere the Christian shrine of David's Tomb (which had nothing to do with the real David but dated from the Crusades), part of the Cenacle, controlled by the Franciscans. The Christians tried to restrict their access, so the Jews complained to Cairo – with unfortunate consequences for both. The sultan of the day, Barsbay, outraged to discover that the Christians held such a site, travelled up to Jerusalem, destroyed the Franciscan chapel and instead built a mosque inside David's Tomb. A few years later, one of his successors, Sultan Jaqmaq, seized the whole of Mount Zion for Islam. And it got worse: old restrictions were enforced, new ones devised. The size of Christian and Jewish turbans was limited; in the baths men had to wear metal neck-rings like cattle; Jewish and Christian women were banned from the baths altogether; Jaqmaq forbade Jewish doctors to treat Muslims.*

---

* Yet Sultan Jaqmaq, who terrorized the Latins, protected the Armenians: his inscription promising his favour can still be read just inside the gate of the Armenian Monastery.

After the collapse of the Ramban Synagogue in a storm, the qadi banned its rebuilding, claiming it belonged to the neighbouring mosque. When Jewish bribes overturned the decision, the local *ulema* demolished it.

On 10 July 1452, the Jerusalemites launched an anti-Christian pogrom, digging up the bones of Christian monks and tearing down a new balustrade in the Sepulchre which was borne in triumph to al-Aqsa. Christians were sometimes insanely provocative. In 1391, four Franciscan monks shouted in al-Aqsa that 'Muhammad was a libertine, murderer, glutton' who believed 'in whoring'! The qadi offered them the chance to recant. When they refused, they were tortured and beaten almost to death. A bonfire was built in the courtyard of the Church where, 'almost drunk with rage', the mob hacked them into pieces 'so that not even a human shape remained', and then kebabbed them.

However, deliverance was at hand and, when a more tolerant sultan came to power, it was a dish of French cuisine that would change the destiny of Christian Jerusalem.

THE SULTAN AND THE CHRISTIAN OMELETTES

Qaitbay, a Circassian slaveboy who became a Mamluk general, had spent years of exile in Jerusalem. Since he was banned from entering a Muslim household, he befriended the Franciscans who introduced him to a French dish: it seems he remained nostalgic about their vegetable omelettes when he ascended the Mamluk throne in 1486, for he welcomed the friars to Cairo and allowed them to build in the Church – and gave them back Mount Zion. They wanted vengeance on the Jews, whom Qaitbay therefore banned from ever approaching the Church or the convent on Mount Zion: Jews were routinely lynched and often killed even for absentmindedly passing the Church, a situation that lasted until 1917. But the sultan also allowed the Jews to rebuild their Ramban Synagogue. And he did not neglect the Temple Mount either: when he visited in 1475, he commissioned his Ashrafiyya madrassa that was so beautiful it was described as 'the third jewel of Jerusalem' while his fountain there, a bellshaped dome resplendent in red and cream *ablaq*, remains the most gorgeous in the whole city.

But for all Qaitbay's interest, the Mamluks were losing their grip. When the qadi of the city, Mujir al-Din, watched the daily sunset parade at the Tower of David, 'it was completely neglected and disorganized'. In 1480, Bedouin attacked Jerusalem, almost capturing the governor who had to gallop across the Temple Mount and out through the Jaffa Gate to escape. 'Jerusalem is mostly desolate', observed Rabbi Obadiah of Bertinoro, just after the Bedouin attack. From the distance, 'I saw a ruined city', agreed one of his disciples, with jackals and lions loping across the hills. Yet Jerusalem was still breathtaking. When Obadiah's follower viewed it from the Olivet, 'my spirit overflowed, my heart mourned and I sat down and wept and rent my garments'. Mujir al-Din, who loved his city, thought it was 'filled with brilliance and beauty – one of the famous wonders.'*

In 1453, the Ottomans finally conquered Constantinople, inheriting the splendour and ideology of the universal Roman empire. For generation after generation, the Ottomans were bedevilled by wars of succession and the challenge of a resurgent Persia. In 1481, Qaitbay welcomed the fugitive Ottoman prince, Jem Sultan. Hoping that a dissident Ottoman kingdom would divide the dynasty, Qaitbay offered Jem the kingdom of Jerusalem. The gambit led to ten years of wasteful warfare. Meanwhile both empires were threatened by rising powers – the Mamluks by Portuguese advances in the Indian Ocean, the Ottomans by the new Persian shah, Ismail, who united his country by imposing the Twelver Shiism that is still revered there. This pushed the Ottomans and Mamluks together in a short-lived, pragmatic embrace: it was to prove the kiss of death.

---

* In the last years of Mamluk Jerusalem, at the same time as those Jewish travellers were weeping on the Mount of Olives, Mujir al-Din compiled his loving, punctilious study of Jerusalem and Hebron. He must have been respected: he was buried in the elegant domed monument that now stands just above the Virgin's Tomb.

PART SEVEN

OTTOMAN

This noble Jerusalem has been the object of desire of the kings of all nations, especially the Christians who, ever since Jesus was born in the city, have waged all their wars over Jerusalem ... Jerusalem was the place of prayer of the tribes of djinn ... It contains the shrines of 124,000 prophets.

Evliya Celebi, Book of Travels

Suleiman saw the Prophet in his dream: 'O Suleiman, you should embellish the Dome of the Rock and rebuild Jerusalem.'

Evliya Celebi, Book of Travels

The great prize contended by several sects is the Holy Sepulchre, a privilege contested with so much fury and animosity that they have sometimes proceeded to blows and wounds, at the door of the Sepulchre mingling their own blood with their 'sacrifices'.

Henry Maundrell, Journey

So part we sadly in this troublous world
To meet with joy in sweet Jerusalem.

William Shakespeare, Henry VI, Part Three

Rather than walk about holy places we can thus pause at our thoughts, examine our heart, and visit the real promised land.

Martin Luther, Table Talk

We shall find that the God of Israel is among us ... for we must consider that we shall be as a City upon a Hill, the eyes of all people upon us.

John Winthrop, A Modell of Christian Charity

31

THE MAGNIFICENCE OF SULEIMAN

1517–1550

THE SECOND SOLOMON AND HIS ROXELANA

On 24 August 1516, the Ottoman sultan, Selim the Grim, routed the Mamluk army not far from Aleppo, the battle that decided Jerusalem's destiny: most of the Middle East would remain Ottoman for the next four centuries. On 20 March 1517, Selim arrived to take possession of Jerusalem. The *ulema* handed him the keys of al-Aqsa and the Dome at which he prostrated himself and exclaimed, 'I am the possessor of the first *qibla*.' Selim confirmed the traditional tolerance of the Christians and Jews and prayed on the Temple Mount. Then he rode on to subjugate Egypt. Selim had defeated Persia, conquered the Mamluks and clarified any succession dilemmas by killing his brothers, his nephews and probably some of his own sons. So when he died in September 1520, he was survived by just one son.

Suleiman was 'only twenty-five years old, tall and slender but tough with a thin and bony face' and he found himself the master of an empire that stretched from the Balkans to the borders of Persia, from Egypt to the Black Sea. 'In Baghdad, I am the Shah, in Byzantine realms, the Caesar; and in Egypt, the Sultan,' he declared and to these titles he added that of caliph. No wonder Ottoman courtiers addressed their monarchs as the Padishah – emperor – who was, one of them wrote, 'the most honoured and respected sovereign the world over.' It was said that Suleiman dreamed he was visited by the Prophet who told him that 'to repulse the Infidels' he must 'embellish the Sanctuary (Temple Mount) and rebuild Jerusalem', but actually he needed no prompting. He was only too aware of himself as the Islamic emperor and, as his Slavic wife Roxelana would repeatedly hail him, 'the Solomon of his age'.

Roxelana shared in Suleiman's projects – and that included Jerusalem. She was probably a priest's daughter kidnapped from Poland and sold into the sultanic harem where she caught Suleiman's eye, bearing him five sons and a daughter. 'Young but not beautiful, although graceful and petite,' a contemporary portrait suggests she was large-eyed, rose-lipped and round-faced. Her letters to Suleiman on campaign catch something of her playful yet indomitable spirit: 'My Sultan, there's no limit to the burning anguish of separation. Now spare this miserable one and don't withhold your noble letters. When your letters are read, your servant and son Mir Mehmed and your slave and daughter Mihrimah weep and wail from missing you. Their weeping has driven me mad.' Suleiman renamed her Hurrem al-Sultan, the Joy of the Sultan, whom he described in poems attributed to him as 'my love, my moonlight, my springtime, my woman of the beautiful hair, my love of the slanted brow, my love of eyes full of mischief' and officially as 'the quintessence of queens, the light of the eye of the resplendent caliphate'. She became a wily politician, intriguing successfully to ensure Suleiman's son by another woman did not succeed to the throne: the son was strangled in Suleiman's presence.

Suleiman inherited Jerusalem and Mecca and believed that his Islamic prestige demanded that he beautify the sanctuaries of Islam: everything about him was on a grand scale, his ambitions boundless, his reign almost half a century long, his horizons vast – he fought almost continental wars from Europe and north Africa to Iraq and the Indian Ocean, from the gates of Vienna to Baghdad. His achievements in Jerusalem were so successful that the Old City today belongs more to him than anyone else: the walls look ancient and to many people they define the city as much as Dome, Wall or Church – but they and most of the gates were the creation of this contemporary of Henry VIII, both to secure the city and add to his own prestige. The sultan added a mosque, an entrance and a tower to the Citadel; he built an aqueduct to bring water into the city and nine fountains from which to drink it – including three on the Temple Mount; and finally he replaced the worn mosaics on the Dome of the Rock with glazed tiles decorated with lilies and lotus in turquoise, cobalt, white and yellow as they are today.*

Roxelana liked to endow charitable foundations close to her husband's projects, she commandeered a Mamluk palace to establish her al-Imara al-Amira al-Khasaki al-Sultan, a foundation known as the Flourishing Edifice that included a mosque, bakery, fifty-five-room hostel and soup-kitchen for the poor. Thus they made the Temple Mount and Jerusalem their own.

In 1553 Suleiman, soi-disant 'Second Solomon and King of the World', decided to inspect Jerusalem, but his far-flung wars intervened and, like Constantine before him, the man who had transformed the city never got to see his achievement. The Sultan's enterprise was on an imperial scale but he clearly supervised it from afar. As the walls arose, the viceroy of Syria presided, Suleiman's imperial architect Sinan probably inspected the work on his way home from Mecca: thousands of workers laboured, new stones were quarried, old stones purloined from ruined churches and Herodian palaces, and the ramparts and gates carefully fused with the Herodian and Umayyad walls around the Temple Mount. The retiling of the Dome required 450,000 tiles, so Suleiman's men created a tile factory next to al-Aqsa to make them, and some of his contractors built mansions in the city and stayed. The local architect founded a dynasty of hereditary architects that reigned for the next two centuries. The city must have resounded with the unfamiliar sounds of hammering masons and the clink of money. The

---

* A legend grew up that Suleiman considered levelling Jerusalem until he dreamed that lions would eat him if he did so, hence he built the Lions' Gate. This is based on a misunderstanding: he did build the Lions' Gate but its lions are actually the panthers of Sultan Baibars from 300 years earlier, borrowed from his Sufi *khanqah* that once stood north-west of the city. Suleiman used the spolia of Jerusalem: his Gate of the Chain fountain is topped with a Crusader rosette and the trough is a Crusader sarcophagus. The new walls did not enclose Mount Zion. It was said that Suleiman was so furious when he looked into a magic cup and saw that David's Tomb was outside the city that he executed the architects. Tour guides point out their graves close to the Jaffa Gate – but this too is a myth: the graves belong to two scholars from Safed.

population almost tripled to 16,000 and the number of Jews doubled to 2,000, boosted by the constant arrival of refugees from the west. A vast, anguished movement of the Jews was in progress, and some of these new arrivals contributed directly to Suleiman's enterprise.

32

MYSTICS AND MESSIAHS

1550–1705

THE SULTAN'S JEWISH DUKE:
PROTESTANTS, FRANCISCANS AND THE WALL

Suleiman assigned the taxes of Egypt to pay for his remodelled Jerusalem, and the man in charge of these revenues was Abraham de Castro, the Master of the Mint and tax-farmer who had proven his loyalty by warning the sultan when the local viceroy planned a rebellion. As his name suggests, Castro was a Jewish refugee from Portugal and his role did not come close to that of the super-rich Portuguese Jew who became Suleiman's adviser and ultimately protector of Palestine and Jerusalem.

The Jewish migration marked the latest chapter in the religious wars. King Ferdinand of Aragon and Sicily and his wife Queen Isabella of Castile had conquered Granada, the last Islamic principality of mainland Europe, in January 1492. Radiating confidence after this triumph, the Catholic Majesties – the title awarded them by the Pope – celebrated their successful Crusade with two decisions that would have world-historical consequences. First, they summoned a white-haired sailor and dreamer named Cristóbal Colón. A Genoese inn-keeper's son, this magnetic and obsessional maverick had for years been soliciting their backing for a voyage across the Atlantic to reach India and China. If one of his dreams was this passage westwards to the Indies, the other was the liberation of Jerusalem from the east: from the start he linked the two. 'I protested to Your Highnesses that everything gained as a result of this voyage would he spent in the conquest of Jerusalem and Your Highnesses laughed and said the idea pleased them.'*

The monarchs backed the enterprise on 17 April 1492, appointing Colón (better known by his anglicized name, Christopher Columbus) Admiral of the Ocean Sea. On 12 October, two months after setting off, Columbus discovered the isles of the West Indies and, during his third voyage, the coast of South America. He probably never realized that he had discovered the New World (which, in 1507, came to be named after the Florentine sailor who did, Amerigo Vespucci). Years later, as his gold-rich discoveries developed into the Spanish Empire, Columbus dreamed quixotically of the End Days, and wrote to the Catholic Majesties in his *Book of Prophecies* that Jerusalem and Mount Zion would be rebuilt by Spaniards. The gold of Ophir – or the Indies – would gild the restored Temple, the court of 'the last world emperor'. But in legion ways unimaginable to Admiral Columbus, who died wealthy but restless as ever in 1506, America and Jerusalem would indeed be interlinked.

On 29 April, twelve days after approving Columbus' voyage, Isabella and Ferdinand turned to their Jewish problem. Many Jews had been forced to convert to Catholicism, but these *conversos* were distrusted: Catholics feared that the 'devilish tricks and seductions' of secret Jews might taint the pure bloodstream of Christendom. The Inquisition, backed by the Catholic Majesties, had already convicted 13,000 people and burned 2,000 for secret Jewish deviations. Now its Inquisitor Tomás de Torquemada advised them to offer the Jews a choice of conversion or expulsion. Isabella was a Crusader-queen, devout, grave, iron-willed; Ferdinand, a cynical, cunning and womanizing manipulator on a Christian mission, was Machiavelli's

---

* Ferdinand, who later claimed the title King of Jerusalem, may have smiled because these ideas coincided with his own messianic-crusader vision: he himself planned to conquer the Holy City by crusading his way along the coast of North Africa. His Maghrebi expeditions, led by a tough cardinal on a mule waving a silver cross, managed to take Oran then Tripoli (in today's Libya) in 1510. Ferdinand and Isabella's grandson, Emperor Charles V, heir to Spain, much of the New World and the Burgundian and Habsburg lands, inherited this crusading ambition and his talk of a campaign to liberate the city was one of the reasons that Suleiman the Magnificent rebuilt her walls.

ideal king. Together the couple, whose marriage created the kingdom of Spain, were the most successful rulers of their age. But in this they miscalculated. Ferdinand had hoped the Jews would convert sincerely. To his surprise, many – somewhere between 75,000 and 150,000 – were instead expelled. He banished them from Naples too, and, in the next fifty years, much of western Europe followed suit. For seven centuries, Spain had been the home of a blossoming Arab–Jewish culture, and the centre of the Jewish Diaspora.

Now, in the most searing Jewish trauma between the fall of the Temple and the Final Solution, these Sephardic Jews (*Sepharad* being Hebrew for Spain) fled eastwards to the more tolerant Holland, Poland-Lithuania and the Ottoman empire where they were welcomed by Suleiman, both to boost his economy and to expose how Christianity had denied its Jewish heritage. The Diaspora moved east. From now until the early twentieth century, the streets of Istanbul, Salonica and Jerusalem would ring with the lyrical tones of their new Judaeo-Spanish language, Ladino.

In 1553, Suleiman's Jewish doctor introduced him to Joseph Nasi, whose family had been forced into a fake conversion to Christianity before they fled via Holland and Italy to Istanbul. There, he won the sultan's trust and became the confidential agent of his son and heir. Joseph, known to European diplomats as the Great Jew, ran a complex business empire, and served as a sultanic envoy and international man of mystery, an arbiter of war and finance, a mediator between east and west. Joseph believed in the return of the Jews to the Promised Land, and Suleiman granted him the lordship of Tiberias in Galilee where he settled Italian Jews, rebuilt the town and planted mulberry trees to foster a silk industry, the first Jew to settle Jews in the Holy Land. He would build his Jerusalem in Galilee because that ultra-sensitive connoisseur of power knew that the real Jerusalem was the reserve of Suleiman.

Nonetheless Joseph patronized the Jewish scholars in Jerusalem where Suleiman promoted the superiority of Islam and diminished the status of the other two religions with a meticulous care that still guides the city now. Suleiman was fighting Emperor Charles V so that his attitude to the Christians was somewhat tempered by the cynical requirements of European diplomacy. The Jews, on the other hand, mattered little.

They still prayed around the walls of the Temple Mount and on the slopes of the Mount of Olives as well as in their main synagogue, the Ramban, but the sultan favoured order in all things. Discouraging anything that diminished the Islamic monopoly on the Temple Mount, he assigned the Jews a 9-foot street along the supporting wall of King Herod's Temple for their prayers. This made some sense, because it was adjacent to their old Cave synagogue and next to the Jewish Quarter where the Jews had started to settle in the fourteenth century, and still the Jewish Quarter today. But the site was overshadowed by the Islamic Maghrebi neighbourhood; Jewish worship there was carefully regulated; and Jews were later required to have a permit to pray there at all. The Jews soon called this place ha-Kotel, the Wall, outsiders called it the Western or Wailing Wall and henceforth its golden, ashlar stones became the symbol of Jerusalem and the focus of holiness.

Suleiman brought the Christians down to size by expelling the Franciscans from David's Tomb where his inscription declares: 'The Emperor Suleiman ordered this place to be purged of infidels and constructed it as a mosque.' Sacred to all three religions, this Byzantine-Crusader site, an early Jewish synagogue and the Christian Coenaculum, now became the Islamic shrine of Nabi Daoud, the Prophet David, where Suleiman appointed a family of Sufi sheikhs called the Dajanis as hereditary guardians, a position they held until 1948.

The politics of the outside world would always reflect back onto the religious life of Jerusalem: Suleiman soon had reason to favour the Franciscans. In the battle for central Europe, he found that he needed Christian allies – the French – to fight the Habsburgs, and the Franciscans were backed by the kings of France. In 1535, the sultan granted France trading privileges and recognized the Franciscans as the custodians of the Christian shrines. This was the first of the so-called capitulations – concessions to European powers – that later undermined the Ottoman empire.

The Franciscans set up headquarters in St Saviour's, close to the Church which ultimately would become a colossal Catholic city-within-a-city, but their rise disturbed the Orthodox. The hatred between Catholics and Orthodox was already venomous but both claimed the paramount custodianship of the Holy Places: the *praedominium*. The Church of the Holy Sepulchre was now shared between eight sects in a Darwinian struggle in which only the strongest could survive. Some were going up, some were going down: the Armenians remained powerful because they were well represented in Istanbul, the Serbs and Maronites were in decline – but the Georgians, who had lost their Mamluk patrons, went into total eclipse.*

The epic conflict between the emperors of Islam and Christendom, the aggressive Catholicism of the Spanish, and the expulsion of the Jews inspired an unsettling feeling that something was not right in the firmament: people questioned their faith, searched for new mystical ways to get closer to God, and they expected the End Days. In 1517, Martin Luther, a theology professor in Wittenberg, protested against the Church's sale of 'indulgences' to limit people's time in purgatory, and insisted God existed only in the Bible, not via the rituals of priests or popes. His brave protest tapped into the widespread resentment of the Church which many believed had lost touch with Jesus' teaching. These Protestants wanted a raw, unmediated faith and, free of the Church, they could find their own way. Protestantism was so flexible that a variety of new sects – Lutherans, the Reform Church, Presbyterians, Calvinists, Anabaptists – soon thrived, while for Henry VIII, English Protestantism was a way to assert

---

* They had to sell their monastery St Saviour's to the Franciscans and that was just the beginning. In 1685, the impoverished Georgians lost their headquarters, the Monastery of the Cross, said to be the origins of the wood for Jesus's cross, to the Orthodox. After the fall of Crusader Jerusalem in 1187, Queen Tamara of Georgia had sent an official, Shota Rustaveli, the author of the national epic, *The Knight in the Panther Skin*, to embellish the Monastery: he is probably buried there and his portrait appeared in its frescoes. But in 2004, Rustaveli's berobbed, white-bearded and high-hatted portrait was vandalized just as the Georgian President Mikheil Saakashvili arrived on a state visit to inspect it. The Russian Orthodox were suspected but nothing was proved. The Serbs passed their last monastery to their Greek brethren in the seventeenth century. The Maronites still maintain a convent near the Jaffa Gate, though the Georgians, Maronites and Serbs have all long since lost their share of the Church.

his political independence. But one thing united all of them: their reverence for the Bible, which restored Jerusalem to the very centre of their faith.*

When after forty-five years on the throne Suleiman died on campaign with his army, his ministers propped him up like a waxwork in his carriage and showed him to his soldiers until the succession was safe for Selim, one of his sons by Roxelana. Selim II, known as the Drunkard, owed much to the intrigues of his friend, Joseph Nasi, the Great Jew, who, now living in splendour in his Belvedere Palace, rich from his monopolies of Polish beeswax and Moldavian wine, was promoted to Duke of Naxos. He almost became King of Cyprus. Such was his championing of persecuted or penurious Jews in Europe and Jerusalem that there were whisperings shortly before his death that this ducal Jewish Croesus must be the Messiah. But little came of his plans. Under Selim and his successors, the Ottoman empire was still expanding and, thanks to vast resources and superb bureaucracy, it remained awesomely powerful for another century – but its emperors soon struggled to control distant provinces ruled by overmighty governors and Jerusalem's tranquillity was periodically shattered by bouts of violence.

In 1590, a local Arab rebel broke into Jerusalem and seized the city, killing the governor. The rebels were defeated and expelled. Jerusalem fell under the sway of two Balkan brothers, Ridwan and Bairam Pasha, Christian slaveboys converted to Islam and trained at the court of Suleiman, and their Circassian henchman, Farrukh. Their families dominated – and abused – Palestine for almost a century. When Farrukh's son, Muhammad, found himself locked

---

* Both Jews and Christians were infected by apocalyptic expectations. In 1523, a dwarfish young Jew, David Reuveni, caused a stir in Jerusalem by declaring himself an Arabian prince leading the Ten Tribes back to Zion, but the Islamic qadi spared him as a lunatic and he then sailed to Rome, where the pope received him, but ultimately Christendom proved less tolerant than Islam and he died in the early 1530s in a Spanish dungeon. In 1534 a radical Protestant sect of Anabaptists seized the German town of Munster which they declared to be the New Jerusalem. Their leader John of Leiden, an illegitimate tailor's apprentice, pronounced himself King of Jerusalem, heir to King David. After eighteen months, this new Zion was recaptured and the Anabaptist leaders executed.

out of Jerusalem in 1625, he stormed the walls with 300 mercenaries then, closing the gates, he proceeded to torture Jews, Christians and Arabs alike to extort money.

Such outrages only encouraged the strongest of the Christian sects, the Armenians, to canvass and bribe the sultans and brawl in the churches of Jerusalem, all part of their campaign to vanquish the Catholics and win the *praedominium*. The Armenians were Ottomans as much as Christians, adept courtiers at the Sublime Porte. While other denominations were backed by European powers, the Armenians were the protégés of the sultans themselves (which is why they have lasted in the Church into the twenty-first century). In the first twenty years of the century, the sultans issued thirty-three decrees to defend the embattled Catholics and in just seven years, the *praedominium* changed hands six times. However, the Christians had become the most lucrative source of business in Palestine: every day, the Custodian of the Church, the chief of the Nusseibeh family, sat on a throne in the courtyard with his armed henchmen charging for access – and the income from the thousands of pilgrims was enormous. At Easter, which Muslims called the Festival of the Red Egg, the governor of Jerusalem set up his throne, and, accompanied by the qadi, the custodian and the entire fully-armed garrison, he charged each of the 20,000 'hell-destined infidels' ten gold pieces that was shared out among the Ottomans and the *ulema*.

Meanwhile something was afoot amongst the Jews. 'Jerusalem', wrote a Jewish pilgrim, 'was more greatly populated than at any time since the first exile' and as Jerusalem's 'fame spread, it became known we lived in peace. Scholars flocked to the gates.' A caravan of Egyptian Jews arrived every Passover. Most of the Jews were Ladino-speaking Sephardis who were secure enough to build the 'four synagogues' that became the centre of life in the Jewish Quarter, but some of the pilgrims were eastern Europeans from the Commonwealth of Poland-Lithuania, known as Ashkenazis (named for Ashkenaz, a descendant of Noah in Genesis, said to be the progenitor of the northern peoples). The turbulence of the world outside encouraged their mysticism: a rabbi named Isaac Luri was teaching the Kabbala, the study of the Torah's secret codes that would bring them closer to the Godhead. Luri was born in Jerusalem but he made his base in the magical mountain city of Safed in Galilee. The trauma of the Spanish persecutions had forced many Jews to fake conversion to Christianity and live clandestine lives – indeed Kabbala's holy text, the Book of Zohar, was written in thirteenth-century Castile. The Kabbalists sought Majesty, Fear and Trembling – 'the ecstatic experience, the tremendous uprush and soaring of the soul to its highest plane, union with God'. On Fridays, the Kabbalists, wearing white robes, would greet the 'bride of God', the Shekinah, outside the city and then escort the divine presence back to their homes. But inevitably the Kabbalists speculated that the Jewish trauma along with their secret codes and incantations contained the key to redemption: surely the Messiah would soon come to Jerusalem?

Notwithstanding occasional anti-Christian riots, Bedouin ambushes and the extortion of Ottoman governors, the city was left to her own rituals. Yet the feuding of the Orthodox, Armenians and Catholics in this Ottoman backwater only served to confirm the prejudices of a new breed of visitor, part-pilgrim, part-merchant-adventurer: the Protestants had arrived. They tended to be English traders, burning with hostility towards the Catholics, and often with links to the new colonies in America.

When the English sea captain and merchant Henry Timberlake arrived, the Ottoman governors had never heard of Protestantism or his Queen Elizabeth and he was thrown into jail next to the Holy Sepulchre, released only on payment of a fine. The exuberant memoir of his adventures, *A True and Strange Discourse*, became a bestseller in Jacobean London. Another of these audacious English-men, John Sanderson, factor of the Levant Company, paid his fee to the Turks to enter the Church but was attacked by the Franciscan monks, whose padre 'accused me to be a Jew'. The Turks then arrested him, tried to convert him to Islam and took him before the qadi, who searched him and then released him as a Christian.

Acts of fanaticism, both Christian and Muslim, unleashed viol-ence that reveals the real limits of the much-vaunted Ottoman tolerance: the Ottoman governor forcibly closed down the beloved Ramban synagogue at the request of the *ulema*: Jews were forbidden to pray there and it was converted into a warehouse. When the Franciscans quietly extended their Mount Zion property, rumours spread that they were burrowing to Malta to let in the Christian armies: they were attacked by the qadi and the mob and only rescued by the Ottoman garrison. A Portuguese nun who baptized Muslim children and denounced Islam was burned on a pyre in the court-yard of the Church.*

At Easter 1610, a young Englishman arrived who represented not only the new Protestantism but the New World too.

GEORGE SANDYS: THE FIRST ANGLO-AMERICAN

George Sandys, son of the Archbishop of York and a scholar who translated Virgil into English, was appalled by the decay of Jeru-salem – 'much of which lies waste, old buildings all ruined, the new, contemptible.' Sandys was half-repulsed, half-amused by the Ladino-speaking Sephardic Jews he saw at the Western Wall: 'their fantastical gestures exceed all barbarity with ridiculous nodding', and he thought it 'impossible not to laugh'. The God-fearing Prot-estant was even more disgusted by what he regarded as the vulgar hucksterism of the Orthodox and Catholics. The city was 'once sacred and glorious, elected by God for his seat', but she was now merely a 'theatre of mysteries and miracles'.

That Easter, Sandys was horrified by Christians and Muslims alike: he saw the pasha of Jerusalem on his throne outside the Church of the Holy Sepulchre. Sandys watched as thousands of pilgrims, each carrying pillow and carpet, flocked to spend the night in the Church. On Good Friday, he followed the procession of the padre of the Franciscans, who carried a life-sized waxen model of Jesus on a sheet along the Via Dolorosa before fixing it

---

* These human bonfires in the courtyard of the Church were not infrequent. In 1557 a Sicilian monk, Brother Juniper, twice invaded the Aqsa before he was killed by the qadi himself – and then incinerated before the Church. A Spanish Franciscan denounced Islam inside al-Aqsa and was beheaded on the Temple Mount before another bonfire. Yet as the case of Reuveni had shown, death was not always the end of the story, and Christianity in Europe was no more civilized: almost 400 heretics were burned in England during the sixteenth century.

to a cross. As thousands filled the Church and camped in its courtyard, he watched the ceremony of the Holy Fire, 'the savage clamours', the clash of cymbals, the 'women whistling' – conduct 'befitting better the solemnities of Bacchus'. When the Fire emerged, the pilgrims ran around 'like madmen thrusting the flame among their clothes and into their bosoms, persuading strangers it will not burn them'.

Yet this composer of hymns was a passionate Protestant who revered Jerusalem just as much as the Catholics and Orthodox. Returning to the fundamentals of the Bible itself, he prayed passionately at the tomb of Christ and the graves of the Crusader kings. On his return, he dedicated his book, *A Relation of a Journey begun AD 1610*, to the young Charles, Prince of Wales, whose father James I had recently commissioned fifty-four scholars to create an English Bible that was entirely accessible to all. In 1611, the scholars delivered their Authorized Version, which, fusing earlier translations by William Tyndale and others, brought the divine scriptures to life in a masterpiece of translation and of poetical English. This Bible became the spiritual and literary heartland of Anglicanism, England's singular Protestantism. The Bible became what one writer called 'the national epic of Britain,' a story that placed the Jews and Jerusalem at the very heart of British and, later, American life.

Sandys was one link between the real city and the Jerusalem of the New World. In 1621, he set off for America as treasurer of the Virginia Company. During his ten years in Jamestown, he led the raid against the Algonquin native Americans during which he slaughtered a considerable number: Protestants were no less capable of killing defiant infidels than any other seventeenth-century faith. Sandys was not the only Jerusalem pilgrim-adventurer to be there: Henry Timberlake was in Virginia at the same time. Their pilgrimages to the new Promised Land of America were at least partly inspired by the Protestant vision of the heavenly Jerusalem.

Sandys' and Timberlake's Virginians were conservative Anglicans of the sort favoured by James I and his son, Charles. However, the kings could not keep a lid on the expectations of a new fervent, radical Protestantism: the Puritans embraced the fundamental truth of the Bible but with immediate messianic expectations. The Thirty Years War between Catholics and Protestants only intensified the feeling that Judgement Day was near. These were strange times which encouraged wild mystical excitement in all three religions. Harvests failed. The grim reaper, in the guise of epidemics, starvation and religious war, scythed through Europe, killing millions.

Thousands of Puritans escaped Charles I's Church to found new colonies in America. As they sailed across the Atlantic to seek religious freedom, they read of Jerusalem and the Israelites in their Bibles and saw themselves as the Chosen People blessed by God to build a new Zion in the wilderness of Canaan. 'Come let us declare in Zion the word of God,' prayed William Bradford as he disembarked from the *Mayflower*. The first governor of the Massachusetts Bay Colony, John Winthrop, believed 'the God of Israel is amongst us' and paraphrased Jeremiah and Matthew to hail his settlement as 'a city on a hill' – America as the new Jerusalem. Soon there would be eighteen Jordans, twelve Canaans, thirty-five Bethels and sixty-six Jerusalems or Salems.

The fear of catastrophe and the anticipation of redemption rose together: civil wars scarred France and England while simultaneously in eastern Europe, the Jews of Poland and Ukraine were slaughtered in tens of thousands by the Cossacks of the marauding Hetman Khmelnytsky. In 1649, Charles I was beheaded and Oliver Cromwell emerged as Lord Protector, a millenarian soldier convinced that his Puritans, like their brethren in New England, were the new Chosen People:

'Truly you are called by God as Judah was, to rule with Him and for Him,' he said. 'You are at the edge of Promises and Prophecies.' Cromwell was a Hebraist who believed that Christ could not come again unless the Jews returned to Zion and then converted to Christianity. Effectively, the Puritans were the first Christian Zionists. Joanna and Ebenezer Cartwright even suggested the Royal Navy should 'transport Izrael's sons and daughters in their ships to the Land promised by their forefathers for an everlasting Inheritance'.

Many Jews earnestly studied the Kabbala, dreaming that the Messiah would transform their Ukrainian tragedy into redemption. A Dutch rabbi, Menasseh ben Israel, petitioned the Lord Protector, pointing out that the Bible stated Jews had to be scattered to *all* corners of the world *before* their Return to Zion would set off the Second Coming – yet they were still banned from England. Therefore Cromwell convened a special Whitehall Conference that ruled it was wrong to exclude 'this mean and despised people from the light and leave them among false teachers, Papists and idolators.' Cromwell allowed the Jews to return. After his death, the monarchy was restored and his Puritanic messianism lost its power but its message endured in the American Colonies and amongst the English Nonconformists ready to blossom again in the evangelical awakening two hundred years later. Just after the Restoration, manic excitement convulsed the Jewish world: the Messiah was in Jerusalem – or was he?

THE MESSIAH: SABBATAI ZEVI

He was Mordecai, the unbalanced son of a Smyrnan poultry-dealer who studied the Kabbala. In 1648 he declared himself the Messiah by uttering the Tetragrammaton. This was the unspeakable name of God based on the Hebrew letters YHWH, only spoken once a year on the Day of Atonement by the high priest in the Temple itself. Now he changed his named to Sabbatai Zevi and proclaimed that Judgement Day would come in 1666. He was expelled from Smyrna but gradually as he worked as a trader around the Mediterranean, he won the devotion of a network of wealthy backers. In 1660, he moved first to Cairo and then travelled on to Jerusalem where he fasted, sang songs, handed sweets to children, and performed strange and unsettling acts.

Sabbatai radiated a reckless but deranged magnetism – he was clearly a manic depressive who swung between bouts of infectious self-belief, desperate melancholia and euphoric exaltation that led him to perform demonic, sometimes shamelessly erotic antics. At any other time, he would have been condemned as an obscene and sinful madman but in those catastrophic days, many Jews were already in a state of Kabbalist anticipation. His craziness was surely the true mark of the sacred.

The Jerusalemite Jews were impoverished by Ottoman taxes so they asked Sabbatai to raise funds from his Cairene patrons, which he did. He succeeded in his mission, but not everyone was convinced as he prepared to declare himself Messiah in Jerusalem. After much debate, the rabbis placed him under a ban. Furious, he moved to Gaza which he chose as his sacred city instead of Jerusalem and then launched his messianic ministry in Aleppo.

If his revelation had started as a slow burn, his fame now exploded and spread like quickfire. Jews across the Diaspora, from Istanbul to Amsterdam, celebrated the arrival of the Messiah. In Ukraine, a pretty Jewish girl named Sarah was orphaned by the Cossack massacres but rescued by Christians and taken to Livorno. There she worked as a prostitute which did not shake her conviction that she was destined to marry the Messiah. When Sabbatai heard about her, he married her (in order to emulate the prophet Hosea, who wed a prostitute) and the two toured the Mediterranean together while Jews across Europe were divided between sceptics and frenzied fans who packed their belongings for the journey to greet the Messiah in Jerusalem, whipped themselves, fasted, and rolled naked in mud and snow. In late 1666, the messianic couple rolled into Istanbul where Jews hailed them. Assuming imperial–universal authority, the King of the Jews had appointed his brothers as kings of Rome and Turkey. Now Sabbatai's ambition to wear the sultan's crown led to his arrest. The Sultan made the 'King of the Jews' an offer he could not refuse: either to perform the miracle of surviving a volley of arrows or to convert to Islam. He chose conversion.

For most, this apostasy* marked the death of the dream even before Sabbatai died in Montenegrin exile – and Jerusalem's Jews

---

* Some of his followers regarded this as the ultimate sacred paradox – and their Sabbatarian Judaeo-Islamic sect, the Donmeh (Turncoats, though they called themselves Mamin, the Believers), particularly the many who lived in Salonica, were to play a role in the Young Turk revolutions between 1908 and the First World War. They still exist in Turkey.

were happy to see the back of this disruptive charlatan. The era of Cromwell and Sabbatai was also the golden age of Islamic mysticism in Jerusalem where the Ottoman sultans were patrons of all the leading orders of Sufis whom the Turks called Dervishes. We have seen how Christians and Jews saw the city. Now a most unconventional Ottoman courtier, Dervish scholar, raconteur and bon vivant named Evliya lovingly describes the city's idiosyncracies from the Islamic angle with the often hilarious flair that makes him probably the greatest of all Islamic travel-writers.

EVLIYA: THE OTTOMAN PEPYS AND FALSTAFF

Even then, Evliya must have been utterly unique: this wealthy traveller, writer, singer, scholar, and warrior was the son of the sultan's goldsmith, born in Istanbul, raised at court, educated by the imperial *ulema*, who was advised by Muhammad in a dream to travel the world. He became, in his own words, 'The World Traveller and Boon Companion to Mankind' and travelled not only the length of the vast Ottoman realm but into Christendom too, obsessively chronicling his adventures in an astonishing ten volumes. Just as Samuel Pepys was writing his diaries in London, Evliya, whether in Istanbul, Cairo or Jerusalem, was compiling his *Book of Travels*, 'the longest and fullest travel account in Islamic literature, perhaps in world literature'. No Islamic writer wrote as poetically about Jerusalem, or as wittily about life.

Evliya lived literally on his wits for he won the favour of Mehmet IV with his irresistible jokes, rhyming couplets, mischievous songs and wrestling and he was able to travel by joining the entourages of Ottoman grandees who recruited him for his religious knowledge and for his exuberant entertainment. His books are partly almanacs of amassed facts, partly anthologies of amazing stories: Evliya Celebi (a title that just means 'gentleman') both fought the Habsburgs and met the Holy Roman Emperor in Vienna, impressing him with his personal knowledge of Jerusalem's Holy Sepulchre. In battle, he self-deprecatingly recorded his own Falstaffian flight – 'fleeing is also an act of courage' – and probably the most 'strange and comic' scatological scene in military history.*

He never married, and refused to take any job in the imperial service that interfered with his free-spirited travelling. He was often given slave-girls and was as witty about sex as he was about everything else: he called it 'the sweet calamity,' and the 'nice wrestling-match,' cheerfully recording his bout of impotence which was finally cured by an Egyptian snakebroth. He daringly joked that sex was the 'greater jihad', and the most striking thing about him to the modern reader is that here was a devout Muslim who constantly made jokes about Islam that would be unthinkable today.

Though this scholar could recite the entire Koran in eight hours and act as muezzin, unusually he was clean-shaven, irreverent, open-minded and an enemy of fanaticism, whether Islamic, Jewish or Christian. As a 'wandering Dervish,' he was fascinated by Jerusalem 'the ancient *qibla*' which 'is at present the Kaaba of the poor (or of the dervishes)' – the capital, the very Mecca of Sufism: he counted seventy Dervish convents, with the largest near the Damascus Gate, varying in origin from India to the Crimea, and described how a contingent from each order performed ecstatic songs and dances of the *zikr* all night until dawn.

Evliya wrote that the city, which boasted 240 prayer-niches and forty madrassas, was 'the object of desire of the kings of all nations' but he was most dazzled by the breathtaking beauty and sanctity of the Dome: 'This humble one has travelled for thirty-eight years through seventeen empires and viewed countless buildings but I've never seen one that so resembled paradise. When a person enters, one stands dumbfounded and amazed with finger to mouth.' In al-Aqsa, where the preacher mounted the pulpit every Friday

* During one of the battles in Transylvania against the Habsburgs, he slipped away from the fray to evacuate his bowels only to be ambushed by an Austrian soldier, 'so I plopped right into my own filth.' As they fought, they rolled 'topsy-turvy' in our hero's excrement until 'I almost became the shitty martyr.' Evliya finally killed the infidel, and managed to pull up his pantaloons 'but I was soaked in blood as well as shit and I had to laugh, seeing that I'd become the shitty Ghazi (Islamic warrior).' Afterwards he presented the Austrian's head to his Pasha, who said, 'My Evliya, you smell strangely of shit!' The officers 'laughed uproariously' and the Pasha gave him fifty gold pieces and a silver turban-crest.

brandishing the sword of Caliph Omar and the rituals were serviced by a staff of 800, Evliya observed how the mosaics reflected the rays of the sun so that 'the mosque becomes light upon light and the congregants' eyes shine with reverence as they pray'.

In the Dome 'all pilgrims circumambulate the Rock outside the railing', while the Temple Mount had become a 'promenading place embellished with roses, hyacinths, myrtle filled with the intoxicating twitter of nightingales' and he happily embraced most of its legends – that King David had started building al-Aqsa while Solomon 'being Sultan of all creatures ordered the demons to complete the construction'. Nonetheless, when he was shown ropes that Solomon had supposedly woven 3,000 years earlier, he could not resist exclaiming to the *ulema*: 'Do you mean to tell me that the ropes used to bind the demons haven't rotted?'

Naturally he visited the Church at Easter where his reaction resembled that of the English Protestants. He worked out the secret of the Holy Fire, claiming that a hidden zinc jar of naphtha was dripped down a chain by a hidden monk to deliver the annual miracle. The festival itself was just 'pandemonium' and the Church 'lacks spirituality, more like a tourist attraction' but he chatted to a Protestant there who blamed it on the Orthodox Greeks, 'a stupid and credulous people'.

Evliya returned several times before he retired to finish his books in Cairo but he never saw anything to compare with the Dome of the Rock – 'verily a replica of a pavilion in paradise'. Not everyone agreed: conservative Muslims were horrified by all the Sufi dancing, miracle-working and the saintly cults that Evliya so enjoyed. 'Some of the women unveil their faces, displaying their beauty, their ornaments and perfumes. By God, they were sitting cheek-to-jowl among men!' observed Qashashi, denouncing 'excited clamours and dancing', the playing of tambourines and merchants selling sweets. 'These are the days of the wedding-feast of Satan.'

The Ottomans were now in full decline, the sultans shoved back and forth between the demands of European powers, each of them backing their own Christian sect. When the Catholic Austrians and French won the *praedominium* for the Franciscans, the Russians, a brash new power in Europe and in Jerusalem, lobbied and bribed the Ottomans until they had regained it for the Orthodox. The Franciscans soon got it back again, but three times actual fighting broke out in the Church.* The daily battle of the Sepulchre was conducted more by sweeping than stabbing, more by broom than by bludgeon: whoever cleaned a part of the Church could claim it. Inch by inch, the sacristans, brooms in hand, tried to advance their territories, watched by their vigilant rival sacred sweepers. In 1699, the Ottomans, defeated on the battlefield, signed the Treaty of Karlowitz, which allowed the Great Powers to protect their brethren in Jerusalem – a disastrous concession.

Meanwhile Istanbul's governors had so repressed Palestine that the peasants rebelled. In 1702, the new Governor of Jerusalem crushed the rebellion and decorated the walls with the heads of his victims. But when he destroyed a village owned by the religious leader – the mufti – of Jerusalem, the city's qadi denounced him at Friday prayers in al-Aqsa and opened the gates to the rebels.

---

* Henry Maundrell, Chaplain of the English Levant Company, who visited in 1697, watched the 'fury' of the monks as they fought bloodily in the Church. He also described the mania of the Holy Fire as even more demented than it had been a century earlier when Sandys visited: the pilgrims 'began to act in such an indecent manner as to expose their nudities, they tumbled about the Sepulchre after the manner of tumblers on stage' lighting their beards – it was 'like Bedlam itself'. As for the priests, Maundrell just called them 'miracle-mongers'.

33

THE FAMILIES

1705–1799

THE HUSSEINIS: THE REVOLT OF THE NAQIB AL-ASHRAF AND THE CANINE POGROM

Armed peasants marauded through the streets. The qadi – the chief judge – backed by the garrison, stormed the prison and took command of Jerusalem. In one of her stranger moments, the city found herself independent: the qadi, in return for bribes, appointed Muhammad ibn Mustafa al-Husseini as head of the city.

Husseini was the chief of Jerusalem's pre-eminent clan who had risen on the coat-tails of the Farrukhs a century earlier, but he was also the Naqib al-Ashraf, the leader of the families descended from the Prophet, via his grandson Hussein: only the Ashraf could wear the green turban and be addressed as Sayyid.

The Ottomans despatched troops to suppress the revolt who camped outside the walls. Husseini showed that he was ready for a siege, and the troops retreated to Gaza. Inside Jerusalem the rebellion had replaced one tyranny with another. Jews were forbidden to wear white on the Sabbath or Muslim headgear or to have nails in their shoes; Christians suffered similar sartorial restrictions; and both had to make way for Muslims in the streets. Outrageous fines were collected with violence. A messianic sect of 500 Polish Jews from Grodno, led by Judah the Pious, had just arrived. But their rabbi died, and they spoke only Polish or Yiddish, leaving them particularly helpless. They were soon impoverished.

When a stray dog wandered on to the Temple Mount, the qadi ordered the killing of every canine in Jerusalem. As a special humiliation, every Jew and Christian had to deliver dead dogs to a collection point outside the Zion Gate. Gangs of children killed dogs and then gave the carcasses to the nearest infidel.

When a stronger Ottoman army approached, the garrison and the Sufi mystics turned against the rebellion and seized the Tower of David. Husseini fortified himself in his mansion, and they fired arrows at each other for three days. In the ensuing battle, the northern streets of the Old City were strewn with corpses – and Husseini lost more support. Outside, the Ottomans bombarded the Temple Mount. In the middle of the night on 28 November 1705, Husseini realized his game was up and escaped, pursued by the Ottomans. The reign of extortion continued under the new governor. Many Jews, robbed again, simply left, and the Polish Ashkenazis were broken, finally in 1720 facing imprisonment, banishment and bankruptcy, their synagogue in the Jewish Quarter burned down.* The Sephardis – the small, old Jewish community at home in the Arab and Ottoman world – survived.

Husseini was captured and beheaded. After much dynastic rivalry, the Husseinis were later succeeded as naqib by Abd al-Latif al-Ghudayya whose family changed its name sometime in the century and purloined that of the prestigious Husseinis. The Ghudayyas became the new Husseinis, the most powerful of Jerusalem's ruling families – right up into the twenty-first century.

THE HUSSEINIS: RISE OF THE FAMILIES

Anyone important who came to Jerusalem during the eighteenth century wished to stay with the chief of this clan, who held open house for peasants, scholars and Ottoman officials alike; it was said he had eighty guests for dinner every night. 'Everyone visits him from near and afar,' wrote one such guest to the 'palace' of Abd al-Latif al-Ghudayya who dominated Jerusalem. 'Strangers find refuge in his home, residing there as they like.' Abd al-Latif's visitors left

---

* This became known as the Ruin – Hurva – Synagogue, and remained a wreck for over a century. It was reconstructed in the nineteenth century – but destroyed by the Jordanians in 1967.

Jerusalem escorted by a squadron of his horsemen.

The resurgence of the Husseinis marked the rise of the great Jerusalem Families. Virtually every position of honour in Jerusalem was hereditary. Most of the Families were descended from Sufi sheikhs who had been favoured by one conqueror or another. Most changed their names, invented grandiose genealogies and alternately feuded and intermarried – not unlike their Western equivalents. Each fiercely defended and strived to expand its own lucrative power-base.* But wealth would have been vulgar without scholarship; pedigree powerless without wealth, and position impossible without Ottoman patronage. Sometimes the Families fought it out: two Nusseibehs were ambushed and killed by a Husseini posse near Abu Ghosh, but, typically, the families made peace by marrying the surviving Nusseibeh brother of the victims to the sister of the Mufti of Jerusalem.

Yet even the Families could not ensure prosperity in a Jerusalem scarred by intermittent fighting between the 500-strong Ottoman garrison notorious for its debauchery, raiding Bedouin, rioting Jerusalemites and venal governors. The population shrank to 8,000, preyed upon by the Governor of Damascus who descended on the city annually with a small army to collect the taxes.†

* These clans were known in English as the Notables, to the Turks as the Effendiya, to the Arabs as the Aya. The Nusseibehs were Custodians of the Church; the Dajanis presided over David's Tomb; the Khalidis ran the *sharia* lawcourts; the Husseinis usually dominated as Naqib al-Ashraf, Mufti and Sheikh of the Haram as well as leading the Nabi Musa festival. The Abu Ghosh, warlords of the mountains around Jerusalem, guardians of the pilgrim route from Jaffa, were allies of the Husseinis. Only recent research by Professor Adel Manna has revealed the true story of how the Ghudayyas took over the identity of the Husseinis. The Nusseibehs changed their name from Ghanim; the Khalidis from Deiri; the Jarallahs (who competed for the muftiship with the Husseinis) from Hasqafi. 'It is disorienting and perplexing to have to endure a change of name,' admits one of these grandees, Hazem Nusseibeh, ex-Foreign Minister of Jordan, in his memoir *The Jerusalemites*, 'even though it occurred seven centuries ago.'

† The powerful Vali (Governor) of the Vilayet (Province) of Damascus usually ruled Jerusalem and was often the Amir al-Haj, Commander of the annual caravan to Mecca which he funded through his *dawra*, an armed expedition. At other times, Jerusalem was controlled by the Vali of Sidon who ruled from Acre. Jerusalem was a small district, a Sanjak, under a Sanjak Bey or Mutasallim. Yet Jerusalem's status changed repeatedly over the next centuries, sometimes becoming an independent district. Ottoman governors ruled with the aid of the qadi, a city judge appointed in

The Jews, without any European backing, suffered bitterly. 'The Arabs', wrote Gedaliah, an Ashkenazi from Poland, 'often wrong the Jews publicly. If one of them gives a Jew a blow, the Jew goes away cowering. While an angry Turk would beat a Jew shamefully and dreadfully with his shoes and not one would deliver the Jew.' They lived in squalor, banned from repairing their houses. Two hundred Jewish families took flight: with 'the persecutions and extortions increasing every day', wrote a Jewish pilgrim in 1766, 'I had to flee from the city at night. Every day somebody was flung into prison.'

The Christians hated each other much more than they hated the infidels – indeed Father Elzear Horn, a Franciscan, simply called the Greeks 'The Vomit'. Each of the sects relished every squalid discomfort and penurious humiliation suffered by their rivals in the Church. Ottoman control and Christian competition meant the 300 permanent residents were locked inside each night; 'more like prisoners' than priests in Evliya's view, living in a state of permanent siege. Food was passed through a hole in the door or winched up via a system of pulleys, to the windows. These monks – most of them Orthodox, Catholic or Armenian – camped in cramped, humid tension, suffering from 'headaches, fevers, tumours, diarrhoea, dysentery'. The latrines of the Sepulchre provided a special source of bitterness – and stench: every sect had its own lavatorial arrangements, but the Franciscans, claimed Father Horn, 'suffer much from the smell'. The Greeks did not have lavatories at all. Meanwhile the poverty-stricken smaller sects, the Copts, Ethiopians and Syriacs, could afford their food only by performing servile tasks such as emptying the Greek slop-buckets. No wonder the French writer Constantin Volney heard Jerusalemites 'have acquired and deserved the reputation of the most evil people in Syria'.

When France again won the *praedominium* for the Franciscans, the Greek Orthodox hit back. On the night before Palm Sunday

Istanbul, and the mufti (the leader appointed by the Grand Mufti of the empire, the Sheikh al-Islam in Istanbul, who wrote *fatwa* judgements on religious questions) drawn from Jerusalem's Families. The pashas of Damascus and Sidon were rivals who sometimes fought mini-wars for control of Palestine.

1757, the Greek Orthodox ambushed the Franciscans in the Rotunda of the Sepulchre, 'with clubs, maces, hooks, poniards, and swords' that had been hidden behind pillars and under their habits, smashing lamps and ripping tapestries. The Franciscans fled to St Saviour's, where they were besieged. These Mafia tactics worked: the sultan switched back to the Greeks, giving them the dominant position in the Church which they still hold today. Now Ottoman power collapsed in Palestine. Starting in Galilee in the 1730s, a Bedouin sheikh, Zahir al-Umar al-Zaydani, carved out a northern fiefdom, which he ruled from Acre – the only time, except for short-lived rebellions, when a native Palestinian Arab ruled an extended part of Palestine.

THE RISE AND FALL OF THE 'KING OF PALESTINE'

In 1770, Ali Bey, an Egyptian general who gloried in the nickname the Cloudsnatcher (which he had won by defeating Bedouin, whom the Ottomans believed were as hard to catch as clouds), allied himself with Sheikh Zahir. Together they conquered most of Palestine, even taking Damascus, but the sultan's pasha held out in Jerusalem. The Russian empress, Catherine the Great, was at war with the Ottomans and now she despatched a fleet to the Mediterranean, where it defeated the sultan's navy. The Cloudsnatcher needed Russian help and Russia was only interested in one prize: Jerusalem. The Russian ships bombarded Jaffa then sailed up to attack Beirut. Zahir occupied Jaffa – but could he and the Cloudsnatcher deliver Jerusalem?

Sheikh Zahir sent his troops to invest the city but they were unable to make any impression on the walls. The Ottomans, defeated on all fronts, sued for peace with the Russians. In the peace treaty in 1774, Catherine and her partner Prince Potemkin forced the Ottomans to recognize Russian protection of the Orthodox – and ultimately the growing Russian obsession with Jerusalem would lead to a European war.* The Ottomans could now retake

* Potemkin devised the 'Greek Project' for Catherine – the Russian conquest of Constantinople (which Russians called Tsargrad) to be ruled by Catherine's grand-

their lost provinces: the Cloudsnatcher was assassinated and Sheikh Zahir, aged eighty-six, had to escape from Acre. As he rode away, he noticed that his favourite concubine was missing – 'this is no time to leave a person behind,' he said – and galloped back. As he scooped her up, the girl dragged her ancient lover from his horse and assassins stabbed and beheaded him. The pickled head of the 'first King of Palestine' was sent to Istanbul. The anarchy now attracted the rising hero of Revolutionary France.

NAPOLEON BONAPARTE:
'A KORAN I COMPOSED MYSELF'

On 19 May 1798, Napoleon Bonaparte, twenty-eight years old, pale and gaunt, with long lank hair, set off with 335 ships, 35,000 troops and an academy of 167 scientists to conquer Egypt. 'I would found a religion', he reflected with megalomaniacal arrogance, 'I saw myself marching on the way to Asia, mounted on an elephant, a turban on my head, in one hand a new Koran I would have composed myself.'

His adventure was inspired by revolutionary science, cold politics and crusading romance. Everyone in Paris had read the bestselling travelogue by the *philosophe*, Constantin Volney, who described the 'battered ruins of Jerusalem' and the decay of the Ottoman Levant as ripe for conquest by the civilizing reason of the Enlightenment. The French Revolution had tried to destroy the Church and replace Christianity with reason, liberty and even a new cult of the Supreme Being. However, Catholicism had endured and Napoleon aspired to heal the wounds of Revolution by fusing together monarchy, faith and science – hence the many scientists on board. Yet it was

son, especially named Constantine. Catherine's partitioning of Poland brought millions of Jews into the Russian empire for the first time, most of whom were confined in miserable poverty to a Pale of Settlement. But Potemkin, one of the most philo-Semitic leaders in Russian history, was a Christian Zionist who saw the liberation of Jerusalem as part of his Greek Project. In 1787, he created the Israelovsky Regiment of Jewish cavalry to take Jerusalem. A witness, the Prince de Ligne, mocked these ringleted cavalrymen as 'monkeys on horseback'. Potemkin died before he could put his schemes into action.

also about empire: France was at war with England. The expedition was the brainchild of the louche, lame ex-bishop and foreign minister, Charles-Maurice de Talleyrand, who hoped it would win control of the Mediterranean and cut off British India. If Bonaparte succeeded, all well and good but if he failed, Talleyrand would destroy a rival. As would happen so often in the Middle East, the Europeans expected the orientals to be grateful for their well-intentioned conquest.

Napoleon landed successfully in Egypt, which was still ruled by a caste of hybrid mamluk–Ottoman officers. He swiftly defeated them at the Battle of the Pyramids, but the English admiral Horatio Nelson obliterated the French fleet at Aboukir Bay. Bonaparte had won Egypt, but Nelson had trapped his army in the East and this encouraged the Ottomans to defy him in Syria. If Napoleon was to survive in Egypt, he had to march north and secure Syria.

In February 1799, he invaded Palestine with 13,000 men and 800 camels. On 2 March, as he advanced on Jaffa, his cavalry under General Damas carried out a raid just three miles from Jerusalem. General Bonaparte fantasized about the conquest of the Holy City, reporting to the revolutionary Directorate in Paris: 'By the time you read this letter, it's possible I will be standing in the ruins of Solomon's Temple.'

PART EIGHT

EMPIRE

How I should like to visit Jerusalem some time.

> Abraham Lincoln, in conversation with his wife

The theatre of the most memorable and stupendous events that have ever occurred in the annals of the world.

> James Barclay, *City of the Great King*

No-where is the arch of heaven more pure, intense and cloudless than above the proud heights of Zion. Yet if the traveller can forget he is treading on the grave of the people from whom his religion has sprung, there is certainly no city he will sooner wish to leave.

> W. H. Bartlett, *Walks*

Yes I am a Jew and when the ancestors of the Rt. Hon. Gentleman were living as savages in an unknown island, mine were priests in the Temple of Solomon.

> Benjamin Disraeli, speech in the House of Commons

See what is done here in the name of religion!

> Harriet Martineau, *Eastern Life*

34

NAPOLEON IN THE HOLY LAND

1799–1806

THE BLUEBEARD OF ACRE

There was nothing between Napoleon and the conquest of Jerusalem – except the Butcher, Ahmet Jazzar Pasha, the warlord of Ottoman Palestine. He had adopted the name Jazzar – Butcher – as a young man and had built his career on the principle that fear motivated men more than anything else.

The Butcher terrorized his territories by mutilating anyone suspected of the slightest disloyalty. An Englishman who visited him at his capital in Acre noticed that he was 'surrounded by persons maimed and disfigured. The persons officiating or standing by the doors' were all missing a limb, nose, ear or eye. His Jewish minister, Haim Farhi, 'had been deprived of both an ear and an eye' just to be sure. 'The number of faces without noses and ears strikes everyone who has visited this part of Syria.' The Butcher called them his 'marked men'. He sometimes had his victims' feet shod with horseshoes. He had walled up some local Christians alive *pour encourager les autres* and once gathered fifty corrupt officials, ordered them to strip naked, and had his troops hack them into pieces. When he suspected his harem of treason, he killed seven of his own wives, becoming notorious as 'the tyrant of Acre, the Herod of his time, the terror of all surrounding nations, the story of Bluebeard realized'.

The Butcher impressed Europeans with his long white beard, his simple robes, the bejewelled dagger at his belt and his rather delicate habit of cutting flowers out of paper which he liked to give as presents. He radiated a macabre charm, telling visitors with a slight smirk: 'I trust you found my name respected, even beloved, notwithstanding my severity.' At night, he locked himself in his harem which starred eighteen Slavic blondes.* This old man now faced Napoleon in his prime. The French besieged Jaffa which was the port of Jerusalem and only 20 miles away. Jerusalem was in panic: the Families armed the Jerusalemites; a mob plundered Christian monasteries; the monks had to be imprisoned for their own safety. Outside the walls, General Damas asked Bonaparte for permission to attack the Holy City.

NAPOLEON: 'GENERAL HEADQUARTERS, JERUSALEM'

Napoleon replied that he had to conquer Acre first and then 'come in person and plant the tree of Liberty at the very spot where Christ suffered, and the first French soldier who fell in the attack would be buried in the Holy Sepulchre'. But Bonaparte and his troops clearly regarded their expedition against the Muslims as falling outside the rules of civilized conduct. When he stormed Jaffa, his 'soldiers hacked to pieces, men and women – the sights were terrible', wrote one of the French scientists, shocked by 'the sound of shots, shrieks of women and fathers, piles of bodies, a daughter being raped on the cadaver of her mother, the smell of blood, the groans of the wounded, the shouts of victors quarrelling about loot'. Finally the French themselves rested, 'sated by blood and gold, on top of a heap of dead'.

Before he marched on towards Acre, Bonaparte ordered the slaughter in cold blood of at least 2,440 but probably more like 4,000 of the Butcher's troops, killing them in batches of 600 a day. On 18 March 1799, he laid siege to Acre, still under the command

---

* He was a Christian slaveboy from Bosnia who, escaping after committing a murder, sold himself to the slave-markets of Istanbul. There he was bought by an Egyptian ruler who converted him to Islam and used him as his chief executioner and hitman. He began his rise as governor of Cairo but made his name defending Beirut against Catherine the Great's navy. Beirut was honourably surrendered to the Russians after a long siege and the sultan rewarded the Butcher with promotion to Governor of Sidon, and sometimes also that of Damascus. He visited Jerusalem, unofficially in his sphere of influence, where the Husseinis owed him allegiance.

of the Butcher, whom Napoleon superciliously called 'an old man whom I don't know'. Yet Bluebeard and his 4,000 Afghans, Albanians and Moors resisted vigorously.

On 16 April, Napoleon defeated the Butcher's cavalry and an Ottoman army at the Battle of Tabor Mountain. Afterwards, finding himself at Ramla, 25 miles from Jerusalem, he issued a pro-Zionist 'Proclamation to the Jews', mendaciously datelined, 'General Headquarters, Jerusalem, 20 April 1799'.

> Bonaparte, Commander in Chief of the Armies of the French Republic in Africa and Asia, to the rightful heirs of Palestine – the unique nation of Jews who have been deprived of the land of your fathers by thousands of years of lust for conquest and tyranny. Arise then with gladness, ye exiled, and take unto yourselves Israel's patrimony. The young army has made Jerusalem my headquarters and will within a few days transfer to Damascus so you can remain there [in Jerusalem] as ruler.

The official French gazette, *Le Moniteur*, claimed that Napoleon had 'already armed a great number [of Jews] to re-establish ancient Jerusalem', but Napoleon could not seize Zion until Acre was his and the Butcher was now reinforced by two Royal Navy ships-of-the-line under a maverick English commodore.

SIR SIDNEY SMITH – 'MOST BRILLIANT OF CHEVALIERS'

Sidney Smith, the son of an eloping heiress and an adventurer, was 'good looking with tremendous moustaches and penetrating black eyes'. He had joined the navy at thirteen, fought the American rebels and then, when he was seconded to the Swedish navy, Catherine the Great's Russians. The King of Sweden knighted him, so English rivals mocked him as the 'Swedish knight'. After the French Revolution, Smith raided France, but was captured and imprisoned in the dreaded Temple. Dashingly he escaped, taunting Bonaparte, whom he particularly despised, in a series of public letters. Not everyone was convinced by Smith: he was, wrote one observer, an 'enthusiast, restlessly active, extravagantly vain with no fixed purpose save that of persuading mankind that Sidney Smith was the most brilliant of chevaliers'. But if he was preposterous in normal life, he was heroic in a crisis.

Smith and the Butcher struck up a rapport. When the Englishman admired the gleaming Damascene sword that the Butcher kept beside him at all times, Jazzar boasted, 'The one I carry never fails. It's taken off dozens of heads.' Smith wanted proof, whereupon the Butcher had an ox brought to him which he then beheaded with a single blow. Smith merged his eighty-eight sailors with the Butcher's multinational garrison. Bonaparte launched three assaults on Acre but Smith and the Butcher managed to repel all three. As Ottoman reinforcements approached and the siege dragged into its third month, the French generals became restless.

On 21 May 1799, with 1,200 troops dead and 2,300 sick or wounded, Napoleon led the retreat towards Egypt. However, 800 French soldiers lay ill in Jaffa. As they would slow the retreat, Napoleon ordered his wounded to be killed by his own doctors. When the French medics refused, a Turkish doctor administered fatal doses of laudanum to the patients. No wonder the French general Jean-Baptiste Kléber reflected, 'We have committed in the Holy Land enormous sins and great stupidities.' Two thousand mounted Jerusalemites under the command of the city's governor pursued and harassed the retreating French. When the peasant fighters of Nablus broke into Jaffa, Smith managed to prevent a massacre of Christians by summoning the Jerusalemites to restore order.

In Egypt, Napoleon, facing the reality of a disastrous campaign that could only be saved by shameless distortion of the truth, abandoned his men and sailed for home. General Kléber, left in command of Egypt, cursed Napoleon: 'That bugger has deserted us with his breeches full of shit.' But in France Napoleon was hailed as a returning conqueror, soon to seize power from the Directory as first consul,* and a romantic song about his expedition – 'Partant pour la Syrie' – became the Bonapartist anthem.

---

* Napoleon blamed his defeat on Smith, 'the man who made me miss my destiny', but he left one legacy in Jerusalem. On taking Jaffa, his sick soldiers (those whom he later had killed) were nursed by Armenian monks, whom he thanked by present-

The Christians of Jerusalem, particularly the Catholics, were in peril from Muslim reprisals. Addicted to grandiose gestures, Smith decided that only a show of English sangfroid would save his brethren. With permission from the Butcher and the sultan, he marched his sailors in dress uniform with beating drums from Jaffa to Jerusalem. Progressing through the streets, he hoisted the British flag over St Saviour's Monastery, whose Franciscan superior declared that 'every Christian in Jerusalem was under the greatest obligation to the English nation and particularly Smith by whose means they have been preserved from the merciless hand of Bonaparte'. In fact it was the Muslims whom they feared. Smith and his crew prayed at the Sepulchre, the first Frankish troops to enter Jerusalem since 1244.

Sultan Selim III showered honours on the Butcher, who was appointed pasha of his native Bosnia as well as of Egypt and Damascus. After a short war with the pasha of Gaza, he again dominated Jerusalem and Palestine. But he had not mellowed, for he cut off his prime minister's nose to spite a face that already lacked an ear and an eye. On his death in 1804, Palestine sank into chaos.

Yet Napoleon and Smith had made the Levant fashionable. Among the adventurers who now started to explore the East and recount their exploits in bestselling books that beguiled the West, the most influential was a French vicomte who in 1806 found Jerusalem bedevilled by fire, rebellion and rapine, at its lowest ebb since the Mongols.

ing them with his tent. The Armenians converted it into chasubles, now used in St Jameses Cathedral in Jerusalem's Armenian Quarter.

35

THE NEW ROMANTICS:
CHATEAUBRIAND AND DISRAELI

1806–1830

THE VICOMTE OF THE ORDER OF THE HOLY SEPULCHRE

'Jerusalem overawes me' declared François-René, Vicomte de Chateaubriand, even though this 'deicidal city' was 'a heap of rubbish' with the 'confused monuments of a cemetery in the midst of a desert'. This bouffant-haired Catholic royalist embraced the romantic view of a shabby Gothic Jerusalem awaiting rescue by the 'genius of Christianity'. To him, the more miserable Jerusalem was, the holier and more poetical she became – and the city was now desperate.

Rebel pashas and hordes of Palestinian peasants repeatedly rebelled and seized a godforsaken Jerusalem which had to be stormed by the governors of Damascus who marched down annually with an army and treated the city as conquered enemy territory. The vicomte arrived to find the governor of Damascus camped outside the Jaffa Gate while his 3,000 soldiers menaced the inhabitants. When Chateaubriand settled in the St Saviour's Monastery, it was occupied by these ruffians who extorted cash from the friars. He strutted the streets armed with several pistols but in the Monastery, one of them caught him unawares and tried to kill him: he only survived by almost throttling the Turk. In the streets, 'we met not a creature! What wretchedness, what desolation for most of the inhabitants had fled to the mountains. Shops are shut, people conceal themselves in cellars or withdraw to the mountains.' When the pasha left, the garrison in David's Tower numbered just a dozen and the city became even more eerie: 'The only noise is the galloping of a steed of the desert – it's a janissary who brings the head of a Bedouin or returns from plundering the unhappy peasants.'

Now the Frenchman could revel in the squalid sacred mysteries of the shrines. Yet this enthusiastic gourmand, who gave his name to his recipe for steak, relished the banquets he shared with his famously plump Franciscan hosts, feasting on 'lentil soup, veal with cucumbers and onions, broiled kid with rice, pigeons, partridges, game, excellent wine'. Armed with several pistols, he retraced every step of Jesus while mocking Ottoman monuments ('not worth notice') and the Jews who were 'covered in rags, sealed in the dust of Zion, with vermin that devoured them'. Chateaubriand was astonished to 'behold these rightful masters of Judaea living as slaves and strangers in their own country'.

In the Sepulchre he prayed on his knees for half an hour, his eyes 'riveted to the stone' of Jesus' tomb, dizzy with the incense, the clash of Ethiopian cymbals and chanting of the Greeks, before kneeling at the tombs of Godfrey and Baldwin, those French paladins who had defeated Islam, 'a religion hostile to civilization that systematically favoured ignorance, despotism and slavery'.

The Franciscans awarded Chateaubriand the Order of the Holy Sepulchre in a solemn ceremony. As they encircled the kneeling vicomte, attaching the spurs of Godfrey to his heels and knighting him with the Crusader's sword, he experienced an almost ecstatic joy:

> If it is considered that I was at Jerusalem, in the Church of Calvary, within a dozen paces of the tomb of Jesus Christ, and thirty from that of Godfrey de Bouillon, that I was equipped with the spurs of the Deliverer of the Holy Sepulchre; and had touched that sword, both long and large, which so noble and so valiant an arm had once wielded, I couldn't remain unmoved.

On 12 October 1808, an Armenian sacristan fell asleep by the stove in the Armenian gallery on the second floor of the Church of the Holy Sepulchre. The stove caught fire, burned him to death and then spread. The Tomb of Jesus was destroyed. In the ensuing chaos, the Christians invited Hassan al-Husseini, the mufti, to camp in the courtyard of the Church to prevent looting. The Greeks accused the Armenians of arson. England and Austria were fighting to contain the apparently invincible Emperor Napoleon so the Greeks, backed by Russia, were able to consolidate their control over the Church. They built the rococo aedicule that stands around the Tomb today. They celebrated by smashing the beautifully decorated sarcophagi of the Crusader kings: Chateaubriand, now back in France, was the last outsider to see them.* A Muslim mob attacked the builders restoring the Church; the garrison mutinied, and the Butcher's successor and son-in-law, Suleiman Pasha – who was known as the Just (though anyone would have seemed clement after his predecessor) – captured the city: forty-six rebels were executed, their heads decorating the gates.

As the real Jerusalem decayed, the imaginary Jerusalem ignited Western dreams, encouraged by Napoleon's nasty little Middle Eastern war, the decline of the Ottomans – and the book that Chateaubriand wrote when he got home. His *Itinerary from Paris to Jerusalem* set the tone of the European attitude to the Orient with its cruel but inept Turks, wailing Jews, and primitive but ferocious Arabs who tended to congregate in picturesque biblical poses. It was such a bestseller that it launched a new genre and even his valet, Julien, wrote his memoirs of the trip.† In London, Sir Sidney

---

* Godfrey's spurs and sword, along with a brick from his French chateau, hang today in the Latin sacristy of the Holy Sepulchre. As for the Crusader tombs, only fragments of the sarcophagus of the boy-king Baldwin V survived this act of sectarian vandalism.

† In 1804, William Blake, poet, painter, engraver and radical, opened his poem *Milton* with the prefatory verses 'And did those feet in ancient times ...' which ends 'Till we have built Jerusalem in England's green and pleasant land.' The poem, printed in about 1808, praises the brief heyday of a heavenly Jerusalem in pre-industrial England, inspired by the mythical visit of young Jesus accompanying Joseph of Arimathea to inspect the latter's Cornish tin-mines. The poem remained little known until 1916 when the Poet Laureate Robert Bridges asked the composer Sir Hubert Parry to set it to music for a patriotic meeting. Edward Elgar later orchestrated it. King George V said he preferred it to 'God Save the King', and it has become an alternative anthem, with universal appeal to plangent patriots, church-goers, Promenaders, sports fans, socialist idealists and generations of drunken, floppy-haired undergraduates. Blake never called it 'Jerusalem' for he also wrote an epic entitled *Jerusalem: The Emanation of the Giant Albion.*

Smith's boasting about his Levantine exploits caught the imagination of his royal mistress – and inspired the most absurd of royal tours.

CAROLINE OF BRUNSWICK AND HESTER STANHOPE: QUEEN OF ENGLAND AND QUEEN OF THE DESERT

Princess Caroline, estranged wife of the English Prince Regent (later King George IV), was much taken with the dashing Smith, and regularly invited his cousin, Lady Hester Stanhope, niece of Prime Minister William Pitt the Younger, to provide cover for their brazen affair.

Lady Hester loathed the coarse, deluded and lecherous Princess Caroline, who showed off to Smith by 'dancing about, exposing herself, like an opera girl' and even gartering below the knee: 'an impudent woman, a downright whore! So low! So vulgar!' Caroline's marriage to the Prince Regent had been a disaster and the so-called 'Delicate Investigation' into her love-life at that time later revealed at least five lovers including Smith, Lord Hood, the painter Thomas Lawrence and various servants. But Smith's stories of Acre and Jerusalem at least found their mark: both women quite separately decided to travel to the East.

Lady Hester had her own Jerusalem destiny. Richard Brothers, an ex-sailor and radical Calvinist, had declared himself a descendant of King David who would be the Ruler of the World until the Second Coming of Christ. His book *Plan for New Jerusalem* revealed that God had 'preordained me to be the King and Restorer of the Jews', and Brothers also asserted that the British people were descended from the Lost Tribes: he would lead them back to Jerusalem. He designed gardens and palaces for the Temple Mount, and uniforms and flags for his new Israelites, but he was eventually imprisoned as a lunatic. This Anglo-Israelite vision was an eccentric one. Yet within thirty years a belief in a sacred return of the Jews to accelerate the Second Coming was almost British government policy.

Brothers expected a heavenly lady to assist in this enterprise and selected Lady Hester Stanhope to be his 'Queen of the Jews'. When she visited him in Newgate Prison, he predicted that 'she would one day go to Jerusalem and lead back the Chosen People!' Stanhope did indeed visit Jerusalem in 1812, dressed fetchingly in Ottoman costume, but Brothers' predictions did not materialize. She stayed in the East – and her fame helped to promote European interest. Most satisfyingly of all, she beat the despised Caroline to Jerusalem by three years.

On 9 August 1814, the princess, aged forty-six, departed on a scandalous Mediterranean tour. Inspired by Smith, Stanhope and the pilgrimages of various crusading ancestors, Caroline declared that 'Jerusalem is my great ambition'.

In Acre, the princess was greeted by Suleiman the Just's 'prime minister, a Jew who wants an eye, an ear and a nose' – for the pasha had inherited not only the Butcher's fiefdom but also his Jewish adviser, Haim Farhi. Ten years after the Butcher's death, Caroline's courtiers were amazed how many 'persons one sees in the streets without noses'. But the princess relished the 'barbarous pomp of Eastern mores'. She arrived with an entourage of twenty-six including a foundling, Willie Austin, whom she had adopted (though he was possibly her own child), and her latest lover, an Italian soldier named Bartholomeo Pergami, sixteen years her junior. Now a baron and her chamberlain, he was 'a man six feet high with a magnificent head of black hair, pale complexion and moustaches that reach from here to London!' as one lady swooningly described him. By the time Caroline left for Jerusalem, her retinue of 200 'presented the appearance of an army'.

She entered Jerusalem on a donkey like Jesus, but she was sufficiently fat to need a servant propping her up on each side. The Franciscans escorted her on her ass to her suite at St Saviour's. 'It would be impossible to paint the scene,' remembered one of her courtiers. 'Men, women and children, Jews and Arabs, Armenians, Greeks, Catholics and infidels all received us. "Ben venute!" they cried!' Illuminated by burning torches, 'many fingers extended towards the Royal Pilgrim' with shouts of 'That's her!' No wonder: Caroline often sported 'a wig (curled at the sides nearly as high as the top of the bonnet), artificial eyebrows (nature having denied her any) and false teeth', with a scarlet dress, cut low at front and back and far too short, scarcely hiding the 'immense protuberance of her ventre'. A courtier had to admit that her entry was both 'solemn and certainly laughable'.

Proud of being the first Christian princess to visit for six centuries, Caroline sincerely wanted to leave 'a proper feeling of her elevated status', so she established an Order of St Caroline with its own banner – a red cross with a riband of lilac and silver. Her lover Pergami was the Order's first (and last) 'Grand Master'. On her return, she commissioned a painting of her pilgrimage: *The Entry of Queen Caroline into Jerusalem.*

The future Queen of England handed out generous donations to the Franciscans, and on 17 July 1815 (four weeks after Napoleon's final defeat at Waterloo) 'quit Jerusalem amid the thanks and regrets of all ranks and degrees' – hardly surprising given the state of the place.

When Damascus trebled the taxes in 1819, the city revolted again. This time, Abdullah Pasha,* the strongman of Palestine, the Butcher's grandson, attacked Jerusalem and when it was captured, the city governor personally strangled twenty-eight rebels – the rest were beheaded the next day, all the bodies lined up outside Jaffa Gate. In 1824, the savage depredations of the Ottoman pasha known as Mustafa the Criminal led to a peasants' revolt. Jerusalem achieved independence for some months until Abdullah bombarded it from the Mount of Olives. By the late 1820s, Jerusalem was 'fallen, desolate and abject', wrote a brave English traveller, Judith Montefiore, visiting with her wealthy husband, Moses. 'Not a single relic', she said, remained of 'the city that was the joy of the whole earth'.

The Montefiores were the first of a new breed of powerful and proud European Jews, determined to help their benighted brethren in Jerusalem. They were fêted by the city's governor but stayed with a Moroccan former slave-trader within the walls and started their philanthropic work by restoring Rachel's Tomb near Bethlehem,

* In 1818, on Suleiman Pasha's death, Abdullah had taken power in Acre and executed the very wealthy, one-eyed, one-eared and noseless Haim Farhi, who had effectively run much of Palestine for thirty years. Abdullah ruled until 1831. The Farhi family still live in Israel.

Judaism's third holiest shrine after the Temple and the Patriarch's Tombs in Hebron, but, like the other two, also holy to Islam. The Montefiores were childless and Rachel's Tomb was said to help women conceive. Jerusalem's Jews welcomed them 'almost like the coming of the Messiah', but begged them not to give too much because the Turks would simply cripple them with higher taxes after they had gone.

Moses Montefiore arrived as an Italian-born, self-made English gentleman and international financier, brother-in-law of Nathaniel Rothschild, but he was not particularly religious. The trip to Jerusalem changed his life. He left as a reborn Jew, having prayed all through his last night there. For him Jerusalem was simply 'the city of our forefathers, the great and long-desired object of our wishes and journey'. He believed it was every Jew's duty to make the pilgrimage: 'I humbly pray to the God of my forefathers that I may henceforth become a more righteous and better man as well as a better Jew.'* He would return to the Holy City many times and he henceforth contrived to combine the life of an English grandee with that of an Orthodox Jew.

No sooner had Montefiore left than a Byronic poseur rode into town: both men were English Sephardic Jews of Italian descent. They did not yet know about each other – but one day both would promote Britain's advance into the Middle East.

DISRAELI: THE SACRED AND THE ROMANTIC

'You should see me in the costume of a Greek pirate. A blood red shirt with silver studs as big as shillings, an immense scarf, girdle full of pistols and daggers, a red cap, red slippers, blue broad striped jacket and trousers. Excessively wicked!' This was how Benjamin

---

* During his voyage home, a fearsome storm struck the Montefiores' ship. The sailors feared that the vessel would sink. Montefiore carried, for luck, from the previous year's Passover, a piece of unleavened matzah, known as the *afikoman*, which, at the height of the tempest, he cast into the waves. The sea instantly became miraculously quiet. Montefiore believed that this was God's blessing on a Jerusalem pilgrimage. The Montefiore family today read his account of this event every Passover.

Disraeli, the twenty-six-year-old fashionable novelist (already author of *The Young Duke*), failed speculator and aspiring politician, dressed on his Oriental tour. Such jaunts were the new version of the eighteenth-century Grand Tour, combining romantic posturing, Classical sightseeing, the smoking of hookah pipes, avid whoring and visits to Istanbul and Jerusalem.

Disraeli had been raised as a Jew but was baptized at twelve. He regarded himself, he later told Queen Victoria, as 'the blank page between the Old and New Testaments'. He looked the part. Slim and pale with a head of black ringleted hair, Disraeli rode through the Judaean hills, 'well mounted and well armed'. When he saw the walls:

> I was thunderstruck. I saw before me apparently a gorgeous city. In the front is the magnificent mosque built on the site of the Temple with its beautiful garden and fantastic gates – a variety of domes and towers arise. Nothing can be conceived more wild and terrible and barren than the surrounding scenery. I never saw anything more essentially striking.

Dining on the roof of the Armenian Monastery, where he was staying, Disraeli was enraptured by the romance of Jewish history as he gazed out at 'Jehovah's lost capital' and was intrigued by that of Islam: he could not resist trying to visit the Temple Mount. A Scottish physician and later an Englishwoman had both penetrated the esplanade – but only in strict disguise. Disraeli was less adept: 'I was detected and surrounded by a crowd of turbaned fanatics and escaped with difficulty!' He regarded the Jews and the Arabs as one people – the Arabs were surely 'Jews on horseback' – and he asked the Christians: 'Where is your Christianity if you don't believe in their Judaism?'

While he was in Jerusalem, he started to write his next novel, *Alroy*, about the doomed twelfth-century 'Messiah' whose uprising he called a 'gorgeous incident in the annals of that sacred and romantic people from whom I derive my blood and name'.

His Jerusalem visit helped him refine his unique hybrid

mystique as a Tory aristocrat and exotic Jewish panjandrum,* convinced him that Britain had a role in the Middle East – and let him dream of a return to Zion. In his novel, David Alroy's adviser declares, 'You ask what I wish. My answer is a national existence. You ask what I wish. My answer is Jerusalem.' In 1851, Disraeli the rising politican reflected that 'restoring the Jews to their land, which could be bought from the Ottomans, was both just and feasible'.

Disraeli claimed Alroy's adventure was 'his ideal ambition' but actually he was far too ambitious to risk his career for anything Jewish: he wanted to be prime minister of the greatest empire on earth. Over thirty years later when he had reached the 'top of the greasy pole', Disraeli did guide British power into the region by gaining Cyprus and buying the Suez Canal.

Not long after Disraeli had returned to embark on his political career, an Albanian warlord who was the ruler of Egypt conquered Jerusalem.

---

* His ideal character, featured in his best novel *Coningsby*, was Sidonia, a Sephardic millionaire who is friends with the emperors, kings and ministers in all the cabinets of Europe. Sidonia was an amalgam of Lionel de Rothschild and Moses Montefiore, both of whom Disraeli knew well.

36

THE ALBANIAN CONQUEST

1830–40

IBRAHIM THE RED

In December 1831, the Egyptian army marched through the city as 'happy and delighted' Jerusalemites 'celebrated with illuminations, dancing and music in every street. For the five days Muslims, Greeks, Franciscans, Armenians and even Jews made merry.' But already the Muslims were worried by the sight of the Egyptian soldiers in 'tight trousers, carrying terrible firearms, music instruments and moving in formation after the European fashion'.

Jerusalem's new master was the Albanian soldier Mehmet Ali, who created a dynasty that still ruled Egypt when the State of Israel was founded over a century later. Now forgotten, he dominated international Near Eastern diplomacy for fifteen years and almost conquered the entire Ottoman empire. The son of a tobacco trader, he was born in what is now Greece, in the same year as Napoleon, and contemporaries saw him as an Eastern Bonaparte: 'Alike distinguished for military genius, the characters of these chieftains are equally marked by insatiable ambition, and unreposing activity.' The white-bearded Albanian, now in his sixties, always dressed simply in white turban, yellow slippers and blue-green gown, ever puffing on a gold and silver seven-foot tall diamond-studded pipe, had a 'Tartar face with high cheekbones', and a 'strange wild fire' in his 'dark grey eyes [which] beam brightly with genius and intelligence'. His power was based on the curved scimitar that always rested by his side. He had arrived in Egypt in time to command his Albanian troops on behalf of the Ottomans against Napoleon. When the French departed, he took advantage of the ensuing power vacuum and seized Egypt. He then summoned his able son (or some say his nephew), Ibrahim, who lured the mamluk–Ottoman elite to a military ceremony and slaughtered them. The Albanians next plundered and raped their way through Cairo, but the sultan appointed Mehmet Ali as vali of Egypt. He needed only four hours' sleep a night and claimed to have learned to read at the age of forty-five. Each night, his favourite concubine read him Montesquieu or Machiavelli, and this brutal modernizer started to create a European army, 90,000 strong, and a fleet.

At first, the Ottoman sultan, Mahmoud II, was glad to exploit this rising power. Embarrassed that the puritanical Wahabi sect, led by the Saudi family, had seized Mecca, the sultan asked for Mehmet Ali's help. The Albanians duly retook Mecca and despatched Abdullah al-Saud's head to Istanbul.* When in 1824 the Greeks rebelled against the sultan, Mehmet Ali sent his forces, which savagely repressed the Greeks. This so alarmed the European Powers that in 1827 the British, French and Russians together destroyed Mehmet Ali's fleet at the Battle of Navarino and sponsored Greek independence. But this did not stop the Albanians for long: encouraged by that earlier visitor to Jerusalem, now French foreign minister, Vicomte de Chateaubriand, they coveted their own empire.

In late 1831, Mehmet Ali conquered present-day Israel, Syria and most of Turkey, defeating every army the sultan threw at him. Soon his armies were poised to take Istanbul. Finally the sultan recognized Mehmet Ali as ruler of Egypt, Arabia and Crete with Ibrahim as governor of greater Syria. This empire now belonged to the Albanians: 'I have now conquered this country with the sword,' declared Mehmet Ali, 'and by the sword will I preserve it.' His sword was his generalissimo, Ibrahim, who had commanded his

* The Wahabis were the followers of an eighteenth-century fundamentalist Salafi preacher Muhammad ibn Abdul Wahab who in 1744 allied himself with the Saudi family. Despite their setback at the hands of Mehmet Ali, the Saudis soon re-established a small state. During the First World War and the 1920s, their chieftain Abdul-Aziz ibn Saud, funded by British subsidies and backed by his fanatical Wahabi army, reconquered Mecca and Arabia. In 1932, he proclaimed himself king of Saudi Arabia, where Wahabi Islam still rules. Ibn Saud fathered at least seventy children and his son Abdullah became king in 2005.

first armies and organized his first massacres as a teenager. It was Ibrahim who had defeated the Saudis, ravaged Greece, conquered Jerusalem and Damascus and marched victoriously almost to the gates of Istanbul.

Now in spring 1834, Ibrahim, known as The Red, and not just for the colour of his beard, set up his headquarters in the palatial compound of David's Tomb. Shocking Muslims by sitting on a European throne instead of cushions and openly drinking wine, he set about reforming Jerusalem. He eased the repression of Christians and Jews, promising them equality under the law, and ended the fees that had to be paid by all pilgrims to the Church: they could now wear Muslim clothes, ride horses in the street and no longer had to pay the *jizaya* tax for the first time in centuries. Yet as Turkish-speaking Albanians, they despised Arabs above all: Ibrahim's father called them 'wild beasts'. On 25 April, Ibrahim met the leaders of Jerusalem and Nablus on the Temple Mount to order the conscription of 200 Jerusalemites. 'I want this order carried out without delay, starting here in Jerusalem,' said Ibrahim. But Jerusalem was defiant: 'It's better to die than give our children to everlasting slavery,' retorted the Jerusalemites.

On 3 May, the Albanian presided over Orthodox Easter: 17,000 Christian pilgrims filled a seething city on the verge of outright revolt. On Good Friday night, the crowds packed the Church of the Holy Sepulchre ready for the Holy Fire, watched by Robert Curzon, an English traveller who left a vivid memoir of what happened next. 'The behaviour of the pilgrims was riotous in the extreme. At one point, they made a racecourse around the Sepulchre and some, almost in a state of nudity, danced about with frantic gestures, yelling and screaming as if possessed.'

Next morning, Ibrahim entered the Church to witness the Holy Fire but the crowd was so dense that the guards cleared the way 'with the butt-ends of their muskets and whips' while three monks played 'crazy fiddles' and women started to ululate 'with a very peculiar shrill cry'.

IBRAHIM: HOLY FIRE, HOLY DEATH

Ibrahim was seated. Darkness fell. The Greek patriarch, in 'magnificent procession', entered the aedicule. The crowd awaited the divine spark. Curzon saw the flicker then the flame of the Miracle which was passed to the pilgrim 'who had paid the highest sum for this honour', but 'a furious battle' broke out for the Fire; pilgrims fell to the floor in ecstatic faints; blinding smoke filled the Church; three pilgrims fell to their deaths from the higher galleries; an old Armenian lady died in her seat. Ibrahim tried to leave the Church but could not move. His guards, attempting to beat a way through the crowd, started a stampede. By the time Curzon 'got as far as the place where the Virgin stood during the Crucifixion', the stones felt soft under his feet.

> There was actually a great heap of bodies on which I trod. All dead. Many of them quite black with suffocation and others all bloody and covered with brains and entrails, trodden to pieces by the crowd. Soldiers with their bayonets killed a number of fainting wretches, the walls splattered with the blood and brains of men who had been felled like oxen.

The frenzied stampede became a 'desperate and savage' fight for survival – Curzon saw people dying all around him. Ibrahim only just escaped with his own life, fainting several times until his guards drew their swords and sliced a path through human flesh.

Bodies were 'lying in heaps even upon the Stone of Unction'. Ibrahim stood in the courtyard 'giving orders for the removal of the corpses and making his men drag out the bodies of those who appeared to be alive'. Four hundred pilgrims perished. When Curzon escaped, many of the bodies were actually 'standing upright quite dead'.

IBRAHIM: THE PEASANTS REVOLT

As news of this disaster spread throughout a shocked Christendom, the Families of Jerusalem, Nablus and Hebron raised the rebellion. On 8 May, 10,000 armed fellahin attacked Jerusalem, but were repulsed by Ibrahim's troops. On 19 May, in a scene that recalled King David's taking of Jerusalem, the villagers of Silwan, below the City of David, showed the rebels a secret tunnel through which they crawled into the city and opened the Dung Gate set in the southern wall. The peasants pillaged the bazaars, the troops attacked them, only to join in the plundering. The Bimbashi – garrison commander – arrested the leaders of the Jerusalemite Families, the Husseinis and Khalidis. But 20,000 peasants were now rampaging through the streets and besieging the Tower. Two young American missionaries, William Thomson and his pregnant wife Eliza, cowered in their digs: he left her to seek help in Jaffa while she locked herself in their room, amid 'the roar of cannon, falling walls, shrieks of the neighbours, terror of the servants and the expectation of massacre'. She gave birth to a boy, but by the time her husband made it back to Jerusalem she was dying. He soon left 'this wreck of a country'.*

Ibrahim, who had retreated to Jaffa, now fought his way across the hills, losing 500 men. On 27 May, encamped on Mount Zion, he attacked, killing 300 rebels. But he was ambushed near the Pools of Solomon, and besieged in David's Tomb. The rebellion flared again led by the Husseinis and the Abu Ghosh. Ibrahim called his father for help.

Mehmet Ali himself and 15,000 reinforcements sailed into Jaffa: 'a fine looking old man', bowing regally on a 'splendid horse, natural, dignified and in perfect keeping with the character of a great man'. The Albanians crushed the rebels and retook Jerusalem; the Husseinis of Jerusalem were exiled to Egypt. The rebels rose again, but Ibrahim the Red slaughtered them outside Nablus,

---

* William Thomson later wrote one of the Evangelical classics that encouraged the American obsession with Jerusalem. *The Land and the Book*, reprinted in thirty editions, presented Palestine as a mystical Eden where the Bible was alive.

sacked Hebron, despoiled the countryside, beheaded his captives –
and launched a reign of terror in Jerusalem. Returning to the city,
he appointed the chieftain Jaber Abu Ghosh as a poacher-turned-
gamekeeper governor, and beheaded anyone found with a weapon.
The walls were bedecked with severed heads; prisoners rotted in
the new Kishleh jail near the Jaffa Gate, since used by the Ottomans,
British and Israelis.

The Albanians were enthusiastic modernizers who needed
European backing if they were to conquer the Ottoman empire.
Ibrahim allowed the minorities to repair their smashed buildings:
the Franciscans restored St Saviour's; the Sephardic Jews started to
rebuild the ben Zakkai Synagogue, one of the four synagogues of the
Jewish Quarter; the Ashkenazis returned to the Hurva Synagogue,
destroyed in 1720. Although the Jewish Quarter was now poverty-
stricken, a few Russian Jews, persecuted at home, started to settle
there.

In 1839, Ibrahim made his bid for Istanbul, smashing the
Ottoman armies. King Louis Philippe's France backed the Alba-
nians, but Britain feared French and Russian influence if the
Ottomans fell. The sultan and his enemy Ibrahim both bid for
Western support. The teenaged Sultan Abdulmecid issued a Noble
Rescript promising equality for minorities, while Ibrahim invited
the Europeans to establish consulates in Jerusalem – and, for the
first time since the Crusades, permitted the ringing of church bells.

In 1839, the first British vice-consul, William Turner Young,
arrived in Jerusalem not only to represent London's new power but
to convert the Jews and accelerate the Second Coming.

37

THE EVANGELISTS

1840–1855

PALMERSTON AND SHAFTESBURY:
THE IMPERIALIST AND THE EVANGELIST

The diplomatic policy relating to Jerusalem was the work of Lord Palmerston, the foreign secretary, but the Godly mission was the achievement of his evangelical stepson-in-law, the Earl of Shaftesbury.* Palmerston, aged fifty-five, was not a Victorian prig or evangelical but an unrepentant Regency buck known as Lord Cupid for his sexual escapades (which he jovially recorded in his diary), as Lord Pam for his jaunty vigour, and as Lord Pumicestone for his gunboat diplomacy. Indeed Shaftesbury joked that Palmerston 'didn't know Moses from Sir Sidney Smith'. His interest in the Jews was pragmatic: the French advanced their power by protecting the Catholics, the Russians by protecting the Orthodox, but there were few Protestants in Jerusalem. Palmerston wanted to diminish French and Russian influence, and saw that British power could be advanced by protecting the Jews. The other mission – the conversion of the Jews – was the result of his son-in-law's evangelical ardour.

Shaftesbury, thirty-nine years old, curly haired and bewhiskered, personified the new Victorian Britain. A pure-hearted aristocrat dedicated to improving the lives of workers, children and lunatics, he was also a fundamentalist who believed that the Bible 'is God's word written from the very first syllable down to the very last'. He

* Anthony Ashley-Cooper, descendant of the first earl, that shrewd minister who had served everyone from Cromwell to William III, still held the courtesy title Lord Ashley and sat in the House of the Commons, succeeding as the 7th earl in 1851. But for simplicity we call him Shaftesbury throughout.

was sure that dynamic Christianity would promote a global moral renaissance and an improvement of humanity itself. In Britain, Puritan millenarianism had long since been overwhelmed by the rationalism of the Enlightenment but it had survived among the Nonconformists. Now it returned to the mainstream: the French Revolution with its guillotine, and the Industrial Revolution with its mobs of workers, had shaped a new British middle class that welcomed the certainties of piety, respectability and the Bible, the antidote to the raging materialism of Victorian prosperity.

The London Society for Promoting Christianity Among the Jews, known as the Jews Society, founded in 1808, now flourished, thanks in part to Shaftesbury. 'All the young people are growing mad about religion,' grumbled another elderly Regency roué, Lord Melbourne, prime minister at Queen Victoria's accession in 1837. Convinced that eternal salvation was attainable through the personal experience of Jesus and his good news (*evangelion* in Greek), these evangelicals expected the Second Coming. Shaftesbury believed, like the Puritans two centuries before, that the return and conversion of the Jews would create an Anglican Jerusalem and the Kingdom of Heaven. He prepared a memorandum for Palmerston: 'There's a country without a nation and God in his wisdom and mercy directs us to a nation without a country.'*

'It will be part of your duty', Palmerston instructed Jerusalem vice-consul Young, 'to afford protection to the Jews generally.' At the same time he told his ambassador to the Sublime Porte that he should 'strongly recommend [the sultan] to hold out every just encouragement to the Jews of Europe to return to Palestine'. In September 1839, Young founded the Jerusalem branch of the London Jews Society. Shaftesbury was exultant, noting in his diary, 'The ancient city of the people of God is about to resume a place among the nations. I shall always remember that God put it into my head to conceive the plan for His honour, gave me the influence to prevail with Palmerston, and provided a man for the situation,

---

* Shaftesbury borrowed the notorious phrase 'a land without a people' from a Scottish minister, Alexander Keith, and it was later attributed (probably mistakenly) to Israel Zangwill, a Zionist who did not believe in settling Palestine, precisely because it was already inhabited by Arabs.

who can remake Jerusalem in her glory.' Shaftesbury's signet ring was inscribed 'Pray for Jerusalem', while (as we have seen) another zealous Victorian fixated with Jerusalem – Sir Moses Montefiore – added Jerusalem to his new coat of arms and inscribed it like a talisman on his carriage, his signet ring and even his bed. Now, in June 1839, Montefiore and his wife Judith returned to Jerusalem, armed with pistols to protect the cash they had raised in London.

Jerusalem was ravaged by the plague, so Montefiore camped outside on the Mount of Olives where he held court, receiving over 300 visitors. When the plague was ebbing, Montefiore entered the city on a white horse, lent him by the governor, and proceeded to hear petitions and distribute alms to the poverty-stricken Jews. He and his wife were welcomed by all three religions in Jerusalem, but while they were visiting the Sanctuary in Hebron to the south, a Muslim mob attacked them. They only escaped with their lives thanks to the intervention of Ottoman troops. Montefiore was not discouraged. As he left, this reborn Jew and dedicated imperialist celebrated a similar though of course different messianic fervour as Shaftesbury: 'O Jerusalem,' he wrote in his diary, 'may the city soon be rebuilt in our days. Amen.'

Shaftesbury and Montefiore both believed in the divine providence of the British empire and the Jewish return to Zion. The righteousness of evangelical zeal and the reborn passion of Jewish dreams of Jerusalem dovetailed neatly to become one of the Victorian obsessions, and it happened that the painter David Roberts returned from Palestine in 1840 just in time to show the public his hugely popular romantic images of a flamboyantly Oriental Jerusalem ripe for British civilization and Jewish restoration. The Jews were in urgent need of British protection because the competing promises of tolerance issued by the sultan and the Albanians provoked a deadly backlash.

JAMES FINN: THE EVANGELICAL CONSUL

In March 1840, seven Jews in Damascus were accused of killing a Christian monk and his Muslim servant to use their blood for a human sacrifice at Passover. This imaginary scenario was the notorious 'blood libel' that had first appeared in Oxford at the time of the Second Crusade in the twelfth century. Sixty-three Jewish children were arrested and tortured to force their mothers to reveal the 'hiding place of the blood'.

Even though he had only just returned to London, Sir Moses Montefiore, backed by the Rothschilds, led the campaign to rescue the Damascene Jews from this medieval persecution. Joining forces with the French lawyer Adolphe Cremieux, Montefiore dashed to Alexandria where he canvassed Mehmet Ali to free the prisoners. But only weeks later, there was another case of the 'blood libel' in Rhodes. Montefiore sailed from Alexandria to Istanbul where he was received by the sultan whom he persuaded to issue a decree that categorically denied the truth of the 'blood libel.' It was Montefiore's finest hour – but his success was due as much to his nationality as to his often ponderous diplomacy. It was a fine time to be an Englishman in the Middle East.

Both the sultan and the Albanians were frantically bidding for British favour as the very existence of the Ottoman empire hung in the balance. Jerusalem remained under Ibrahim the Red who ruled much of the Middle East. While France backed the Albanians, Britain tried to satisfy their appetite while preserving the Ottomans. They offered Palestine as well as Egypt if Ibrahim would withdraw from Syria. It was a good offer but Mehmet Ali and Ibrahim could not resist the supreme prize: Istanbul. Ibrahim defied Britain so Palmerston put together an Anglo-Austrian-Ottoman coalition and despatched his gunboats, under Commodore Charles Napier, cannons blazing. Ibrahim crumbled before British might.

Ibrahim the Red had opened up Jerusalem to the Europeans and changed her for ever but now, in return for hereditary rule in Egypt, he abandoned Syria and the Holy City.* The French, humiliated by Palmerston's triumph, considered a 'Christian Free City at

---

* The Albanians never again held Jerusalem but they ruled Egypt for a century, first as khedives (nominally Ottoman viceroys but actually independent), then as sultans of Egypt and finally as kings. When Mehmet Ali became senile, Ibrahim became his regent but he himself died in 1848 just before his father. The last of the Albanian dynasty was King Farouk who was overthrown in 1952.

Jerusalem', the first proposal for an internationalized Zion, but on 20 October, 1840, the sultan's troops marched back into Jerusalem. Within the walls, a third of the city was wasteland, covered in thickets of prickly-pear cacti, and there were only 13,000 inhabitants, but 5,000 of them were now Jews, their numbers boosted by Russian immigrants and refugees from an earthquake that had struck Safed in Galilee.

Even when Palmerston lost the Foreign Office to Lord Aberdeen, who ordered the vice-consul to desist from evangelical Jewish schemes, Young continued regardless. When Palmerston returned to power he ordered the Jerusalem consul to 'receive under British Protection all Russian Jews who apply to you'.

Meanwhile Shaftesbury had persuaded the new prime minister, Robert Peel, to back the creation of the first ever Anglican bishopric and church in Jerusalem. In 1841, Prussia (whose king had proposed a Christian international Jerusalem) and Britain jointly appointed the first Protestant bishop, Michael Solomon Alexander, a Jewish convert – Protestant Germany too was experiencing an evangelical awakening. British missionaries became increasingly aggressive in their Jewish mission. They created an Anglican compound with a church, run by the Jews' Society, and British consulate, near the Jaffa Gate, opposite the Citadel: an island of Victorian gothic architecture and missionary evangelism. However, Christ Church was – and remains – unique in the Protestant world: there was no cross, just a menorah; all the writing was in Hebrew, even the Lord's Prayer. It was a Protestant church designed for Jews. At its opening, three Jews were baptized before Consul Young. The Jewish plight in Jerusalem was pitiful: the Jews lived 'like flies who have taken up their abode in a skull', wrote the American novelist Herman Melville. The swelling Jewish community lived in almost theatrical poverty without any medical care, but they did have access to the free doctors provided by the London Jews Society. This tempted a few converts.

'I can rejoice in Zion for a capital,' mused Shaftesbury, 'in Jerusalem for a church and in Hebrew for a King!' Jerusalem went overnight from a benighted ruin ruled by a shabby pasha in a tawdry seraglio to a city with a surfeit of gold-braided and bejewelled dignitaries. There had not been a Latin patriarch since the thirteenth century and the Orthodox patriarch had long resided in Istanbul, but now the French and the Russians sponsored their return to Jerusalem. However, it was the seven European consuls, puffed-up minor officials representing imperial ambitions, who could scarcely contain their high-handed grandiosity. Escorted by towering body-guards, the kavasses, wearing bright scarlet uniforms, wielding sabres and heavy gold wands that they banged on the cobbles to clear the streets, the consuls paraded solemnly through the city, craving any pretext to impose their will on the beleaguered Ottoman governors. Ottoman soldiers even had to stand in the presence of the consul's children. The pretensions of the Austrian and Sardinian consuls were all the haughtier because their monarchs claimed to be kings of Jerusalem. But none were more arrogant or petty than the British and the French.

In 1845, Young was replaced by James Finn, who for twenty years was almost as powerful as the Ottoman governors, yet this sanctimonious meddler offended everyone from English lords and Ottoman pashas to every other foreign diplomat. Regardless of orders from London, he offered British protection to the Russian Jews but never ceased his mission to convert them. When the Ottomans allowed foreign purchase of land, Finn bought and developed his farm at Talbieh and then another at Abraham's Vineyard, funded by a Miss Cook of Cheltenham, and aided by a team of dedicated English evangelical ladies, as a means to proselytize more Jews by teaching them the joys of honest work.

Finn regarded himself as a cross between imperial proconsul, saintly missionary and property magnate, unscrupulously buying lands and houses with suspiciously large amounts of money. He and his wife, another fanatical evangelical, learned fluent Hebrew and the widely spoken Ladino. On one hand, they aggressively protected the Jews, who were brutally oppressed in Jerusalem. Yet at the same time his pushy mission provoked violent Jewish resist-ance. When he converted a boy called Mendel Digness, he caused mayhem as 'the Jews climbed over the terraces and made great disturbances'. Finn called the rabbis 'fanatics', but back in Britain, the powerful Montefiore, hearing that the Jews were being harassed, sent a Jewish doctor and pharmacy to Jerusalem to foil the Jews Society, which in turn founded a hospital on the edge of the Jewish Quarter.

In 1847, a Christian Arab boy attacked a Jewish youth who threw back a pebble which grazed the Arab boy's foot. The Greek Orthodox, traditionally the most anti-Semitic community, quickly backed by the Muslim mufti and qadi, accused the Jews of procuring Christian blood to bake the Passover biscuits: the blood libel had come to Jerusalem, but the sultan's ban, granted to Montefiore after the Damascus affair, proved decisive.

Meanwhile the consuls were joined by perhaps the most extraordinary diplomat in American history. 'I doubt,' observed William Thackeray, the English author of *Vanity Fair*, who was visiting Jerusalem, 'that any government has received or appointed so queer an ambassador.'

WARDER CRESSON, US CONSUL: THE AMERICAN HOLY STRANGER

On 4 October 1844, Warder Cresson arrived in Jerusalem as the US consul-general of Syria and Jerusalem – his chief qualification for the job being his certainty that the Second Coming was due in 1847. Cresson took the consular hauteur of his European colleagues to a new level: he galloped around Jerusalem in a 'cloud of dust' surrounded by 'a little American army' who belonged in a 'troop of knights and paladins' from a Walter Scott novel – 'a party of armed and glittering horsemen led by an Arab followed by two Janissaries with silver maces shining in the sun'.

At his interview with the pasha, Cresson explained that he had arrived for the coming Apocalypse and the return of the Jews. A Philadelphian landowner, child of rich Quakers, Cresson had spent twenty years spinning from one apocalyptic cult to another: after writing his first manifesto, *Jerusalem, the Centre of the Joy of the Whole World*, and abandoning his wife and six children, Cresson persuaded Secretary of State John Calhoun to appoint him consul: 'I left everything near and dear to me on earth in pursuit of truth.'

The US president John Tyler was soon informed by his diplomats that his first Jerusalem consul was a 'religious maniac and madman', but Cresson was already in Jerusalem. And he was not alone in his apocalyptic views: he was an American of his time.

The American Constitution was secular, carefully not mentioning Christ and separating state and faith, yet on the Great Seal, the Founding Fathers, Thomas Jefferson and Ben Franklin, had depicted the Children of Israel led by cloud and fire towards the Promised Land. Cresson personified how that cloud and fire were attracting many Americans to Jerusalem. Indeed the separation of Church and state liberated American faith and generated a blossoming of new sects and fresh millennial prophecies.

The early Americans, inheriting the Hebraist fervour of the English Puritans, had enjoyed a Great Awakening of religious joy. Now, in the first half of the nineteenth century, a Second Awakening was driven by the evangelical energy of the frontier. In 1776, some 10 per cent of Americans were church-goers; by 1815, it was a quarter; by 1914, it was half. Their passionate Protestantism was American in character – gritty, exuberant and swashbuckling. At its heart was the belief that a person could save himself and accelerate the Second Coming by righteous action and heartfelt joy. America was itself a mission disguised as a nation, blessed by God, not unlike the way Shaftesbury and the English evangelicals saw the British empire.

In little wooden churches in one-horse mining towns, farmsteads on boundless prairies and gleaming new industrial cities, the preachers in the New Promised Land of America cited the literal biblical revelations of the Old. 'In no country,' wrote Dr Edward Robinson, an evangelical academic who became the founder of biblical archaeology in Jerusalem, 'are the Scriptures better known.' The first American missionaries believed that the Native Americans were the Lost Tribes of Israel and that every Christian must perform acts of righteousness in Jerusalem and help the Return and Restoration of the Jews: 'I really wish the Jews again in Judaea an independent nation,' wrote the second US president John Adams. In 1819, two young missionaries in Boston prepared to put this into action: 'Every eye is fixed on Jerusalem,' preached Levi Parsons in

Boston, 'indeed the centre of the world.' Their congregation wept as Pliny Fisk announced: 'I go bound in spirit to Jerusalem.' They made it there but their early deaths in the east did not discourage others because 'Jerusalem', insisted William Thomson, the American missionary whose wife died there during the revolt of 1834, 'is the common property of the whole Christian world.'

Consul Cresson had ridden the wave of this flowering of prophecies: he had been a Shaker, a Millerite, a Mormon and a Campbellite before a local rabbi in Pennsylvania convinced him that 'salvation was of the Jews' whose return would bring the Second Coming.* One of the first to arrive in Jerusalem was Harriet Livermore. Daughter and granddaughter of New England congressmen, she set off in 1837, after years preaching to the Sioux and Cheyenne tribes that they were the Lost Tribes of Israel who should accompany her back to Zion. She rented rooms on Mount Zion to prepare her sect, the Pilgrim Strangers, for the Apocalypse that she expected in 1847 – but it did not come and she ended up begging in Jerusalem's streets. At the same time, Joseph Smith, prophet of the new revelation of Latter Day Saints – the Mormons – sent his Apostle to Jerusalem: he built an altar on the Olivet to prepare 'to restore Israel with Jerusalem as capital.'

By the time Cresson became the US consul, a growing number of American evangelists were visiting Jerusalem to prepare for the End Days. The US government eventually dismissed him, but he continued defiantly to issue visas of protection to Jews for several years and then, changing his name to Michael Boaz Israel, converted to Judaism. For his long-abandoned wife this was a revelation too far. She sued to have Cresson declared insane, citing his pistol-waving, street-haranguing, financial incompetence, cultic

---

* William Miller was one of the most popular of these new American prophets. An ex-army officer from Massachusetts, he calculated that Christ would come again in Jerusalem in 1843: 100,000 Americans became Millerites. He converted the assertion in Daniel 8.14 that the 'sanctuary would be cleansed' in 'two thousand and three hundred days' into years by claiming that a prophetic day was really a year. Hence starting in 457 BC, which Miller believed was the date of Persian King Artaxerxes I's order to restore the Temple, he arrived at 1843. When nothing happened that year, he suggested 1844. The Millerite successor churches, the Seventh Day Adventists and the Jehovah's Witnesses, still number 14 million members worldwide.

eclecticism, plans to rebuild the Jewish Temple and sexual deviance. He sailed back from Jerusalem for the Inquisition of Lunacy in Philadelphia, a cause célèbre, for Mrs Cresson was challenging the constitutional right of American citizens to believe whatever they wished, the essence of Jeffersonian liberty.

At the trial Cresson was found to be insane, but he appealed and was awarded a retrial. Mrs Cresson had to 'deny either her Saviour or her Husband' while he had to deny 'either the One, Only God or My Wife'. The wife lost the second case, confirming American freedom of worship, and Cresson returned to Jerusalem. He created a Jewish model farm near the city, studied the Torah, divorced his American wife and married a Jewess, all the while completing his book *The Key of David*. He was honoured by local Jews as 'the American Holy Stranger'. On his death he was buried in the Jewish cemetery on the Mount of Olives.

Jerusalem was now so overrun by apocalyptic Americans that the *American Journal of Insanity* compared its hysteria to the California Gold Rush. When Herman Melville visited, he was fascinated yet repulsed by the 'contagion' of American Christian millenarianism – 'this preposterous Jewmania', he called it, 'half-melancholy, half-farcical'. 'How am I to act when any crazy or distressed citizen of the US comes into the country?' the American consul in Beirut asked his secretary of state. 'There are several of late going to Jerusalem with strange ideas in their heads that Our Saviour is coming this year.' But Melville grasped that such majestic world-shaking hopes were impossible to satisfy: 'No country will more quickly dissipate romantic expectations than Palestine particularly Jerusalem. To some the disappointment is heart-sickening.'

Jerusalem was essential to the American and English evangelical vision of the Second Coming. Yet even their urgency was dwarfed by the obsessive Russian passion for Jerusalem. Now in the late 1840s, the Russian emperor's aggressive ambitions were about to place Jerusalem at what the English visitor, William Thackeray, called 'the centre of the world's past and future history' and ignite a European war.

THE GENDARME OF EUROPE AND THE SHOOT-OUT IN
THE SEPULCHRE: THE RUSSIAN GOD IN JERUSALEM

On Good Friday, 10 April 1846, the Ottoman governor and his soldiers were on alert at the Church. Unusually, that year the Orthodox and Catholic Easters fell on the same day. The monks were not just priming their incense-burners: they smuggled in pistols and daggers, secreting them behind the pillars and under robes. Who would hold their service first? The Greeks won the race to place their altar-cloth on the altar of Calvary. The Catholics were just behind them – but too late. They challenged the Greeks: did they have the sultan's authority? The Greeks challenged the Catholics – where was their sultanic *firman* giving them the right to pray first? There was a stand-off. Fingers must have hovered over triggers under chasubles. Suddenly, the two sides were fighting with every weapon they could improvise from the ecclesiastical paraphernalia at their disposal: they wielded crucifixes, candlesticks and lamps until cold steel flashed and the shooting started. Ottoman soldiers waded in to stop the fighting but forty lay dead around the Holy Sepulchre.

The killing resounded around the world but above all in St Petersburg and Paris: the aggressive confidence of the coenobite brawlers reflected not just the religions but the empires behind them. New railways and steamships had eased the journey to Jerusalem from all over Europe but particularly by sea from Odessa to Jaffa: the vast majority of the 20,000 pilgrims were now Russians. A French monk noticed that in a typical year, out of 4,000 Christmas pilgrims, only four were Catholics, the rest being Russian. This Russian adoration flowed from the devout Orthodoxy to be found from the very bottom of society, the shaggy peasants in the smallest, remotest Siberian villages, to the very top, the Emperor-Tsar Nicholas I himself. The Orthodox mission of Holy Russia was shared by both.

When Constantinople fell in 1453, the grand princes of Muscovy had seen themselves as the heirs of the last Byzantine emperors, Moscow as the Third Rome. The princes adopted the Byzantine double-headed eagle and a new title, Caesar or Tsar. In their wars against the Islamic Crimean khans and then the Ottoman sultans, the tsars promoted the Russian empire as a sacred Orthodox crusade. In Russia, Orthodoxy had developed its own singularly Russian character, spread through its vastness both by tsars – and peasant hermits, all of whom specially revered Jerusalem. It was said that the distinctive onion-shaped domes of Russian churches were an attempt to copy those in paintings of Jerusalem. Russia had even built its own mini-Jerusalem* but every Russian believed that the pilgrimage to Jerusalem was an essential part of the preparation for death and salvation. As the poet Alexander Pushkin, the personification of Russia's soul, expressed this in 1836, shortly before his death in a duel: 'Is not Jerusalem the cradle of us all?'

Nicholas I had imbibed this tradition – he was very much the grandson of Catherine the Great and heir of Peter the Great, both of whom had promoted themselves as protectors of the Orthodox and the Holy Places, and the Russian peasants themselves linked the two: when Nicholas' elder brother Alexander I died unexpectedly in 1825, they believed that he had gone to Jerusalem as an ordinary hermit, a modern version of the Last Emperor legend.

Now Nicholas, harshly conservative, deeply anti-Semitic and shamelessly philistine in all matters artistic (he had appointed himself as Pushkin's personal censor), regarded himself as answerable only to what he called 'The Russian God' in the cause of 'Our Russia entrusted to Us by God.' This martinet, who prided himself on sleeping on a military cot, ruled Russia like a stern drillmaster. As a young man, the strapping, blue-eyed Nicholas had dazzled British society where one lady described him as 'devilish handsome, the handsomest man in Europe!' By the 1840s, his hair was gone and a paunch bulged out of his still high-waisted and skintight military breeches. After thirty years of happy marriage – spiced up

* In 1656, Patriarch Nikon built the New Jerusalem Monastery in Istra, near Moscow, to promote the universal mission of Russian Orthodoxy and Autocracy. Its centrepiece was a replica of the actual Sepulchre in Jerusalem which is valuable since the original was destroyed in the fire of 1808. In 1818, before he ascended the throne, Nicholas I visited the New Jerusalem and was deeply moved, ordering its restoration. The Nazis damaged it but it is now being restored.

by frequent affairs – he took a young lady-in-waiting as his regular mistress. For all Russia's vast power, he feared impotence, personally and politically.

For years he had cautiously wielded his personal charm to persuade Britain to agree to the partition of the Ottoman empire, which he called 'the sick man of Europe,' hoping to liberate the Orthodox provinces of the Balkans and oversee Jerusalem. Now the British were no longer impressed. Twenty-five years of autocracy had desensitized him and made him impatient: 'very clever, I don't think him,' wrote the shrewd Queen Victoria, 'and his mind is an uncivilized one.'

In Jerusalem, the streets glittered with the gold braid and shoulderboards of Russian uniforms, worn by princes and generals, while teeming with the sheepskins and smocks of thousands of peasant pilgrims, all encouraged by Nicholas who also despatched an ecclesiastical mission to compete with the other Europeans. The British consul warned London that 'the Russians could in one night during Easter arm 10,000 pilgrims within the walls of Jerusalem' and seize the city. Meanwhile the French pursued their own mission to protect the Catholics. 'Jerusalem', reported Consul Finn in 1844, 'is now a central point of interest to France and Russia.'

GOGOL: THE JERUSALEM SYNDROME

Not all Russia's pilgrims were soldiers or peasants and not all found the salvation they sought. On 23 February 1848, a Russian pilgrim entered Jerusalem who was both typical in his soaring religious fever and utterly atypical in his flawed genius. The novelist Nikolai Gogol, famed for his play *The Inspector-General* and for his novel *Dead Souls*, arrived by donkey in a quest for spiritual ease and divine inspiration. He had envisaged *Dead Souls* as a trilogy, yet he was struggling to write the second and third parts. God was surely blocking his writing to punish his sins. As a Russian, only one place offered redemption: 'until I've been to Jerusalem,' he wrote, 'I'll be incapable of saying anything comforting to anyone.'

The visit was disastrous: he spent a single night praying beside the

Sepulchre, yet he found it filthy and vulgar. 'Before I had time to pull my wits together, it was over.' The gaudiness of the holy sites and the barrenness of the hills crushed him: 'I have never been so little content with the state of my heart as in Jerusalem and afterwards.' On his return, he refused to talk about Jerusalem but fell under the power of a mystic priest who convinced him that his works were sinful. Gogol manically destroyed his manuscripts then starved himself to death – or at least into a coma – for when his coffin was opened in the twentieth century, his body was found face down.

The special madness of Jerusalem had been called 'Jerusalem fever' but in the 1930s, it was recognized as Jerusalem Syndrome, 'a psychotic decompensation related to religious excitement induced by proximity to the holy places of Jerusalem'. The *British Journal of Psychiatry*, in 2000, diagnosed this demented disappointment as: 'Jerusalem Syndrome Subtype Two: those who come with magical ideas of Jerusalem's healing powers – such as the writer Gogol.'

In a sense, Nicholas was suffering from his own strain of Jerusalem Syndrome. There was madness in his family: 'as the years have passed,' wrote the French ambassador to Petersburg, 'it is now the qualities of [his father Emperor] Paul which come more to the fore.' The mad Paul had been assassinated (as had his grandfather Peter III). If Nicholas was far from insane, he started to display some of his father's obstinately impulsive over-confidence. In 1848, he planned to make the pilgrimage to Jerusalem but he was forced to cancel when revolutions broke out across Europe. He triumphantly crushed the Hungarian revolt against his neighbour, the Habsburg emperor: he enjoyed the prestige of being the 'Gendarme of Europe' but Nicholas, wrote the French ambassador, became 'spoiled by adulation, success and the religious prejudices of the Muscovite nation'.

On 31 October 1847, the silver star on the marble floor of the Grotto of Bethlehem's Church of the Nativity, was cut out and stolen. The star had been donated by France in the eighteenth century; now it had obviously been stolen by the Greeks. The monks fought in Bethlehem. In Istanbul, the French claimed the right to replace the Bethlehem star and to repair the roof of the Church in Jerusalem; the Russians claimed it was their right; each cited eighteenth-century treaties. The row simmered until it became a duel of two emperors.

In December 1851, the French president Louis-Napoleon Bonaparte, the inscrutably bland yet politically agile nephew of the great Napoleon, overthrew the Second Republic in a coup d'état and prepared to crown himself Emperor Napoleon III. This womanizing adventurer whose sharply-waxed moustaches could not distract attention from an oversized head and an undersized torso was in some ways the first modern politician and he knew his brash, fragile new empire required Catholic prestige and victory abroad. Nicholas, on the other hand, saw the crisis as the chance to crown his reign by saving the Holy Places for 'the Russian God'. For these two very different emperors, Jerusalem was the key to glory in heaven and on earth.

JAMES FINN AND THE CRIMEAN WAR: MURDERED EVANGELISTS AND MARAUDING BEDOUIN

The sultan, squeezed between the French and Russians, tried to settle the dispute with his decree of 8 February 1852, confirming the Orthodox paramountcy in the Church, with some concessions to the Catholics. But the French were no less committed than the Russians. They traced their claims back to the great Napoleon's invasion, the alliance with Suleiman the Magnificent, the French Crusader kings of Jerusalem, and to Charlemagne. When Napoleon III threatened the Ottomans, it was no coincidence that he sent a gunboat called the *Charlemagne*. In November, the sultan buckled and granted the paramountcy to the Catholics. Nicholas was outraged. He demanded the restoration of Orthodox rights in Jerusalem and an 'alliance' that would reduce the Ottoman empire to a Russian protectorate.

When Nicholas' bullying demands were rejected, he invaded the Ottoman territories on the Danube – today's Romania – advancing towards Istanbul. Nicholas had convinced himself that he had charmed the British into agreement, denying he wanted to swallow Istanbul, let alone Jerusalem, but he fatally misjudged both London and Paris. Faced with Russian menace and Ottoman collapse, Britain and France threatened war. Nicholas stubbornly called their bluff because, he explained, he was 'waging war for a solely Christian purpose, under the banner of the Holy Cross'. On 28 March, 1853, the French and British declared war on Russia. Even though most of the fighting was far away in the Crimea, this war placed Jerusalem at the centre of the world stage where she has remained ever since.*

As Jerusalem's garrison marched off to fight the Russians, James Finn watched them present arms on the Maidan parade ground outside the Jaffa Gate where the 'Syrian sun glistened along the moving steel for they marched with fixed bayonets'. Finn could not forget that the 'kernel of it all lay with us in the Holy Places' and that Nicholas 'aimed still at an actual possession of [Jerusalem's] Sanctuaries'.

Instead of the usual devout Russians, a new breed of often sceptical Western visitors – 10,000 a year, by 1856 – poured into the city to see the Holy Places that had sparked a European war. Yet a visit to Jerusalem was still an adventure. There were no carriages, just covered litters. She possessed virtually no hotels or banks: visitors stayed in the monasteries, the most comfortable being the Armenian with its elegant, airy courtyards. However in 1843, a Russian Jew named Menachem Mendel founded the first hotel, the Kaminitz, which was soon followed by the English Hotel; and in 1848 a Sephardic family, the Valeros, opened the first European bank in a room up some stairs off David Street. This was still a provincial Ottoman town, usually governed by a scruffy pasha who resided in a ramshackle seraglio – residence, harem and prison – just north of the Temple Mount.† Westerners were 'astonished at

* The Crimean war saw another attempt to arm the Jews. In September 1855, the Polish poet Adam Mickiewicz travelled to Istanbul to organize Polish forces known as Ottoman Cossacks, to fight the Russians. These included the Hussars of Israel, recruited from Russian, Polish and Palestinian Jews. Mickiewicz died three months later and the Hussars were never tested in the valley of death.

† The seat of the Ottoman governors was al-Jawailiyya, built by one of Nasir Mohammad's Mamluk amirs, on the site of Herod's Antonia Fortress and the first station of the Via Dolorosa. Under Crusader rule, the Templars had built a chapel there and part of its domed porch stood until the 1920s. A modern school stands there today.

the beggarly meanness of that mansion,' wrote Finn, and repulsed by the mangy concubines and 'ragamuffin officials'. As visitors sipped coffee with the pasha, they could hear the clank of prisoners' chains and groans of the tortured from the dungeons below. During the war, the pasha tried to ensure tranquillity in Jerusalem – but the Greek Orthodox monks attacked the newly appointed Catholic patriarch and herded camels into his residence, all to the delight of the great writers who came to see those very shrines for which so many soldiers were dying in the grinding battles and putrid hospitals of the Crimea. They were not impressed.

THE WRITERS: MELVILLE, FLAUBERT AND THACKERAY

Herman Melville, then aged thirty-seven, had made his name with three novels based on his own breathtaking whaling adventures in the Pacific but *Moby Dick*, published in 1851, had sold just 3,000 copies. Melancholic and tormented, not unlike Gogol, he arrived in Jerusalem in 1856 to restore his health – and to investigate the nature of God. 'My object – saturation of my mind with the atmosphere of Jerusalem, offering myself as a passive subject to its weird impressions' – and he was stimulated by the 'wreck' that was Jerusalem, beguiled by the 'unleavened nakedness of desolation'. As we saw earlier, he was fascinated by the 'fanatical energy and spirit' and 'Jewmania' of the many 'crazy' Americans. They inspired his epic *Clarel* – at 18,000 lines, the longest American poem, which he wrote when he got home as he toiled in the US Customs Office.

Melville was not the only novelist looking for restoration and consolation for literary disappointment in the Orient: Gustave Flaubert, accompanied by his wealthy friend Maxime du Camp, and funded by the French government to report on trade and agriculture, was on a cultural and sexual tour to recover from the reception of his first novel. He saw Jerusalem as a 'charnelhouse surrounded by walls, the old religions rotting in the sun'. As for the Church, 'a dog would have been more moved than me. The Armenians curse the Greeks who detest the Latins who execrate the Copts.' Melville agreed that the Church was a 'half-ruinous pile of mouldering grottoes that smelled like death' but recognized that wars were started in what he called the 'thronged newsroom and theology exchange of Jerusalem'.*

The coenobite fighting was only one aspect of the violent theatre of Jerusalem. The tensions between the new visitors – Anglo-American evangelicals and Russian Jews and Orthodox peasants on one hand, and the older world of the Ottomans, Arab Families, Sephardic Jews and Bedouin and *fellahin* on the other – led to a series of murders. One of James Finn's evangelical ladies, Mathilda Creasy, was found with her head smashed in; and a Jew was found stabbed down a well. The poisoning of a rich rabbi, David Herschell, led to a sensational court case but the suspects, who were his own grandsons, were acquitted for lack of evidence. The British consul James Finn was the most powerful official in Jerusalem at a time when the Ottomans were so indebted to Britain, hence he took it upon himself to intervene wherever he saw fit. Considering himself to be the Sherlock Holmes of the Holy City, he set about investigating each of these crimes, but despite his powers of detection (and the aid of six African necromancers), no killers were ever found.

Finn was the courageous champion and proselytizing irritant for the Jews who still needed his protection. Their plight was, if anything, getting worse. Most of the Jews lived in the 'stinking ruins of the Jewish Quarter, venerable in filth', wrote Thackeray, and their 'wailings and lamentations of the lost glory of their city' haunted Jerusalem on Friday nights. 'None equals the misery and suffering of the Jews at Jerusalem,' Karl Marx wrote in the *New York Daily Tribune* in April 1854, 'inhabiting the most filthy quarter, constant object of Musulman oppression and intolerance, insulted by the Greeks, persecuted by the Latins.' A Jew who walked past the gate leading to the Church of the Holy Sepulchre, was, as Finn reported,

---

* These writers were following a fashion for oriental travelogues. Between 1800 and 1875, about 5,000 books were published in English about Jerusalem. Many of these works are remarkably similar, either breathless repetitions of biblical stories by evangelicals (sometimes reinforced by archaeology) or travelogues mocking Ottoman incompetence, Jewish wailing, Arab simplicity and Orthodox vulgarity. The witty *Eothen* by Alexander Kinglake, who later reported on the Crimean War, is probably the best.

'beaten by a mob of pilgrims' because it was still illegal for a Jew to pass it. Another was stabbed by an Ottoman soldier. A Jewish funeral was attacked by Arabs. In each case, Finn swooped on the Ottoman governor and forced him to intervene and see British justice done.

The pasha himself was more interested in controlling the Palestinian Arabs whose rebellions and clan wars, partly a response to the centralizing reforms of the Ottoman empire, were often fought out with the gallop of camels, the swish of spears and the whistle of bullets around the walls of Jerusalem. These thrilling scenes played into the European view of Palestine as a biblical theatre crossed with a Wild West stage set, and they gathered on the walls to spectate the skirmishes which to them must have resembled surreal sporting events – with the added spice of the occasional fatality.

THE WRITERS: DAVID DORR, AN AMERICAN SLAVE ON TOUR

At their Talbieh evangelical farm for converting Jews, the Finns frequently found themselves caught in the crossfire. As bullets flew, Mrs Finn was often amazed to identify women amongst the warriors. She did her best to negotiate peace between the sheikhs. But the Bedouin were only part of the problem: the sheikhs of Hebron and Abu Ghosh fielded private armies of 500 warriors and fought full-scale wars against the Ottomans. When one of these sheikhs was captured and brought to Jerusalem in chains, the dashing warrior managed to escape and gallop away to fight again, like an Arab Robin Hood. Finally Hafiz Pasha, the aged governor of Jerusalem, had to lead an expedition with 550 troops and two brass field-guns to suppress the warlord of Hebron.

Yet despite such melodrama, on summer evenings, Jerusalemites of all creeds – Muslim and Christian Arabs along with the Sephardic Jews – picnicked on the Damascus road. The American explorer, Lieutenant William Lynch, observed a 'picturesque scene – hundreds of Jews enjoying the fresh air, seated outside the walls under enormous olive trees, the women all in white shrouds, the men in broad-brimmed black hats'. James Finn and the other consuls, preceded by Ottoman soldiers and kavasses with silver-mounted batons, promenaded with their wives. 'As the sun set, everyone hurried inside the walls that were still locked every night.'

'Ah the sadness of Jerusalem,' sighed Finn who had to admit that the city seemed 'monastically dull to a person imbued with the gay habits of other places. French visitors have been known to utter the ejaculation which ever accompanies the shrug of the shoulders at the contrast between Jerusalem and Paris.' This was certainly not the sort of ejaculation which the priapic Flaubert expected and he expressed his frustration at the Jaffa Gate, 'I let a fart escape as I crossed the threshold,' even if 'I was annoyed by the Voltaireanism of my anus.' That sexual gourmand Flaubert celebrated escape from Jerusalem with a five-girl orgy in Beirut: 'I screwed three women and came four times – three times before lunch and once after dessert. Young Du Camp came only once, his member still sore with the remnant of a chancre given him by a Wallachian whore.'

One unique American visitor, David Dorr, a young black slave from Louisiana who called himself a 'quadroon', agreed with Flaubert: on tour with his master, he arrived 'with submissive heart' filled with awe for Jerusalem but soon changed his mind: 'When I heard all the absurdities of these ignorant people, I was more inclined to ridicule right over these sacred dead bodies and spots than pay homage. After seventeen days in Jerusalem, I leave never wishing to return again.'*

* Dorr's young master, plantation owner Cornelius Fellowes, decided to set off on a three-year tour of the world from Paris to Jerusalem. Fellowes offered a deal to his intelligent and literate young slave. If Dorr served him on the trip, he would be freed on his return. In his effervescent travelogue, Dorr recorded everything from the gorgeous ladies of Paris to the 'scarce towers and charred walls' of Jerusalem. On his return, his master refused to manumit him so Dorr escaped to the north and in 1858 published *A Colored Man Round the World by a Quadroon*. It was the American Civil War, which started soon afterwards, that finally gave him his freedom. The winner of that war, President Abraham Lincoln, was not formally religious, but longed to visit Jerusalem, perhaps because as a young man he had lived in one of the American Jerusalems, New Salem, Illinois; he knew the Bible by heart and he

Yet for all their irreverence, the writers could not help but be awed by Jerusalem. Flaubert considered her 'diabolically grand'. Thackeray sensed 'there's not a spot at which you may look but where some violent deed has been done, some massacre, some visitors murdered, some idol worshipped with bloody rites.' Melville almost admired the 'plague-stricken splendour' of the place. Standing at the Golden Gate, gazing out at Muslim and Jewish cemeteries, Melville saw a 'city besieged by armies of the dead' and asked himself: 'is the desolation the result of the fatal embrace of the Deity?'

As Russian forces were repeatedly defeated in the Crimea, Nicholas fell ill under the strain and died on 18 February 1855. In September, the Russian naval base at Sebastopol fell to the British and French. Russia had been thoroughly humiliated. After staggering military incompetence on all sides in a campaign that cost 750,000 lives, the new Russian emperor, Alexander II, sued for peace, surrendering his imperial ambitions for Jerusalem, but winning at least a restoration of the dominant Orthodox rights in the Sepulchre, the status quo that still remains in force today.

On 14 April 1856, the cannons of the Citadel saluted the signing of peace. But twelve days later, James Finn, attending the Holy Fire, watched 'Greek pilgrims, provided with sticks, stones and cudgels, concealed beforehand behind the columns and dropped from the gallery,' attack the Armenians. 'Dreadful conflict ensued,' he observed, 'missiles were flung upwards to the galleries, demolishing rows of lamps, glass and oil pouring down upon heads.' When the pasha rushed down from his throne in the gallery, he 'received blows to the head' and had to be carried out before his soldiers charged in with fixed bayonets. Minutes later, the Orthodox patriarch appeared with the Holy Fire to screams of exultation, the beating of chests, and flickering of flames.

had probably heard the stories of his Secretary of State, William H. Seward who had visited Jerusalem on his world tour. On the way with his wife to Ford's Theatre, on 14 April 1865, he proposed a 'special pilgrimage to Jerusalem'. At the theatre, moments before he was shot, he whispered: 'How I should like to visit Jerusalem.' Afterwards Mary Todd Lincoln decided he 'was in the midst of the Heavenly Jerusalem'.

The garrison celebrated the sultan's victory with a parade on the Maidan which was ironic because soon afterwards, Alexander II bought this parade ground, once the site of Assyrian and Roman camps, to build a Russian Compound. Henceforth Russia would pursue cultural dominance in Jerusalem.

The victory was bitter sweet for the Ottomans, their weak Islamic realm saved by Christian soldiers. To show his gratitude and keep the West at bay, Sultan Abdulmecid was forced, in measures known as Tanzimat – reform – to centralize his administration, decree absolute equality for all minorities regardless of religion, and allow the Europeans all manner of once-inconceivable liberties. He presented St Anne's, the Crusader church that had become Saladin's madrassa, to Napoleon III. In March 1855, the Duke of Brabant, the future King Leopold II of Belgium, exploiter of the Congo, was the first European allowed to visit the Temple Mount: its guards – club-wielding Sudanese from Darfur – had to be locked in their quarters for fear they would attack the infidel. In June, Archduke Maximilian, the heir to the Habsburg empire – and ill-fated future Emperor of Mexico – arrived with the officers of his flagship. The Europeans started to build hulking imperial-style Christian edifices in a Jerusalem building boom. Ottoman statesmen were unsettled and there would be a violent Muslim backlash but, after the Crimean War, the West had invested too much to leave Jerusalem alone.

In the last months of the Crimean War, Sir Moses Montefiore had bought the trains and rails of the Balaclava Railway, built specially for British troops in the Crimea, to create a line between Jaffa and Jerusalem. Now, endowed with all the prestige and power of a British plutocrat after the Crimean victory, he returned to the city, the harbinger of her future.

38

THE NEW CITY

1855-60

MOSES MONTEFIORE: 'THIS CROESUS'

On 18 July 1855, Montefiore ritually ripped his clothes when he saw the lost Temple and then set up his camp outside the Jaffa Gate where he was mobbed by thousands of Jerusalemites firing off guns in the air and cheering. James Finn, whose schemes to convert Jews he had repeatedly foiled, tried to undermine his reception but the liberal-minded governor, Kiamil Pasha, sent an honour guard to present arms. When Montefiore became the first Jew to visit the Temple Mount, the pasha had him escorted by a hundred soldiers – and he was borne in a sedan-chair so he would not break the law that banned Jews from the holy mountain lest they stood on the Holy of Holies. His life's mission of helping Jerusalem's Jews was never easy: many of them lived on charity and were so infuriated when Montefiore tried to wean them off his handouts that they rioted in his camp. 'Really,' wrote his niece Jemima Sebag, who was in his entourage, 'If this continues, we'll scarcely be safe in our tents!' Not all his schemes worked either: he never managed to build his Crimean railway from Jaffa, but it was this trip that changed the destiny of Jerusalem. On his way, he had persuaded the sultan to let him rebuild the Hurva Synagogue, destroyed in 1720, and even more important, to buy land in Jerusalem to settle Jews. He paid for the restoration of the Hurva and started to look for a place to buy.

Melville described Sir Moses Montefiore as 'this Croesus – a huge man of 75 carried from Joppa on a litter borne by mules'. He was 6 foot 3 and not quite seventy-five, but he was old to make such a trip. He had already risked his life on three visits to Jerusalem and his doctors had advised him not to go again – 'his heart was feeble and there was poison in his blood' – but he and Judith came anyway, accompanied by an entourage of retainers, servants and even his own kosher butcher.

To the Jews of Jerusalem and across the Diaspora, Montefiore was already a legend who combined the proconsular prestige of a rich Victorian baronet at the height of the British empire with the dignity of a Jew who always rushed to the aid of his brethren and had never compromised his Judaism. It was his unique position in Britain that gave him his power: he straddled the old and new societies, as much at home with royal dukes, prime ministers and bishops as he was with rabbis and financiers. In a London dominated by staid morality and evangelical Hebraism, Montefiore was the ideal of what Victorians thought a Jew should be: 'That grand old Hebrew', wrote Lord Shaftesbury, 'is better than many Christians.'

He had been born in Livorno, Italy but he made his fortune as one of the 'Jew brokers' on the London Stock Exchange, an ascent helped by his happy marriage to Judith Cohen, sister-in-law of the banker Nathaniel Rothschild. His social rise and wealth were only a means to help others. When he received a knighthood from Queen Victoria in 1837, she described him in her diary as 'a Jew, an excellent man' while in his journal, he prayed that the honour 'may prove the harbinger of future good to the Jews generally. I had besides the pleasure of my banner with "Jerusalem" floating proudly in the hall.' Once he was rich, he scaled down his business and, often campaigning with his brother-in-law or his nephew Lionel de Rothschild, he devoted himself to winning political rights for British Jews.* But he was most needed abroad, where he was

* Practising Jews could not sit in the House of Commons until 1858. Then a new Act of Parliament finally allowed Lionel de Rothschild to take his seat as the first practising Jew ever to sit in the House. Interestingly, Shaftesbury had repeatedly spoken against this – as a Christian Zionist, his interest was really in the return and conversion of the Jews in preparation for the Second Coming. But much later he graciously proposed to Prime Minister William Gladstone, 'It would be a glorious day for the House of Lords when that grand old Hebrew [Montefiore] were enrolled on the lists of the hereditary legislators of England.' But it was too soon. The first Jewish peerage was awarded to Lionel Rothschild's son, Nathaniel, in 1885, after Montefiore's death.

received like a British ambassador by emperors and sultans, displaying tireless courage and ingenuity while often in personal danger. As we have seen, it was his Damascus mission to Mehmet Ali and the sultan that made him famous.

Montefiore found himself admired even by the most eminent anti-Semites: when Nicholas I, in his crusade for Orthodoxy and Autocracy, was starting to repress the millions of Russian Jews, Montefiore travelled to St Petersburg to insist that Russian Jews were loyal, brave and honourable. 'If they resembled you,' replied Nicholas with ominous courtesy.* However he was more than capable of holding his own with anyone: when he rushed to Rome to intervene in an anti-Semitic intrigue, a cardinal asked him how much of Rothschild's gold had paid for the sultan's ban on the 'blood libel.' 'Not as much as I gave your lackey for hanging up my coat in your hall,' Montefiore replied.

His partner in all his enterprises was the vivacious, curly-haired Judith who always called him 'Monty', but they were not destined to found a dynasty: despite their prayers at Rachel's Tomb, they never had children. Yet apart from his Jewishness and the Hebrew letters of Jerusalem on his coat of arms, Montefiore had the virtues and faults of a typical Victorian grandee. He lived in splendour in a Park Lane mansion and a crenellated Gothic Revival villa in Ramsgate where he built his own synagogue and a unique if grandiose mausoleum based exactly on Rachel's Tomb. His tone was ponderously orotund, his righteousness was scarcely leavened with humour, there was a certain vanity in his autocratic style, and behind the façade, there were mistresses and illegitimate children. Indeed his modern biographer reveals that while in his eighties, he fathered a

* On the way to St Petersburg he was welcomed to Vilna, a semi-Jewish city filled with so many Talmudic scholars that it was known as 'the Jerusalem of Lithuania', by thousands of enthusiastic Jews, but Nicholas did not moderate his polices and as Jewish life worsened, Montefiore later returned to meet Alexander II. It was said that every Jewish shack in Russia had a portrait, almost a Jewish icon, of their champion. 'At breakfast (in Motol, a village near Pinsk) my grandpa used to tell me stories of the deeds of mighty figures,' wrote Chaim Weizmann, a future Zionist leader. 'I was particularly impressed by the visit of Sir Moses Montefiore to Russia, a visit only a generation before my birth but the story was already a legend. Indeed Montefiore was himself, though then still living, already a legend.'

child with a teenage maid, yet another sign of his astonishing energy.

Now his search for a place to buy in Jerusalem was helped by the Jerusalem Families whom he had always befriended: even the qadi called him 'the pride of the people of Moses'. Ahmed Duzhdar Aga, whom he had known for twenty years, sold him a plot outside the walls between the Zion and Jaffa gates for 1,000 gold English sovereigns. Montefiore immediately moved his tents to his new land where he planned a hospital and a Kentish windmill so that Jews could make their own bread. Before he left he asked the pasha for a special favour: the stench of the Jewish Quarter, cited in every Western travelogue, was caused by a Muslim abattoir, its very presence a sign of the inferior status of the Jews. Montefiore asked for it to be moved and the pasha agreed.

In June 1857, Montefiore returned for the fifth time with the materials for his windmill and in 1859, construction started. Instead of a hospital, he built the almshouses for poor Jewish families that became known as the Montefiore Cottages, unmistakably Victorian like a red-brick, crenellated, mock-medieval clubhouse in English suburbia. In Hebrew they were called Mishkenot Sha'ananim – the Dwellings of Delight – but initially they were preyed on by bandits and their inhabitants were so undelighted they used to creep back into the city to sleep. The windmill did at first produce cheap bread but it soon broke down due to the lack of Judaean wind and Kentish maintenance.

Christian evangelists and Jewish rabbis alike dreamed of the Jewish return – and this was Montefiore's contribution. The colossal wealth of the new Jewish plutocrats, especially the Rothschilds, encouraged the idea that, as Disraeli put it at just this time, the 'Hebrew capitalists' would buy Palestine. The Rothschilds, arbiters of international politics and finance at the height of their power, as influential in Paris and Vienna as they were in London, were unconvinced but they were happy to contribute money and help to Montefiore whose 'constant dream' was that 'Jerusalem is destined to become the seat of a Jewish empire.'* In 1859, after a suggestion

---

* Montefiore was the most famous but not the richest of Jerusalem's philanthropists. He was often the channel for Rothschild money and his almshouses were funded by Judah Touro, an American tycoon from New Orleans who in 1825 had backed a

from the Ottoman ambassador in London, Montefiore discussed the idea of buying Palestine but he was sceptical, knowing that the rising Anglo-Jewish elite were busy buying country estates to live the English dream and had no interest in such a scheme. Ultimately Montefiore believed that his beloved 'national restoration of the Israelites' was beyond politics and best left to 'Divine Agency' – but the opening in 1860 of his little Montefiore Quarter was the beginning of the new Jewish city outside the walls. This was far from Montefiore's last visit but after the Crimean War, Jerusalem was once again an international object of desire: Romanovs, Hohenzollerns, Habsburgs and British princes vied with one another to combine the new science of archaeology with the old game of empires.

Jewish homeland on Grand Island in the Niagara river, upstate New York. The project failed and in his will, he left $60,000 for Montefiore to spend in Jerusalem. In 1854, the Rothschilds built a much-needed Jewish hospital. During his 1856 visit, Montefiore created a Jewish girls' school, to the disapproval of the Orthodox Jews, and this was later taken over by his nephew Lionel de Rothschild who renamed it after his late daughter Evelina. But the greatest project was the Tiferet Israel Synagogue close to the Hurva in the Jewish Quarter. Funded by Jews all over the world, but chiefly by the Reuben and Sassoon families of Baghdad, this splendidly domed synagogue, the highest building in the Jewish Quarter, became the centre of Palestinian Jewry until it was destroyed in 1948. Meanwhile the Armenians had their own Rothschilds: the oil-rich Gulbenkian family regularly came on pilgrimage and created the Gulbenkian Library in the Armenian Monastery.

39

THE NEW RELIGION

1860–70

EMPERORS AND ARCHAEOLOGISTS: INNOCENTS ABROAD

In April 1859, Emperor Alexander II's brother Grand Duke Konstantin Nikolaevich was the first of the Romanovs to visit Jerusalem – 'finally my triumphant entry', he recorded in his laconic diary, 'Crowds and dust'. When he walked to the Holy Sepulchre: 'Tears and emotions'; and when he left the city, 'we couldn't stop crying'. The emperor and the grand duke had planned a Russian cultural offensive. 'We must establish our presence in the East not politically but through the church,' declared a Foreign Ministry report. 'Jerusalem is the centre of the world and our mission must be there.' The grand duke founded a Palestine Society and the Russian Steamship Company to bring Russian pilgrims from Odessa. He inspected the 18 acres of the Russian Compound where the Romanovs were starting to build a little Muscovite town.* Soon there were so many Russian pilgrims that tents had to be pitched to house them.

The British were every bit as committed as the Russians. On 1 April 1862, Albert Edward, the plump, twenty-year-old Prince of Wales (the future Edward VII), rode into Jerusalem, escorted by a hundred Ottoman cavalrymen.

The prince, who stayed in a grand encampment outside the

---

* The Russian Compound contained the consulate, a hospital, the multidomed Holy Trinity Church with four belltowers, the archimandrite's residence, apartments for visiting aristocrats and pilgrim hostels, to house over 3,000 pilgrims. Its buildings resembled huge but elegant modern fortresses and during the British Mandate they served as military strongholds.

walls, was very excited about getting a Crusader tattoo on his arm and his visit made an indelible impression both in Jerusalem and back home. Not only did his presence accelerate the recall of James Finn, accused of financial improprieties after twenty years of his domineering presence, but it intensified the feeling that Jerusalem was somehow a little piece of England. The prince was guided around the sites by the Dean of Westminster, Arthur Stanley, whose immensely influential book of biblical history and archaeological speculation convinced a generation of British readers that Jerusalem was 'a land more dear to us from our childhood even than England'. In the mid-nineteenth century, archaeology suddenly became not just a new historical science to study the past but a way to control the future. No wonder archaeology was immediately political – not only a cultural fetish, social fashion and royal hobby, but empire-building by other means and an extension of military espionage. It became Jerusalem's secular religion and also, in the hands of imperialist Christians such as Dean Stanley, a science in the service of God: if it confirmed the truth of the Bible and the Passion, Christians could reclaim the Holy Land itself.

The Russians and British were not alone. The consuls of the Great Powers, many of them religious ministers, also fancied themselves as archaeologists, but it was American Christians who really created modern archaeology.* The French and Germans were not far behind, pursuing archaeological spectaculars with ruthless national esprit, their emperors and premiers keenly backing their digs. Like the space race in the twentieth century with its heroic astronauts, archaeology quickly became a projection of national power with celebrity archaeologists who resembled swashbuckling

---

* Edward Robinson, a missionary and Professor of Biblical Literature in New York, yearned to uncover the geography of the Bible. He used his knowledge of other sources such as Josephus to make some astonishing finds. In 1852, he noticed, at ground level, the top of what he guessed was one of the monumental arches across the valley into the Temple – known ever since as Robinson's Arch. Another American, Dr James Barclay, a missionary to convert the Jews and an engineer advising the Ottomans on the preservation of the Mamluk buildings, spotted the lintel that had topped one of Herod's gates – today's Barclay's Gate. The two Americans might have started as Christian missionaries, but as archaeologists they proved that the Muslim Haram al-Sharif was the Herodian Temple.

historical conquistadors and scientific treasure hunters. One German archaeologist called it 'the peaceful crusade'.

The Prince of Wales' visit encouraged the expedition of a red-coated British officer and archaeologist, Captain Charles Wilson, who, in the tunnels close to the Western Wall under the Gate of the Chain Street, discovered the monumental Herodian arch of the great bridge reaching across the Tyropaean Valley to the Temple. It is still known as Wilson's Arch, and this was just the start.

In May 1865, an array of patricians, from Earl Russell the foreign secretary to the Duke of Argyll, founded the Palestine Exploration Fund with contributions from Queen Victoria and Montefiore. Shaftesbury would later serve as its president. The visit to Palestine of the first heir to the British throne since Edward I 'opened the whole of Syria to Christian research', explained the Society's prospectus. At its first session, the Archbishop of York, William Thomson, declared that the Bible had given him 'the laws by which I try to live' and 'the best knowledge I possess'. He went further: 'This country of Palestine belongs to you and me. It was given to the Father of Israel. It's the land whence comes news of our redemption. It's the land where we look with as true a patriotism as we do this dear old England.'

In February 1867, Lieutenant of Royal Engineers Charles Warren, twenty-seven years old, began the Society's survey of Palestine. However, the Jerusalemites were hostile to any excavations around the Temple Mount so he hired plots nearby and sank twenty-seven shafts deep into the rock. He uncovered the first real archaeological artefacts in Jerusalem, the pottery of Hezekiah marked 'Belonging to the King'; forty-three cisterns under the Temple Mount; Warren's Shaft in the Ophel hill that he believed was King David's conduit into the city; and his Warren's Gate in the tunnels along the Western Wall was one of Herod's main entrances to the Temple – and later the Jewish Cave. This adventurous archaeologist personified the glamour of the new science. In one of his subterranean exploits he uncovered the ancient Struthion Pool and sailed on it on a raft made of doors. Fashionable Victorian ladies were lowered in baskets down his shafts, swooning at the biblical sights as they loosened their corsets.

Warren sympathized with the Jews, angered by the boorish European tourists who mocked their 'most solemn gathering' at the Wall as if it were a 'farce'. On the contrary, the 'country must be governed for them' so that ultimately 'the Jewish principality might stand by itself as a separate kingdom guaranteed by the Great Powers'.* The French were just as aggressive in their archaeological aspirations – though their chief archaeologist, Félicien de Saulcy, was a bungler who declared that the Tomb of Kings just north of the walls belonged to King David. In fact it was the tomb of the Queen of Adiabene dating from a thousand years later.

In 1860, Muslims massacred Christians in Syria and Lebanon, furious at the sultan's laws in favour of Christians and Jews, but this only attracted further Western advances: Napoleon III sent troops to save the Maronite Christians of the Lebanon, refreshing French claims to the area that had survived from Charlemagne, the Crusades and King Francis in the sixteenth century. In 1869, Egypt, backed by French capital, opened the Suez Canal at a ceremony attended by the French empress Eugénie, the Prussian crown prince Frederick and the Austrian emperor Franz Joseph. Not to be outdone by the British and Russians, the Prussian Frederick sailed up to Jaffa and rode to Jerusalem, where he vigorously promoted a Prussian presence in the race to grab churches and archaeological prizes: he bought the site of the Crusader St Mary of the Latins, close to the Church, and Frederick (the father of the future Kaiser Wilhelm II) backed the aggressive archaeologist Titus Tobler, who declared: 'Jerusalem must be ours.' As Frederick headed back to Jaffa, he almost rode into Franz Joseph, the Emperor of Austria and titular King of Jerusalem, who had only recently been defeated by the Prussians at the Battle of Sadowa. They greeted one another coldly.

Franz Joseph galloped into Jerusalem escorted by a thousand Ottoman guards, including Bedouin with lances, Druze with rifles,

---

* After Jerusalem, Warren became famous as the inept Metropolitan Police Commissioner who failed to catch Jack the Ripper and as a dud military commander during the Boer War. His successors, Lieutenants Charles Conder and Herbert Kitchener (the latter subsequently the conqueror of Sudan), surveyed the country so successfully that General Allenby used their maps to conquer Palestine in 1917.

and cameleers, and accompanied by an enormous silver bed, a present from the sultan. 'We dismounted,' the emperor recorded, 'and I knelt in the road and kissed the earth' as the cannon of David's Tower boomed a salute. He was overcome by 'how everything seemed to be just like one imagined it from one's childhood stories and the Bible'. But the Austrians, like all the Europeans, were buying buildings to promote a new Christian city: the emperor inspected the huge earth-works to build an Austrian Hospice on the Via Dolorosa.

'I shall never concede any road improvements to these crazy Christians,' wrote the Ottoman grand vizier Fuad Pasha, 'as they would then transform Jerusalem into a Christian madhouse.' But the Ottomans did build a new Jaffa road especially for Franz Joseph. The momentum of the 'Christian madhouse' was unstoppable.

MARK TWAIN AND THE 'PAUPER VILLAGE'

Captain Charles Warren, the young archaeologist, was passing the Jaffa Gate when he was amazed to witness a beheading. The execution was horribly botched by a clumsy headman: 'You're hurting me,' cried the victim as the executioner hacked at his neck sixteen times until he just climbed onto the unfortunate's back and sawed through his spinal column as if he was sacrificing a sheep. Jerusalem had at least two faces and a multiple personality disorder: the gleaming, imperial edifices, built by the Europeans in pith helmets and redcoats as they rapidly Christianized the Muslim Quarter, existed alongside the old Ottoman city where black Sudanese guards protected the Haram and guarded condemned prisoners whose heads still rolled in public executions. The gates were still closed each sundown; Bedouin surrendered their spears and swords when they came into the city. A third of the city was a wasteland and a photograph (taken by the Armenian Patriarch no less) showed the Church surrounded by open country in the midst of the city. The two worlds frequently clashed: when in 1865, the first telegraph opened between Jerusalem and Istanbul, the Arab horseman who charged the telegraph-pole was arrested and hanged from it.

In March 1866, Montefiore, now a widower of eighty-one, arrived on his sixth visit and could not believe the changes. Finding that the Jews at the Western Wall were exposed not only to the rain but to occasional pelting from the Temple Mount above, he received permission to set up an awning there – and tried unsuccessfully to buy the Wall, one of many attempts by the Jews to own their holy site. As he left Jerusalem, he felt 'more deeply than ever impressed'. It was not his last trip: when he returned in 1875 aged ninety-one, 'I beheld almost a new Jerusalem springing up with buildings, some of them as fine as any in Europe.' As he left for the last time, he could not help but muse that 'surely we're approaching the time to witness the realization of God's hallowed promises unto Zion.'*

Guidebooks warned against 'squalid Polish Jews', and a 'miasma of filth', but to some it was the Protestant pilgrims who tainted the place. 'Lepers, cripples, the blind and idiotic, assail you on every hand,' observed Samuel Clemens, the journalist from Missouri who wrote as 'Mark Twain'. Travelling the Mediterranean aboard the *Quaker City*, Twain, celebrated as the 'Wild Humorist', was on a pilgrim cruise called the Grand Holy Land Pleasure Excursion which he renamed the Grand Holy Land Funeral Expedition. He treated pilgrimage as a farce, mocking the sincerity of American pilgrims whom he called 'innocents abroad'. 'It's a relief to steal a walk for a hundred yards', he wrote, without encountering another 'site'. He was most amused to find the column in the Church that was the centre of the world made of the dust from which Adam was conjured: 'No man has been able to prove that the dirt was NOT procured here.' Overall he hated the Church's 'trumpery, geegaws and tawdry ornamentation', and the city: 'Renowned Jerusalem, the

* Montefiore died in 1885 aged over 100. He and Judith were buried with Jerusalem earth in their own Rachel's Tomb in Ramsgate. The Montefiore Windmill still stands and the Montefiore Quarter, know as Yemin Moshe, is one of the city's most elegant neighbourhoods and one of five named after him. His baronetcy was inherited by his nephew Sir Abraham who was childless (his wife went insane on their wedding night) but Moses left his estates to his Moroccan-born nephew Joseph Sebag who became Sebag-Montefiore. The Ramsgate mansion burned down in the 1930s. An almost forgotten figure (except in Israel), his tomb was neglected for a long time, threatened by urban sprawl and graffiti, but in the twenty-first century, his tomb has become a shrine: thousands of ultra-Orthodox Jews make a pilgrimage there on the anniversary of his death.

stateliest name in history has become a pauper village – mournful dreary and lifeless – I wouldn't want to live here.'* Yet even the Wild Humorist quietly bought his mother a Jerusalem Bible and sometimes reflected, 'I am sitting where a god has stood.'

The tourists, whether religious or secular, Christian or Jewish, Chateaubriand, Montefiore or Twain, were good at seeing where gods had stood but almost blind when it came to seeing the actual people who lived there. Throughout her history, Jerusalem existed in the imagination of devotees who lived faraway in America or Europe. Now that these visitors were arriving on steamships in their thousands, they expected to find the exotic and dangerous, picturesque and authentic images they had imagined with the help of their Bibles, their Victorian stereotypes of race, and, once they arrived, their translators and guides. They saw only the diversity of costumes in the streets and dismissed the images they did not like as Oriental filth and what Baedeker called 'wild superstition and fanaticism'. Instead, they would build the 'authentic' grand Holy City they had expected to find. It was these views that would drive the imperial interest in Jerusalem. As for the rest – the vibrant, half-veiled, ancient world of the Arabs and Sephardic Jews – they could scarcely see it. But it was very much there.

---

* Ironically Twain stayed in the Mediterranean Hotel in the Muslim Quarter, the very building which the Israeli Likud leader and general Ariel Sharon bought in the late 1980s in his bid to judaize the Muslim Quarter. Today it is a Jewish seminary. Twain's book *The Innocents Abroad* was an instant classic for sceptics: when ex-President Ulysses Grant visited Jerusalem, he used it as his guidebook.

40

ARAB CITY, IMPERIAL CITY

1870–80

YUSUF KHALIDI: MUSIC, DANCING, DAILY LIFE

The real Jerusalem was like a Tower of Babel in fancy dress with a hierarchy of religions and languages. Ottoman officers wore embroidered jackets coupled with European uniforms; Ottoman Jews, Armenians and Arab Christians and Muslims sported frock-coats or white suits with a new piece of headgear that symbolized the new reformed Ottoman empire: the tarbush, or fez; the Muslim *ulema* wore turbans and robes that were almost identical to those worn by many of the Sephardic Jews and Orthodox Arabs; the growing numbers of penurious Polish Hasidic Jews* wore gaberdine coats and fedoras; the kavasses – the bodyguards of the Europeans – were often Armenians who still wore scarlet jackets, white pantaloons and packed big pistols. Shoeless black slaves served ice sherbet to their masters, the old Arab or Sephardic families whose men often wore a smattering of all the above costumes – turbans or fezzes but with long coats tied with a sash, wide Turkish trousers and a black Western jacket on top. The Arabs spoke Turkish and Arabic; the Armenians Armenian, Turkish and

---

* The Hasidim – 'the pious' in Hebrew – are a growing presence in Jerusalem. The inheritors of seventeenth-century mysticism they still wear the distinctive black garb of that era. In the 1740s, a faith-healer in Ukraine named Israel ben Eliezer, adopting the name Baal Shem Tov (Master of the Good Name), created a mass movement that challenged Talmudic studies, advocating trance-like movements in prayer, singing, dancing and mystical practices to get closer to God. Their chief opponent was the Vilna Gaon who rejected all this as folk superstition and stressed the need for traditional Talmudic studies. Their conflict resembles that between the mystical Sufis and the harsh Islamic conservatives of, say, the Saudi Wahabis.

Arabic; Sephardis, Ladino, Turkish and Arabic; the Hasids, Yiddish, that mitteleuropean argot of German and Hebrew which spawned its own great literature.

If this seemed chaotic to the outsiders, the sultan-caliph presided over a Sunni empire: the Muslims were at the top; the Turks ruled; then came the Arabs. The Polish Jews, much mocked for their poverty, 'wailing' and the trance-like rhythms of their prayers, were at the bottom; but in between, in a half-submerged folk culture, there was much blending, despite the stringent rules of each religion.

At the end of the Ramadan fast, all the religions celebrated with a feast and a fair outside the walls, with merry-go-rounds and horseraces, while vendors exhibited obscene peepshows and sold Arab sweets, Maidens Hair and Turkish Delight. During the Jewish festival of Purim, Muslim and Christian Arabs dressed up in the traditional Jewish costumes, and all three religions attended the Jewish Picnic held at the tomb of Simon the Just north of the Damascus Gate. Jews presented their Arab neighbours with matzah and invited them to the Passover Seder dinner, while the Arabs returned the favour by giving the Jews newly baked bread when the festival ended. Jewish *mohels* often circumcised Muslim children. Jews held parties to welcome their Muslim neighbours back from the *haj*. The closest relations were between Arabs and Sephardic Jews. Indeed the Arabs called the Sephardis '*Yahud, awlad Arab –* Jews, son of Arabs', their own Jews and some Muslim women even learned Ladino. During droughts, the *ulema* asked the Sephardic rabbis to pray for rain. The Sephardic, Arab-speaking Valeros, the city's leading bankers, were business partners with many of the Families. Ironically, the Arab Orthodox Christians were the most hostile to Jews, whom they insulted in traditional Easter songs and lynched as they approached the Church.

Although Baedeker warned tourists that 'there are no places of public amusement in Jerusalem', this was a city of music and dancing. The locals met in the coffee houses and cellar bars to smoke *narghileh* water pipes, play backgammon, watch wrestling matches and belly dancing. At weddings and festivals, there was circle-dancing (*dabkah*), while singers performed such love songs as 'My lover, your beauty hurt me'. Arab love songs alternated with the Andalusian Ladino songs of the Sephardis. Dervishes danced their *zikr* wildly to the *mazhar* drums and cymbals. In private houses, music was played by mixed Jewish and Arab musicians on the lute (*oud*), fiddle (*rababa*), double clarinets (*zummara* and *arghul*) and kettledrum (*inaqqara*). These instruments echoed through the six hammam bathhouses that were central to Jerusalem life. The men (who used them between 2 a.m. and midday) enjoyed massages and had their moustaches trimmed; the women dyed their hair with henna and drank coffee. The brides of Jerusalem were led by singing, drumming girlfriends to the hammam where all their body hair was festively removed using *zarnikh*, a pitch-like syrup. The wedding night itself started at the baths, then the groom and his party collected the bride from her home and, if this was a wedding of the Families, they walked under a canopy held by servants, illuminated by torches and followed by a drummer and a band of pipers, up to the Temple Mount.

The Families were the apex of Jerusalem society. The first municipal leader was a Dajani, and in 1867, Yusuf al-Diya al-Khalidi, aged twenty-five, became the first mayor of Jerusalem. Henceforth the post was always held by the Families – there would be six Husseinis, four Alamis, two Khalidis, three Dajanis. Khalidi, whose mother was a Husseini, had run away as a boy to attend Protestant school in Malta. Later he worked for the liberal grand vizier in Istanbul. He regarded himself first as an 'Utsi' – a Jerusalemite (he called Jerusalem his 'homeland') – second as an Arab (and a Shami, an inhabitant of Shams al-Bilad, greater Syria), third as an Ottoman. He was an intellectual, one of the stars of the *nahda*, the Arab literary renaissance that saw the opening of cultural clubs, newspapers and publishers.* Yet the first mayor discovered his was a fighting as well as municipal job: the governor despatched him with forty horsemen to suppress fighting at Kerak, perhaps the only mayor of modern history to lead a cavalry expedition.

---

* Ever since the 1760s, the Khalidis had been forming a library – collecting 5,000 Islamic books, some dating from the tenth century, and 1,200 manuscripts. In 1899, Raghib Khalidi merged his collection with those of Yusuf and his cousins and opened the Khalidi Library the next year around the Mamluk tomb of Barka Khan on Silsila Street, where it remains.

The Families each had their own banners and their own special role in the city's festivals. At the Holy Fire, the thirteen leading Arab Christian families paraded their banners but the Nabi Musa was the most popular festival. Thousands arrived on horseback and foot from all over Palestine to be greeted by the mufti, usually a Husseini, and the Ottoman governor. There was boisterous dancing and singing to cymbals and drums. Sufi dervishes whirled – 'some ate live coals, others forced spikes through their cheeks' and there were punch-ups between Jerusalemites and Nablusites. Jews and Christians were sometimes beaten up by over-excited Arab bravos. When the crowds had assembled on the Temple Mount, they were saluted by a cannonade and then the Husseinis on horseback, brandishing their own green banners, led the cavalcade towards Baibars' shrine near Jericho. The Dajanis waved their own purple Banner of David's Tomb. Yet the Families, each with their own dynastic domain – the Husseinis had the Temple Mount, the Khalidis the lawcourts, and they all competed for the mayoralty – were still struggling for supremacy and playing the perilous game of Istanbul politics.

The Orthodox Slavs of the Balkans, backed by Russia, wanted independence; the Ottoman empire struggled to survive. The accession of a new and more forceful sultan, Abdul-Hamid II, was marked by massacres of Bulgarian Christians. Under Russian pressure, Abdul-Hamid accepted a constitution and the election of a parliament: in Jerusalem, the Husseinis backed the old autocracy and the Khalidis were the new liberals. Mayor Khalidi was elected to represent Jerusalem and headed off to Istanbul, yet the constitution was a feint. Abdul-Hamid cancelled it and started to promote a new Ottoman nationalism combined with an pan-Islamic loyalty to the caliphate. This intelligent but neurotic sultan, diminutive with a bleating voice and a tendency to fainting-fits, enforced his rule with the *Khafiya* secret police who murdered his ex-grand vizier and one of his slavegirls amongst others. While he enjoyed the traditional privileges – his harem contained 900 odalisques – he lived in fear, checking under his bed for assassins each night, but he was also a skilled carpenter, a reader of Sherlock Holmes, and the impresario of his own theatre.

His crackdown was immediately felt in Jerusalem: Yusuf Khalidi was expelled from Istanbul, sacked as mayor and replaced by Umar al-Husseini. When the Khalidis were down, the Husseinis were up. Meanwhile, Russia prepared finally to destroy the Ottomans. The British prime minister, Benjamin Disraeli, intervened to save them.

JERUSALEM TATTOOS:
BRITISH PRINCES AND RUSSIAN GRAND DUKES

He had just bought the Suez Canal, borrowing £4 million from Lionel de Rothschild. 'What is your security?' asked Rothschild.

'The British government,' replied Disraeli's secretary.

'You shall have it.' Now in 1878 at the Congress of Berlin, Disraeli guided the cabinets of Europe to curb Russia and enforce a settlement, in which Britain was able to occupy Cyprus. His performance was admired by the German chancellor Prince Bismarck, who pointing at Disraeli remarked, 'The old Jew – he's the man.' The Ottomans had to give up much of their European, Christian territory and were forced to confirm the rights of Jews and other minorities. In 1882, the British took control of Egypt, which remained nominally under the Albanian dynasty. Two representatives of Britain's forward position in the Middle East visited Jerusalem on their world tour: the young heirs to the British throne – Prince Albert Victor, known as Prince Eddy, the future Duke of Clarence, aged eighteen, and his brother George, aged sixteen, the future George V.*

They pitched their camp on the Mount of Olives, 'the very same that Papa camped on,' wrote Prince George, who thought it 'a capital place'. The camp boasted eleven luxurious tents, borne by ninety-five pack-animals and served by sixty servants – all marshalled by the king of travel agents, Thomas Cook, a Baptist minister from Melbourne, Derbyshire, who in 1841 had started a travel business

---

* Guided around Jerusalem by Captains Charles Wilson and Conder, archaeologists of the Palestine Exploration Fund, the princes attended a Sephardic Passover dinner, and were 'much impressed by the complete domesticity' of this 'happy family gathering'. They were even more excited by their tattoos. 'I was tattooed', wrote Prince George, 'by the same man who tattooed Papa [the Prince of Wales].'

conveying temperance campaigners from Leicester to Lough-borough. Now Cook and his sons – one of whom accompanied the princes – were pioneers of the new tourism, hiring small armies of servants, guards and dragomans (translator-fixers) to protect against any attack by Bedouin or the Abu Ghosh clan, who still dominated the road from Jaffa and had to be either bribed or co-opted. These impresarios of travel laid out encampments of sumptuous silk tents, decorated in exotic reds and turquoise arabesques with dining rooms and receiving rooms, and even hot and cold water. The desired effect was to deliver an Oriental fantasy for the well-heeled English traveller – like something out of the *Thousand and One Nights*.

Thomas Cook's offices were at the Jaffa Gate, which was the hub of a new tourist-friendly Jerusalem, symbolized by the opening of the Grand New Hotel, just over Bathsheba's Pool, supposedly where Uriah's wife was seen bathing by King David,* and Joachim Fast's hotel just outside the gate. In 1892, the railway finally reached Jerusalem, truly opening up the city to tourism.

Photography developed alongside tourism. It was unexpected if fitting that the high priest of Jerusalem's photographic boom was Yessayi Garabedian, the Armenian patriarch, 'probably the hand-somest potentate in the world', who studied the art in Manchester. His two protégés left the Armenian priesthood and founded photo-graphic studios on the Jaffa Road that offered tourists the chance to buy photographs of Arabs in 'biblical poses' or to pose themselves in biblical costume. In a typical moment, a group of bearded and sheepskin-clad Russian peasants gathered in amazement to watch 'a blue-eyed fair-haired English lady' wearing 'an embroidered scarlet costume' with a brass circlet on her head and 'tight corsets' framing a 'finely-developed bust,' striking poses in front of David's Tower. The Russians were half-horrified, half-dazzled.

The growing New City was so architecturally eclectic that today

---

* The sign outside Cook's office read: 'Thomas Cook and Son have the largest staff of dragomans and muleteers, the best landaus, carriages, camp, saddlery etc in Palestine!' The building of the Grand New Hotel revealed Roman remains: a part of the Second Wall, tiles inscribed with the Tenth Legion's insignia and a column erected by a legate of Augustus, used for decades as the base of a streetlamp.

The red-bearded Albanian generalissimo Ibrahim Pasha conquered Syria in 1831 and almost took Istanbul on behalf of his father Mehmet Ali. He crushed rebellious Jerusalem brutally and opened up the city to Europeans.

Mehmet Ali received the Scottish painter David Roberts on his way to Jerusalem: his paintings of Oriental scenes, such as this interior of the Church of the Holy Sepuchre, influenced the European view of Palestine.

The plutocrat and Jewish philanthropist Sir Moses Montefiore visited Jerusalem seven times and was one of the first to build outside the Old City. In 1860, he started his windmill and cottages (*below*). He was what Victorians thought a 'noble Hebrew' should be like, but he had his secret scandals too: he fathered a child with his teenaged maid in his eighties.

Below Much of the Old City was surprisingly empty in this period. This photograph taken in 1861 by the pioneering photographer Yessayi, the Armenian Patriarch, shows the deserted landscape behind the Church of the Holy Sepulchre.

From the 1830s, the Sephardic Arab-speaking Jews of Jerusalem were joined by Yiddish-speaking immigrants from the Russian Empire and more Sephardis from the Arab world. European visitors were appalled and fascinated by the squalor and exoticism of Yemenite (*left*) and Ashkenazi (*right*) Jews.

Jerusalem was also dominated by Russian Orthodox peasants (*above left*, outside the Church at Easter), who prayed and caroused with equal fervour, while Jaffa Gate and David Street (*above right*) became the hub of European Jerusalem.

Theodore Herzl, assimilated Viennese journalist and brilliant publicist, was the organizer of political Zionism. In 1898, he approached Kaiser Wilhelm II who ordered Herzl to meet him in Jerusalem. Regarding himself as a German Crusader, the Kaiser wore a specially designed white uniform with a full-length veil attached to his pickelhauber.

The Kaiser visits the Tomb of Kings. In the archaeological race between the Great Powers, the Frenchman de Saulcy had claimed this was King David's tomb. It is actually the tomb of the first-century Queen of Adiabene.

Above The American Colonists arrived as a millenarian Christian sect but they soon became beloved philanthropists: here, Bertha Spafford, a daughter of the founders, poses with Bedouin friends.

Above Jerusalem's mayor Selim al-Husseini: the very model of an aristocratic Jerusalemite.

Above Ne'er-do-well aristocratic rogue and huckster, Montagu Parker, later Earl of Morley, whose three-year project to uncover the Ark of the Covenant ended in the sole riot in Jerusalem's history to unite Jews and Muslims. He only just escaped with his life.

Above For almost half a century the fixer, aesthete, socialite and *oud*-player Wasif Jawhariyyeh knew everyone, saw everything, and recorded it all in his peerlessly vivid diary.

Jemal Pasha, the dictator of Jerusalem during the First World War, was a Turkish nationalist with a taste for cigars, champagne, beautiful Jewish courtesans and brutal executions (*below*).

Born in a Russian shtetl, Chaim Weizmann (*left*) was at home with kings and lords. His passionate charm helped convert Britain's imperial panjandrums, Lloyd George, Churchill (*centre*) and Balfour, to Zionism, while Lawrence of Arabia (*right*) promoted the Arab cause.

Surrender, 1917: Hussein al-Husseini, mayor of Jerusalem (centre, with walking stick), tried six times to surrender to the British with a sheet tied to a broom.

Mandate: conqueror of Jerusalem, General 'the Bull' Allenby (right), and military governor Ronald Storrs celebrate the Fourth of July with Bertha Spafford (left) at the American Colony in 1918.

Lawrence of Arabia and Amir Abdullah follow Winston Churchill through the gardens of Augusta Victoria in 1921: the British Colonial Secretary created the new realm of Transjordan for the Hashemite Abdullah.

The glories of Imperial Jerusalem: Prince Arthur, Duke of Connaught, son of Queen Victoria, hands out awards in Barracks Square, though he grumbled when some recipients wore Ottoman and German medals.

High Commissioner of Palestine Herbert Samuel (seated, centre) and Jerusalem governor Storrs (standing, fourth from the right) host the religious hierarchs of the city after a service to celebrate British liberation in 1924.

Jerusalem has houses and entire suburbs that look as if they belong anywhere other than in the Middle East. The new Christian edifices added at the end of the century included twenty-seven French convents, ten Italian and eight Russian.* After Britain and Prussia ended their shared Anglo-Prussian bishopric, the Anglicans constructed their own sturdily English St George's Cathedral, the see of an Anglican bishop. But in 1892, the Ottomans were still building too: Abdul-Hamid had added new fountains, created the New Gate to allow access directly to the Christian Quarter and in 1901, celebrating his twenty-fifth jubilee, he added a belltower to the Jaffa Gate that looked as if it belonged in a suburban English railway station.

Meanwhile Jews and Arabs, Greeks and Germans were colonizing the New City outside the walls. In 1869, seven Jewish families founded the Nahalat Shiva – Quarter of the Seven – outside the Jaffa Gate; in 1874, ultra-Orthodox Jews settled in Mea Shearim, now a Hassidic quarter. By 1880, the 17,000 Jews formed a majority and there were nine new Jewish suburbs while the Arab Families built their own Husseini and Nashashibi quarters in Sheikh Jarrah, the area north of the Damascus Gate.† The Families' Arab mansions boasted decorated ceilings in hybrid Turkish–European styles. One Husseini built the Orient House with its entry hall painted in flowers and geometric patterns, while another, Rabah Effendi Husseini, created a mansion featuring the Pasha Room with a high dome painted celestial blue, framed by gilded acanthus leaves. Orient House became a hotel then the Palestine Authority's Jerusalem headquarters in the 1990s and Rabah Husseini's mansion became the home of Jerusalem's most eminent American family.

* The German architect and archaeologist Conrad Schick was the most prolific architect of his time, but his buildings defy any pigeon-holing – his home, Thabor House, and chapel contain vestiges of Germanic, Arab and Graeco-Roman styles.
† The Husseinis and the other Families such as the newer Nashashibis became much richer, embracing the commercial boom; one of the Husseinis provided the wooden sleepers for the new railway. In 1858, the Ottoman Land Law privatized many of the ancient *waqfs*, which suddenly made the Families into rich landowners and traders in grain. The losers were the Arab fellahin, the peasants, now at the mercy of feudal absentee landlords. Hence Rauf Pasha, the last Hamidian governor, called the Families 'parasites'.

THE AMERICAN OVERCOMERS:
KEEPING JESUS' MILK WARM

On 21 November 1873, Anna Spafford and four of her daughters were crossing the Atlantic on the *Ville de Havre* when it was struck by another ship. As the ship sank, all four children were drowned, but Anna survived. When she learned, after her rescue, that they were dead, she wanted to throw herself into the water after them. Instead she sent her husband, Horatio, a prosperous Chicago attorney, the heartbreaking telegram: 'SAVED ALONE. WHAT SHALL I DO?' What the Spaffords did was to give up their conventional life and come to Jerusalem. First they faced more tragedy: their son died of scarlet fever, leaving them one child, Bertha, out of six. Anna Spafford believed herself 'spared for a purpose', but the couple was also outraged by their Presbyterian Church, which regarded their fate as divine punishment. Forming their own messianic sect, which the US press called the Overcomers, they believed that good works in Jerusalem and the restoration of the Jews to Israel – followed by their conversion – would hasten the imminent Second Coming.

In 1881, the Overcomers – thirteen adults and three children, who became the nucleus of the American Colony – settled in a large house just inside the Damascus Gate until, in 1896, they were joined by the farmers of the Swedish Evangelical Church and needed a larger headquarters. They then leased Rabbah Husseini's mansion in Sheikh Jarrah on the road to Nablus. Horatio died in 1888, but the sect thrived as they preached the Second Coming, converted Jews and developed their colony into a philanthropic, evangelical beehive of hospitals, orphanages, soup-kitchens, a shop, their own photography studio and a school. Their success attracted the hostility of the long-serving American consul-general, Selah Merrill, an anti-Semitic Massachusetts Congregationalist clergyman, Andover professor and inept archaeologist. For twenty years Merrill tried to destroy the Colonists, accusing them of charlatanism, anti-Americanism, lewdness and child-kidnapping. He threatened to send his guards to horsewhip them.

The US press claimed that the Colonists made tea on the Olivet every day ready for the Second Coming: 'They keep milk warm at all times', explained the *Detroit News*, 'in case the Lord and Master should arrive and asses are kept saddled in case Jesus appeared and some said they would never die.' They also played a special part in the city's archaeology: in 1882, they befriended a British imperial hero who symbolized the empire's embrace of Bible and sword.

After helping suppress the Taiping Rebellion in China and governing the Sudan, General Charles 'Chinese' Gordon settled in John the Baptist's village, Ein Kerem. But he came into town to study the Bible and enjoy the view from the roof of the Colony's original house. There he became convinced that the skull-like hill opposite was the true Golgotha, an idea he promoted with such energy that his so-called Garden Tomb became a Protestant alternative to the Sepulchre.* Meanwhile the Overcomers were generous to the many mentally fragile pilgrims whom Bertha Spafford called 'Simples in the Garden of Allah'. 'Jerusalem', she wrote in her memoirs, 'attracts all kinds of religious fanatics and cranks of different degrees of derangement.' There were fellow Americans who regarded themselves as 'Elijah, John the Baptist or another of the prophets [and] there were several messiahs wandering around Jerusalem'. One of the Elijahs tried to kill Horatio Spafford with a rock; a Texan named Titus thought he was a world-conqueror but had to be restrained after he groped the maids. Then there was a rich Dutch countess designing a mansion to house the 144,000 ransomed souls of Revelation 7.4. Yet not all the Americans in Jerusalem were Christian Hebraists. Consul-General Merrill hated the Jews as much as he hated the Overcomers, calling them an arrogant, money-obsessed 'race of weaklings of whom neither soldiers, colonists nor citizens can be made'.

Gradually the American Colony's cheerful hymn-singing and

* His year in Jerusalem was cut short by the Mahdi's rebellion in Sudan. Recalled to govern Sudan, Gordon was besieged and then killed in Khartoum, reputedly holding his Bible. The Garden Tomb was not the only archaeological achievement of the Colony: as we saw much earlier, it was Jacob Eliahu, the child of a Jew converted by the London Jews Society who defected to the Colony, who found the inscription left by the workers in the Siloam tunnel.

charitable deeds made them friends among all sects and religions, and the first port of call for every well-connected writer, pilgrim and potentate. Selma Lagerlöf, a Swedish writer who stayed with the Spaffords, made the Colony famous with her novel *Jerusalem*, winning the Nobel Literature Prize. In 1902, Baron Plato von Ustinov (grandfather of the actor Peter), who ran a hotel in Jaffa, asked if his guests could stay at the Colony, the start of its transformation into a hotel.* Yet if the city had been transformed by Westerners, by the end of the century she was dominated by Russia, empire of Orthodox peasants and persecuted Jews, both drawn irresistibly towards Jerusalem – and both travelling from Odessa on the same ships.

* In 1904, the founders' daughter Bertha Spafford married a fellow Colonist Frederick Vester, and their heirs still own the hotel.

41

RUSSIANS

1880–98

GRAND DUKE SERGEI AND GRAND DUCHESS ELLA

Russian peasants, many of them women, often walked all the way from their villages southwards to Odessa for the voyage to Zion. They wore 'deeply padded overcoats and furlined jackets with sheep-skin caps', the women adding 'bundles of four or five petticoats and grey shawls over their heads'. They brought their death shrouds and felt, wrote Stephen Graham, an English journalist who travelled with them disguised by perfect Russian, shaggy beard and peasant smock, 'that when they have been to Jerusalem, the serious occupations of their life are all ended. For the peasant goes to Jerusalem to *die* in a certain way in Russia – just as the whole concern of the Protestant centres round *life*.'

They sailed in the 'dark and filthy holds' of subsidized ships: 'In one storm, when the masts were broken, the hold where the peasants rolled over one another like corpses, or grasped at one another like madmen, was worse than any imagined pit, the stench worse than any fire!' In Jerusalem, they were welcomed 'by a giant Montenegrin guide in the magnificent uniform of the Russian Palestine Society – scarlet and cream cloak and riding knickers – and conducted through the Jerusalem streets' crowded with 'Arab beggars, almost naked and ugly beyond words, howling for coppers', to the Russian Compound. There they lived in capacious, crowded dormitories for 'threepence-a-day' and ate *kasha*, cabbage soup and mugs of *kvass* root-beer in the refectories. There were so many Russians that the 'Arab boys ran alongside shouting in Russian "Muscovites are good!"'

Throughout the journey, rumours would spread: 'There is a mysterious passenger on board.' When they arrived, crying 'Glory be to Thee O God!', they would say, 'There's a mysterious pilgrim in Jerusalem,' and claim to have seen Jesus at the Golden Gate or by Herod's wall. 'They spend a night in the Sepulchre of Christ,' explained Graham, 'and receiving the Holy Fire, extinguish it with their caps that they will wear in their coffins.' Yet they were increasingly shocked by 'Jerusalem the earthly, a pleasure-ground for wealthy sightseers', and particularly by 'the vast strange ruined dirty verminous' Church, 'the womb of death'. They would reassure themselves by reflecting, 'We find Jesus really when we cease looking at Jerusalem and allow the Gospel to look into us.' Yet their Holy Russia itself was changing: Alexander II's liberation of the serfs in 1861 unleashed expectations of reform that he could not satisfy: anarchist and socialist terrorists hunted him down in his own empire. During one attack, the emperor himself drew his pistol and fired at his would-be killers. But in 1881 he was finally assassinated in St Petersburg, his legs blown off by bomb-throwing radicals.

Rumours quickly spread that Jews were implicated (there was a Jewish woman in the terrorists' circle but none of the assassins was Jewish) and these unleashed bloody attacks against Jews across Russia, encouraged and sometimes organized by the state. These predations gave the west a new word: pogrom, from the Russian *gromit* – to destroy. The new emperor, Alexander III, a bearded giant with blinkered, conservative views, regarded the Jews as a 'social cancer' and he blamed them for their own persecution by honest Orthodox Russians. His May Laws of 1882 effectively made anti-Semitism* a state policy, enforced by secret-police repression.

The emperor believed Holy Russia would be saved by autocracy and Orthodoxy encouraged by the cult of pilgrimage to Jerusalem. He therefore appointed his brother Grand Duke Sergei Alexandrovich to the presidency of the Imperial Orthodox Palestine Society 'to strengthen Orthodoxy in the Holy Land'.

* This word was coined in 1879 by Wilhelm Marr, a German journalist, in his book *The Victory of Judaism over Germandom*, in time to describe the new racial breed of hatred that was replacing the old religious version.

On 28 September 1888, Sergei and his twenty-three-year-old wife Elizabeth, nicknamed Ella, pretty granddaughter of Queen Victoria, consecrated their Church of Mary Magdalene, with white limestone and seven glistening gold onion-domes, on the Mount of Olives. Both were moved by Jerusalem. 'You can't imagine what a profound impression it makes', Ella reported to Queen Victoria, 'when entering the Holy Sepulchre. It's such an intense joy being here and my thoughts constantly turn to you.' Ella, born a Protestant princess of Hesse-Darmstadt, had passionately embraced her conversion to Orthodoxy. 'How happy' it made her to 'see all these holy places one learns to love from tender infancy.' Sergei and the emperor had carefully overseen the design of the church, with Ella commissioning its paintings of Magdalene. Dazzled by the beauty of the church's Russian character and gorgeous setting opposite the Golden Gate, the Grand Duchess declared she wanted to be buried there – so as to rise first at the Last Judgement. 'It's like a dream to see all these places where our Lord suffered for us,' Ella told Victoria, 'and such an intense comfort to pray here.' Ella needed comfort.

Sergei, thirty-one years old, was a military martinet and domestic tyrant haunted by rumours of a secret gay life that clashed with his severe belief in autocracy and Orthodoxy. 'Without redeeming features, obstinate, arrogant and disagreeable, he flaunted his peculiarities,' claimed one of his cousins. His marriage to Ella placed him at the centre of European royalty: her sister Alexandra was about to marry the future tsar Nicholas II.

Before they left, Sergei's interests – empire, God and archaeology – merged in his new church, the St Alexander Nevsky, right next to the Church of the Sepulchre. When he bought this prime site, Sergei and his builders had uncovered walls dating from Hadrian's Temple and Constantine's Basilica, and when he built his church, he incorporated these archaeological finds into the building. In the Russian Compound, he commissioned Sergei's House, a luxury hostel with turreted neo-Gothic towers for Russian aristocrats.* The lives of Sergei and Ella would be tragic; yet, apart

* Sergei's House remained technically owned by his estate until President Putin admired it on his 2005 visit to Israel and was said to have been so moved that he wept. Israel returned the hostel to Russia in 2008.

from these buildings and the thousands of Russian pilgrims they attracted, his defining contribution was as one of the proponents of the official anti-Semitism that drove Russia's Jews towards the sanctuary of Zion.

GRAND DUKE SERGEI:
RUSSIAN JEWS AND THE POGROMS

In 1891, Alexander III appointed Sergei governor-general of Moscow. There, he immediately expelled 20,000 Jews from the city, surrounding their neighbourhood in the middle of the first night of Passover with Cossacks and police. 'I can't believe we won't be judged for this in the future,' Ella wrote, but Sergei 'believes this is for our security. I see nothing in it but shame.'*

The six million Russian Jews had always honoured Jerusalem, praying towards the eastern walls of their houses. But now the pogroms pushed them either towards revolution – many embraced socialism – or towards escape. Thus was triggered a vast exodus, the first Aliyah, a word that meant flight to a higher place, the Holy Mountain of Jerusalem. Two million Jews left Russia between 1888 and 1914, but 85 per cent of them headed not for the Promised Land but the Golden Land of America. Nonetheless thousands looked to Jerusalem. By 1890, Russian Jewish immigration was starting to change the city: there were now 25,000 Jews out of 40,000 Jerusalemites. In 1882 the sultan banned Jewish immigration and in 1889 decreed that Jews were not allowed to stay in Palestine more than three months, measures scarcely enforced. The Arab Families, led by Yusuf Khalidi, petitioned Istanbul against Jewish immigration, but the Jews kept coming.

Ever since the writers of the Bible created their narrative of

---

* Alexander III died in 1894 and was succeeded by his inexperienced, inept and unlucky son Nicholas II, who shared his father's rigid belief in autocracy. He liked and trusted 'Uncle Sergei'. As governor-general, Sergei was responsible for the coronation festivities in Moscow during which thousands of celebrating peasants died in a stampede. Sergei advised his nephew to continue with the celebrations and evaded responsibility.

Jerusalem, and ever since that biography of the city had become the universal story, her fate had been decided faraway – in Babylon, Susa, Rome, Mecca, Istanbul, London and St Petersburg. In 1896, an Austrian journalist published the book that would define twentieth-century Jerusalem: *The Jewish State*.

PART NINE

ZIONISM

O Jerusalem: the one man who has been present all this while, the lovable dreamer of Nazareth, has done nothing but increase the hate.

Theodor Herzl, *Diary*

The angry face of Yahweh is brooding over the hot rocks which have seen more holy murder, rape, and plunder than any other place on this earth.

Arthur Koestler

If a land can have a soul, Jerusalem is the soul of the land of Israel.

David Ben-Gurion, press interview

No two cities have counted more with mankind than Athens and Jerusalem.

Winston Churchill, *The Second World War*, vol 6: *Triumph and Tragedy*

It's not easy to be a Jerusalemite. A thorny path runs alongside its joys. The great are small inside the Old City. Popes, patriarchs, kings all remove their crowns. It is the city of the King of Kings; and earthly kings and lords are not its masters. No human can ever possess Jerusalem.

John Tleel, 'I am Jerusalem', *Jerusalem Quarterly*

And burthened Gentiles
    o'er the main
Must bear the weight
    of Israel's hate
Because he is not
    brought again
In triumph to Jerusalem.

Rudyard Kipling, 'The Burden of Jerusalem'

42

THE KAISER

1898–1905

HERZL

Theodor Herzl, a literary critic in Vienna, was said to be 'extraordinarily handsome', his eyes were 'almond-shaped with heavy, black melancholy lashes', his profile that of 'an Assyrian Emperor'. An unhappily married father of three, he was a thoroughly assimilated Jew who wore winged collars and frock-coats; 'he was not of the people', and had little connection to the shabby, ringletted Jews of the *shtetls*. He was a lawyer by training, spoke no Hebrew or Yiddish, put up Christmas trees at home and did not bother to circumcise his son. But the Russian pogroms of 1881 fundamentally shocked him. When, in 1895, Vienna elected the anti-Semitic rabble-rouser Karl Lueger as mayor, Herzl wrote: 'The mood among the Jews is one of despair.' That same year, he was in Paris covering the Dreyfus Affair, in which an innocent Jewish army officer was framed as a German spy, and he watched Parisian mobs shrieking 'Mort aux Juifs' in the country that had emancipated Jews. This reinforced his conviction that assimilation had not only failed but was provoking more anti-Semitism. He even predicted that anti-Semitism would one day be legalized in Germany.

Herzl concluded that Jews could never be safe without their own homeland. At first, this half-pragmatist, half-utopian dreamed of a Germanic aristocratic republic, a Jewish Venice ruled by a senate with a Rothschild as princely doge and himself as chancellor. His vision was secular: the high priests 'will wear impressive robes'; the Herzl army would boast cuirassiers with silver breastplates; his modern Jewish citizens would play cricket and tennis in a modern

Jerusalem. The Rothschilds, initially sceptical of any Jewish state, rejected Herzl's approaches, but these early notes soon matured into something more practical. 'Palestine is our ever-memorable historic home,' he proclaimed in *The Jewish State* in February 1896. 'The Maccabees will rise again. We shall live at last as free men on our own soil and die peacefully in our own homes.'

There was nothing new about Zionism – even the word had already been coined in 1890 – but Herzl gave political expression and organization to a very ancient sentiment. Jews had envisaged their very existence in terms of their relationship to Jerusalem since King David and particularly since the Babylonian Exile. Jews prayed towards Jerusalem, wished each other 'Next Year in Jerusalem' each year at Passover, and commemorated the fallen Temple by smashing a glass at their weddings and keeping a corner of their houses undecorated. They went on pilgrimage there, wished to be buried there and prayed whenever possible around the Temple walls. Even when they were grievously persecuted, Jews continued to live in Jerusalem and were absent only when they were banned on pain of death.

The new European nationalism inevitably provoked racial hostility towards this supranational and cosmopolitan people – but simultaneously the same nationalism, along with the liberty won by the French Revolution, was bound to inspire the Jews too. Prince Potemkin, Emperor Napoleon and US President John Adams all believed in the return of the Jews to Jerusalem as had Polish and Italian nationalists, and of course the Christian Zionists in America and Britain. Yet the Zionist pioneers were Orthodox rabbis who saw the Return in the light of messianic expectation. In 1836, an Ashkenazi rabbi in Prussia, Zvi Hirsch Kalischer, approached the Rothschilds and Montefiores to fund a Jewish nation, and later wrote his book *Seeking Zion*. After the Damascus 'blood-libel', Rabbi Yehuda Hai Alchelai, a Sephardic rabbi in Sarajevo, suggested Jews in the Islamic world should elect leaders and buy land in Palestine. In 1862, Moses Hess, a comrade of Karl Marx, predicted that nationalism would lead to racial anti-Semitism, in *Rome and Jerusalem: the Last National Question*, which proposed a socialist Jewish society in Palestine. Yet it was the Russian pogroms that were decisive.

'We must re-establish ourselves as a living nation,' wrote Leo Pinsker, an Odessan physician, in his book, *Auto-Emancipation*, writing at the same time as Herzl. He inspired a new movement of Russian Jews, 'The Lovers of Zion', *Hovevei Zion*, to develop agricultural settlements in Palestine. Even though many of them were secular, 'our Jewishness and our Zionism,' explained a young believer, Chaim Weizmann, 'were interchangeable'. In 1878, Palestinian Jews had founded Petah Tikvah (Gateway of Hope) on the coast but now even the Rothschilds, in the person of the French Baron Edmond, started to fund agricultural villages such as Rishon-le-Zion (First in Zion) for Russian immigrants – altogether he would donate the princely sum of £6.6 million. Like Montefiore, he tried to buy the Wall in Jerusalem. In 1887, the mufti, Mustafa al-Husseini, agreed a deal but it fell through. When Rothschild tried again in 1897, the Husseini Sheikh al-Haram blocked it.

In 1883, long before Herzl's book, 25,000 Jews started to arrive in Palestine in the first wave – Aliyah – of immigration. Most but not all were from Russia. But Jerusalem also attracted Persians in the 1870s, Yemenites in the 1880s. They tended to live together in their own communities: Jews from Bokhara, including the Moussaieff family of jewellers who had cut diamonds for Genghis Khan, settled their own Bokharan Quarter that was carefully laid out in a grid, its grand often neo-Gothic, neo-Renaissance, sometimes Moorish mansions designed to resemble those of Central Asian cities.*

In August 1897, Herzl presided over the first Zionist Congress in Basle and afterwards he boasted to his diary: 'L'état c'est moi. At Basle, I founded the Jewish state. If I said this out loud today, I would be greeted by universal laughter. Perhaps in five years and certainly in fifty, everyone will know it.' They did – and he was only five years out. Herzl became a new species of politician and publicist, riding the new railways of Europe to canvass kings, ministers and press barons. His relentless energy aggravated, and defied, a weak heart, liable to kill him at any moment.

* Jerusalem's so-called 'Polish Jews' were mainly Hasidim from the Russian empire but some of their sects were opposed to Zionism, believing it was sacrilege for mere men to decide God's timing for the Return and Judgement Day.

Herzl believed in a Zionism, not built from the bottom by settlers, but granted by emperors and financed by plutocrats. The Rothschilds and Montefiores initially disdained Zionism but the earliest Zionist Congresses were ornamented by Sir Francis Montefiore, Moses' nephew, 'a rather footling English gentleman' who 'wore white gloves in the heat of the Swiss summer because he had to shake so many hands'. However, Herzl needed a potentate to intervene with the sultan. He decided that his Jewish state should be German-speaking – and so he turned to the very model of a modern monarch, the German Kaiser.

Wilhelm II was planning an Oriental tour to meet the sultan and then proceed to Jerusalem for the dedication of a new church built close to the Sepulchre on the land granted to his father, Kaiser Frederick. But there was more to the Kaiser's plan: he prided himself on his diplomacy with the sultan and saw himself as a Protestant pilgrim to the Holy Places. Above all he hoped to offer German protection to the Ottomans, promote his new Germany and counter British influence.

'I shall go to the German Kaiser [to say] "Let our people go"', decided Herzl, and resolved to base his state on 'this great, strong, moral, splendidly governed, tightly organized Germany. Through Zionism, it will again become possible for Jews to love this Germany.'

WILHELM: THE PARASITES OF MY EMPIRE

The Kaiser was an unlikely Jewish champion. When he heard that Jews were settling in Argentina, he said, 'Oh if only we could send ours there too,' and hearing about Herzl's Zionism, he wrote, 'I'm very much in favour of the Mauschels going to Palestine. The sooner they clear off the better!' Although he regularly met Jewish industrialists in Germany, and became friends with the Jewish shipowner Albert Ballin, he was at heart an anti-Semite who ranted against the poisonous hydra of Jewish capitalism. Jews were the 'parasites of my empire' who he believed were 'twisting and corrupting' Germany. Years later, as a deposed monarch, he would propose mass extermination of the Jews using gas. Yet Herzl sensed that 'the anti-Semites are becoming our most reliable friends'.

Herzl had to penetrate the Kaiser's court. First he managed to meet the Kaiser's influential uncle, Grand Duke Friedrich of Baden, who was interested in a scheme to find the Ark of the Covenant. Baden wrote to his nephew, who in turn asked Philipp, Prince of Eulenburg, to report on the Zionist plan. Eulenburg, the Kaiser's best friend, ambassador to Vienna and political mastermind, was 'fascinated' by Herzl's pitch: Zionism was a way to extend German power. The Kaiser agreed that 'the energy, creativity and efficiency of the tribe of Shem would be diverted to worthier goals than the sucking dry of Christians'. Wilhelm, like most of the ruling class of that time, believed that the Jews possessed a mystical power over the workings of the world:

> Our dear God knows even better than we do that the Jews killed Our Saviour and he punished them accordingly. It shouldn't be forgotten that, considering the immense and extremely dangerous power which International Jewish capital represents, it would be a huge advantage to Germany if the Hebrews looked up to it in gratitude.

Here was the good news for Herzl: 'Everywhere the hydra of the ghastliest anti-Semitism is raising its dreadful head and the terrified Jews are looking around for a protector. Well then, I shall intercede with the Sultan.' Herzl was ecstatic: 'Wonderful, wonderful.'

On 11 October 1898, the Kaiser and Kaiserin embarked on the imperial train with a retinue including his foreign minister, twenty courtiers, two doctors and eighty maids, servants and bodyguards. Anxious to impress the world, he had personally designed a special white-grey uniform with a full-length white Crusader-style veil. On 13 October, Herzl, with four Zionist colleagues, set out from Vienna on the Orient Express, packing a wardrobe that included white tie and tails as well as pith-helmet and safari suit.

In Istanbul, Wilhelm finally received the Zionist, whom he judged to be 'an idealist with an aristocratic mentality, clever, very intelligent with expressive eyes'. The Kaiser said he supported Herzl because 'there are usurers at work. If these people went to settle in the colonies, they could be more useful.' Herzl protested at this calumny. The Kaiser inquired what he should ask the sultan for. 'A chartered company under German protection,' replied Herzl. The Kaiser invited Herzl to meet him in Jerusalem.

Herzl was impressed. The Hohenzollern personified imperial power with 'his great sea blue eyes, his fine serious face, frank, genial and yet bold', but the reality was different. Wilhelm was certainly intelligent, knowledgeable and energetic, but he was also so restless and inconsistent that even Eulenburg feared he was mentally ill. After sacking Prince Bismarck as chancellor, he took control of German politics, but he was too unstable to sustain it. His personal diplomacy was disastrous; his written notes to his ministers were so outrageous that they had to be locked in a safe; his alarmingly articulate speeches, in which he encouraged his troops to shoot German workers or to massacre enemies like Huns, were embarrassing.* Already by 1898, Wilhelm was regarded as half-buffoon, half-warmonger.

Nonetheless he proposed the Zionist plan to Abdul-Hamid. The sultan rejected it firmly, telling his daughter, 'The Jews may spare their millions. When my empire is divided, perhaps they will get Palestine for nothing. But only our corpse can be divided.' Meanwhile Wilhelm, dazzled by the vigour of Islam, lost interest in Herzl.

At 3 p.m. on 29 October 1898, the Kaiser rode through a breach specially opened in the wall next to the Jaffa Gate and entered Jerusalem on a white charger.

---

* Wilhelm's unpredictable behaviour frequently alarmed his own entourage. His early sex life with its outré tastes, including glove-wearing and sado-masochistic fetishes, had to be concealed. One courtier, a middle-aged Prussian general, died of a heart attack while dancing for the Kaiser in nothing but a tutu and feather-boa, and another entertained him dressed as a begging poodle 'in shaved tights with, under a real poodle-tail, a marked rectal opening. I can already see His Majesty laughing with us.' Ultimately his friend Eulenburg was destroyed in a sex scandal when his secret gay life was exposed. Yet Wilhelm was also a priggish Victorian when it came to the morals of others: he never spoke to Eulenburg again.

THE KAISER AND HERZL:
THE LAST CRUSADER AND THE FIRST ZIONIST

The Kaiser sported the white uniform with the full-length gold-threaded burnous veil sparkling in the sunlight, flowing from a spiked helmet surmounted with a burnished golden eagle, escorted by a cavalcade of giant Prussian hussars in steel helmets waving Crusader-style banners and the Sultan's lancers in red waistcoats, blue pantaloons and green turbans and armed with lances. The Kaiserin, in a patterned silk dress with a sash and a straw hat, followed on behind him in a carriage with her two ladies-in-waiting.

Herzl watched the Kaiser's performance from a hotel filled with German officers. The Kaiser had grasped that Jerusalem was the ideal stage on which to advertise his newly minted empire, but not everyone was impressed: the Dowager Russian Empress thought his performance 'revolting, perfectly ridiculous, disgusting!' The Kaiser was the first head of state to appoint an official photographer for a state visit. The Crusader uniform and the pack of photographers revealed what Eulenburg called the Kaiser's 'two totally different natures – the knightly, reminiscent of the finest days of the Middle Ages, and the modern'.

The crowds, reported the *New York Times*, were 'dressed in holiday clothes, the city men in white turbans, gaily striped tunics, the wives of Turkish army officers in gorgeous silken *milayes*, the well-to-do peasants in flowing kaftans of flaming red', while Bedouin on fine steeds 'wore large clumsy red boots, a leather girdle over a tunic filled with an arsenal of small arms' and a *keffiyeh*. Their sheikhs carried spears with a burst of ostrich feathers around the blade.

At the Jewish triumphal arch, the chief Sephardic rabbi, a bearded nonagenarian in white kaftan and blue turban, and his Ashkenazi counterpart presented Wilhelm with a copy of the Torah, and he was welcomed by the mayor, Yasin al-Khalidi, in a royal purple cloak and a gold-encircled turban. Wilhelm dismounted at David's Tower, and from there he and the empress walked into the city, the crowds cleared for fear of anarchist assassins (Empress

Elisabeth of Austria had recently been assassinated). As the patriarchs in the effulgence of their jewel-encrusted regalia showed him
the Sepulchre, the Kaiser's heart was beating 'faster and more
fervently' as he trod in Jesus' footsteps.

While Herzl waited for his summons and explored the city, the
Kaiser dedicated the Church of the Redeemer with its Romanesque
tower, a structure that he had personally designed 'with particular
care and love'. When he visited the Temple Mount, the Kaiser,
another enthusiastic archaeologist, asked the mufti to allow excavations, but the latter politely demurred.

On 2 November, Herzl was finally summoned for his imperial
audience – the five Zionists were so nervous that one of them
suggested taking bromide. Dressing appropriately in white tie,
tails and top hats, they arrived north of the Damascus Gate at
the Kaiser's encampment. This was a luxury Thomas Cook village
with 230 tents, which had been transported in 120 carriages,
borne by 1,300 horses, served by 100 coachmen, 600 drivers,
twelve cooks and sixty waiters, all guarded by an Ottoman
regiment. It was, said the tour maestro John Mason Cook, 'the
largest party gone to Jerusalem since the Crusades. We swept the
country of horses and carriages and almost of food.' *Punch*
mocked Wilhelm as 'Cook's Crusader'.

Herzl found the Kaiser posing 'in a grey colonial uniform, veiled
helmet, brown gloves and holding – oddly enough – a riding crop'.
The Zionist approached, 'halted and bowed. Wilhelm held out his
hand very affably' and then lectured him, declaring, 'The land needs
water and shade. There is room for all. The idea behind your
movement is a healthy one.' When Herzl explained that laying on
a water supply was feasible but expensive, the Kaiser replied, 'Well,
you have plenty of money, more money than all of us.' Herzl
proposed a modern Jerusalem, but the Kaiser then ended the
meeting, saying 'neither yes nor no'.

Ironically, both the Kaiser and Herzl loathed Jerusalem: 'a dismal
arid heap of stones,' wrote Wilhelm, 'spoilt by large quite modern
suburbs formed by Jewish colonies. 60,000 of these people are
there, greasy and squalid, cringing and abject, doing nothing but
trying to fleece their neighbours for every farthing – Shylocks by

the score.'* But he wrote to his cousin, Russian Emperor Nicholas II, that he despised the 'fetish adoration' of the Christians even more – 'in leaving the Holy City I felt profoundly ashamed before the Muslims'. Herzl almost agreed: 'When I remember you in days to come, O Jerusalem, it won't be with delight. The musty deposits of 2,000 years of inhumanity, intolerance and foulness lie in your reeking alleys.' The Western Wall, he thought, was pervaded by 'hideous, miserable, scrambling beggary'.

Instead Herzl dreamed that 'if Jerusalem is ever ours, I'd clear up everything not sacred, tear down the filthy ratholes,' preserving the Old City as a heritage site like Lourdes or Mecca. 'I'd build an airy comfortable properly sewered, brand new city around the Holy Places.' Herzl later decided that Jerusalem should be shared: 'We shall extra-territorialize Jerusalem so that it will belong to nobody and everybody, its Holy Places the joint possession of all Believers.'

As the Kaiser departed down the road to Damascus, where he declared himself the protector of Islam and endowed Saladin with a new tomb, Herzl saw the future in three burly Jewish porters in kaftans: 'If we can bring here 300,000 Jews like them, all of Israel will be ours.'

Yet Jerusalem was already very much the Jewish centre in Palestine: out of 45,300 inhabitants, 28,000 were now Jewish, a rise that was already worrying the Arab leadership. 'Who can contest the rights of the Jews to Palestine?' old Yusuf Khalidi told his friend Zadok Kahn, Chief Rabbi of France, in 1899. 'God knows, historically it is indeed your country' but 'the brute force of reality,' was that 'Palestine is now an integral part of the Ottoman Empire and, what is more serious, it is inhabited by other than Israelites.' While the letter predates the idea of a Palestinian nation – Khalidi was a Jerusalemite, an Arab, an Ottoman and ultimately a citizen of the world – and the necessity to deny the Jewish claim to Zion,

* The Kaiser's Teutonic gigantism changed the modern Jerusalem skyline. His Augusta Victoria Hospice, a German medieval fortress with a hideous tower so high that it was visible from the Jordan, dominated the Mount of Olives, and his Catholic Dormition Church, on Mount Zion, modelled outside on Worms Cathedral and inside on Charlemagne's chapel at Aachen, had 'massive towers more suited to the Rhine Valley'.

he foresaw that Jewish return, ancient and legitimate as it was, would clash with the ancient and legitimate presence of the Arabs.

In April 1903, the Kishinev pogrom, backed by the tsar's interior minister Viacheslav von Plehve, launched a spree of anti-Semitic slaughter and terror across Russia.* In panic, Herzl travelled to St Petersburg to negotiate with Plehve himself, the ultimate anti-Semite, but, getting nowhere with the Kaiser and the sultan, he started to look for a provisional territory outside the Holy Land.

Herzl needed a new backer: he proposed a Jewish homeland either in Cyprus or around El Arish in Sinai, part of British Egypt, both of them locations close to Palestine. In 1903, Natty, the first Lord Rothschild, who had finally come round to Zionism, introduced Herzl to Joseph Chamberlain, the British colonial secretary, who ruled out Cyprus but agreed to consider El Arish. Herzl hired a lawyer to draft a charter for the Jewish settlement. The lawyer was the forty-year-old Liberal politician David Lloyd George, whose decisions would later alter Jerusalem's fate more than those of anyone since Saladin. The application was turned down, much to Herzl's disappointment. Chamberlain and Prime Minister Arthur Balfour came up with another territory – they offered Uganda or rather part of Kenya as a Jewish homeland. Herzl, who was short of alternatives, provisionally accepted.

Regardless of his failed attempts to win over emperors and sultans, Herzl's Zionism had inspired the persecuted Jews of Russia, particularly a boy in a well-off lawyer's family in Płońsk. The eleven-year-old David Grün thought Herzl was the Messiah who would lead the Jews back to Israel.

---

* It was around this time that one of the tsar's top secret policemen, the Okhrana director in Paris, Piotr Rachkovsky, ordered the forging of a book claiming to be a secret record of Herzl's Congress in Basle in 1897: *The Protocols of the Elders of Zion* was adapted (and much of it lifted directly) from an 1864 French satire against Emperor Napoleon III and an 1868 anti-Semitic German novel by Hermann Goedsche. The *Protocols* was a preposterous though diabolical plan for Jews to infiltrate governments, churches and the media and incite wars and revolution, in order to create a world empire ruled by a Davidic autocrat. Published in 1903, it was designed to provoke anti-Semitism within Russia where tsardom was threatened by Jewish revolutionaries.

43

THE *OUD*-PLAYER OF JERUSALEM

1905–1914

DAVID GRÜN BECOMES DAVID BEN-GURION

David Grün's father was already a local leader of the Lovers of Zion, forerunner of the Zionist movement, and a keen Hebraist, so the boy was taught Hebrew from an early age. But David, like many other Zionists, was shocked when he read that Herzl had accepted the Ugandan offer. At the Sixth Zionist Congress, Herzl tried to sell his so-called Ugandaism but he succeeded only in splitting his movement. His rival, the English playwright Israel Zangwill, coiner of the phrase 'melting pot' to describe the assimilation of immigrants in America, decamped to found his Jewish Territorialist Organization and pursue an array of quixotic non-Palestinian Zions. The Austrian plutocrat Baron Maurice de Hirsch was financing Jewish colonies in Argentina, and the New York financier Jacob Schiff was promoting the Galveston Plan, a Lone Star Zion for Russian Jews in Texas. There was more support for El Arish because it was close to Palestine and Zionism was nothing without Zion, but none of these schemes* flourished and Herzl, exhausted by his peripatetic travels, died soon afterwards, aged just forty-four. He

---

* There would be at least thirty-four different plans in locations as diverse as Alaska, Angola, Libya, Iraq and South America. The plan for Alaska during the Second World War was satirized by Michael Chabon in his thriller, *The Yiddish Policeman's Union*. Politicians from Churchill and FDR to Hitler and Stalin pursued other plans: before attacking the Soviet Union in 1941, Hitler planned to deport the Jews to a death-colony in Madagascar. During the 1930s and 1940s, Churchill proposed a Jewish homeland in Libya while in 1945, his colonial secretary Lord Moyne suggested East Prussia for the Jews. As we will see, Stalin actually set up a Jewish homeland and during the 1940s considered a Jewish Crimea.

had successfully established Zionism as one of the solutions to the Jewish plight, particularly in Russia.

Young David Grün mourned his hero Herzl even though 'we concluded the most effective way to combat Ugandaism was by settling in the Land of Israel'. In 1905, Emperor Nicholas II faced a revolution that almost cost him the throne. Many of the revolutionaries were Jews – Leon Trotsky being the most prominent – yet they were actually internationalists who despised both race and religion. Nonetheless, Nicholas felt that the forged anti-Semitic tract, *The Protocols of the Elders of Zion*, was coming true: 'How prophetic!' he wrote, 'This year 1905 had been truly dominated by the Jewish Elders.' Forced to accept a constitution, he tried to restore his damaged autocracy by encouraging anti-Semitic massacres by nationalistic revanchists nicknamed the Black Hundreds.

The pogroms encouraged David Grün, a member of the socialist party Poalei Zion – Workers of Zion – to board one of the pilgrim ships from Odessa and set out for the Holy Land. The boy from Płońsk was typical of the Second Aliyah, a wave of secular pioneers, many of them socialist, who regarded Jerusalem as a nest of medieval superstition. In 1909, these settlers founded Tel Aviv on the sand dunes next to the ancient port of Jaffa; in 1911, they created a new collective farm – the first kibbutz – in the north.

Grün did not visit Jerusalem for many months after his arrival; instead he worked in the fields of Galilee, until, in mid-1910 the twenty-four-year-old moved to Jerusalem to write for a Zionist newspaper. Diminutive, skinny, curly-haired and always clad in a Russian *rubashka* smock to emphasize his socialist credentials, he adopted the nom de plume 'Ben-Gurion', borrowed from one of Simon bar Kochba's lieutenants. The old shirt and the new name revealed the two sides of the emerging Zionist leader.

Ben-Gurion believed, like most of his fellow Zionists at this time, that a socialist Jewish state would be created without violence and without dominating or displacing the Palestinian Arabs; rather it would exist alongside them. He was sure that the Jewish and Arab working classes would cooperate. After all, the Ottoman *vilayets* of Sidon and Damascus and the *sanjak* of Jerusalem – as Palestine was then known – were poverty-stricken backwaters, sparsely populated by the 600,000 Arabs. There was much space to be developed. The Zionists hoped the Arabs would share the economic benefits of Jewish immigration. But there was little mixing between the two and it did not occur to the Zionists that most of these Arabs had no wish for the benefits of their settlement.

In Jerusalem, Ben-Gurion rented a windowless cellar but he spent his time in the Arab cafés of the Old City listening to the gramophones that played the latest Arabic songs. At the same time, a Christian Arab boy, a native Jerusalemite already a connoisseur of beauty and pleasure, was listening to the same songs in the same cafés and learning to play them on his lute.

THE *OUD*-PLAYER: WASIF JAWHARIYYEH

Wasif Jawhariyyeh started to learn the lute – or *oud* – as a boy, and soon he was the best *oud*-player in a town that lived for music: it gave him access to everyone, high and low. Born in 1897, the son of a respected Greek Orthodox town councillor, close to the Families, he was too felinely artistic to develop into a local worthy. He was apprenticed as a barber but soon defied his parents to become a musician. Witnessing everything and knowing everybody, from the Jerusalemite grandees and Ottoman pashas to Egyptian chanteuses, hash-smoking musicians and promiscuous Jewesses, useful to the elite but not quite of it, Wasif Jawhariyyeh started to write a diary at the age of seven that is one of the masterpieces of Jerusalem's literature.*

When he began his diary, his father still rode to work on a white donkey, but he saw the first horseless conveyance, a Ford automobile driven by one of the American Colonists on the Jaffa Road; having been used to a life without electricity, soon he loved watching the new cinematograph in the Russian Compound ('entry fee was one Ottoman bishlik paid at the door').

Wasif revelled in the cultural mix. A Christian educated at the

---

* Ironically, while Westerners reread the superficial memoirs of European visitors, this superlative chronicle of the city, covering forty years up to the creation of Israel and beyond, is still published only in Arabic.

English public school of St George's, he studied the Koran and enjoyed picnics on the Temple Mount. Regarding Sephardic Jews as 'Yahud, awlad Arab' (Jews, son of Arabs), he dressed up for Jewish Purim and attended the annual Jewish Picnic at Simon the Just's tomb, where he sang Andalusian songs to *oud* and tambourine. At a typical gig, he played a Jewish version of a well-known Arab song to accompany an Ashkenazi choir in the house of a Jewish tailor in the Montefiore Quarter.

In 1908, Jerusalem celebrated the Young Turk Revolution which overthrew the tyrannical Abdul-Hamid and his secret police. The Young Turks – the Committee of Union and Progress – restored the 1876 Constitution and called parliamentary elections. In the excitement, Albert Antebi, a local businessman known to his fans as the Jewish Pasha and to his enemies as Little Herod, threw hundreds of free loaves to the delighted crowds at the Jaffa Gate. Children acted out the Young Turk coup in street plays.

The Arabs believed that at last they would be liberated from Ottoman despotism. The early Arab nationalists were unsure if they wanted a kingdom centred in Arabia or a Greater Syria, but already the Lebanese writer Najib Azouri had noticed how Arab and Jewish aspirations were developing simultaneously – and were bound to collide. Jerusalem elected the grandees Uthman al-Husseini and Yusuf Khalidi's nephew, Ruhi, a writer, politician and man of the world, as Members of Parliament. In Istanbul, Ruhi Khalidi became deputy speaker, using his position to campaign against Zionism and Jewish land purchases.

The ever-richer Families thrived. Their boys were educated with Wasif at the English St George's, the girls at the Husseini girls' school. Now women wore both Arab and Western fashions. The British school brought football to Jerusalem: there was a match every Saturday afternoon on a pitch outside Bab al-Sahra: the Husseini boys were especially keen players – some would play in their tarbushes. Before the Great War, Wasif was still a schoolboy, yet he was already living a Bohemian double life. He played his *oud* and served as trusted fixer and party-giver, perhaps even a subtle pimp for the Families, who now lived outside the walls in new mansions in Sheikh Jarrah. The grandees customarily rented an *odah* or garçonnière, a small apartment to play cards and keep their concubines, and they would let him have their spare keys. Wasif's patron, the mayor's son Hussein Effendi al-Husseini, kept the most lissom of the concubines, Persephone, a Greek-Albanian seamstress, in his *odah* off the Jaffa Road, whence this entrepreneurial temptress traded in cattle and sold her own brand of medicinal thyme oil. Persephone loved to sing and she was accompanied by young Wasif on the *oud*. When Husseini himself became mayor in 1909, he married off Persephone.

The mistresses of the grandees had traditionally been Jewish, Armenian or Greek, but now the thousands of Russian pilgrims became the richest resource for Jerusalem's hedonists. Wasif recorded that in the company of the future mayor Ragheb al-Nashashibi and Ismail al-Husseini he arranged secret parties 'for the Russian ladies'. It just happened that at this time an unusual Russian pilgrim to Jerusalem was complaining about the astonishing decadence and whoring in the city of his fellow countrymen. Arriving in March 1911, this sybaritic monk was the spiritual adviser and comfort of the Russian emperor and empress, whose haemophiliac son, Alexei, only he could heal.

RASPUTIN: THE RUSSIAN NUNS BEWARE

'I can't describe the joyful impressions, ink is useless as your soul joyfully sings "Let God rise from the dead",' wrote Grigory Rasputin, a forty-four-year-old Siberian peasant turned itinerant holy man. He had first come to Jerusalem in 1903 as an unknown pilgrim and still remembered the misery of the sea voyage from Odessa, 'stuffed in the hold like cattle, as many as 700 people at a time'. But Rasputin had risen in the world since then. This time, Nicholas II, who called Rasputin 'our friend', had sponsored his pilgrimage to remove him from St Petersburg and deflect the increasing criticism of this sacred sinner, who partied with prostitutes, exposed himself and urinated in restaurants. Now Rasputin stayed in style at the palatial residence of Jerusalem's Orthodox patriarch, but he counted himself a champion of the ordinary pilgrim, expressing 'the inexplicable joy' of Easter: 'It is all as it was: you see the people dressed the same as in [biblical] times, wearing the same coats and strange dress of the Old Testament. It makes me melt into tears.' Then there was the sex and drink, on which Rasputin was an expert.

By 1911, over 10,000 Russians, mostly unruly peasants, came for Easter, staying in the ever-expanding dormitories in the Russian Compound, praying in Grand Duke Sergei's Mary Magdalene and the new Alexander Nevsky next to the Church.* These visitors brought their nation into increasing disrepute: even in the early days their consul had described Bishop Cyril Naumov as 'an alcoholic and buffoon who surrounds himself with Arab comedians and women'. As for the pilgrims, 'Many of them live in Jerusalem in a manner that corresponds neither to the holiness of the place nor to the aim of their pilgrimage, falling prey to various temptations.'

As the numbers grew, the pilgrims, who indulged in fighting and drinking, became harder to control, and Rasputin revealed how much he hated the Catholics and Armenians, not to mention the Muslims. In 1893, the Russian bodyguard of a rich pilgrim shot and killed a Latin sacristan and three others when a Catholic asked him to make way in the Church.'The booze is everywhere and they drink it because it's cheap, mostly made by Athenian nuns,' explained Rasputin. Worse was the promiscuity: as we have seen, Russian pilgrims were easily procured by the grandees of Jerusalem for their parties, and some stayed behind as concubines. Rasputin knew what he was talking about when he warned:

Nuns mustn't travel there! Most of them earn their living away from the Holy City itself. Not to explain further, anyone who has been there understands how many mistakes are made by young

* Sergei himself, patron of the Russian presence, was long dead. In 1905, he finally resigned his post as governor-general of Moscow, but was blown to smithereens by terrorists within the Kremlin. His wife Ella rushed outside and crawled across the ground collecting the body parts of her husband, though only an armless chunk of torso and a fragment of the skull and jaw were identifiable. She visited his killer in prison before his execution. Afterwards she succeeded Sergei as president of the Palestine Society, which Nicholas II now personally supervised. But Ella fell out with her sister Empress Alexandra over the growing power of Rasputin. And tragically, she would return to Jerusalem (see footnote on p. 533).

brothers and sisters! It's very hard for the girls, they are forced to stay longer, the temptation is great, the enemy [Catholics? Muslims?] are tremendously envious. Many of them become concubines and women of the markets. It happens that they tell you 'we have our own sugar-daddy' and they add you to the list!*

The traffic in pleasure travelled both ways. Stephen Graham, the English journalist who accompanied the peasant pilgrims at roughly the same time as Rasputin was there, described how 'Arab women found their way into the hostelry in Holy Week despite the regulations and sold bottles of gin and cognac to the peasants. Jerusalem began to overflow with pilgrims and sightseers and also with mountebanks, showmen and hawkers, Montenegrin policemen, mounted Turkish gendarmes, pilgrims on asses, pilgrims on carts,' Englishmen and Americans, but 'the Holy City is delivered into the hand of Russians, Armenians, Bulgarians and Christian Arabs'.

Russian hucksters debauched the visitors. Philip, 'a tall peasant, broad-shouldered but fat, with a large dirty black-haired unshaven face, a bushy moustache that hung in a sensual sort of droop over thick red sluggish lips' was typical – 'a pander to the monks, a tout for ecclesiastical shopkeepers, a smuggler of goods, an immoralist and a trader in articles of religion' manufactured in a so-called Jew Factory. Fallen priests ended their Jerusalem days in 'drunkenness, religious hysteria and corpse-washing' – for many Russians died (happily) in Jerusalem. Meanwhile, just to add to this incendiary mix, Marxist propagandists preached revolution and atheism to the Russian peasants.

On the Palm Sunday of Graham's visit, as Turkish soldiers beat back the pilgrims, the crowds poured out of the Church to 'much

---

* On his return to Russia, Rasputin resumed his intimate role in the imperial family. He published *My Thoughts and Reflections: Brief Description of a Journey to the Holy Places* in the midst of the Great War in 1915 when Nicholas II was commanding the Russian army, leaving Alexandra, advised by Rasputin, as effective ruler of the home front – with disastrous consequences. He was illiterate; the book reads as if it had been dictated, and it was said that the empress herself corrected it. Designed to promote his image as a respectable pilgrim when he was at the height of his power and unpopularity, it was too late: he was assassinated shortly afterwards.

shrieking and skirling from the Orthodox Arabs, crying out in religious frenzy' until suddenly they were attacked by 'a band of redcapped Turks and beturbaned Muslims who made a loud whoop and struck their way with blows, threw themselves on the bearer of the olive branch and gained possession, broke the branch to bits and ran off. An American girl snapped her Kodak. The Christian Arabs swore vengeance.' Afterwards the Russians awaited the Second Coming of 'the great conqueror' at the Golden Gate. But the climax as ever was the Holy Fire: when the flame emerged, 'exalted easterners plunged sheaves of lighted candles into their bosoms, and cried out in joy and ecstasy. They sang as if under the influence of some extraordinary drug' with 'one guiding cry: *KYRIE ELEISON*: CHRIST IS RISEN!' But 'there was a regular stampede' that had to be suppressed with the whips and rifle butts.

That night Graham recorded how his companions – 'excited, feverish, and fluttering like so many children' – filled their bags with Jerusalem earth, Jordan water, palms, death shrouds, stereoscopes – 'and we kissed each other all over again!'

> What embracing and kissing there were this night; smacking of hearty lips and tangling of beards and whiskers. There commenced a day of uproarious festivity. The quantity of wine, cognac and arak [aniseed-flavoured liqueur] consumed would appal most English. And the drunken dancing would be rather foreign to Jesus!

That year, Easter coincided with Passover and Nabi Musa. While Rasputin policed the morals of the Orthodox sisterhood whom Wasif was busy debauching, an English aristocrat unleashed riots and made headlines across the world.

THE HON. CAPTAIN MONTY PARKER
AND THE ARK OF THE COVENANT

Monty Parker, a twenty-nine-year-old nobleman with a plumage of luxuriant moustaches and pointed Edward VII beard, expensive tastes and minimal income, was an opportunistic but credulous rogue, always on the lookout for an easy way to make his fortune – or at least find someone else to pay for his luxuries. In 1908, this Old Etonian son of a Cabinet minister in Gladstone's last government, younger brother of the Earl of Morley, ex-Grenadier Guards officer and veteran of the Boer War, encountered a Finnish hierophant who convinced him that together they could discover in Jerusalem the most valuable treasure of world history.

The Finn was Dr Valter Juvelius, a teacher, poet and spiritualist with a taste for dressing up in biblical robes and deciphering biblical codes. After working for years on the Book of Ezekiel, encouraged by séances with a Swedish psychic, Juvelius believed he had uncovered what he called 'The Cipher of Ezekiel'. This revealed that in 586 BC, when Nebuchadnezzar was about to destroy Jerusalem, the Jews had hidden what he dubbed 'the Temple Archive' – the Ark of the Covenant – in a tunnel south of the Temple Mount. But he needed a man of action who could also help him raise the funds required to find the Ark. Who better than a dim but energetic English aristocrat with the best connections in Edwardian London?

Juvelius showed his secret prospectus to Parker, who excitedly read this revelation:

> I now believe I have empirically proved the extremely ingenious deduction that the entrance to the Temple Archive is the Akeldama and that Temple Archive stands untouched in its hiding place. It ought to be a simple matter to produce the Archive of the Temple from its 2500 year old hiding-place. The existence of the Cipher proves the Temple Archive remains untouched.

Parker was convinced by this crank's closely argued thesis – even if it was scarcely more rational than the plot of *The Da Vinci Code*. At a time when even the Kaiser was attending séances and when many believed in the Jewish conspiracy, Juvelius had no trouble finding converts. As one of his adepts wrote to him, 'the Jews are a somewhat secretive race' – so naturally they had hidden the Ark rather well.

Parker had Juvelius' document translated from Finnish and bound in a glossy brochure. Then he told his pals, a disreputable crew of indebted aristocrats and military mountebanks,* about this astonishing opportunity to make a fortune: surely this cache would be worth $200 million? Parker was a glib salesman who soon attracted more investors than he could handle. British, Russian and Swedish aristocrats threw money at him, as did wealthy Americans such as Consuelo Vanderbilt, the Duchess of Marlborough. Parker's syndicate needed free access to the Temple Mount and the City of David, which he was convinced could be arranged 'by dint of liberal baksheesh!' In spring 1909, Parker, Juvelius and their Swedish bodyguard-cum-fixer Captain Hoffenstahl visited the sites in Jerusalem, then sailed for Istanbul where Monty, offering ministers 50 per cent of the treasure and cash up front, managed to corrupt much of the new Young Turk regime from the grand vizier down, signing a contract between Djavid Bey, the finance minister, and 'Honourable M. Parker of the Turf Club, London'.

The Sublime Porte advised Parker to hire an Armenian called Mr Macasadar as his fixer and sent two commissioners to supervise the dig. In August 1909 Captain Hoffenstahl collected the 'Cipher' from Juvelius then headed to meet Parker and his friends in Jerusalem, where they made their headquarters in the Kaiser's Augusta Victoria Fortress on the Mount of Olives and stayed at the Hotel Fast (the best in town). Monty and his friends behaved like a stag-party of hearty public-schoolboys, giving 'gay dinners' and holding shooting competitions using oranges for target-practice. 'One morning, we heard unusual noises,' remembered Bertha Spafford, the American Colonist, 'and saw the worthy archaeologists playing at being donkeyboys, running alongside the donkeys and imitating the yelling, usually made by Arab boys who were mounted in the Englishmen's place.' Parker's gang

* Parker's friends were Captain Clarence Wilson, Major Foley, who had participated in the Jameson Raid in Transvaal, the Hon. Cyril Ward, third son of the Earl of Dudley, Captain Robin Duff, cousin of the Duke of Fife, and Captain Hyde Villiers, cousin of the Earl of Jersey, along with the Scandinavians Count Herman Wrangel and a certain van Bourg, a mystic who irritated the group when he suggested that the treasure might actually be on Mount Ararat, not in Jerusalem at all.

bribed many of the potentates of Jerusalem, suborned the governor Azmey Pasha, hired a huge retinue of workers, guides, maids and bodyguards and started to excavate on the Ophel hill. This was and remains the archaeological fulcrum in the quest for ancient Jerusalem: here Charles Warren had dug in 1867. Later the American archaeologists Frederick Bliss and Archibald Dickie found more tunnels which together suggested that this was the site of King David's Jerusalem. Parker was guided spiritually from afar by Juvelius, and by another member of the expedition, the Irish 'thought-reader, Lee'. Even when he found nothing, Parker did not lose his faith in Juvelius.

Jerusalem's Jews, backed by Baron Edmond de Rothschild (who was himself financing a dig for the Ark of the Covenant), claimed that Parker was abusing sacred Jewish ground. Muslims too were anxious, but the Ottomans kept them at arm's length. To ease their suspicions, Parker hired the archaeological scholar Père Vincent of the Ecole Biblique to supervise his excavation – which did in fact find more evidence that this was the site of a very early settlement. Vincent was oblivious to the real purpose of the dig.

In late 1909, the rains halted Parker's work, but in 1910 he sailed back into Jaffa on Clarence Wilson's yacht, the *Water Lily*, and continued his excavations. The Arab workers went on strike several times. When the courts threatened to back the Arabs, Monty and his partners decided that only a dazzling display of British Trooping of the Colour pageantry would overawe the natives: they decided to confront the mayor (Wasif the *oud*-player's patron) 'in full uniform'. Captain Duff, wearing helmet, cuirass and the white gauntlets of the Life Guards, and Monty Parker in scarlet tunic and bearskin were, recalled Major Foley, 'the star turns. We created a sensation!'

When the strikers were dismissed, this farcical parade headed triumphantly through the Old City, led, in Foley's words, by 'a troop of Turkish lancers, then the Mayor and Commandant, some holy men, then Duff, Parker, me, Wilson, Macasadar and Turkish gendarmes in the rear.' Suddenly Duff's mule bolted through the bazaars with the captain hanging on until he was thrown into a shop and buried in peanuts, much to the hilarity of his friends. 'An old Jew', said Foley, 'thought it was the end of the world and started to wail in Yiddish.'

This display – or more likely 'liberal baksheesh' – worked for now. Parker meticulously sent secret reports to the syndicate, covertly named FJMPW after some of its members, and accounts for the bribes, which on his first visit cost £1,900. He spent £3,400 in the first year, and when he had to return in 1910 his accounts reveal 'Payments to Jerusalem officials: £5,667'. The mayor, Hussein Husseini, received £100 a month. These lavish bribes must have been a blessing for the Jerusalem grandees, but Parker realized that the Young Turk government was in flux and that Jerusalem was a sensitive place: 'The utmost caution must be used for the smallest mistake may involve serious difficulties!' he reported. Yet even he did not really understand that he was playing on a volcano. When he resumed digging in the spring of 1911, Parker paid out even more but he was now desperate: he decided to dig on the Temple Mount, bribing Sheikh Khalil al-Ansari, hereditary Custodian of the Haram, and his brother.

Parker and his gang, disguised in pantomime Arab garb, crept on to the Temple Mount and, in the precinct of the Dome itself, they broke open the pavement to dig into the secret tunnels beneath. However, on the night of 17 April, a Muslim nightwatchman, unable to sleep in his crowded home, decided to camp out on the Haram, where he surprised the English and ran into the streets, shouting that disguised Christians were digging up the Dome of the Rock.

The mufti turned back the entire Nabi Musa procession and denounced this wicked Ottoman and British conspiracy. A mob, reinforced by the pilgrims of Nabi Musa raced to defend the Noble Sanctuary. Captain Parker and his friends galloped for their lives to Jaffa. The crowd, which for the one and only time combined Muslims and Jews, both equally outraged, tried to lynch Sheikh Khalil and Macasadar whose lives were saved only when the Ottoman garrison intervened and arrested them. They and Parker's police guards were all imprisoned in Beirut. In Jaffa, Monty Parker just made it on board the *Water Lily*. But the police there were alerted that he might have the Ark of the Covenant about his person. They searched him and his baggage, but found no Ark. Parker knew he had to escape – so, bamboozling the Ottoman gendarmes by playing the English gentleman, he illuminated the *Water Lily* and announced that he was going 'to hold a reception on board for the Jaffa officials'. He then sailed away as they were about to board.

Back in Jerusalem, the crowds threatened to kill the governor and slaughter anyone British as rumours spread that Parker had stolen the Crown of Solomon, the Ark of the Covenant and the Sword of Muhammad. The governor was in hiding for fear of his life. By the morning of 19 April, the London *Times* reported, 'there was a tremendous row throughout the city. Shops closed, peasants bolting out of the place and rumours spreading'. The Christians were terrified that 'Mahomedan pilgrims from Nabi Musa' were coming 'to assassinate all Christians'. Simultaneously the Muslims were petrified that '8,000 Russian pilgrims were armed to massacre the Mahomedans'. All sides believed that 'the Solomonic regalia' had been 'transferred to Captain Parker's yacht'.

Europeans stayed indoors and locked their gates. 'The wrath of the people of Jerusalem was so great', remembered Bertha Spafford, 'that patrols were posted on every street.' Then on the last day of the Nabi Musa, with 10,000 Jerusalemites on the Temple Mount, the mob 'stampeded. A fearful panic ensued, peasant women and pilgrims pouring out of the walls and running toward the city gates crying "Massacre!" Every family armed itself and barricaded its home. The "Parker fiasco",' wrote Spafford, 'came nearer to causing anti-Christian riots and even massacre than anything that had happened during our long residence in Jerusalem.' The *New York Times* informed the world: 'Gone with Treasure that was Solomon's. English Party Vanishes on Yacht After Digging under Mosque of Omar: SAID TO HAVE FOUND KING'S CROWN. Turkish Government Sends High Officials to Jerusalem to Investigate!'

Monty Parker, who never grasped the gravity of all this, sailed back to Jaffa that autumn but was advised not to land 'or else there might be more trouble'. He told the syndicate that he would 'proceed to Beirut' to visit the prisoners. His plan was then to go on: 'To Jerusalem to quiet the press and get hold of the Notables to see a little bit of reason. Once all is quiet, get the Governor to write to the Grand Vizier and say it's safe for us to return!' Jerusalem never did 'see a little bit of reason' but Parker kept trying until 1914.*

There were diplomatic complaints between London and Istanbul, Jerusalem's governor was sacked, Parker's accomplices were tried but acquitted (because nothing had been stolen), the money was gone, the treasure chimerical, and the 'Parker fiasco' brought down the curtain on fifty years of European archaeology and imperialism.

---

* The full story of Parker is told here for the first time, based not only on his letters and accounts but also Juvelius' prophecies. Even in 1921, Parker's agents in Jerusalem were still suing him for unpaid fees. The Flashman-esque Parker skulked at headquarters and avoided the trenches in the Great War, never married but kept multiple mistresses, inherited the earldom of Morley and the stately home in 1951 and proudly told his family that he meant to spend every penny of his inheritance. Even in old age, he remained in the words of one of the family 'a vain, venal, unreliable blacksheep who left nothing, a namedropper and boaster'. He lived until 1962, but he never mentioned Jerusalem and there were no papers – until in 1975 the Parker lawyers found a file that they returned to the Sixth Earl of Morley. For many years, the papers were forgotten, but the earl and his brother Nigel Parker kindly made them available to this author. Juvelius, becoming a librarian in Vyborg, wrote a novel based on the story and died of cancer in 1922. This episode left little trace in Jerusalem, but in the tunnels of Ophel, now the site of Ronny Reich's excavation of those huge Canaanite towers, a small cave leads to an abandoned bucket that once belonged to Monty Parker.

44

WORLD WAR

1914–1916

JEMAL PASHA: THE TYRANT OF JERUSALEM

Parker's adventure had exposed the realities of the Young Turks'
rule over Jerusalem: they were no less venal and inept than their
predecessors, but they had raised Arab expectations of autonomy,
if not more. A nationalist newspaper, *Filastin*, was founded in
Jaffa to express this new consciousness. But soon it became
clear that the Young Turks remained a ruthless and secretive
organization with only a democratic façade. They were Turkish
nationalists who were determined to suppress not just Arab hopes
but even the teaching of Arabic. Arab nationalists started to found
secret clubs to plot for independence and even the Husseinis
and other scions joined them. Meanwhile the Zionist leaders
encouraged their new immigrants to create 'Jewish towns, particularly in Jerusalem, the head of the nation', and they now
bought the land for the future Hebrew University on Mount
Scopus. This alarmed the Families – even though the Husseinis
and other landowners such as the Sursocks of Lebanon were all
quietly selling land to the Zionists.

Ruhi Khalidi, French-speaking intellectual and now deputy
speaker of the Parliament in Istanbul, was an Ottoman liberal, not
an Arab nationalist. But he carefully studied Zionism, even writing
a book about it, and decided that it was a threat. In Parliament, he
tried to ban any Jewish land purchases in Palestine. The richest
scion of the Families, Ragheb al-Nashashibi, an elegant playboy,
ran for Parliament too, promising, 'I'll dedicate all my energies to
removing the danger awaiting us from Zionism.' The editor of

Filastin warned, 'If this state of affairs continues, the Zionists will gain mastery over our country.'*

On 23 January 1913, a thirty-one-year-old Young Turk officer, Ismail Enver, a veteran of the 1908 Revolution who had made his name fighting the Italians in Libya, burst into the Sublime Porte, shot the war minister and seized power. He and two comrades, Mehmet Talaat and Ahmet Jemal, formed the triumvirate of the Three Pashas. Enver won a small victory in the Second Balkan War which convinced him he was the Turkish Napoleon, destined to restore the empire. In 1914, he emerged as Ottoman strongman and war minister – and even married the sultan's niece. The Three Pashas believed that only the Turkization of the empire could stop the final rot. Their programme anticipated Fascism and the Holocaust in its barbarity, racism and warmongering.

On 28 June 1914, Serbian terrorists assassinated the Austrian heir Archduke Franz Ferdinand and the Great Powers staggered then stampeded into the First World War. Enver Pasha was eager to fight, pushing for a German alliance to provide the necessary military and financial backing. Kaiser Wilhelm, remembering his trip to the East, backed the Ottoman alliance. Enver appointed himself vice-generalissimo under his puppet sultan and entered the war by bombarding Russian ports from his newly supplied German battleships.

On 11 November, Sultan Mehmet V Rashid declared war on Britain, France and Russia – and in Jerusalem jihad was proclaimed in al-Aqsa. At first there was some enthusiasm for war. When the commander of the Ottoman troops in Palestine, the Bavarian general Baron Friedrich Kress von Kressenstein, arrived, the Jews of Jerusalem welcomed his units with a triumphal arch. The Germans assumed protection of the Jews from the British. Meanwhile Jerusalem awaited the arrival of her new master.

On 18 November Wasif Jawhariyyeh, the *oud*-player, still only seventeen years old, watched Ahmet Jemal, minister of the marine and one of the Three Pashas, drive into Jerusalem as effective dictator of Greater Syria and supreme commander of the Fourth

---

* Ruhi Khalidi died of typhoid later that year and many were convinced that he had been poisoned by the Young Turks.

Ottoman Army. Jemal set up his headquarters in the Augusta Victoria on the Mount of Olives. On 20 December, an elderly sheikh arrived at the Damascus Gate in a stately carriage bearing the Prophet's green banner from Mecca. His entrance into the city caused 'indescribable commotion' as 'an orderly and picturesque train of soldiers followed the flag through the Old City' as they sprinkled rosewater. The whole population of Jerusalem followed in his wake 'singing Allahu akhbar in the most beautiful parade I ever saw,' wrote Wasif Jawhariyyeh. Outside the Dome, Jemal declared jihad. 'Jubilation took possession,' agreed Kress von Kressenstein, 'of the entire population' – until the ancient Meccan sheikh suddenly died just before Christmas, an embarrassing augur for the Ottoman jihad.

Jemal, forty-five years old, squat and bearded, always protected by a camel-mounted squadron of guards, combined brutish, paranoid cruelty with charm, intelligence and grotesque buffoonery. A bon vivant with 'a weakness for pomp and circumstance', and for beautiful Jewesses, he had a sense both of his own greatness and of his own absurdity. While he terrorized Jerusalem, he liked to play poker, race horses through the Judaean hills, drink champagne and smoke cigars with his friend, Count Antonio de Ballobar, the Spanish consul. Ballobar, an elegant aristocrat in his late twenties, described the pasha as a *'sale type'* but *'bon garçon'* – a filthy type but a good boy. Bertha Spafford thought Jemal 'a strange man and one to be feared', but also 'a man of dual personality' capable of charm and kindness. Once, without anyone seeing, he gave a diamond-studded medal to a little girl whose parents found her with it when they returned home. One of his German officers, Franz von Papen, simply judged him 'an extremely intelligent Oriental despot'.

Jemal ruled his fiefdom almost independently: 'That man of limitless influence' relished his power, asking jovially: 'What are laws? I make them and unmake them!' The Three Pashas were rightly suspicious of Arab loyalty. Enjoying a cultural renaissance, a flowering of nationalistic aspirations, the Arabs hated the new Turkish chauvinism. Yet they formed 40 per cent of the Ottoman population, and many of the Ottoman regiments were entirely Arab.

Jemal's mission was to hold the Arab provinces and suppress any Arab – or for that matter Zionist – stirrings, using first menacing charm and then just menace.

Soon after arriving in the Holy City, he called in a delegation of Arabs suspected of nationalist beliefs. He studiously ignored them as they grew paler and paler. Finally he asked, 'Do you appreciate the gravity of your crimes?' He cut off their answer: 'SILENCE! Do you know the punishment? Execution! Execution!' He waited as they quaked, then added quietly: 'But I shall content myself with exiling you and your families to Anatolia.' When the terrified Arabs had trooped out, Jemal turned laughing to his adjutant: 'What can one do? That's how we get things done here.' When he needed new roads built, he told the engineer, 'If the road isn't finished in time, I shall have you executed *at the point when the last stones have been laid!*' He would sigh rather proudly: 'Everywhere there are people groaning because of me.'

As Jemal mustered his forces, commanded mainly by German officers, for his offensive against British Egypt, he found that Syria was seething with intrigue, and Jerusalem, 'a nest of spies'. The pasha's policy was simple: 'For Palestine, deportation; for Syria, terrorization; for the Hejaz, the army.' In Jerusalem his approach was to line up 'patriarchs, princes and sheikhs in rows, and to hang Notables and deputies'. As his secret police tracked down traitors, he deported anyone suspected of nationalist agitation. He commandeered Christian sites such as St Anne's Church and started to expel the Christian hierarchs while he prepared to attack Egypt.

The pasha paraded his 20,000 men through Jerusalem on the way to the front. 'We'll meet on the other side of the [Suez] Canal or in Heaven!' he boasted, but Count Ballobar noticed an Ottoman soldier pushing his water rations in a stolen pram, surely not the mark of a daunting military machine. Jemal, on the other hand, travelled with 'magnificent tents, hat stands, commodes'. On 1 February 1915, Jemal, moved by hearing his men singing 'The Red Flag Flies over Cairo', attacked the Canal with 12,000 troops; they were easily repelled. He claimed that the attack had only been a reconnaissance in force, but he failed again in the summer. Military defeat, Western blockade and Jemal's growing repression brought desperate suffering and wild hedonism to Jerusalem. It was not long before the killing started.

TERROR AND DEATH: JEMAL THE SLAUGHTERMAN

Within a month of Jemal's arrival, Wasif Jawhariyyeh saw the body of an Arab in a white cloak hanging from a tree outside the Jaffa Gate. On 30 March 1915, the pasha executed two Arab soldiers at the Damascus Gate as 'British spies', and then executed the Mufti of Gaza and his son, whose hanging at the Jaffa Gate was watched by a full crowd in respectful silence. Hangings were staged at the Damascus and Jaffa Gates after Friday prayers to ensure the largest audience. Soon the gates seemed to be permanently festooned with swaying cadavers, deliberately left for days on Jemal's orders. On one occasion, Wasif was horrified by the sadistic incompetence:

The hanging process was not studied scientifically or medically enough so that the victim stayed alive, suffering a lot and we watched but couldn't say or do anything. An officer ordered a soldier to climb up and hang on the victim but this extra weight made the victim's eyes bulge out of his face. This was the cruelty of Jemal Pasha. My heart cries out from the memory of this sight.

In August 1915, after uncovering evidence of Arab nationalist plots, 'I decided', wrote Jemal, 'to take ruthless action against the traitors.' He hanged fifteen prominent Arabs near Beirut (including a Nashashibi from Jerusalem), and then, in May 1916, another twenty-one in Damascus and Beirut, winning the soubriquet the Slaughterman. He joked to the Spaniard Ballobar that he could hang him too.

Jemal also suspected the Zionists of treason. Yet Ben-Gurion, sporting a tarboush, was recruiting Jewish soldiers for the Ottomans. Jemal had not quite given up on charm: in December 1915 he sponsored two unique meetings between the Husseinis and Zionist leaders including Ben-Gurion, to rally support for a joint homeland under the Ottomans. But afterwards, Jemal deported 500 foreign Jews, arrested Zionist leaders and banned their symbols. The deportations provoked uproar in the German and Austrian newspapers, whereupon Jemal called in the Zionists to warn against any sabotage: 'You can choose. I am prepared to deport you as was done with the Armenians. Anyone who lays a finger on a single orange, I shall execute. But if you want the second option, the entire Vienna and Berlin press must be silent!' Later, he ranted: 'I've no trust in your loyalty. Had you no conspiratorial designs you wouldn't have come to live here in this desolate land among Arabs who hate you. We deem Zionists deserving of hanging but I'm tired of hangings. [Instead] we'll disperse you around the Turkish state.'*

Ben-Gurion was deported, switching his hopes to the Allies. Arabs were conscripted into the army; Jews and Christians were forced into labour battalions to build roads, many of them perishing from hunger and exposure. Then came disease, insects and starvation. 'The locusts were thick as clouds,' remembered Wasif, mocking Jemal's attempts to solve the plague 'by ordering every person over 12 to bring 3 kilos of locust eggs', since this simply led to an absurd trade in locust eggs.

Wasif saw 'starvation spread all around the country', along with 'typhus, malaria, and many people died'. By 1918, the Jewish population of Jerusalem had fallen, from epidemic, starvation and deportation, by 20,000. Yet Wasif's voice, his *oud* and his ability to rustle up pretty guests for wild parties, were never more valued.

WAR AND SEX IN THE CITY: WASIF JAWHARIYYEH

Jemal, his officers and the Family grandees enjoyed a life of feverish pleasure while the Jerusalemites just struggled to survive the calamities of war. The poverty was such that young prostitutes, many of

* Jemal loathed Jewish nationalism or anything that threatened Turkish dominance but at the same time, he tried to court Jewish support: he offered Henry Morganthau, US ambassador to Istanbul, the chance to buy the Western Wall and repeated the offer to Jerusalem's Jews.

them war widows charging just two piastres a trick, patrolled the Old City. In May 1915, some teachers were sacked when they were found entertaining prostitutes during school hours. Women even sold their babies. 'Old men and women' – particularly the poor Hasidic Jews in Mea Shearim – 'were bloated with hunger. On their faces and all over their bodies, slime, filth, disease and sores.'

Wasif's every night was an adventure: 'I only went home to change my clothes, sleeping in a different house every night, my body totally exhausted from drinking and merrymaking. In the morning I'm picnicking with the Jerusalem Notable Families, next I'm holding an orgy with thugs and gangsters in the alleys of the Old City.' One night Wasif Jawhariyyeh found himself in a convoy of four limousines, containing the governor, his Jewish mistress from Salonica, various Ottoman beys and Family grandees includ- ing Mayor Hussein Husseini, being driven out to Artas near Beth- lehem for an 'international picnic' at the Latin monastery: 'It was a lovely day for everyone during the hard time when hunger and war were making people suffer. No one hung on ceremony, everyone drank wine, and the ladies were so beautiful that night, there was no time to eat and they all sang like one choir.'

The governor's Jewish mistress 'so adored Arabic music' that Wasif agreed to teach her the *oud*. He seems to have existed in a dizzy parade of orgies with his patrons, attended by 'the most beautiful Jewish women' and sometimes Russian girls trapped in Jerusalem by the war. Once, the Fourth Army quartermaster, Raushen Pasha, got 'so drunk that the beautiful Jewish women made him lose consciousness!'

Wasif did not need to work because the grandees, first Hussein Husseini and later Ragheb Nashashibi, arranged sinecures for him in the city administration. Husseini was head of the Red Crescent charity. As so often, charity was the shameless pretext for extrava- gance and social climbing: the 'attractive ladies' of Jerusalem were asked to dress up in fetchingly figure-hugging Ottoman military uniforms decorated with Red Crescents, a look that proved irre- sistible for the supremo Jemal: his mistress was Leah Tennenbaum, whom Wasif considered 'one of the most beautiful women in Pal- estine'. Sima al-Magribiyyah, another Jewess, became mistress of the garrison commander; an Englishwoman, Miss Cobb, serviced the governor.

Sometimes, the *oud*-player himself enjoyed a tidbit from high table. When he and his band were invited to play at a party in a Jewish house, he found a 'huge hall, and a group of [Ottoman] officers prowling around the ladies', who included a certain Miss Rachel. Suddenly the drunken Turks started to fight, shooting their pistols first at the lights and then at each other. The demi-mondaines and musicians ran for their lives. Wasif's beloved lute was broken but the pretty Miss Rachel pulled him into a cupboard that led through a hidden doorway into another house – 'she saved my life', and, perhaps just as joyously, 'I stayed the night with her.'

On 27 April 1915, the anniversary of Sultan Mehmet's succession, Jemal invited Ottoman and German commanders and the Jerusalemite grandees to staff headquarters in the commandeered Notre Dame outside the New Gate: fifty 'prostitutes' accompanied the Ottoman officers while the grandees brought their wives.

Even as Jerusalem deteriorated, Count Ballobar's dinner parties for Jemal remained banquets: the menu for one feast on 6 July 1916 included Turkish soup, fish, steak, meat pies and stuffed turkey, followed by ice cream, pineapple and fruit. While they ate, Jemal talked about girls, power and his new Jerusalem. He fancied himself a city planner and wanted to knock down the walls of Jerusalem and cut a boulevard through the Old City from the Jaffa Gate to the Temple Mount. Then he boasted that he had married the glamorous Leah Tennenbaum: 'Do you know I've married an Austrian Jewess?'* Jemal often turned up chez Ballobar without warning – and, as things got more desperate, the Spaniard used his influence to restrain the Slaughterman's despotism. At their feasts, Jemal would jovially tease Ballobar and the Greek consul that 'he would hang them across from the Holy Sepulchre' if Spain or Greece entered the war.

While Jemal oversaw this evanescent Jerusalem, his colleague,

---

* Leah Tennenbaum later married a Christian lawyer, Abcarius Bey, who built her a mansion, Villa Leah, in Talbieh; she was thirty years younger than him. She left him, but he rented the Villa Leah to the exiled Ethiopian emperor, Haile Selassie. Later the house belonged to Moshe Dayan.

Vice-Generalissimo Enver, lost 80,000 men in his inept Russian offensive. He and Talaat blamed their disasters on the Christian Armenians, who were systematically deported and killed. A million perished in a barbaric crime that would later encourage Hitler to begin the Holocaust: 'No one now remembers the Armenians,' he reflected. Jemal claimed to disapprove of this massacre. Certainly he allowed refugees to settle in Jerusalem, and the number of Armenians there doubled during the war.

There were secret negotiations with the British: Jemal told Ballobar that London wanted him to assassinate his colleague Talaat Pasha. At some point, Jemal secretly approached the Allies, offering to march on Istanbul, overthrow Enver, save the Armenians and become hereditary sultan himself: as the Allies did not take him seriously, Jemal fought on. He hanged twelve Arabs in Jerusalem, their bodies displayed around the walls, while Enver toured the east to emphasize his Islamic credentials, intimidate Arab dissidents and keep an eye on his colleague. Wasif watched the Ottoman strongman drive into Jerusalem with Jemal. After visiting the Dome, David's Tomb and the Church, and opening Jemal Pasha Street, Enver was entertained at the Fast Hotel by Mayor Hussein Husseini, accompanied by Jawhariyyeh who as usual arranged the party.

The two pashas set out for Mecca to see off any potential Arab rebellion. But Enver's *haj* could not save Arabia for the Ottomans.

45

ARAB REVOLT, BALFOUR DECLARATION

1916–17

LAWRENCE AND THE SHERIF OF MECCA

Just before the Great War began, a young princeling from Mecca, Abdullah ibn Hussein, on his way back from Istanbul, visited Field Marshal Lord Kitchener, the reigning British Agent in Cairo, to ask for military aid for his father.

Abdullah's father was Hussein, the Sherif of Sherifs and the Amir of Mecca, the grandest potentate in Arabia, a Hashemite in direct descent from the Prophet. The family were traditionally amirs of Mecca but the Ottoman sultan Abdul-Hamid had kept him in luxurious limbo in Istanbul for over fifteen years while appointing other members of the family. Then in 1908, the Young Turks, faced with a lack of other candidates, despatched him to Mecca (where his telephone number was Mecca 1). Faced with Enver Pasha's aggressive Turkish nationalism and the rivalry of the Saudis and other Arabian chieftains, Hussein wished to prepare for either war in Arabia or revolt against Istanbul.

Abdullah proudly showed Kitchener a flesh wound gained fighting a southern Arabian sheikh, and Kitchener revealed his scars from the Sudan. 'Your Lordship', the squat Arabian told the towering Kitchener, 'is a target that cannot be missed but, short as I am, a Bedouin hit me.' Despite Abdullah's charm, Kitchener refused to arm the Sherifians.

A few months later, the start of the Great War changed everything. Kitchener returned to London to serve as secretary of state for war – and to launch the steely-eyed recruiting poster that read 'Your Country Needs You' – but he remained Britain's pre-eminent

Eastern expert. When the Ottoman sultan-caliph declared jihad against the Allies, he remembered Hussein and proposed appointing him as Britain's own caliph to launch an Arab revolt. He ordered Cairo to contact the Sherif.

At first there was no reply. Then suddenly, in August 1915, Sherif Hussein offered to lead an Arab revolt – in return for certain promises. The British, confronting the failure of their Gallipoli expedition, designed to break the Western Front stalemate by knocking the Ottomans out of the war, and the disastrous encirclement of an army at Kut in Iraq, were afraid that Jemal Pasha would conquer Egypt unless he was restrained by Arab unrest. London therefore ordered Sir Henry McMahon, high commissioner in Egypt, to agree whatever necessary to keep the Arabs on side without promising anything that clashed with French and of course British ambitions.

Sherif Hussein, now over sixty, was described by no less an observer than Lawrence of Arabia as 'conceited to a degree, greedy and stupid' and 'pitifully unfit' to rule a state, but nonetheless 'such an old dear' and at this point the British badly needed his help. Guided by his canny second son Abdullah, he now demanded a Hashemite* empire of all of Arabia, Syria, Palestine and Iraq, an outrageously exorbitant gambit and an imperium on a scale that had not existed since the Abbasids. In return he would lead a revolt against the Ottomans not only in his native Arabia but also in Syria through the network of secret Arab nationalist societies such as al-Fatat and al-Ahd. None of this was quite true: he commanded only a few thousand warriors and did not even rule all of the Hejaz. Much of Arabia was controlled by rival chieftains like the Saudis and his position was precarious. The secret societies were tiny, with just a few hundred active members between them, and would soon be decimated by Jemal.

McMahon was unsure how much to concede to these 'tragi-comic pretensions', but, while he agonized, Hussein

---

* They took the name of the dynasty from Hashem, great-grandfather of the Prophet. They were descended from Muhammad through his daughter Fatima and grandson Hassan, hence their title of sherif. They called themselves the Hashemites, the British called them the Sherifians.

simultaneously offered the Three Pashas the chance to outbid the British, asking for hereditary possession of the Hejaz and an end to Jemal's terror. The sherif sent his third son Faisal to negotiate with Jemal, but the tyrant forced him to attend the hangings of Arab nationalists.

The sherif had much more success with the British. London's Eastern experts based in Cairo knew the contours of Palestine intimately through the espionage archaeology of the last century and Kitchener himself had photographed Jerusalem and mapped the country, sometimes in full Arab disguise. But many understood the clubs of Cairo better than the souks of Damascus: they were patronizing about the Arabs and prejudiced against the Jews whom they saw as behind every enemy conspiracy. While London ran one policy, negotiating with the sherif, the British viceroy of India ran his own quite different policy, backing the sherif's enemy, the Saudis. Britain's often amateurish experts found themselves living the real version of John Buchan's novel *Greenmantle*, adrift on the subtle, treacherous currents of Arab politics in the vast Ottoman sea.

Fortunately, McMahon had one officer who really did know Syria. The twenty-eight-year-old T. E. Lawrence, described by his fellow Arabist Gertrude Bell as 'exceedingly intelligent', was an eccentric outsider who hailed from the ambiguous heart of the British establishment and never quite reconciled his tormented allegiances to his two flawed masters – the empire and the Arabs. He was illegitimate: his father was Thomas Chapman, heir to a baronetcy who had left his wife to raise a new family with his mistress Sarah Lawrence and adopted her surname.

'As a boy, TE always thought he was going to do great things, both active and reflective and determined to achieve both.' He trained himself to improve his powers of physical endurance while writing his Oxford thesis on Crusader fortresses. Afterwards, he perfected his Arabic by travelling throughout Syria, and worked as an archaeologist at Hittite sites in Iraq, where his young Arab assistant Dahoum became his companion and perhaps the guiding passion of his life. His sexuality, like so much else about him, remains mysterious, but he mocked 'our comic reproductive processes' and his friend Ronald Storrs said, 'He was not a mis-ogynist though he'd have kept his composure if he'd suddenly been informed he'd never see a woman again.' While in Iraq, he planned a book of 'adventures' on Jerusalem and six other Arab cities which he would call *The Seven Pillars of Wisdom* after a verse in Proverbs. He never published this, but he later used the title for another book.

'A rather short, strongly built man with sandy complexion, a typical English face bronzed by the desert, remarkable blue eyes,' as an American later described him, Lawrence stood 5 foot 5 inches – Gertrude Bell called him the Imp. 'My brain', he wrote, 'was quick and silent as a wild cat.' Super-sensitive to every human nuance, superb writer and keen observer, and abruptly rude to those he disliked, he suffered from 'a craving to be famous', he admitted, 'and a horror of being known to like being known'. He did it all for 'egotistical curiosity'. This believer in chivalry and justice was also a serpentine intriguer and self-mythologizer with what the journalist Lowell Thomas called 'a genius for backing into the limelight'. Vanity competed with masochism: 'I like the things underneath me and took my pleasures and adventures downwards. There seemed a certainty in degradation.'

Now in Cairo, McMahon turned to this junior officer who became 'a moving spirit in the negotiations with the sherif'. As Lawrence wrote his reports, he always found himself 'thinking of Saladin and Abu Ubayda', but he shared the view of many British Arabists that the desert Arabs were pure and noble – unlike those of Palestine. While he defined Damascus, Aleppo, Homs and Hama as the Arab heartland of Syria, he did not recognize Jerusalem as really Arab – she was a 'squalid town', whose people, he wrote, 'were characterless as hotel servants, living on the crowd of visitors passing through. Questions of Arabs and their nationality are as far from them as bimetallism from the life of Texas.' Such places as Jerusalem or Beirut were 'shop-soiled – as representative of Syria as Soho of the Home Counties'.

On 24 October 1915, McMahon replied to Hussein. Laced with deliberate vagueness, the reply was designed to be read differently by both parties. McMahon agreed to Hussein's empire, east of the Syrian cities specified by Lawrence, but excluded the fuzzy area to the west. Palestine was not mentioned and nor was Jerusalem. The sherif would be unlikely to accept Jerusalem's exclusion but the British had their own interests there, so not mentioning the city sidestepped the problem. Besides, McMahon insisted that all French interests were excluded – and France had ancient claims on Jerusalem too. In fact, the high commissioner planned to place Jerusalem nominally under the Albanian dynasty of Egypt so that the Holy City would be Muslim but under British control.

Britain needed the Arab Revolt immediately so it made the necessary promises as unclearly as possible. Yet McMahon's promises were not ambiguous enough, for they raised Arab expectations just before Britain and France began the real negotiation to divide up the Ottoman empire.

The British negotiator, Sir Mark Sykes, MP and Yorkshire baronet, was a creative and irrepressible amateur who had travelled in the East and therefore become a towering expert – though Lawrence called him 'a bundle of prejudices, intuitions and half-sciences'. His real talent was an ambitious ebullience that was so attractive that his superiors happily allowed him to dabble in any eastern policies he chose. Sykes and his French counterpart, François Georges-Picot, who had served as consul in Beirut, agreed that France would receive Syria and Lebanon, Britain, Iraq and some of Palestine. There would be an Arab confederation, under British and French supervision – and Jerusalem would be internationalized under France, Britain and Russia.* This all made sense to the three empires that had been striving to control Jerusalem for the last seventy years – and it allowed for an Arab state of sorts. But it was soon outdated because Britain secretly coveted Jerusalem and Palestine for itself.

On 5 June 1916, Sherif Hussein, oblivious to the secret of Sykes–Picot but aware that the Ottomans were about to overthrow him, raised his red banner in Mecca and launched his Arab Revolt. He declared himself 'King of All the Arabs', a title that alarmed the British, who persuaded him to downgrade it to 'King of Hejaz'. This

---

* At first Sykes had considered giving Jerusalem to Russia whose pilgrims had dominated the city until the war. Russia had already been promised Istanbul to which Sykes–Picot added swathes of eastern Anatolia, Armenia and Kurdistan.

was just the beginning: few families in history would wear so many crowns in so many kingdoms in such a short time. King Hussein appointed each of his sons to command his small armies but the military results were disappointing and revolts in Syria never materialized. The British found it hard to work out whether the Sherifians could ever be effective. So, in October, Ronald Storrs, who would later govern Jerusalem, and his subordinate, Lawrence, arrived in Arabia.

LAWRENCE OF ARABIA: THE SHERIFIANS – ABDULLAH AND FAISAL

Lawrence had a good look at the king's four sons in order to find the ideal Arab ruler, but he quickly realized that the second and third, Abdullah and Faisal, were the only ones that mattered. He dismissed Abdullah as 'too clever' and Abdullah dismissed Lawrence as 'a strange creature', but the moment Lawrence set eyes upon Prince Faisal, he almost swooned: 'tall, graceful, vigorous, almost regal. Aged thirty-one, very quick and restless. Is clear-skinned as a pure Circassian, with dark hair, vivid black eyes. Looks like a European and very like the monument of Richard I at Fontevraud. A popular idol.' Lawrence gushed that he was 'an absolute ripper!' but Faisal was also 'a brave, weak, ignorant spirit – I served him out of pity'.

The Arab Revolt was failing even in the Sherifian fiefdom of Hejaz and Lawrence saw that Faisal's few thousand cameleers could be defeated by 'one company of Turks'. Yet if they raided outposts and sabotaged the railways, they could tie down an entire Ottoman army. When he was posted to Faisal, Lawrence put this into practice and created the prototype of the modern insurgency. But it was Faisal who dressed the Lawrence of legend, 'fitting me out in splendid, white silk and gold-embroidered wedding garments'. As he wrote in his guide to Arab insurgency – required reading for American officers in twenty-first-century Iraq and Afghanistan – 'If you wear Arab things, wear the best. Dress like a sherif.' Lawrence had no military training and the spirit of an ascetic poet, but he understood that 'the beginning and end of the secret of handling Arabs is unremitting study of them. Get to know their families, clans and tribes, friends and enemies by listening and indirect inquiry.' He learned to ride camels and to live like a Bedouin. But he never forgot that doling out vast sums of British gold was what kept his army together – 'this is the fattest time the tribes have ever known' – and even fifty years later they remembered him as 'the man with the gold'.

The slaughter and grit of war both horrified and excited him. 'I hope this sounds the fun it is,' he wrote feverishly after one successful raid. 'It's the most amateurish, Buffalo-Bill sort of performance and the only people who did it well are the Bedouin.' When one of his men murdered another, Lawrence had to execute the murderer himself, to avoid a blood feud. After a slaughter of Turks, he hoped 'this nightmare ends when I'll wake up and become alive again. This killing and killing of Turks is horrible.'

Lawrence knew the secret of the Sykes–Picot carve-up of the Middle East and it shamed him: 'We are calling them to fight for us on a lie and I can't stand it.' There were times he risked his life in a fit of despair, 'hoping to get killed on the way'. He described himself as 'strongly pro-British and pro-Arab', but he despised imperial conquest, preferring an independent Arabia as a dominion – but under British protection. 'I presumed I would survive and be able to defeat not merely the Turk on the battlefield but my own country and its allies in the council-chamber.'

Lawrence confided the secret of Sykes–Picot to Faisal together with his plan to remedy it. If they were to avoid a French Syria, they had to liberate it themselves and they had to begin with a spectacular piece of military élan that would earn the Arabs the right to Syria: Lawrence led Faisal's forces on a circular 300-mile escapade through the punishing Jordanian desert to seize the port of Aqaba.

FALKENHAYN TAKES COMMAND: GERMAN JERUSALEM

After Jemal's third offensive against Egypt had failed, the British counter-attacked across Sinai. In spring 1917, they were twice severely defeated at Gaza by 16,000 Germans backed by Austro-Hungarian artillery. Jemal realized that they would attack again. Palestine now seethed with anti-Ottoman intrigue. The pasha's secret police uncovered a pro-British Jewish spy-ring, NILI, whose members were tortured – their nails ripped out, their skulls squeezed in vices until they cracked – and then hanged. In Jerusalem, Jemal's police were hunting down another Jewish spy, Alter Levine, a poet, businessman and fixer born in Russia, whom they claimed had set up a chain of brothels-cum-spy-nests. Levine turned up at the house of his friend, Khalil Sakakini, the respected teacher, in Jerusalem, who agreed to protect him. The Zionist spy-rings outraged the Slaughterman, who in April summoned the foreign consuls to a menacing soliloquy at the Augusta Victoria Fortress: he threatened to deport the entire population of Jerusalem – and after the dystopic Armenian 'deportations', that would mean the death of thousands.

'We'll find ourselves compelled to fight for Jerusalem,' Jemal told Enver. They invited Field Marshal Erich von Falkenhayn, the former German Chief of Staff who had commanded the Verdun offensive, to come to Jerusalem and advise on how to defeat the British. But Enver went over Jemal's head and placed the German in supreme command. 'Falkenhayn's Verdun was disastrous for Germany', Jemal warned Enver, 'and his Palestinian offensive will be disastrous for us.'

In June 1917, a crestfallen Jemal met Falkenhayn at Jerusalem station and they posed awkwardly together on the steps of the Dome of the Rock. Falkenhayn set up his headquarters in the kaiserine Augusta Victoria. The cafés of the city were filled with German soldiers of the Asienkorps and their officers took over the Fast Hotel. 'We were in the Holy Land,' wrote a typical young German soldier in the city, Rudolf Hoess.* 'The old familiar names from

---

* Hoess, the future SS Commandant of Auschwitz, where millions of Jews were gassed and cremated during the Holocaust, was considering a career in the Catholic priesthood. Jerusalem 'played a decisive part in my subsequent renunciation of my faith. As a devout Catholic, I was disgusted by the cynical manner in which trade in allegedly holy relics was carried on by the representatives of the many churches there.' Wounded in the knee and awarded the Iron Cross, Hoess, who 'shunned all demonstrations of affection', was seduced in Jerusalem by one of his German

religious history and the stories of the saints were all around us. And how different from my youthful dreams!' Austrian troops marched through the city; Jewish Austrian soldiers prayed at the Western Wall. Jemal Pasha left the city and governed his provinces from Damascus. The Kaiser finally controlled Jerusalem – but it was too late.

On 28 June, Sir Edmund Allenby arrived in Cairo as the new British commander. Just a week later, Lawrence and the Sherifians seized Aqaba. It took him just four days, riding camels, trains and ships, to reach Cairo and report his triumph to Allenby, who, despite being a bluffly conventional cavalryman, was immediately impressed by this gaunt Englishman dressed in Bedouin robes. Allenby ordered Lawrence and his Sherifian Camel Corps to serve as the maverick right wing of his army.

In Jerusalem, British aeroplanes bombed the Mount of Olives. Falkenhayn's adjutant, Colonel Franz von Papen, arranged the defences and planned to counter-attack. The Germans underestimated Allenby and they were taken by surprise when on 31 October 1917, he launched his offensive to capture Jerusalem.

LLOYD GEORGE, BALFOUR AND WEIZMANN

As Allenby massed his 75,000 infantry, 17,000 cavalry and a handful of new tanks, Arthur Balfour, the British foreign secretary, was negotiating a new policy with a Russian-born scientist named Dr Chaim Weizmann. It is a remarkable story: a Russian immigrant, wandering around Whitehall and dropping into the offices of the most powerful statesmen in the world for romantic conversations on ancient Israel and the Bible, managed to win the backing of the British empire for a policy that would change

---

nurses: 'I fell under the magic spell of love.' He was hanged in April 1947. By coincidence an 'obstreperous' young German boy, helping the American Colony with its Casualty Clearing Station near the Notre Dame, was the son of the German Vice Consul: Rudolf Hess was the future deputy Führer of Nazi Germany, who flew to Scotland on an insane peace mission in 1941 and spent the rest of his life as a prisoner.

Jerusalem as radically as any decision by Constantine or Saladin and define the Middle East to this day.

They had first met ten years earlier but their relationship was an unlikely one. Balfour was nicknamed Niminy Piminy and Pretty Fanny for his rosy cheeks and willowy limbs, but also Bloody Balfour for his harshness when chief secretary for Ireland. He was the scion of both Scottish mercantile wealth and English aristocracy – his mother being the sister of the Victorian prime minister, Robert Cecil, Marquess of Salisbury. He had accompanied his uncle and Disraeli to the Congress of Berlin in 1878 and when he succeeded Salisbury in 1902, wits coined the expression 'Bob's your uncle!' A philosopher, poetaster and enthusiastic tennis-player, he was a foppish romantic who never married and a frivolous improviser whose favourite expression was 'nothing matters much and very little matters at all'. David Lloyd George mused scathingly that history would remember Balfour 'like the scent on a pocket-handkerchief' while, in fact, he is most definitely remembered for his relationship with Weizmann and the Declaration that bears his name.

The two could not have come from more alien worlds. Weizmann was a timber merchant's son from a tiny Jewish village near Pinsk who had embraced Zionism as a boy and escaped Russia to study science in Germany and Switzerland. When he was thirty, he moved to Manchester to teach chemistry at the university.

Weizmann was simultaneously 'Bohemian and aristocratic, patriarchal and sardonic, with the caustic and self-mocking wit of a Russian intellectual'. He 'was one of nature's aristocrats who was at home with kings and prime ministers' and managed to win the respect of men as different as Churchill, Lawrence and President Truman. His wife Vera, being the daughter of one of the few Jewish officers in the tsarist army, regarded most Russian Jews as plebeian, preferred the company of English nobility and made sure her 'Chaimchik' dressed like an Edwardian gentleman. Weizmann, this passionate Zionist, hater of tsarist Russia and despiser of anti-Zionist Jews, resembled 'a well-nourished Lenin' and was sometimes mistaken for him. A 'brilliant talker', his perfect English was always spiced with a Russian accent and his 'almost feminine charm

[was] combined with feline deadliness of attack, burning enthu-siasm and prophetic vision'.

The Old Etonian and the graduate of Pinsk *chever* first met in 1906. Their chat was short but unforgettable. 'I remember Balfour sat in his usual pose, legs stretched out, an imperturbable expres-sion.' It was Balfour, who as prime minister in 1903, had offered Uganda to the Zionists, but now he was out of power. Weizmann feared that his languid interest was just 'a mask', so he explained that if Moses had heard about Ugandaism 'he would surely have broken the tablets again'. Balfour appeared bemused.

'Mr Balfour, supposing I were to offer you Paris instead of London, would you take it?'

'But, Dr Weizmann, we have London,' said Balfour.

'True, but we had Jerusalem', replied Weizmann, 'when London was a marsh.'

'Are there many Jews who think like you?'

'I speak the mind of millions of Jews.'

Balfour was impressed but added, 'Curious. The Jews I meet are quite different.'

'Mr Balfour,' answered Weizmann, who knew that most Anglo-Jewish grandees scorned Zionism, 'you meet the wrong kind of Jews.'

This conversation led nowhere, but Weizmann had met his first imperial statesman. Balfour lost the general election and spent years out of power. Meanwhile, Weizmann campaigned to build a Hebrew university in Jerusalem, which he visited for the first time shortly after meeting Balfour. The dynamic Zionist farms in Pal-estine thrilled him, but Weizmann was horrified by Jerusalem, 'a city living on charity, a miserable ghetto', where 'we hadn't a single decent building – all the world had a foothold in Jerusalem except the Jews. It depressed me and I left the city before nightfall.' Back in Manchester, Weizmann made his name as a chemist and became friends with C. P. Scott, editor – proprietor of the *Manchester Guardian*, a pro-Zionist who himself resembled a biblical prophet. 'Now Dr Weizmann,' Scott said in 1914, 'tell me what you want me to do for you.'

At the start of the Great War, Weizmann was summoned to the

Admiralty by the First Lord, 'the brisk, fascinating, charming and energetic' Winston Churchill, who said: 'Well, Dr Weizmann, we need 30,000 tons of acetone.' Weizmann had discovered a new formula to manufacture acetone, the solvent used in the making of cordite explosives. 'Can you make it?' asked Churchill. Weizmann could and did.

A few months later, in December 1914, C. P. Scott took Weizmann to a breakfast with Lloyd George, who was then chancellor of the exchequer, and his colleague Herbert Samuel. Weizmann noted how the ministers discussed the war with a flippant humour that concealed their deadly seriousness, but 'I was terribly shy and suffered from suppressed excitement'. Weizmann was amazed to discover that the politicians were sympathetic to Zionism. Lloyd George admitted, 'When Dr Weizmann was talking of Palestine, he kept bringing up place-names more familiar to me than those on the Western Front,' and he offered to introduce him to Balfour – not realizing they had already met. Weizmann was wary of Samuel – an Anglo-Jewish banking scion related to the Rothschilds and Montefiores, and the first practising Jew to serve in a British cabinet – until he revealed that he was preparing a memorandum on the Jewish Return.

In January 1915, Samuel delivered his memorandum to the prime minister, Herbert Asquith: 'There is already a stirring among the twelve million scattered,' wrote Samuel. '[There is] widespread sympathy with the idea of restoring the Hebrew people to their land.' Asquith mocked the idea that the Jews 'could swarm back' and sneered 'what an attractive community' they would be. As for Samuel, his memorandum 'reads like a new edition of *Tancred*.* I'm not attracted by the proposal but it is a curious illustration of Dizzy's favourite maxim that "race is everything" to find this almost lyrical outburst proceeding from the well-ordered and methodical brain of HS.' Asquith was even more surprised to discover that 'curiously enough, the only other partisan of this proposal is Lloyd George and he doesn't give a damn for the Jews but thinks it will be an outrage to let the Holy Places pass into the possession of

* In one of Disraeli's most popular novels, *Tancred*, a duke's son travels to Jerusalem where a Jew says, prophetically, 'The English will take this city; they will keep it.'

"agnostic and atheistic" France.' Asquith was right that Lloyd George wanted Jerusalem for Britain but wrong about his attitude to the Jews.

Lloyd George, a blue-eyed Welsh Baptist schoolmaster's son and reckless womanizer whose shock of raffishly long white hair made him more resemble an artist than a statesman, cared greatly about the Jews, and had represented the Zionists as a lawyer ten years earlier. 'I was taught more in school about the history of the Jews than about my own land,' said this silver-tongued orator and intuitive showman who had started as a radical reformer, anti-imperial pacifist and persecutor of dukes. Once the Great War had started, he mutated into a vigorous war minister and romantic imperialist, influenced by the Greek classics and the Bible.

Lloyd George reintroduced Weizmann to Balfour. 'Weizmann needs no introduction,' scribbled Balfour. 'I still remember our conversation in 1906.' He greeted the Zionist with, 'Well, you haven't changed much,' and then mused, almost misty-eyed, 'You know, when the guns stop firing, you may get your Jerusalem. It's a great cause you're working for. You must come again and again.' They started to meet regularly, strolling around Whitehall by night and discussing how a Jewish homeland would serve, by the quirks of fate, the interests of historical justice and British power.

Science and Zionism overlapped even more because Balfour was now First Lord of the Admiralty and Lloyd George was minister of munitions, the two portfolios most concerned with Weizmann's work on explosives. He found himself 'caught up in a maze of personal relations' with the panjandrums of the world's most expansive empire, prompting him to reflect on his humble background: 'starting with nothing, I, Chaim Weizmann, a Yid from Motelle and only an almost professor at a provincial university!' To the panjandrums themselves, he was what they thought a Jew should be: 'Just like an Old Testament prophet,' Churchill later remarked, though one dressed in a frock-coat and top hat. In his memoirs, Lloyd George frivolously claimed that his gratitude for Weizmann's war work led to his support for the Jews, but actually there was strong Cabinet backing much earlier.

Once again, the Bible, Jerusalem's book, influenced the city over two millennia after it was written. 'Britain was a Biblical nation,' wrote Weizmann. 'Those British statesmen of the old school were genuinely religious. They understood as a reality the concept of the Return. It appealed to their tradition and their faith.' Along with America, 'Bible-reading and Bible-thinking England,' noted one of Lloyd George's aides, 'was the only country where the desire of the Jews to return to their ancient homeland' was regarded 'as a natural aspiration not to be denied.'

There was something more lurking in their attitude to the Jews: the British leaders were genuinely sympathetic to the plight of the Russian Jews, and tsarist repression had intensified during the war. The European upper classes had been dazzled by the fabulous wealth, exotic power and sumptuous palaces of Jewish plutocrats such as the Rothschilds. However this had confused them too, for they could not decide if the Jews were a noble race of persecuted biblical heroes, every one of them a King David and a Maccabee, or a sinister conspiracy of mystically brilliant, hook-nosed hobbits with almost supernatural powers. In an age of uninhibited theories of racial superiority, Balfour was convinced Jews were 'the most gifted race mankind has known since fifth century BC Greece' and Churchill thought them 'the most formidable and gifted race', yet simultaneously he called them a 'mystic and mysterious race chosen for the supreme manifestations both of the divine and the diabolical'. Lloyd George privately criticized Herbert Samuel for having 'the worst characteristics of his race'. Yet all three were genuine philo-Semites. Weizmann appreciated that the line between racist conspiracy-theory and Christian Hebraism was a thin one: 'we hate equally anti-Semitism and philo-Semitism. Both are degrading.'

Yet timing is everything in politics. In December 1916, Asquith's government fell, Lloyd George became prime minister, and he appointed Balfour as foreign secretary. Lloyd George was described as the 'greatest warleader since Chatham' and he and Balfour would do whatever was necessary to win the war. At this vital moment in a long and terrible struggle against Germany, their peculiar attitudes to the Jews and the special concatenation of circumstances of

1917 merged to convince Lloyd George and Balfour that Zionism was essential to help Britain achieve victory.

'IT'S A BOY, DR WEIZMANN': THE DECLARATION

In the spring of 1917, America entered the war and the Russian Revolution overthrew Emperor Nicholas II. 'It's clear Her Majesty's Government were mainly concerned how Russia was to be kept in the ranks of the Allies,' explained one of the key British officials, and as for America, 'it was supposed American opinion might be favourably influenced if the return of the Jews to Palestine became a purpose of British policy'. Balfour, about to visit America, told his colleagues that 'the vast majority of Jews in Russia and America now appear favourable to Zionism.' If Britain could make a pro-Zionist declaration, 'we should be able to carry on extremely useful propaganda both in Russia and America'.

If Russia and America were not urgent enough, the British learned that the Germans were considering a Zionist declaration of their own: after all, Zionism was a German-Austrian idea and until 1914, the Zionists had been based in Berlin. When Jemal Pasha, the tyrant of Jerusalem, visited Berlin in August 1917, he met the German Zionists, and the Ottoman grand vizier, Talaat Pasha, reluctantly agreed to promote 'a Jewish national home'. Meanwhile, on the borders of Palestine, General Allenby was secretly preparing his offensive.

These, not Weizmann's charm, were the real reasons that Britain embraced Zionism and now time was of the essence. 'I'm a Zionist,' declared Balfour and it may be that Zionism became the only true passion of his career. Lloyd George and Churchill, now munitions minister, became Zionists too and that effervescent gadfly, Sir Mark Sykes, now in the Cabinet Office, was suddenly convinced that Britain needed 'the friendship of the Jews of the World' because 'with Great Jewry against us, there's no possibility of getting the thing through' – the thing being victory in the war.

Not everyone in the Cabinet agreed and battle was joined. 'What is to become of the people of the country?' asked Lord Curzon, former viceroy of India. Lloyd George argued 'the Jews might be able to render us more assistance than the Arabs'. The secretary of state for India, Edwin Montagu, tormented Jew, banking heir and cousin of Herbert Samuel, argued strongly that Zionism was likely to arouse more anti-Semitism. Many of Britain's Jewish magnates agreed: Claude Goldsmith Montefiore, Sir Moses' great-nephew, backed by some of the Rothschilds, led the campaign against Zionism and Weizmann complained he 'considered nationalism beneath the religious level of Jews except as Englishmen'.

Montagu and Montefiore delayed the Declaration but Weizmann fought back and conquered the drawing-rooms and country houses of Jewish grandees and English aristocrats as he had the cabinet-rooms of Whitehall. He won the support of the twenty-year-old Dolly de Rothschild who introduced him to the Astors and Cecils. At one dinner-party, the Marchioness of Crewe was heard telling Lord Robert Cecil, 'We all in this house are Weizmannites.' The support of Walter, Lord Rothschild, uncrowned king of British Jewry, helped Weizmann to defeat his Jewish opponents. In Cabinet, Lloyd George and Balfour got their way. 'I have asked Ld Rothschild and Professor Weizmann to submit a formula,' minuted Balfour, putting Sykes in charge of the negotiations.

The French and then the Americans gave their approval, making way for the decision at the end of October: on the very day that General Allenby captured Beersheba, Sykes came out and spotted Weizmann waiting nervously in the anteroom of the Cabinet Office. 'Dr Weizmann,' cried Sykes, 'it's a boy.'

On 9 November, Balfour issued his Declaration, addressed to Lord Rothschild, which proclaimed: 'His Majesty's Government view with favour the establishment in Palestine of a national home for the Jewish people ... it being clearly understood that nothing shall be done which may prejudice the civil and religious rights of existing non-Jewish communities.' Britain was later accused by the Arabs of cynical betrayal – simultaneously promising Palestine to the sherif, the Zionists and the French, perfidy that became part of the mythology of the Great Arab Revolt. It was certainly cynical but the promises to the Arabs and the Jews were both the result of short-term, ill-considered and urgent political expediency in wartime and *neither* would have been proffered in other circumstances. Sykes cheerfully insisted 'we're pledged to Zionism, Armenian liberation and Arabian independence', yet there were serious contradictions: Syria was specifically promised both to the Arabs and the French. As we saw, Palestine and Jerusalem had not been mentioned in the letters to the sherif nor was the city promised to the Jews. Sykes–Picot specified an international city and the Zionists agreed: 'we wanted the Holy Places internationalised,' wrote Weizmann.*

The Declaration was designed to detach Russian Jews from Bolshevism but the very night before it was published, Lenin seized power in St Petersburg. Had Lenin moved a few days earlier, the Balfour Declaration may never have been issued. Ironically, Zionism, propelled by the energy of Russian Jews – from Weizmann in Whitehall to Ben-Gurion in Jerusalem – and Christian sympathy for their plight, was now cut off from Russian Jewry until the fall of the Soviet Union in 1991.

The Declaration should really be named for Lloyd George, not Balfour. It was he who had already decided that Britain had to possess Palestine – 'oh, we must grab that!' he said – and this was the precondition for any Jewish homeland. He was not going to share it with France or anyone else but Jerusalem was his ultimate prize. As Allenby broke into Palestine, Lloyd George flamboyantly demanded the capture of Jerusalem 'as a Christmas present for the British nation'.

---

* Lloyd George's mission was to win the war and everything else was subordinate to that. So it was no surprise that he was also considering a fourth Middle Eastern option: he was negotiating indirectly and very secretly with the Three Pashas over a separate Ottoman peace that would betray Jews, Arabs and French by leaving Jerusalem under the sultan. 'Almost the same week that we've pledged ourselves to secure Palestine as a national home for the Jewish People,' wrote an exasperated Curzon, 'are we to contemplate leaving the Turkish flag flying over Jerusalem?' The talks came to nothing.

46

THE CHRISTMAS PRESENT

1917–1919

THE MAYOR'S ATTEMPT TO SURRENDER

Allenby took Gaza on 7 November 1917; Jaffa fell on the 16th. There were desperate scenes in Jerusalem. Jemal the Slaughterman, ruling his provinces from Damascus, threatened a *Götterdämmerung* in Jerusalem. First he ordered the deportation of all Christian priests. Christian buildings, including St Saviour's Monastery, were dynamited. The patriarchs were sent to Damascus but Colonel von Papen, a Catholic, rescued the Latin patriarch and kept him in Nazareth. Jemal hanged two Jewish spies in Damascus, then he announced the deportation of all Jerusalem's Jews: there would be no Jews left alive to welcome the British. 'We're in a time of anti-Semitic mania,' Count Ballobar noted in his diary before rushing to Field Marshal von Falkenhayn to complain. The Germans, now in control of Jerusalem, were dismayed. Jemal's anti-Semitic threats were 'insane', believed General Kress, who intervened at the highest level to save the Jews. It was Jemal's last involvement in Jerusalem.*

On 25 November, Allenby took Nabi Samuel just outside the Holy City. The Germans were unsure what to do. 'I begged Falkenhayn to evacuate Jerusalem – the city had no strategic value', recalled Papen, 'before it came under direct attack for which we'd be

---

* Jemal returned to Istanbul in 1917, but on the Ottoman surrender the following year he fled to Berlin where he wrote his memoirs. He was assassinated by Armenians in Tbilisi in 1922 as revenge for the Armenian genocide, even though he claimed, 'I was convinced the deportations of all Armenians was bound to cause great distress,' and it may well be true, as he said, that 'I was able to bring nearly 150,000 to Beirut and Aleppo.' Talaat was also assassinated; Enver was killed in battle, leading a Turkic revolt against the Bolsheviks in Central Asia.

blamed.' He imagined the headlines: 'HUNS BLAMED FOR RAZING HOLY CITY!' 'I lost Verdun,' cried Falkenhayn, 'and now you ask me to evacuate the city which is the cynosure of the world's attention. Impossible!' Papen rang his ambassador in Constantinople, who promised to talk to Enver.

British planes bombed German headquarters in the Augusta Victoria and Allenby's intelligence chief dropped opium cigarettes for the Ottoman troops, hoping that they would be too stoned to defend Jerusalem. Refugees poured out of the city. Removing the portrait of the Kaiser from the Augusta Victoria Chapel, Falkenhayn finally left the city himself and moved his headquarters to Nablus. British and German planes fought a quick dogfight over Jerusalem. Howitzers bombarded enemy positions; the Ottomans counter-attacked three times at Nabi Samuel; savage fighting raged for four days. 'The war was at its height,' wrote the teacher Sakakini, 'shells falling all around, total pandemonium, soldiers running around, and fear ruling all.'* On 4 December, British planes bombed Ottoman headquarters in the Russian Compound. In the Fast Hotel, German officers drank their last *schnapps* and laughed until the final moment, while the Ottoman generals debated whether to surrender or not; the Husseinis met secretly in one of their mansions. The Turks started to desert. Cartloads of wounded soldiers and shattered corpses rumbled through the streets.

On the evening of 7 December, the first British troops saw Jerusalem. A heavy fog hung over the city; rain darkened the hills. The next morning, Governor Izzat Bey smashed his telegraph instruments with a hammer, handed over his writ of surrender to the mayor, 'borrowed' a carriage with two horses from the American Colony which he swore to return,† and galloped away towards Jericho. All night thousands of Ottoman troops trudged through

---

* On 3 December, Ottoman secret police raided the house of Sakakini, who was hiding the Jewish adventurer and spy, Alter Levine, a kindness that was almost the last example of the old Ottomanist tolerance between Jews and Arabs. Both were arrested and despatched to Damascus: they had to walk the whole way.

† Two years later, the Colonists were still trying to get their carriage returned or the cost reimbursed, writing to Military Governor Storrs: 'On 8th December 1917 the late Governor borrowed our wagon complete with oil, cloth cover and spring seat, whip, pole and two horses.'

the city and out of history. At 3 a.m. on the 9th, German forces withdrew from the city on what Count Ballobar called a day of 'astounding beauty'. The last Turk left St Stephen's Gate at 7 a.m. By coincidence, it was the first day of Jewish Hanukkah, the festival of lights that celebrated the Maccabean liberation of Jerusalem. Looters raided the shops on Jaffa Road. At 8.45 a.m., British soldiers approached the Zion Gate.

Hussein Husseini, Mayor of Jerusalem, the hedonistic patron of Wasif the *oud*-player, rushed to break the glad tidings to the American Colony, where the Holy Colonists sang 'Alleluia'. The mayor sought a white flag – even though in his society, it proclaimed the home of a marriageable virgin. A woman offered him a white blouse, but this seemed inappropriate, so Husseini finally borrowed a bedsheet from the American Colony which he tied to a broom, and, gathering a delegation that contained several Husseinis, he mounted his horse and set off through Jaffa Gate to surrender, all the while brandishing this farcical banner.

Jerusalem proved surprisingly hard to surrender. First the mayor and his fluttering sheet found two Cockney mess-cooks near the north-western Arab village of Lifta, looking for eggs in a chicken coop. He offered to surrender Jerusalem to them. But the Cockneys refused; the sheet and broom looked like a Levantine trick and their major was waiting for his eggs; they hurried back to their lines.

The mayor met the teenaged son of a friend from a respected Jewish family, Menache Elyashar. 'Witness a historical event you'll never forget,' he said to the boy. Like a scene from *The Wizard of Oz*, Elyashar too joined the gang, which now included Muslims, Jews and Christians. Then two sergeants from another London regiment cried 'Halt!' and emerged from behind a wall with guns cocked; the mayor waved his sheet. Sergeants James Sedgewick and Fred Hurcombe refused the surrender, 'Hey, don't any of you Johnnies speak English?' they exclaimed. The mayor spoke it fluently but preferred to save it for more senior Englishmen. But they agreed to be photographed by a Swede from the American Colony with the mayor and his merry men and accepted some cigarettes.

The Jerusalemites next found two artillery officers, who also refused the honour but offered to inform headquarters. The mayor then came upon Lieutenant-Colonel Bayley who passed the offer on to Brigadier-General C. F. Watson, commander of the 180th Brigade. He summoned Major-General John Shea, General Officer Commanding the 160th Division, who galloped up on horseback. 'They've come!' cried the mayor's group, waiting on the steps outside the Tower of David.* Bertha Spafford, the American Colonist, kissed the general's stirrup. Shea accepted the surrender in the name of General Allenby, who heard the news in his tent near Jaffa where he was talking to Lawrence of Arabia. But Mayor Husseini had one surrender left.

ALLENBY THE BULL: THE SUPREME MOMENT

The guns were still booming when General Sir Edmund Allenby rode down the Jaffa Road to the Jaffa Gate. Inside his saddlebag, he kept a book entitled *Historical Geography of the Holy Land* by George Adam Smith, a present from Lloyd George. In London, the prime minister was elated. 'The capture of Jerusalem has made a most profound impression throughout the whole civilised world,' he declaimed in a rodomontade a few days later. 'The most famous city in the world, after centuries of strife and vain struggle, has fallen into the hands of the British army, never to be restored to those who so successfully held it against the embattled hosts of Christendom. The name of every hill thrills with sacred memories.'

The Foreign Office telegraphed Allenby to avoid any kaiserine grandiosity or Christ-like pretension as he entered the city: 'STRONGLY SUGGEST DISMOUNTING!' The general walked through the gate, accompanied by American, French and Italian legates and watched by all the patriarchs, rabbis, muftis and consuls, to be greeted by the Mayor of Jerusalem who for the seventh time surrendered the city as 'many wept for joy' and 'strangers greeted and congratulated each other'.

---

* The Arab boy holding the historic bedsheet stuck the broomstick into the ground, but it was purloined by the Swedish photographer. The British threatened to arrest him at which he surrendered it to Allenby, who gave it to the Imperial War Museum, where it remains.

Allenby was accompanied by Lawrence of Arabia, who had just survived the greatest trauma of his life. In late November, on a solitary recce behind enemy lines, he had been captured at Deraa in Syria by the sadistic Ottoman governor Hajim Bey who, with his myrmidons, had subjected the 'absurdly boyish' Englishman to a homosexual rape. Lawrence managed to escape and seemingly recover but the psychological damage was profound and, after the war, he described feeling 'maimed, imperfect, only half-myself. Probably it had been the breaking of the spirit by that frenzied nerveshattering pain which degraded me to beast level and which had journeyed with me ever since, a fascination and terror and morbid desire.' When he reached Aqaba after his escape, Allenby summoned him just as Jerusalem fell.

Lawrence, eschewing his Bedouin gear, borrowed a captain's uniform for the day. 'For me,' he wrote in *Seven Pillars of Wisdom*, 'my appointment in the ceremony of the Jaffa Gate' was 'the supreme moment of the war, the one which for historical reasons made a greater appeal than anything on earth.' He still regarded Jerusalem as 'a squalid town' of 'hotel servants', but now he bowed to the 'mastering spirit of the place'. Naturally, the diarist Wasif Jawhariyyeh was also watching from the crowd.

Allenby was nicknamed the Bloody Bull for his force, dignity and stature – 'the last of the paladins' – and even Jemal Pasha admired his 'alertness, discretion and brains'. An amateur naturalist, he knew 'all there was to know about birds and beasts' and had 'read everything and quoted in full at dinner one of the lesser known sonnets of Rupert Brooke'. He had a cumbersome sense of humour – his horse and his pet scorpion were both named Hindenburg after the German military supremo – but even the fastidious Lawrence worshipped the 'gigantic, red and merry' general, who was 'morally so great that the comprehension of our littleness came slow to him. What an idol that man was.'

Allenby climbed the steps to the platform to read his proclamation about 'Jerusalem the Blessed', which was then repeated in French, Arabic, Hebrew, Greek, Russian and Italian – carefully not mentioning the word that was on everyone's mind: Crusade. But when Mayor Husseini finally handed over the city's keys

Allenby is supposed to have said: 'The Crusades have now ended.'
The mayor and the mufti, both Husseinis, stalked off angrily.
However, for the millenarian American Colonists, it was different:
'We thought we were witnessing the triumph of the last Crusade,'
said Bertha Spafford. 'A Christian nation had conquered Palestine!' No one could share Lawrence's thoughts for, as he listened
to Allenby, he imagined himself a few days earlier: 'It was
strange to stand before the Tower with the Chief listening to his
proclamation and to think how a few days earlier I had stood
before [his rapist] Hajim.'

Allenby then marched out of the Jaffa Gate and remounted
Hindenburg.* 'Jerusalem cheered us mightily. It was impressive,'
wrote Lawrence, but the Ottomans were counter-attacking with,
Lawrence noted, 'an accompaniment of machine-gun fire with aeroplanes circling over us continually. Jerusalem has not been taken
for so long nor has it ever fallen so tamely before.' In spite of
himself, he felt 'shame-faced with triumph'.

Afterwards, recalled Lawrence, there was a luncheon at General
Shea's headquarters, which was spoiled when the French envoy
Picot made a bid for France to share Jerusalem. 'And tomorrow,
my dear general,' he told Allenby in his 'fluting voice', 'I'll take the
necessary steps to set up civil government in this town.'

A silence followed. Salad, chicken mayonnaise and foie gras
sandwiches hung in our wet mouths unmunched while we turned
to Allenby and gaped. His face grew red, he swallowed, his chin
coming forward (in the way we loved) whilst he said grimly: 'The
only authority is that of the Commander-in-Chief – MYSELF!'

Lawrence flew black to join Faisal and the Sherifian Camel Corps.
The French and Italians were allowed to share guard duties at the
Sepulchre, but the Church was, as always, locked and unlocked by

---

* One of Allenby's officers was Captain William Sebag-Montefiore MC, aged thirty-
two, great-nephew of Sir Moses Montefiore, who used to tell how, near Jerusalem,
he was beckoned by a beautiful Arab woman who led him to a cave where he found
and arrested a group of Ottoman officers.

its hereditary Nusseibeh.* Allenby placed Indian Muslim troops on guard at the Temple Mount.

After an audience with King George V in London, the white-suited Weizmann arrived in the Holy City with his Zionist Commission, assisted by Vladimir Jabotinsky, a bombastic nationalist and sophisticated intellectual from Odessa where he had organized a Jewish militia to resist pogroms. Allenby's advance stalled just north of Jerusalem. The Ottomans were by no means finished in Palestine, and it took him almost a year to muster his forces to relaunch his offensive, so Jerusalem was a front-line city, crowded with British and colonial troops preparing for the big push. Jabotinsky and Major James de Rothschild helped recruit a Jewish Legion to serve with them, while the Sherifians, under Lawrence and Prince Faisal, keenly awaited the opportunity to capture Damascus – and spoil French ambitions.

Jerusalem was tawdry and freezing; its population had shrunk by 30,000 since 1914 to around 55,000; many were still dying of hunger and malaria, tormented by venereal diseases (the city was patrolled by 500 teenaged Jewish prostitutes); there were 3,000 Jewish orphans. Weizmann, not unlike Lawrence, was astonished by the squalor: 'anything done to desecrate and defile the sacred has been done. It's impossible to imagine so much falsehood and blasphemy.' But, like Montefiore and Rothschild before him, he now twice tried to buy the Western Wall for £70,000 from the mufti. The money would pay for the rehousing of the Maghrebi Quarter. The Maghrebis were interested but the Husseinis prevented any deal.

Jerusalem's deputy police chief, the assistant provost marshal, newly appointed by Allenby, was a great-nephew of Montefiore who would have been appointed chief if he had not been Jewish. 'There is a great prevalence of venereal disease in the Jerusalem Area,' reported Major Geoffrey Sebag-Montefiore, who deployed guards

---

* When the Nusseibehs showed Allenby round the Church, they claimed that he asked for the keys. 'Now the Crusades have ended,' he said. 'I return you the keys but these are not from Omar or Saladin but from Allenby.' Hazem Nusseibeh, Jordanian foreign minister in the 1960s, tells the story in his memoirs, published in 2007.

around the Holy Places. He raided bawdy houses, which were usually full of Australian soldiers, and had to waste much of his time investigating cases where soldiers were accused of sleeping with local girls. 'The brothels in Jerusalem are still giving considerable trouble,' he informed Allenby in June 1918. He moved them into an allotted area, the Wazzah, which made policing easier. In October he wrote, 'there's been trouble keeping Australians out of brothels. A squadron now provide a picquet [patrol] for the Wazzah.' Major Sebag-Montefiore's reports usually read: 'Venereal Disease is rampant. Otherwise nothing of note to report.'

Among the cafés at the Jaffa Gate, Arabs and Jews debated the future of Palestine: there was a capacious breadth of opinions on both sides. On the Jewish side, this extended from the ultra-Orthodox who despised sacrilegious Zionism, via those who envisaged Jewish colonies fully integrated across an Arab-ruled Middle East, to extreme nationalists who wanted an armed Hebrew state ruling a submissive Arab minority. Arab opinion varied from nationalists and Islamicist fundamentalists who wanted Jewish immigrants expelled, to democratic liberals who welcomed Jewish aid in building an Arab state. Arab intellectuals discussed whether Palestine was part of Syria or Egypt. During the war, a young Jerusalemite called Ihsan Turjman wrote that 'The Egyptian Khedive should be joint king of Palestine and the Hejaz,' yet Khalil Sakakini noted that 'the idea of joining Palestine to Syria is spreading powerfully'. Ragheb Nashashibi founded the Literary Society, demanding union with Syria; the Husseinis set up the Arab Club. Both were hostile to the Balfour Declaration.

On 20 December 1917, Sir Ronald Storrs arrived as military governor of Jerusalem – or, as he put it, 'the equivalent of Pontius Pilate'.

ORIENTAL STORRS: BENEFICENT DESPOT

In the lobby of the Fast Hotel, Storrs bumped into his predecessor, General Barton, in his dressing-gown: 'The only tolerable places in Jerusalem are bath and bed,' declared Barton. Storrs, who favoured white suits and flamboyant buttonholes, found 'Jerusalem on star-vation rations' and remarked that 'the Jews have as usual cornered the small change.' He was enthused by his 'great adventure' in Jerusalem which 'stands alone among the cities of the world', yet like many Protestants he disliked the theatricality of the Church* and regarded the Temple Mount as a 'glorified union of the Piazza San Marco and the Great Court of Trinity [College, Cambridge].' Storrs felt he was born to rule Jerusalem: 'To be able by a word written or even spoken to right wrong, to forbid desecration, to promote ability and goodwill is to wield the power of Aristotle's Beneficent Despot.'

Storrs was not the average Colonial Office bureaucrat. This imperial peacock was a vicar's son and Cambridge classicist with 'a surprisingly cosmopolitan outlook – for an Englishman'. His friend Lawrence, who despised most officials, described him as 'the most brilliant Englishman in the Near East, and subtly efficient, despite his diversion of energy in love of music and letters, of sculpture, painting, of whatever was beautiful in the world's fruit'. He remem-bered hearing Storrs discuss the merits of Wagner and Debussy in Arabic, German and French, but his 'intolerant brain rarely stooped to conquer'. In Egypt, his catty barbs and serpentine intrigues earned him the nickname Oriental Storrs after Cairo's most dis-honest shop. This unusual military governor set about restoring battered Jerusalem, through a motley staff that included:

> a cashier from a bank in Rangoon, an actor-manager, 2 assistants from Thomas Cook, a picture-dealer, an army-coach, a clown, a land-valuer, a bosun from the Niger, a Glasgow distiller, an organ-ist, an Alexandria cotton-broker, an architect, a junior London postal official, a taxi driver from Egypt, 2 schoolmasters, and a missionary.

---

* Storrs made an exciting discovery in the Church. Much to the fury of the Greek priests, he found the last Crusader grave at the south door – that of a signatory of Magna Carta and tutor to Henry III named Philip d'Aubeny, a three-times Crusader who died in Jerusalem in 1236 during the rule of Frederick II. Storrs had the grave guarded by English soldiers.

In just a few months, Storrs founded the Pro-Jerusalem Society, funded by the Armenian arms-dealer Sir Basil Zaharoff and the American millionaires, Mrs Andrew Carnegie and J. P. Morgan Jr. Its aims were to prevent Jerusalem becoming 'a second-rate Baltimore'.

No one was more delighted than Storrs by the titles, costumes and colours of the city. He initially became friends not only with the Husseinis* but also with Weizmann and even Jabotinsky. Storrs thought there was 'no more gallant officer, no one more charming and cultivated' than Jabotinsky. Weizmann agreed that Jabotinsky was 'utterly unJewish in manner and deportment, rather ugly, immensely attractive, well spoken, theatrically chivalresque, with a certain knightliness'.

Yet Storrs found Zionist tactics 'a nightmare, reflecting the Turkish proverb: "The non-crying child gets no milk".' The Zionists soon suspected that he was unsympathetic. Many Britons despised Jabotinsky and the Russian Jews swaggering around Jerusalem in paramilitary khaki belts, and considered the Balfour Declaration unworkable. A sympathetic British general handed Weizmann a book – the Zionist leader's first encounter with the *Protocols of the Elders of Zion*† – 'You'll find it in the haversack of a great many British officers here and they believe it,' warned the general. Not yet exposed as a forgery, the *Protocols* was at its most plausible, with Britain backing Zionism and Bolshevik Russia apparently dominated by Jewish commissars.

Storrs was 'much more subtle', observed Weizmann. 'He was

---

* The Husseinis were prospering; they now owned over 12,500 acres of Palestine. Mayor Husseini was popular with Arabs and Jews alike. Storrs liked Mufti Kamil al-Husseini. Until then, the mufti was actually only leader of the Hanafi school of Islamic law (favoured by the Ottomans); there are four such schools. Storrs now promoted him to Grand Mufti not just of all four schools in Jerusalem but of all Palestine. The mufti requested that his younger brother Amin al-Husseini join Prince Faisal in Damascus when the city fell; Storrs agreed.

† When the *Protocols* was published in English, it became influential in Britain and America (backed by Henry Ford), until in August 1921 the London *Times* exposed it as a forgery. It had been published in German in 1919, and Hitler believed that it contained the truth about the Jews, explaining in *Mein Kampf* that the forgery claim 'is the surest proof they are genuine'. When it was published in Arabic in 1925, the Latin Patriarch of Jerusalem recommended the book to his congregants.

everyone's friend.' But the governor protested that he was being 'pogrommed' and that these obstreperous 'samovar Zionists' had nothing in common with Disraeli. When the governor told the prime minister about Arab and Jewish complaints, Lloyd George snapped, 'Well, if either one side stops complaining, you'll be dismissed.'

Despite Arab alarm about the Balfour Declaration, Jerusalem was quiet for two years. Storrs supervised the restoration of the walls and the Dome, the installation of street lights, the creation of the Jerusalem Chess Club and the dynamiting of Abdul-Hamid's Jaffa Gate watchtower. He especially relished his power to rename Jerusalem: 'When the Jews wished to rename Fast's Hotel [as] *King Solomon* and the Arabs [as] *Sultan Sulaiman* [Suleiman the Magnificent], either of which would have excluded half Jerusalem, one could order it to be called The Allenby.' He even established a nuns' choir which he conducted himself, and tried to mediate the Christian brawling in the Church, adhering to the sultan's 1852 division. This satisfied the Orthodox but displeased the Catholics. When Storrs visited the Vatican, the pope accused him of polluting Jerusalem by introducing ungodly cinemas and 500 prostitutes. The British never managed to solve the viciously petty feuds.*

The actual status of Palestine, to say nothing of Jerusalem, was far from decided. Picot again pushed the Gallic claim on Jerusalem. The British had no idea, he insisted, how much the French had rejoiced over the capture of Jerusalem. 'Think what it must have been like for us who took it!' retorted Storrs. Picot next tried to assert French protection of the Catholics by presiding on a special throne at a Te Deum in the Church, but the scheme collapsed when the Franciscans refused to co-operate.

---

* The Greeks argued with the Armenians over the division of the Virgin's Tomb. The Armenians feuded with the Syriac Jacobites over the cemetery on Mount Zion and ownership of the St Nicodemus Chapel in the Church, where the Orthodox and Catholics fought over the use of the northern staircase at Calvary and ownership of a strip floor at the eastern arch between the Orthodox and the Latin chapels there. The Armenians fought the Orthodox over the ownership of the staircase on the east of the main entrance – and over the right to sweep it. The Copts fought the Ethiopians over the latter's precarious rooftop monastery.

When the mayor died unexpectedly of pneumonia (perhaps contracted by surrendering too often in the pouring rain), Storrs appointed his brother, Musa Kazem al-Husseini. But the impressive new mayor, who had served as the governor of Ottoman provinces from Anatolia to Jaffa, gradually assumed leadership of the campaign against the Zionists. The Arab Jerusalemites placed their hopes in a Greater Syrian kingdom ruled by Prince Faisal, Lawrence's friend. At the First Congress of Muslim–Christian Associations, held in Jerusalem, the delegates voted to join Faisal's Syria. The Zionists, who were still unrealistically adamant that most Arabs were reconciled to their settlement, tried to appease local fears. The British encouraged friendly gestures by both sides. Weizmann met and reassured the grand mufti that the Jews would not threaten Arab interests, presenting him with an ancient Koran.

In June 1918, Weizmann travelled across the desert to meet Faisal, attended by Lawrence, at his encampment near Aqaba. It was the start of what Weizmann exaggerated as 'a lifelong friendship'. He explained that the Jews would develop the country under British protection. Privately, Faisal saw a big difference between what Lawrence called 'the Palestine Jews and the colonist Jews: to Faisal the important point is that the former speak Arabic and the latter German Yiddish'. Faisal and Lawrence hoped that the Sherifians and Zionists could cooperate to build the kingdom of Syria. Lawrence explained: 'I look upon the Jews as the natural importers of Western leaven so necessary for countries in the Near East.' Weizmann recalled that Lawrence's 'relationship to Zionism was a very positive one', as he believed that 'the Arabs stood to gain much from a Jewish Homeland'.

At their oasis summit, Faisal 'accepted the possibility of future Jewish claims to territory in Palestine'. Later, when the three men met again in London, Faisal agreed that Palestine could absorb '4–5 million Jews without encroaching on the rights of the Arab peasantry. He did not think for a moment there was any scarcity of land in Palestine,' and approved a Jewish majority presence in Palestine within the Kingdom of Syria – providing he received the crown. Syria was the prize and Faisal was happy to compromise to secure it.

Weizmann's diplomacy at first bore fruit. He had joked that 'a Jewish state without a university is like Monaco without the casino', so on 24 July 1918 Allenby drove him in his Rolls-Royce up Mount Scopus. There the foundation-stones were laid for the Hebrew University by the mufti, the Anglican bishop, two chief rabbis and Weizmann himself. But observers noticed that the mufti looked sick at heart. In the distance, the Ottoman artillery boomed as the guests sang 'God Save the King' and the Zionist anthem Hatikvah. 'Below us lay Jerusalem,' said Weizmann, 'gleaming like a jewel.'

The Ottomans were still fighting powerfully in Palestine, while on the Western Front there was as yet no sign of victory. During these months, Storrs was sometimes told by his manservant that 'a Bedouin' was waiting for him. He would find Lawrence there, reading his books. The English Bedouin then disappeared just as mysteriously. In Jerusalem that May, Storrs introduced Lawrence to the American journalist Lowell Thomas, who thought 'he might be one of the younger apostles returned to life'. Thomas would later help create the legend of Lawrence of Arabia.

Only in September 1918 did Allenby retake the offensive, defeating the Ottomans at the Battle of Megiddo. Thousands of German and Ottoman prisoners were marched through the streets of Jerusalem. Storrs celebrated 'by playing upon my Steinway a medley of "Vittoria" from La Tosca, Handel's Marches from Jephthah and Scipio, Parry's "Wedding March" from the Birds of Aristophanes'. On 2 October, Allenby allowed Faisal, King-designate of Syria, and Colonel Lawrence to liberate Damascus with their Sherifians. But, as Lawrence suspected, the real decision-making had started far away. Lloyd George was determined to keep Jerusalem. Lord Curzon later complained: 'The Prime Minister talks about Jerusalem with almost the same enthusiasm as about his native hills.'

Even as Germany finally buckled, the lobbying had already started. On the day the armistice was signed, 11 November, Weizmann, who had an appointment arranged before this momentous development, found Lloyd George weeping in 10 Downing Street reading the Psalms. Lawrence canvassed officials in London to help the Arab cause. Faisal was in Paris to put his case to the French.

But when the British and French clashed in Paris over the division of the East, Lloyd George protested that it was Britain that had conquered Jerusalem: 'The other governments had only put a few nigger policemen to see we didn't steal the Holy Sepulchre.'

47

THE VICTORS AND THE SPOILS

1919–20

WOODROW WILSON AT VERSAILLES

Meeting in London a few weeks later, Lloyd George and the French Premier Georges Clemenceau traded chips in the Middle East. In return for Syria, Clemenceau was accommodating:

CLEMENCEAU: 'Tell me what you want.'
LLOYD GEORGE: 'I want Mosul.'
CLEMENCEAU: 'You shall have it. Anything else?'
LLOYD GEORGE: 'Yes I want Jerusalem too!'
CLEMENCEAU: 'You shall have it.'

In January 1919, Woodrow Wilson, the first US president ever to leave the Americas while in office, arrived in Versailles to settle the peace with Lloyd George and Clemenceau. The protagonists of the Middle East came to lobby the victors, with Faisal, accompanied by Lawrence, striving to prevent French control of Syria; and Weizmann hoping to keep Britain in Palestine and win international recognition for the Balfour Declaration. The very presence of Lawrence, as Faisal's adviser, wearing British uniform combined with Arab headdress, outraged the French. They tried to get him banned from the conference.

Wilson, that idealistic Virginian professor turned Democratic politician and now international arbiter, proclaimed that 'every territorial settlement involved in this war must be made in the interests and for the benefit of the populations concerned'. He refused to countenance an imperial carve-up of the Middle East. The three potentates soon came to resent each other. Wilson regarded Lloyd George as 'slippery'. The seventy-eight-year-old Clemenceau, squeezed between the self-righteous Wilson and the land-grabbing Lloyd George, complained, 'I find myself between Jesus Christ and Napoleon Bonaparte.' The playful Welshman and the buttoned-up American got on best: Lloyd George admired the latter's idealism – providing Britain got what he wanted. In a wood-panelled room in Paris, lined with books, these Olympians would shape the world, a prospect that amused the cynical Balfour as he superciliously watched 'three all-powerful, all-ignorant men carving up continents'.

Clemenceau's ambitions were as shameless as those of Lloyd George. When Clemenceau agreed to meet Lawrence, he justified his claim to Syria by explaining that the French had ruled Palestine in the Crusades: 'Yes,' answered Lawrence, 'but the Crusades failed.' Besides, the Crusaders never took Damascus, Clemenceau's primary target and the heart of Arab national aspirations. The French still hoped to share Jerusalem under Sykes–Picot, but the British now rejected that entire treaty.

The US president, son of a Presbyterian minister, had endorsed the Balfour Declaration: 'To think that I, the son of the manse,' said Wilson, 'should be able to help restore the Holy Land to its people.' He was influenced by both Protestant Hebraism and his adviser, Louis Brandeis, a Jew from Kentucky who had been nominated by Wilson to the Supreme Court. Brandeis, known as 'the People's Lawyer', was an incorruptible paragon of American scholarship and public service but in 1914, only 15,000 of 3 million American Jews were members of his US Zionist Federation. By 1917, hundreds of thousands of American Jews had become involved; evangelical Christians were lobbying for Zionism; and ex-President Teddy Roosevelt, who had visited the Holy City with his parents as a boy, was backing 'a Zionist State around Jerusalem'.

Nonetheless Wilson faced a painful contradiction between Zionism and the self-determination of the Arabs. The British had at one point suggested an American mandate – a new word to describe something between a protectorate and a province. Wilson actually considered the possibility. But, faced with the Anglo-French grab for Palestine and Syria, he despatched an American commission to investigate Arab aspirations. The King–Crane Commission, led by a Chicago valve-manufacturer and the president of Oberlin College, reported back that most Palestinian and Syrian Arabs wished to live in Faisal's Kingdom of Greater Syria – under American protection. But these findings proved irrelevant when Wilson failed to restrain his imperialist allies. It still took two years for the new League of Nations to confirm that the British got Palestine and the French, Syria – which Lawrence called 'the mandate swindle'.

On 8 March 1920, Faisal was proclaimed king of Syria (including Lebanon and Palestine) and appointed Jerusalem's Said al-Husseini as his foreign minister, while the mufti's brother Amin had for a short time served in the royal court. The excitement generated by the creation of this new kingdom emboldened the Palestinian Arabs to stand up to the Zionist threat. Weizmann warned that there could be trouble. Jabotinsky and the former Russian revolutionary Pinkhas Rutenberg,* created a Jewish self-defence force, 600 strong. But Storrs ignored the alarm bells.

STORRS: THE NABI MUSA RIOTS – FIRST SHOTS

On the morning of Sunday 20 April 1920, in a city tense with Jewish and Christian pilgrims, 60,000 Arabs gathered for the Nabi Musa festival, led by the Husseinis. The diarist Wasif Jawhariyyeh watched them singing songs in protest against the Balfour Declaration. The mufti's younger brother, Haj Amin al-Husseini, incited the crowds, holding up a picture of Faisal: 'This is your King!' The mob shouted, 'Palestine is our land, the Jews are our

---

* Storrs called Rutenberg, a Russian Socialist Revolutionary whom Kerensky had in 1917 appointed Deputy Governor of Petrograd, 'the most remarkable of them all'. He had commanded the Winter Palace before it was stormed by Trotsky's Red Guards. Rutenberg was 'thickset, powerful, dressed always in black, head strong as granite, utterances low and menacing, brilliant and fascinating' but also 'versatile and violent.' In 1922, Churchill supported Rutenberg, an engineer, in his bid to found the hydroelectric works that powered much of Palestine.

dogs!' and poured into the Old City. An old Jew was beaten with sticks.

Suddenly, recalled Khalil Sakakini, 'the furore turned into madness'. Many drew daggers and clubs, crying, 'The religion of Muhammad was founded by the sword!' The city, observed Jawhariyyeh, 'became a battlefield'. The crowd chanted 'Slaughter the Jews!' Both Sakakini and Wasif hated violence but were starting to loathe not just the Zionists but the British too.

Storrs came out of the morning service in the Anglican Church to find Jerusalem out of control. He rushed to his headquarters in the Austrian Hospice, feeling as though someone 'had thrust a sword into my heart'. Storrs had only 188 policemen in Jerusalem. As the riot intensified in the course of the next day, the Jews feared they would be wiped out. Weizmann burst into Storrs' office to demand help; Jabotinsky and Rutenberg grabbed their pistols and mustered 200 men at police headquarters in the Russian Compound. When Storrs banned this, Jabotinsky patrolled outside the Old City, exchanging shots with Arab gunmen – that was the day the shooting really started. In the Old City, some streets of the Jewish Quarter were under siege, and Arab intruders gang-raped some Jewish girls. Meanwhile the British were trying to police the Holy Fire ceremony but when a Syriac moved a Coptic chair 'all hell broke loose', and the doors of the Church caught fire in the brawl. As a British official left the Church of the Holy Sepulchre, a little Arab girl fell from a nearby window, hit by a stray bullet.

One of Jabotinsky's recruits, Nehemia Rubitzov, and a colleague covered their pistols with medical white coats and entered the Old City in an ambulance to organize the defence. Rubitzov, Ukrainian-born, had been recruited by Ben-Gurion into the Jewish Legion, changing his name to Rabin. Now, as he calmed the terrified Jews, he encountered and rescued 'Red Rosa' Cohen, a spirited ex-Bolshevik newly arrived from Russia: they fell in love and married. 'I was born in Jerusalem' said their son, Yitzhak Rabin, who as Israeli chief of staff many years later would capture Jerusalem.

HERBERT SAMUEL: ONE PALESTINE, COMPLETE

By the time the riots ebbed, five Jews and four Arabs were dead, 216 Jews and 23 Arabs wounded. Thirty-nine Jews and 161 Arabs were tried for their part in what came to be known as the Nabi Musa riots. Storrs ordered raids on Weizmann's and Jabotinsky's homes: Jabotinsky was found guilty of possessing guns and sentenced to fifteen years. Young Amin Husseini – 'the chief fomenter' of the riots, in Storrs' words – was sentenced to ten years, but escaped from Jerusalem. Storrs sacked Mayor Musa Kazem Husseini, though the British naively blamed Jewish Bolsheviks from Russia for the violence.

The liberal Weizmann and socialist Ben-Gurion continued to hope for a gradually evolving homeland and a modus vivendi with the Arabs. Ben-Gurion refused to recognize Arab nationalism: he wanted Arab and Jewish workers to share 'a life of harmony and friendship', but sometimes he exclaimed, 'There's no solution! We want the country to be ours. The Arabs want it to be theirs.' The Zionists now started to reorganize their old Hashomer – the Watchmen – into a more efficient militia, Haganah – the Defence.

Each act of violence fed the extremists on both sides. Jabotinsky absolutely recognized that Arab nationalism was as real as Zionism. He argued implacably that the Jewish state, which he believed should encompass both banks of the Jordan, would be violently opposed and could be defended only with an 'iron wall'. In the mid-twenties, Jabotinsky split off to form the Union of Zionist-Revisionists with a youth movement, Betar, that wore uniforms and held parades. He wanted to create a new sort of activist Jew, no longer dependent on the genteel lobbying of Weizmann. Jabotinsky was adamant that his Jewish commonwealth would be built with 'absolute equality' between the two peoples and without any displacement of the Arabs. When Benito Mussolini came to power in 1922, Jabotinsky mocked the cult of Il Duce – 'the most absurd of all English words – leader. Buffaloes follow a leader. Civilised men have no "leaders".' Yet Weizmann called Jabotinsky 'Fascistic' and Ben-Gurion nicknamed him 'Il Duce'.

King Faisal, the hope of the Arab nationalists – was doomed by French determination to possess Syria. The French forcibly expelled the king and smashed his ragtag army, completing the collapse of Lawrence's plans. The end of Greater Syria and the riots helped form a Palestinian national identity.*

On 24 April 1920, at the San Remo Conference, Lloyd George accepted the Mandate to rule Palestine, based on the Balfour Declaration, and appointed Sir Herbert Samuel as the first high commissioner. He arrived at the station in Jerusalem on 30 June, resplendent in a white uniform, pith helmet with feathers, and a sword, to the boom of a seventeen-gun salute. Samuel may have been Jewish and a Zionist but he was no dreamer: Lloyd George found him 'dry and cold'. A journalist thought he was 'as free from passion as an oyster' and one of his officials noted he was 'stiffish – never seems able to forget his office'. When the military governor handed over control of Palestine, Samuel managed one of his few recorded jokes, signing a chit that read 'Received from Major-General Sir Louis J Bols KCB, One Palestine, complete.' He then added 'E and O [Errors and Omissions] excepted', but there would be many of both.

Initially Samuel's calm tact soothed Palestine after the shock of Nabi Musa. Setting up Government House in the Augusta Victoria on the Mount of Olives, he released Jabotinsky, pardoned Amin Husseini, temporarily limited Jewish immigration and reassured the Arabs. British interests were no longer the same as they had been in 1917. Curzon, now foreign secretary, was opposed to full-blown support for Zionism and watered down Balfour's promises. There would be a Jewish home but no state then or later. Weizmann felt betrayed but the Arabs regarded even this as disastrous. By 1921, a total of 18,500 Jews had arrived in Palestine. During the next eight years, Samuel allowed in another 70,000.

In the spring of 1921, Samuel's boss Winston Churchill, the

---

* The word 'Palestinian' came to mean the Palestinian Arab nation, but for the first half of the twentieth century the Jews there were known as Palestinians or Palestinian Jews; the Arabs known as Palestinian Arabs. In Weizmann's memoirs (published 1949) when he writes 'Palestinian' he means Jewish. A Zionist newspaper was called *Palestine*, an Arab one *Filistin*.

secretary of state for colonial affairs, arrived in Jerusalem accompanied by his adviser Lawrence of Arabia.

CHURCHILL CREATES THE MODERN MIDDLE EAST: LAWRENCE'S SHERIFIAN SOLUTION

'I liked Winston so much,' said Lawrence afterwards, 'and have such respect for him.' Churchill had already enjoyed a career of swashbuckling adventure, bumptious self-promotion and irrepressible success. Now in his late forties, the colonial secretary was confronted with the punishing cost in blood and treasure of garrisoning a new empire: Iraq was already in the grip of a bloody insurgency against British rule. Churchill therefore called a conference in Cairo to hand over a certain amount of power to Arab rulers under British influence. Lawrence proposed granting a new kingdom of Iraq to Faisal.

On 12 March 1920, Churchill convened his Arab experts in the Semiramis Hotel while a pair of Somalian lion cubs played around their feet. Churchill enjoyed the luxury, having no wish to experience 'thankless deserts', but Lawrence hated it. 'We lived in a marble bronze hotel,' he wrote. 'Very expensive, and luxurious – horrible place. Makes me Bolshevik. Everybody in the Middle East is here. Day after tomorrow, we go to Jerusalem. We're a very happy family: agreed upon everything important' – in other words, Churchill had accepted the 'Sherifian solution': Lawrence finally saw some honour restored in the wake of the broken British promises to the sherif and his sons.

The old sherif, King Hussein of Hejaz, was no match for the Wahabi warriors led by the Saudi chieftain Ibn Saud.* When his

---

* The ageing Hussein became the King Lear of Arabia, obsessed with filial ingratitude and British perfidy. Lawrence, on his last mission, was sent to persuade the bitter king to compromise with Anglo-French hegemony or lose his British funding. He wept, raged and refused. Soon afterwards, Hussein was defeated by Ibn Saud and abdicated in favour of his eldest son, who became King Ali. But the Saudis conquered Mecca, Ali was ejected and Ibn Saud declared himself king of Hejaz, then of Saudi Arabia. The two kingdoms are still ruled by their families – Saudi Arabia and Hashemite Jordan.

son Abdullah tried to repel the Saudis with 1,350 fighters, they were routed: Abdullah had to flee through the back of his tent in his underwear, surviving 'by a miracle'. They had planned that Faisal would rule Syria-Palestine and Abdullah would be king of Iraq. Now that Faisal was getting Iraq, this left nothing for Abdullah.

While Churchill's conference was proceeding in Cairo, Abdullah led thirty officers and 200 Bedouin into today's Jordan – technically part of the British Mandate – to seize his own meagre fiefdom – even though Lord Curzon thought he was 'much too big a cock for so small a dunghill'. The news of this escapade presented Churchill with a fait accompli. Lawrence advised Churchill to back Abdullah. Churchill despatched Lawrence to invite the prince to meet him in Jerusalem.

At midnight on 23 March, Churchill and his wife Clementine set off for Jerusalem by train, and were greeted at Gaza by enthusiastic crowds crying 'Cheers for the minister' and 'Down with Jews! Cut their throats!' Churchill, understanding nothing, waved back with oblivious bonhomie.

In Jerusalem he stayed with Samuel at the Augusta Victoria Fortress where he met four times with 'the moderate and friendly' Abdullah, hopeful occupier of Transjordan, escorted by Lawrence. Abdullah, who hoped for a Hashemite empire, thought the best way for Jews and Arabs to live together would be in one kingdom under him with Syria added later. Churchill offered him Transjordan provided he recognized French Syria and British Palestine. Abdullah reluctantly agreed, whereupon Churchill created a new country: 'Amir Abdullah is in Transjordania,' he remembered, 'where I put him one Sunday afternoon in Jerusalem.' The mission of Lawrence, who had finally shepherded Faisal and Abdullah to two thrones, was complete.*

* The twenty-five-year-old American Lowell Thomas of Colorado made his fortune launching *Last Crusade*, a travelling show that told the legendary adventures of 'Lawrence of Arabia'. A million people saw it in London alone and even more in America. Lawrence despised and loved it, watching the show five times. 'I saw your show and thank god the lights were out,' he wrote. 'He's invented some silly phantom thing, a matinee idol in fancy dress.' Lawrence finished his memoirs, using that old title, *Seven Pillars of Wisdom*, a creamily baroque yet poetical work that was a mix of

The Palestinian Arabs petitioned Churchill, alleging, in the tradition of the forged *Protocols of the Elders of Zion*, that 'the Jew is a Jew the world over', that 'Jews have been among the most active advocates of destruction in many lands' and the Zionists wanted to 'control the world'. Churchill received the Jerusalemites under the ex-mayor, Musa Kazim al-Husseini, but insisted 'it's manifestly right that Jews should have a National Home, a great event in the world's destiny'.

Churchill's father* had imbued him with an admiration for Jews and he saw Zionism as just outcome after two millennia of suffering. During the Red scare after Lenin created Soviet Russia, he believed that the Zionist Jew was 'the antidote' to 'the foul baboonery of Bolshevism' which was 'a Jewish movement' led by a diabolical bogeyman called the 'International Jew'.

Churchill loved Jerusalem, where, he declared, opening the British Military Cemetery on Mount Scopus, 'lies the dust of the Caliphs and Crusaders and Maccabees!' He was drawn to the Temple Mount, which he visited whenever possible, begrudging every moment away from it. Before he returned to England, he was still holding court on the Mount of Olives when the mufti of Jerusalem died unexpectedly. Storrs had already sacked the Husseini mayor so it seemed rash to upset the family further by also taking away the post of mufti. Besides, the British were attracted to the ascendancy of the Families who resembled their own gentry. Samuel and Storrs therefore arranged that the mayor and the mufti should each be chosen from the two pre-eminent Families: their feud would make them the Montagues and Capulets of Jerusalem.

---

history, confession and mythology – 'I prefer lies to truth, particularly where they concern me,' he joked. Yet for all its faults it is surely a masterpiece. Afterwards, Lawrence changed his name, joined the air force and retired into obscurity, dying in a motorcycle accident in 1935.

* Lord Randolph Churchill became friends with the Rothschilds and others when this was still risqué amongst aristocrats. When he arrived at a house party, an aristocrat greeted him, 'What Lord Randolph, you've not brought your Jewish friends?' at which Randolph replied, 'No, I didn't think they'd be amused by the company.'

48

THE BRITISH MANDATE

1920–36

THE MUFTI VERSUS THE MAYOR:
AMIN HUSSEINI VERSUS RAGHEB NASHASHIBI

The man they chose as mayor was the very personification of the Arab boulevardier: Ragheb Nashashibi smoked cigarettes in a holder, carried a cane and was the first Jerusalemite to own an American limousine, a green Packard, always driven by his Armenian chauffeur. The debonair Nashashibi, the heir to the orange-groves and mansions of the most recent but richest of the Families,* fluent in French and English, had represented Jerusalem in the Ottoman Parliament, and had hired Wasif to arrange his parties and give *oud* lessons to him and his mistress. Now that he was mayor, he gave two parties a year, one for his friends, and one for the high commissioner. As a veteran campaigner against Zionism, he took his role seriously as Jerusalemite seigneur and Palestinian leader.

The man they chose as grand mufti was Nashashibi's wealthy cousin, Haj Amin Husseini. Storrs introduced the young rabble-rouser of the Nabi Musa riots to the high commissioner who was impressed. Husseini was 'soft, intelligent, well-educated, well-dressed with a shiny smile, fair hair, blue eyes, red beard and a wry sense of humour,' recalled the mayor's nephew Nassereddin

---

* The Nashashibis claimed descent from a thirteenth-century Mamluk potentate, Nasir al-Din al-Naqashibi, who had served as Superindentant of the Two Harams (Jerusalem and Hebron). In fact they were descended from eighteenth-century merchants who manufactured bows and arrows for the Ottomans. Ragheb's father had made a huge fortune and married a Husseini.

Nashashibi. 'Yet he told his jokes with cold eyes.' Husseini asked Samuel, 'Which do you prefer – an avowed opponent or an unsound friend?' Samuel replied, 'An avowed opponent.' Weizmann commented drily that, 'in spite of the proverb, poachers-turned-game-keepers are not always a success.' Husseini turned out be, in the words of the Lebanese historian Gilbert Achcar 'a megalomaniac who presented himself as the leader of the whole Islamic world'.

Inconveniently, Husseini did not win the first ever election for mufti, which was won by a Jarallah. He only came fourth so the British, who prided themselves on their 'totalitarianism tempered with benevolence,' simply overruled the election and appointed him even though he was only twenty-six and had never finished his religious studies in Cairo. Samuel then doubled his political and financial power by sponsoring his election as president of a new Supreme Muslim Council.

Husseini belonged to the Islamic tradition; Nashashibi to the Ottoman. Both opposed Zionism but Nashashibi believed that, faced with British power, the Arabs should negotiate; Husseini, in a meandering and capricious journey, ended up as an intransigent nationalist opposing any compromise. At first, Husseini played the passive British ally, but he would ultimately reach far beyond the anti-British stance of many Arabs to become a racial anti-Semite and embrace Hitler's Final Solution to the Jewish problem. The most enduring achievement of Samuel was to promote the most energetic enemy of Zionism and Britain. Yet one could argue that no one proved such a divisive calamity for his own people, and such an asset for the Zionist struggle.

THE MUFTI: THE BATTLE OF THE WALL

The first generation of British proconsuls congratulated themselves that they had tamed Jerusalem. In June 1925, Samuel returned to London, declaring, with Olympian delusion, that 'the spirit of lawlessness has ceased.' A year later, Storrs left a peaceful, much embellished city and was promoted to the governorships of Cyprus and then of Northern Rhodesia – though he sighed, 'There's no promotion after Jerusalem.' The new high commissioner was Viscount Plumer, a walrus-moustached field marshal nicknamed the Old Plum or Daddy Plummer. Thanks to cuts in his funding, the Old Plum had to keep order with fewer soldiers than Samuel, but he radiated a reassuring calm by cheerfully walking on his own around Jerusalem. When his officials reported on political tensions, he embraced ostrichism. 'There *is* no political situation,' he replied. 'Don't create one!'

The Old Plum retired due to ill-health but the new commissioner had not yet arrived when the 'political situation' duly materialized. On Kol Nidre, eve of the Jewish Day of Atonement, in 1928, the Jewish *shames* – beadle – at the Western Wall (who gloried in the name William Ewart Gladstone Noah) put up a small screen to divide men and women worshippers in accordance with Jewish law. The screen and chairs for elderly worshippers had been allowed in previous years, but now the mufti protested that the Jews were changing the status quo.

The Muslims believed that the Wall was the place Muhammad tied up his steed with the human face, Buraq, during the Night Journey, yet in the nineteenth century, the Ottomans had used the adjacent tunnel as a donkey stable. Legally it had belonged to the Abu Maidan *waqf* dating back to Saladin's son Afdal. Therefore it was 'purely Muslim property'. The Muslim fear, however, was that Jewish access to the Wall would lead to a Third Temple on the Islamic Haram, the Jewish Har-haBayit. Yet the Wall – the Kotel – was Judaism's holiest site and Palestinian Jews believed that the British restrictions, and indeed the cramped space available for worship, were relics of centuries of Muslim oppression that demonstrated why Zionism was necessary. The British even banned the blowing of the *shofar* – the ram's horn – on the Jewish High Holy Days.

The next day, Storrs' successor as governor, Edward Keith-Roach, who liked to call himself the Pasha of Jerusalem, ordered his police to raid the Wall during the Yom Kippur service, the holiest of the Jewish year. The policemen beat praying Jews and pulled chairs from under elderly worshippers. It was not Britain's finest hour. The mufti was jubilant but warned that 'the Jews' aim is to take possession of the Mosque of al-Aqsa gradually.' He therefore launched a campaign against Jewish worshippers, who were bombarded with stones, beaten up and harassed with loud music. Jabotinsky's Betar youths demonstrated for access to the Wall.

Both sides were changing the Ottoman status quo, which no longer reflected reality. Jewish immigration and land purchases had understandably raised Arab anxieties. Since the Declaration, some 90,000 Jews had arrived in Palestine. In 1925 alone, Jews had bought 44,000 acres from the Families. A tiny minority of Jewish religious nationalists did dream of a Third Temple, but the overwhelming majority simply wanted to pray at their own holy site. The new high commissioner, Sir John Chancellor, who was said to resemble 'a good-looking Shakespearian actor', asked the mufti to sell the Wall in order that the Jews could built a courtyard there. The mufti refused. To the Jews, the Kotel was the symbol of their freedom to pray and exist in their own homeland, to the Arabs, the Buraq became the symbol of resistance and nationhood.

Foreboding and claustrophobia hung over the city. 'It is the haughty and desolate beauty of a walled-in mountain fortress in the desert, of tragedy without catharsis,' observed Arthur Koestler, a young Hungarian Zionist living in Jerusalem and writing for Jabotinsky's newspaper. The 'tragic beauty' and 'inhuman atmosphere' gave him 'Jerusalem sadness'. Koestler longed to escape to kitsch Tel Aviv. In Jerusalem he felt 'the angry face of Yahweh, brooding over the hot rocks'.

In the summer of 1929, the mufti ordered the opening of a doorway that made the Jewish Wall an Arab thoroughfare for donkeys and passers-by while muezzin calls to prayer and Sufi chanting were amplified over the Jewish prayers. Jews were attacked in the nearby alleyways. Across Palestine, thousands of Jews demonstrated under the slogan 'The Wall is Ours'. Chancellor was away when, on 15 August, a 300-strong Zionist demonstration, led by the historian Joseph Klausner (the uncle of Amos Oz, the Israeli writer) and including members of Betar, marched to the Wall in silence, guarded by British police, and raised a Zionist flag and sang songs. The next day, after Friday prayers, 2,000 Arabs descended from al-Aqsa and attacked Jewish worshippers, chasing them from the Wall and beating up any they caught. On the 17th, a Jewish boy kicked a football into an Arab garden and, on going to fetch it, was murdered. At his funeral, Jewish youths tried to attack the Muslim Quarter.

At Friday prayers on 23 August, encouraged by the mufti, thousands of worshippers swept out of al-Aqsa to attack Jews. The mufti and his Nashashibi rivals tried variously to incite and to restrain the crowds: some brave Arab leaders stood up to the mob – to no avail. They attacked the Jewish Quarter, the Montefiore neighbourhood and the suburbs, where thirty-one Jews were killed. In one Jerusalem household, five members of the same family were slaughtered; in Hebron, fifty-nine Jews were massacred. The Haganah, the Zionist militia founded in 1920, fought back. There were only 292 British policemen in the whole of Palestine, so troops were flown in from Cairo. Altogether, 131 Jews were killed by Arabs, while the 116 Arabs who died were mainly shot by British troops.

The riots, which the Arabs called Thawrat al-Buraq – the Buraq Uprising – confounded the British. 'I know of no one who would be a good high commissioner of Palestine except God,' Chancellor told his son. The Balfour policy was unravelling. In October 1930, the White Paper of Colonial Secretary Lord Passfield (formerly Sidney Webb, the Fabian socialist) proposed restricting Jewish immigration and retreat from a Jewish national home. The Zionists despaired. The Buraq Uprising inflamed extremism on both sides. The violence and Passfield's White Paper discredited Weizmann's Anglophile style: the Zionists could no longer depend on the British and many turned instead to Jabotinsky's harsher nationalism. At the Seventeenth Zionist Congress, Jabotinsky attacked Weizmann who was canvassing the British prime minister Ramsay Macdonald to overturn the White Paper. Macdonald wrote him a letter, read out in Parliament, reconfirming the Balfour Declaration and reopening Jewish immigration. The Arabs called it 'the Black Letter' but it was too late to save Weizmann who was then deposed as Zionist president. Immensely hurt, he returned temporarily to science. The Haganah still concentrated on guarding the rural settlements, but it started to arm itself. Frustrated with this restraint, militant nationalists splintered off and founded the Irgun Zvai Leumi, National Military Organization, inspired by Jabotinsky, though it remained

very small. Jabotinsky was expelled from Palestine for his provocative speeches, but became increasingly popular among Jewish
youths in Palestine and eastern Europe. But it was not he who
replaced Weizmann: it was David Ben-Gurion who emerged as the
strongman of the Jewish community just as the mufti became the
strongman of the Arabs.

In December 1931, the mufti emerged onto the world stage when
he presided as a pan-Islamic and unrivalled national leader at his
World Islamic Conference on the Temple Mount: it was his finest
hour and it went to his head. He remained radically opposed to any
Zionist colony in Palestine, yet his rivals, Mayor Nashashibi, the
Dajanis and the Khalidis argued that conciliation would be better
for Arabs and Jews. The mufti would tolerate no opposition and
accused his rivals of being pro-Zionist traitors and the Nashashibis
of secretly having Jewish blood. Nashashibi tried to unseat him on
the Supreme Muslim Council but failed and the mufti started to
exclude his opponents from all the organizations he controlled. The
British, weak and unsure, leant towards the radicals instead of
the moderates: in 1934, the new high commissioner, Sir Arthur
Wauchope, withdrew his backing from Nashashibi and backed the
election of one of the Khalidis as mayor. The rivalry between
Husseinis and Nashashibis became ever more vicious.

The world was darkening, the stakes rising. The growth of
Fascism made compromise seem weak, and violence not just
acceptable but attractive. On 30 January 1933, Hitler was appointed
chancellor of Germany.* On 31 March, just two months later, the
mufti secretly visited the German consul in Jerusalem, Heinrich
Wolff, to declare that 'Muslims inside Palestine welcome the new
regime, hope for the spread of Fascist antidemocratic leadership';
he added that 'Muslims hoped for a boycott of the Jews in Germany.'

European Jews were alarmed by Hitler. Immigration, which had

---

* He was aided by von Papen, the officer who in 1917 had so wanted to save
Germany's reputation in Jerusalem. Papen, who had already served as chancellor,
advised President Hindenburg to appoint Hitler, convinced he and his aristocratic
camarilla could control the Nazis: 'Within two months, we'll have pushed Hitler so
far in the corner, he'll squeak.' Papen became Hitler's vice-chancellor but soon
resigned, becoming German ambassador to Istanbul. He was tried at Nuremburg,
served a few years in prison, and died in 1969.

slowed down, now accelerated in a way that forever changed the demographic balance. In 1933, 37,000 Jews arrived in Palestine; 45,000 in 1934. By 1936, there were 100,000 Jews in Jerusalem, compared to 60,000 Christian and Muslim Arabs. Just as Nazi aggression and anti-Semitism threatened Europe, and the tension in Palestine intensified,* Sir Arthur Wauchope presided over a new Jerusalem, capital of the short-lived Golden Age of the British Mandate.

WAUCHOPE'S CAPITAL:
HUNTS, CAFÉS, PARTIES AND WHITE SUITS

Wauchope, a wealthy bachelor, loved to entertain. Flanked by two scarlet-clad *kavasses* brandishing gilded wands, the feather-helmeted general welcomed guests to the new Government House, a baronial-cum-Moorish palace on the Hill of Evil Counsel, south of the city, with an octagonal tower, all set amid fountains, and groves of acacia and pine. The mansion was a mini English world with its parquet-floored ballroom, crystal chandeliers and a gallery for the police band, dining halls, billiard rooms, separate bathrooms for English and locals – and Jerusalem's only ever dog cemetery for a nation of dog lovers. The guests wore uniforms or top hat and tails. 'Money and champagne', recalled one, 'flowed like water.'

Wauchope's residence was the centrepiece of a modernist Jerusalem created by the British at dizzying speed. The old Earl

---

* As the British contemplated limiting immigration to Zion, Joseph Stalin was building his own Soviet Jerusalem. 'The Tsar gave the Jews no land but we will,' he announced. His views on the Jews were contradictory. In a famous 1913 article on nationality, Stalin declared that Jews were not a nation but 'mystical, intangible and otherworldly'. Once in power, he banned anti-Semitism, which he called 'cannibalism', and in 1928, approved the creation of a secular Jewish homeland with Yiddish and Russian as official languages. Inaugurated in May 1934, Stalin's Zion, the Jewish Autonomous Region, was a wasteland, Birobidzhan, on the Chinese border. After the Second World War and the Holocaust, his foreign minister Vyacheslav Molotov and others backed the creation of another Jewish homeland in the more attractive Crimea – a Stalinist California – which ultimately aroused Stalin's vicious anti-Semitism. Yet by 1948 Birobidzhan contained 35,000 Jews. Today it survives with a few thousand Jews and all its signs still in Yiddish.

of Balfour himself had come for the opening of the Hebrew University on Mount Scopus, near the new Hadassah Hospital. A YMCA in the form of a phallic tower was built by the architect of the Empire State Building. The Rockefellers raised a Gothic-Moorish museum just north of the walls. King George V Avenue, with its 'splendid shops, cafés with high chandeliers, and rich stores', reminded a young Jewish Jerusalemite, Amos Oz, later a famous Israeli writer, of 'that wonderful London Town I knew from films where culture-seeking Jews and Arabs mixed with cultivated Englishmen, where dreamy long-necked ladies floated in evening dress'. This was the Jazz Age in Jerusalem, where flappers combined fast cars with millenarian evangelism. 'HAREM BEAUTIES DRIVE FORDS THROUGH JERU-SALEM' declared the *Boston Herald*, interviewing Bertha Spafford – who, it reported, was 'introducing Flivvers [American cars] and Vacuum bottles to the Turk and says God not Balfour will send the Jews back to Palestine'.

Jerusalem still lacked the luxuries of a major city, but in 1930, she got her first world-class hotel. The majestic King David Hotel, backed by wealthy Egyptian Jews and the Anglo-Jewish financier Frank Goldsmith (father of Sir James), which instantly became the city's stylish hub, noted for its 'biblical style' with Assyrian, Hittite and Muslim ornamentation, and its 'tall Sudanese waiters in white pantaloons and red tarboush'. One American tourist supposedly believed that it was the renovated Temple of Solomon. Ragheb Nashashibi had his hair cut there every day. The hotel helped make Jerusalem a luxury resort for the rich Arabs of Lebanon and Egypt, whose decadent royal family were often in residence. Abdullah, Amir of Transjordan, stayed regularly – the King David could cope with his camels and horses. In October 1934, Churchill came to stay with his wife and his friend Lord Moyne, himself later a victim of the Palestinian conflict. Not to be outdone, the mufti built his own hotel, the Palace, using Jewish contractors, on the site of the ancient Mamilla cemetery.

When an American Jewess, a former nurse, opened the first beauty parlour, peasants stood and stared, expecting the man-nequins in the window to speak. The best bookshop in town was run by Boulos Said, father of the intellectual Edward, and his brother, near the Jaffa Gate, while the finest haute couture emporium belonged to Kurt May and his wife, typical German Jews fleeing Hitler. When he created the shop – the name 'May' was emblazoned above the door in Hebrew, English and Arab – he imported all the fixtures from Germany and soon it attracted the rich wives of Jewish businessmen and British proconsuls – and of Abdullah of Jordan. Emperor Haile Selassie and his entourage once took over the entire shop. The Mays were more cultured Germans than Zionists – Kurt had won the Iron Cross in the Great War – and they were totally irreligious. The Mays lived over the shop: when their daughter Miriam was born, she was breastfed by an Arab wetnurse but when she grew up, her parents discouraged her from playing with the Polish Jews next door who were 'not sufficiently cultured'. Jerusalem was still small though: sometimes in spring, Miriam's father would take her on walks out of the city to pick cyclamen on the blooming Judaean hills. Friday nights were the height of their social week: when the ultra-Orthodox Jews were praying, the Mays went dancing at the King David Hotel.

The British behaved as if Palestine were a real imperial province: Brigadier Angus McNeil founded the Ramle Vale Jackal Hounds Hunt which chased the fox and the jackal with a pack of hounds. At the Officers Club, Zionist guests noticed that all conversation was about duck shooting, if not the latest polo game or race meeting. One young officer flew into town in his own private aeroplane.

The British public schoolboys, raised on the complexities of their own aristocracy, revelled in the hierarchies of Jerusalem, especially the social etiquette required for dinner parties at Government House, where Sir Harry Luke, John Chancellor's deputy, remembered how the toastmaster welcomed high commissioners, chief rabbis, chief judges, mayors and patriarchs: 'Your Excellency, Your Honour, Your Beatitudes, Your Eminences, Your Lord Bishops, Your Paternity, Your Reverends, Your Worship, Ladies and Gentlemen.'

This thriving new Jerusalem, with 132,661 inhabitants by 1931, proved that British rule and Zionist immigration did help create a flourishing economy – and rising Arab immigration: more Arabs immigrated to Palestine than Jews and the Arab population of Palestine increased by 10 per cent, twice as fast of that of Syria or Lebanon.* In ten years, Jerusalem attracted 21,000 new Arabs and 20,000 new Jews – and this was the glamorous heyday of the Families. The British sympathized with the Arab dynasties, Nusseibehs and Nashashibis, who still owned 25 per cent of the land, and who 'fitted into the social order imported by the British as if tailor-made', wrote Sari Nusseibeh, later the Palestinian philosopher. 'The men belonged to the same gentleman's society and in private English officers tended to prefer them to the Russian Jewish upstarts.'

The Families had never lived more luxuriously: Hazem Nusseibeh's father owned two 'palatial residences, each one with 20–30 rooms.' The fathers had been educated in Constantinople, the sons would attend St George's public school in Sheikh Jarrah and then Oxford. Hazem Nusseibeh, who was Sari's uncle, recalled that 'It was amusing to watch the *effendi* aristocracy of Arab Jerusalem, attired during summer in well-pressed white silk suits with polished shoes and silk ties.' Hazem's brother, Anwar Nusseibeh, cruised Jerusalem in a gleaming Buick, the city's first.

Many of the Arab middle class, Muslims and Orthodox, worked for the Mandate. They lived in pink stone villas in the Ottoman world of Sheikh Jarrah, Talbieh, Bakaa and Katamon, the suburbs of what Amos Oz called 'a veiled city, heavy with crosses, turrets, mosques, and mysteries' and filled with 'monks and nuns, qadis and muezzins, Notables, veiled women and cowled priests'. When Oz visited a well-off Arab family, he admired the 'moustachioed men, jewelled women' and 'charming young girls, slim-hipped, red-nailed with elegant hair-dos and sporty skirts'.

'Sumptuous parties, lunches, dinners and receptions, the year round' were held by the historian George Antonius, an aesthetic 'Syrian patriot with the lucidity of a Cambridge don', and his 'charming, beautiful' and irrepressible wife, Katy, daughter of a Lebanese

* The Woodhead Commission of 1938 stated that between 1919 and 1938, the Arab population of Palestine had increased by 419,000; the Jewish population by 343,000.

proprietor of Egyptian newspapers.* Their Sheikh Jarrah villa,
which was owned by the mufti and filled with 12,000 books, was the
social headquarters for Arab grandees, British elites and celebrity
visitors, as well as a political salon for Arab nationalists. 'Pretty
women, delicious food, clever conversation: everyone who was
anyone was there at the best parties in Jerusalem,' remembered
Nassereddin Nashashibi, 'and they always had the most delightfully
louche atmosphere'. Their marriage was said to be open and Katy
was notoriously flirtatious, with a taste for Englishmen in uniform:
'She was naughty, curious about everything,' recalled an old
Jerusalemite; 'she would start gossip; she was always matching
people up.' Antonius later told his daughter about a party with a
dance band given by a local socialite where he shocked and thrilled
the other guests by proposing a swinging Jerusalem party game of
his own: he would invite ten couples but each person would bring
a member of the opposite sex who was not their spouse – and then
they would see what happened.

The cooling of British enthusiasm for Zionism increasingly
alienated the Jews. Perhaps High Commissioner Sir John Chancellor was typical when he complained that Jews were 'ungrateful
people'. Each Jewish neighbourhood belonged in a different
country: Rehavia, home of secular German professors and British
officials, was the most desirable suburb, civilized, calm and European; the Bokharan Quarter belonged in Central Asia; the Hasidic
Mea Shearim was shabby, impoverished and redolent of seventeenth-century Poland; Zikhron Zion was heady with the 'poor
Ashkenazi cooking smells, of borscht, garlic and onion and sauer-
kraut,' recalled Amos Oz; Talpiot was 'a Jerusalemite replica of a
Berlin garden suburb', while his own home was in Kerem Avraham,
built around the old house of the British consul James Finn, which
was so Russian 'it belonged to Chekhov'.

---

* Antonius, son of a rich Christian Lebanese cotton-trader, born in Alexandria and
educated at Victoria College and Cambridge and a friend of E. M. Forster, was
assistant education director for the Mandate. He was chronicling the Arab Revolt
and the British betrayal in his book *The Arab Awakening*, one of the seminal texts of
Arab nationalism. Antonius advised both the mufti and the British high commissioners. Antonius' daughter Soraya later wrote probably the best novel about this
period based on her parents' milieu, *Where the Jinn Consult*.

Weizmann had called Jerusalem 'a modern Babel' but all these different worlds continued to mix, despite spasms of violence and clouds of foreboding. That cosmopolitan Jerusalem, wrote Hazem Nusseibeh, was 'one of the most exhilarating cities in the world to live in'. Cafés opened all the time, enjoyed by a new class of intellectuals, boulevardiers, and flâneurs, funded by family orange groves, newspaper articles and civil service salaries. The cafés presented respectable belly-dancing, as well as the saucier *suzi* version, cabaret-singers and traditional balladeers, jazz bands, and Egyptian popular singers. During early Mandate years, just inside the Jaffa Gate next to the Imperial Hotel, the flamboyant intellectual Khalil Sakakini held court at the Vagabond Café, where over puffs of *nargileh* water pipes and shots of Lebanese *arak* firewater, this soi-disant 'Prince of Idleness' discussed politics and expounded his hedonistic philosophy, the Manifesto of Vagabonds – 'Idleness is the motto of our party. The working-day is made up of two hours' – after which he indulged 'in eating, drinks and merriment'. However, his indolence was limited when he became Palestine's inspector of education.

Wasif Jawhariyyeh, the *oud*-player with the municipal sinecure, had long embraced laziness: his brother opened the Café Jawhariyyeh on Jaffa Road by the Russian Compound where a cabaret and band performed. One regular denizen of the nearby Postal Café recalled 'the cosmopolitan clientele; a Tsarist officer with a white beard, a young clerk; an immigrant painter, an elegant lady who kept talking about her properties in Ukraine, and many young men and women immigrants'.

Many of the British enjoyed this 'real blend of cultures', not least Sir Harry Luke, who presided over a typical Jerusalem household: 'The nanny was from south England, the butler a White Russian,*

---

* Jerusalem was still filled with White Russians but one Grand Duchess returned posthumously. In 1918, the widow of Grand Duke Sergei, Ella, who had become a nun, was arrested by the Bolsheviks. Her skull was smashed in and she was tossed down a mineshaft in Alapaevsk, just hours after the Bolsheviks had also murdered her sister, Empress Alexandra, Emperor Nicholas II and all their children. When the Whites took Alapaevsk, they discovered the bodies: Ella's had scarcely decayed. Her body and that of her devoted fellow nun Sister Barbara travelled via Peking,

the servant a Cypriot Turk, Ahmed the cook was a rascally black Berber, the kitchenboy was an Armenian who surprised us by turning out to be a girl; the housemaid is Russian.' But not everyone was so charmed. 'I dislike them *all* intensely,' said General Sir Walter 'Squib' Congreve. 'Beastly people. The whole lot are not worth a single Englishman.'

BEN-GURION AND THE MUFTI: THE SHRINKING SOFA

The mufti was at the height of his prestige but he struggled to control the wide range of Arab views. There were liberal Westernizers like George Antonius, there were Marxists, there were secular nationalists and there were Islamic fundamentalists. Many Arabs loathed the mufti but the majority were becoming convinced that only armed struggle could stop Zionism. In November 1933, the ex-mayor Musa Kazem Husseini, who was no fan of his cousin the mufti, led demonstrations in Jerusalem that sparked riots in which thirty Arabs were killed. When Musa Kazem died the next year, the Arabs lost an elder statesman respected by all: 'people wept a lot over Musa Kazem,' wrote Ahmed Shuqayri, a later Palestinian leader, 'whereas Haj Amin (the mufti) made a lot of people weep.' More than a quarter of a million Jews arrived in Palestine during the second decade of the Mandate, twice as many as during the first. The Arabs, whether they were the most sophisticated of the Jerusalem elite, educated at Oxford, or whether

Bombay and Port Said to Jerusalem where they were received in January 1921 by Sir Harry Luke who had to change their route through the city to avoid pro-Bolshevik protests by Jewish immigrants. 'Two unadorned coffins were lifted from the train. The little cavalcade wound its way sadly, unobtrusively to the Olivet', wrote Louis, Marquess of Milford Haven who, with his wife Victoria, helped bear the coffins. 'Russian peasant women, stranded pilgrims, sobbing and moaning, were almost fighting to get some part of the coffin.' The Milford Havens were the grandparents of Prince Philip, Duke of Edinburgh. Elizabeth the New Martyr was canonized and rests in a glass-topped white marble sarcophagus in the Church of Mary Magdalene she and her husband had built. As she wished, her remains, covered in a shroud with dainty white slippers peeking out, rest there opposite the Golden Gate, ready to rise again at the Last Judgement. Some of her saintly relics have been returned to her Martha and Mary Convent in Moscow.

they were the Islamicist radicals of the Muslim Brotherhood, all now sensed that the British would never halt the immigration, nor hold back the ever more sophisticated organization of the Yishuv, as the Jewish community was known. They were running out of time. In 1935, at the height of the immigration, 66,000 Jews arrived. In that morbid age when war was often regarded as a purifying national ritual, even the intellectual Sakakini and the aesthete Jawhariyyeh now believed that only violence could save Palestine. The answer, wrote Hazem Nusseibeh, was 'armed rebellion'.

This was confronted by the ageing Weizmann, again Zionist president, but the real power lay with David Ben-Gurion, recently elected chairman of the Executive of the Jewish Agency, the highest authority for the Yishuv. Both men were autocratic and intellectual in style, dedicated to Zionism and Western democracy. But they were opposites. Ben-Gurion was a gruff working-class man of action, equipped to lead in war and peace. He lacked all small talk (except about history and philosophy) and was humourless – the only joke the diminutive Ben-Gurion told was about Napoleon's height. Its punchline was: 'no one was bigger than Napoleon, just taller.' Married with two children, a dissatisfied husband, he enjoyed a discreet love-affair with a tall, blue-eyed Englishwoman in London. But he was a brooding loner and thoughtful strategist, always obsessed with the cause, who collected books, spending any spare time in second-hand bookshops. The Old Man, as he was already known, learned Spanish to read Cervantes and Greek to study Plato; when he planned statehood, he read Greek philosophy; when he made war, he read Clausewitz.

Weizmann was Zionism's *grand seigneur*, dressed in Savile Row suits, more at home in the salons of Mayfair than on the sunbeaten farms of Galilee and now well off from founder-shares in Marks & Spencer, donated by his friends, the Sieff family. 'You're now King of Israel,' Ben-Gurion told him, but he would soon turn against 'Weizmann's regime of personal fetishism'. As for Weizmann, he knew that, unlike Ben-Gurion, he was not cut out to be a warlord, but he half respected, half disdained the younger man's militancy. In his 600-page memoirs, he mentioned Ben-Gurion's name just twice. Weizmann was mistaken for Lenin in looks but Ben-Gurion emulated the Bolshevik's ruthless pragmatism.

He had started as a socialist, risen in the labour movement and had not quite lost his belief that a new Palestine should be created through the cooperation of the Jewish and Arab working classes. Ben-Gurion may have dreamed of a Jewish state but that seemed totally unlikely and remote. Since he appreciated that 'the Arab national movement was born at almost the same time as political Zionism,' he believed that an Arab–Jewish confederation was the best the Jews could hope for at that time. Both he and the mufti probed each other with plans for a shared state: in retrospect, a compromise was still possible. In August 1934, Ben-Gurion started to meet Musa al-Alami,* a lawyer working for the British, and George Antonius, the writer – both moderate advisers to the mufti. Ben-Gurion proposed either a Jewish–Arab shared government or a Jewish entity within an Arab federation that would include Transjordan and Iraq. Surely, Ben-Gurion argued, Palestine was like a sofa: there was room for both. The mufti was impressed, but noncommittal. Later Alami reflected that the mufti and Ben-Gurion shared the same harsh nationalism but the Jewish leader was much more flexible and skilful. He regretted that the Arabs never produced their own Ben-Gurion. Meanwhile, the mufti and his fellow aristocrats were losing control of their movement.

In November 1935, a Syrian preacher named Sheikh Izzat al-Din al-Qassam, who worked as a junior official in the mufti's *sharia* court in Haifa and was constantly urging him to reject any political compromise, rebelled against the British. He was far more radical than the mufti, a puritan fundamentalist who believed in the sanctity of martyrdom, a precursor of al-Qaeda and today's Jihadists. Now he led the thirteen *mujahidin* of his Black Hand cell into hills where, on 20 November, he was cornered by 400 British police and

* He was a member of one of the grandest Families. The Alamis' house remains the most extraordinary in Jerusalem: in the seventeenth century the family bought a house right next to the Church which actually shares and owns part of its roof; the view from there is astonishing. The building, with Byzantine, Crusader and Mamluk vestiges, is still owned by Mohammad al-Alami. A cousin still serves as sheikh of Saladin's Salahiyya *khanqah* next door.

killed. Qassam's martyrdom* jolted the mufti closer to revolt. In April 1936, Qassam's successor launched an operation outside Nablus that killed two Jews – but released a German who claimed to be a Nazi 'for Hitler's sake'. This lit the spark. The Irgun, Jewish nationalists, killed two Arabs in response. As the shooting started, Sir Arthur Wauchope was totally unqualified to respond. A young officer noticed that he 'doesn't know what to do.'

* Hamas, the Islamic Palestinian organization in Gaza, was inspired by Qassam hence it named its armed wing the Qassam Brigade, and its missiles are Qassam rockets.

49

THE ARAB REVOLT

1936–45

THE MUFTI'S TERROR

One cool night in Jerusalem in early 1936, 'scattered rifle shots rang out in the clear evening sky' and Hazem Nusseibeh realized that 'the armed rebellion had begun'. The Revolt escalated slowly. In April that year, Arabs killed sixteen Jews in Jaffa. The Palestinian parties formed a Higher Arab Committee under the mufti and called a national strike that swiftly spun out of anyone's control. The mufti declared this a sacred struggle and called his forces the Holy War Army as volunteers started to arrive to fight the British and Jews from Syria, Iraq and Transjordan.

On 14 May, two Jews were shot in the Jewish Quarter, and the mufti insisted, 'The Jews are trying to expel us from the country, murdering our sons and burning our houses.' Two days later, Arab gunmen killed three Jews in the Edison Cinema.

The Yishuv began to panic, but Ben-Gurion embraced a policy of self-restraint. Meanwhile British ministers now questioned the entire basis of the Mandate and commissioned Earl Peel, an ex-Cabinet minister, to report. The mufti called off the strike in October 1936, though he refused to recognize Peel. But Weizmann charmed the commissioners. On Amir Abdullah's insistence the mufti testi-fied that the Palestinians demanded independence, the annulment of the Balfour Declaration and, ominously, the removal of the Jews.

In July 1937, Peel proposed a two-state solution, the partition of Palestine into an Arab area (70 per cent of the country) joined to Amir Abdullah's Transjordan and a Jewish area (20 per cent). In addition, he suggested a population transfer of the 300,000 Arabs in the Jewish area. Jerusalem would remain a special entity under British control. The Zionists accepted – they had realized they would never be given Jerusalem in a partition. Weizmann was not disappointed by the small size of the Jewish entity, musing that 'King David's [kingdom] was smaller.'

Peel complained that, in contrast to the Zionists, 'not once since 1919 has any Arab leader said that cooperation with the Jews was even possible'. Only Abdullah of Transjordan enthusiastically supported Peel's plan and, in retrospect, this would have prevented Israel in its present form but at the time, all Palestinians were inflamed by an English earl's idea of creating a Jewish state: both the mufti and his rival Nashashibi rejected it.

The Revolt exploded again, but this time, the mufti embraced and organized the violence; he was seemingly more interested in murdering his Palestinian rivals than the British or Jews. 'It seems', writes the latest historian of the Husseinis, 'he was personally responsible for establishing internecine terror as a means of control.' Over his favourite meal of lentil soup, the mufti, always accompanied by his Sudanese bodyguards descended from the Haram's traditional watchmen, behaved like a Mafia boss as he ordered assassinations that in two years of fratricide wiped out many of his most decent and moderate compatriots. Nine days after Peel, the mufti called on the German consul-general in Jerusalem to state his sympathy for Nazism and his wish to cooperate. The next day, the British tried to arrest him but he sought sanctuary in al-Aqsa.

The British did not dare storm the Sanctuary. Instead they besieged Husseini on the Temple Mount, denouncing him as the organizer of the Revolt. But not all the Arab gangs were under his control: the Jihadi followers of Qassam also enthusiastically killed any Arabs suspected of cooperating with the authorities. Nothing less than a brutal civil war broke out among the Arabs themselves. It was now that it was said that the mufti made many families weep.

After supporting the Revolt initially, Ragheb Nashashibi opposed the mufti both for his terror and his strategy. Nashashibi's villa was raked with machinegun fire; a young cousin was killed watching a football game. When Fakhri Bey Nashashibi, his nephew, accused the mufti of destructive egotism, his death warrant was published in the newspapers: he was later assassinated in Baghdad. Nashashibi armed his retainers, known as 'the Nashashibi units' or 'peace-bands', and they fought the mufti's men. Arab headwear became the shibboleth of the Revolt: Husseini supporters wore the *keffiyeh* checked scarf; the Nashashibis, the *tarboush* of compromise. The mufti set up rebel courts to try traitors and issued rebel stamps.

In Jerusalem, the Revolt was commanded by Abd al-Kadir Husseini, thirty-year-old commander of the Holy War Army. He was the son of the late Musa Kazem Husseini (he used the nom de guerre Abu Musa), and received the best education at the Anglican Bishop Gobat's school on Mount Zion. He had used his graduation at Cairo University to denounce British perfidy and Zionist conspiracy. After being expelled from Egypt, he organized the mufti's Palestine Arab Party, edited its newspapers and founded, under cover of the boy scouts, his own Green Hand militia that became its military wing.

At home he was an elegant grandee with his pencil moustache and English suit but he was in his element on the run, in the field, riding shotgun, fighting. He often 'humiliated the colonial forces around Jerusalem,' noted Wasif Jawhariyyeh the *oud*-player. He was wounded in 1936 in a battle against British tanks near Hebron but after his wounds were treated in Germany, he returned to fight on from his base in John the Baptist's village, Ein Kerem. In the city, he organized the assassination of a British police chief. Wounded again in RAF strafing, Husseini's admirers regarded him as an Arab knight who eschewed luxury to fight amongst Arab peasants against infidel intruders – but his Palestinian enemies regarded him as one of the worst of the mufti's warlords, whose henchmen terrorized villages that did not support the Husseinis.

On 26 September 1937, the British district commissioner in Galilee, Lewis Andrews, was assassinated. On the 12th, the mufti escaped from Jerusalem dressed as a woman, an undignified exit that weakened his power in Palestine. In exile in Lebanon, he directed operations in a war that was still escalating. He mercilessly enforced obedience to himself personally and his rigidly intransigent policies.

The British were struggling to hold Palestine: Nablus, Hebron, swathes of Galilee were often out of control – and they even lost the Old City for short periods. The British recruited Jewish auxiliaries from the Haganah to join their so-called Jewish Settlement Police, but the latter could scarcely defend their far-flung villages. The Zionist nationalists were disgusted by Ben-Gurion's policy of restraint. The Irgun Zvai Leumi, the National Military Organization, still only mustering about 1,500 men at the beginning of the Revolt, answered Arab attacks with atrocities against Arab civilians, tossing grenades into cafés in Jerusalem. On Black Sunday in November 1937, they launched coordinated bombings, much to the horror of Weizmann and Ben-Gurion, but recruits poured into the Irgun. Just as the Arab moderates were being annihilated by the mufti's thugs, so the Revolt destroyed the credibility of conciliatory Jews such as Judah Magnes, the American president of the Hebrew University, who wanted a binational state with a bicameral congress of Jews and Arabs and no Jewish entity at all. Ben-Gurion's self-restraint was soon exhausted and the British now took off their gloves to crush the Arabs by all and any means: they collectively punished villages and at one point destroyed a whole neighbourhood of Jaffa. In June 1937, they brought in the death penalty for anyone bearing arms. In October, Sir Charles Tegart, who had stringently policed Calcutta for thirty years, arrived in Jerusalem. He built fifty 'Tegart forts', erected security fences around the borders and took charge of counter-insurgency and intelligence, creating Arab Investigation Centres. Tegart ran a school in west Jerusalem to instruct his interrogators how to torture suspects – including the 'water-can' technique in which prisoners had water forced down their noses from coffeepots, a method now known as 'water-boarding' – until the city governor Keith-Roach demanded it be moved. An RAF officer, Arthur Harris – later famed as the 'Bomber' of Dresden – supervised air attacks on rebel villages. Yet as the crisis with Hitler developed in Europe, the British could not bring in enough troops to destroy the Revolt, so they needed more Jewish help.

A well-connected young counter-insurgency expert named Orde Wingate was posted to Jerusalem where he was invited to stay by High Commissioner Wauchope. Wingate observed that Wauchope

'takes everyone's advice and has lost all grasp of affairs'. His rec-
ommendation was to train Jewish fighters and take the insurgency
to the insurgents. He would become the Zionist version of
Lawrence – Weizmann called him 'Lawrence of Judaea'. By chance,
these two unconventional English Arabists were cousins.

ORDE WINGATE AND MOSHE DAYAN:
THE FALL OF THE OLD CITY

The son of a well-off colonial colonel with an evangelical mission
to convert the Jews, raised on Bible and empire, Wingate was a
fluent Arabic-speaker, and, like Lawrence, earned his spurs commanding Arab irregulars – a unit of the East Arab Corps in Sudan.
'There was in him', wrote Weizmann, 'a fusion of the student and
man of action that reminded me of Lawrence.' But on arrival in
Jerusalem he underwent an almost Damascene conversion, impressed by the energy of the Zionists, and repulsed by the mufti's
bullyboy tactics and the anti-Semitism of British officers: 'Everyone's against the Jews,' he declared, 'so I'm for them!'

Wingate inspected the beleaguered British troops and Jewish
farms. In the depths of the night, they would receive visits from an
'extraordinary figure' wearing a Borsalino hat or a Wolseley topee,
a battered Palm Beach suit and a Royal Artillery tie, who looked
'like the kind of lowlife you saw hanging around dubious cafés in Tel
Aviv'. Always armed to the teeth, the thirty-three-year-old Captain
Wingate, who had 'very piercing blue eyes, aquiline features and a
faraway ascetic look with a scholarly air', arrived in a Studebaker
sedan 'filled with weapons, maps, Lee Enfield rifles, Mills grenades – and a Bible'. Wingate decided that 'the Jews will provide
better soldiery than ours.' In March 1938, the British commander,
Sir Archibald Wavell, impressed by this 'remarkable personality',
ordered Wingate to train Jewish special forces and deploy these so-
called Special Night Squads against the rebels. Wavell did not know
what he was dealing with: 'I wasn't then aware of the connection
with T. E. Lawrence.'

Setting up headquarters in the Fast Hotel, near the Jaffa Gate,

Wingate learned fluent Hebrew and was soon known as 'the Friend' by the Zionists – but he was regarded as an enemy by the Arabs and a reckless freak by many of his British brother-officers. Moving out of Government House, he set up home in Talpiot with his wife Lorna, who was 'very young and very beautiful like a porcelain doll. People didn't take their eyes off her', recalled Ruth Dayan. Her husband Moshe Dayan, the twenty-two-year-old son of Russian immigrants, born in the first kibbutz, had (secretly) joined the Haganah and was (openly) serving in the Jewish Settlement Police, when 'one evening, a Haganah man from Haifa turned up accompanied by a strange visitor. Wingate was a slender man, a heavy revolver at his side, carrying a small Bible. Before going on an action, he'd read the passage in the Bible relating to the place where we'd be operating.' This military heir of the bibliolatrist evangelicals led his Night Squads against the Arab gunmen who were 'forced to realize they could no longer find any path secure for them: they were likely to be caught in a surprise ambush anywhere.' During the Revolt and later during the Second World War, the British trained 25,000 Jewish auxiliaries, including other commando units led by Yitzhak Sadeh, a Russian Red Army veteran who became Haganah's chief of staff. 'You are the sons of the Maccabees,' Wingate told them, 'You are the first soldiers of a Jewish army!' Their expertise and spirit later formed the basis of the Israel Defence Forces.

In September 1938, Prime Minister Neville Chamberlain's Munich Agreement, which appeased Adolf Hitler's aggression and allowed him to dismember Czechoslovakia, freed British troops: 25,000 reinforcements arrived in Palestine. Yet in Jerusalem, the rebels pulled off a daring *coup de main*: on 17 October, they seized the entire Old City, barricading the gates, driving out British troops and even issuing postage stamps marked al-Quds. Wasif Jawhariyyeh, who lived near the Jaffa Gate, proudly saw an Arab flag fluttering from the Tower of David. A beleaguered rabbi at the Western Wall was terrorized by Arab gunmen. But on 19 October, the British stormed the gates and retook the city, killing nineteen gunmen as Wasif watched from his home. 'I can't describe the night of the battle with the British army and the rebels. We saw the explosions and heard the incredible smashing of bombs and bullets.'

Though he was a hero to the Jews, Wingate's operations were increasingly regarded as counter-productive by British officers, who heard that he opened his front door to guests stark naked, and was having an affair with a Jewish opera singer. Even Dayan had to admit: 'Judged by ordinary standards he wouldn't be regarded as normal. [After operations] he'd sit in the corner stark naked reading the Bible, and munching raw onions.' Wingate's divisional commander, Major-General Bernard Montgomery, disliked his military recklessness and Zionist partisanship. Wingate, Montgomery later told Dayan, 'was mentally unstable'. He was ordered back to the British headquarters in Jerusalem. Now the British had the forces, they no longer needed Jewish commandos.

'I don't care whether you're Jews or gentiles,' Montgomery told representatives of both sides. 'My duty is to maintain law and order. I intend to do so.' Montgomery declared the Revolt 'definitely, finally smashed'. Five hundred Jews had been killed and 150 Britons, but the Revolt had taken the most terrible toll on Palestinian society which has yet to recover: one-tenth of all males between 20 and 60 had been killed, wounded or exiled. One hundred and forty-six were sentenced to death, 50,000 arrested, and 5,000 homes destroyed. Around 4,000 were killed, many of them by fellow Arabs. It was just in time, as British forces were soon likely to be needed in Europe. 'I shall be sorry to leave Palestine in many ways,' said Montgomery, 'as I have enjoyed the war out here.'*

Neville Chamberlain, whose father had proposed a Jewish homeland in Uganda, decided to reverse the Balfour Declaration. If there was a war, the Jews had no choice but to back Britain against the Nazis. But the Arabs had a real choice. 'If we must offend one side,' said Chamberlain, 'let us offend the Jews rather than the Arabs.' He therefore invited both sides, and the Arab states, to a conference

* Wingate had made his name in Palestine. He was admired by Churchill who later backed his career. In 1941, Wingate's Gideon Force helped liberate Ethiopia from the Italians and then as a major general, he created and commanded the Chindits, the largest Allied special forces of the war, to fight behind Japanese lines in Burma. He was killed in a plane crash in 1944.

in London. The Arabs named the mufti as chief delegate, but since the British would not tolerate his presence, his cousin Jamal al-Husseini led one Arab delegation; Nashashibi led the moderates. The Husseinis stayed at the Dorchester, the Nashashibis at the Carlton. Weizmann and Ben-Gurion represented the Zionists. On 7 February 1939, Chamberlain had to open the conference in St James's Palace twice, because Arabs and Zionists refused to negotiate directly.

Chamberlain hoped to persuade the Zionists to agree to a cessation in immigration, but to no avail. On 15 March, the hollowness of his appeasement of Hitler was exposed when the Führer invaded the rump of Czechoslovakia. Two days later, Malcolm MacDonald, the colonial secretary, issued a White Paper that proposed limiting Jewish land purchases and restricting immigration to 15,000 people annually for five years, after which Arabs would have a veto, Palestinian independence within ten years and no Jewish state. This was the best offer the Palestinians were to receive from the British or anyone else during the entire twentieth century, but the mufti, displaying spectacular political incompetence and megalomaniacal intransigence, rejected it from his Lebanese exile.

Ben-Gurion prepared his Haganah militia for war against the British. Jews rioted in Jerusalem. On 2 June, the Irgun bombed the market outside the Jaffa Gate, killing nine Arabs. On the 8th, the last night of his stay in Jerusalem on an Eastern tour, a young American visitor, John F. Kennedy, son of the US ambassador to London, heard fourteen explosions ignited by the Irgun, knocking out electricity across the Holy City. Many now shared General Montgomery's view that 'The Jew murders the Arab and the Arabs murder the Jews and it will go on for the next 50 years in all probability.'

THE MUFTI AND HITLER: WORLD WAR IN JERUSALEM

As Adolf Hitler seemed to carry all before him, the mufti of Jerusalem saw an opportunity to strike at their common enemies, the British and the Jews. France had collapsed, the Wehrmacht was advancing towards Moscow, and Hitler had started the killing of 6 million Jews in his Final Solution.* The mufti had moved to Iraq to direct anti-British intrigues but, after organizing yet more defeats, had to flee to Iran and then, pursued by British agents, he embarked on an adventurous voyage that finally brought him to Italy. On 27 October 1941, Benito Mussolini received him at the Palazzo Venezia in Rome, backing the creation of a Palestinian state: if the Jews wanted their own country, 'they should establish Tel Aviv in America', said Il Duce. 'We have here in Italy 45,000 Jews and there will be no place for them in Europe.' The mufti – 'very satisfied by the meeting' – flew to Berlin.

At 4.30 p.m. on 28 November, the mufti was received by a tense Adolf Hitler: the Soviets had halted the Germans on the outskirts of Moscow. The mufti's interpreter suggested to the Führer that, by Arab tradition, coffee should be served. Hitler jumpily replied that he did not drink coffee. The mufti inquired if there was a problem. The interpreter soothed the mufti, but explained to the Führer that the guest still expected coffee. Hitler replied that even the High Command was not allowed to drink coffee in his presence: he then left the room, returning with an SS guard bearing lemonade.

Husseini asked Hitler to support the 'independence and unity of Palestine, Syria and Iraq' and the creation of an Arab Legion to fight with the Wehrmacht. The mufti, speaking to the apparent master of the world, was bidding not just for Palestine but for an Arab empire under his own rule.

Hitler was happy that he and the mufti shared the same enemies:

* In Greece, a princess with a special link to Jerusalem was one of those brave gentiles who protected Jews. Princess Andrew of Greece, born Princess Alice of Battenberg, great-granddaughter of Queen Victoria, risked her life by hiding the Cohen family of three while 60,000 Greek Jews were murdered. In 1947, her son Prince Philip, a lieutenant in the Royal Navy, married Princess Elizabeth, who succeeded to the throne four years later. Princess Andrew became a nun and founded her own order, like her aunt Grand Duchess Ella. She lived in London but decided to be buried in Jerusalem. When her daughter grumbled that this was a long trip for visitors, the princess retorted, 'Nonsense, there's a perfectly good bus service from Istanbul!' She died in 1969, but not until 1988 was she buried in the Church of Mary Magdalene close to her aunt Ella. In 1994, Prince Philip, Duke of Edinburgh, attended the ceremony at Yad Vashem, the Holocaust memorial in Jerusalem, that honoured his mother as one of the 'Righteous among the nations'.

'Germany was engaged in a life-and-death struggle with two citadels of Jewish power – Britain and the Soviet Union' – and naturally there would be no Jewish state in Palestine. Indeed the Führer hinted at his Final Solution to the Jewish problem: 'Germany was resolved, step by step, to ask one European nation after another to solve its Jewish problem.' As soon as 'German armies reached the southern exit of Caucasia', Hitler said, 'Germany's objective would then solely be the destruction of the Jewish element residing in the Arab sphere.'

However, until Russia and Britain were defeated, the mufti's ambitious bid for the entire Middle East would have to wait. Hitler said he 'had to think and speak coolly and deliberately as a rational man', careful not to offend his Vichy French ally. 'We were troubled about you,' Hitler told Husseini. 'I know your life story. I followed with interest your long and dangerous journey. I'm happy that you're with us now.' Afterwards, Hitler admired Husseini's blue eyes and reddish hair, deciding he definitely had Aryan blood.

Yet the mufti shared with Hitler not just a strategic hostility to Britain but racial anti-Semitism at its most lethal – and even in memoirs written long afterwards, he remembered that Reichführer-SS Heinrich Himmler, whom he liked greatly, confided to him in the summer of 1943 that the Nazis had 'already exterminated more than three million Jews.' The mufti chillingly boasted that he supported the Nazis 'because I was persuaded and still am that if Germany had carried the day, no trace of the Zionists would have remained in Palestine'.*

* 'He entered into the Nazis' criminal delirium about "the Jews"', writes Professor Gilbert Achcar in his book *Arabs and the Holocaust*, 'as it burgeoned into the greatest of all crimes against humanity.' Achcar adds, 'it is undeniable that the mufti espoused the Nazis' anti-Semitic doctrine which was easily compatible with a fanatical anti-Judaism cast in the Pan-Islamic mould.' In a speech in Berlin on the 1943 anniversary of the Balfour Declaration, he said 'they live rather as parasites amongst the peoples, suck their blood, pervert their morals . . . Germany has very clearly resolved to find a definitive solution for the Jewish danger that will eliminate the scourge that the Jews represent in the world.' In his memoirs written in his Lebanese exile, he revelled in the fact that Jewish 'losses in the course of the Second World War represented more than 30 per cent of the total number of their people whereas the Germans' losses were less significant' and, citing the *Protocols* and the World War One 'stab in the back' myth, he justified the Holocaust since there was no other way to scientifically reform the Jews.

He had come a long way from multi-national Jerusalem where, unsurprisingly, Jews were disheartened by his presence in Berlin. The mufti's views are indefensible – but it is wrong to use them to claim that Arab nationalists were Hitlerite anti-Semites. Wasif Jawhariyyeh, who, as we will see, was very sympathetic to the Jewish plight, was typical, writing in his diary that Arab Jerusalemites, loathing the British for 'their injustice, dishonesty and the Balfour Declaration, hoped Germany would win the war. They used to sit, listening to the news, waiting for headlines of German victory, grieving over good news for England.'

'Strange as it may sound', recalled Hazem Nusseibeh, wartime 'Jerusalem enjoyed unprecedented peace and prosperity'. The British clamped down on the Jewish militias: Moshe Dayan and his Haganah comrades were arrested and imprisoned in Acre Fortress. But in May 1941, as British Palestine was potentially pincered between the Axis forces in North Africa and Vichy French Syria, the British created the Palmach, a small Jewish commando force, out of Wingate's and Sadeh's fighters, ready to fight the Nazis.

Dayan, released from prison, was sent on raids to prepare for the British invasion of Vichy Syria and Lebanon. During a firefight in southern Lebanon, Dayan was checking on French positions through his binoculars 'when a rifle bullet smashed into them splintering a lens and the metal casing which became embedded in the socket of my eye'. He hated the eyepatch he now had to wear, feeling like 'a cripple. If only I could get rid of my black eyepatch. The attention it drew was intolerable to me. I preferred to shut myself up at home, rather than encounter the reactions of people wherever I went.' Dayan and his young wife moved to Jerusalem so that he could receive treatment. He 'loved to wander around the Old City, especially to walk the narrow path along the top of its encircling walls. The New City was somewhat strange to me. But the Old City was an enchantment.' The Haganah, with British help, was preparing to go underground if the Germans took Palestine.

Jerusalem was a favourite refuge for exiled kings – George II of Greece, Peter of Yugoslavia and the Ethiopian emperor Haile Selassie all stayed at the King David. The emperor walked barefoot through the streets and placed his crown at the foot of the altar in the Sepulchre. Indeed his prayers were answered: he was restored to his throne.*

Day and night, the corridors and bars of the King David were so crowded with Egyptian, Lebanese, Syrian, Serbian, Greek and Ethiopian princelings, aristocrats, racketeers, courtiers, loafers, tycoons, pimps, gigolos, courtesans, film stars and Allied, Axis, Zionist and Arab spies, as well as officers and diplomats in French, British, Australian and American uniforms, that visitors had to fight their way through its corridors even to reach its bar and get the desired dry martini. In 1942, a new guest checked in who was one of the most renowned Arab stars of her time and personifies the decadence of Jerusalem as Levantine entrepot. She sung under the name Asmahan; everywhere she went, this dangerous but irresistible woman, who contrived to be, among other things, a Druze princess, Egyptian film star, Arabic popular singer, *grande horizantale* and spy for all sides, managed to create her own breed of gorgeous havoc and mystery.

The scion of a princely but impoverished family, who had fled in 1918 to Egypt, Amal al-Altrash, born a Druze in Syria, was discovered as a singer aged fourteen and made her first record at sixteen, achieving instant fame on the radio and then in movies, always recognizable by the beauty spot on her chin. In 1933 she married her cousin, the amir of Mount Druze in Syria, for the first time (she married and divorced him twice). She insisted on living as a liberated, Western woman, even in his mountain palace, though she spent much time at the King David. In May 1941, the princess – or amira – was recruited by British intelligence to return to Vichy Damascus to charm and bribe Syrian leaders into backing the Allied powers. When the Allies retook Syria and Lebanon, she was personally thanked by General Charles de Gaulle. With her singing, invincible chic and utterly uninhibited libido (with bisexual tastes), Asmahan soon beguiled the Free French and British generals in

---

* In the 1930s, the emperor, known as Ras Tafar before his accession, inspired the Rastafarians, founded in Jamaica and made famous by the reggae singer Bob Marley, who hailed him as the Lion of Judah and the Second Coming of Jesus Christ. Ethiopia and Africa were the new Zion. Haile Selassie was murdered by the Marxist Dergue in 1974.

Beirut, playing them against each other and being paid by both as
an agent of influence. Churchill's envoy, General Louis Spears, was
so smitten, he said 'she was and will always be one the most
beautiful women I've ever seen. Her eyes were immense, green as
the sea you cross to paradise. She bowled over British officers with
the speed and accuracy of a machine gun. Naturally enough she
needed money.' It was said that if you were her lover it was impossible to be lonely in her boudoir, where you were liable to find one
general under the bed, one in the bed, and Spears dangling from
the chandelier.

Furious at Allied betrayal of the promise to grant immediate
Arab independence, the princess stole military secrets from a
British lover and tried to offer them to the Germans; when she was
stopped at the Turkish border, she bit the officer who arrested her.
When the Free French broke off her salary, she moved to Jerusalem.
Still only twenty-four, she became 'the Lady of the Lobbies' in the
King David, staying up all night drinking her favourite whisky-
champagne cocktail, seducing Palestinian grandees, more British
officers (and their wives) and Prince Aly Khan. A French friend
recalled: 'she was all woman. *Elle était diabolique avec les hommes.*'
As her surname was Altrash, the English women called her Princess
Trash, and she so shocked her Druze compatriots that they fired
shots at the screen when her first film was shown in the cinema –
she was years ahead of her time. She could be her own worst enemy:
she tried to throw the Egyptian Queen Mother Nazli out of the
best suite while starting an affair with the royal chamberlain. A
competition with an Egyptian dancer for a man culminated in the
ritual mutilation of each other's dresses. She regarded Zionism as
a fashion opportunity: 'Thank God for these Viennese furriers – at
least it means you can get a decent fur coat in Jerusalem.' After over
a year in the city, and marrying a third husband, an Egyptian
playboy, in 1944 she went to Egypt to star in the movie *Love and
Vengeance*, but before the film was finished she drowned in the Nile
in a mysterious car crash arranged, it was said, by MI6, the Gestapo,
King Farouk (whom she refused) or her rival, Umm Kulthum, the
pre-eminent Egyptian singer. If her brother Farid was the Arab
world's Sinatra, she was its Monroe. Asmahan's angelic singing,

particularly in her hit song 'Magical Nights in Vienna', is still much loved.

The streets teemed with American and Australian soldiers. The main challenge for the 'Pasha of Jerusalem', Governor Edward Keith-Roach, was to control the Australians, who were provided with a brothel under a Madame Zeinab in the old Hensmans Hotel in the centre of the New City. But the medical inspections completely failed to limit the spread of VD, so Keith-Roach sent 'Zeinab and her motley crew out of my district'.

In 1942, the Germans pushed deep into the Caucasus, while General Erwin Rommel's Afrika Korps advanced on Egypt. The very existence of the Yishuv in Palestine was in jeopardy. Across the Mediterranean, in Greece, SS Einsatzkommando Afrika under SS-Obersturmbannführer Walter Rauff, had been assigned to exterminate the Jews of Africa and Palestine. 'The faces of the Jews showed the grief, sadness and fear especially when the Germans reached Tobruk,' recorded Wasif Jawhariyyeh. An Arab pedlar loudly hawking sand – ramel in Arabic sounds like Rommel – made Jews fear that the Germans were approaching. 'They started crying and made efforts to flee', recalled Wasif. As his doctor was Jewish, Wasif offered to hide him and his family if the Nazis arrived. But the doctor had taken his own precautions: he showed his patient two poison-filled syringes for himself and his wife.

In October 1942, General Montgomery smashed the Germans at El Alamein, a miracle which Weizmann compared to Sennacherib's mysterious withdrawal from Jerusalem. But in November the first terrible news of the Holocaust reached Jerusalem: 'Mass Butchery of Polish Jews!' reported the Palestine Post. Jewish Jerusalem mourned for three days, culminating in a service at the Wall.

The British crackdown on Jewish immigration, announced in the 1939 White Paper, could not have been worse timed: while European Jewry was being slaughtered in Nazi Europe, British troops were turning back shiploads of desperate refugees. The Arab Revolt, Hitler's Final Solution and the White Paper convinced many Zionists that violence was the only way to force Britain to grant the promised Jewish homeland.

The Jewish Agency controlled the largest militia, the Haganah, with its 2,000-strong special forces, the Palmach, and its 25,000 militiamen trained by the British. Ben-Gurion was now the unrivalled Zionist leader, 'a short tubby man with a prophetic shock of silvery hair' around his bald patch, in Amos Oz's words, 'thick bushy eyebrows, a wide coarse nose, the prominent defiant jaw of an ancient mariner' and the laser-beam willpower of a 'visionary peasant'. But it was the more belligerent Irgun, under an implacable new leader, that now waged war against the British.

50

THE DIRTY WAR

1945–7

MENACHEM BEGIN: THE BLACK SABBATH

'I fight; therefore I am,' said Menachem Begin, adapting Descartes. Born in Brest-Litovsk, this child of the *shtetl* had joined Jabotinsky's Betar movement in Poland, but he had clashed with his hero, throwing out his subtleties, to forge his own harsher ideology of military Zionism – a 'war of liberation against those who hold the land of our fathers', combining maximalist politics with emotional religion. After the Nazis and Soviets had carved up Poland at the start of the Second World War, Begin was arrested by Stalin's NKVD and sentenced to the Gulag as a British spy: 'What became of this British agent?' he joked. 'He soon had on his head the largest reward offered by the British police.'

Released after Stalin's 1941 pact with the Polish leader General Sikorski, Begin joined the Polish Army which brought him via Persia to Palestine. Formed in the dark continent of Stalin's meat-grinder and Hitler's slaughterhouse – in which his parents and brother perished – he came from a harsher school than Weizmann or Ben-Gurion: 'It's not Masada,' he said, 'but Modin [where the Maccabees started their rebellion] that symbolizes the Hebrew revolt.' Jabotinsky had died of a heart attack in 1940 and now in 1944, Begin was appointed commander of the Irgun with its 600 fighters. The older Zionists regarded Begin as 'plebeian or provincial'. With his rimless glasses, 'soft restless hands, thinning hair and wet lips',* Begin looked more like a provincial Polish

---

* The description is that of Arthur Koestler, the writer who had come to Jerusalem as a Revisionist Zionist in 1928 but had soon left. In 1948, Koestler returned to cover the War of Independence and interviewed Begin and Ben-Gurion.

schoolmaster than a revolutionary mastermind. Yet he had 'the patience of a hunter in ambush'.

Although the Irgun had joined the Allied war against the Nazis, some extremists, led by Abraham Stern, had split off. Stern was killed by the British in 1942. But his faction, the Lehi, Fighters for the Freedom of Israel, nicknamed the Stern Gang, now launched their own revolt against the British. As Allied victory became more likely, Begin started to test British resolve in Jerusalem: the blowing of the *shofar*, the ram's horn, on The Day of Atonement, had been banned at the Wall since 1929. But Jabotinsky had annually challenged the rule. In October 1943, Begin ordered the blowing of the *shofar*: British police immediately attacked the praying Jews but in 1944, the British desisted. Begin took this as a sign of weakness.

This impresario of violence declared war on Britain and in September 1944, the Irgun attacked British police stations in Jerusalem and then assassinated a CID officer as he walked through the city. Begin, nicknamed the Old Man (the same nickname enjoyed by Ben-Gurion), even though he was about thirty, descended into the underground, constantly moving address and adopting the disguise of a bearded Talmudic scholar. The British placed a £10,000 bounty on his head, dead or alive.

The Jewish Agency condemned terrorism, but as the Allies launched the D-Day invasion of German-occupied Europe,* the Lehi twice tried to assassinate the high commissioner Harold Mac-Michael in the streets of Jerusalem. In Cairo that November, they killed Walter Guinness, Lord Moyne, Minister Resident in Egypt and friend of Churchill, who had tactlessly suggested to Ben-Gurion that the Allies should establish a Jewish state in East Prussia, instead of Zion. Churchill called the Zionist extremists the 'vilest gangsters'. Ben-Gurion condemned the murders and, during 1944–5, helped the British hunt down the Jewish 'dissident' militias – 300

---

* That summer, Churchill wrote to Stalin suggesting an allied conference in Jerusalem – 'There are first class hotels, Government houses etc. Marshal Stalin could come by special train with every form of protection from Moscow to Jerusalem' – and the British prime minister helpfully enclosed the route: 'Moscow Tbilisi Ankara Beirut Haifa Jerusalem'. Instead they met (with President Roosevelt) at Yalta.

insurgents were arrested. The Zionists called this 'la saison', the hunting season.

On 8 May 1945, Victory in Europe Day, the new high commissioner, Field Marshal Viscount Gort, took the salute outside the King David Hotel and issued an amnesty for Jewish and Arab political prisoners while Jerusalemites partied. However, the reality of sectarian politics reared up again the next day: both Jews and Arabs demonstrated – and both were already effectively boycotting the city's mayoralty.

In Britain, Churchill was defeated in the general election. The new prime minister, Clement Attlee, had adopted William Blake's anthem as his Labour Party campaign song, promising his people a 'New Jerusalem' – though he proved quite incapable of governing the old one.

The British anxiously steeled themselves for the coming struggle. Should the city with 100,000 Jews, 34,000 Muslims and 30,000 Christians be a British-run State of Jerusalem, as suggested by MacMichael, or partitioned, with the holy sites run by the British, as proposed by Gort? Either way, the British were determined to stop Jewish immigration into Palestine – even though many of the immigrants were survivors of Hitler's death-camps. Now confined in miserable Displaced Person camps across Europe, shiploads of desperate Jewish refugees were harassed and turned away by British forces. The Exodus was stormed by the British, who roughed up its refugees, many of them death-camp survivors (three of whom were killed), and then, with scarcely credible insensitivity, sent them back to camps in Germany. Even the moderate Jewish Agency found this morally repugnant.

Ben-Gurion, Begin and the Lehi therefore agreed to form a United Resistance Command to smuggle in Jewish immigrants from Europe and coordinate the struggle against the British, attacking trains, airfields, army bases and police stations across the country. But the two small factions paid only lip-service to the more moderate Haganah. The Russian Compound, its majestic hostels now converted into a police stronghold, was a favoured target of the Irgun. On 27 December, they destroyed the CID police headquarters, the former Nikolai pilgrims hostel. Begin travelled by bus from Tel Aviv to Jerusalem to view his handiwork. In January 1946, the Irgun attacked the prison inside the Russian Compound which had once been the Marianskaya Hostel for female pilgrims.*

The British, battered by these attacks, drew America into their dilemmas. The American Jewish community was increasingly pro-Zionist but President Franklin D. Roosevelt had never publicly backed a Jewish state. At Yalta, Roosevelt and Stalin had discussed the Holocaust. 'I'm a Zionist,' said Roosevelt. 'Me too, in principle,' replied Stalin, who boasted that he had 'tried to establish a national home for the Jews in Birobidzhan but they had stayed there two or three years and then scattered'. The Jews, added that visceral anti-Semite, were 'middlemen, profiteers and parasites' – but secretly he hoped that any Jewish state would be a Soviet satellite.

FDR died in April 1945. His successor, Harry S. Truman, wanted to settle Holocaust survivors in Palestine and asked the British to let them in. Truman, raised as a Baptist, a former farmer, bank-clerk, Kansas City haberdasher, was a mediocre Missouri senator with a sympathy for the Jews and a sense of history. When the new president toured the dynamited moonscape of Berlin in 1945, he 'thought of Carthage, Baalbek, Jerusalem, Rome, Atlantis'. Now his longstanding friendship with his Jewish ex-haberdashery partner, Eddie Jacobson, and the influence of pro-Zionist aides, along with 'his own reading of ancient history and the Bible, made him a supporter of a Jewish homeland', recalled his adviser Clark Clifford. Yet Truman, facing the resistance of his own State Department, was frequently irritated by Zionist lobbying and was wary of any sign of the Jewish underdogs becoming the bullying overdogs: 'Jesus Christ couldn't please them when he was on earth,' he snapped, 'so how on earth could anyone expect that I would have any luck?' But he agreed to create an Anglo-American commission of inquiry.

The commissioners stayed in the King David Hotel where one of them, Richard Crossman, a Labour MP, found 'the atmosphere terrific, with private detectives, Zionist agents, Arab sheikhs, special

---

* This is now a museum to the Jewish resistance fighters who were imprisoned there. The Nikolai Hostel was the last Russian pilgrim hostel to be built, with room for 1,200 pilgrims, opened by the Romanov Prince Nikolai in 1903.

correspondents, all sitting about discreetly overhearing each other'. At night, Arab grandees and British generals gathered at Katy Antonius' villa. She was now alone. The Antoniuses' decadent marriage had started to collapse at the same time as the Arab Revolt. During the war, Katy had divorced her ailing husband – who died unexpectedly just two weeks later. He was buried on Mount Zion: 'Arise ye Arabs and awake' was written on his headstone. But Katy's soirées were still legendary. Crossman, enjoying 'the evening dress, Syrian food and drink, and dancing on the marble floor', reported that the Arabs gave the best parties: 'It's easy to see why the British prefer the Arab upper class to the Jews. This Arab intelligentsia has a French culture, amusing, civilized, tragic and gay. Compared with them, the Jews seem tense, bourgeois, central European.'

Attlee had hoped that Truman would support his policies against Jewish immigration, but the Anglo-American Commission unhelpfully recommended that the British admit 100,000 refugees immediately: Truman publicly backed their recommendations. Attlee furiously rejected American interference. The Jewish Agency stepped up the secret immigration of refugees from the Holocaust, bringing in 70,000 in three years while its Palmach harassed the British, culminating in an explosive spectacular – the Night of the Bridges.

The British had crushed the Arabs; now they would crush the Jews. In June 1946, Viscount Montgomery of Alamein, now field marshal and Chief of the Imperial General Staff, returned to Jerusalem, complaining that 'British rule existed only in name; the true rulers seemed to me to be the Jews, whose unspoken slogan was – "You dare not touch us".' But Montgomery dared, sending in reinforcements.

On Saturday 29 June, his commander, General Evelyn 'Bubbles' Barker, launched Operation Agatha, an attack on the Zionist organizations. He arrested 3,000 Jews – though failed to pick up Ben-Gurion who happened to be in Paris. Barker fortified three 'security zones' in Jerusalem, turning the Russian Compound into a fortress that the Jews nicknamed Bevingrad, after the British foreign secretary Ernest Bevin. To the Jews the operation came to be known as Black Sabbath, and Barker was at once the hated symbol of

British oppression. The general was a regular at Katy Antonius' parties. Now the hostess became his mistress: his love letters were passionate, indiscreet and hate-filled, featuring British military secrets and foam-flecked rants against Jews: 'Why should we be afraid of saying we hate them?' Lehi attempted to assassinate Barker, using a bomb disguised as a baby in a pram. Menachem Begin of the Irgun, assisted by the Lehi, planned a response to Barker's Black Sabbath to resound across the world. The Haganah, though not Ben-Gurion and the Jewish Agency, approved.

The King David Hotel was the secular temple of Mandate Jerusalem, and one wing had been requisitioned by the British administration and intelligence agencies. On 22 July 1946, the Irgun, disguised as Arabs and hotel staff in Nubian costumes, stowed milkchurns filled with 500 pounds of explosives in the basement.

MONTGOMERY'S CRACKDOWN:
THE CASE OF MAJOR FARRAN

The Irgun made anonymous calls to the hotel, to the *Palestine Post* and to the French Consulate, to warn of the imminent attack so that the King David could be evacuated. But the calls were ignored – and they were too late. It is unclear if the mishandling of these warnings was by accident or design. Begin waited nearby: 'each minute seemed like a day. Twelve-thirty-one, thirty-two. Zero hour drew near. The half-hour was almost up. Twelve-thirty-seven. Suddenly the whole town seemed to shudder!' The bombs shattered an entire wing of the King David, killing ninety-one, including Britons, Jews and Arabs.* Five MI5 operatives were among the dead, but the Secret Service 'London Ladies' survived, staggering from the wreckage, their hair white with plaster dust, 'looking like the wrath of God'. Ben-Gurion denounced the bombing; he regarded Begin as a threat to the Jewish community, and the Jewish Agency quit the United Resistance Command.

The King David bombing intensified the severity of the British

---

* One of those killed was Julius Jacobs, a cousin of the author and a British civil servant who happened to be Jewish.

counter-attack – but it succeeded in accelerating London's retreat from the Mandate. In Jerusalem, the mixing of Jews and Arabs ceased. 'It felt', sensed Amos Oz, 'as though an invisible muscle was suddenly flexed. Everyone prophesied war. A curtain had begun to divide Jerusalem.' The Jews were terrified by rumours of imminent massacre. British civilians were evacuated from Jerusalem.

In October, the Irgun blew up the British Embassy in Rome. In November, Montgomery flew back into Jerusalem. 'I saw Monty at one of Katy Antonius' parties,' remembers Nassereddin Nashashibi. The field marshal planned a harsh response to the Irgun's outrage. A new police chief, Colonel Nicol Gray, recruited hard men, ex-policemen and former members of the special forces, to join new counter-insurgency Special Squads. Major Roy Farran DSO, MC was a typical recruit, an Irish SAS commando whose record revealed a history of trigger-happy exploits.

On arrival in Jerusalem, Farran was driven to the Russian Compound for briefing followed by dinner at the King David Hotel. Farran and the Special Squads started to drive around Jerusalem, looking for suspects to interrogate, if not shoot on sight. These Special Squads had no experience in covert operations, no local languages or knowledge, so, unsurprisingly, Farran had been almost comically unsuccessful until, driving through Rehavia on the 6 May 1947, his team spotted an unarmed schoolboy, Alexander Rubowitz, pasting up Lehi posters. Farran kidnapped the boy but, in the scuffle, dropped his trilby, marked with his ill-spelt name 'FARAN'. He hoped that the scared teenager would betray bigger Lehi fish. He drove Rubowitz out of Jerusalem, down the Jericho Road into the hills, tied him to a tree, roughed him up for an hour, then he went too far and smashed his skull with a rock. The body was stabbed and stripped and probably eaten by jackals.

While Jewish Jerusalem frantically searched for the missing boy, Major Farran confessed to his superior officer at the police mess in Katamon, then suddenly disappeared, fleeing Jerusalem. There was first a cover-up, then an outcry across the world. The Lehi started to kill random British soldiers, until Farran returned to Jerusalem and gave himself up at the Allenby Barracks. On 1 October, 1947, he was court-martialled in a fortified court in Talbieh, but was acquitted for lack of admissible evidence. Rubowitz's body was never found. Farran was bundled away by two officers in an armoured car and driven into the night towards Gaza. The Lehi was determined to kill him. In 1948, a parcel, addressed to 'R. FARRAN' but opened by his brother, who shared the same initial, exploded: the brother was killed.*

The case confirmed everything the Yishuv hated about the British. When the authorities condemned an Irgun man to death for terrorist offences, Begin bombed the British Officers Club in Goldsmid House, Jerusalem, killing fourteen, and pulled off a breakout from Acre Prison. When his men were flogged, he flogged British soldiers, and when his men were hanged at Acre Prison for terrorism, he hanged two random British soldiers for 'anti-Hebrew activities'.

Churchill, now leader of the Opposition, denounced Attlee's conduct of this 'senseless squalid war with the Jews in order to give Palestine to the Arabs or God knows who'. Even during the war, Churchill had considered a crackdown on 'anti-Semites and others in high places' among his administrators in Palestine. Now a combination of outrage at the violence of Irgun and Lehi, traditional Arabism and anti-Semitism had turned the British firmly against the Jews. British deserters and sometimes serving troops aided Arab forces.

The new high commissioner, General Sir Alan Cunningham, privately described Zionism as 'nationalism accompanied by the psychology of the Jew which is something quite abnormal and unresponsive to rational treatment'. General Barker banned British troops from all Jewish restaurants, explaining that he would be 'punishing the Jews in a way the race dislikes as much as any, by striking at their pockets'. Barker was reprimanded by the prime minister, but the hatred was now visceral. In Barker's love letters

---

* Farran remained a war hero to British security forces. He failed to win a Scottish seat in Parliament as a Conservative in 1949 and then moved to Canada. There he took up farming, was elected to the Alberta legislature, becoming minister of telephones, solicitor-general and a professor of political science. He died in 2006 aged eighty-six. A street in East Talpiot, Jerusalem, was recently named after Rubowitz.

to Katy Antonius, he said he hoped the Arabs would kill more 'bloody Jews ... loathsome people .... Katy, I love you so much.'

On 14 February 1947, Attlee, worn down by the bloodshed, agreed in Cabinet to get out of Palestine. On 2 April, he asked the newly formed United Nations to create a Special Committee on Palestine (UNSCOP) to decide on its future. Four months later UNSCOP proposed the partition of Palestine into two states with Jerusalem as an international trusteeship under a UN governor. Ben-Gurion accepted the plan, despite its unworkable boundaries. He felt that Jerusalem was 'the heart of the Jewish people' but losing her was 'the price paid for statehood'. The Arab Higher Committee, backed by Iraq, Saudi Arabia and Syria, rejected partition, demanding 'a unified independent Palestine'. On 29 November the UN voted on the proposal. After midnight, the Jerusalemites gathered around their radios to listen in nerve-jangling silence.

ABD AL-KADIR HUSSEINI: THE JERUSALEM FRONT

Thirty-three countries voted in favour of Resolution 181, led by the United States and the Soviet Union, thirteen voted against, and ten, including Britain, abstained. 'After a couple of minutes of shock, of lips parted as though in thirst and eyes wide open,' recalled Amos Oz, 'our faraway street on the edge of northern Jerusalem roared all at once, not a shout of joy, more like a scream of horror, a cataclysmic shout that could shift rocks.' Then 'roars of joy' and 'everyone was singing'. Jews even kissed 'startled English policemen'.

The Arabs did not accept that the UN had authority to carve up the country. There were 1.2 million Palestinians who still owned 94 per cent of the land; there were 600,000 Jews. Both sides prepared to fight, while Jewish and Arab extremists competed in a flint-hearted tournament of mutual savagery. Jerusalem was 'at war with itself'.

Arab mobs poured into the city centre, lynching Jews, firing into their suburbs, looting their shops, shrieking 'Butcher the Jews!' Anwar Nusseibeh, heir to orange groves and mansions, a

Cambridge-educated lawyer, sadly watched this descent into 'dust, noise and chaos' as 'professors, doctors and shopkeepers on both sides traded fire with people who, under different circumstances, would have been house guests'.

On 2 December, three Jews were shot in the Old City; on the 3rd, Arab gunmen attacked the Montefiore Quarter, then a week later the Jewish Quarter, where 1,500 Jews waited nervously, outnumbered within the walls by 22,000 Arabs. Jews and Arabs moved out of mixed areas. On 13 December, the Irgun tossed bombs into the bus station outside the Damascus Gate, killing five Arabs and wounding many more. Anwar Nusseibeh's uncle just survived the Irgun attack, seeing a 'torn human limb stuck to the city wall.' Within two weeks, 74 Jews, 71 Arabs and 9 Britons had been killed.

When Ben-Gurion travelled down from Tel Aviv to meet the high commissioner on 7 December, his convoy was ambushed on the road. The Haganah called up all reservists between the ages of seventeen and twenty-five. The Arabs prepared for war. Irregulars volunteered to fight in the various militias: Iraqis, Lebanese, Syrians, Bosnians, some were nationalist veterans of earlier struggles; others were Jihadi fundamentalists. The largest militia, the Arab Liberation Army, boasted about 5,000 fighters. On paper, the Arab forces, backed by the regular armies of seven Arab states, were overwhelming. General Barker, who had now left Palestine, gleefully predicted to Katy Antonius 'as a soldier' that 'the Jews will be eradicated'. In fact, the Arab League, the organization of newly independent Arab states formed in 1945, was divided between the territorial ambitions and dynastic rivalries of its members. Abdullah, freshly minted Hashemite King of Jordan, still wanted Palestine within his kingdom; Damascus coveted a Greater Syria; King Farouk of Egypt regarded himself as the rightful leader of the Arab world and hated the Hashemites of both Jordan and Iraq, who in turn loathed King Ibn Saud who had ejected them from Arabia. All the Arab leaders distrusted the mufti who, returning to Egypt, was determined to place himself at the head of the Palestinian state.

Amid so much corruption, betrayal and incompetence, Jerusalem supplied the Arab heroes of the war. Anwar Nusseibeh, disgusted by the 'sordid round of intrigues and debacles', founded the Herod's Gate Committee with other dynasts, the Khalidis and Dajanis, to buy arms. His cousin Abd al-Kadir Husseini, who had fought the British in Iraq in 1941, then had lain low during the war in Cairo, took command of the Arab headquarters called the Jerusalem Front.

Husseini emerged as the Arab hero personified, always dressed in *keffiyeh*, khaki tunic and crossed bandoliers, the revolutionary scion of Jerusalem's aristocracy, son and grandson of mayors, descendant of the Prophet, a graduate in chemistry, amateur poet, newspaper editor and a warrior of proven courage. 'As a child,' says his cousin Said al-Husseini, 'I remember seeing him arrive at a safe apartment in one of our houses and I can still remember his charisma and grace and that air of urgent heroic excitement that followed him everywhere. He was admired by everyone high and low.' A teenage student from Gaza named Yasser Arafat, who was proud that his mother was related to the Husseinis, served on Abd al-Kadir's staff.

Zionist gunmen in the Jewish Quarter fired over the Temple Mount; Arabs fired at Jewish civilians from Katamon. On 5 January, the Haganah attacked Katamon and destroyed the Semiramis Hotel, killing eleven innocent Christian Arabs. This outrage accelerated the Arab flight from the city. Ben-Gurion sacked the Haganah officer in charge. Two days later, the Irgun bombed an Arab outpost at the Jaffa Gate which was denying provisions to the Jewish Quarter. On 10 February, 150 of Husseini's militiamen attacked the Montefiore Quarter; the Haganah fought back but came under fire from British snipers in the nearby King David Hotel, who killed a young Jewish fighter there. There was still four months left of British rule but Jerusalem was already mired in a full-scale if asymmetrical war. In the previous six weeks, 1,060 Arabs, 769 Jews and 123 Britons had been killed. Each atrocity had to be avenged twofold.

The Zionists were vulnerable in Jerusalem: the road from Tel Aviv passed through 30 miles of Arab territory and Abd al-Kadir Husseini, who commanded the 1,000-strong Jerusalem brigade of the mufti's Holy War Army, attacked it constantly. 'The Arab plan', recalled Yitzhak Rabin, the Palmach officer born in the Holy City, 'was to choke Jerusalem's 90,000 Jews into submission' – and it soon began to work.

On 1 February, Husseini's militiamen, aided by two British deserters, blew up the offices of the *Palestine Post*; on the 10th, he attacked Montefiore again but was repelled by the Haganah after a six-hour gun battle. The British set up a command post below the Jaffa Gate to defend Montefiore. On 13 February, the British arrested four Haganah fighters and then released them unarmed to an Arab mob, who murdered them. On the 22nd, Husseini sent British deserters to blow up Ben Yehuda Street, an atrocity that killed fifty-two Jewish civilians. The Irgun shot ten British soldiers.

Trying to defend the Arab areas in Jerusalem, recalled Nusseibeh, 'was like a worn-out water hose repaired in one place only to burst in two more.' The Haganah blew up the old Nusseibeh castle. The former Arab mayor Hussein Khalidi complained, 'Everyone's leaving. I won't be able to hold out much longer. Jerusalem is lost. No one is left in Katamon. Sheikh Jarrah has emptied. Everyone who has a cheque or a little money is off to Egypt, off to Lebanon, off to Damascus.' Soon refugees were pouring out of the Arab suburbs. Katy Antonius left for Egypt; her mansion was blown up by the Haganah, but only after they had found her love-letters from General Barker. Nonetheless Abd al-Kadir Husseini had successfully cut off Jewish west Jerusalem from the coast.

Ironically the Jews, like the Arabs, felt they were losing Jerusalem. By early 1948, the Jewish Quarter in the Old City was under siege and defence was made more difficult by the number of non-combatant ultra-Orthodox Jews. 'Well, what about Jerusalem?' Ben-Gurion asked his generals on 28 March at his headquarters in Tel Aviv. 'That's the decisive battle. The fall of Jerusalem could be a deathblow to the Yishuv.' The generals could spare only 500 men. The Jews had been on the defensive since the UN vote, but now Ben-Gurion ordered Operation Nachshon to clear the road to Jerusalem, the start of a wider offensive, Plan D, designed to secure the UN-assigned Jewish areas but also west Jerusalem. 'The plan', writes the historian Benny Morris, 'explicitly called for the destruction of resisting Arab villages and the expulsion of their inhabitants' but 'nowhere does the document speak of a policy or desire to expel "the Arab inhabitants" of Palestine.' In some places, the Palestinians remained in their homes; in some places they were expelled.

The village of Kastel controlled the road from the coast to Jerusalem. On the night of 2 April, the Haganah seized the stronghold, but Husseini massed his militiamen (including Iraqi irregulars) to retake it. He and Anwar Nusseibeh realized, however, that they needed reinforcements. The two of them hurried to Damascus to demand artillery only to be exasperated by the incompetence and intrigues of the Arab League generals. 'Kastel has fallen,' said the Iraqi commander-in-chief. 'It's your job to get it back, Abd al-Kadir.'

'Give us the weapons I requested and we will recover it,' answered Husseini furiously.

'What's this, Abd al-Kadir? No cannon?' said the general, who offered nothing.

Husseini stormed out: 'You traitors! History will record that you lost Palestine. I'll take Kastel or die fighting with my *mujahidin*!' That night he wrote a poem for his seven-year-old son Faisal who, decades later, would become Yasser Arafat's Palestinian 'minister' for Jerusalem:

This land of the brave is the land of our forefathers
The Jews have no right to this land.
How can I sleep while the enemy rules it?
Something burns in my heart. My homeland beckons.

The commander reached Jerusalem next morning and mustered his fighters.

GUN SALUTES ON THE HARAM: ABD AL-KADIR HUSSEINI

On 7 April, Abd al-Kadir led 300 fighters and three British deserters up to Kastel. At 11 o'clock that night, they attacked the village but were repelled. At dawn the next day, Husseini moved forward to replace a wounded officer, but as he approached in the fog, unsure who held the actual village, a Haganah sentry, thinking the new arrivals were Jewish reinforcements, called in Arabic slang: 'Up here, boys!'

'Hello, boys,' retorted Husseini in English. The Jews often used Arabic – but never English. The Haganah sentry sensed danger and let slip a volley that hit Husseini. His comrades fled, leaving him on the ground, moaning, 'Water, water.' Despite attention from a Jewish medic, he died. The gold watch and the ivory-handled pistol revealed that he was a leader, but who was he?

On the radio, the exhausted Haganah defenders eavesdropped on the anxious Arabic talk of regaining the body of the lost commander. His brother Khaled assumed the command. As word spread, Arab militiamen streamed into the area on buses, donkeys and trucks and retook the village, the Palmach troops dying in position. The Arabs killed their fifty Jewish prisoners and mutilated the bodies. The Arabs had retaken the key to Jerusalem – with Husseini's body.

'What a sad day! His martyrdom depressed everyone,' recorded Wasif Jawhariyyeh. 'A warrior of patriotism and Arab nobility!' On Friday 9 April, 'no one stayed in their house. Everyone walked in the procession. I was at the funeral,' Wasif noted. Thirty thousand mourners – Arab fighters waving their rifles, Arab Legionaries from Jordan, peasants, the Families – attended as the fallen Husseini was buried on the Temple Mount next to his father and near King Hussein in Jerusalem's Arab pantheon. There was an eleven-cannon salute; gunmen fired into the air and a witness claimed that more mourners were killed than had died in the storming of Kastel. 'It sounded as if a major battle was in progress. Church bells rang, voices cried for revenge; everyone feared a Zionist attack,' remembered Anwar Nusseibeh, who was 'despondent'. But the Arab fighters were so keen to attend Husseini's burial that they left no garrison in Kastel. The Palmach destroyed the stronghold.

As Husseini was being buried, 120 fighters of the Irgun and Lehi jointly attacked an Arab village just west of Jerusalem named Deir Yassin, where they committed the most shameful Jewish atrocity of the war. They were under specific orders not to harm women, children or prisoners. As they entered the village, they came under fire. Four Jewish fighters were killed and several dozen wounded.

Once they were in Deir Yassin, the Jewish fighters tossed grenades into houses and slaughtered men, women and children. The number of victims is still debated, but between 100 and 254, including entire families, were murdered. The survivors were then paraded in trucks through Jerusalem until the Haganah released them. The Irgun and Lehi were undoubtedly aware that a spectacular massacre would terrify many Arab civilians and encourage flight. The Irgun commander, Begin, contrived to deny that the atrocity had taken place while boasting of its utility: 'The legend [of Deir Yassin] was worth half a dozen battalions to the forces of Israel. Panic overwhelmed the Arabs.' But Ben-Gurion apologized to King Abdullah, who rejected the apology.

Arab vengeance was swift. On 14 April, a convoy of ambulances and food trucks set off for the Hadassah Hospital on Mount Scopus. Bertha Spafford watched as 'a hundred and fifty insurgents, armed with weapons varying from blunderbusses and old flintlocks to modern Sten and Bren guns, took cover behind a cactus patch in the grounds of the American Colony. Their faces were distorted by hate and lust for revenge,' she wrote. 'I went out and faced them. I told them, "To fire from the shelter of the American Colony is the same as firing from a mosque,"' but they ignored her rollcall of sixty years' philanthropy and threatened to kill her if she did not withdraw. Seventy-seven Jews, mainly doctors and nurses, were killed and twenty wounded before the British intervened. 'Had it not been for Army interference,' declared the Arab Higher Committee, 'not a single Jewish passenger would have remained alive.' The gunmen mutilated the dead and photographed each other with the corpses splayed in macabre poses. The photographs were mass-produced and sold as postcards in Jerusalem.

Deir Yassin was one of the pivotal events of the war: it became the centrepiece of a bloodcurdling Arab media campaign that amplified Jewish atrocities. This was designed to fortify resistance, but instead it encouraged a psychosis of foreboding in a country already at war. By March, before Deir Yassin, 75,000 Arabs had left their homes. Two months later, 390,000 had gone. Wasif Jawhariyyeh, living with his wife and children in western Jerusalem, close to the King David Hotel, was probably typical – and he recorded his thoughts and actions in the diary that is a unique and under-used record.

'I was in a very bad way,' he writes after these events in mid-April, 'depressed, physically and mentally', so much so that he abandoned his job in the Mandate administration and 'stayed at home trying to decide what to do'. Finally, the diarist records the 'reasons that made me decide to leave my home'. First was the 'dangerous position of our house', where he was under fire from the Arabs at the Jaffa Gate, the Jews in Montefiore and the British Bevingrad security zone: 'there was non-stop shooting day and night so it was hard even to reach the house. The fighting between Arabs and Jews, the blowing up of buildings, continued day and night around us.' The British fired on Montefiore, blowing off the top of Sir Moses' windmill, but to no avail. Wasif wrote that the Jewish snipers in Montefiore, 'shot at anyone walking in the streets and it was a miracle we survived.' He considered how to save his collection of ceramics, diaries and his beloved *oud*. His health was deteriorating too: 'My body became so weak I couldn't handle the pressure and the doctor told me to leave.' The family debated: 'What will happen when the Mandate ends? Will we be under the Arabs or the Jews?' Wasif's neighbour, the French consul-general, promised to protect the house and the collection. 'Even if we never come back,' Wasif felt they should pack their bags 'to save ourselves and our children': 'We thought we would not leave the house for more than two weeks because we knew how soon the seven [sic] Arab armies will enter the country not to occupy it but to free it and return it to its people and we are its people!' He left in the last days of the Mandate, never to return. Wasif's story is that of the Palestinians. Some were expelled by force, some departed to avoid the war, hoping to return later – and approximately half remained safely in their homes to become Israeli Arabs, non-Jewish citizens in the Zionist democracy. But altogether 600,000–750,000 Palestinians left – and lost – their homes. Their tragedy was the Nakhba – the Catastrophe.

Ben-Gurion summoned the chief of the Jerusalem Emergency Committee, Bernard Joseph, to Tel Aviv to decide how to supply the now starving Jerusalem. On 15 April the convoys broke through, and food trickled into the city. On the 20th, Ben-Gurion insisted on visiting Jerusalem to celebrate Passover with the troops: Rabin, commander of the Palmach's Harel Brigade, protested at Ben-Gurion's grandstanding. Soon after the convoy set off with Ben-Gurion in an armoured bus, the Arabs attacked. 'I even ordered two stolen British armoured cars to be brought out of concealment and sent into action', said Rabin. Twenty were killed – but the food and Ben-Gurion reached Jewish Jerusalem – which he described, with grim humour but acute observation, as '20 per cent normal people; 20 per cent privileged (university etc), 60 per cent weird (provincial, medieval etc)' – by which he meant the Hasidim.

British rule was now in its last days. On 28 April, Rabin captured the Arab suburb Sheikh Jarrah, home of the Families, but the British forced him to relinquish it. As the British took the last salute, the Jews held the western part of the city, the Arabs the Old City and the east. At 8 a.m. on Friday 14 May, Cunningham, the last high commissioner, marched out of Government House in full uniform, reviewed a guard of honour, mounted his armoured Daimler and drove to inspect his troops at the King David Hotel.

51

JEWISH INDEPENDENCE,
ARAB CATASTROPHE

1948–51

THE BRITISH DEPART; BEN-GURION: WE DID IT!

General Cunningham headed out of Jerusalem through streets deserted except for a few Arab children. British troops manned machine-gun posts on street corners. As the Daimler sped past, the young onlookers 'clapped childishly and one saluted. The salute was returned.' From Kalandia airport, the high commissioner flew out of Jerusalem to Haifa whence, at midnight, he sailed for England.

British troops evacuated their Bevingrad fortress in the Russian Compound: 250 trucks and tanks rumbled out along King George V Avenue, watched by silent Jewish crowds. The race to control the Russian Compound started instantly. The Irgun stormed the Nikolai Hostel. Gunfire ricocheted across the town. Nusseibeh rushed to Amman to beg King Abdullah to save the city, 'once sacked in the Crusades' and about to be sacked again. The king promised.

At 4.00 p.m. on 14 May 1948, just outside Jerusalem, Rabin and his Palmach soldiers, exhausted by their fight to keep the road open, were listening to a radio announcement from David Ben-Gurion, chairman of the Jewish Agency. Standing beneath a portrait of Herzl, before an audience of 250 in the Tel Aviv Museum, Ben-Gurion proclaimed, 'I shall read from the scroll of the Declaration of the Establishment of the State of . . .' He and his aides had debated what the name of the state should be. Some had suggested Judaea or Zion – but these names were associated with Jerusalem and the

Zionists were struggling to hold even part of the city. Others had proposed Ivriya or Herzliya, but Ben-Gurion had argued for Israel and that was agreed: 'The Land of Israel', he read out, 'was the birthplace of the Jewish people.' They sang the national anthem, Hatikvah (The Hope):

> Our hope is not lost
> The hope of two thousand years;
> To be a free people in our land,
> The land of Zion and Jerusalem!

Ben-Gurion beamed at the journalists. 'We did it!' he said, but he eschewed jubilation. He had repeatedly accepted two-state partition, but now the Jews had to resist an invasion by the regular Arab armies with the openly stated object of annihilation. The very survival of the State of Israel was in jeopardy. On the other hand, his views had evolved since he had hoped in the 1920s and early 1930s for a shared socialist Palestine or a federated state. Now, faced with total war, everything was up for grabs.

At the Jerusalem front, Rabin's soldiers of the Harel Brigade were too weary to listen to Ben-Gurion on the radio. 'Hey men, turn it off,' pleaded one of them. 'I'm dying for some sleep. Fine words tomorrow!'

'Someone got up and turned the knob, leaving a leaden silence,' recalled Rabin. 'I was mute, stifling my own mixture of emotions.' Most people did not hear the Declaration anyway, because Arab forces had cut off the electricity.

Eleven minutes later, President Truman announced *de facto* recognition of Israel. Encouraged by Eddie Jacobson, Truman had secretly reassured Weizmann that he backed partition. Yet he had almost lost control of the administration when his UN diplomats tried to suspend partition. His secretary of state, George Marshall, wartime chief of staff and doyen of American public service, outspokenly opposed recognition. But Truman backed the new state while Stalin was the first to recognize Israel officially.

In New York, Weizmann, now almost blind, waited in his room at the Waldorf Astoria, delighted by independence yet feeling abandoned and forgotten, until Ben-Gurion and his colleagues asked him to be the first president. Truman invited Weizmann to make his first formal visit to the White House. When the US president was later praised by Eddie Jacobson for having 'helped create Israel', he retorted: 'What do you mean "helped create"?' I am Cyrus! I am Cyrus!' When the chief rabbi of Israel thanked him, Truman wept.*

President Weizmann travelled to Israel, while he feared 'the Jewish shrines in Jerusalem, which had survived the attacks of barbarians in medieval times, were now being laid waste.' In Jerusalem, Anwar Nusseibeh and a few irregulars, mainly ex-policemen, did their best to defend the Old City until the real armies arrived. Nusseibeh was shot in the thigh, and had to have his leg amputated. But the irregular war was over.

The real war was now starting and Israel's position was dire. The armies of the Arab League states, Egypt, Jordan, Iraq, Syria and Lebanon, invaded Israel with the specific mission of liquidating the Jews. 'This will be a war of extermination and a momentous massacre,' announced Azzam Pasha, secretary of the League, 'which will be spoken of like the Mongolian massacres and the Crusades.' Their commanders were overconfident. The Jews had been inferior subjects of Islamic empires, sometimes tolerated, often persecuted, but always submissive, for over a thousand years. 'The Arabs believed themselves to be a great military people and regarded the Jews as a nation of shopkeepers', recalled General Sir John Glubb, the English commander of King Abdullah's Arab Legion. 'The Egyptians, Syrians and Iraqis assumed they'd have no difficulty defeating the Jews.' Secular nationalism merged with the fervour of holy war: it was unthinkable that Jews could defeat Islamic armies, and many of the Jihadist factions that fought beside

---

* One American Jerusalemite was infuriated by Truman's policy. Although the American Colony, flying the Red Cross flag, was already famed for its neutrality, in fact Bertha Spafford no longer regarded the Return of the Jews to Zion as a step towards the Second Coming and opposed Zionism: 'How can we as Americans in Palestine vindicate such an action? We're ashamed to acknowledge that American statesmen can be moved either way to acquire votes.' In June, backed by Jerusalem's Arab leaders and the commander of the Arab Legion, she travelled to Washington to lobby Truman against Israel. The president refused to meet her.

the regular armies had long since embraced a fanatical anti-Semitism. Half the Egyptian forces were *mujahidin* of the Muslim Brotherhood, among them young Yasser Arafat.

Yet the intervention with its blood-curdling hopes and political cynicism would be a disaster for the Palestinians and help forge a much larger and stronger Israel than would otherwise have emerged. On paper there were 165,000 troops in the Arab armies but such was the disorganization that, during May, they fielded about 28,000 – roughly the same as the Israelis. Since Abdullah's 9,000-strong British-trained Arab Legion were the best of them, he was officially appointed Supreme Commander of Arab League forces.

King Abdullah stood on the Allenby Bridge and, drawing his pistol, fired into the air. 'Forward!' he shouted.

ABDULLAH THE HASTY

The king, recalled his grandson Hussein, 'was a full-blooded extrovert'. When we last saw Abdullah, he was in Jerusalem receiving his desert kingdom from Winston Churchill. Lawrence had described him as 'short, thick-built, strong as a horse, with merry, dark brown eyes, a smooth round face, full but short lips, straight nose' – and he had led an adventurous life, shocking Lawrence with his raffish exploits: 'once Abdullah shot a coffee-pot off his court-fool's head thrice from twenty yards'. As a Sherifian, thirty-seventh in line from the Prophet, he could tease the *ulema*. 'Is it wrong to look at a pretty woman?' he asked a mufti. 'A sin, Your Majesty.' 'But the Holy Koran says "If you see a woman, avert your eyes" but you can't avert the gaze unless you've been looking!' He was both a proud Bedouin and a child of the Ottoman sultanate, he had commanded armies as a teenager and been 'the brains' of the Great Arab Revolt. His ambitions were as boundless as they were urgent, hence his nickname 'the Hasty'. Yet he had waited a long time for this chance to conquer Jerusalem.

'He was more than a soldier and diplomat but also a classical scholar', remembered Sir Ronald Storrs, who was impressed when 'he intoned for me the Seven Suspended Odes of Pre-Islamic Poetry'. The British ambassador in Amman, Sir Alec Kirkbridge, always called him 'the king with a twinkle in his eye'. As a diplomat Abdullah was witty. Asked when he would ever receive a diplomat he disliked, he answered, 'When my mule foals.'

Now that his mule *was* foaling, he was realistic about the Zionists, citing the Turkish proverb: 'If you meet a bear crossing a rotten bridge, call her "Dear Auntie".' Over the years, he often talked to Weizmann and Jewish businessmen, offering the Jews a homeland if they would accept him as king of Palestine. He had often visited Jerusalem, meeting up with his ally Ragheb Nashashibi, but he detested the mufti, believing that Zionism flourished all the more thanks to 'those partisans of the Arabs who'll accept no solution'.

The king had secretly negotiated a non-aggression pact with the Zionists: he would occupy the parts of the West Bank assigned to the Arabs in return for not opposing the UN borders of the Jewish state: and the British had agreed to his annexation. 'I don't want to create a new Arab state that will allow the Arabs to ride on me', he explained to the Zionist envoy Golda Myerson (later Meir). 'I want to be the rider not the horse.' But the horse had now bolted: the war, particularly, the Deir Yassin massacre, obliged him to fight the Jews. Besides, the other Arab states were as determined to limit Abdullah's ambitions as they were to rescue Palestine, and the Egyptians and Syrians planned to annex their own conquests. Abdullah's commander Glubb Pasha, who had devoted his life to providing the Hashemites with a decent army, was now loath to risk it.

His Arab Legion advanced cautiously through the Judaean hills towards Jerusalem, where the irregular Arab Liberation Army attacked the Jewish suburbs. By nightfall on 16 May, the Haganah had captured the Mea Shearim police station and Sheikh Jarrah to the north and all the New City south of the walls as well as the former British strongholds in the centre, the Russian Compound and the YMCA. 'We have conquered almost all of Jerusalem, apart from the Augusta Victoria and the Old City,' claimed an overwhelmed Ben-Gurion.

'SOS! The Jews are near the walls!' Anwar Nusseibeh rushed

back to the king to beg for his intervention. Abdullah never forgot his place in history: 'By God I am a Muslim ruler, a Hashemite king, and my father was king of all the Arabs.' Now he wrote to his English commander: 'My dear Glubb Pasha, the importance of Jerusalem in the eyes of the Arabs and the Muslims and Arab Christians is well known. Any disaster suffered by the people of the city at the hands of the Jews would have far-reaching consequences for us. Everything we hold today must be preserved – the Old City and the road to Jericho. I ask you to execute this as quickly as possible my dear.'

ABDULLAH: THE BATTLE OF JERUSALEM

The king's 'troops were in jubilation, many of the vehicles decorated with green branches or bunches of pink oleander flowers'. The procession of the Arab Legion towards Jerusalem 'seemed more like a carnival than an army going to war', observed Glubb. On 18 May, the first Legionaries took up positions around the walls of the Old City whence, he wrote, 'nearly 1900 years ago the Jews themselves had cast their darts at the advancing legions of Titus'. But the king was 'haggard with anxiety lest the Jews enter the Old City and the Temple where his father the late King Hussein of the Hejaz was buried.' Glubb's forces smashed through the Israeli-held Sheikh Jarrah to the Damascus Gate.

Within the Old City, first irregulars and then Arab Legionaries surrounded the Jewish Quarter, home of some of the oldest Jewish families in Palestine, many of them aged Hasidic scholars, and all defended by just 190 Haganah and Irgun fighters. Rabin was furious to learn that only meagre forces could be spared to rescue the Old City. Was this, he shouted at the commander of Jerusalem, David Shaltiel, 'the only force the Jewish people can muster for the liberation of its capital?'

Rabin tried unsuccessfully to storm the Jaffa Gate, but simultaneously other troops broke through the Zion Gate into the Old City. Eighty Palmachniks joined the defenders before losing the Zion Gate. But now, the Arab Legion arrived in force. The battle for the Old City would be desperate; the fighting, noted Glubb, was 'room to room, down dark passages, up and down tiny staircases cut into courtyards and down in cellars' through the 'teeming rabbit-warren of the Jewish Quarter on top of the spoils and rubble of millennia.' Glubb now ordered the systematic reduction of the Jewish Quarter. Its rabbis appealed for help. Ben-Gurion became frantic: 'Jerusalem can fall at any minute! Attack whatever the cost!'

On 26 May, the Legionaries took the Hurva Square, and dynamited its magnificent synagogues. Two days later, 'two old rabbis, their backs bent with age, came forward down a narrow lane carrying a white flag', observed Glubb. Across the lines, and just a few hundred feet away in this tiny theatre of war, Rabin watched the same 'shattering scene' from Mount Zion: 'I was horrified.' Thirty-nine of the 213 defenders were dead, 134 wounded. 'So the City of David fell to the enemy,' wrote Begin. 'Mourning descended over us.' Glubb was elated: 'I've an intense love of Jerusalem. The Bible lives before our eyes.' Yet he allowed the ransacking of the Jewish Quarter: twenty-two of the twenty-seven synagogues were demolished. For the first time since the Muslim reconquest in 1187, the Jews lost access to the Western Wall.

Glubb used the Latrun Fortress to close the road to west Jerusalem. Ben-Gurion repeatedly ordered the taking of Latrun, at a punishing cost in Israeli lives, but the attacks failed. Jewish Jerusalemites, already living in their cellars, began to starve until the Israelis created a new route for provisions, the so-called Burma Road south of Latrun.

On 11 June, the UN mediator Count Folke Bernadotte, grandson of a Swedish king who had negotiated with Himmler to rescue Jews in the last months of the war, successfully mediated a truce and proposed a new version of the partition giving all of Jerusalem to King Abdullah. Israel rejected Bernadotte's plans. Meanwhile Ben-Gurion defeated a near-mutiny when Menachem Begin, having already agreed to merge his Irgun forces with those of the State, attempted to land his own shipment of arms: the Israeli Army sank the ship. Instead of starting a civil war, Begin retired from the underground to enter regular politics.

When Bernadotte's truce ended; war resumed. The next day an Egyptian Spitfire bombed western Jerusalem. The excited Legionaries attacked the New City through the Zion Gate and then advanced towards Notre Dame: 'By turning their heads, they could see the Dome of the Rock and al-Aqsa,' wrote Glubb. 'They were fighting in the path of God', as the Israelis again tried to capture the Old City.

'Can we hold Jerusalem?' Abdullah asked Glubb.

'They'll never take it, sir!'

'If you ever think the Jews will take Jerusalem, you tell me,' said the king. 'I'll go there and die on the walls of the city.' The Israeli counterattack failed. But Israel's military strength was increasing: the new State was now fielding 88,000 troops in all, against the Arabs' 68,000. In the ten days before a second truce, the Israelis took Lydda and Ramla.

Such was the Zionist fury at Bernadotte's proposal that the Swede now suggested that Jerusalem should be internationalized. On 17 September, the Swedish count flew into the Holy City. But the Lehi extremists, led by Yitzhak Shamir (a future Israeli prime minister), decided to annihilate both the man and his plans. As Bernadotte drove from his headquarters in Government House through Katamon to meet the Israeli governor Dov Joseph in Rehavia, his jeep was waved to a halt at a checkpoint. Three men dismounted from another jeep brandishing Stens; two shot out the tyres; the third machine-gunned Bernadotte in the chest before they sped off. The count died in Hadassah Hospital. Ben-Gurion suppressed and dismantled the Lehi, but the killers were never caught.

Abdullah had secured the Old City. On the West Bank, the king held the south, the Iraqis held the north. South of Jerusalem, the Egyptian vanguard could see the Old City and was pounding the southern suburbs. In mid-September, the Arab League recognized a Gaza-based Palestinian 'government' that was dominated by the mufti and the Jerusalemite Families.* But when the fighting resumed, the Israelis defeated and encircled the Egyptians, conquering the Negev desert. Humiliated, the Egyptians sent the mufti

---

* Two Husseini cousins served as foreign and defence ministers, Anwar Nusseibeh as cabinet secretary – and the mufti as president of the Palestine National Council.

back to Cairo, his political career finally discredited. At the end of November, 1948, Lieutenant-Colonel Moshe Dayan, now military commander of Jerusalem, agreed a cease fire with the Jordanians. During the first half of 1949, Israel signed armistices with all five of the Arab states, and in February 1949, the Knesset, the Israeli Parliament, met in the Jewish Agency building on Jerusalem's George V Avenue to elect Weizmann formally to the largely ceremonial post of president. Weizmann, aged seventy-five, found himself ignored by Prime Minister Ben-Gurion and was frustrated by his non-executive role. 'Why do I have to be a Swiss president?' Weizmann asked. 'Why not an American president?' He jokingly called himself 'the Prisoner of Rehovoth' – referring to the town where he had set up the Weizmann Institute of Science. Even though he had his official residence in Jerusalem, 'I remained prejudiced against the city and even now I feel ill at ease in it.' He died in 1952.

The Armistice, signed in April 1949 and supervised by the UN, who were based in the British Government House, divided Jerusalem: Israel received the west with an island of territory on Mount Scopus, while Abdullah kept the Old City, eastern Jerusalem and the West Bank. The agreement promised the Jews access to the Wall, the Mount of Olives cemetery and the Kidron Valley tombs but this was never honoured. Jews were not allowed to pray at the Wall for the next nineteen years,* and the tombstones in their cemeteries were vandalized.

The Israelis and Abdullah both feared losing their halves of Jerusalem. The UN persisted in debating the internationalization of the city, so both sides occupied Jerusalem illegally and only two countries recognized Abdullah's hold on the Old City. Weizmann's chief of staff, George Weidenfeld, a young Viennese who had recently founded his own publishing house in London, launched a campaign to convince the world that Israel should keep west Jerusalem. On 11 December, Jerusalem was declared the capital of Israel.

---

* In a classic example of Jerusalem's religious competitiveness and its ability to create sanctity out of necessity, Jewish pilgrims, robbed of the Wall, prayed at the Tomb of David on Mount Zion and created the country's first Holocaust Museum there.

The Arab victor was Abdullah the Hasty, who, thirty-two years after the Arab Revolt, had finally won Jerusalem: 'Nobody', he said, 'will take over Jerusalem from me unless I'm killed.'

52

DIVIDED

1951–67

KING OF JERUSALEM: BLOOD ON THE TEMPLE MOUNT

'A fortified strip of barbed wire, minefields, firing positions and observation posts crossed [the city],' wrote Amos Oz. 'A concrete curtain came down and divided us from Sheikh Jarrah and the Arab neighbourhoods.' There was often sniper fire: in 1954, nine people were killed in this way and fifty-four wounded. Even when the two sides cooperated, it was agonizing: in 1950, the UN mediated the feeding of the one tiger, one lion and two bears of the Biblical Zoo on Israeli-controlled Mount Scopus and officially explained that 'Decisions had to be taken whether (a) Israeli money should be used to buy Arab donkeys to feed the Israeli lion or (b) whether an Israeli donkey should pass through Jordan-held territory to be eaten by the lion in question.' Eventually the animals were escorted in a UN convoy through Jordanian territory to west Jerusalem.

Across the barbed wire, the Nusseibehs mourned the Catastrophe: 'I suffered what amounted to a nervous breakdown,' admitted Hazem Nusseibeh. His nephew Sari missed 'the English and Arab aristocrats, the free-wheeling parvenus, the middle-class tradesmen, the demi-monde catering to soldiers, the rich blend of cultures, the bishops, Muslim clerics and black-bearded rabbis crowding the same streets'.

In November, Abdullah was, bizarrely, crowned king of Jerusalem by the Coptic bishop – the first king to control the city since Frederick II. On 1 December, he had himself declared king of Palestine in Jericho, renaming his realm the United Kingdom of Jordan. The Husseinis and the Arab nationalists denounced

Left Sherif of Mecca, King of Hejaz, Hussein (right) meets the early Palestinian nationalist leader Musa Kazem Husseini (left) in Jerusalem.

Right The sherif never forgave his ambitious sons, Faisal (left), king first of Syria then Iraq, and Abdullah (right), later king of Jordan (seen here in Jerusalem in 1931) for seizing kingdoms of their own.

David Ben-Gurion, working on new Jewish housing in 1924 (*left*), emerged as the tough Zionist leader just as the Mufti, Amin al-Husseini (*right*), emerged as Arab nationalist leader: here he leads the annual Nabi Musa, Jerusalem's main Islamic festival, on horseback in 1937.

The annual Easter ritual of the Holy Fire (seen from the dome of the Church of the Holy Sepulchre) was crowded, passionate and often fatal.

The prayers at the Western Wall in 1944 to commemorate the dead of the Holocaust show the tiny, constrained area permitted for Jewish worship.

Asmahan: Arab singer, Druze princess, Egyptian film star, spy and temptress of the wartime King David Hotel.

Above left The Mufti Amin al-Husseini meets Hitler, who admired his fair hair and blue eyes. His cousin, Abd al-Kadir Husseini (*above right*), was an aristocratic warrior and Arab hero of 1947–8, whose death was a blow to Palestinian hopes. His funeral on the Temple Mount (*below*) was a chaotic, tense occasion: some mourners were killed by guns fired in the air.

Jerusalem Bomb Outrage by Fanatical Zionists

1946–8: as Arabs and Jews massacred each other's civilians, Menachem Begin's Irgun bombed the British headquarters in the King David Hotel. British General Bubbles Barker (bottom right on newspaper) already loathed the Jews, encouraged by his charming, exuberant mistress, the leading Palestinian hostess Katy Antonius (*below*).

KING DAVID HOTEL, where British military H.Q. and government offices in Jerusalem were located, was the scene of a bomb outrage by Jewish terrorists on July 22, 1946. Worse work continued until August 1, when all the debris was cleared, the final death-toll—British, Arab and Jewish—being 91. Sir John Shaw (left), Chief Secretary to the Palestine Government, and Lieut.-Gen. Sir Evelyn Barker (right), G.O.C. Palestine, escaped uninjured. This incident coincided with Anglo-American consultations in London on Palestine's future. On July 31 it was announced that the British Government was willing to accept the experts' recommendations that Palestine should be divided into an Arab province, a Jewish province, a district of Jerusalem and a divert area to the south, implementation of this plan depending on United States co-operation.

The battle of Jerusalem in 1948 (*facing page, below*): Arab soldiers escorting a Jewish prisoner during the fight for the Jewish Quarter (*above left*); a Jewish girl fleeing from the fighting (*above right*); Arab Legionaries behind sandbag barricades (*below*).

Israeli government in crisis: Israeli Chief of Staff Yitzhak Rabin (left) collapsed under the pressure and had to be sedated; Moshe Dayan (right), brought in as Defence Minister, seen here with Rabin at a cabinet meeting as the crisis intensifies in 1967. Dayan thrice warned Hussein not to attack but held back until Syria and Egypt were defeated. *Below* Israeli paratroopers advance towards Lions' Gate.

Clockwise from top right: Minutes after its capture in June 1967, Israeli soldiers pray at the Western Wall; the sheikh of the Haram al-Sharif watches from the Maghrebi Gate; behind him, Israeli jeeps fight across the Haram, before celebrating the reunification of Jerusalem in front of the Dome.

Abdullah for his compromises and could not forgive him for being the only Arab to have succeeded in the Palestinian Catastrophe.

The king turned to the Families of Jerusalem, who now enjoyed a strange renaissance. He offered Ragheb Nashashibi the premiership of Jordan. Nashashibi refused, but agreed to become a minister. The king also appointed him governor of the West Bank and Custodian of the Two Harams (Jerusalem and Hebron) as well as presenting him with a Studebaker car and the title 'Ragheb Pasha'. (The Jordanians were still awarding Ottoman titles in the 1950s.) His dandyish nephew, Nassereddin Nashashibi, became royal chamberlain.* In a satisfying dismissal of the hated mufti, Abdullah officially sacked him and appointed Sheikh Husam al-Jarallah, the very man cheated of the title back in 1921.

Abdullah was warned of assassination plots, but he always replied, 'Until my day comes, nobody can harm me; when the day comes, no one can guard me.' Whatever the dangers, Abdullah, now sixty-nine, was proud of his possession of Jerusalem. 'When I was a boy,' recalled his grandson Hussein, 'my grandfather used to tell me that Jerusalem was one of the most beautiful cities in the world.' As time went on he noticed that the king 'grew to love Jerusalem more and more'. Abdullah was disappointed in his eldest son Talal, but he adored his grandson whom he educated to be king. During school holidays, they breakfasted together every day. 'I'd become the son he always wanted,' wrote Hussein.

On Friday 20 July 1951, Abdullah drove to Jerusalem with Hussein, a sixteen-year-old Harrow schoolboy, whom he ordered to wear his military uniform with medals. Before they left, the king told him, 'My son, one day you will have to assume responsibility,' adding 'When I have to die, I'd like to be shot in the head by a nobody. That's the simplest way.' They stopped in Nablus to meet the mufti's cousin, Dr Musa al-Husseini, who had served the mufti in Nazi Berlin: he bowed and expressed loyalty.

* But Ragheb Nashashibi was dying of cancer. The king visited him in the Augusta Victoria Hospital. 'In this building,' said Abdullah, 'in the spring of 1921, I had my first meeting with Winston Churchill.' In April 1951, Nashashibi died and was buried in a small tomb near his villa – which was later knocked down to build the Ambassador Hotel.

Just before midday, Abdullah arrived in Jerusalem for Friday prayers with his grandson, Glubb Pasha, Royal Chamberlain Nassereddin Nashashibi and the unctuous Musa Husseini. The crowd was sulky and suspicious; his nervous Arab Legion body-guard was so numerous that Hussein joked 'What is this, a funeral procession?' Abdullah visited his father's tomb, then walked to al-Aqsa and told the guards to pull back, but Musa Husseini stayed very close. As Abdullah stepped into the portico, the sheikh of the mosque kissed the royal hand, and simultaneously a young man emerged from behind the door. Raising a pistol, the youth pressed the barrel against the king's ear and fired, killing him instantly. The bullet exited through the eye, and Abdullah collapsed, his white turban rolling away. Everyone threw themselves to the ground, 'doubled up like bent old terrified women,' observed Hussein 'but I must have lost my head for at that moment, I lunged towards the assassin', who turned on Hussein: 'I saw his bared teeth, his dazed eyes. He had the gun and I watched him point it at me then saw the smoke, heard the bang and felt the shot on my chest. Is this what death is like? His bullet hit metal.' Abdullah had saved his grandson's life by ordering him to wear the medals.

The bodyguards, firing haphazardly, killed the assassin. Holding the dead king in his arms as blood gushed from his nose, Nashashibi kissed his hand repeatedly. The Legionaries started to rampage through the streets, and Glubb struggled to restrain them. Kneeling by the king, Hussein undid his robe, and then walked with the body as it was borne to the Austrian Hospice. There Hussein himself was sedated before being hurriedly flown back to Amman.

HUSSEIN OF JORDAN: LAST KING OF JERUSALEM

The mufti and King Farouk of Egypt were said to be behind the assassination. Musa Husseini was arrested and tortured before he and three others were executed. The assassination was just one of the killings and coups precipitated by the Arab defeat. In 1952, King Farouk, last of Mehmet Ali's Albanians, was overthrown by a junta of Free Officers, led by General Muhammad Neguib and Colonel Gamal Abdul Nasser.

Abdullah of Jordan was succeeded by his son, King Talal, who suffered violent attacks of schizophrenia that led to his almost killing his wife. On 12 August 1952, young Hussein was holidaying at a hotel in Geneva when a waiter entered with an envelope on a silver platter: it was addressed to 'His Majesty King Hussein'. His father had abdicated. Still just seventeen, Hussein liked fast cars and motorcycles, planes and helicopters, which he flew himself, and beautiful women – he married five. While his grandfather had never lost the dream of a greater Hashemite kingdom, risking everything to win Jerusalem, Hussein realized gradually that it would be an achievement even to survive as king of Jordan.

A Sandhurst-trained officer, this debonair monarch was pro-Western, his regime funded first by Britain then by America, yet he survived only by trimming between the forces at play in the Arab world. At times he had to endure the suffocating embrace of hostile radical tyrants such as Nasser of Egypt and Saddam Hussein of Iraq. Like his grandfather, he was able to work with the Israelis; much later, he came to like Rabin especially.

The octogenarian Churchill, who had returned to office as prime minister in 1951, muttered to one of his officials, 'You ought to let the Jews have Jerusalem – it was they who made it famous.' But the city remained divided between east and west, 'a jarring series of ad hoc fences, walls and bails of barbed wire' with 'signs in Hebrew, English and Arabic reading *STOP! DANGER! FRONTIER AHEAD*'. The nights crackled with machine-gun fire, the only gateway was the Mandelbaum Gate, which became as famous as Berlin's Checkpoint Charlie. Yet it was neither a gate nor the house of the Mandelbaums. The long-departed Simchah and Esther Mandelbaum had been Belorussian-born manufacturers of stockings whose sturdy home had become a Haganah stronghold that was blown up by the Arab Legion in 1948. The Mandelbaum checkpoint stood on its ruins.

Through these mined and barbed barriers the Jewish teenager Amos Oz and the Palestinian child Sari Nusseibeh, the son of

Anwar, were living close to each other. Later Oz and Nusseibeh, both fine writers and opponents of fanatacism, became friends. 'Islam', wrote Nusseibeh, 'was no different for families like ours than I would learn later that Judaism was for Amos Oz a couple of hundred feet away, just beyond No-Man's-Land.' The boys watched as a new influx of immigrants changed Jerusalem yet again. The Arabs, particularly Iraq, had avenged themselves on their own Jewish communities: 600,000 of them now migrated to Israel. But it was the survivors of the ultra-Orthodox sects known as the Haredim (Awestruck) who changed the look of Jerusalem, bringing with them the culture and clothes of seventeenth-century Mitteleuropa and a faith in mystical and joyous prayer. 'Hardly a day would go by', recalled Sari Nusseibeh, 'when I didn't spy into the streets beyond No-Man's-Land' and there in Mea Shearim, 'I saw blackclad men. Sometimes the bearded creatures looked back at me.' Who were they, he wondered?

The Haredim were split between those who embraced Zionism and the many, such as the Toldot Haron of Mea Shearim, who were devoutly anti-Zionist. They believed that only God could restore the Temple. These introspective, rigid and ritualistic sects were divided between Hasidics and Lithuanians, all speaking Yiddish. The Hasidim are in turn divided into many sects originating from seven principal 'courts', each ruled by a dynasty descended from a miracle-working rabbi known as the *admor* (an acronym deriving from 'Our Master Teacher and Rabbi'). Their costumes and the arcane differences between sects contributed to the complexity of Israeli Jerusalem.*

The Israelis built a modern capital in Western Jerusalem,† which was an uneasy blend of secular and religious. 'Israel was socialist

---

* The largest court, the Ger, named after a village in Poland and ruled by the Alter family, wear *shtreimel* fur hats; the Belzers, from Ukraine, wear kaftans and fur hats; the Breslavers worship with mystic and exhibitionistic dancing and singing, and are known as the 'Hasidic hippies'.

† In 1957, Yad Vashem, 'A Place and a Name', the memorial to the 6 million Jews killed in the Holocaust, was created on Mount Herzl. In 1965, the Israel Museum was opened, followed by the new Knesset, both funded by James de Rothschild who had helped recruit the Jewish Legion in Allenby's army.

and secular,' recalls George Weidenfeld, 'high society was in Tel
Aviv but Jerusalem revolved around the old Jerusalem of the rabbis,
the German intellectuals of Rehavia who discussed art and politics
after dinner in the kitchen and the Israeli elite of senior civil servants
and generals like Moshe Dayan.' While the Haredim lived their
separate lives, secular Jews like Weidenfeld dined out at the
smartest restaurant in Jerusalem – Fink's, with its non-kosher
goulash and sausages. Amos Oz felt uneasy in this kaleidoscopic
city, with its peculiar mix of restored antiquities and modern ruins.
'Can one ever feel at home in Jerusalem, I wonder, even if one lives
here for a century?' he asked in his novel *My Michael*. 'If you turn
your head you can see in the midst of all this building a rocky field.
Olive trees. A barren wilderness. Herds grazing around the newly
built prime minister's office.' Oz left Jerusalem, but Sari Nusseibeh
stayed.

On 23 May 1961, Ben-Gurion summoned one of his young aides,
Yitzhak Yaacovy, into his office. The prime minister looked up at
Yaacovy: 'Do you know who Adolf Eichmann is?'

'No,' replied Yaacovy.

'He is the man who organized the Holocaust, killed your family
and deported you to Auschwitz,' replied Ben-Gurion, who knew
that Yaacovy, child of Orthodox Hungarian parents, had been sent
to the death-camp by SS-Obersturmbannführer Eichmann in 1944.
There he had survived the selection of those allowed to live as slave
labourers and those to be gassed at once by SS Dr Josef Mengele
himself, perhaps because of his blond hair and blue eyes. Afterwards he emigrated to Israel, fought and was wounded in the War
of Independence and settled in Jerusalem where he worked in the
prime minister's office.

'Today,' Ben-Gurion went on, 'you will take a car to the Knesset
and you will sit as my guest and watch me announce that we have
brought Eichmann to stand trial in Jerusalem.'

The Israeli secret service Mossad had kidnapped Eichmann from
his hiding-place in Argentina, and in April his trial started in a
courthouse in downtown Jerusalem. He was hanged in Ramla
prison.

On the other side of the border, King Hussein called the city his 'second capital', but his regime was too precarious to risk moving the real capital from Amman. The Holy City was effectively demoted to a 'provincial town with barbed-wire in the centre'. Nonetheless, Hashemite Jerusalem regained some of its old charm. The king's brother, Prince Muhammad, governed the West Bank. He had just married the beautiful sixteen-year-old Palestinian: Firyal al-Rashid, 'We spent six months of the year in Jerusalem,' remembers Princess Firyal, 'in the most delightful small villa that had belonged to the Dajanis, but my husband spent most of his time negotiating with the Christians, trying to make peace between the warring Orthodox, Catholics and Armenians!'

King Hussein appointed Anwar Nusseibeh as governor and custodian of the Sanctuaries. The Nusseibehs were more prominent than they had been for many centuries: Anwar at times served as Jordanian defence minister, his brother Hazem as foreign minister. All of the Families had lost their money and their olive groves, but many continued to live in their villas in Sheikh Jarrah. Anwar Nusseibeh now lived opposite the American Colony in an old-style villa with 'Persian carpets, gold-embossed academic degrees, crystal decanters for after-dinner drinks and dozens of tennis trophies'. Nusseibeh had to practise 'a tolerant ecumenicalism', praying at al-Aqsa every Friday and every Easter leading his whole family to join 'the high clergy in robes holding golden crosses to circle the Holy Sepulchre three times', as his son Sari recalled. 'My brothers and I liked this [Easter celebration] the most because the Christian girls were the prettiest in town.' But the Temple Mount itself was quiet. 'There were few Muslim visitors to the Haram,' noticed Oleg Grabar, the pre-eminent scholar of Jerusalem, who started to explore the city during those years.

Sari Nusseibeh investigated the Old City, 'full of smug shop-keepers with their golden pocketwatches, old women hawking wares, whirling dervishes' and cafés resonating 'with the bubbling sound of people smoking water pipes'. Jordanian Jerusalem was, observed Eugene Bird, the US vice-consul, a tiny world: 'I've never seen such a small big town before. The eligible society restricted it to about 150 people.' Some of the Families embraced tourism: the Husseinis opened Orient House as a hotel. The white-haired Bertha Spafford converted her American Colony into a luxury hotel and the brooch-wearing grande dame herself became one of the sights of the city, having known everybody from Jemal Pasha to Lawrence of Arabia: she even featured twice on the British television show *This is Your Life*. Katy Antonius had returned and set up an orphanage in the Old City and, in her home, 'an upscale restaurant-cum-salon' named Katakeet after a local gossip column. She was 'something out Eliot's *Cocktail Party*', wrote the US vice-consul; 'she's gossipy and thoroughly affected'. Always in 'the latest fashions and a string of pearls, black hair cut fairly short' with 'a distinctive white streak', she was, thought the vice-consul's son, the writer Kai Bird, 'part dragon-lady and part-flirt'. But she had not lost her political anger, remarking: 'Before the Jewish State, I knew many Jews in Jerusalem. Now I will slap the face of any Arab friend who tries to trade with a Jew. We lost the first round; we haven't lost the war.'

The Great Powers had always backed their own sects so it was no surprise that the Cold War was waged furtively beneath the robes and behind the altars of Jerusalem 'as ardently as in the back alleys of Berlin', that other divided city. US Vice-Consul Bird advised the CIA to contribute $80,000 to repair the golden onion-domes of Grand Duke Sergei's Church of Mary Magdalene. If the CIA did not pay, the KGB just might. Russian Orthodoxy was divided between the CIA-backed Church based in New York and the KGB-backed Soviet version in Moscow. The Jordanians, staunch American allies, gave their Russian churches to the anti-Communist Church, while the Israelis, remembering that Stalin had been the first to recognize their new state, granted their Russian properties to the Soviets, who set up a mission in west Jerusalem led by a 'priest', actually a KGB colonel who had formerly been an adviser to North Korea.

In a backwater still dominated by 'Husseinis, Nashashibis, Islamic scholars and Christian bishops, if you could ignore No-Man's-Land and the refugee camps,' wrote Sari Nusseibeh, 'it was as if nothing had ever happened'. Yet nothing was the same –

and even this hybrid Jerusalem was now under threat. The rise of Nasser, President of Egypt, changed everything, imperilling King Hussein and risking his very possession of Jerusalem.

53

SIX DAYS

1967

Born in obscurity, Nasser was the beau idéal of the Arab statesman – a young officer wounded in the Israeli encirclement of 1948 and determined to restore Arab pride. He became the most popular Arab leader for centuries, yet he also ruled as a dictator, supported by the secret police. Known as El Rais – the Boss – across the Arab world, Nasser promulgated a socialist pan-Arabism that inspired his people to defy Western domination and Zionist victory and raised soaring hopes that their defeats could be avenged.

Nasser supported Palestinian raids against Israel, which responded with increasing violence. His leadership of the most powerful Arab nation, Egypt, alarmed Israel. In 1956, he challenged the vestiges of the Anglo-French empires by nationalizing the Suez Canal and backing the Algerian rebels against France. London and Paris, determined to destroy him, made a secret alliance with Ben-Gurion. The successful Israeli attack on Sinai, planned by Chief of Staff Dayan, provided the Anglo-French pretext to invade Egypt, ostensibly to separate the two neighbours. However, Britain and France lacked the power to sustain this last imperial adventure: the United States forced them to withdraw. Soon afterwards, King Hussein dismissed Glubb as commander of his army. Nineteen-fifty-six was the twilight of British Middle Eastern imperium and the dawn of American ascendancy.

Nasser targeted the two Hashemite kingdoms, where his pan-Arabist radicalism was increasingly popular on the streets and in the officer corps. In 1958, Hussein's cousin and schoolfriend

Faisal II of Iraq was murdered in a military coup. The family had been kings of the Arabs, Hejaz, Syria, Palestine, Iraq – and Hussein was now the last royal Hashemite. Nasser officially merged Egypt with Syria in the United Arab Republic, encircling Israel and dominating Jordan, but his UAR, which twice fell apart and was twice put together again, remained fragile.

'Growing up in Jerusalem was like being in a fairy tale invaded by Detroit and modern armies, though its magical quality remained, and the dangers merely added to the mysteries,' wrote Sari Nusseibeh. Gradually 'Jerusalem recovered much of the life it had lost in 1948,' again becoming the 'world capital of pilgrimage'. In 1964, King Hussein regilded the lead of the Dome of the Rock that had been a dull grey for centuries in preparation for the pilgrimage of Pope Paul VI. The supreme pontiff was met by Prince Muhammad and Princess Firyal, who accompanied him into the city where he was welcomed by the governor Anwar Nusseibeh. But the pope had to cross the lines at the Mandelbaum Gate like everyone else. When he asked permission to pray in the Greek chapel of Calvary, the Orthodox patriarch ordered him to make the request in writing and then turned it down. 'The pope's visit', wrote Sari Nusseibeh, 'sparked a boom': the Husseinis and Nusseibehs knocked down their elegant villas and built hideous hotels.

Yet King Hussein was now struggling for survival, crushed between radical Nasserite Egypt and Syria, between the Arabs and the Israelis, and between his own dynastic ambitions and the passionate bitterness of the Palestinians who felt he had betrayed them. As Nasser plotted to overthrow the king, Jerusalem and the West Bank repeatedly rioted against the Hashemites.

In 1959, Yasser Arafat, a veteran of the 1948 war,* founded a militant liberation movement called Fatah – Conquest. In 1964, Nasser held a summit in Cairo that created a United Arab Command for the coming war against Israel and founded the Palestine Liberation Organization under Ahmed al-Shuqayri. That May in Jerusalem, King Hussein reluctantly opened the Palestinian

* Arafat claimed to have been born in Jerusalem. His mother was a Jerusalemite, but he was in fact born in Cairo. In 1933, at the age of four, he went to live with relatives for four years in the Maghrebi Quarter next to the Wall.

Congress, which launched the PLO. The following January, Arafat's Fatah carried out a small raid into Israel from Jordan. It was a disaster and the only casualty was a Palestinian guerrilla shot dead by the Jordanians. But Fatah's exploit caught the Arab imagination and marked the beginning of Arafat's campaign to place the Palestinian cause at the centre of the global stage. The rise of the pistol-packing, khaki-clad, *keffiyeh*-wearing radicals of Fatah had eclipsed the haughty Families, discredited by the mufti and by 1948. In a sign of the times, Anwar Nusseibeh's son Sari joined Fatah.

The Palestinians were losing patience with Hussein. When Governor Nusseibeh refused a royal order, the king sacked him and appointed a Jordanian in his place. In September 1965, following in his grandfather's footsteps, Hussein secretly met the Israeli foreign minister, Golda Meir, who suggested that one day 'we could put aside arms and create a monument in Jerusalem that would signify peace between us'.

When Ben-Gurion retired as prime minister in 1963, his successor was the sixty-seven-year-old Levi Eshkol, born near Kiev, a bespectacled plodder whose chief achievement had been founding the Israeli water utility: he was no Ben-Gurion. In early 1967, Syrian attacks on northern Israel led to a dogfight in which the Syrian air force was decimated over Damascus. Syria backed more Palestinian raids into Israel.*

The Soviet Union warned Nasser – wrongly as it turned out – that Israel planned to attack Syria. It is still unclear why Moscow pushed this false intelligence and why Nasser chose to believe it when he had weeks to verify or disprove it. For all the strength of Egypt, his own charisma and the popularity of pan-Arabism, Nasser had been humiliated by Israeli reprisal raids and exposed by Syrian brinkmanship. He moved his troops into the peninsula to show that he would not tolerate an attack on Syria.

On 15 May, an anxious Eshkol and his chief of staff, General Rabin, met at the King David in Jerusalem before the Independence Day parade: how should they react to Nasser's threats? The next

---

* As the tension rose, an old man visited the city for the last time and the world scarcely noticed: Haj Amin Husseini, the ex-mufti, prayed at al-Aqsa and then returned to his Lebanese exile, where he died in 1974.

day, Egypt asked the UN to remove its peacekeepers from Sinai. Nasser probably hoped to escalate the crisis while yet avoiding war. If so, his actions were either hopelessly clumsy or reckless. As the Arab leadership and the crowds on the street hailed the coming extermination of the Jewish state, Eshkol dithered nervously. A crisis of foreboding and existential fear swept over Israel, which had lost the initiative to Nasser. Surviving on coffee, chain-smoking seventy cigarettes a day, aware that the survival of Israel rested on his shoulders, General Rabin started to crack up.

RABIN: THE BREAKDOWN BEFORE BATTLE

Nasser called the odds as he convened his Cabinet and closely questioned his vice-president and military supremo, Field-Marshal Abdel-Hakim al-Amer, a deluded, drug-taking bon vivant, who remained the president's oldest friend.

NASSER: 'Now with our concentrations in Sinai the chances of war are 50–50. If we close the Strait of Tiran, war will be 100 per cent. Are the armed forces ready, Abdel Hakim (Amer)?'

AMER: 'On my own head be it, Boss! Everything's in tiptop shape.'

On 23 May, Nasser closed the Straits of Tiran, the seaway to Israel's key port of Eilat. Syria mobilized for war. King Hussein reviewed his forces. Rabin and the generals advised Eshkol to launch a pre-emptive strike against Egypt or face annihilation. But Eshkol refused until he had exhausted all political options: his foreign minister Abba Eban carried out painstaking diplomacy to prevent war – or win support if it came. Yet Rabin was tormented by guilt that he had not done enough to save Israel: 'I had the feeling, rightly or wrongly, that I had to carry everything on my own. I had sunk into a profound crisis. I had eaten almost nothing for almost nine days, hadn't slept, was smoking nonstop and was physically exhausted.'

With its drifting prime minister, its chief of staff under sedation, its generals on the verge of mutiny and the nation itself in panic, there was nothing fake about Israel's trauma. In Washington,

President L. B. Johnson refused to back any Israeli strike; in Moscow, Premier Alexei Kosygin strongly advised Nasser to pull back from war. In Cairo, Field Marshal Amer, boasting that 'This time we'll be the ones to start the war,' prepared to attack the Negev. Just in time, Nasser ordered Amer to hold back.

In Amman, King Hussein felt he had little choice but to join Nasser: if Egypt attacked, he had to support his Arab brother; otherwise, if Egypt lost, he would be regarded as a traitor. On 30 May, Hussein, wearing a field marshal's uniform and packing a .357 Magnum, piloted his own plane to Cairo where he was met by Nasser. 'Since your visit is a secret,' said Nasser, towering over the diminutive king, 'what would happen if we arrested you?' 'The possibility never crossed my mind,' replied Hussein, who agreed to place his 56,000-strong army under the Egyptian General Riyad. 'All the Arab armies now surround Israel,' declared the king. Israel faced war on three fronts. On 28 May, Eshkol had given a rambling radio address that only intensified Israeli anxiety. In Jerusalem, bomb shelters were dug, air-raid drills practised. The Israelis feared annihilation, another Holocaust. Eban had exhausted diplomacy and the generals, the politicians and the public had lost confidence in Eshkol. He was forced to call in Israel's most respected soldier.

DAYAN TAKES COMMAND

On 1 June, Moshe Dayan was sworn in as defence minister and Menachem Begin also joined the new National Government as minister without portfolio. Dayan, who always wore his trademark black eyepatch, was a disciple of Ben-Gurion and despised Eshkol, who privately nicknamed him Abu Jildi after a slippery one-eyed Arab bandit.

Wingate's pupil, chief of staff during the Suez war and now an MP, Dayan was a contradiction – an archaeologist and looter of artefacts, an avenging wielder of military might and a believer in tolerant coexistence, a vanquisher of the Arabs and a lover of Arab culture. He was 'supremely intelligent,' recalls his friend Shimon Peres, 'his mind was brilliant and he never said a foolish thing'.

His fellow general Ariel Sharon thought Dayan 'would wake up with a hundred ideas. Of them ninety-five were dangerous; three more were bad; the remaining two however were brilliant.' He 'despised most people', recalled Sharon, 'and took no pains to conceal it'. His critics called him 'a partisan and adventurer' and Dayan once admitted to Peres, 'Remember one thing: I am unreliable.'

Dayan radiated the charisma of the new dashing Jew 'not because he followed rules,' says Peres, 'but because he discarded them with ability and charm.' A classmate described him as 'a liar, a braggart, a schemer, and a prima donna and in spite of that, the object of deep admiration'. He was a loner without friends, an inscrutable showman and a priapic womanizer, which Ben-Gurion excused because Dayan was 'cast from biblical material' like King David – or Admiral Nelson: 'You have to get used to it', he told Dayan's heartbroken wife, Ruth. 'Great men's private and public lives are often conducted on parallel planes that never meet.'

As Eban reported that America did not approve military action, but nor would it move to prevent it, Dayan showed his cool grasp of strategy. He stressed that Israel had to strike the Egyptians at once while avoiding any confrontation with Jordan. His Jerusalem commander Uzi Narkiss challenged him: what if Jordan attacked Mount Scopus? 'In that case,' replied Dayan drily, 'bite your lip and hold the line!'

Nasser already believed he had won a bloodless victory but the Egyptians continued to plan their attack in Sinai. The Jordanians, backed by an Iraqi brigade, drew up Operation Tariq to encircle Jewish west Jerusalem. The Arab world, now fielding 500,000 men, 5,000 tanks and 900 planes, had never been so united. 'Our basic aim will be the destruction of Israel,' said Nasser. 'Our goal', explained President Aref of Iraq, 'is to wipe Israel off the face of the map.' The Israelis fielded 275,000 men, 1,100 tanks and 200 planes.

At 7.10 a.m. on 5 June, Israeli pilots surprised and wiped out the Egyptian air force. At 8.15, Dayan ordered the Israeli Defence Forces into Sinai. In Jerusalem, General Narkiss waited nervously, fearful that the Jordanians would take the vulnerable Mount Scopus and encircle the 197,000 Jews in west Jerusalem, but he was hoping that the Jordanians would make only a symbolic contribution to the Egyptian war. Just after 8 a.m., the air-raid sirens rang. The Dead Sea Scrolls were securely stored. Reservists were called up. Three times, Israel warned King Hussein, through the US State Department, the UN in Jerusalem and the British Foreign Office, that 'Israel will not, repeat *not*, attack Jordan if Jordan maintains the quiet. But if Jordan opens hostilities, Israel will respond with all its might.'

'Your Majesty, the Israeli offensive has begun in Egypt,' King Hussein's aide-de-camp informed him at 8.50 a.m. Telephoning headquarters, Hussein learned that Field Marshal Amer had smashed Israeli forces and was successfully counter-attacking. At 9 a.m., Hussein entered the headquarters to find that his Egyptian general Riyad had ordered attacks on Israeli targets and the seizure of Government House in south Jerusalem. Nasser called to confirm Egyptian victories and the destruction of the Israeli air force.

At 9.30, the sombre king told his people: 'The hour of revenge has come.'

5–7 JUNE 1967: HUSSEIN, DAYAN AND RABIN

At 11.15 a.m., Jordanian artillery launched a 6,000-shell barrage against Jewish Jerusalem, hitting the Knesset and the prime minister's house as well as the Hadassah Hospital and the Church of Dormition on Mount Zion. Following Dayan's orders, the Israelis responded only with small arms. At 11.30, Dayan ordered a strike against the Jordanian air force. Watching from the roof his palace with his eldest son, the future King Abdullah II, Hussein saw his planes destroyed.

In Jerusalem, Israel offered a ceasefire but the Jordanians were not interested. The muezzin loudspeakers on the Dome of the Rock cried, 'Take up your weapons and take back your country stolen by the Jews.' At 12.45, the Jordanians occupied Government House: it happened to be the UN headquarters but it dominated Jerusalem. Dayan immediately ordered it to be stormed, and it fell after four hours' fighting. To the north, Israeli mortars and artillery fired on the Jordanians.

Dayan revered Jerusalem, but he understood that its political complexities could threaten Israel's very existence. When the Israeli Cabinet debated whether to attack the Old City or simply silence the Jordanian guns, Dayan argued against the conquest, anxious about the responsibilities of governing the Temple Mount, but he was overruled. He delayed any action until Sinai was conquered.

'That night was hell,' wrote Hussein. 'It was clear as day. The sky and earth glowed with the light of rockets and the explosions of bombs pouring from Israeli planes.' At 2.10 a.m. on 6 June, Israeli paratroopers mustered in three squads, encouraged by General Narkiss to 'atone for the sin of '48' when he himself had fought for the city. The first squad crossed no-man's-land towards Mandelbaum Gate to take Ammunition Hill – where Allenby had stored his arsenal – in a fierce battle in which seventy-one Jordanians and thirty-five Israelis were killed. The paratroopers advanced swiftly through Sheikh Jarrah past the American Colony towards the Rockefeller Museum, which fell at 7.27.

The king still held the commanding Augusta Victoria Hospital between Mount Scopus and the Mount of Olives, and he desperately tried to save the Old City by offering a ceasefire, but it was too late. Nasser called to tell Hussein that they should claim that the US and Britain had defeated the Arabs, not just Israel on its own.

Hussein sped in a jeep down into the Jordan Valley, where he encountered his troops retreating from the north. Within the Old City, the Jordanians, who had had their headquarters in the Armenian Monastery since 1948, posted fifty men at each of the gates and waited. The Israelis planned to capture the Augusta Victoria, but their Sherman tanks took a wrong turn down into the Kidron Valley and were fiercely attacked from the Lions' Gate, losing five men and four tanks close to the Garden of Gethsemane. The Israelis sheltered in the sunken courtyard of the Virgin's Tomb. The Old City was still not surrounded.

Dayan joined Narkiss on Mount Scopus overlooking the Old City: 'What a divine view!' said Dayan, but he refused to allow any attack. However, at dawn on 7 June, the UN Security Council prepared to order a ceasefire. Menachem Begin called Eshkol to encourage an urgent assault on the Old City. Dayan was suddenly in danger of running out of time. In the War Room, he ordered Rabin to take 'the most difficult and coveted target of the war'.

First the Israelis bombarded the Augusta Victoria ridge, using napalm; the Jordanians fled. Then Israeli paratroopers took the Mount of Olives and moved down towards the Garden of Gethsemane. 'We occupy the heights overlooking the Old City,' the paratroop commander Colonel Motta Gur told his men. 'In a little while we will enter it. The ancient city of Jerusalem which for generations we have dreamed of and striven for – we'll be the first to enter it. The Jewish nation is awaiting our victory. Be proud. Good luck!'

At 9.45 a.m., the Israeli Sherman tanks fired at the Lions' Gate, smashing the bus that was blocking it, and blew open the doors. Under raking Jordanian fire, the Israelis charged the gate. The paratroopers broke into the Via Dolorosa, and Colonel Gur led a group on to the Temple Mount. 'There you are on a half-track after 2 days of fighting with shots still filling the air, and suddenly you enter this wide open space that everyone has seen before in pictures,' wrote intelligence officer Arik Akhmon, 'and though I'm not religious, I don't think there was a man who wasn't overwhelmed with emotion. Something special had happened.' There was a skirmish with Jordanian troops before Gur announced over the radio: 'The Temple Mount is in our hands!'

Meanwhile on Mount Zion, a company of the Jerusalem Brigade burst through a portal in the Zion Gate into the Armenian Quarter, hurtling down the steep hill into the Jewish Quarter, just as soldiers of the same unit broke through the Dung Gate. All headed for the Wall. Back on the Temple Mount, Gur and his paratroopers did not know how to reach it, but an old Arab showed them the Maghrebi Gate and all three companies converged simultaneously on the holy place. Holding his *shofar* and a Torah, the bearded Rabbi Shlomo Goren, chief chaplain of the Israeli Army, strode to the Wall and began to recite the Kaddish mourning prayer as the soldiers prayed, wept, applauded, danced and some sang the city's new anthem 'Jerusalem of Gold'.

At 2.30 p.m., Dayan, flanked by Rabin and Narkiss, entered the city, passing 'smouldering tanks', and walking through 'alleys totally deserted, an eerie silence broken by sniper fire. I remembered my childhood,' said Rabin, and reported feeling 'sheer excitement as we got closer' to the Kotel. As they proceeded across the Temple Mount, Dayan saw an Israeli flag atop the Dome of the Rock and 'I ordered it removed immediately.' Rabin was 'breathless' as he watched the 'tangle of rugged battle-weary men, eyes moist with tears', but 'it was no time for weeping – a moment of redemption, of hope'.

Rabbi Goren wanted to accelerate the messianic era by dynamiting the mosques on the Temple Mount, but General Narkiss replied: 'Stop it!'

'You'll enter the history books,' said Rabbi Goren.

'I've already recorded my name in the history of Jerusalem,' answered Narkiss.

'This was the peak of my life,' recalled Rabin. 'For years I had secretly harboured the dream that I might play a role in restoring the Western Wall to the Jewish people. Now that dream had come true and suddenly I wondered why I of all men should be privileged.' Rabin was granted the honour of naming the war: always modest and dignified, gruff and laconic, he chose the simplest name: the Six Day War. Nasser had another name for it – al-Naksa, the Reversal.

Dayan wrote a note on a piece of the paper – it read 'May peace descend on the whole house of Israel' – which he placed between Herod's ashlars. He then declared, 'We've reunited the city, the capital of Israel, never to part it again.' But Dayan – always the Israeli who most respected, and was most respected by, the Arabs, who called him Abu Musa (son of Moses) – continued, 'To our Arab neighbours, Israel extends the hand of peace and to all peoples of all faiths, we guarantee full freedom of worship. We've not come to conquer the holy places of others but to live with others in harmony.' As he left he plucked 'some wild cyclamen of a delicate pink mauve sprouting between the Wall and the Maghrebi Gate' to give to his long-suffering wife.

Dayan thought hard about Jerusalem and created his own policy. Ten days later, he returned to al-Aqsa where, sitting in his socks with the sheikh of the Haram and the *ulema*, he explained that Jerusalem now belonged to Israel but the *Waqf* would control the Temple Mount. Even though, after 2,000 years, Jews could now finally visit the Har ha-Bayit, he ruled that they were forbidden to pray there. Dayan's statesmanlike decision stands today.

President Nasser resigned temporarily but never relinquished power and even forgave his friend Field Marshal Amer. But the latter planned a coup d'état and, after his arrest, died mysteriously in prison. Nasser insisted that 'Al-Quds can never be relinquished,' but he never recovered from the defeat, dying of a heart attack three years later. King Hussein later admitted that 5–10 June 'were the worst days of my life'. He had lost half his territory – and the prize of Jerusalem. Privately, he wept for al-Quds: 'I cannot accept that Jerusalem is lost in my time.'

EPILOGUE

Everybody has two cities, his own and Jerusalem.

Teddy Kollek, interview

Through a historical catastrophe, the destruction of Jerusalem by the emperor of Rome – I was born in one of the cities of the Diaspora. But I always deemed myself a child of Jerusalem.

S. Y. Agnon, Nobel Prize acceptance speech 1966

The Jerusalem I was raised to love was the terrestrial gateway to the divine world where Jewish, Christian and Muslim prophets, men of vision and a sense of humanity, met – if only in the imagination.

Sari Nusseibeh, *Once Upon a Country*

O Jerusalem, fragrant with prophets
The shortest path between heaven and earth ...
A beautiful child with burned fingers and downcast
   eyes ...
O Jerusalem, city of sorrow,
A tear lingering in your eye ...
Who will wash your bloody walls?
O Jerusalem, my beloved
Tomorrow the lemon-trees will blossom; the olive-
   trees rejoice; your eyes will dance; and the doves
   fly back to your sacred towers.

Nizar Qabbani, *Jerusalem*

The Jewish people were building in Jerusalem 3,000 years ago and the Jewish people are building in Jerusalem today. Jerusalem's not a settlement. It is our capital.

Binyamin Netanyahu, speech, 2010

Once again the centre of international storms. Neither Athens nor Rome aroused so many passions. When a Jew visits Jerusalem for the first time, it's not the first time, it's a homecoming.

Elie Wiesel, open letter to Barack Obama, 2010

MORNING IN JERUSALEM:
FROM THEN UNTIL NOW

The conquest transformed, elevated and complicated Jerusalem in a flash of revelation that was simultaneously messianic and apocalyptic, strategic and nationalistic. And this new vision itself altered Israel, the Palestinians and the Middle East. A decision that had been taken in panic, a conquest that was never planned, a military victory stolen from the edge of catastrophe, changed those who believed, those who believed nothing and those who craved to believe in something.

At the time none of this was clear but, in retrospect, the possession of Jerusalem gradually changed Israel's ruling spirit, which was traditionally secular, socialist, modern, and if the state had a religion it was as much the historical science of Judaean archaeology as Orthodox Judaism.

The capture of Jerusalem elated even the most secular Jews. The craving for Zion was so deep, so ancient, so ingrained in song, prayer and myth, the exclusion from the Wall so longstanding and so painful, and the aura of holiness so powerful that even the most irreligious Jews, across the world, experienced a sensation of exhilaration that approached a religious experience and in the modern world was as close as they would ever come to one.

For the religious Jews, the heirs of those who for thousands of years, from Babylon to Cordoba and Vilna, had, as we have seen, expected imminent messianic delivery, this was a sign, a deliverance, a redemption and the fulfilment of the biblical prophecies, and the end of the Exile and Return to the gates and courts of the Temple in David's restored city. For the many Israelis who embraced nationalistic, military Zionism, the heirs of Jabotinsky, this military victory was political and strategic – the singular, God-given chance to secure a Greater Israel with safe borders. Religious and nationalistic Jews alike shared the conviction that they must energetically embrace the exciting mission to rebuild and forever keep the Jewish Jerusalem. During the 1970s, these battalions of the messianic and the maximalist became every bit as dynamic as the majority of Israelis, who remained secular and liberal and whose centre of life was Tel Aviv, not the Holy City. But the nationalist–redemptionist programme was God's urgent work and this divine imperative would soon alter the physiognomy and bloodstream of Jerusalem.

It was not only Jews who were affected: the much more numerous and powerful Christian evangelicals, especially those of America, also experienced this instant of almost apocalyptic ecstasy. Evangelicals believed that two of the preconditions had been met for Judgement Day: Israel was restored and Jerusalem was Jewish. All that remained was the rebuilding of the Third Temple and seven years of tribulation, followed by the battle of Armageddon when St Michael would appear on the Mount of Olives to fight the Anti-Christ on the Temple Mount. This would culminate in the conversion or destruction of the Jews and the Second Coming and Thousand Year Reign of Jesus Christ.

The victory of the small Jewish democracy against the Soviet-armed legions of Arab despotism convinced the United States that Israel was its special friend in the most dangerous of neighbourhoods, its ally in the struggle against Communist Russia, Nasserite radicalism and Islamicist fundamentalism. America and Israel shared more than that, for they were countries built on an ideal of freedom touched by the divine: one was the new Zion, the 'city on a hill', the other the old Zion restored. American Jews were already avid supporters but now American evangelists believed that Israel had been blessed by Providence. Polls consistently claim that over 40 per cent of Americans sometime expect the Second Coming in Jerusalem. However exaggerated this may be, American Christian Zionists threw their weight behind Jewish Jerusalem, and Israel was grateful even though the role of the Jews in their doomsday scenario was a tragic one.

Israelis from west Jerusalem, from all Israel and the breadth of the Diaspora, crowded into the Old City to touch the Wall and pray there. The possession of the city was so intoxicating that giving her up became henceforth unbearable and unthinkable – and vast resources were now mobilized to make such a thing very difficult indeed. Even the pragmatic Ben-Gurion proposed from his retirement that Israel should give up the West Bank and Gaza in return for peace – but never Jerusalem.

Israel officially united the city's two halves, expanding the municipal borders to encompass 267,800 citizens – 196,800 Jews and 71,000 Arabs. Jerusalem became larger than it had ever been in its history. Scarcely before the gunbarrels had cooled, the inhabitants of the Maghrebi Quarter, founded by Saladin's son Afdal, were evacuated to new homes, their houses demolished to open the space before the Wall for the first time. After centuries of cramped, confined, harassed worship in a 9-foot-long alleyway, the airy, light space of the new plaza at the paramount Jewish shrine was itself a liberation; Jews flocked to pray there. The dilapidated Jewish Quarter was restored, its dynamited synagogues rebuilt and resanctified, its ravaged squares and alleys repaved and embellished, Orthodox religious schools – yeshivas – were created or repaired, all in gleaming golden stone.

Science was celebrated too: Israeli archaeologists started to excavate the united city. The long Western Wall was divided between the rabbis, who controlled the praying area to north of the Maghrebi Gate, and the archaeologists, who could dig to the south. Around the Wall, in the Muslim and Jewish Quarters, and in the City of David, they uncovered such astounding treasures – Canaanite fortifications, Judaean seals, Herodian foundations, Maccabean and Byzantine walls, Roman streets, Umayyad palaces, Ayyubid gates, Crusader churches – that their scientific finds seemed to fuse with the political-religious enthusiasm. The stones they uncovered – from the wall of Hezekiah and Herod's ashlars tossed down by the Roman soldiers to the paving of Hadrian's Cardo – became permanent displays in the restored Old City.

Teddy Kollek, the mayor of west Jerusalem who was re-elected to run the united city for twenty-eight years, worked hard to reassure the Arabs, becoming the face of the liberal Israeli instinct to unify the city under Jewish rule but also to respect Arab Jerusalem.* As

* Kollek, born in Hungary, raised in Vienna, and named after Theodor Herzl, had specialized in secret missions for the Jewish Agency, liaising with the British secret service during the campaign against the Irgun and the Stern Gang, and then buying

under the Mandate, the prosperous Jerusalem attracted Arabs from the West Bank – their population doubled in ten years. Now the conquest encouraged Israelis of all parties, but especially nationalists and redemptionist Zionists, to secure the conquest by creating 'facts on the ground'; the building of new Jewish suburbs around Arab east Jerusalem began immediately.

At first, Arab opposition was muted; many Palestinians worked in Israel or with Israelis, and, as a young boy visiting Jerusalem, I remember days spent with Palestinian and Israeli friends in their houses in Jerusalem and the West Bank, never realizing that this period of goodwill and mixing would very soon become the exception to the rule. Abroad, things were different. Yasser Arafat and his Fatah took over the PLO in 1969. Fatah intensified its guerrilla attacks on Israel while another faction, the Marxist-Leninist Popular Front for the Liberation of Palestine, pioneered the new spectacle of hijacking aeroplanes as well as embracing the more traditional killing of civilians.

The Temple Mount, as Dayan had understood, brought with it an awesome responsibility. On 21 August 1969, an Australian Christian, David Rohan, who seems to have suffered from the Jerusalem Syndrome,* set fire to al-Aqsa Mosque to accelerate the Second Coming. The blaze destroyed Nur al-Din's *minbar* placed

arms for the Haganah. He then served as director of Ben-Gurion's private office. Meanwhile, the grande dame of the American Colony, Bertha Spafford Vester, now ninety, was reconciled to Israel: 'I've lived under Turks, British, Jordanians and we've got along with everyone. We shall do the same with the Israelis.' She died in June 1968. Mayor Kollek became a regular visitor to the Colony.

* The chief academic work on Jerusalem madness describes the typical patients as 'individuals who strongly identify with characters from the Old or New Testament or are convinced they are one of these characters and fall victim to a psychotic episode in Jerusalem.' Tour guides should look out for '1. Agitation. 2. Split away from group. 3. Obsession with taking baths; compulsive fingernail/toe-nail clipping. 4. Preparation, often with aid of hotel bed-linen, of toga-like gown, always white. 5. The need to scream, sing out loud biblical verses. 6. Procession to one of Jerusalem's holy places. 7. Delivery of a sermon in a holy place.' Jerusalem's Kfar Shaul Mental Centre specializes in the Syndrome: it stands on the site of Deir Yassin, its secure walls containing the last houses from that tragic village. Around 100 patients are admitted annually (though more during the messianic excitement of the new Millennium) but only one or two suffer the Syndrome in its purest form, often believing they are John the Baptist or Virgin Mary.

there by Saladin, and kindled rumours of a Jewish conspiracy to seize the Temple Mount, which in turn unleashed Arab riots.

In 'Black September' 1970, King Hussein defeated and expelled Arafat and the PLO, who had challenged his control of Jordan. Arafat moved his headquarters to Lebanon and Fatah embarked on an international campaign of hijacking and killing of civilians to bring the Palestinian cause to the attention of the world – this was carnage as political theatre. In 1972, Fatah gunmen, using 'Black September' as a front, murdered eleven Israeli athletes at the Munich Olympics. In response, Mossad, Israel's secret service, hunted down the perpetrators across Europe.

On the Day of Atonement in October 1973, Nasser's successor, President Anwar Sadat of Egypt, launched a successful surprise attack, in collusion with Syria, against an overconfident Israel. The Arabs scored early successes, discrediting defence minister Moshe Dayan who almost lost his nerve after two days of reverses. However, the Israelis, supplied by an American airlift, rallied and the war made the name of General Ariel Sharon who led the Israeli counter-attack across the Suez Canal. Soon afterwards, the Arab League persuaded King Hussein to recognize the PLO as the sole representative of the Palestinians.

In 1977, thirty years after the bombing of the King David, Menachem Begin and his Likud finally swept aside the Labour party that had ruled since 1948 and came to power with a nationalist–messianic programme for a Greater Israel with Jerusalem as its capital. Yet it was Begin who, on 19 November, welcomed President Sadat on his courageous flight to Jerusalem. Sadat stayed in the King David Hotel, prayed at al-Aqsa, visited Yad Vashem and offered peace to the Knesset. Hopes soared. With the help of Moshe Dayan whom he had appointed foreign minister, Begin restored Sinai to Egypt in return for a peace treaty. Yet, unlike Dayan who soon resigned, Begin knew little of the Arab world, remaining the son of the Polish *shtetl*, a harsh nationalist with a Manichaean view of the Jewish struggle, an emotional attachment to Judaism and a vision of biblical Israel. Negotiating with Sadat under the aegis of President Jimmy Carter, Begin insisted 'Jerusalem will remain the eternal united capital of Israel and that is that', and the Knesset voted a similar formula into Israeli law. Driven by the bulldozer-like energy of his agriculture minister, Ariel Sharon, and determined 'to secure Jerusalem as permanent capital of the Jewish people', Begin accelerated the building of what Sharon called 'an outer ring of development around the Arab neighbourhoods' to 'develop a greater Jerusalem'.

In April 1982, an Israeli reservist named Alan Goodman shot two Arabs in a rampage across the Temple Mount. The mufti had constantly warned that the Jews wanted to rebuild the Temple on the site of al-Aqsa so now Arabs wondered if there really was such a secret plan. The vast majority of Israelis and Jews utterly reject any such thing and most ultra-Orthodox believe that men should not meddle with God's work. There are only about a thousand Jewish fundamentalists in groups, such as the Temple Mount Faithful, who demand the right to pray on the Temple Mount, or the Movement for the Establishment of the Temple, which claims to be training a priestly caste for the Third Temple. Only the tiniest factions within the most extreme cells of fanatics have conspired to destroy the mosques, but so far, Israeli police have foiled all their plots. Such an outrage would be a catastrophe not just for Muslims but for the State of Israel itself.

In 1982, Begin responded to PLO attacks on Israeli diplomats and civilians by invading Lebanon where Arafat had built up a fiefdom. Arafat and his forces were forced out of Beirut, moving to Tunis. The war, masterminded by defence minister Sharon, became a quagmire which culminated in Christian militias massacring between 300 and 700 Palestinian civilians in the Sabra and Shatila camps. Sharon, bearing indirect responsibility for the atrocity, was forced to resign and Begin's career ended in depression, resignation and isolation.

The raised hopes of 1977 were dashed by the intransigence of both sides, the killing of civilians, and the expansion of Jewish settlements in Jerusalem and the West Bank. In 1981, the assassination of Sadat, punishment for his flight to Jerusalem, by fundamentalists, was an early sign of a new power rising in Islam. In December 1987 a spontaneous Palestinian revolt – the Intifada, the Uprising – broke out in Gaza and spread to Jerusalem. Israeli police fought protesters in pitched battles on the Temple Mount. The youths in the streets of Jerusalem slinging stones at uniformed Israeli soldiers replaced the murderous hijackers of the PLO as the image of the persecuted but defiant Palestinians.

The energy of the Intifada created a power vacuum that was filled by new leaders and ideas: the PLO elite was out of touch with the Palestinian street, and fundamentalist Islam was replacing Nasser's obsolete pan-Arabism. In 1987, Islamicist radicals founded the Islamic Resistance Movement, Hamas, a branch of the Egyptian Muslim Brotherhood, which was dedicated to the jihad to destroy Israel.

The Intifada also altered Jewish Jerusalem, admitted Kollek, 'in a fundamental way' – it destroyed the dream of a united city. Israelis and Arabs ceased to work together; they no longer walked through each other's suburbs. The tension spread not only between Muslim and Jew but also among the Jews themselves: the ultra-Orthodox rioted against secular Jews, who began to move out of Jerusalem. The old world of Christian Jerusalem was shrinking fast: by 1995 there were only 14,100 Christians left. Yet the Israeli nationalists did not deviate from their plan to Judaize Jerusalem. Sharon provocatively moved into an apartment in the Muslim Quarter and in 1991, religious ultra-nationalists started to settle in Arab Silwan, next to the original City of David. Kollek, who saw his life's work overwhelmed by aggressive redemptionists, denounced Sharon and these settlers for their 'messianism which has always been extremely harmful to us in history'.

The Intifada led indirectly to the Oslo peace talks. In 1988, Arafat accepted the idea of a two-state solution and renounced the armed struggle to destroy Israel. King Hussein gave up his claim on Jerusalem and the West Bank where Arafat planned to build a Palestinian state with al-Quds as its capital. In 1992, Yitzhak Rabin became prime minister and crushed the Intifada; with his plain-spoken toughness, he possessed the only qualities Israelis would trust in a peacemaker. The Americans had presided over abortive talks in Madrid but, unbeknown to most of the major players, there was another, secret process that would bear fruit.

This began with informal talks between Israeli and Palestinian academics. There were meetings at the American Colony which was regarded as neutral territory, in London and then in Oslo. The talks were initially run without Rabin's knowledge by the foreign minister Shimon Peres and his deputy Yossi Beilin. It was only in 1993 that they informed Rabin, who backed the talks. On 13 September, Rabin and Peres signed the treaty with Arafat at the White House, genially supervised by President Clinton. The West Bank and Gaza were partly handed over to a Palestinian Authority which took over the old Husseini mansion, Orient House, as its Jerusalem headquarters, run by the most respected Palestinian in the city, Faisal al-Husseini, son of the hero of 1948.* Rabin signed a peace treaty with King Hussein of Jordan and confirmed his special Hashemite role as custodian of the Islamic Sanctuary in Jerusalem which continues today. Israeli and Palestinian archaeologists negotiated their own academic version of the peace and enthusiastically started to work together for the first time.

The conundrum of Jerusalem was set aside until later in the negotiations and Rabin intensified the building of settlements in Jerusalem before any agreement. Beilin and Arafat's deputy Mahmoud Abbas negotiated to divide Jerusalem between Arab and Jewish areas under a united municipality and to give the Old City a 'special status,' almost like a Middle Eastern Vatican City – but nothing was signed.

The Oslo Accords perhaps left too much detail undecided and were violently opposed on both sides. Mayor Kollek, aged eighty-two, was defeated in elections by the more hardline Ehud Olmert, backed by nationalists and ultra-Orthodox. On 4 November 1995, just four days after Beilin and Abbas had come to an informal understanding on Jerusalem, Rabin was assassinated by a Jewish

---

* Faisal Husseini, the son of Abd al-Kadir, emerged as one of the leaders of the Intifada. Husseini had trained as a Fatah explosives expert and spent years in Israeli jails, the essential badges of honour for any Palestinian leader, but, released from prison, he was one of the first to come round to talks with the Israelis, even learning Hebrew to put his case more clearly. Husseini attended the Madrid talks and now became Arafat's Palestinian minister for Jerusalem. When the Oslo Accords fell apart, the Israelis confined him to Orient House before eventually closing it down. When he died in 2001, buried like his father on the Haram, the Palestinians lost the only leader who could have replaced Arafat.

fanatic. Born in Jerusalem, Rabin returned there to be buried on Mount Herzl. King Hussein delivered a eulogy; the American president and two of his predecessors attended. President Mubarak of Egypt visited for the first time, and the Prince of Wales made the only formal royal visit to Jerusalem since the foundation of Israel.

The peace began to fall apart. The Islamic fundamentalists of Hamas launched a campaign of suicide bombings that wrought random carnage on Israeli civilians: an Arab suicide bomber killed twenty-five people on a Jerusalem bus. A week later another suicide bomber killed eighteen on the same bus route. Israeli voters punished Prime Minister Peres for the Palestinian violence, instead electing Binyamin Netanyahu, leader of Likud, on the slogan: 'Peres will divide Jerusalem.' Netanyahu questioned the principle of land-for-peace, opposed any division of Jerusalem and commissioned more settlements.

In September 1996, Netanyahu opened a tunnel that ran from the Wall alongside the Temple Mount to emerge in the Muslim Quarter.* When some Israeli radicals tried to excavate upwards towards the Temple Mount, the Islamic authorities of the *Waqf* quickly cemented up the hole. Rumours spread that the tunnels were an attempt to undermine the Islamic Sanctuary and seventy-five were killed and 1,500 wounded in riots that proved that archaeology is worth dying for in Jerusalem. It was not only the Israelis who politicized their archaeology: history was paramount. The PLO banned Palestinian historians from admitting there had ever been a Jewish Temple in Jerusalem – and this order came from Arafat himself: he was a secular guerrilla leader but as with the Israelis, even the secular national narrative was underpinned by the religious

---

* Archaeologists had started exploring tunnels beneath the Arab homes that bordered the entire western wall of the Temple Mount during the 1950s and Professor Oleg Grabar, the future doyen of Jerusalem scholars, remembers how they would frequently appear as if by magic out of the floors in the kitchens of the surprised residents. Under Israeli archaeologists, the tunnel yielded – and continues to do so – the most breathtaking finds from the immense stones of the foundations of Herod's Temple, via Maccabee, Roman, Byzantine and Umayyad buildings, to a new Crusader chapel. But the tunnel also contained the place closest to the Temple's Foundation Stone where Jews could now pray – and it united Jerusalem by linking the Jewish and Muslim Quarters.

one. In 1948, Arafat had fought with the Muslim Brotherhood –
their forces were called the Al-Jihad al-Muqadas, Jerusalem Holy
War – and he embraced the Islamic significance of the city: he
called Fatah's armed wing the Aqsa Martyrs Brigade. Arafat's aides
admitted Jerusalem was his 'personal obsession'. He identified
himself with Saladin and Omar the Great, and denied any Jewish
connection to Jerusalem. 'The greater the Jewish pressure on the
Temple Mount,' says Palestinian historian Dr Nazmi Jubeh, 'the
greater the denial of the First and Second Temples.'

In the tense days after the Tunnel riots and amid rumours of
plans to open a synagogue in the Stables of Solomon, the Israelis
allowed the *Waqf* to clear the ancient halls under al-Aqsa and then
use bulldozers to dig a stairway and build a new, capacious subterranean mosque, the Marwan, in the hallways of Herod. The
debris was simply thrown away. Israeli archaeologists were aghast
at the crude bulldozing of the most delicate site on earth: archaeology was the loser in the battle of religions and politics.*

Israelis had not quite lost their faith in peace. At the presidential
retreat of Camp David, Clinton brought together the new prime
minister Ehud Barak and Arafat in July 2000. Barak boldly offered
a 'final' deal: 91 per cent of the West Bank with the Palestinian
capital in Abu Dis and all the Arab suburbs of east Jerusalem. The
Old City would remain under Israeli sovereignty but the Muslim
and Christian Quarters and the Temple Mount would be under
Palestinian 'sovereign custodianship'. The earth and tunnels
beneath the Sanctuary – above all the Foundation Stone of the
Temple – would remain Israeli and for the first time, Jews would
be allowed to pray in limited numbers somewhere on the Temple
Mount. The Old City would be jointly patrolled but demilitarized
and open to all. Already offered half the Old City's quarters, Arafat
demanded the Armenian Quarter. Israel agreed, effectively offering

* These struggles reveal the complexities of both sides, sometimes bringing
Israelis and Arabs together: when Rabbi Goren tried to commandeer the Khalidi
house overlooking the Wall for a yeshiva, Mrs Haifa Khalidi was defended in
Israeli courts by two Israeli historians, Amnon Cohen and Dan Bahat, and still
lives today in her house above the famous Khalidiyyah Library. When religious
Jews tried to expand their digs and settlement in Silwan below the City of David,
they were stopped by lawsuits brought by Israeli archaeologists.

three-quarters of the Old City. Despite Saudi pressure to accept, Arafat felt he could neither negotiate a final settlement of the Palestinians' right of return nor approve Israeli sovereignty over the Dome which belonged to all Islam.

'Do you want to attend my funeral?' he exclaimed to Clinton. 'I won't relinquish Jerusalem and the Holy Places.' But his rejection was much more fundamental: during the talks, Arafat shocked the Americans and Israelis when he insisted that Jerusalem had never been the site of the Jewish Temple, which had in fact existed only on the Samaritan Mount Gerizim. The city's holiness for Jews was a modern invention. In talks later that year in the last weeks of Clinton's presidency, Israel offered full sovereignty on the Temple Mount keeping only a symbolic link to the Holy of Holies beneath, but Arafat rejected this.

On 28 September 2000, Sharon, leader of the Likud opposition, added to Barak's problems by swaggering on to the Temple Mount, guarded by phalanxes of Israeli police, with a 'message of peace' that clearly menaced Islam's beloved Aqsa and Dome. The resulting riots escalated into the Aqsa Intifada, partly another stone-throwing insurgency and partly a pre-planned campaign of suicide bombings aimed by Fatah and Hamas at Israeli civilians. If the first Intifada had helped the Palestinians, this one destroyed Israeli trust in the peace process, led to the election of Sharon, and fatally split the Palestinians themselves.

Sharon suppressed the Intifada by smashing the Palestinian Authority, besieging and humiliating Arafat. He died in 2004 and the Israelis refused to allow his burial on the Temple Mount. His successor Abbas lost the 2006 elections to Hamas. After a short conflict, Hamas seized Gaza while Abbas's Fatah continued to rule the West Bank. Sharon built a security wall through Jerusalem, a depressing concrete eyesore which did, however, succeed in stopping the suicide bombings.

The seeds of peace not only fell on stony ground but poisoned it too; the peace discredited its makers. Jerusalem today lives in a state of schizophrenic anxiety. Jews and Arabs dare not venture into each other's neighbourhoods; secular Jews avoid ultra-Orthodox who stone them for not resting on the Sabbath or for wearing disrespectful clothing; messianic Jews test police resolve and tease Muslim anxiety by attempting to pray on the Temple Mount; and the Christian sects keep brawling. The faces of Jerusalemites are tense, their voices are angry and one feels that everyone, even those of all three faiths who are convinced that they are fulfilling a divine plan, is unsure of what tomorrow will bring.

TOMORROW

Here, more than anywhere else on earth, we crave, we hope and we search for any drop of the elixir of tolerance, sharing and generosity to act as the antidote to the arsenic of prejudice, exclusivity and possessiveness. It is not always easy to find. Today, Jerusalem has not been so large, so embellished, nor has she been so over-whelmingly Jewish for two millennia. Yet she is also the most populous Palestinian city.* Sometimes her very Jewishness is presented as somehow synthetic and against the grain of Jerusalem, but this is a distortion of the city's past and present.

Jerusalem's history is a chronicle of settlers, colonists and pilgrims, who have included Arabs, Jews and many others, in a place that has grown and contracted many times. During more than a millennium of Islamic rule, Jerusalem was repeatedly colonized by Islamic settlers, scholars, Sufis and pilgrims who were Arabs, Turks, Indians, Sudanese, Iranians, Kurds, Iraqis and Maghrebis, as well as Christian Armenians, Serbs, Georgians and Russians – not so different from the Sephardic and Russian Jews who later settled there for similar reasons. It was this character that convinced Lawrence of Arabia that Jerusalem was more a Levantine city than an Arab one, and this is utterly intrinsic to the city's character.

It is often forgotten that all the suburbs of Jerusalem outside the walls were new settlements built between 1860 and 1948 by Arabs

---

* In 2009/2010, the population of Greater Jerusalem was 780,000: 514,800 Jews (who include 163,800 ultra-Orthodox) and 265,200 Arabs. There were around 30,000 Arabs in the Old City and 3,500 Jews. There are around 200,000 Israelis living in new suburbs in eastern Jerusalem.

as well as Jews and Europeans. The Arab areas, such as Sheikh Jarrah, are no older than the Jewish ones, and no more, or less, legitimate.

Both Muslims and Jews have unimpeachable historical claims. Jews have inhabited, and revered this city for 3,000 years, and have the same right to live in, and settle around, an equitable Jerusalem as Arabs do. Yet there are times when even the most harmless Jewish restoration is presented as illegitimate: in 2010, the Israelis finally consecrated the restored Hurva Synagogue in the Jewish Quarter, which had been demolished by the Jordanians in 1948, yet this provoked European media criticism and minor riots in eastern Jerusalem.

However, it is a very different matter when the existing Arab inhabitants find themselves removed, coerced and harassed, their property expropriated with dubious legal rulings to make way for new Jewish settlements, backed by the full power of state and mayoralty, and fiercely promoted by people with the urgent determination of those on a divine mission. The aggressive building of settlements, designed to colonize Arab neighbourhoods and sabotage any peace deal to share the city, and the systematic neglect of services and new housing in Arab areas, have given even the most innocent Jewish projects a bad name.

Israel faces two paths – the Jerusalemite, religious-nationalist state versus a liberal, westernized Tel Aviv which is nicknamed 'the Bubble'. There is a danger that the nationalistic project in Jerusalem, and the obsessive settlement-building on the West Bank, may so distort Israel's own interests that they do more harm to Israel itself than any benefit they may bring to Jewish Jerusalem.*

---

* In Israel's dysfunctional democracy, with weak coalition governments, national-religious organizations have become ever more powerful in questions of Jerusalem's planning and archaeology. In 2003, Israeli building started in the vital East One (E1) section, east of the Old City, which would have effectively cut off east Jerusalem from the West Bank, undermining the creation of a Palestinian state. Israeli liberals and America persuaded Israel to stop this, but plans to build Jewish settlements in the Arab neighbourhoods of Sheikh Jarrah and Silwan continue. The latter stands next to the much-excavated ancient City of David where a Jewish nationalist-religious foundation, Elad, funds the invaluable archaeological excavations and runs a visitors' centre telling the story of Jewish Jerusalem. It also plans to move Palestinian residents to nearby housing to make way for more Jewish settlers and a King

However the tides of opinion ebb and flow, Israel has the same right to security and prosperity as any other country – though Jerusalem is not just any capital. Some of the settlements undermine Israel's record, uniquely impressive by historical standards, as guardian of a Jerusalem for all faiths. 'Today for the first time in history, Jews, Christians and Muslims all may freely worship at their shrines,' the writer Elie Wiesel wrote in an open letter to US President Obama in 2010 and, under Israel's democracy, this is for the most part true.

It is certainly the first time Jews have been able to worship freely there since AD 70. Under Christian rule, Jews were forbidden even to approach the city. During the Islamic centuries, Christians and Jews were tolerated as *dhimmi* but frequently repressed. The Jews, who lacked the protection of the European powers enjoyed by the Christians, were often treated badly – though never as badly as they were treated in Christian Europe at its worst. Jews could be killed for approaching the Islamic or Christian holy places – but anyone could drive a donkey through the passageway next to the Wall, which technically they could only attend with a permit. Even in the twentieth century, Jewish access to the Wall was severely restricted by the British and totally banned by the Jordanians. However, thanks to what Israelis called 'the Situation', Wiesel's claim about freedom of worship is not always true for non-Jews who endure a multitude of bureaucratic harassments while the security wall makes it harder for West Bank Palestinians to reach Jerusalem to pray at the Church or Aqsa.

When they are not in conflict, Jews, Muslims and Christians return to the ancient Jerusalem tradition of ostrichism – burying their heads in the sand and pretending The Others do not exist. In September 2008, the overlapping of Jewish Holy Days and

David park called the King's Gardens. Such situations can challenge archaeological professionalism. Archaeologists, writes Dr Raphael Greenberg, a historian who has campaigned against this project, represent 'a secular academic approach', yet their backers hope for 'results that legitimise their concepts of the history of Jerusalem'. So far his fears have not materialized. The integrity of the archaeologists is high and as we saw earlier, the present dig has uncovered Canaanite not Jewish walls. Nonetheless these sites have become flashpoints for protests by Palestinians and Israeli liberals.

Ramadan created a 'monotheistic traffic jam' in the alleyways as Jews and Arabs came to pray at Sanctuary and Wall but 'it would be wrong to call these *tense encounters* because there are essentially no encounters at all,' reported Ethan Bronner in the *New York Times*. 'Words are not exchanged; [they] look past one another. Like parallel universes with different names for every place and moment they both claim as their own, the groups pass in the night.'

By the bile-spattered standards of Jerusalem, this ostrichism is a sign of normality – particularly since the city has never been so globally important. Today Jerusalem is the cockpit of the Middle East, the battlefield of Western secularism versus Islamic fundamentalism, not to speak of the struggle between Israel and Palestine. New Yorkers, Londoners and Parisians feel they live in an atheistic, secular world in which organized religion, and its believers, are at best gently mocked, yet the numbers of fundamentalist millenarian Abrahamic believers – Christian, Jewish and Muslim – are increasing.

Jerusalem's apocalyptic and political roles become ever more fraught. America's exuberant democracy is raucously diverse and secular yet it is simultaneously the last and probably the greatest ever Christian power – and its evangelicals continue to look to the End Days in Jerusalem, just as US governments see a calm Jerusalem as key to any Middle Eastern peace and strategically vital for relations with their Arab allies. Meanwhile Israel's rule over al-Quds has intensified Muslim reverence: on Iran's annual Jerusalem Day, inaugurated by Ayatollah Khomeini in 1979, the city is presented as more than an Islamic shrine and Palestinian capital. In Tehran's bid for regional hegemony backed by nuclear weapons, and its cold war with America, Jerusalem is a cause that conveniently unites Iranian Shiites with Sunni Arabs sceptical of the ambitions of the Islamic Republic. Whether for Shiite Hezbollah in Lebanon or Sunni Hamas in Gaza, the city now serves as the rallying totem of anti-Zionism, anti-Americanism and Iranian leadership. 'The Occupation Regime over Jerusalem,' says President Mahmoud Ahmadinejad, 'should vanish from the page of history.' And Ahmadinejad too is a millenarian who believes that the imminent return of the 'righteous, perfect human Al-Madhi the

Chosen', the 'occulted' Twelfth Imam, will liberate Jerusalem, the setting for what the Koran calls 'The Hour'.

This eschatological–political intensity places twenty-first-century Jerusalem, Chosen City of the three faiths, in the crosshairs of all these conflicts and visions. Jerusalem's apocalyptic role may be exaggerated but, as changes sweep the Arab world, this unique combination of power, faith and fashion, all played out under the hothouse glare of twenty-four-hour TV news, heaps the pressure on to the delicate stones of the Universal City, again, in some ways, the centre of the world.

'Jerusalem is a tinderbox that could go off at any time,' warned King Abdullah II of Jordan, great-grandson of Abdullah the Hasty, in 2010. 'All roads in our part of the world, all the conflicts, lead to Jerusalem.' This is the reason that American presidents need to bring the sides together even at the most inauspicious moments. The peace-party in Israeli democracy is in eclipse, its fragile governments influenced by overmighty religious-nationalist parties while the fractious Palestinian factions, encouraged by the Arab Spring, try to reconcile their very different programmes – that of Fatah, conciliatory and secular, that of Hamas, militant and Islamicist – to form a united Palestinian government. If Fatah's West Bank is increasingly prosperous, the most dynamic Palestinian organization is the fundamentalist Hamas, which rules Gaza and remains dedicated to Israel's annihilation. It embraces suicide bombings as its weapon of choice and period- ically fires missiles onto southern Israel, provoking Israeli incur- sions. Europeans and Americans regard it as a terrorist organization and so far conciliatory signals of a willingness to support a settlement based on 1967 borders have been mixed. At some point, elections will hopefully choose a democratic Pal- estinian government, although it is unclear whether the two factions can work together to provide a stable interlocutor with Israel and whether Hamas can become a trusted partner in a peace process with Israel. At some point in the negotiations, Hamas will need to renounce violence and recognize the Jewish State. Furthermore, as always in her history, Jerusalem will be affected by the turbulent destinies of Egypt, Syria and the other revolutions that began to remould the Middle East in the Arab Spring of 2011.

The history of the negotiations since 1993, and the difference in spirit between noble words and distrustful, violent acts, suggest unwillingness on both sides to make the necessary compromises to share Jerusalem permanently. At the best of times, the reconciliation of the celestial, national and emotional in Jerusalem is a puzzle within a labyrinth: during the twentieth century, there were over forty plans for Jerusalem which all failed, and today there are at least thirteen different models just for sharing the Temple Mount.

In 2010, President Obama forced Netanyahu, back in power in coalition with Barak, to freeze Jerusalem settlement-building temporarily. At the cost of the bitterest moment in US–Israeli relations, Obama at least got the two sides to talk again, though progress was glacial and short-lived.

Israel has often been diplomatically rigid and risked its own security and reputation by building settlements, but the latter are negotiable. The problem on the other side seems equally fundamental. Under Rabin, Barak and Olmert, Israel offered to share Jerusalem, including the Old City. Despite exasperating negotiations during the almost two decades since 1993, the Palestinians have never formally agreed to share the city, though there is hope: they did so secretly and informally in 2007/8. Yet when each made their most flexible offer and their positions were very close, it was at the wrong time for the other. And the revelation in leaked documents of such a Palestinian offer provoked furious accusations of betrayal on the Arab side.

Jerusalem may continue for decades in its present state, but whenever, if ever, a peace is signed, there will be two states, which is essential for the survival of Israel as state and as democracy, and justice and respect for the Palestinians. The shape of a Palestinian state and a shared Jerusalem is known to both sides. 'Jerusalem will be the capital for both states, Arab suburbs will be Palestinian, Jewish suburbs will be Israeli,' said Israeli President Shimon Peres, architect of the Oslo Accords, who knows the picture as well as anyone. The Israelis will get their twelve or so settlements in eastern

Jerusalem, following the parameters set by Clinton, but the Pal-
estinians will be compensated with Israeli land elsewhere, and
Israeli settlements will be removed from most of the West Bank.
So far so simple, 'but the challenge,' explains Peres, 'is the Old City.
We must distinguish between sovereignty and religion. Everyone
would control their own shrines but one can hardly slice the Old
City into pieces.'

The Old City would be a demilitarized Vatican, run by an international committee, policed by joint Arab-Israeli patrols or an international trustee, perhaps even a Jerusalemite version of the
Vatican's Swiss Guards. The Arabs might not accept America, the
Israelis distrust the UN and the EU, so perhaps the job could be
done by NATO with Russia, which is once again keen to play a role
in Jerusalem.* It is hard to internationalize the Temple Mount
itself because no Israeli politician could totally surrender any claim
to the Foundation Stone of the Temple and live to tell the tale, while
no Islamic potentate could acknowledge full Israeli sovereignty over
the Noble Sanctuary and survive. Besides, international or free
cities, from Danzig to Trieste, have usually ended badly.

The Temple Mount is difficult to divide. The Haram and the
Kotel, the Dome, the Aqsa and the Wall are all part of the same
structure: 'no one can monopolize holiness,' added Peres. 'Jerusalem is more a flame than a city and no one can divide a flame.'
Flame or not, someone has to hold the sovereignty, so the various
plans give the surface to the Muslims and the tunnels and cisterns
beneath (and therefore the Foundation Stone) to Israel. The minute
complexities of the twilight world of subterranean caverns, pipes
and waterways there are breathtaking, if peculiarly Jerusalemite:
who owns the earth, who owns the land, who owns the heavens?

---

* The Russian reverence for Jerusalem has been modernized to suit the authoritarian
nationalism fostered by Vladimir Putin who in 2007 oversaw the reunion of the ex-
Soviet Moscow Patriarchate and the White Russian Orthodox Church Outside
Russia. Thousands of singing Russian pilgrims again fill the streets. The Holy Fire
is flown back to Moscow on a plane, chartered by an organization called the Centre for
National Glory and the Apostle Andrei Foundation, headed by a Kremlin potentate. A
kitsch life-sized golden statue of 'Tsar David' has appeared outside David's Tomb.
An ex-prime minister, Stephan Stepashin, is the chief of the restored Palestine
Society: 'a Russian flag in the centre of Jerusalem,' he says, 'is priceless.'

No deal can be agreed nor will it endure without something else. Political sovereignty can be drawn on a map, expressed in legal agreements, enforced with M-16s but it will be futile and meaningless without the historic, mystical and emotional. 'Two thirds of the Arab–Israeli conflict is psychology,' said Sadat. The real conditions for peace are not just the details of which Herodian cistern will be Palestinian or Israeli but the heartfelt intangibles of mutual trust and respect. On both sides, some elements deny the history of the Other. If this book has any mission, I passionately hope that it might encourage each side to recognize and respect the ancient heritage of the Other: Arafat's denial of Jewish history in Jerusalem was regarded as absurd by his own historians (who all happily accept that history in private), but none would risk contradicting him. As late as 2010, only the philosopher Sari Nusseibeh had the courage to admit that the Haram al-Sharif was the site of the Jewish Temple. Israeli settlement-building undermines Arab confidence and the practicality of a Palestinian state. Yet the firing of missiles into Israel by Hamas is an act of war, while Palestinian denial of the ancient Jewish heritage and the Jewishness of the modern state are just as disastrous to peacemaking. And this is before we reach an even greater challenge: each must recognize the Other's sacred modern narratives of tragedy and heroism. This is a lot to ask since both of these stories star the Other as arch-villain – yet this too is possible.

This being Jerusalem, one could easily imagine the unthinkable: will Jerusalem even exist five or forty years on? There is always the possibility that extremists could destroy the Temple Mount at any moment, break the heart of the world and convince fundamentalists of every persuasion that Judgement Day is nigh and the war of Christ and Anti-Christ is beginning.

Amos Oz, the Jerusalemite writer who now lives in the Negev, offers this droll solution: 'We should remove every stone of the Holy Sites and transport them to Scandinavia for a hundred years and not return them until everyone has learned to live together in Jerusalem.' Sadly this is slightly impractical.

For 1,000 years, Jerusalem was exclusively Jewish; for about 400 years, Christian; for 1,300 years, Islamic; and not one of the three faiths ever gained Jerusalem without the sword, the mangonel or the howitzer. Their nationalistic histories tell a rigid story of inevitable progressions to heroic triumphs and abrupt disasters, but in this history I have tried to show that nothing was inevitable, there were always choices. The fates and identities of Jerusalemites were rarely clear cut. Life in Herodian, Crusader, or British Jerusalem was always just as complex and nuanced as life is for us today.

There were quiet evolutions as well as dramatic revolutions. Sometimes it was dynamite, steel and blood that changed Jerusalem, sometimes it was more the slow descent of generations, of songs sung and passed down, stories told, poems recited, sculptures carved, and the blurred half-conscious routines of families over many centuries taking small steps down winding stairways, quick leaps over neighbouring thresholds and the smoothing of rough stones until they shone.

Jerusalem, so loveable in many ways, so hate-filled in others, always bristling with the hallowed and the brash, the preposterously vulgar and the aesthetically exquisite, seems to live more intensely than anywhere else; everything stays the same yet nothing stays still. At dawn each day, the three shrines of the three faiths come to life in their own way.

THIS MORNING

At 4.30 a.m., Shmuel Rabinowitz, rabbi of the Western Wall and the Holy Sites, wakes up to begin his daily ritual of prayer, reading the Torah. He walks through the Jewish Quarter to the Wall which never closes, its colossal layers of Herodian ashlar stones glowing in the darkness. Jews pray there all day and all night.

The rabbi, forty years old and descended from Russian immigrants who arrived in Jerusalem seven generations ago, comes from families in the Gerer and Lubavitcher courts. The father of seven children, bespectacled, bearded and blue-eyed, in black suit and skullcap, proceeds down through the Jewish Quarter, whether it is cold or hot, raining or snowing, until he sees Herod the Great's Wall rising up before him. Each time 'his heart skips a beat' as he gets closer to 'the biggest synagogue in the world. There's no earthly way to describe the personal connection to these stones. That is spiritual.'

High above Herod's stones is the Dome of the Rock and al-Aqsa Mosque on what Jews call the Mountain of the House of God, but 'there is room for all of us,' says the rabbi who firmly rejects any encroachment on the Temple Mount. 'One day God may rebuild the Temple – but it is not for men to interfere. This is only a matter for God.'

As rabbi, he is in charge of keeping the Wall clean: the cracks between the stones are filled with notes written by worshippers. Twice a year – before Passover and Rosh Hashanah – the notes are cleared out; they are considered so sacred, he buries them on the Mount of Olives.

When he reaches the Wall, the sun is rising and there are already around 700 Jews praying there, but he always finds the same prayer group – *minyan* – who stand at the same spot beside the Wall: 'It's important to have a ritual so that one can concentrate on the prayers.' But he does not greet this *minyan*, he may nod but there is no talking – 'the first words will be for God' – while he wraps the *tefillin* around his arm. He recites the morning prayers, the *shacharit*, which finish: 'God bless the nation with peace.' Only then does he greet his friends properly. The day at the Wall has started.

Shortly before 4 a.m., just as Rabbi Rabinowitz is rising in the Jewish Quarter, a pebble skims across the window of Wajeeh al-Nusseibeh in Sheikh Jarrah. When he opens his door, Aded al-Judeh, aged eighty, hands Nusseibeh a heavy, medieval 12-inch key. Nusseibeh, now sixty, scion of one of the grandest Jerusalem Families,* already dressed in suit and tie, sets off briskly through the Damascus Gate, down to the Church of the Holy Sepulchre.

---

* The Families remain important in Jerusalem. After the death of Faisal Husseini, Arafat appointed the philosopher Sari Nusseibeh (cousin of Weejah), as Palestinian representative in Jerusalem, but sacked him after he rejected suicide bombings. The founder of al-Quds University, Nusseibeh remains the city's intellectual maverick, admired by both sides. At the time of writing, the Palestinian representative for Jerusalem is Adnan al-Husseini. As for the Khalidis, Rashid Khalidi, the Edward Said Professor of Modern Arab Studies at Columbia University in New York, advises Barack Obama.

Nusseibeh, who has been the Custodian of the Holy Sepulchre for more than twenty-five years, arrives at 4.00 a.m. precisely and knocks on the towering ancient doors set in Melisende's Roman-esque façade. Inside the Church, which he locked at 8 p.m. the night before, the sextons of the Greeks, Latins and Armenians have already negotiated who is to open the doors that particular day. The priests of the three reigning sects have spent the night in jovial companionship and ritual prayer. At 2 a.m. the dominant Orthodox, who are first in all things, start their Mass, with eight priests chant-ing in Greek, around the Tomb, before they hand over to the Armenians, for their *badarak* service in Armenian which is just starting as the gates are opened; the Catholics get their chance at about 6 a.m. Meanwhile all the sects are singing their Matins services. Only one Copt is allowed to stay the night but he prays alone in ancient Coptic Egyptian.

As the gate opens, the Ethiopians, in their rooftop monastery and St Michael's Chapel, its entrance just to the right of the main portal, start to chant in Amharic, their services so long that they lean on the shepherd's crooks that are piled up in their churches ready to support their weary worshippers. By night, the Church resounds to a euphonic hum of many languages and chants like a stone forest in which many species of bird are singing their own choruses. This is Jerusalem and Nusseibeh never knows what is going to happen: 'I know thousands depend on me and I worry if the key won't open or something goes wrong. I first opened it when I was fifteen and thought it was fun but now I realize it's a serious matter.' Whether there is war or peace, he must open the door and says his father often slept in the lobby of the Church just to be sure.

Yet Nusseibeh knows there is likely to be a priestly brawl several times a year. Even in the twenty-first century, the priests veer between accidental courtesy, born of good manners and the tedium of long sepulchral nights, and visceral historical resentment that can explode any time but usually at Easter. The Greeks, who control most of the Church and are the most numerous, fight the Catholics and Armenians and usually win the battles. The Copts and Ethiopians, despite their shared Monophysitism, are especially ven-omous: after the Six Day War, the Israelis in a rare intervention gave the Coptic St Michael's Chapel to the Ethiopians, to punish Nasser's Egypt and support Haile Selassie's Ethiopia. In peace negotiations, support for the Copts usually features in Egyptian demands. The Israeli High Court decided that St Michael's belongs to the Copts though it remains in the possession of the Ethiopians, a very Jerusalemite situation. In July 2002, when a Coptic priest sunned himself near the Ethiopians' dilapidated rooftop eyrie, he was beaten with iron bars as punishment for the Copts' mean treatment of their African brethren. The Copts rushed to their priest's aid: four Copts and seven Ethiopians (who seem to lose every brawl here) were hospitalized.

In September 2004, at the Feast of the Holy Cross, the Greek patriarch Ireneos asked the Franciscans to close the door of the Chapel of the Apparition. When they refused, he led his bodyguards and priests against the Latins. The Israeli police intervened but were attacked by the priests who as adversaries are often just as tough as Palestinian stone throwers. At the Holy Fire in 2005, there was a punch-up when the Armenian superior almost emerged with the flame instead of the Greeks.* The pugilistic patriarch Ireneos was finally deposed for selling the Imperial Hotel at the Jaffa Gate to Israeli settlers. Nusseibeh shrugs wearily: 'Well, as brothers, they have their upsets and I help settle them. We're neutral like the United Nations keeping the peace in this holy place.' Nusseibeh and Judeh play complex roles at each Christian festival. At the feverish and crowded Holy Fire, Nusseibeh is the official witness.

* On a last visit to Jerusalem in 1992 before his death, Edward Said called the Church 'an alien, run-down, unattractive place full of frumpy middle-aged tourists milling about in a decrepit and ill-lit area where Copts, Greeks, Armenians and other Christian sects nurtured their unattractive ecclesiastical gardens in sometimes open combat with each other'. The most famous sign of that open combat is a little ladder belonging to the Armenians on the balcony outside the right-hand window in the façade of the Church which tour guides claim can never be moved without other sects seizing it. In fact, the ladder leads to a balcony where the Armenian superior used to drink coffee with his friends and tend his flower garden: it is there so that the balcony can be cleaned. To the right of the façade stands a small grey door to the storeroom which holds the full collection of life-sized crosses to be rented out and borne by pilgrims along the Via Dolorosa. At Easter, these crosses are in such demand that runners fetch them in relays and return them to the start of the Via so they are ready for the next group to re-enact Jesus's journey to Crucifixion.

Now the sexton opens a small hatch in the right-hand door and hands through a ladder. Nusseibeh takes the ladder and leans it against the left-hand door. He unlocks the lower lock of the right door with his giant key before climbing the ladder and unlocking the top one. When he has climbed down, the priests swing open the immense door before they open the left leaf themselves. Inside, Nusseibeh greets the priests: 'Peace!'

'Peace!' they reply optimistically. The Nusseibehs and Judehs have been opening the Sepulchre doors at least since 1192 when Saladin appointed the Judehs as 'Custodian of the Key' and the Nusseibehs as 'Custodian and Doorkeeper of the Church of the Holy Sepulchre' (as specified on Wajeeh's business-card). The Nusseibehs, who were also appointed hereditary cleaners of the Sakhra (the Rock) in the Dome, claim that Saladin was simply restoring them to a position they had been granted by Caliph Omar in 638. Until the Albanian conquest in the 1830s, they were extremely rich but now they earn a scanty living as tour guides.

Yet the two families exist in vigilant rivalry. 'The Nusseibehs have nothing to do with us,' says the octogenarian Judeh, who has held the key for twenty-two years, 'they are merely, just door-keepers!' Nusseibeh insists 'the Judehs aren't allowed to touch the door or the lock,' suggesting that Islamic rivalries are just as vivid as those among the Christians. Wajeeh's son, Obadah, a personal trainer, is his heir.

Nusseibeh and Judeh spend some of the day sitting in the lobby as their ancestors have for eight centuries – but they are never there at the same time. 'I know every stone here, it's like home,' muses Nusseibeh. He reveres the Church: 'We Muslims believe Muhammad, Jesus and Moses are prophets and Mary is very holy so this is a special place for us too.' If he wishes to pray, he can pop next door to the neighbouring mosque, built to overawe the Christians, or walk the five minutes to al-Aqsa.

At precisely the same time as the Rabbi of the Wall is waking up and Custodian Nusseibeh hears the pebble on the window announcing the delivery of the Sepulchre key, Adeb al-Ansari, forty-two years old, a father of five in a black leather jacket, is coming out of his Mamluk house, owned by his family *waqf*, in the Muslim Quarter and starting the five-minute walk down the street, up to the north-eastern Bab al-Ghawanmeh. He passes through the checkpoint of blue-clad Israeli police, ironically often Druze or Galilean Arabs charged with keeping out Jews, to enter the Haram al-Sharif.

The sacred esplanade is already electrically illuminated but it used to take his father two hours to light all the lanterns. Ansari greets the Haram security and begins to open the four main gates of the Dome of the Rock and the ten gates of al-Aqsa. This takes an hour.

The Ansaris, who trace their family back to the Ansaris who emigrated with Muhammad to Medina, claim that they were appointed Custodians of the Haram by Omar but they were certainly confirmed in the post by Saladin. (The black sheep of the family was the Sheikh of the Haram, bribed by Monty Parker.)

The mosque is open one hour before the dawn prayer. Ansari does not open the gates every dawn – he has a team now – but before he succeeded as hereditary Custodian, he fulfilled this duty every morning and with pride: 'It's firstly just a job, then it's a family profession, and an enormous responsibility, but above all, it's noble and sacred work. But it is not paid well. I also work on the front desk of a hotel on the Mount of Olives.'

The hereditary posts are gradually disappearing on the Haram. The Shihabis, another one of the Families, descended from Lebanese princes, who live in their own family *waqf* close to the Little Wall, used to be Custodians of the Prophet's Beard. The beard and job have disappeared yet the pull of this place is magnetic: the Shihabis still work on the Haram.

Just as the rabbi walks down to the Wall, just as Nusseibeh is tapping on the doors of the Church, just as Ansari opens the gates of the Haram, Naji Qazaz is leaving the house on Bab al-Hadid Street that his family have owned for 225 years, to walk the few yards along the old Mamluk streets up the steps through the Iron Gate and on to the Haram. He proceeds directly into al-Aqsa, where he enters a small room equipped with a microphone and bottles of mineral water. Until 1960, the Qazaz family used the minaret but now they use this room to prepare like athletes for the call. For twenty minutes, Qazaz sits and stretches, an athlete of holiness, he then breathes and gargles the water. He checks that the microphone is on and when the clock on the wall shows it is time, he faces the *qibla* and starts to chant the *adhan* that reverberates across the Old City.

The Qazaz have been the muezzins at al-Aqsa for 500 years since the reign of Mamluk Sultan Qaitbay. Naji, who has been muezzin for thirty years, shares his duties with his son Firaz and two cousins.

It is now one hour before dawn on a day in Jerusalem. The Dome of the Rock is open: Muslims are praying. The Wall is always open: the Jews are praying. The Church of the Holy Sepulchre is open: the Christians are praying in several languages. The sun is rising over Jerusalem, its rays making the light Herodian stones of the Wall almost snowy – just as Josephus described it two thousand years ago – and then catching the glorious gold of the Dome of the Rock that glints back at the sun. The divine esplanade where Heaven and Earth meet, where God meets man, is still in a realm beyond human cartography. Only the rays of the sun can do it and finally the light falls on the most exquisite and mysterious edifice in Jerusalem. Bathing and glowing in the sunlight, it earns its auric name. But The Golden Gate remains locked, until the coming of the Last Days.

THE MACCABEES: KINGS AND HIGH PRIESTS
160 BC–37 BC

Rulers are in capitals; dates refer to the dates of their reigns

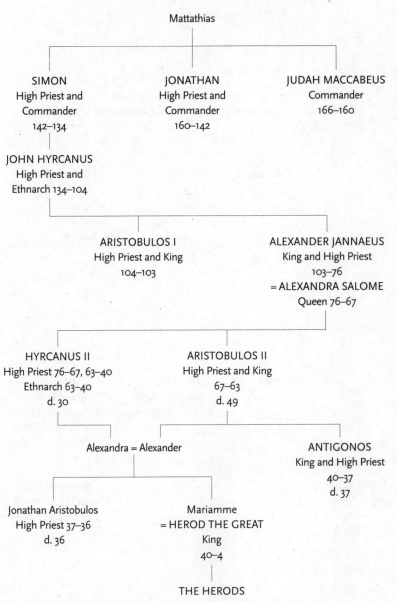

Mattathias

SIMON
High Priest and
Commander
142–134

JONATHAN
High Priest and
Commander
160–142

JUDAH MACCABEUS
Commander
166–160

JOHN HYRCANUS
High Priest and
Ethnarch 134–104

ARISTOBULOS I
High Priest and King
104–103

ALEXANDER JANNAEUS
King and High Priest
103–76
= ALEXANDRA SALOME
Queen 76–67

HYRCANUS II
High Priest 76–67, 63–40
Ethnarch 63–40
d. 30

ARISTOBULOS II
High Priest and King
67–63
d. 49

Alexandra = Alexander

ANTIGONOS
King and High Priest
40–37
d. 37

Jonathan Aristobulos
High Priest 37–36
d. 36

Mariamme
= HEROD THE GREAT
King
40–4

THE HERODS

THE HERODS

37 BC–AD 100

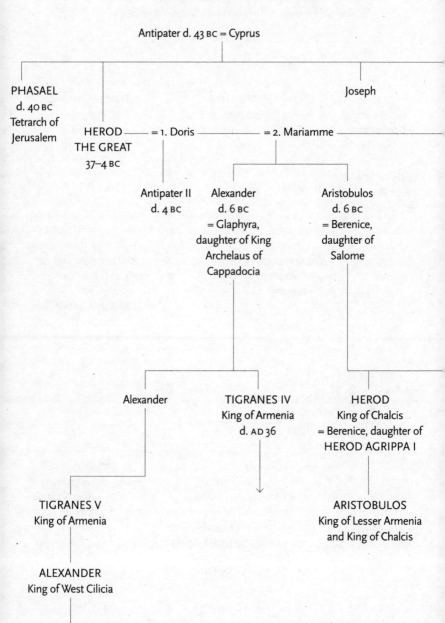

Antipater d. 43 BC = Cyprus

PHASAEL
d. 40 BC
Tetrarch of
Jerusalem

Joseph

HEROD —— = 1. Doris —————— = 2. Mariamme ——————
THE GREAT
37–4 BC

Antipater II
d. 4 BC

Alexander
d. 6 BC
= Glaphyra,
daughter of King
Archelaus of
Cappadocia

Aristobulos
d. 6 BC
= Berenice,
daughter of
Salome

Alexander

TIGRANES IV
King of Armenia
d. AD 36

HEROD
King of Chalcis
= Berenice, daughter of
HEROD AGRIPPA I

TIGRANES V
King of Armenia

ARISTOBULOS
King of Lesser Armenia
and King of Chalcis

ALEXANDER
King of West Cilicia

Rulers are in capitals; dates refer to the dates of their reigns.
This family tree shows only the Herodian rulers. The Herodians frequently
intermarried making a full family tree extremely complex.

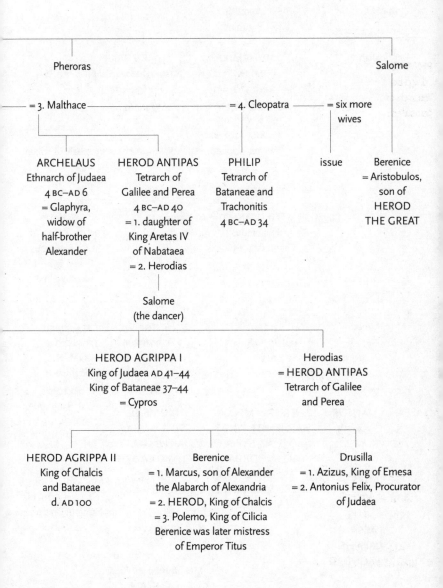

Pheroras

Salome

= 3. Malthace

= 4. Cleopatra

= six more
wives

ARCHELAUS
Ethnarch of Judaea
4 BC–AD 6
= Glaphyra,
widow of
half-brother
Alexander

HEROD ANTIPAS
Tetrarch of
Galilee and Perea
4 BC–AD 40
= 1. daughter of
King Aretas IV
of Nabataea
= 2. Herodias

PHILIP
Tetrarch of
Bataneae and
Trachonitis
4 BC–AD 34

issue

Berenice
= Aristobulos,
son of
HEROD
THE GREAT

Salome
(the dancer)

HEROD AGRIPPA I
King of Judaea AD 41–44
King of Bataneae 37–44
= Cypros

Herodias
= HEROD ANTIPAS
Tetrarch of Galilee
and Perea

HEROD AGRIPPA II
King of Chalcis
and Bataneae
d. AD 100

Berenice
= 1. Marcus, son of Alexander
the Alabarch of Alexandria
= 2. HEROD, King of Chalcis
= 3. Polemo, King of Cilicia
Berenice was later mistress
of Emperor Titus

Drusilla
= 1. Azizus, King of Emesa
= 2. Antonius Felix, Procurator
of Judaea

THE PROPHET MUHAMMAD AND
THE ISLAMIC CALIPHS AND DYNASTIES

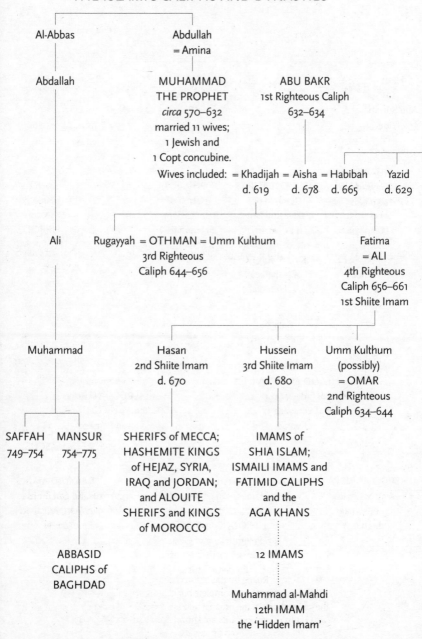

Al-Abbas

Abdallah

Abdullah
= Amina

MUHAMMAD
THE PROPHET
circa 570–632
married 11 wives;
1 Jewish and
1 Copt concubine.

ABU BAKR
1st Righteous Caliph
632–634

Wives included: = Khadijah = Aisha = Habibah   Yazid
                  d. 619   d. 678   d. 665   d. 629

Ali

Rugayyah = OTHMAN = Umm Kulthum
3rd Righteous
Caliph 644–656

Fatima
= ALI
4th Righteous
Caliph 656–661
1st Shiite Imam

Muhammad

Hasan
2nd Shiite Imam
d. 670

Hussein
3rd Shiite Imam
d. 680

Umm Kulthum
(possibly)
= OMAR
2nd Righteous
Caliph 634–644

SAFFAH   MANSUR
749–754 754–775

SHERIFS of MECCA;
HASHEMITE KINGS
of HEJAZ, SYRIA,
IRAQ and JORDAN;
and ALOUITE
SHERIFS and KINGS
of MOROCCO

IMAMS of
SHIA ISLAM;
ISMAILI IMAMS and
FATIMID CALIPHS
and the
AGA KHANS

ABBASID
CALIPHS of
BAGHDAD

12 IMAMS

Muhammad al-Mahdi
12th IMAM
the 'Hidden Imam'

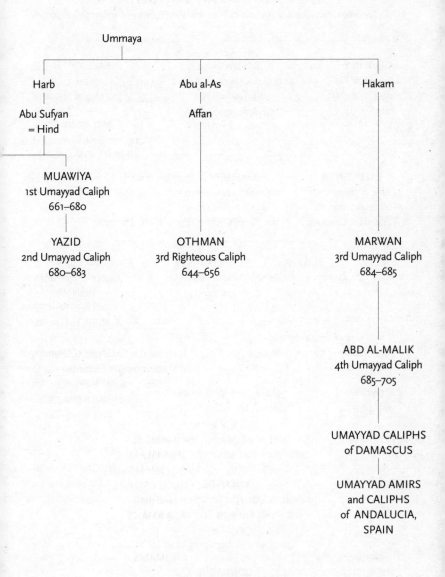

Ummaya

Harb   Abu al-As   Hakam

Abu Sufyan   Affan
= Hind

MUAWIYA
1st Umayyad Caliph
661–680

YAZID   **OTHMAN**   **MARWAN**
2nd Umayyad Caliph   3rd Righteous Caliph   3rd Umayyad Caliph
680–683   644–656   684–685

ABD AL-MALIK
4th Umayyad Caliph
685–705

UMAYYAD CALIPHS
of DAMASCUS

UMAYYAD AMIRS
and **CALIPHS**
of **ANDALUCIA,**
SPAIN

Ruling caliphs are in capitals.
This family tree is not complete but is designed to show
the connections of the Prophet and the dynasties of Islam.
Ali and Fatima's descendants are known as the Sherifs (Ashraf)
and as sayyids.

CRUSADER KINGS OF JERUSALEM

1099–1291

Ruling kings and queens are in bold capitals; consort titular kings are in roman capitals

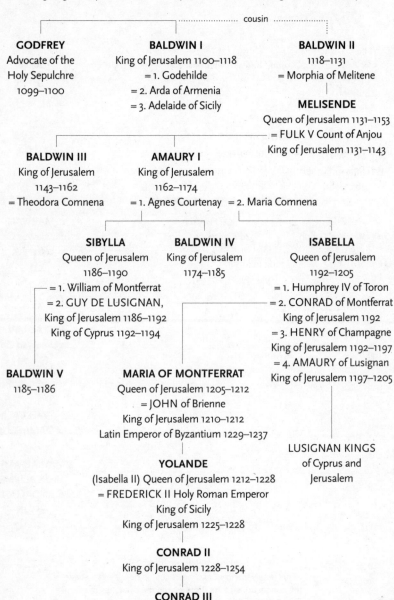

·············· cousin ··············

GODFREY
Advocate of the
Holy Sepulchre
1099–1100

BALDWIN I
King of Jerusalem 1100–1118
= 1. Godehilde
= 2. Arda of Armenia
= 3. Adelaide of Sicily

BALDWIN II
1118–1131
= Morphia of Melitene

MELISENDE
Queen of Jerusalem 1131–1153
= FULK V Count of Anjou
King of Jerusalem 1131–1143

BALDWIN III
King of Jerusalem
1143–1162
= Theodora Comnena

AMAURY I
King of Jerusalem
1162–1174
= 1. Agnes Courtenay = 2. Maria Comnena

SIBYLLA
Queen of Jerusalem
1186–1190
= 1. William of Montferrat
= 2. GUY DE LUSIGNAN,
King of Jerusalem 1186–1192
King of Cyprus 1192–1194

BALDWIN IV
King of Jerusalem
1174–1185

ISABELLA
Queen of Jerusalem
1192–1205
= 1. Humphrey IV of Toron
= 2. CONRAD of Montferrat
King of Jerusalem 1192
= 3. HENRY of Champagne
King of Jerusalem 1192–1197
= 4. AMAURY of Lusignan
King of Jerusalem 1197–1205

BALDWIN V
1185–1186

MARIA OF MONTFERRAT
Queen of Jerusalem 1205–1212
= JOHN of Brienne
King of Jerusalem 1210–1212
Latin Emperor of Byzantium 1229–1237

LUSIGNAN KINGS
of Cyprus and
Jerusalem

YOLANDE
(Isabella II) Queen of Jerusalem 1212–1228
= FREDERICK II Holy Roman Emperor
King of Sicily
King of Jerusalem 1225–1228

CONRAD II
King of Jerusalem 1228–1254

CONRAD III
King of Jerusalem 1254–1265

THE HASHEMITE
(SHERIFIAN) DYNASTY 1916–

Rulers are in capitals; dates refer to the dates of their reigns

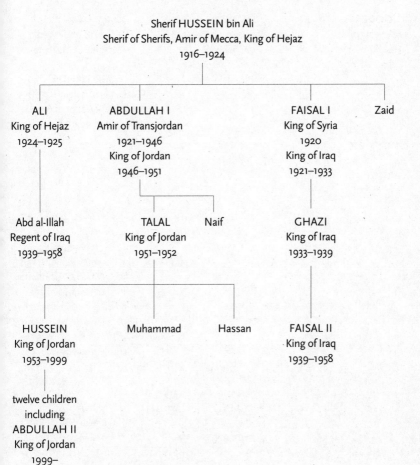

Sherif HUSSEIN bin Ali
Sherif of Sherifs, Amir of Mecca, King of Hejaz
1916–1924

ALI
King of Hejaz
1924–1925

ABDULLAH I
Amir of Transjordan
1921–1946
King of Jordan
1946–1951

FAISAL I
King of Syria
1920
King of Iraq
1921–1933

Zaid

Abd al-Illah
Regent of Iraq
1939–1958

TALAL
King of Jordan
1951–1952

Naif

GHAZI
King of Iraq
1933–1939

HUSSEIN
King of Jordan
1953–1999

Muhammad

Hassan

FAISAL II
King of Iraq
1939–1958

twelve children
including
ABDULLAH II
King of Jordan
1999–

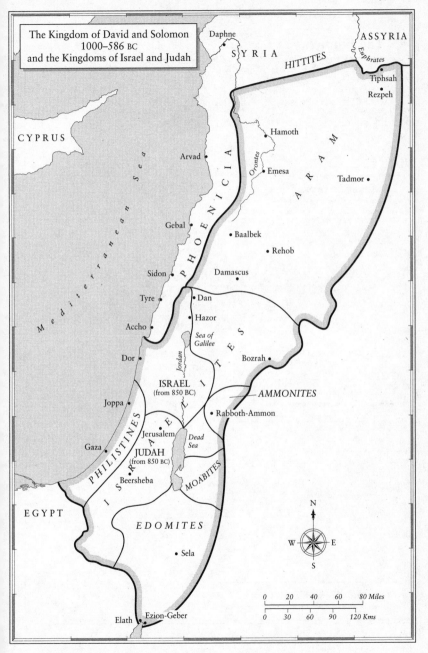

The Kingdom of David and Solomon
1000–586 BC
and the Kingdoms of Israel and Judah

ASSYRIA

Daphne

SYRIA

HITTITES

Euphrates

Tiphsah
Rezpeh

Hamoth

CYPRUS

Arvad

ARAM

Orontes

Emesa

Tadmor

P
H
O
E
N
I
C
I
A

Gebal

Baalbek

Rehob

*M
e
d
i
t
e
r
r
a
n
e
a
n
  S
e
a*

Sidon

Damascus

Tyre

Dan

Accho

Hazor

*Sea of
Galilee*

Bozrah

Dor

*J
o
r
d
a
n*

I
S
R
A
E
L
I
T
E
S

ISRAEL
(from 850 BC)

AMMONITES

Joppa

P
H
I
L
I
S
T
I
N
E
S

Rabboth-Ammon

Jerusalem

*Dead
Sea*

Gaza

JUDAH
(from 850 BC)

I
S
R
A
E
L
I
T
E
S

Beersheba

MOABITES

EGYPT

EDOMITES

Sela

N

W   E

S

0   20   40   60   80 Miles

0   30   60   90   120 Kms

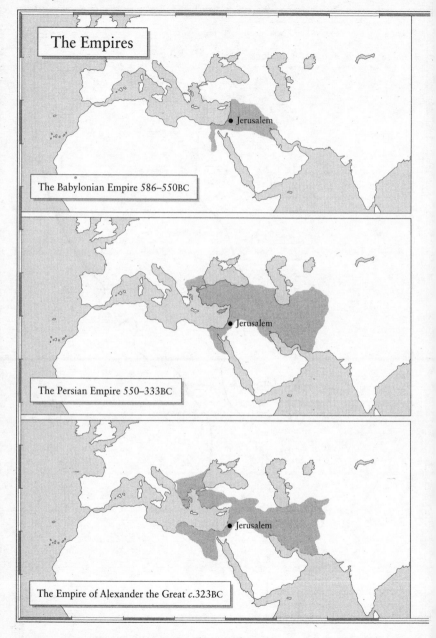

The Empires

The Babylonian Empire 586–550BC

● Jerusalem

The Persian Empire 550–333BC

● Jerusalem

The Empire of Alexander the Great c.323BC

● Jerusalem

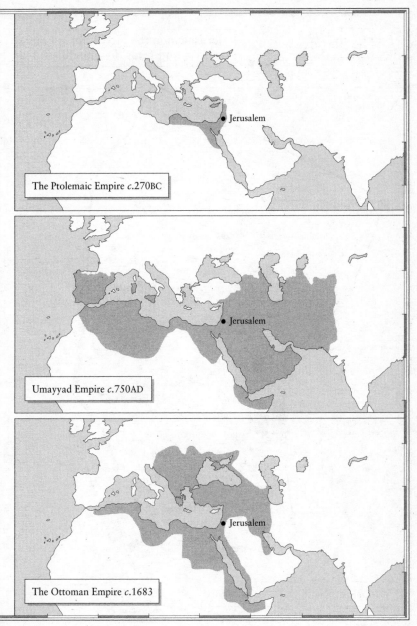

The Ptolemaic Empire c.270BC

Umayyad Empire c.750AD

The Ottoman Empire c.1683

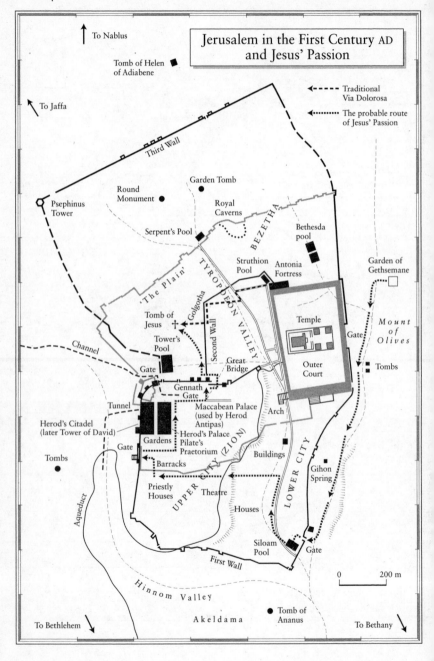

Jerusalem in the First Century AD and Jesus' Passion

To Nablus

Tomb of Helen of Adiabene

To Jaffa

◄----- Traditional Via Dolorosa

◄········ The probable route of Jesus' Passion

Third Wall

Psephinus Tower

Round Monument

Garden Tomb

Royal Caverns

BEZETHA

Serpent's Pool

Struthion Pool

Antonia Fortress

Bethesda pool

Garden of Gethsemane

'The Plain'

TYROPOEON VALLEY

Golgotha

Tomb of Jesus

Second Wall

Temple

Gate

Mount of Olives

Channel

Tower's Pool

Great Bridge

Outer Court

Tombs

Gate

Gennath Gate

Maccabean Palace (used by Herod Antipas)

Herod's Palace

Pilate's Praetorium

Arch

Tunnel

Herod's Citadel (later Tower of David)

Gardens

Buildings

UPPER CITY (ZION)

Gate

Tombs

Barracks

Priestly Houses

Theatre

Houses

Gihon Spring

LOWER CITY

Aqueduct

Siloam Pool

Gate

First Wall

0   200 m

Hinnom Valley

To Bethlehem

Akeldama

● Tomb of Ananus

To Bethany

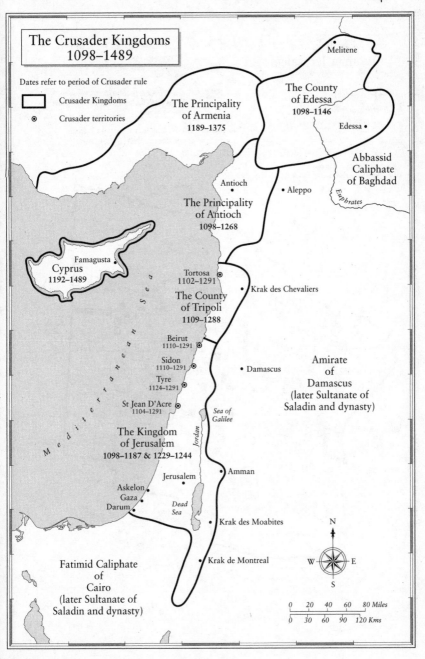

The Crusader Kingdoms
1098–1489

Dates refer to period of Crusader rule

☐ Crusader Kingdoms

◉ Crusader territories

Melitene

The County
of Edessa
1098–1146

Edessa •

The Principality
of Armenia
1189–1375

Abbassid
Caliphate
of Baghdad

• Antioch

• Aleppo

Euphrates

The Principality
of Antioch
1098–1268

Mediterranean Sea

Famagusta •

Cyprus
1192–1489

Tortosa
1102–1291 ◉

• Krak des Chevaliers

The County
of Tripoli
1109–1288

Beirut
1110–1291 ◉

Sidon
1110–1291 ◉

• Damascus

Amirate
of
Damascus
(later Sultanate of
Saladin and dynasty)

Tyre
1124–1291 ◉

St Jean D'Acre
1104–1291 ◉

*Sea of
Galilee*

Jordan

The Kingdom
of Jerusalem
1098–1187 & 1229–1244

• Amman

Askelon •
Gaza •
Darum •

Jerusalem •

*Dead
Sea*

• Krak des Moabites

N

Fatimid Caliphate
of
Cairo
(later Sultanate of
Saladin and dynasty)

• Krak de Montreal

W ✦ E

S

| 0 | 20 | 40 | 60 | 80 Miles |
| 0 | 30 | 60 | 90 | 120 Kms |

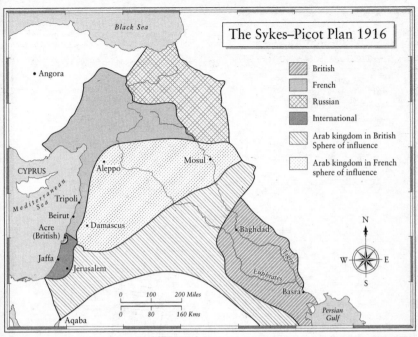

The Sykes–Picot Plan 1916

British
French
Russian
International
Arab kingdom in British Sphere of influence
Arab kingdom in French sphere of influence

Black Sea

Angora

CYPRUS

Mediterranean Sea

Tripoli
Beirut
Acre (British)
Jaffa
Jerusalem

Aleppo

Damascus

Mosul

Baghdad

Tigris

Euphrates

Basra

Persian Gulf

Aqaba

0   100   200 Miles
0   80   160 Kms

N
W   E
S

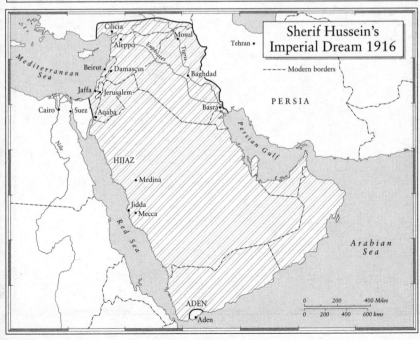

Sherif Hussein's Imperial Dream 1916

---·--- Modern borders

Cilicia
Aleppo
Mosul
Tehran •
Euphrates
Tigris
Beirut
Damascus
Baghdad
Jaffa
Jerusalem
Basra
Cairo
Suez
Aqaba

PERSIA

Mediterranean Sea

Persian Gulf

HIJAZ

Medina

Nile

Jidda
Mecca

Red Sea

Arabian Sea

ADEN
Aden

0   200   400 Miles
0   200   400   600 kms

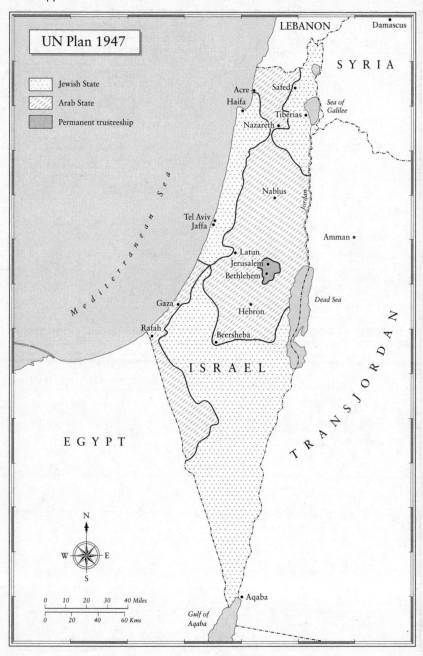

UN Plan 1947

Jewish State

Arab State

Permanent trusteeship

LEBANON

Damascus

SYRIA

Acre · Safed ·
Haifa ·
Tiberias · *Sea of Galilee*
Nazareth ·

Mediterranean Sea

Nablus ·

Jordan

Tel Aviv ·
Jaffa ·

Amman ·

· Latun
Jerusalem ·
Bethlehem ·

Gaza ·
Rafah ·

Hebron ·

Dead Sea

· Beersheba

I S R A E L

E G Y P T

T R A N S J O R D A N

N
W E
S

0 10 20 30 40 Miles
0 20 40 60 Kms

· Aqaba

Gulf of Aqaba

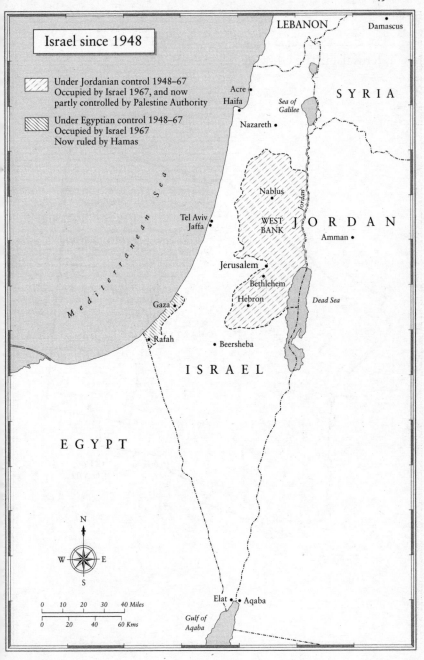

Israel since 1948

Under Jordanian control 1948–67
Occupied by Israel 1967, and now
partly controlled by Palestine Authority

Under Egyptian control 1948–67
Occupied by Israel 1967
Now ruled by Hamas

Jerusalem: The Old City

The Temple Tunnel (opened 1996)

○ The underground place closest to the Holy of Holies

□ Wilson's Arch

△ Warren's Gate / the 'Cave'

✳ Robinson's Arch

0   100   200 Metres

Herod's Gate

Damascus Gate

St Stephen's Gate (Lions' Gate)

Church of St Anne

Old City Wall

Convent of the Sisters of Zion

Church of the Flagellation

Ecce Homo Basilica

Via Dolorosa

St Anne Seminary

New Gate

CHRISTIAN QUARTER

Greek Orthodox Patriarchate

Coptic Patriarchate

Via Dolorosa

Al-Haram al-Sharif

Solomon's Throne

Golden Gate

Church of St Veronica

MUSLIM QUARTER

Dome of the Rock

Dome of the Chain

Greek Catholic Patriarchate

Church of the Holy Sepulchre

Street of the Gate of the Chain

Temple Mount

Latin Patriarchate St Saviour's Monastery

Church of St John the Baptist

Jaffa Gate

David's Tower

The Citadel

Western Wall

Islamic Museum

Al-Aqsa Mosque

Maghrebi Gate

ARMENIAN QUARTER

JEWISH QUARTER

Cathedral of St James

Armenian Patriarchate

Dung Gate

CITY OF DAVID

Zion Gate

Valley of Kidron

Valley of Hinnom

Mount Zion

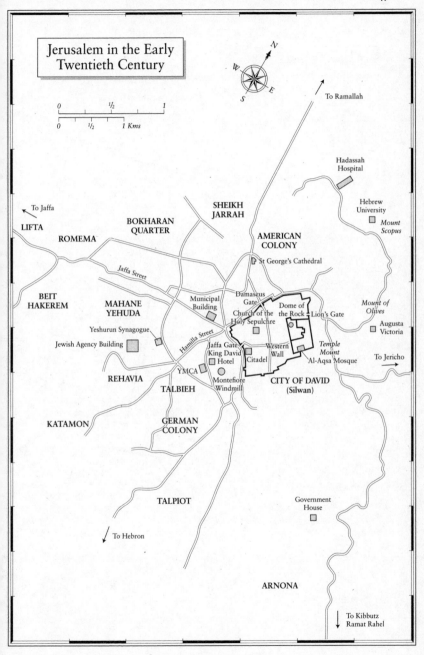

Jerusalem in the Early Twentieth Century

N W E S

To Ramallah

0   ½   1
0   ½   1 Kms

To Jaffa

LIFTA

ROMEMA

BOKHARAN QUARTER

SHEIKH JARRAH

Hadassah Hospital

Hebrew University

Mount Scopus

AMERICAN COLONY

St George's Cathedral

Jaffa Street

BEIT HAKEREM

MAHANE YEHUDA

Municipal Building

Damascus Gate

Church of the Holy Sepulchre

Dome of the Rock

Lion's Gate

Mount of Olives

Augusta Victoria

Yeshurun Synagogue

Jewish Agency Building

Hamilla Street

Jaffa Gate

King David Hotel

YMCA

Citadel

Western Wall

Temple Mount

Al-Aqsa Mosque

To Jericho

REHAVIA

TALBIEH

Montefiore Windmill

CITY OF DAVID (Silwan)

KATAMON

GERMAN COLONY

TALPIOT

Government House

To Hebron

ARNONA

To Kibbutz Ramat Rahel

NOTES

The full and extremely extensive references for this book are available in the hardback edition and also on the author's website at: http://www.simonsebagmontefiore.com

In order to make the paperback a manageable and readable size, the author and publishers have decided not to include the notes in the paperback. We hope readers will agree that, for most, the balance of convenience is best served by this policy.

BIBLIOGRAPHY

The Jerusalem literature is vast and this bibliography is not exhaustive but lists the main sources used in the book.

The Authorized Version of the Bible and the New Translation of the Koran by M. A. S. Abdel Haleem (Oxford 2004) are used throughout.

JOURNALS

Al-Fajr al-Adabi
American Journal of Semitic Languages and Literatures
Associated Christian Press
Biblical Archaeologist
Biblical Archaeology Review
British Journal of Psychiatry
Bulletin of the American Schools of Oriental Research
Conservation and Management of Archaeological Sites
Crusades
Eastern Christian Art
The Economist
English Historical Review
Graeco-Arabia
History Today
Israel Exploration Journal
Jerusalem Quarterly (Institute of Jerusalem Studies, al-Quds University) (JQ)
Jewish Chronicle, London
Jewish Quarterly
Journal of Asian and African Studies
Journal of the Royal Asiatic Society (JRAS)
Liber Annuus (Studium Biblicum Franciscanum, Jerusalem)
Middle Eastern Studies
New York Times

The New Yorker
Palestine Exploration Fund Annual
Palestine Exploration Quarterly
Pravoslavny Palomnik
Revue des Etudes Juives
Saudi Aramco World
Standpoint
Tadias Magazine
The Times, London

ARTICLES

Abu Zaida, Sufian, '"A Miserable Provincial Town": The Zionist Approach to Jerusalem 1897–1937', *JQ* 32, Autumn 2007

Amitai, Reuven, 'Mongol Raids into Palestine (AD 1260 and 1300)', *Journal of Royal Asiatic Society of Great Britain and Ireland*, No. 2, 1987, 236–55.

Anon., 'Where Piety Meets Power (Russia in Jerusalem)', *Economist* 19 December 2009

Ayele, Negussay, 'Deir Sultan, Ethiopia and the Black World', *Tadias Magazine* August 2008

Bar-El, Yair et al, 'Jerusalem Syndrome', *British Journal of Psychiatry* 176 (2000)

Bronner, Ethan, 'Jews and Muslims Share Holy Season in Jerusalem', *New York Times* 28 September 2008

Budeiri, Musa, 'A Chronicle of a Defeat Foretold: The Battle for Jerusalem in the Memoirs of Anwar Nusseibeh', *JQ* 3, Winter/Spring 2001

Conybeare, F., 'Antiochus Strategos: Account of the Sack of Jerusalem', *English Historical Review* 25 (1910) 502–16

Curtis, Sarah, 'Sarah Palin's Jerusalem and Pentecostal Faith: A Hysteric Symptom of American Utopianism', *Colloquy Text Theory Critique* 17 (2009)

Der Matossian, Bedross, 'The Young Turk Revolution: Its Impact on Religious Politics of Jerusalem (1908–1912)', *JQ* 40, Winter 2009

Dixon, Simon, 'A Stunted International: Russian Orthodoxy in the Holy Land in the 19th Century', unpublished ms, January 2009

Dorfmann-Lazarev, Igor, 'Historical Itinerary of the Armenian People in Light of its Biblical Memory', unpublished ms, 2009

Dumper, Michael, 'Two State Plus: Jerusalem and the Binational Debate', *JQ* 39, Autumn 2009

Gilboa, Ayelet and Sharon, Ilan, 'An Archaeological Contribution to the Early Iron Age Chronological Debate: Alternative Chronologies for Phoenicia and their Effects on the Levant, Cyprus and Greece', *Bulletin of the American Schools of Oriental Research* 332, November 2003

Glass, Joseph B. and Kark, Ruth, 'Sarah la Preta: A Slave in Jerusalem', *JQ* 34, Spring 2009

Gonen, Rivka, 'Was the Site of the Jerusalem Temple Originally a Cemetery?', *Biblical Archaeology Review* May–June 1985

Greenberg, Raphael, 'Extreme Exposure: Archaeology in Jerusalem, 1967–2007', *Conservation and Management of Archaeological Sites*, vol 11, no. 3–4, 2009

Gross, Miriam, 'A Jerusalem Childhood', *Standpoint* September 2010

Hintlian, George, 'Armenians of Jerusalem', *JQ* 2, Autumn 1998

Housley, Norman, 'Saladin's Triumph over the Crusader States: The Battle of Hattin, 1187', *History Today* 37 (1987)

Ji, C. C., 'A New Look at the Tobiads in Iraq al-Amir', *Liber Annuus* 48 (1998) 417–40

Al-Jubeh, Nazmi, 'The Khalidiyah Library', *JQ* 3, Winter 1999

Kark, Ruth and Glass, Joseph B., 'The Valero Family: Sephardi–Arab Relations in Ottoman and Mandatory Jerusalem', *JQ* 21, August 2004

Kedar, Benjamin Z., 'The Jerusalem Massacre of 1099 in the Western Historiography of the Crusades', *Crusades* 3 (2004) 15–75

Loupo, Yakov and Chen, Nitzan, 'The Jerusalem Area Ultra-Orthodox Population', unpublished ms

Lutfi, Huda, 'Al-Quds Al-Mamelukiyya: A History of Mamluk Jerusalem Based on the Haram Documents', *JQ* 2, Autumn 1998

Manna, Adel, 'Yusuf Diyaddin al-Khalidi', *Al-Fajr al-Adabi* 35–6 (1983)

Manna, Adel, 'Scholars and Notables Tracing the Effendiya's Hold on Power in 18th Century Jerusalem', *JQ* 32, Autumn 2007

Manna, Adel, 'Between Jerusalem and Damascus: The End of Ottoman Rule as Seen by a Palestinian Modernist', *JQ* 22–23, Autumn/Winter 2005

Mazza, Roberto, 'Antonio de la Cierva y Lewita: Spanish Consul in Jerusalem 1914–1920', and 'Dining Out in Times of War', *JQ* 40, Winter 2009, and 41, Spring 2010

Meuwese, Martine, 'Representations of Jerusalem on Medieval Maps and Miniatures', *Eastern Christian Art* 2 (2005) 139–48

Mouradian, Clare, 'Les Chrétiens: Un enjeu pour les Puissances', in Catherine Nicault (ed.), *Jérusalem, 1850–1948: Des Ottomans aux Anglais, entre coexistence spirituelle et déchirure politique*, Paris, 1999, pp. 177–204

Al-Natsheh, Yusuf Said, 'Uninventing the Bab al-Khalil Tombs: Between the Magic of Legend and Historical Fact', *JQ* 22–23, Autumn/Winter 2005

Pappe, Ilan, 'The Rise and Fall of the Husaynis', Part 1, *JQ* 10, Autumn 2000

Pappe, Ilan, 'The Husayni Family Faces New Challenges: Tanzimat, Young Turks, the Europeans and Zionism, 1840–1922', Part 2, *JQ* 11–12, Winter 2001

Pappe, Ilan, 'Haj Amin and the Buraq Revolt', *JQ* 18, June 2003

Peters, F. E., 'Who Built the Dome of the Rock?', *Graeco-Arabia* 2 (1983)

Reich, Ronny, 'The Roman Destruction of Jerusalem in 70 CE: Flavius Josephus' Account and Archaeological Record', in Gerd Theissen et al. (eds), *Jerusalem und die Länder*, Göttingen 2009

Reich, Ronny, Shukron, Eli and Lernau, Omri, 'Recent Discoveries in the City of David, Jerusalem: Findings from the Iron Age II Rock-Cut Pool Near the Spring', *Israel Exploration Journal* 57/2 (2007)

Riley-Smith, Jonathan, 'The Death and Burial of Latin Christian Pilgrims to Jerusalem and Acre, 1099–1291', *Crusades* 7 (2008)

Robson, Laura C., 'Archeology and Mission: The British Presence in Nineteenth-Century Jerusalem', *JQ* 40, Winter 2009

Rood, Judith M., 'The Time the Peasants Entered Jerusalem: The Revolt against Ibrahim Pasha in the Islamic Court Sources', *JQ* 27, Summer 2006

Rood, Judith M., 'Intercommunal Relations in Jerusalem during Egyptian Rule', Parts 1 and 2, *JQ* 32, Autumn 2007, and 34, Spring 2009

Rozen, Minna, 'The Naqib al-Ashraf Rebellion in Jerusalem and its Repercussions on the City's Dhimmis', *Journal of Asian and African Studies* 18/2, November 1984, 249–70

Rozen, Minna and Witztum, Eliezer, 'The Dark Mirror of the Soul: Dreams of a Jewish Physician in Jerusalem at the End of the 17th Century', *Revue des Etudes Juives* 151 (1992) 5–42

Scholch, Alexander, 'An Ottoman Bismarck from Jerusalem: Yusuf Diya al-Khalidi', *JQ* 24, Summer 2005

Tamari, Salim, 'Ottoman Jerusalem in the Jawhariyyeh Memoirs', *JQ* 9, Summer 2000

Tamari, Salim, 'Jerusalem's Ottoman Modernity: The Times and Lives of Wasif Jawhariyyeh', *JQ* 9, Summer 2000

Tamari, Salim, 'The Last Feudal Lord in Palestine', *JQ* 16, November 2002

Tamari, Salim, 'The Vagabond Café and Jerusalem's Prince of Idleness', *JQ* 19, October 2003

Tamari, Salim, 'The Short life of Private Ihsan: Jerusalem 1915', *JQ* 30, Spring 2007

Tamari, Salim, 'With God's Camel in Siberia: The Russian Exile of an Ottoman Officer from Jerusalem', *JQ* 35, Autumn 2008

Tleel, John, 'I am Jerusalem: Life in the Old City from the Mandate Period to the Present', *JQ* 4, Spring 1999

Vereté, M., 'Why was a British Consulate Established in Jerusalem?', *English Historical Review* 75 (1970)

Vereté, M., 'The Restoration of the Jews in English Protestant Thought, 1790–1840', *Middle Eastern Studies* 8/1 (1972)

Voropanov, V. A., 'Gogol v Ierusalime', *Pravoslavnyy Palomnik* (2006) 2

Wright, Lawrence, 'Letter from Jerusalem', *The New Yorker* 20 July 1998

Zias, Joe, 'Crucifixion in Antiquity', www.joezias.com

Zweig, Zachi, 'New Substantial Discoveries in Past Waqf Excavations on Temple Mount: New Information from Various Temple Mount Digs', New Studies on Jerusalem, Conference of Ingeborg Rennert Center for Jerusalem Studies at Bar-Ilan University, November 2008

PRIMARY SOURCES

Abdullah bin Hussein, King of Jordan, *Memoirs*, London 1950

Ahima'as, *The Chronicle of Ahima'as*, ed. and trans. M. Salzman, New York 1924

Albert of Achen, *Historia Iherosolimitana*, ed. and trans. S. B. Edgington, London 2007

Anon., *Le Pèlerinage de Charlemagne à Jérusalem et à Constantinople*, trans. G. S. Burgess and A. E. Cobbs, New York 1988

Antonius, Soroya, *Where the Jinn Consult*, London 1987

Arculf, Saint Adamnan, *The Pilgrimage of Arculfus in the Holy Land*, ed. and trans. J. R. Macpherson, London 1895

Aristeas, *Letter of Aristeas*, ed. and trans. H. S. J. Thackeray, London 2009

Al-Athir, *The Chronicle of Ibn Al-Athir for the Crusading Period from Al-Kamil Fi'l-Ta'rikh: Years 589–629/1193–1231: The Ayyubids after Saladin and the Mongol Menace Part 3*, Aldershot 2008

Baedeker, Karl, *Palestine and Syria*, Leipzig/London 1876 and 1912

Al-Baladhuri, *The Origins of the Islamic State*, trans. P. Hitti and F. Murgotten, New York 1916–24

Ballobar, Conde de, *Diario de Jerusalén*, Madrid 1996

Ballobar, Conde de, *Jerusalem in World War One: The Palestine Diary of a European Diplomat*, Edwards Manzano Moreno and Roberto Mazza (eds), London 2011

Barclay, James Turner, *City of the Great King*, Philadelphia 1858

Begin, Menachem, *The Revolt*, Jerusalem 1952/1977

Ben-Gurion, David, *Recollections*, London 1970

Benjamin of Tudela, *The Itinerary of Benjamin of Tudela*, ed. and trans. M. N. Adler, London 1907

Bird, Kai, *Crossing Mandelbaum Gate: Coming of Age between the Arabs and Israelis 1956–78*, London 2010

Blyden, Edward Wilmot, *From West Africa to Palestine*, Freetown 1873

Bordeaux Pilgrim, *Itinerary from Bordeaux to Jerusalem*, trans. Aubrey Stewart, London 1987

Brothers, Richard, *Plan of the Holy City the New Jerusalem*, London 1800

Cassius Dio, *Roman History* LXIX, New York 1925/1989

Celebi, Evliya, see Evliya

Chateaubriand, F. R. de, *Journal de Jérusalem: Notes inédites*, Paris 1950

Chateaubriand, F. R. de, *Travels in Greece, Palestine, Egypt and Barbary during the Years 1806 and 1807*, London 1812

Clarke, Edward Daniel, *Travels in Various Countries of Europe, Asia and Africa*, London 1810

Cresson, Warder, *Jerusalem: Centre and Joy of the Universe*, Philadelphia 1844

Cresson, Warder, *The Key of David*, Philadelphia 1852

Conquest of Jerusalem and the Third Crusade: Old French Continuation of William of Tyre and Sources in Translation, ed. Peter W. Edbury, Aldershot 1998

Curzon, R., *Visits to the Monasteries of the Levant*, London 1849

Daniel the Abbot, *Pilgrimage of the Russian Abbot Daniel in the Holy Land*, New York 1917

Dayan, Moshe, *Story of My Life*, London 1976

Diodorus, *Library of History*, New York 1989

Djemal Pasha, *Memoirs of a Turkish Statesman 1913–19*, London 1922

Dorr, David F., *A Colored Man Round the World by a Quadroon*, Cleveland 1858

Egeria/Sylvia, *Pilgrimage of Saint Sylvia of Aquitaine to the Holy Places*, trans. J. Bernard, London 1891

Eusebius of Caesarea, *Church History* [and] *Life of Constantine the Great*, trans. A. C. McGiffert and others, New York 1890

Evliya, Celebi, *An Ottoman Traveller: Selections from the Books of Travels of Evliya Celebi*, ed. and trans. Robert Dankoff and Sooying Kim, London, 2010

Fabri, Felix, *The Book of Wanderings of Brother Felix Fabri*, ed. and trans. Aubrey Stewart, London 1887–97

Finn, E. A., *Reminiscences of Mrs Finn*, London 1929

Finn, James, *Stirring Times*, London 1878

Finn, James and Elizabeth, *View from Jerusalem, 1849–58: The Consular Diary of James and Elizabeth Anne Finn*, ed. Arnold Blumberg, Madison NJ 1981

Flaubert, G., *Les Oeuvres complètes de Gustave Flaubert*, vol. 19: *Notes de voyage*, Paris 1901

Florence of Worcester, *Chronicle*, ed. T. Forester, London 1854

Fosdick, H. E., *A Pilgrimage to Palestine*, London 1930

Fulcher of Chartres, *A History of the Expedition to Jerusalem*, trans. F. R. Ryan, Knoxville TN 1969

Gabrieli, Francesco, *Arab Historians of the Crusades*, London 1969

Gesta Francorum et Aliorum Hierosolimitanorum, ed. and trans. R. Hill, London 1962

Glubb, John, *A Soldier with the Arabs*, London 1957

Gogol, N. V., *Polnoe sobranie sochineniy*, vol. 14: *Pisma, 1848–52*, Moscow 1952

Graham, Stephen, *With the Russian Pilgrims to Jerusalem*, London 1913

Hadi, Mahdi Abdul (ed.) *Documents on Jerusalem*, Jerusalem 1996

Haggard, Rider, *A Winter Pilgrimage*, London 1900

Halevi, Judah, *Selected Poems*, trans. Nina Salaman, Philadelphia 1946

Halevi, Judah, *Selected Poems*, ed. H. Brody, New York 1924/1973

Harff, Arnold von, *Pilgrimage of Arnold von Harff*, London 1946

Al-Harizi, Judah, *The Tahkemoni: The 28th Gate*, trans. V. Reichert, Jerusalem 1973

Al-Harawi, Abu al-Hasan, *Guide des Lieux de Pèlerinage*, trans. J. Sourdel-Thomime, Damascus 1957

Herodotus, *Histories*, London 1972

Herzl, Theodor, *The Complete Diaries of Theodor Herzl*, London/New York 1960

Hess, Moses, *Rome and Jerusalem*, New York 1943

Hill, R. (ed. and trans.), *The Deeds of the Franks and Other Pilgrims to Jerusalem*, London 1962

Hodgson, William Brown, *An Edited Biographical Sketch of Mohammed Ali, Pasha of Egypt, Syria, and Arabia*, Washington DC 1835

Hoess, Rudolf, *Commandant of Auschwitz*, London 1959

Horn, Elzear, *Ichnographiae Monumentorum Terrae Sanctae 1724–44*, ed. and trans. E. Hoade, Jerusalem 1962

Hussein bin Talal, King Hussein of Jordan, *Uneasy Lies the Head*, London 1962

Hussein bin Talal, King Hussein of Jordan, *My War with Israel*, London 1969

Ibn Battutah, *Travels of Ibn Battutah*, ed. Tim Mackintosh-Smith, London 2002

Ibn Ishaq, *The Life of Muhammad*, ed. A. Guillaume, Oxford 1955

Ibn Khaldun, *The Muqaddimah: An Introduction to History*, Princeton 1967

Ibn Shaddad (Baha al-Din Ibn Shaddad), *The Rare and Excellent History of Saladin*, trans. D. S. Richards, Aldershot 2002

Ibn al-Qalinisi, *Continuation of the Chronicle of Damascus: The Damascus Chronicle of the Crusades*, ed. and trans. H. A. R. Gibb, London 1932

Ingrams, Doreen (ed.), *Palestine Papers 1917–1922: Seeds of Conflict*, London 1972/2009

Jawhariyyeh, Wasif, *Al Quds Al Othmaniyah Fi Al Muthakrat Al Jawhariyyeh* (The Jawhariyyeh Memoirs: Ottoman Jerusalem, 1904–1917), vol. 1, and *Al Quds Al Intedabiyeh Fi Al Muthakrat al Jawhariyyeh* (The Jawhariyyeh Memoirs: British Mandate Jerusalem, 1918–1948), vol. 2, ed. Salim Tamari and Issam Nassar, Jerusalem 2001

Jemal Pasha, see Djemal

John of Wurzburg, *Description of the Holy Land*, ed. and trans. Aubrey Stewart, London 1896

Joinville and Villehardouin, *Chronicles of the Crusades*, ed. and trans. Caroline Smith, London 2008

Joseph, B., *Faithful City: Siege of Jerusalem, 1948*, New York 1960

Josephus, *The New Complete Works of Josephus*, ed. Paul L. Maier, trans. William Whiston, Grand Rapids MI 1999

Julien, *Itinéraire de Paris à Jérusalem par Julien, domestique de M. de Chateaubriand*, Paris 1904

Keith-Roach, Edward, *Pasha of Jerusalem*, London 1994

Kinglake, A. W., *Eothen*, London 1844

Ha-Kohen, Solomon ben Joseph, 'The Turkoman Defeat at Cairo', ed. Julius Greenstone, *American Journal of Semitic Languages and Literatures* January 1906

Kollek, Teddy, *For Jerusalem*, New York 1978

Krey, August C., *The First Crusade: The Accounts of Eyewitnesses and Participants*, Princeton/London 1921

Kulish, P. A., *Zapiski iz zhizni N. V. Gogolya, sostavlennye iz vospominaniy ego druzey i znakomykh i iz ego sobstvennykh pisem*, St Petersburg 1856

Lagerlöf, Selma, *Jerusalem*. Dearborn MI 2009

Lamartine, Alphonse de, *Travels in the East Including Journey to the Holy Land*, Edinburgh 1839

Lawrence, T. E., *Seven Pillars of Wisdom*, London 1926

Le Strange, Guy, *Palestine under the Moslems: A Description of Syria and the Holy Land from A.D. 650 to 1500*, London 1890

Lisovoy, N. N., *Russkoe dukhovnoe i politicheskoe prisutstvie v Svyatoy Zemle i na Blizhnem Vostoke v XIX–nachale XXv*, Moscow 2006

Lisovoy, N. N. and Stegniy, P. V., *Rossia v Svyatoy Zemle: Dokumenty i materialy*, Moscow 2000

Luke, Harry, *Cities and Men: An Autobiography*, London 1953–6

Lynch, William, *Narrative of the US Expedition to the River Jordan and the Dead Sea*, Philadelphia 1853

Maimonides, Moses, *Code of Maimonides*, Book 8: *Temple Service*, trans. M. Lewittes, New Haven 1957

Martineau, Harriet, *Eastern Life: Present and Past*, London 1848.

Massy, Colonel P. H. H., *Eastern Mediterranean Lands: Twenty Years of Life, Sport and Travel*, London 1928

Maundrell, Henry, *A Journey from Aleppo to Jerusalem in 1697*, Beirut 1963

Melville, Herman, *Journal of a Visit to Europe and the Levant*, Princeton/New York 1955

Melville, Herman, *Journals*, ed. Howard C. Horsford and L. Horth, Chicago 1989

Melville, Herman, *Clarel: A Poem and Pilgrimage to the Holy Land*, Chicago 1991

Montefiore, Moses and Judith, *Diaries of Sir Moses and Lady Montefiore*, London 1983

Morgenthau, Henry, *United States Diplomacy on the Bosphorus: The Diaries of Ambassador Morgenthau*, ed. Ara Sarafian, Princeton 2004

Mujir al-Din, *Histoire de Jérusalem et d'Hébron: Fragments de la Chronique de Mujir al-Din*, ed. and trans. Henry Sauvaire, Paris 1876

Al-Muqaddasi, *A Description of Syria Including Palestine*, ed. and trans. Guy Le Strange, London 1896

Nashashibi, Nasser Eddin, *Jerusalem's Other Voice: Ragheb Nashashibi and Moderation in Palestinian Politics 1920–1948*, Exeter 1990

Nasir-i-Khusrau, *Diary of a Journey through Syria and Palestine*, ed. and trans. Guy Le Strange, London 1893

Niccolo of Poggibonsi, *A Voyage Beyond the Sea 1346–50*, trans. T. Bellorini and E. Hoade, Jerusalem 1945

Noor, Queen of Jordan, *Leap of Faith*, London 2003

Nusseibeh, Hazem Zaki, *The Jerusalemites: A Living Memory*, Nicosia/London 2009

Nusseibeh, Sari, with Anthony David, *Once Upon a Country: A Palestinian Life*, London 2007

Oz, Amos, *My Michael*, London 1984

Oz, Amos, *A Tale of Love and Darkness*, London 2005

Papen, Franz von, *Memoirs*, London 1952

Parsons, Levi, *Dereliction and Restoration of the Jews: A Sermon, Sabbath Oct 31 1819*, Boston 1819

Parsons, Levi, *Memoir of Rev. Levi Parsons*, New York 1977

Peters, F. E (ed.), *Jerusalem: The Holy City in the Eyes of Chroniclers, Visitors, Pilgrims and Prophets from the Days of Abraham to the Beginning of Modern Times*, Princeton 1985

Peters, F. E. (ed.), *The First Crusade: Chronicle of Fulcher of Chartres and Other Source Materials*, Philadelphia 1998

Philo, *Works*, trans. F. H. Colson, Cambridge MA 1962

Pliny the Elder, *Historia Naturalis*, trans. H. T. Riley, London 1857

Plutarch, *Makers of Rome*, London 1965

Polybius, *The Histories*, Oxford 2010

Procopius, *Of the Buildings of Justinian*, ed. and trans. Aubrey Stewart, London 1896

Procopius, *The Secret History*, London 2007

Rabin, Yitzhak, *The Rabin Memoirs*, London 1979

Rasputin, G., *Moi mysli i razmyshleniya: kratkoe opisanie puteshestviya po svyatym mestam i vyzvannye im razmyshleniya po religioznym voprosam* (My Thoughts and Reflections: Brief Description of a Journey to the Holy Places and Reflections on Religious Matters Caused by This Journey), Petrograd 1915

Raymond of Aguilers, *Le 'Liber' de Raymond d'Aguilers*, ed. and trans. J. H. Hill and L. L. Hill, Paris 1969

Robinson, Edward, *Biblical Researches in Palestine, Mount Sinai and Arabia Petraea*, Boston 1841

Rose, John H. Melkon, *Armenians of Jerusalem: Memories of Life in Palestine*, London/New York 1993

Saewulf, *Pilgrimage to Jerusalem and the Holy Land*, ed. and trans. Rt Rev. Bishop of Clifton, London 1896

Said, Edward, *Out of Place*, London 1999

Samuel, Herbert, *Memoirs*, London 1945

Sanderson, John, *The Travels of John Sanderson in the Levant*, ed. W. Forster, London 1931

Sandys, George, *A Relation of a Journey begun AD 1610*. London 1615

Saulcy, F. de, *Les Derniers Jours de Jérusalem*, Paris 1866

Sebeos, *Histoire d'Heraclius*, trans. F. Macler, Paris 1904

Suchem, Ludolp von, *Description of the Holy Land and the Way Thither*, ed. and trans. Aubrey Stewart, London 1895

Sharon, Ariel, *Warrior: An Autobiography*, New York 1989

Spafford, Bertha, see Vester

Stanley, Arthur, *Sinai and Palestine in Connection with their History*, London 1856

Storrs, Ronald, *Orientations*, London 1939

Suetonius, *The Twelve Caesars*, London 1957

Al-Tabari, *Tarikh: The History of al-Tabari*, ed. Y. Yarshater, Albany 1985–98

Tacitus, *The Annals of Imperial Rome*, London 1956

Tacitus, *The Histories*, London 1964

Thackeray, William, *Notes on a Journey from Cornhill to Grand Cairo*, London 1888

Theodorich, *Description of the Holy Places*, ed. and trans. Aubrey Stewart, London 1896

Thomson, William M., *The Land and the Book*, New York 1859

Timberlake, Henry, *A True and Strange Discourse of the Travels of Two English Pilgrims*, London 1616/1808

Twain, Mark, *The Innocents Abroad, or the New Pilgrims' Progress*, New York 1911

Usama ibn Munqidh, *The Book of Contemplation: Islam and the Crusades*, ed. and trans. Paul M. Cobb, London 2008

Vester, Bertha Spafford, *Our Jerusalem*, Jerusalem 1988

Vincent, H. and Abel, F. M., *Jérusalem: Recherches de topographie, d'archéologie et d'histoire*, Paris 1912/1926

Volney, C.-F., *Travels through Syria and Egypt*, London 1787

Warren, C., *Underground Jerusalem*, London 1876

Warren, C. and Conder, C. R., *Survey of Western Palestine*, Jerusalem 1884

Weidenfeld, George, *Remembering my Good Friends*, London 1995

Weizmann, Chaim, *Trial and Error*, London 1949

Wilkinson, J., *Jerusalem Pilgrims before the Crusades*, Jerusalem 1977

Wilkinson, J., *Egeria's Travels to the Holy Land*, Warminster 1918

William of Tyre, *A History of Deeds Done beyond the Sea*, trans. E. A. Babcock and A. C. Krey, New York 1943

Wilson, C. *Ordnance Survey of Jerusalem*, London 1865

Wilson, C. (ed.), *Palestine Pilgrims Text Society*, ed. Aubrey Stewart, New York 1971

Wright, Thomas, *Early Travels in Palestine*, Mineola NY 1848/2003

Yizhar, S., *Khirbet Khizeh*, Jerusalem 1949

Zakharova, L. G., *Perepiska Imperatora Aleksandra II s Velikim Kniazem Konstantinom Nikolaevichem; Dnevnik Velikogo Kniazia Konstantina Nikolaevicha*. Moscow 1994

SECONDARY SOURCES

Aaronovitch, David, *Voodoo Histories*, London 2009

Abel, F. M., *Histoire de la Palestine*, Paris 1952

Abulafia, David, *Frederick II: A Medieval Emperor*, London 2002

Abulafia, David, *The Great Sea: A Human History of the Mediterranean*, London 2011

Abu-Manneh, Butros, 'The Husaynis: Rise of a Notable Family in 18th-Century Palestine', in David Kushner (ed.), *Palestine in the Late Ottoman Period: Political, Social and Economic Transformation*, Leiden/Boston 1983

Abu Sway, Mustafa, 'Holy Land, Jerusalem and the Aqsa Mosque in Islamic Sources', in Oleg Grabar and Benjamin Z., Kedar (eds), *Where Heaven and Earth Meet: Jerusalem's Sacred Esplanade*, Jerusalem/Austin 2009

Achcar, Gilbert, *The Arabs and the Holocaust: The Arab–Israeli War of Narratives*, London 2010

Adams, R. J. Q., *Balfour, The Last Grandee*, London 2007

Ahimeir, O., and Bar-Simon-Tov, Y. (eds), *Forty Years in Jerusalem*, Jerusalem 2008

Ahlstrom, Gosta W., *History of Ancient Palestine*, Minneapolis 1993

Al-Alami, Muhammad Ali, 'The Waqfs of the Traditional Families of Jerusalem during the Ottoman Period', in Sylvia Auld and Robert Hillenbrand (eds), *Ottoman Jerusalem: The Living City, 1517–1917*, London 2000

Al-Khalili, Jim, *The House of Wisdom*, London 2010

Allmand, Christopher, *Henry V*, New Haven/London 1998

Andrew, Christopher, *Defence of the Realm: The Authorized History of MI5*, London 2009

Ansary, Tanim, *Destiny Disrupted: A History of the World through Islamic Eyes*, London 2009

Antonius, George, *The Arab Awakening: The Story of the Arab National Movement*, London 1938

Archer, Thomas, *Crusade of Richard I*, London 1988

Armstrong, Karen, *The First Christian: St Paul's Impact on Christianity*, London 1983

Armstrong, Karen, *Muhammad: A Biography of the Prophet*, London 2001

Armstrong, Karen, *A History of Jerusalem: One City, Three Faiths*, London 2005

Asali, K. J. (ed.), *Jerusalem in History*, New York 1990

Asali, K. J., 'The Cemeteries of Ottoman Jerusalem' and 'The Libraries of Ottoman Jerusalem', in Sylvia Auld and Robert Hillenbrand (eds), *Ottoman Jerusalem: The Living City, 1517–1917*, London 2000

Asbridge, Thomas, *The First Crusade: A New History*, London 2005

Asbridge, Thomas, *The Crusades: The War for the Holy Land*, London 2010

Ascalone, Enrico, *Mesopotamia*, Berkeley 2007

Ashton, Nigel, *King Hussein of Jordan: A Political Life*, London 2008

Atallah, Mahmud, 'The Architects in Jerusalem in the 10th–11th/16th–17th Centuries', in Sylvia Auld and Robert Hillenbrand (eds), *Ottoman Jerusalem: The Living City, 1517–1917*, London 2000

Auld, Graeme and Steiner, Margreet, *Jerusalem 1: From Bronze Age to Maccabees*, Cambridge 1996

Auld, Sylvia and Hillenbrand, Robert (eds), *Ottoman Jerusalem: The Living City, 1517–1917*, London 2000

Auld, Sylvia and Hillenbrand, Robert (eds), *Ayyubid Jerusalem: The Holy City in Context, 1187–1250*, London 2009

Avigad, N., *Discovering Jerusalem*, Nashville 1983

Avi-Yonah, Michael, *The Jews of Palestine: A Political History from the Bar Kochba War to the Arab Conquest*, Oxford 1976

Avi-Yonah, Michael, *The Madaba Mosaic Map*, Jerusalem 1954

Azarya, V., *Armenian Quarter of Jerusalem*, Berkeley/Los Angeles/London 1984

Bahat, Dan, with Chaim T. Rubinstein, *Illustrated Atlas of Jerusalem*, New York 1990

Bahat, Dan, 'Western Wall Tunnels', in H. Geva (ed.), *Ancient Jerusalem Revealed*, Jerusalem 2000

Bahat, Dan, *The Western Wall Tunnels: Touching the Stones of our Heritage*, Jerusalem 2007

Baldwin, M. W., *Raymond III of Tripoli and the Fall of Jerusalem*, Princeton 1936

Baldwin, M. W. (ed.), *The First Hundred Years*, vol. 1 of K. M. Setton (ed. in chief), *A History of the Crusades*, Madison WI 1969

Barr, James, *Setting the Desert on Fire: T. E. Lawrence and Britain's Secret War in Arabia 1916–18*, London 2006

Barrow, J., *The Life and Correspondence of Admiral Sir William Sidney Smith*, London 1848

Bar-Zohar, Michael, *Ben-Gurion*, New York 1977

Bar-Zohar, Michael, *Shimon Peres*, New York 2007

Ben-Ami, Shlomo, *Scars of War, Wounds of Peace: The Arab–Israel Tragedy*, London 2005

Ben-Arieh, Y., *Jerusalem in the 19th Century: The Old City*, New York 1984

Ben-Arieh, Y., *Jerusalem in the 19th Century: Emergence of the New City*, Jerusalem 1986

Ben-Arieh, Y., *The Rediscovery of the Holy Land in the 19th Century*, Jerusalem 2007

Ben-Dov, Meir, *The Western Wall*, Jerusalem 1983

Bentwich, Norman and Shaftesley, John M., 'Forerunners of Zionism in the Victorian Era', in John M. Shaftesley (ed.), *Remember the Days: Essays on Anglo-Jewish History Presented to Cecil Roth*, London 1966

Benvenisti, Meron, *Jerusalem: The Torn City*, Jerusalem 1975

Benvenisti, Meron, *Sacred Landscape: The Buried History of the Holy Land since 1948*, Berkeley 2000

Berlin, Andrea and Overman, J. A., *The First Jewish Revolt: Archaeology, History, and Ideology*, London 2002

Bermant, Chaim, *The Cousinhood: The Anglo-Jewish Gentry*, London 1971

Bevan, Edwyn, *The House of Seleucus*, London 1902

Bevan, Edwyn, *Jerusalem under the High Priests*, London 1904

Bianquis, Thierry, 'Autonomous Egypt from Ibn Tulun to Kafur 868–969', in Carl F. Petry (ed.), *The Cambridge History of Egypt*, vol. 1: *Islamic Egypt 640–1517*, Cambridge 1998

Bickermann, E. J., *Jews in the Greek Age*, Cambridge MA/London 1988

Bierman, John and Smith, Colin, *Fire in the Night: Wingate of Burma, Ethiopia and Zion*, London 1999

Birley, Anthony R., *Hadrian: the Restless Emperor*, London 1997

Blake, R., *Disraeli*, London 1967

Blake, R., *Disraeli on the Grand Tour*, London 1982

Bliss, F. J. and Dickie, A., *Excavations at Jerusalem*, London 1898

Boas, Adrian, *Crusader Archeology: The Material Culture of the Latin East*, London/New York 1999

Boas, Adrian, *Jerusalem in the Time of the Crusades*, London/New York 2001

Bosworth, C. E., *The Islamic Dynasties*, Edinburgh 1967

Bowen, Jeremy, *Six Days: How the 1967 War Shaped the Middle East*, London 2004

Brenner, Michael, *A Short History of the Jews*, Princeton 2010

Brook, Kevin Alan, *The Jews of Khazaria*, Lanham MD 1999

Brown, David, *Palmerston: A Biography*, Yale 2010

Brown, Frederick, *Flaubert: A Life*, London 2007

Burgoyne, Michael Hamilton, with Richards, D. S., *Mamluk Jerusalem: an Architectural Survey*, London 1987

Burgoyne, Michael Hamilton, '1187–1260: The Furthest Mosque (al-Masjid al-Aqsa) under Ayyubid Rule', in Oleg Grabar and Benjamin Z. Kedar (eds), *Where Heaven and Earth Meet: Jerusalem's Sacred Esplanade*, Jerusalem/Austin 2009

Burgoyne, Michael Hamilton, 'The Noble Sanctuary under Mamluk Rule', in Oleg Grabar and Benjamin Z. Kedar (eds), *Where Heaven and Earth Meet: Jerusalem's Sacred Esplanade*, Jerusalem/Austin 2009

Burns, Ross, *Damascus: A History*, London 2005

Butcher, Kevin, *Roman Syria and the Near East*, London 2003

Campbell Jr, Edward F., 'A Land Divided: Judah and Israel from the Death of Solomon to the Fall of Samaria', in Michael Coogan (ed.), *The Oxford History of the Biblical World*, Oxford 1998

Carswell, John, 'Decoration of the Dome of the Rock', in Sylvia Auld, and Robert Hillenbrand (eds), *Ottoman Jerusalem: The Living City, 1517–1917*, London 2000

Cesarani, David, *Major Farran's Hat: Murder, Scandal, and Britain's War against Jewish Terrorism 1945–8*, London 2009

Chamberlain, Michael, 'The Crusader Era and the Ayyubid Dynasty', in Carl F. Petry (ed.), *The Cambridge History of Egypt*, vol. 1: *Islamic Egypt 640–1517*, Cambridge 1998

Cline, Eric H., *Jerusalem Besieged: From Ancient Canaan to Modern Israel*, Ann Arbor 2004

Cogan, Mordecai, 'Into Exile: From the Assyrian Conquest of Israel to the Fall of Babylon', in Michael Coogan (ed.), *The Oxford History of the Biblical World*, Oxford 1998

Cohen, A. and Baer, G. (eds), *Egypt and Palestine: A Millennium of Association (868–1948)*, Jerusalem 1984

Cohen, Amnon, *Palestine in the 18th Century*, Jerusalem 1973

Cohen, Amnon, *Jewish Life under Islam: Jerusalem in the 16th Century*, Cambridge MA/London 1984

Cohen, Amnon, *Economic Life in Ottoman Jerusalem*, Cambridge 2002

Cohen, Amnon, '1517–1917 Haram-al-Sherif: The Temple Mount under Ottoman Rule', in Oleg Grabar and Benjamin Z. Kedar (eds), *Where Heaven and Earth Meet: Jerusalem's Sacred Esplanade*, Jerusalem/Austin 2009

Cohn, Norman, *The Pursuit of the Millennium: Revolutionary Millenarians and Mystical Anarchists of the Middle Ages*, London 1958/1993

Conrad, L., 'The Khalidi Library', in Sylvia Auld and Robert Hillenbrand (eds), *Ottoman Jerusalem: The Living City, 1517–1917*, London 2000

Coogan, Michael, 'In the Beginning: The Earliest History', in Michael Coogan (ed.), *The Oxford History of the Biblical World*, Oxford 1998

Coogan, Michael (ed.) *The Oxford History of the Biblical World*, Oxford 1998

Couasnon, Charles, *The Church of the Holy Sepulchre in Jerusalem*, London 1974

Coughlin, Con, *A Golden Basin Full of Scorpions: The Quest for Modern Jerusalem*, London 1997

Courret, A., *La Prise de Jérusalem par les Perses*, Orleans 1876

Curtis, J. E. and Reade, J. E. (eds), *Art and Empire: Treasures from Assyria in the British Museum*, London 1995

Cust, L. G. A., *The Status Quo in the Holy Place*, Jerusalem 1929

Dalrymple, William, *From the Holy Mountain: A Journey in the Shadow of Byzantium*, London 1998

Daly, M. W. (ed.), *Modern Egypt from 1517 to the End of the Twentieth Century*, vol 2 of *The Cambridge History of Egypt*, Cambridge 1998

Dan, Yaron, 'Circus Factions in Byzantine Palestine', in Lee I. Levine (ed.), *Jerusalem Cathedra: Studies in the History, Geography and Ethnology of the Land of Israel*, vol. 1. Jerusalem 1981

Daniel-Rops, Henri, *Daily Life in Palestine at the Time of Christ*, London 1962

Dankoff, Robert, *An Ottoman Mentality: The world of Evliya Celebi*, Leiden/Boston 2006

De Vaux, Ronald, *Ancient Israel: Its Life and Institutions*, New York/London 1961

Donner, Fred M., *The Early Islamic Conquests*, Princeton 1981

Donner, Fred M., *Muhammad and the Believers: At the Origins of Islam*, Cambridge MA 2010

Donner, H., *The Mosaic Map of Madaba: An Introductory Guide*, Kampen 1992

Douglas, David C. *William the Conqueror*, New Haven/London 1964

Dow, Martin, 'The Hammams of Ottoman Jerusalem', in Sylvia Auld and Robert Hillenbrand (eds), *Ottoman Jerusalem: The Living City, 1517–1917*, London 2000

Drory, J., 'Jerusalem during the Mamluk Period', in Lee I. Levine (ed.), *Jerusalem Cathedra: Studies in the History, Geography and Ethnology of the Land of Israel*, vol. 1, Jerusalem 1981

Duri, Abdul Aziz, 'Jerusalem in the Early Islamic Period', in K. J. Asali (ed.), *Jerusalem in History*, New York 1990

Egremont, Max, *Balfour*, London 1980

Elior, Rachel, 'From Priestly and Early Christian Mount Zion to Rabbinic Temple Mount', in Oleg Grabar and Benjamin Z. Kedar (eds) *Where Heaven and Earth Meet: Jerusalem's Sacred Esplanade*, Jerusalem/Austin 2009

Ellenblum, Ronnie, *Crusader Castles and Modern Histories*, Cambridge 2007

Ellis, Kirsten, *Star of the Morning: The Extraordinary Life of Lady Hester Stanhope*, London 2008

Elon, Amos, *Herzl*, New York 1975

Elon, Amos, *Jerusalem: A City of Mirrors*, London 1991

Farrokh, Kaveh, *Shadows in the Desert: Ancient Persia at War*, London 2007

Ferguson, Niall, *The World's Banker: The History of the House of Rothschild*, London 1998

Figes, Orlando, *Crimea: the Last Crusade*, London 2010.

Finkel, Caroline, *Osman's Dream: The Story of the Ottoman Empire 1300–1923*, London 2005

Finkel, I. L. and Seymour, M. J., *Babylon: Myth and Reality*, London 2008

Finkelstein, Israel and Silberman, Neil Asher, *The Bible Unearthed: Archeology's New Vision of Ancient Israel and the Origin of its Sacred Text*, New York 2002

Finucane, R., *Soldiers of the Faith*, London 1983

Fischel, Walter J., *Ibn Khaldun and Tamerlane*, Berkeley 1952

Folda, Jaroslav, *Crusader Art: The Art of the Crusaders in the Holy Land 1099–1291*, Farnham 2008

Folda, Jaroslav, *Crusader Art in the Holy Land: From the Third Crusade to the Fall of Acre*, Cambridge 2005

Ford, Roger, *Eden to Armageddon: World War I in the Middle East*, London 2009

Franken, H. J., 'Jerusalem in the Bronze Age', in K. J. Asali, (ed.), *Jerusalem in History*, New York 1990

Fraser, Flora, *The Unruly Queen: The Life of Queen Caroline*, London 1997

Freely, John, *Storm on Horseback: Seljuk Warriors of Turkey*, London 2008

Freeman, Charles, *A New History of Early Christianity*, New Haven 2009

Freeman, Charles, *Holy Bones, Holy Dust*, New Haven 2011

Frenkel, Miriam, 'The Temple Mount in Jewish Thought', in Oleg Grabar and Benjamin Z. Kedar (eds), *Where Heaven and Earth Meet: Jerusalem's Sacred Esplanade*, Jerusalem/Austin 2009

Friedman, Thomas L., *From Beirut to Jerusalem*, New York 1989

Fromkin, David, *A Peace to End All Peace: The Fall of the Ottoman Empire and the Creation of the Modern Middle East*, New York 1989

Garcin, J. C., 'The Regime of the Circassian Mamluks', in Carl F. Petry (ed.), *The Cambridge History of Egypt*, vol. 1: *Islamic Egypt 640–1517*, Cambridge 1998

Gelvin, James, *Divided Loyalties: Nationalism and Mass Politics in Syria at the Close of Empire*, Berkeley 1998

Geniesse, Jane Fletcher, *American Priestess: The Extraordinary Story of Anna Spafford and the American Colony in Jerusalem*, New York 2008

Geva, H. (ed.), *Ancient Jerusalem Revealed*, Jerusalem 2000

Gibb, Hamilton A. R., 'The Career of Nur-ad-Din', in *A History of the Crusades*, vol. 1: *The First Hundred Years*, ed. M. W. Baldwin, Madison WI 1969–89

Gibb, Hamilton, A. R., 'Zengi and the Fall of Edessa', in *A History of the Crusades*, vol. 1: *The First Hundred Years*, ed. M. W. Baldwin, Madison WI 1969–89

Gibson, Shimon, *The Final Days of Jesus*, New York 2009

Gil, Moshe, 'Aliyah and Pilgrimage in Early Arab Period', in Lee I. Levine (ed.), *Jerusalem Cathedra: Studies in the History, Geography and Ethnology of the Land of Israel*, vol. 3, Jerusalem 1983

Gil, Moshe, *A History of Palestine*, Cambridge 1992

Gilbert, Martin, *Jerusalem: Illustrated History Atlas*, London 1977

Gilbert, Martin, *Jerusalem: Rebirth of a City*, London 1985

Gilbert, Martin, *Churchill: A Life*, London 1991

Gilbert, Martin, *Jerusalem in the Twentieth Century*, London 1996

Gilbert, Martin, *Israel: A History*, London 1998

Gilbert, Martin, *Churchill and the Jews*, London 2007

Gilbert, Martin, *In Ishmael's House: A History of the Jews in Muslim Lands*, London/New Haven 2010

Gillingham, John, *Richard I*, London 1999

Glass, Charles, *Tribes with Flags: A Journey Curtailed*, London 1990

Glass, Charles, *The Tribes Triumphant: Return Journey to the Middle East*, London 2010

Goitein, S. D., *A Mediterranean Society*, 5 vols, Berkeley 1967–88

Goitein, S.D., 'Jerusalem in the Arab Period 638–1099', in Lee I. Levine (ed.), *Jerusalem Cathedra: Studies in the History, Geography and Ethnology of the Land of Israel*, vol. 2, Jerusalem 1982

Goldhill, Simon, *The Temple of Jerusalem*, London 2005

Goldhill, Simon, *Jerusalem: A City of Longing*, London/Cambridge MA 2008

Goldsworthy, Adrian, *Antony and Cleopatra*, London 2010

Goodman, Martin, *Rome and Jerusalem: The Clash of Ancient Civilisations*, London 2007

Gorton, T. J. and A. F. (eds.), *Lebanon Through Writers' Eyes*, London 2009

Grabar, Oleg, *The Shape of the Holy: Early Islamic Jerusalem*, Princeton 1996

Grabar, Oleg, *The Dome of the Rock*, Cambridge MA 2006

Grabar, Oleg, *Jerusalem*, Aldershot 2005

Grabar, Oleg and Kedar, Benjamin Z. (eds), *Where Heaven and Earth Meet: Jerusalem's Sacred Esplanade*, Jerusalem/Austin, Texas 2009

Grabbe, Lester L., *Ancient Israel*, New York 2007

Grabbe, Lester L., *Good Kings and Bad Kings: The Kingdom of Judah in the Seventh Century BCE*, London 2007

Grant, Michael, *Herod the Great*, New York 1971

Grant, Michael, *Cleopatra*, London 1972

Grant, Michael, *History of Ancient Israel*, London 1984

Grant, Michael, *Emperor Constantine*, London 1993

Green, Abigail, *Moses Montefiore: Jewish Liberator, Imperial Hero*, London 2010

Greenberg, Raphael and Keinan, Adi, *Present Past of Israeli–Palestinian Conflict: Israeli Archaeology in the West Bank and East Jerusalem since 1967*, Tel Aviv 2007

Grigg, J. *Lloyd George: War Leader*, London 2002

Haag, Michael, *The Templars: History and Myth*, London 2008

Hackett, Jo Ann, 'There Was No King in Israel: The Era of the Judges', in Michael Coogan (ed.), *The Oxford History of the Biblical World*, Oxford 1998

Hadi, Mahdi Abdul, *Dialogue on Jerusalem*, PASSIA Meetings 1990–8, Jerusalem 1998

Hadi, Mahdi Abdul, *100 Years of Palestinian History: A 20th Century Chronology*, Jerusalem 2001/2005

Hadi, Mahdi Abdul, *Palestinian Personalities: A Biographical Dictionary*, Jerusalem 2005

Halpern, Ben, *A Clash of Heroes: Brandeis, Weizmann and American Zionism*, New York 1987

Hamilton, Bernard, *The Leper King and his Heirs: Baldwin IV and the Crusader Kingdom of Jerusalem*, Cambridge 2000

Hamilton, R. W., *The Structural History of the Aqsa Mosque: A Record of Archaeological Gleanings from the Repairs of 1938–42.* Jerusalem/London/Oxford 1949

Hare, David, *Via Dolorosa*, London 1998

Harrington, D., *The Maccabee Revolt: Anatomy of a Biblical Revolution*, Wilmington DE 1988

Hassan bin Talal, Crown Prince of Jordan, *A Study on Jerusalem*, London 1979

Hassan, Isaac, 'Muslim Literature in Praise of Jerusalem', in Lee I. Levine (ed.), *Jerusalem Cathedra: Studies in the History, Geography and Ethnology of the Land of Israel*, vol. 1, Jerusalem 1981

Hawari, M., 'The Citadel (Qal'a) in the Ottoman Period: An Overview', in Sylvia Auld and Robert Hillenbrand (eds), *Ottoman Jerusalem: The Living City, 1517–1917*, London 2000

Hawting, G. R., *The First Dynasty of Islam: The Umayyad Caliphate, AD 661–750*, London 2000

Heaton, E. W., *Everyday Life in Old Testament Times*, London 1956

Herf, Jeffrey, *Nazi Propaganda for the Arab World*, New Haven 2009

Herrin, Judith, *Byzantium: The Surprising Life of a Medieval Empire*, London 2007

Hillenbrand, Carole, *The Crusades: Islamic Perspectives*, New York 2000

Hintlian, George, 'The First World War in Palestine and Msgr. Franz Fellinger', in Marian Wrba (ed.), *Austrian Presence in the Holy Land in the 19th and Early 20th Century*, Tel Aviv 1996

Hintlian, George, 'Commercial Life of Ottoman Jerusalem', in Sylvia Auld and Robert Hillenbrand (eds), *Ottoman Jerusalem: The Living City, 1517–1917*, London 2000

Hintlian, Kevork, *History of the Armenians in the Holy Land*, Jerusalem 1989

Hintlian, Kevork, 'Travellers and Pilgrims in the Holy Land: The Armenian Patriarchate of Jerusalem in 17th and 18th Century', in Anthony O'Mahony (ed.), *The Christian Heritage in the Holy Land*, London 1995

Hirst, David, *The Gun and the Olive Branch*, London 2003

Hiyari, M. A., 'Crusader Jerusalem', in K. J. Asali (ed.), *Jerusalem in History*, New York 1990

Hoffmeier, J. K., *The Archaeology of the Bible*, London 2008

Holbl, Gunther, *A History of the Ptolemaic Empire*, London 2001

Holland, Tom, *Persian Fire: The First World Empire, Battle for the West*, London 2005

Holland, Tom, *Millennium: The End of the World and the Forging of Christianity*, London 2008

Hopwood, Derek *The Russian Presence in Syria and Palestine 1843–1914: Church and Politics in the Near East*, Oxford 1969

Hourani, Albert, *The Emergence of the Modern Middle East*, Berkeley/Los Angeles 1981

Hourani, Albert, *History of the Arab Peoples*, London 2005

Housley, Norman, *Fighting for the Cross: Crusading to the Holy Land*, London/New Haven 2008

Howard, Edward, *The Memoirs of Sir Sidney Smith*, London 2008

Hudson, M. C., 'Transformation of Jerusalem', in K. J. Asali (ed.), *Jerusalem in History*, New York 1990

Hummel, Ruth and Thomas, *Patterns of the Sacred: English Protestant and Russian Orthodox Pilgrims of the Nineteenth Century*, Jerusalem 1995

Hummel, Ruth Victor-, 'Culture and Image: Christians and the Beginning of Local Photography in 19th Century Ottoman Palestine', in Anthony O'Mahony (ed.), *The Christian Heritage in the Holy Land*, London 1995

Hummel, Ruth, 'Imperial Pilgrim: Franz Josef's Journey to the Holy Land in 1869', in Marian Wrba, (ed.), *Austrian Presence in the Holy Land in the 19th and Early 20th Century*, Tel Aviv 1996

Hummel, Ruth Victor-, 'Reality, Imagination and Belief: Jerusalem in Photography', in Sylvia Auld and Robert Hillenbrand (eds), *Ottoman Jerusalem: The Living City, 1517–1917*, London 2000

Humphreys, R. Stephen, *From Saladin to the Mongols: The Ayyubids of Damascus 1193–1260*, Albany 1977

Humphreys, R. Stephen, *Muawiya ibn Abi Sufyan: From Arabia to Empire*, Oxford 2006

Huneidi, Sahar and Khalidi, Walid, *A Broken Trust: Herbert Samuel, Zionism and the Palestinians*, London 1999

Hurowitz, V. A., 'Tenth Century to 586 BC: House of the Lord', in Oleg Grabar and Benjamin Z. Kedar (eds), *Where Heaven and Earth Meet: Jerusalem's Sacred Esplanade*, Jerusalem/Austin 2009

Irwin, Robert, *The Middle East in the Middle Ages: The Early Mamluk Sultanate 1250–1382*, Carbondale and Edwardsville IL 1986

James, Lawrence, *Golden Warrior: The Life and Legend of Lawrence of Arabia*, New York 1993

Jeffery, Keith, *MI6: History of the Secret Intelligence Service 1909–1949*, London 2010

Johnson, Paul, *History of the Jews*, London 1987

Joudah, A. H., *Revolt in Palestine in the Eighteenth Century: The Era of Shaykh Zahir al-Umar*, Princeton 1987

Al-Jubeh, Nazmi, 'Basic Changes But Not Dramatic: Al-Haram al-Sherif in the Aftermath of 1967', in Oleg Grabar and Benjamin Z. Kedar (eds), *Where Heaven and Earth Meet: Jerusalem's Sacred Esplanade*, Jerusalem/ Austin 2009

Kaegi, Walter, *Heraclius: Emperor of Byzantium*, Cambridge 2003

Kaplony, Andreas, 'The Mosque of Jerusalem', in Oleg Grabar and Benjamin Z. Kedar (eds), *Where Heaven and Earth Meet: Jerusalem's Sacred Esplanade*, Jerusalem/Austin 2009

Kark, Ruth, *American Consuls in the Holy Land 1932–1914*, Jerusalem 1994

Karsh, Efraim, *Palestine Betrayed*, New Haven 2010

Karsh, Efraim and Karsh, Inari, *Empires of the Sand: The Struggle for Mastery in the Middle East 1789–1923*, Cambridge MA 2001

Kasmieh, Khairia, 'The Leading Intellectuals of Late Ottoman Jerusalem', in Sylvia Auld and Robert Hillenbrand (eds), *Ottoman Jerusalem: The Living City, 1517–1917*, London 2000

Kedar, Benjamin Z. (ed.), *Jerusalem in the Middle Ages: Selected Papers*, Jerusalem 1979

Kedar, Benjamin Z., 'A Commentary on the Book of Isaiah Ransomed from the Crusaders', in Lee I. Levine (ed.), *Jerusalem Cathedra: Studies in the History, Geography and Ethnology of the Land of Israel*, vol. 2, Jerusalem 1982

Kedar, Benjamin Z. (ed.), *The Horns of Hattin*, London 1992

Kedar, Benjamin Z, Mayer H. E. and Smail, R. C. (eds), *Outremer: Studies in the History of the Crusading Kingdom of Jerusalem, Presented to Joshua Prawer*, Jerusalem 1982

Kedar, Benjamin Z. and Pringle, Denys, '1099–1187: The Lord's Temple (Templum Domini) and Solomon's Palace (Palatium Salominis)', in Oleg Grabar and Benjamin Z. Kedar (eds), *Where Heaven and Earth Meet: Jerusalem's Sacred Esplanade*, Jerusalem/Austin 2009

Kedourie, Elie, *In the Anglo-Arab Labyrinth: The McMahon–Husayn Correspondence and its Interpretations*, Cambridge 1976

Kennedy, Hugh, *Armies of the Caliphs*, London 2001

Kennedy, Hugh, *The Court of the Caliphs: The Rise and Fall of Islam's Greatest Dynasty*, London 2004

Kennedy, Hugh, *The Great Arab Conquests: How the Spread of Islam Changed the World We Live In*, London 2007

Kenyon, K. M., *Digging Up Jerusalem*, London 1974

Khalidi, Rashid, *British Policy towards Syria and Palestine 1906–14*, London 1980

Khalidi, Rashid, *Palestinian Identity: The Construction of Modern National Consciousness*, New York 1998

Khalidi, Rashid, 'Intellectual Life in Late Ottoman Jerusalem', in Sylvia Auld and Robert Hillenbrand (eds), *Ottoman Jerusalem: The Living City, 1517–1917*, London 2000

Khalidi, Rashid, *The Iron Cage: The Story of the Palestinian Struggle for Statehood*, London 2009

Khalidi, Walid, *From Haven to Conquest: readings in Zionism and the Palestinian Problem until 1948*, Beirut 1987

Khoury, Philip S., *Urban Notables and Arab Nationalism: The Politics of Damascus 1860–1920*, Cambridge 2003

Kister, Meir, 'A Comment on the Antiquity of Traditions Praising Jerusalem', in Lee I. Levine (ed.), *Jerusalem Cathedra: Studies in the History, Geography and Ethnology of the Land of Israel*, vol. 1, Jerusalem 1981

Kokkinos, Nikos, *The Herodian Dynasty: Origins, Role in Society and Eclipse*, Sheffield 1998

Kollek, Teddy and Pearlman, Moshe, *Jerusalem, Sacred City of Mankind: A History of Forty Centuries*, Jerusalem 1968

Kraemer, Joel L., *Maimonides: The Life and World of One of Civilisation's Greatest Minds*, New York 2008

Krämer, Gudrun, *A History of Palestine: From the Ottoman Conquest to the Founding of the State of Israel*, Princeton 2008

Kroyanker, David, *Jerusalem Architecture*, New York 1994

Kushner, David (ed.), *Palestine in the Late Ottoman Period: Political, Social and Economic Transformation*, Leiden/Boston 1983

La Guardia, Anton, *Holy Land, Unholy War*, London 2001

Lane Fox, Robin, *Alexander the Great*, London 1973

Lane Fox, Robin, *The Unauthorized Version: Truth and Fiction in the Bible*, London 1991

Leach, John, *Pompey the Great*, London 1978

LeBor, Adam, *City of Oranges: Arabs and Jews in Jaffa*, London 2006

Leith, Mary Joan Winn, 'Israel among the Nations: The Persian Period', in Michael Coogan (ed.), *The Oxford History of the Biblical World*, Oxford 1998

Levine, Lee I. (ed.), *Jerusalem Cathedra: Studies in the History, Geography and Ethnology of the Land of Israel*, Jerusalem 1981–3

Levy, Y., 'Julian the Apostate and the Building of the Temple', in Lee I. Levine (ed.), *Jerusalem Cathedra: Studies in the History, Geography and Ethnology of the Land of Israel*, vol. 3, Jerusalem 1983

Lewis, Bernard, *The Arabs in History*, New York 1966

Lewis, Bernard, *The Middle East*, London 1995

Lewis, David Levering, *God's Crucible: Islam and the Making of Europe 570–1215*, New York 2010

Lewis, Donald M., *The Origins of Christian Zionism: Lord Shaftesbury and Evangelical Support for a Jewish Homeland*, Cambridge 2009

Lewis, Geoffrey, *Balfour and Weizmann: The Zionist, the Zealot and the Declaration which Changed the World*, London 2009

Lewis, Geoffrey, 'An Ottoman Officer in Palestine 1914–18', in David Kushner (ed.), *Palestine in the Late Ottoman Period: Political, Social and Economic Transformation*, Leiden/Boston 1983

Lincoln, W. Bruce, *Nicholas I*, London 1978

Little, Donald P., 'Jerusalem under the Ayyubids and Mamluks', in K. J. Asali (ed.), *Jerusalem in History*, New York 1990

Little, Donald P., '1260–1516: The Noble Sanctuary under Mamluk Rule', in Oleg Grabar and Benjamin Z. Kedar (eds), *Where Heaven and Earth Meet: Jerusalem's Sacred Esplanade*, Jerusalem/Austin 2009

Loupo, Yakov and Chen, Nitzan, 'The Ultra-Orthodox', in O. Ahimeir and Y. Bar-Simon-Tov (eds), *Forty Years in Jerusalem*, Jerusalem 2008

Lubetski, Meir (ed.), *New Seals and Inscriptions, Hebrew, Idumean and Cuneiform*, Sheffield 2007

Luke, Harry Charles and Keith-Roach, Edward, *The Handbook of Palestine*, London 1922

Lyons, Jonathan, *House of Wisdom*, London 2009

Lyons, M. C. and Jackson, D. E. P., *Saladin: Politics of Holy War*, Cambridge 1982

Maalouf, Amin, *Crusades through Arab Eyes*, London 1973

McCullough, David, *Truman*, New York, 1992

MacCulloch, Diarmaid, *A History of Christianity: The First Three Thousand Years*, London 2010

Mackowiak, P. A., *Post Mortem: Solving History's Great Medical Mysteries*, New York 2007

McLynn, Frank, *Lionheart and Lackland*, London 2008

McLynn, Frank, *Marcus Aurelius: Warrior, Philosopher, Emperor*, London 2009

McMeekin, Sean, *The Berlin–Baghdad Express: The Ottoman Empire and Germany's Bid for World Power, 1898–1918*, London 2010

MacMillan, Margaret, *Peacemakers: The Paris Peace Conference of 1919 and its Attempt to End War*, London 2001

Mamluk Art: Splendour and Magic of the Sultans, Museum with No Frontiers, Cairo 2001

Mann, J., *The Jews in Egypt and Palestine under the Fatimid Caliphs*, 2 vols, New York 1970

Manna, Adel, *Liwa' al Quds fi Awasit al Ahd al othmani al idarah wa al mujtama mundhu awasit al qarn al thamin ashar hatta hamlat Mohammad Ali Basha sanat 1831* (The District of Jerusalem in the Mid-Ottoman Period: Administration and Society, from the Mid-Eighteenth Century to the Campaign of Mohammad Ali Pasha in 1831), Jerusalem 2008

Mansel, Philip, *Levant: Splendour and Catastrophe on the Mediterranean*, London 2010

Mansel, Philip, *Asmahan: Siren of the Nile* (unpublished ms)

Maoz, M. (ed.), *Studies on Palestine during the Ottoman Period*, Jerusalem 1975

Marcus, Amy Dockser, *Jerusalem 1913: Origins of the Arab–Israeli Conflict*, New York 2007

Mattar, Philip, *The Mufti of Jerusalem: Al-Hajj Amin al-Hussayni and the Palestinian National Movement*, New York 1988

Mazar, Benjamin, *The Mountain of the Lord*, New York 1975

Mazar, Benjamin, 'Jerusalem in Biblical Times', in Lee I. Levine (ed.), *Jerusalem Cathedra: Studies in the History, Geography and Ethnology of the Land of Israel*, vol. 2, Jerusalem 1982

Mazower, Mark, *Salonica, City of Ghosts: Christians, Muslims and Jews*, London 2005

Mazza, Roberto, *Jerusalem from the Ottomans to the British*, London 2009

Mendenhall, G. E., 'Jerusalem from 1000–63 BC', in K. J. Asali (ed.), *Jerusalem in History*, New York 1990

Merkley, P. C., *The Politics of Christian Zionism 1891–1948*, London 1998

Meyer, Karl E. and Brysac, S. B., *Kingmakers: The Invention of the Modern Middle East*, New York 2008

Meyers, Carol, 'Kinship and Kingship: The Early Monarchy', in Michael Coogan (ed.), *The Oxford History of the Biblical World*, Oxford 1998

Miles, Richard, *Carthage Must Be Destroyed*, London 2009

Miles, Richard, *Ancient Worlds: The Search for the Origins of Western Civilization*, London 2010

Mitchell, T. C., *The Bible in the British Museum*, London 1998

Morris, Benny, *The Road to Jerusalem: Glubb Pasha, Palestine and the Jews*, London 2002

Morris, Benny, *1948: A History of the First Arab–Israeli War*, London 2008

Murphy-O'Connor, J., *The Holy Land: An Archaeological Guide*, Oxford 1986

Murray, Alan V., *Clash of Cultures on the Medieval Baltic Frontier*, Farnham 2009

Myres, David, 'An overview of the Islamic Architecture of Ottoman Jerusalem', 'Restorations on Masjid Mahd Isa (the Cradle of Jesus) during the Ottoman Period', 'Al-Imara al-Amira, The Charitable Foundation of

Khassaki Sultan' and 'A Grammar of Ottoman Ornament in Jerusalem', in Sylvia Auld and Robert Hillenbrand (eds), *Ottoman Jerusalem: The Living City, 1517–1917*, London 2000

Nashashibi, Nasser Eddin, *Jerusalem's Other Voice: Ragheb Nashashibi and Moderation in Palestinian Politics 1920–1948*, Exeter 1990

al-Natsheh, Yusuf Said, 'The Architecture of Ottoman Jerusalem', in Sylvia Auld and Robert Hillenbrand (eds), *Ottoman Jerusalem: The Living City, 1517–1917*, London 2000

Netanyahu, Benzion, *The Origins of the Inquisition in Fifteenth-Century Spain*, New York 1995

Neuwirth, Angelika, 'Jerusalem in Islam: The Three Honorific Names of the City', in Sylvia Auld and Robert Hillenbrand (eds), *Ottoman Jerusalem: The Living City, 1517–1917*, London 2000

Newby, Martine S., *The Shlomo Moussaieff Collection: Byzantine Mould-Blown Glass from the Holy Land*, London 2008

Nicault, Catherine (ed.), *Jérusalem, 1850–1948: Des Ottomans aux Anglais, entre coexistence spirituelle et déchirure politique*, Paris 1999

Northrup, Linda S., *From Slave to Sultan: The Career of Al-Mansur Qalawun and the Consolidation of Mamluk Rule in Egypt and Syria (678–689 A.H./1279–1290 A.D.)*, Wiesbaden 1998

Northrup, Linda S., 'The Bahri Mamluk Sultanate', in Carl F. Petry (ed.), *The Cambridge History of Egypt*, vol. 1: *Islamic Egypt 640–1517*, Cambridge 1998

Norwich, John Julius, *The Normans in the South* (two volumes), London 1967

Norwich, John Julius, *Byzantium: The Early Centuries*, London 1988

Nusseibeh, Sari, 'The Haram al-Sharif', in Oleg Grabar and Benjamin Z. Kedar (eds), *Where Heaven and Earth Meet: Jerusalem's Sacred Esplanade*, Jerusalem/Austin 2009

Obenzinger, Hilton, *American Palestine: Melville, Twain and the Holy Land Mania*, Princeton 1999

Olmstead, A. T., *History of the Persian Empire*, Chicago 1948

O'Mahoney, Anthony, *Christian Heritage in the Holy Land*, London 1995

Opper, Thorsten, *Hadrian: Empire and Conflict*, London 2008

Oren, Michael B., *Six Days of War: June 1967 and the Making of the Modern Middle East*, New York 2002

Oren, Michael B., *Power, Faith, and Fantasy: America in the Middle East 1776 to the Present*, New York 2007

Ott, Claudia, 'Songs and Musical Instruments', in Sylvia Auld and Robert Hillenbrand (eds), *Ottoman Jerusalem: The Living City, 1517–1917*, London 2000

Pappe, Ilan, *The Rise and Fall of a Palestinian Dynasty: The Husaynis, 1700–1948*, London 2010

Pappe, Ilan, *The Making of the Arab-Israeli Conflict 1947–51*, London 1994

Pappe, Ilan, *A History of Modern Palestine: One Land, Two Peoples*, London 2006

Pappe, Ilan, *Ethnic Cleansing of Palestine*, London 2007

Peters, F. E., *Jesus and Muhammad: Parallel Tracks, Parallel Lives*, Oxford 2010, see primary sources

Parfitt, Tudor, *The Jews of Palestine 1800–82*, London 1987

Patrich, J., '538 BCE–70 CE: The Temple (Beyt ha-Miqdash) and its Mount', in Oleg Grabar and Benjamin Z. Kedar (eds), *Where Heaven and Earth Meet: Jerusalem's Sacred Esplanade*, Jerusalem/Austin 2009

Perowne, Stewart, *Herod the Great*, London 1956

Perowne, Stewart, *The Later Herods*, London 1958

Peters, F. E., *The Distant Shrine: Islamic Centuries in Jerusalem*, New York 1993

Petry, Carl F. (ed.), *The Cambridge History of Egypt*, vol. 1: *Islamic Egypt 640–1517*, Cambridge 1998

Phillips, Jonathan, *The Second Crusade: Extending the Frontiers of Christendom*, London 2007

Phillips, Jonathan, *Holy Warriors: A Modern History of the Crusades*, London 2009

Pitard, Wayne T., 'Before Israel: Syria–Palestine in the Bronze Age', in Michael Coogan (ed.), *The Oxford History of the Biblical World*, Oxford 1998

Plokhy, S. M., *Yalta: The Price of Peace*, New York 2010

Pocock, Tom, *A Thirst for Glory: The Life of Admiral Sir Sidney Smith*, London 1996

Pollock, John, *Kitchener: Saviour of the Realm*, London 2001

Prawer, Joshua, *The Latin Kingdom of Jerusalem*, London 1972

Prawer, Joshua, *The History of the Jews in the Latin Kingdom of Jerusalem*, Oxford 1988

Prestwich, Michael, *Edward I*, New Haven/London 1988

Pringle, Denys, *The Churches of the Crusader Kingdom of Jerusalem: A Corpus*, Cambridge 1993–9

Rabinowitz, E., *Justice Louis D. Brandeis: The Zionist Chapter of his Life*, New York 1968

Rafeq, Abdul-Karim, *The Province of Damascus 1723–83*, Beirut 1966

Rafeq, Abdul-Karim, 'Political History of Ottoman Jerusalem', in Sylvia Auld and Robert Hillenbrand (eds), *Ottoman Jerusalem: The Living City, 1517–1917*, London 2000

Rafeq, Abdul-Karim, 'Ulema of Ottoman Jerusalem', in Sylvia Auld and

Robert Hillenbrand (eds), *Ottoman Jerusalem: The Living City, 1517–1917*, London 2000

Raider, M. A., *The Emergence of American Zionism*, New York 1998

Read, Piers Paul, *The Templars*, London 1999

Redford, Donald P., *Egypt, Canaan and Israel in Ancient Times*, Princeton 1992

Redmount, Carol A., 'Bitter Lives: Israel in and out of Egypt', in Michael Coogan (ed.), *The Oxford History of the Biblical World*, Oxford 1998

Reich, Ronny, Avni, Gideon and Winter, Tamar, *The Jerusalem Archeological Park*, Jerusalem 1999

Reiter, Y. and Seligman, J., 'Al-Haram al-Sherif/Temple Mount (Har ha-Bayit) and the Western Wall', in Oleg Grabar and Benjamin Z. Kedar (eds), *Where Heaven and Earth Meet: Jerusalem's Sacred Esplanade*, Jerusalem/Austin 2009

Richardson, Peter, *Herod the Great: King of the Jews, Friend of the Romans*, New York 1999

Ridley, Jane, *Young Disraeli*, London 1995

Riley-Smith, Jonathan, *The Knights of St John in Jerusalem and Cyprus 1050–1310*, London 1967

Riley-Smith, Jonathan, *The Feudal Nobility and the Kingdom of Jerusalem 1174–1277*, London 1973

Riley-Smith, Jonathan, *The First Crusade and the Idea of Crusading*, London 1987

Riley-Smith, Jonathan, *The Crusades: A Short History*, London 2005

Roaf, Susan, 'Life in 19th-Century Jerusalem', in Sylvia Auld and Robert Hillenbrand (eds), *Ottoman Jerusalem: The Living City, 1517–1917*, London 2000

Robinson, Chase F., *Abd al-Malik*, Oxford 2007

Rogan, Eugene, *The Arabs: A History*, London 2009

Rogerson, Barnaby, *The Heirs of the Prophet Muhammad and the Roots of the Sunni–Shia Schism*, London 2006

Rohl, John C. G., *The Kaiser and his Court*, Cambridge 1987

Rohl, John C. G., *Wilhelm II: The Kaiser's Personal Monarchy 1888–1900*, Cambridge 2004

Rood, Judith, *Sacred Law in the Holy City: The Khedival Challenge to the Ottomans as Seen from Jerusalem, 1829–1841*, Leyden/Boston 2004

Rose, Norman, *A Senseless Squalid War: Voices from Palestine 1945–8*, London 2009

Rose, Norman, *Chaim Weizmann: A Biography*, London 1986

Roth, Cecil, *The House of Nasi: The Duke of Naxos*, Philadelphia 1948

Roux, G., *Ancient Iraq*, London 1864

Royle, Trevor, *Glubb Pasha*, London 1992

Rozen, Minna, 'The Relations between Egyptian Jewry and the Jewish Community of Jerusalem in the 17th Century', in A. Cohen and G. Baer (eds), *Egypt and Palestine: A Millennium of Association (868–1948)*, Jerusalem 1984

Rozen, Minna, *Jewish Identity and Society in the Seventeenth Century: Reflections on the Life and Works of Refael Mordekhai Malki*, Tübingen 1992

Rozen, Minna, 'Pedigree Remembered, Reconstructed, Invented: Benjamin Disraeli between East and West', in Martin Kramer (ed.), *The Jewish Discovery of Islam*, Tel Aviv 1999

Rubin, Zeev, 'Christianity in Byzantine Palestine – Missionary Activity and Religious Coercion', in Lee I. Levine (ed.), *Jerusalem Cathedra: Studies in the History, Geography and Ethnology of the Land of Israel*, vol. 3, Jerusalem 1983

Ruderman, David B., *Early Modern Jewry: A New Cultural History*, Princeton NJ 2011

Runciman, Steven, *A History of the Crusades*, 3 vols, Cambridge 1951–4

Sabbagh, Karl, *Palestine: A Personal History*, London 2006

Said, Edward, *Orientalism*, New York 1978

Sand, Shlomo, *The Invention of the Jewish People*, London 2009

Sanders, Paula A., 'The Fatimid State', in Carl F. Petry (ed.), *The Cambridge History of Egypt*, vol. 1: *Islamic Egypt 640–1517*, Cambridge 1998

Sanders, Ronald, *The High Walls of Jerusalem: A History of the Balfour Declaration and the Birth of the British Mandate for Palestine*, London 1989

Sartre, Maurice, *The Middle East under Rome*, Cambridge MA 2005

Satloff, Robert, *Among the Righteous: Lost Stories from the Holocaust's Long Reach into Arab Lands*, London 2007

Sattin, Anthony, *A Winter on the Nile: Florence Nightingale, Gustave Flaubert and the Temptations of Egypt*, London 2010

Scammell, Michael, *Koestler: The Indispensable Intellectual*, London 2010

Schäfer, Peter, *The History of the Jews in the Greco-Roman World*, London 1983

Schneer, Jonathan, *The Balfour Declaration: The Origins of the Arab–Israeli Conflict*, London 2010

Scholch, A., 'Jerusalem in the 19th Century', in K. J. Asali (ed.), *Jerusalem in History*, New York 1990

Scholem, G., *Major Trends in Jewish Mysticism*, New York 1961

Scholem, G., *Sabbatai Zevi: The Mystical Messiah*, Princeton 1973

Schreiber, Nicola, *Cypro-Phoenician Pottery of the Iron Age*, Leiden/Boston 2003

Schur, Nathan, *Napoleon in the Holy Land*, London 1999

Schürer, E., *The History of the Jewish People in the Age of Jesus Christ*, Edinburgh 1973/1979

Schwartz, Daniel, 'Josephus, Philo and Pontius Pilate', in Lee I. Levine (ed.), *Jerusalem Cathedra: Studies in the History, Geography and Ethnology of the Land of Israel*, vol. 3, Jerusalem 1983

Schwartz, Daniel, *Agrippa the First, the Last King of Judaea*, Tübingen 1990

Segev, Tom, *One Palestine Complete: Jews and Arabs under The British Mandate*, London 2000

Segev, Tom, *1967: Israel, the War and the Year that Transformed the Middle East*, London 2007

Shanks, Hershel, *Jerusalem's Temple Mount*, New York/London 2007

Shepherd, Naomi, *The Zealous Intruders: The Western Rediscovery of Palestine*, London 1987

Sherman, A. J., *Mandate Days: British Lives in Palestine 1918–48*, London 1997

Shindler, Colin, *A History of Modern Israel*, Cambridge 2008

Shindler, Colin, *The Triumph of Military Zionism*, London 2010

Shlaim, Avi, *Collusion across the Jordan: King Abdullah, the Zionist Movement and the Partition of Palestine*, New York 1988

Shlaim, Avi, *Lion of Jordan: The Life of King Hussein in War and Peace*, London 2007

Shlaim, Avi, *Israel and Palestine*, London 2009

Sievers, J., *The Hasmoneans and their Supporters: From Mattathias to the Death of John Hyrcanus*, Atlanta 1990

Silberman, Neil Asher, *Digging for God and Country: Exploration, Archaeology and the Secret Struggle for the Holy Land 1799–1917*, New York 1990

Slater, Robert, *Rabin of Israel*, London 1996

Smail, R. C., 'The Predicaments of Guy of Lusignan', in Benjamin Z. Kedar, H. E. Mayer and R. C. Smail (eds), *Outremer: Studies in the History of the Crusading Kingdom of Jerusalem, Presented to Joshua Prawer*, Jerusalem 1982

Soskice, Janet, *Sisters of Sinai: How Two Lady Adventurers Found the Hidden Gospels*, London 2009

Stager, Lawrence E., 'Forging an Identity: The Emergence of Ancient Israel', in Michael Coogan (ed.), *The Oxford History of the Biblical World*, Oxford 1998

Stern, M., 'Judaea and her Neighbours in the Days of Alexander Jannaeus', *Jerusalem Cathedra: Studies in the History, Geography and Ethnology of the Land of Israel*, vol. 1, Jerusalem 1981

Stewart, Desmond, *Theodor Herzl*, London 1974

Stillman, Norman A., 'The Non-Muslim Communities: The Jewish Community', in Carl F. Petry (ed.), *The Cambridge History of Egypt*, vol. 1: *Islamic Egypt 640–1517*, Cambridge 1998

Strathern, Paul, *Napoleon in Egypt*, London 2007

Stroumsa, G. G., 'Christian Memories and Visions of Jerusalem in the Jewish and Islamic Context', in Oleg Grabar and Benjamin Z. Kedar (eds), *Where Heaven and Earth Meet: Jerusalem's Sacred Esplanade*, Jerusalem/Austin 2009

Tabor, James D., *The Jesus Dynasty*, London 2006

Tamari, Salim, *Mountain Against the Sea: Essays on Palestinian Society and Culture*, Berkeley/Los Angeles/London 2009

Tchamkerten, Astrig, *The Gulbenkians in Jerusalem*, Lisbon 2006

Thomas, Hugh, *Rivers of Blood: The Rise of the Spanish Empire*, London 2010

Thompson, Thomas L., *The Bible in History: How Writers Create a Past*, London 1999

Thubron, Colin, *Jerusalem*, London 1986

Tibawi, A., *British Interests in Palestine*, Oxford 1961

Tibawi, A., *Jerusalem: Its Place in Islam and Arab History*, Beirut 1967

Tibawi, A., *The Islamic Pious Foundations in Jerusalem: Origins, History and Usurpation by Israel*, London 1978

Treadgold, Warren T., *A History of Byzantine State and Society*, Stanford 1997

Tsafrir, Yoram (ed.), *Ancient Churches Revealed*, Jerusalem 1993

Tsafrir, Yoram, 'The Templeless Mountain', in Oleg Grabar and Benjamin Z. Kedar (eds), *Where Heaven and Earth Meet: Jerusalem's Sacred Esplanade*, Jerusalem/Austin 2009

Tuchman, Barbara, *Bible and Sword*, London 1998

Turner, R. V., *Eleanor of Aquitaine*, New Haven 2009

Tveit, Odd Karsten, *Anna's House: The American Colony in Jerusalem*, Nicosia 2011

Tyerman, Christopher, *God's War: A New History of the Crusades*, London 2007

The Umayyads: The Rise of Islamic Art, Museum with No Frontiers, Amman/Vienna 2000

Van Creveld, Martin, *Moshe Dayan*, London 2004

Vermes, Geza, *The Dead Sea Scrolls in English*, London 1987

Vermes, Geza, *Jesus and the World of Judaism*, London 1993

Vermes, Geza, *The Changing Faces of Jesus*, London 2000

Vermes, Geza, *The Story of the Scrolls: The Miraculous Discovery and True Significance of the Dead Sea Scrolls*, London 2010

Vincent, L. H. and Abel, F. M., *Jérusalem nouvelle*, Paris 1914–26

Walker, Paul E., 'The Ismaili Dawa and Fatimid Caliphate', in Carl F. Petry (ed.), *The Cambridge History of Egypt*, vol 1: *Islamic Egypt 640–1517*, Cambridge 1998

Wallach, Janet, *Desert Queen: The Extraordinary Life of Gertrude Bell*, London 1997

Warren, W. L., *King John*, New Haven/London 1981

Warwick, Christopher, *Ella: Princess, Saint and Martyr*, London 2006

Wasserstein, Bernard, *The British in Palestine: Mandatory Government and the Arab–Jewish Conflict 1917–29*, Oxford 1991

Wasserstein, Bernard, *Herbert Samuel: A Political Life*, Oxford 1992

Wasserstein, Bernard, *Divided Jerusalem: The Struggle for the Holy City*, London 2001

Watt, W. Montgomery, *Muhammad: Prophet and Statesman*, Oxford 1961

Watt, W. Montgomery, *Muhammad's Mecca: History in the Quran*, Edinburgh 1988

Whitelam, Keith, *The Invention of Ancient Israel: The Silencing of Palestinian History*, London 1997

Wickham, Chris, *The Inheritance of Rome: A History of Europe from 400 to 1000*, London 2009

Wilkinson, J., *Jerusalem Pilgrims before the Crusades*, Warminster 1977

Wilkinson, J., 'Jerusalem under Rome and Byzantium', in K. J. Asali, *Jerusalem in History*, New York 1990

Wilkinson, Toby, *The Rise and Fall of Ancient Egypt: The History of a Civilization from 3000 BC to Cleopatra*, London 2010

Williams, Hywel, *Emperor of the West: Charlemagne and the Carolingian Empire*, London 2010

Wilson, A. N., *Jesus*, London 1993

Wilson, A. N., *Paul: The Mind of the Apostle*, London 1998

Wrba, Marion, *Austrian Presence in the Holy Land in the Nineteenth and Twentieth Centuries*, Tel Aviv 1996

Ze'evi, Dror, *An Ottoman Century: The District of Jerusalem in the 1600s*, New York 1996

INDEX